LISTENING TO
MUSIC
FOURTH EDITION

CRAIG WRIGHT

YALE UNIVERSITY

Australia • Canada • Mexico • Singapore • Spain
United Kingdom • United States

THOMSON

★

™

SCHIRMER

Publisher: Clark Baxter
Development Editor: Sharon Adams Poore
Assistant Editor: Julie Yardley
Editorial Assistant: Eno Sarris
Technology Project Manager: Jennifer Ellis
Marketing Manager: Mark Orr
Marketing Assistant: Kristi Bostock
Advertising Project Manager: Brian Chaffee
Project Manager, Editorial Production: Trudy Brown

Print/Media Buyer: Barbara Britton
Permissions Editor: Joohee Lee
Production Service: Johnstone Associates
Photo Researcher: Roberta Broyer
Text and Cover Designer: Diane Beasley
Cover Image: "Liszt at the Grand Piano" by Josef Danhauser, 1840
(Bildarschiv Preussischer Kulturbesitz, Berlin)
Compositor: Thompson Type
Text and Cover Printer: CTPS

Printed in China by CTPS
4 5 6 7 07 06

> For more information about our products, contact us at:
> **Thomson Learning Academic Resource Center**
> **1-800-423-0563**
> For permission to use material from this text, contact us by:
> **Phone:** 1-800-730-2214   **Fax:** 1-800-730-2215
> **Web:** http://www.thomsonrights.com

Library of Congress Control Number: 2003103614

ISBN 0-534-60372-6
Instructor's Edition: ISBN 0-534-60373-4

Wadsworth Group/Thomson Learning
10 Davis Drive
Belmont, CA 94002-3098
USA

Asia
Thomson Learning
5 Shenton Way #01-01
UIC Building
Singapore 068808

Australia/New Zealand
Thomson Learning
102 Dodds Street
Southbank, Victoria 3006
Australia

Canada
Nelson
1120 Birchmount Road
Toronto, Ontario M1K 5G4
Canada

Europe/Middle East/Africa
Thomson Learning
High Holborn House
50/51 Bedford Row
London WC1R 4LR
United Kingdom

Latin America
Thomson Learning
Seneca, 53
Colonia Polanco
11560 Mexico D.F.
Mexico

Spain/Portugal
Paraninfo
Calle/Magallanes, 25
28015 Madrid, Spain

www.wadsworth.com

wadsworth.com is the World Wide Web site for Wadsworth and is your direct source to dozens of online resources.

At *wadsworth.com* you can find out about supplements, demonstration software, and student resources. You can also send e-mail to many of our authors and preview new publications and exciting new technologies.

wadsworth.com
Changing the way the world learns®

Contents

Chapter 1

Listening to Music   1

Chapter 2

Rhythm, Melody, and Harmony   13

Chapter 3

Musical Color, Texture, and Form   42

Chapter 7

Late Baroque Music: Bach and Handel 135

Chapter 11

The Bridge to Romanticism: Ludwig van Beethoven   228

Chapter 12

The Romantic Spirit (1820–1900)   248

Chapter 13

The Early Romantics   264

Chapter 14

Romantic Opera 297

Chapter 15

Late Romanticism 320

Chapter 16

From Romantic to Modern: Impressionism   341

Chapter 17

The Twentieth Century   356

Chapter 18

American Popular Music: Blues, Jazz, and Rock   399

Listening Exercises

Boxes

Preface

The painting that serves as the cover for this book is a fascinating artifact. Indeed, one could write a book about it alone. Executed in 1840 by a minor Austrian painter, Josef Danhauser, it is a fanciful depiction of a gathering of some of the greatest artistic luminaries of the nineteenth century. Engaged at the piano is the imposing figure of Franz Liszt, perhaps the most formidable pianist who ever lived. Standing immediately behind him are Gioachino Rossini, the famous opera composer, and Niccolò Paganini, a violin virtuoso whose playing was so extraordinary that he was widely thought to be in league with the devil. With arm on chair, book in hand, is the French nineteenth-century lion of letters, Victor Hugo. Below him sits Alexandre Dumas, author of *The Three Musketeers* and *The Count of Monte Cristo*. To his left, cigar in hand, is Aurore Dudevant, the prototype of the nineteenth-century feminist and novelist of more than two dozen volumes under her pen name George Sand. Reclining under the sway of the music is Marie d'Agoult, herself a feminist author, playwright, and prize-winning historian. If one looks carefully at the painting on the wall, the profile of the recently deceased poet Lord Byron, the romantic figure *par excellence*, comes into view. Finally, radiating the very spirit of music from Olympian heights, a bust of the great Beethoven sits atop the piano—Beethoven the law-giver surrounded by his apostles. Although most of the listeners are poets, playwrights, and novelists, they have put down their books. It is the art of music that dominates the scene. From the faces of the guests we can see that they are profoundly affected by what they hear. Music touches their emotions. They are transfixed by its power.

PEDAGOGICAL GOALS

The aim of this textbook is to encourage students, too, to become transfixed by the expressive power of music. As Danhauser's scene suggests, music can be the most compelling of the arts. Yet ironically, most beginning students feel more comfortable with the visual arts than with music. The reason for this is not difficult to fathom: Painting, sculpture, and architecture have an immediate appeal to our visual senses. But music cannot be seen or held. It is intangible, ephemeral, and mysterious. Because of this, our ways of thinking and talking about music are different from those used to address the visual arts. A new and separate set of concepts and vocabulary is needed. The notion of scales, chords, meters, and rhythms, for example, involves a technical understanding that can be intimidating initially. To help clarify things, this book will use the language of the visual arts whenever possible to explain musical concepts. In this Fourth Edition nearly 300 color illustrations help transfer ideas already understood in the visual arts to the process of hearing music.

Most music appreciation textbooks treat music, not as an opportunity for personal engagement through listening but as a history of music. The student is required to learn something of the technical workings of music (what a tonic chord is, for example) and specific facts (how many symphonies Beethoven wrote) but is not asked to become personally engaged in the act of listening to music. What listening there is is passive, not active. *Listening to Music*, however, is different. Here the student is encouraged, indeed required, to become an active participant in a musical dialogue. The dialogue is made possible by several pedagogical aids.

PEDAGOGICAL AIDS

Listening Exercises

Listening to Music is the only music appreciation text on the market to include Listening Exercises within the book. For the Fourth Edition, forty-four wholly new or refashioned exercises have been prepared. By means of these, the student will embrace hundreds of specific passages of music and make critical decisions about them. The exercises begin by developing basic listening skills—recognizing rhythmic patterns, distinguishing major keys from minor, and differentiating various kinds of textures. The exercises then move on to entire pieces in which the student is required to become a participant in an artistic exchange, the composer communicating with the listener, and the listener reacting over a long span of time. Ultimately, equipped with these newly developed listening skills, the student will move comfortably to the concert hall, listening to classical and popular music with greater confidence and enjoyment. To be sure, this book is for the present course, but its aim is to prepare the student for a lifetime of musical listening and enjoyment.

The instructor's enjoyment of the Fourth Edition has been enhanced as well, for now it is possible to have these Listening Exercises graded electronically and the results returned to the instructor's electronic grade book via Web Tutor or Blackboard (for details, please contact your Thomson/ Schirmer sales representative). Instructors will also find additional drills, self-tests, and lists of Internet sites, as well as suggestions for further listening and reading in the excellent Study Guide prepared by Professor Timothy Roden of Ohio Wesleyan University.

Listening Guides

In addition to the Listening Exercises, more than eighty Listening Guides appear regularly throughout the text to help the novice enjoy extended musical compositions. Within each guide is a "time log" that allows the listener to follow along as the piece unfolds. The compact disc makes this especially easy, since all that is required is a glance at the minute and second counter to know how far the piece has progressed. The discussion in the text, the Listening Exercises, and the Listening Guides have been carefully coordinated, minute by minute, second by second, with the CDs.

Interactive Web Site

A new feature with the Fourth Edition is an interactive Web site at which the student can download an interactive listening guide for each piece of music in the book. At this site students will also find additional listening quizzes and an audio comparison of musical styles: Baroque compared to Romantic, for example.

Introductory CD

The Fourth Edition comes with an introductory CD that contains the music for the first part of the course, specifically Chapters 1 through 3. Included here is a new feature called "Instruments of the Orchestra" in which the primary instruments of the Western symphony orchestra are exemplified through specially recorded examples. Following a demonstration of the various instruments and instrumental techniques, students may undertake a series of graduated Listening Exercises that test their ability to recognize the instruments.

Cultural Contexts

New with the Fourth Edition is a series of boxed essays appearing throughout the book entitled "Cultural Context." They discuss aspects of the music of Ghana (West Africa), China, India, Indonesia, Argentina, Cuba, and Pakistan, as well as Jewish klezmer music. Their aim is to set off in clear relief, and thereby call attention to, the special and often peculiar qualities of Western classical and popular music. Certainly it is important to know something of non-Western music. But equally important, by studying the musics of these other cultures we can often learn much about our own.

Musical Terminology and the Glossary

As with medicine, law, and architecture, for example, music has its own vocabulary to express concepts unique to this discipline. To engage in a lively dialogue about music, we must all understand and be conversant with this musical vocabulary. All musical terms used in this book are defined in the Glossary (beginning on page 425). They appear in the text with an asterisk to remind the reader that definitions can be found in this glossary. They also are set in boldface type, usually at their first appearance in the text, and are included in the appropriate list of Key Words found at the ends of chapters. Finally, the Schirmer Web site now includes an aural dictionary, including both audio and visual examples of musical terms.

Repertoire

Every book about music aims to present the very best musical repertoire. But some musical works make better teaching pieces than others. In this regard Tchaikovsky's *The 1812 Overture*, new to this edition, is typical. It may not be Tchaikovsky's finest work, but it is a piece that students frequently hear—at pops concerts and on the Fourth of July, for example. Whenever possible it is important to emphasize that what students learn in this book is relevant to the music they hear in the real world. To this end there are ten works new to the Fourth Edition, spanning the centuries, from Dufay to Miles Davis.

Students also need to know that not all music worth hearing was composed by "dead white men." Thus the coverage of women both as composers and patrons of music has again been expanded. Among the women treated in the Fourth Edition are Hildegard of Bingen, Beatriz of Dia, Barbara Strozzi, Clara Schumann, and Ellen Taaffe Zwilich. Similarly, the coverage of jazz, rock, and pop music has been enlarged in Chapter 18. These expanded repertoires, when added to the new feature of "Cultural Context" boxes, makes for a much broader treatment of music of the world's people.

ANCILLARIES FOR STUDENTS

Introductory CD

Automatically packaged with each new copy of the book, and not sold separately—this CD contains all of the music discussed in Chapters 1–3 on the elements, as well as a new interactive guide to "Instruments of the Orchestra," which presents the instruments and then tests the student's ability to recognize the instruments by themselves and in various combinations.

2-CD Set

Includes a core repertoire of music discussed in the book. Each selection works with an interactive multimedia Listening Guide (available via Web site download) that demonstrates visually what the students hear.

6-CD Set

Includes all musical selections discussed in the book. Each selection works with an interactive multimedia Listening Guide (available via Web site download) that demonstrates visually what the students hear.

Study Guide

by Timothy Roden, Ohio Wesleyan University
Includes chapter reviews, quizzes, and additional listening and reading assignments.

The Young Person's Guide to the Orchestra Video

With music by Benjamin Britten, this video corresponds to Chapter 3 of the text. This video discusses, then allows students to see, each instrument played alone and in ensembles.

FOR INSTRUCTORS

Instructor's Manual and Test Bank

by Timothy Roden, Ohio Wesleyan University
Contains chapter summaries, teaching suggestions, objective and essay questions, and answers to the Listening Exercises in the text.

Instructor's Resource CD

Includes ExamView computerized testing, as well as an electronic version of the Instructor's Manual/Test Bank, and PowerPoint slides, all on one convenient CD.

FOR STUDENTS AND INSTRUCTORS

Web Site

The *Listening to Music* companion Web site offers additional tools to aid in student comprehension. Special features of this site include the free multimedia downloads that accompany the intro, 2-CD, and 6-CD sets. The multimedia downloads work with the audio CDs to provide an interactive learning environment for students and feature the following components: listening guides, elements of music tutorial, music style comparisons, and more. Visit *http://music.wadsworth.com* to find an aural dictionary that includes both audio and visual examples of musical terms, an Internet library of Web links, and other additional text-specific pedagogical devices.

WebTutor, for Blackboard and WebCT

This Web-based teaching and learning tool is rich with study and mastery tools, communication tools, and course content. Use Web Tutor to provide virtual office hours, post syllabi, set up threaded discussions, track student progress with the quizzing material, and more. For students, Web Tutor offers real-time access to a full array of study tools, including flashcards (with audio), practice quizzes, online tutorials, and Web links. Professors can customize the content by uploading images and other resources, adding Web links, or creating their own practice materials. Web Tutor also provides rich communication tools, including a course calendar, asynchronous discussion, "real-time" chat, and an integrated e-mail system. Available to qualified adopters. Please contact your local sales representative for details.

ACKNOWLEDGMENTS

Part of the fun of teaching music appreciation comes from discussing with colleagues ways in which to introduce classical music to students who know little about music. What can students be reasonably expected to hear? What is the best terminology to use? Profs. Keith Polk (University of New Hampshire) and Tilden Russell (Southern Connecticut State University) have gently taken me to task for using the term "ternary form" where "rounded binary" is more correct; they are right, yet for fear of overloading the beginning student with too many new formal concepts, here I simplify and call both rounded binary and ternary forms just ternary. I am, nevertheless, grateful for their continuing support and attention to matters of detail. So too I am indebted to Profs. Anne Robertson and Robert Kendrick of the University of Chicago for their input on matters large and small. Three former students, Profs. Jess Tyre (SUNY at Potsdam), Marica Tacconi (Pennsylvania State University) and Laura Nash (Fairfield University) continue to provide me with valuable criticisms and suggestions. Several colleagues made suggestions for specific improvements in content, for which I am grateful, namely Profs. James Ladewig (University of Rhode Island), Carlo Caballero (University of Colorado, Boulder), Mary Ann Smart (University of California, Berkeley), and Michael Tenzer (University of British Columbia). Finally, Prof. Timothy Roden (Ohio Wesleyan University), the author of the Study Guide and Instructor's Manual, has corrected errors and saved me from myself on numerous occasions.

The following reviewers also evaluated material or provided helpful information during the writing of this book:

Wesley Ball
Hope College

D. E. Bussinaeau-King
University of the Incarnate Word

Andrew Byrne
Columbia University

Ann B. Caldwell
Georgia College and State University

Cheong L. Chuah
Cerro Cosso Community College

Kyle Cheong Chuah
Los Medanos College

Ginger Covert
Colla Modesto Junior College

Joseph Darby
Keene State College

Hollie Duvall
Westmoreland County Community College

Harry Faulk
Fairmont State College

Fenton G. Fly
Alabama State University

Nancy M. Gamso
Ohio Wesleyan University

Benjamin K. Gish
Walla Walla College

Stephanie B. Graber
University of Wisconsin–Stout

Larry N. Graham
Valencia Community College

Patricia L. Hales
Purdue University, Calumet

Marymal L. Holmes
Bowie State University

David Lee Jackson
Baylor University

Tido Janssen
Hardin-Simmons University

Benjamin M. Korstvedt
University of St. Thomas

Walter Kreiszig
University of Saskatchewan

Charles S. Larkowski
Wright State University

Gary Lewis
Midwestern State University

Bernard C. Lemoine
Mary Washington College

Ed Macan
College of the Redwoods

Michael Moss
Southern Connecticut State University

Sharon H. Nelson
Wright State University

Laurie H. Ongley
Southern Connecticut State University

Mustak Zafer Ozgen
Baruch College

Diane M. Paige
University of California, Santa Barbara

Linda Pohly
Ball State University

Thomas C. Polett
Culver-Stockton College

Ronald Rabin
University of Michigan

Daniel Ratelle
San Diego Mesa College

Laurie A. Reese
Lebanon Community College

Steven Roberson
Butler University

Timothy J. Roden
Ohio Wesleyan University

Karl Schmidt
Towson University

Chirstine Larson Seitz
Indiana University South Bend

John Sinclair
Rollins College

Richard Shillea
Fairfield University

Jayme Stayer
Owens Community College

Janet L. Sturman
University of Arizona

Gary R. Sudano
Purdue University

Timothy P. Urban
Rutgers University

Melva Villard
Louisiana State University at Alexandria

Susan Weiss
Johns Hopkins University

Cynthia Wong
Columbia University

Annette H. Zalanowski
Pennsylvania State University, Altoona

Ray H. Ziegler
Salisbury State University

Finally, I owe a debt of gratitude to many colleagues at Yale, including Profs. Leon Plantinga, James Hopokoski, Ellen Rosand, Michael Veal, and Kathryn Alexander, as well as graduate students Padma Newsome, Craig Harwood, and Jessica Wiscus. In addition, I benefited greatly from the help and good will of the staff of the Yale Music Library: Kendall Crilly, librarian, and Suzanne Eggleston, Richard Boursy, and Eva Heater. Karl Schrom, record librarian at Yale, has been a source of good advice regarding the availability and quality of recordings for twenty years. Within my own family, my wife Sherry, sons Evan, Andrew, and Chris, daughter Stephanie, daughter-in-law Melanie, and esteemed brother-in-law Sterling Murray provided many good ideas and a noisy counterpoint to my own. This time more than ever it has been a privilege to work with publisher Clark Baxter and his experienced team at Schirmer—Sharon Adams Poore, Julie Yardley, Eno Sarris, Mark Orr, Jennifer Ellis, Trudy Brown, and especially my editorial soulmate Judy Johnstone, as well as Wayne Olsen at Universal Records. My heartiest thanks to all of you!

© Corbis

Listening to Music

*"It is perhaps in music that the dignity of art is most eminently apparent,
for it elevates and ennobles everything that it expresses."*

Johann Wolfgang von Goethe (1749–1832)

"It don't mean a thing if it ain't got that swing."

Edward Kennedy "Duke" Ellington (1899–1974)

Why do we listen to music? Because it gives us pleasure. Why does it give us pleasure? We don't know, though psychologists have spent a great deal of time trying to find out. By some inexplicable means, music has the power to intensify and deepen our feelings, to calm our jangled nerves, to make us sad or cheerful, to incite us to dance, and even, perhaps, to march proudly off to war. Long ago, the ancient Greeks recognized the powers of music; indeed, Plato thought exposure to the proper sort of music would encourage the young men of Athens to study diligently and avoid the eternal temptations of wine and women. Taking a page from the ancient Greeks, two modern governments (the clerical party in Iran in 1979 and the Taliban in Afghanistan in 1996) banned all non-religious music for fear of its potentially corruptive powers. But since time immemorial people around the world have made music an indispensable part of their most important religious, social, and artistic activities. Music adds to the solemnity of our ceremonies, arts, and entertainments, and thus "moves" (heightens the feelings) of all who watch and participate. If you doubt this, try looking at a motion picture without listening to the musical score, or

AP/Wide World Photos

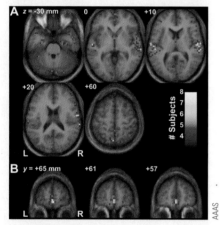

AAAS

FIGURE 1–1

Virtuoso Hilary Hahn performing on the violin. A musical instrument, such as the violin, produces regular waves of sound that radiate through the air to the ear of the listener and ultimately to the brain. Scientists at Dartmouth have recently identified the part of the brain that sorts and tries to make sense of these musical patterns—the rostromedial prefrontal cortex! As these same scientists have said about music: "It's not necessary for human survival, yet something inside us craves it."

imagine a parade, a wedding, or a funeral without music and think how empty these events would be.

Consciously or not, we all know that music affects our moods and behavior. Most people have a sense of what music they like and what music to choose so as to feel a certain way. Those who design radio programs and commercial broadcasts know this too, and they select different kinds of music for different times and places. In the morning, energetic, upbeat music is needed to get us off to work, but coming home we prefer mellow, relaxing sounds. Music in shopping malls is designed to encourage people to take their time and feel at ease, and here classical music is often heard to suggest the pleasures of rich living and stylish elegance. Music is all around us, and it is often used to manipulate our thinking in ways that we are not aware.

When we listen to music, physically speaking, we are reacting to an organized disturbance of our environment (Fig. 1–1). A voice or an instrument emits energized sounds that set the air in motion, creating waves that carry the sound to our ears. In the inner ear, these vibrations are transformed into electrochemical impulses that, in turn, are transferred to the brain. What happens there is not certain, but it appears that the impulses are sorted and recognized as patterns and shapes, perhaps not unlike visual patterns or geometric shapes. In the end, the way we perceive a musical composition may not be much different from our perception of a harmonious work of architecture, the colorful relationships within a tapestry, or the gently moving contours of a lovely landscape. We respond emotionally to, and are moved by, musical relationships that are pleasing, novel, or even disturbing. Responding to the endless patterns of music—by tapping our feet, moving our bodies, or humming along—is an experience common to us all.

BECOMING A GOOD LISTENER

Listening to music is an art, and like all the arts it requires preparation and discipline. Part of the preparation involves learning what to listen for and what to expect in music. To do this, we must have some knowledge of how music works. How do melodies unfold? How do musical phrases work together to mark the progress of a piece? How does a composer, classical or pop, get from one section to the next, and how does he or she signal that the conclusion is near? One of the aims of this book is to give you an understanding of what these common musical processes are, so that you can make sense out of what you hear and can even anticipate what may come next. In this way, knowledge will increase your enjoyment.

Along with learning how music works comes the development of good listening skills. We should be able to recognize which instruments are playing, sort out the melody from the harmony, identify how many distinctive layers or lines there are in the musical texture, feel the meter and the rhythm of the piece, and sense where we are in the formal design of the work. This will require active, not passive, listening. But once such skills have been mastered, they can be applied equally well to both classical and popular music. Hearing a bass line in a tune of R.E.M. or U2, for example, is not much different from hearing one in a symphony by Beethoven.

Focus Solely on the Music

The first step toward improving your listening skills is to focus solely on the music. Most of us use music as a backdrop for other activities. You may be in the habit of listening to the radio or a CD while doing your class assignments. Some music, specifically the "easy listening" music that floods the FM airwaves, is in fact designed *not* to be heard, or at least not to be the object of any heavy thinking. But, for more serious music, this sort of background listening won't do. Similarly, the superficial hearing we give to most popular music is anything but deep and penetrating. We respond emotionally with our hearts (and bodies, if we wish to dance), but not with our minds. Classical music and jazz require that we engage our intellect and think critically about what we hear. Popular music, too, often has surprises that reward the attentive listener, if we choose to look beneath the surface. But whether for classical or pop, we have to recognize specific musical events, retain these in our memory, and relate them to one another over a span of time. For this, we must devote our full attention to the music.

be an active listener

Improve Your Memory

Memory is essential to good listening. Unlike the visual arts, music passes through time. When we look at a painting, for example, it stands still before us, to be taken in all at once. If we relate this painting to anything, it is to other, similar paintings that we know. Our approach to a musical composition, however, is much different. We are not given the entire object at once. Rather, it comes to us gradually, bit by bit, as the seconds and minutes go by. To make sense of what we hear *now*, we have to remember what we heard *before*. Trying to remember and relate sounds that seem to pass by all too quickly is the greatest challenge for the beginning listener. How do we deal with this rush of music? Simply said, we should try to seize upon a few key events and hold them firmly in mind. The Listening Exercises in this book are designed to improve your capacity to remember sounds. And, like most physical and mental exercises, the more you use your musical memory, the better it becomes.

Grasp the Important Sounds

Mozart had an extraordinary musical ear. In April 1771, at the age of fourteen, he heard a two-minute religious work performed in Rome and then later that day wrote it down in all parts by memory, note for note, on just this one hearing. But few of us possess Mozart's gift of musical memory. So, if we can't remember everything, we must try to remember the important things. Some aspects of the music should be strongly locked in our consciousness and other parts we can let go.

FIGURE 1–2
A violinist sets sound waves in motion in a recording studio.

A violinist records music in a studio.

Incoming analog sound is sampled 44,100 times a second.

A digital version of the sound is created, by converting music into numerical "words" of 16 bits each. The encoded sound is then stored as digital data along an extremely narrow (1/100th the thickness of a human hair) spiral track. The track, if uncoiled, would extend for three miles.

The finished CD is coated with aluminum to give it a reflective surface and covered with ultraviolet lacquer.

Finally, a digital analog converter within the CD player changes numbers to electrical impulses that can be amplified and pushed through audio speakers.

CD player and speakers.

seize the important ideas

Being able to differentiate between the important and the unimportant in music is thus the listener's first task. The Listening Guides in this book are designed to sharpen your critical faculties by showing you what the author thinks is important. The Listening Exercises at the end of the chapters, however, are intended to get you actively involved in the decisionmaking process. Later, you yourself will make all the critical judgments about music when you buy a new CD, hear a new piece on the radio, or attend a concert.

CLASSICAL MUSIC–POPULAR MUSIC

There is an astonishing variety of music in the world, both good and bad. Most of the music that will be discussed in this book is what we refer to as "classical" music. It is also called "art" music or "serious" music. Someone said that classical music is music that was written by "dead white men." That's not entirely accurate: no small amount of it has been written by women, and many classical composers, of both sexes, are very much alive and well today. But in truth, most of what we hear in the way of classical music—the music of Bach, Handel, Mozart, Haydn, Beethoven, Schubert, and Tchaikovsky, for example—was written by composers working in Europe or Russia between 1700 and 1900, and thus was created at least a century ago. Indeed, one thing that makes a cultural artifact a "classic" is that it possesses certain qualities of expression, proportion, and balance that are timeless in their appeal.

Popular music embraces the sounds that most people want to hear. Pop and rock CDs outsell those of classical music by more than ten to one. Popular music can be just as artful and just as serious as classical music, and often the musicians who perform it are just as talented and skilled as classical musicians. But popular music, unlike classical, rarely contains multiple levels of musical activity, and for this reason does not require, and does not reward, intensely active listening. What we hear the first time is (more or less) what we get. Perhaps this inability to reward repeated hearings or to allow for a different interpretation each time we listen is why the listening public quickly tires of particular popular songs and moves on to new ones. Only when a popular song does give pleasure to more than one generation, over a span of twenty or thirty years do we say that that tune has become a "classic."

Popular music can be useful in learning good listening skills. When trying to hear how and when chords change in a piece by Bach, for example, it can be helpful to listen first to a rock song, say one by U2, in which the chords are uncomplicated, the chords change at regular time intervals, and the bass, which carries the chords, is very loud and thus easy to hear. What we learn in one style can easily be transferred to another.

ATTENDING A CONCERT OF CLASSICAL MUSIC

Compared to pop or rock concerts, a performance of classical music may seem strange indeed. People dress up, not down. They sit quietly, saying nothing to friends or performers. No one sways or dances to the music. Only at the very end of each composition does the audience express itself, by respectfully clapping.

FIGURE 1-3

Trumpeter Wynton Marsalis can record a Baroque trumpet concerto one week and an album of New Orleans-style jazz the next. He has won nine Grammy awards, seven for various jazz categories and two for classical discs.

© Lynn Goldsmith/Corbis

But classical concerts weren't always so formal. In the eighteenth century the audience talked during the performance and yelled words of encouragement to the players. People clapped at the end of each movement of a symphony and often in the middle of the movement as well. After an exceptionally pleasing performance, the audience would demand that the piece be repeated immediately (an **encore**). But if the audience didn't like what it heard, it would show displeasure by throwing fruit and other debris toward the stage. Our modern, more dignified classical concert was a creation of the nineteenth century (see page 255).

Attending a classical concert requires forethought. Get familiar with the pieces in advance. Go to a music library and listen to a CD of the pieces that will be performed. Read the liner notes that accompany the CD to learn something about the history and cultural context of the works. Having heard a professional-quality recording, you will be prepared to judge the merits of a live (perhaps student) performance.

preparation for a concert

Choosing the right seat is also important. What is best for seeing may not be best for hearing. In some concert halls the sound sails immediately over those seated in the front rows and coalesces at the back (Fig. 1–4). Often the optimal place for sound (the best in terms of acoustics) is at the back of the hall, in the first balcony. Sitting closer, of course, allows you to enjoy watching the interplay of the performers on stage. If you attend a concert of a symphony orchestra, follow the gestures of the conductor to the various soloists and sections of the orchestra. Like a movie director, he or she turns directly to the soloist of the moment. The conductor conveys not only to the players but also to the audience the essential lines and themes of the music.

© Corbis

FIGURE 1–4
Symphony Hall in Boston. The best seats for hearing the music are not up front, but at the back in the middle of the balcony.

VISUALIZING CLASSICAL MUSIC

Many people feel more comfortable looking at the visual arts than listening to classical music. They prefer to visit an art museum rather than attend a classical concert. But why is music thought to be more inaccessible? Probably because we cannot see or touch it. Music is difficult to measure and quantify. It wafts through the air and works its magic in mysterious ways. Our inability to hold on to music makes it just a little bit intimidating. To get to the heart of classical music, an entirely new vocabulary—that of music theory—has to be learned; this is what music majors study in universities. But for the beginning listener there is a simpler, more immediately satisfying way: visualizing the music. We can picture—make a mental image—of the music as it passes. Here in this text we will do so by means of listening exercises and visual aids. This book contains more than 300 color illustrations. Most of these amplify

make a mental image of the music

themes discussed in the text. Many, however, offer visual illustrations of phenomena that occur in music. They show the workings of music by drawing analogies to identical practices in architecture, painting, and design. "Analogies decide nothing that is true," Sigmund Freud (1856–1939) said, "but they can make one feel more at home." Let us begin to feel more at home with classical music by listening to a work composed with the aim of capturing in sound the emotions present in a series of paintings.

PICTURES AT AN EXHIBITION (1874), MODEST MUSORGSKY

In February 1874 an exhibition of the works of designer and architect Victor Hartmann (1833–1873) was held at the Academy of Artists in St. Petersburg, Russia. Hartmann had died unexpectedly of a stroke the previous year, and a group of his friends organized a show of 400 of his works to honor his memory. One of Hartmann's closest colleagues, the Russian composer Modest Musorgsky, paid further homage to the artist in 1874 by transforming ten of these pictures into a musical work. The classic that Musorgsky created is called *Pictures at an Exhibition.*

Novosti Information Agency, London

FIGURE 1–5
Modest Musorgsky.

Modest Musorgsky (1839–1881) was born into a land-rich, aristocratic family near St. Petersburg. As a youth he showed great musical talent, performing a piano concerto at the age of nine. But the life of a professional musician was not deemed an appropriate vocation for a member of the aristocracy, and so he trained half-heartedly to be a military officer, receiving a commission in 1856. When Czar Alexander II emancipated the serfs in 1859, the Russian leader simultaneously separated the Musorgsky family from the source of its wealth. Having resigned his commission in the army and finding himself suddenly penniless, Musorgsky took a job as a clerk in the forestry department to put food on the table. But his real love—indeed obsession—remained music, and he composed during all of his spare moments.

Support for his music came to Musorgsky from a group of other young composers then active in St. Petersburg. Contemporaries dubbed this musical club "The Mighty Handful" or, less grandiosely, **The Russian Five**. It included Alexander Borodin (1833–1887), César Cui (1835–1918), Mily Balakirev (1837–1910), Nikolai Rimsky-Korsakov (1844–1908), and Musorgsky himself. Sadly, Musorgsky's brief, chaotic life was marked by increasing poverty, depression, and alcoholism. Still he managed to create a small but influential collection of works that includes a boldly inventive symphonic poem, *Night on Bald Mountain* (1867) and an operatic masterpiece, *Boris Godunov* (1874). Musorgsky is best remembered today, however, for his *Pictures at an Exhibition.*

from piano to orchestra

Musorgsky created his musical response to Hartmann's art at the piano, to be performed on the piano. Yet, there are times in the history of music when a densely packed composition written at the keyboard cries out for a more colorful presentation that only a full symphonic orchestra can provide. Musorgsky's inventive *Pictures at an Exhibition* was one work that demanded an orchestral presentation to reach its fullest potential. When music conceived at the keyboard is allocated to the various instruments of the orchestra, an **orchestration** results. The most successful orchestration of *Pictures at an Exhibition* was effected in 1922 by French composer Maurice Ravel (on Ravel, see page 351). To the usual symphony orchestra, Ravel added a saxophone and novel percussion instruments for special effects. The result is astonishing. Just as the addition of color radically alters the impact of a motion picture filmed in black and white (Figs. 1–6 and 1–7), so Ravel's orchestration intensifies Musorgsky's originally monochromatic music. The effect of Ravel's orchestration is to make Musorgsky's musical pictures both more powerful and more vivid. Let us begin our visit to the Musorgsky-Ravel musical museum.

© Bettmann/Corbis

FIGURE 1–6
Still from the motion picture *The Wizard of Oz* (1939) in black and white.

FIGURE 1–7
Still from the motion picture *The Wizard of Oz*, color-enhanced version. Just as color can enrich the art of film, so a full orchestra can add color to a musical score created at the piano.

Photofest

PROMENADE Here the composer portrays himself (and by extension us, the listeners) as wandering through an exhibition of Hartmann's paintings. The first piece, Promenade, later returns between pictures to create the sense of moving through a gallery from one painting to the next. Immediately, we are transported musically into a world of purely Russian art. Promenade is marked "Fast but resolute, in the Russian manner" (Allegro guisto, nel modo russico). This is an indication of the **tempo**, the speed at which the beat of a piece is to proceed. The music unfolds in purposeful, evenly spaced sounds as the viewer marches resolutely up to each picture. Let us call this marching melody the Promenade theme. The musical notation for it is given in the Listening Guide. This notation may seem alien to you, but don't panic—musical notation will be explained fully in Chapter 2. For the moment, simply put on the CD and follow the music as it unfolds according to the minute and second counter on your CD player. The featured instrument here is a single trumpet. When just one performer plays by him- or herself that performance is called a **solo**. Thus Promenade begins with a trumpet solo.

a world of Russian art

Listening Guide   Modest Musorgsky   Intro CD/1
                    Promenade from *Pictures at an Exhibition* (1874)
                    (orchestrated by Maurice Ravel, 1922)

0:00   Solo trumpet begins Promenade theme
0:08   Full brasses respond
0:15   Trumpet and full brass continue to alternate
0:30   Full strings and then woodwinds and brass enter
1:22   Brasses briefly restate Promenade theme

PICTURE 4 Now we stand before a painting in the exhibition. Alas, this particular tableau, called *Polish Ox-Cart,* has not survived, so we will have to picture it in our mind's eye. Imagine an overloaded wagon pulled by oxen, lumbering down a dirt road in rural Russia. The rocking of the cart is suggested by a bass that alternates, back and forth, between just two notes (down-up-down-up-down-up). A rhythm, melody, or harmony that repeats over and over in this fashion is called an **ostinato** (from the Italian word meaning "obstinate" or "stubborn"). Here the ostinato helps create a sense of motion. Thus a musical composition has the capacity to project a feeling of movement in a way that a painting cannot. The viewer stands stationary as the cart appears **pianissimo** (very softly), hence in the distance; it moves closer and closer by means of a **crescendo** (a gradual increase in the volume of sound). Now the cart shakes the earth **fortissimo** (very loud) as it rumbles past, and then it slowly disappears as the orchestra effects a **diminuendo** (a gradual reduction of the volume of sound).

art imitates nature

Creating this sense of motion (coming and going) required a knowledge of the physics of music. Musorgsky knew that longer sound waves (those of the low-sounding pitches) travel farther than shorter waves (high-sounding pitches). In other words, sounds made by low instruments go farther than those made by high ones. We have all experienced this law of musical acoustics: when listening to a marching band approaching from the distance we hear the sounds of the bass drum and tubas long before the higher ones of the trumpets and clarinets. Thus, in *Polish Ox-Cart,* Musorgsky begins and ends with the very lowest sounds (orchestrated by Ravel with tuba and double basses), to give the impression that the sound comes from a distance and then disappears again into the distance. By changing musical dynamics (soft to loud to soft) and by shifting ranges of sound (low to high to low), Musorgsky makes the ox-cart move before our eyes.

Listening Guide   Modest Musorgsky   Intro CD/2
                    Pictures at an Exhibition
                    Polish Ox-Cart

0:00   Solo tuba plays Ox-Cart melody against backdrop of a two-note
       ostinato
0:51   Strings, and soon full orchestra, join in
1:33   Full orchestra plays Ox-Cart theme (rattle of tambourine suggests
       cart shaking the earth)
1:54   Tuba returns with Ox-Cart theme
2:24   Diminuendo and fadeout

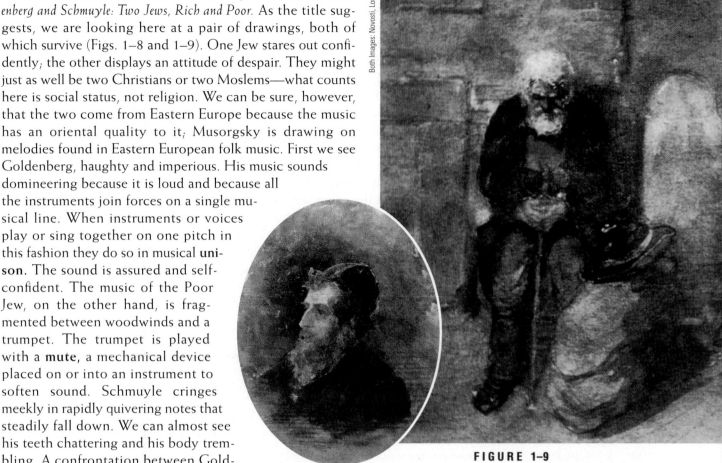

Both Images: Novosti, London

PICTURE 6 Let's walk now to the next picture, *Samuel Goldenberg and Schmuyle: Two Jews, Rich and Poor.* As the title suggests, we are looking here at a pair of drawings, both of which survive (Figs. 1–8 and 1–9). One Jew stares out confidently; the other displays an attitude of despair. They might just as well be two Christians or two Moslems—what counts here is social status, not religion. We can be sure, however, that the two come from Eastern Europe because the music has an oriental quality to it; Musorgsky is drawing on melodies found in Eastern European folk music. First we see Goldenberg, haughty and imperious. His music sounds domineering because it is loud and because all the instruments join forces on a single musical line. When instruments or voices play or sing together on one pitch in this fashion they do so in musical **unison**. The sound is assured and self-confident. The music of the Poor Jew, on the other hand, is fragmented between woodwinds and a trumpet. The trumpet is played with a **mute**, a mechanical device placed on or into an instrument to soften sound. Schmuyle cringes meekly in rapidly quivering notes that steadily fall down. We can almost see his teeth chattering and his body trembling. A confrontation between Goldenberg and Schmuyle follows, as the musics of the two characters sound simultaneously. Musorgsky not only makes the characters come alive in music but also causes them to interact in a way portrait paintings cannot. As you listen, ask yourself who has the last word in this musical encounter.

FIGURE 1–8

Victor Hartmann. Pencil drawing, *A Rich Jew.* The subject wears a comfortable fur skull cap, the symbol of his religion.

FIGURE 1–9

Victor Hartmann. Pencil and watercolor, *A Poor Jew.* The subject sits downcast, a sack containing his worldly possessions placed nearby. Musorgsky created appropriately downcast music to characterize this figure.

Listening Guide

Modest Musorgsky
Pictures at an Exhibition
Goldenberg and Schmuyle: Two Jews, Rich and Poor

Intro CD/3

WWW

0:00	Strings in unison play imposing music of Goldenberg
0:45	Trumpet (with mute), accompanied by woodwinds, plays trembling music of Schmuyle
1:23	Strings loudly interject the music of Goldenberg
1:51	The music of Schmuyle slithers away in the strings

FIGURE 1–10

Victor Hartmann's vision *The Great Gate of Kiev*, which inspired the last of the musical paintings in Musorgsky's *Pictures at an Exhibition*. Note the bells in the tower, a motif that is featured prominently at the very end of Musorgsky's musical evocation of this design.

PICTURE 10 Finally, we arrive at the last painting in this musical exhibition, *The Great Gate of Kiev*. The stimulus for the majestic conclusion to *Pictures at an Exhibition* was Victor Hartmann's design for a new and grandiose gate to the ancient Ukrainian city of Kiev, then part of Russia (Fig. 1–10). The gate, which was designed by Hartmann but never constructed, was to celebrate an event in the life of Czar Alexander II. It was to be the Russian equivalent of the Arch of Triumph in Paris and the Brandenburg Gate in Berlin, both of which Hartmann had seen in his travels to Europe (Fig. 1–11). This vision of a great triumphal arch accounts for the grand and majestic sound of the music.

Musorgsky disposes his musical material to give the impression of a parade passing beneath the giant gate. The music of the gate itself (music **A**) alternates with a Russian Orthodox hymn for a procession of pilgrims (music **B**), and even the composer-viewer walks beneath the gate as the Promenade theme (music **C**) appears, before a final return to a panoramic view of the gate (**A**), now with Hartmann's bells ringing triumphantly. Taken in sum, the events in *The Great Gate of Kiev* constitute a pleasing musical form (**ABABXCA**) in which a refrain (**A**) provides unity and coherence. Here in this final tableau, the full orchestra is able to create a strong feeling of the local color and, at the same time, of the great power of old Russia.

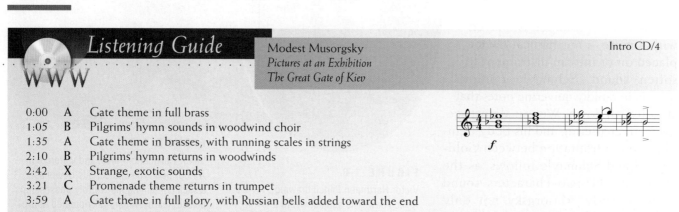

Listening Guide

Modest Musorgsky
Pictures at an Exhibition
The Great Gate of Kiev

Intro CD/4

0:00	A	Gate theme in full brass
1:05	B	Pilgrims' hymn sounds in woodwind choir
1:35	A	Gate theme in brasses, with running scales in strings
2:10	B	Pilgrims' hymn returns in woodwinds
2:42	X	Strange, exotic sounds
3:21	C	Promenade theme returns in trumpet
3:59	A	Gate theme in full glory, with Russian bells added toward the end

FIGURE 1–11

The Brandenburg Gate in Berlin, built by King Frederic Wilhelm II in 1791, likely provided inspiration for Hartmann's design for the Gate of Kiev.

Musorgsky's *Pictures at an Exhibition* has remained popular with audiences down to the present day—with those who attend "pops" as well as classical concerts. In addition, the rock group Emerson, Lake, and Palmer has fashioned a version aimed at pleasing more modern listeners (*Pictures at an Exhibition*, Rhino Records R2 72225). If you have occasion to hear this rock rendering of *Pictures at an Exhibition*, you may prefer this more "with-it" version for rock band in place of orchestra. On the other hand, you may not. Instead, you may come away from this classical encounter with a new-found respect for the ingenuity of both Musorgsky and Ravel, as well as the power and beauty of classical music generally.

a rock version

Listening Exercises

Modest Musorgsky   Intro CD/1–4
Pictures at an Exhibition (1874)
(orchestrated by Maurice Ravel, 1922)

Be sure that you have read the discussion of this work in the text (pages 6–10) and listened to it following the Listening Guides (pages 7–10). Now listen to it once again and answer the following questions. They are intended to introduce you to some of the instruments of the orchestra. Should you have difficulties, CD technology allows you to move quickly back and forth to rehear passages as many times as you wish. This first exercise is designed to be user-friendly—the questions are not too difficult.

Promenade Intro CD/1

1. (0:00–0:07) What brass instrument(s) opens the work?
   a. trumpets and trombones   b. a group of trumpets   c. a solo trumpet
2. (0:08–0:30) Which statement is true regarding this next passage?
   a. Other brass instruments enter and the trumpet continues playing.
   b. Other brass instruments enter and the trumpet stops playing.
3. The sound of the trumpet can be said to be
   a. at the bottom of the sound of the brass family
   b. at the middle of the sound of the brass family
   c. at the top of the sound of the brass family
4. (1:30–1:37) At the end of the movement, do the strings join with the brasses in playing the Promenade theme?
   a. yes   b. no

Polish Ox-Cart Intro CD/2

5. (0:00–0:50) How many parts, or musical lines, do you hear here?
   a. two: tuba and supporting harmony in the bass
   b. two: trumpet and supporting harmony in the bass
   c. three: trumpet on top, tuba in middle, supporting harmony in the bass
6. (0:00–0:50) Focus now on the bass, which is played by the large string double basses (Fig. 3–6). Which of the following statements is true?
   a. The double basses alternately play sounds that are short and long.

b. The double basses constantly play sounds of the same duration.

c. The double basses alternately play sounds that are long and short.

Goldenberg and Schmuyle: Two Jews, Rich and Poor Intro CD/3

7. (0:45–1:14) The character of Schmuyle is depicted in music by means of a fluttering trumpet (played with a softening mute) supported by members of the woodwind family. The woodwinds play notes moving
   a. at the same speed as those of the trumpet
   b. more rapidly than those of the trumpet
   c. more slowly than those of the trumpet

8. (2:10–2:12) Which character ultimately has the last word, Goldenberg (loud, unison writing for the string family) or Schmuyle (fluttering trumpet)?
   a. Goldenberg   b. Schmuyle

The Great Gate of Kiev Intro CD/4

9. The Gate theme is heard in full three times in this movement (at 0:00, 1:35, and 3:35). When it appears the second time (1:36–2:09) the texture is enriched by means of running scales in the strings. Which of the following is true?
   a. Low strings play racing scales while the Gate theme sounds in the high brasses. Then at 1:51 the roles are reversed. High strings play racing scales while the Gate theme sounds in the low brasses.
   b. High strings play racing scales while the Gate theme sounds in the low brasses. Then at 1:51 the roles are reversed. Low strings play racing scales while the Gate theme sounds in the high brasses.

10. The Gate theme is briefly recalled toward the very end (5:01–5:20), and it sounds very grand indeed! The composer creates this feeling of grandeur in several ways. Identify which of the following does **not** occur in this final statement.
    a. The Gate theme moves more slowly, in notes twice as long as before.
    b. All of the orchestra is playing, and doing so *fortissimo.*
    c. The trumpet plays a solo.
    d. Percussion (drums and cymbals and bells) are added for emphasis.
    e. The last chords are very drawn out.

Key Words

crescendo (7)	mute (9)	the Russian Five (6)
diminuendo (8)	orchestration (6)	solo (9)
encore (5)	ostinato (7)	tempo (7)
fortissimo (7)	*pianissimo* (7)	unison (9)

Musée Nationale de L'Arte Moderne, Paris

Chapter 2

Rhythm, Melody, and Harmony

Music can be defined as sound that moves through time in some organized fashion. Sounds and silences can be shaped, given a profile, as they pass through time. Durations can be organized in patterns to form rhythms. And musical pitches can be placed one after the other in a purposeful way to form a melody. When more than one pitch sounds at a time, the potential exists for musical harmony. Rhythm, melody, and harmony, then, are the most basic musical elements. They are the building blocks of music, and how they are arranged determines the color, texture, and form of every musical composition.

In discussing rhythm, melody, and harmony, we depend greatly on a terminology that has grown up around the practice of notating music. Musical notation is simply music put down on paper by means of special signs or symbols. Two simple concepts are at work here. The vertical axis (top to bottom) indicates pitch in music, high to low. The horizontal one (left to right) specifies duration; black notes show pitches that move more quickly than white notes. By recording a piece in musical notation, we, in effect, "freeze dry" the musical work so that it can be exactly reproduced by performers at some later date. In addition, musical notation allows us to stop at any point, to look at a composition as it is standing still, talk about its various parts, and learn something about how it is put together. You do not have to know musical notation to derive great pleasure from listening to music, nor will you have to read it to be highly successful in using this book. But the enjoyment of music can be enhanced if we understand how music works, and to explain this we need to know something of the technical language of music.

RHYTHM

Rhythm is arguably the most fundamental element of music. When asked to sing a favorite song, most of us will recall the rhythm better than the melody. Similarly, when hearing a piece of music for the first time, we are more likely to be struck by, and remember, a catchy rhythm than a catchy tune. We have a direct, even physical, response to rhythm.

Rhythm, in its broadest definition, is the organization of time in music. It divides up long spans of time into smaller, more easily comprehended units. It gives a shape, or profile, to the melody or tune. Basic to rhythm is the principle of the beat. The **beat** is an even pulse that divides the passing of time into equal segments. It may be strongly felt, as in a waltz or a straight-ahead rock 'n' roll tune, or it may be only dimly heard (because no instrument plays it strongly), as in much of the Impressionistic music of the late nineteenth century (Chapter 16). But whether immediately or distantly heard, almost all music has a beat to it. When we tap our foot to music, we are reacting to such a beat.

The beat in music is most often carried by a unit of measurement called the quarter note (♩), a basic duration in music. Normally, the quarter note will move along roughly at the rate of the average person's heartbeat, sometimes faster, sometimes slower. As you might suspect from its name, the quarter note is shorter in length than the half and the whole note, but longer than the eighth and the sixteenth note. These other note values account for durations that are longer or shorter than the beat. Here are the symbols for the most-used musical notes and an indication of how they relate to one another in length:

EXAMPLE 2–1

note values

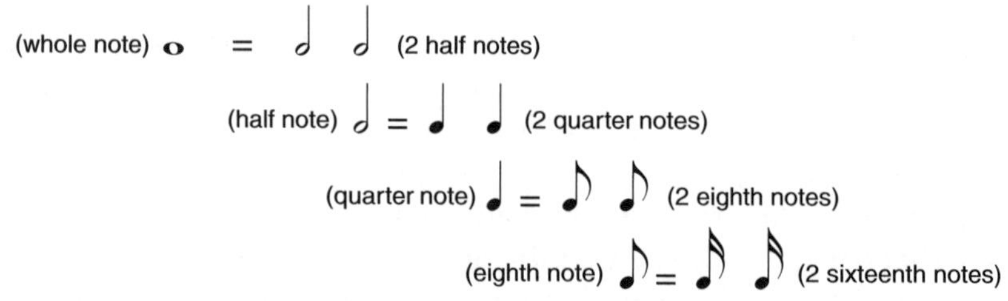

(whole note) 𝅝 = 𝅗𝅥 𝅗𝅥 (2 half notes)

(half note) 𝅗𝅥 = ♩ ♩ (2 quarter notes)

(quarter note) ♩ = ♪ ♪ (2 eighth notes)

(eighth note) ♪ = ♬ ♬ (2 sixteenth notes)

To help the performer keep the beat when playing or singing, the smaller note values, specifically, those with flags on the vertical stem, are beamed, or joined together, in groups of two or four:

FIGURE 2–1
The popular Afro-Cuban band Buena Vista Social Club is especially adept at playing two or more rhythms simultaneously.

EXAMPLE 2–2

 *becomes*

In vocal music, however, the beaming is broken when a syllable of text is placed below a note:

EXAMPLE 2–3

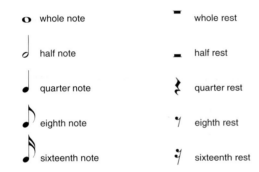

Jin - gle bells, jin - gle bells, jin - gle all the way

In addition to notes that signify the duration of sound, there are other signs, called rests, that indicate silence. For each note there is a corresponding rest of the same value:

EXAMPLE 2–4

o	whole note	—	whole rest
♩	half note	—	half rest
♩	quarter note	𝄽	quarter rest
♪	eighth note	𝄾	eighth rest
♬	sixteenth note	𝄿	sixteenth rest

You will have noticed that, in their basic form, adjacent note values (and rests) in music all have a 2:1 ratio to one another: One half note equals two quarter notes, and so on. But triple relationships can and do exist, and these are created by means of the addition of a dot after a note, which increases the duration of the note to one and one-half its original value:

EXAMPLE 2–5

$$o \cdot \ = \ o \ + \ \text{half}$$
$$\text{half} \cdot \ = \ \text{half} \ + \ \text{quarter}$$
$$\text{quarter} \cdot \ = \ \text{quarter} \ + \ \text{eighth}$$

Let's take a look at how the various note values can reflect the rhythm of an actual piece of music. For this we choose a simple, well-known tune, *Yankee Doodle*. First the text is given to refresh your memory as to how the song goes, next the rhythm of the tune indicated by horizontal lines of different lengths to show how long each pitch lasts, then the rhythm in musical notation, and finally the position of the beat in *Yankee Doodle* as indicated by quarter notes:

FIGURE 2-2

Rhythms of a Russian Dance (1918) by Theo van Doesburg. Rhythm in music is the rational organization of time into longer and shorter durations. The same process can be at work in the visual arts. Here the painter places units of color of different length to form complementary patterns.

EXAMPLE 2–6

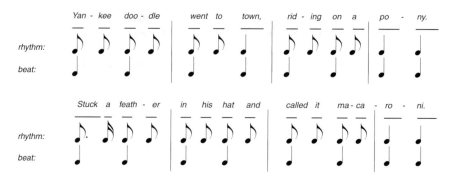

Here's the patriotic song *America* (first known in England and Canada as *God Save the King*—or *Queen*) arranged the same way:

EXAMPLE 2–7

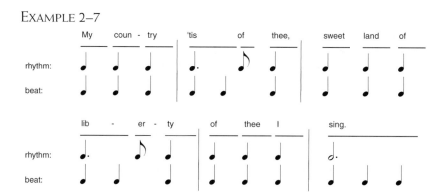

Listening Exercise 2a at the end of the chapter will help you to focus on the many musical rhythms you already have in your ear.

Meter

Notice how in the preceding examples vertical lines divide the music into groups of two beats, in the case of *Yankee Doodle*, and into groups of three beats in *America*. These strokes are called measure lines, or bar lines. A **measure**, or bar, is a group of beats. Usually, there are two or three, sometimes four or more beats per measure. The gathering of beats into regular groups produces **meter**. Instead of having a steady stream of undifferentiated beats, we instinctively stress some more than others in a regular and repeating fashion. If we stress every other beat— ONE two, ONE two, ONE two—we have two beats per measure and therefore duple meter. The stressed beats are called strong beats and the unstressed beats weak beats. Similarly, if we emphasize every third beat—ONE two three, ONE two three, ONE two three—we have three beats per measure and thus triple meter. Triple meter has one strong beat and two weak beats per bar. In addition, there are other meters with four or six beats per measure. Here is a familiar folk song in the more common quadruple meter (four beats per measure):

FIGURE 2–3

Eve Queler is music director and conductor of the Opera Orchestra of New York. Conductors have traditional beating patterns to indicate the meter to the orchestra. The listener can use these same patterns to hear more easily the meter of the music.

Steve J. Sherman/Photofest

EXAMPLE 2–8

And here is an equally well-known tune in sextuple meter:

EXAMPLE 2–9

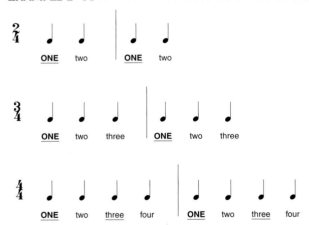

Most music, however, is written in duple ($\frac{2}{4}$), triple ($\frac{3}{4}$), or quadruple ($\frac{4}{4}$) meter.

Meter in music is indicated by a **meter signature** (also called a **time signature**), two numbers, one on top of the other, placed at the beginning of the music to tell the performer how the beats of the music are to be grouped. The top number of the signature indicates how many beats there are per measure; the bottom number tells what note value is the beat. Since, as we have said, the quarter note most often carries the beat, most time signatures have a "4" on the bottom. The three most frequently encountered time signatures are given here:

time signatures

EXAMPLE 2–10

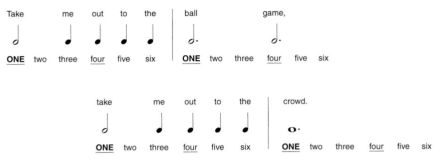

Having a time signature at the beginning of the music may be of great value to the performer, but it doesn't help the listener, unless he or she happens to be following along with the musical notation—following the **score**, as musicians call it. Without a score, the listener must of necessity hear and feel the meter. Most music, as we have said, is written in $\frac{2}{4}$, $\frac{3}{4}$, or $\frac{4}{4}$. Since $\frac{4}{4}$ is in most (but not all) ways merely a multiple or extension of $\frac{2}{4}$, there are really only two meters that the beginning listener should be aware of: duple meter ($\frac{2}{4}$) and triple meter ($\frac{3}{4}$). But how do we hear these and differentiate between them?

duple and triple meters

FIGURE 2–4
Leonard Bernstein (1918–1990), one of the most forceful, and flamboyant, conductors of the twentieth century.

Hearing Meters

One way you can more easily come to hear a given meter is to establish some sort of physical response to the music: Obvious as it seems, start tapping the beat with your foot and moving with the music in a way that groups beats into measures of two or three. Perhaps the most graceful way to move with the music is to adopt the same patterns of motion that conductors use to lead symphony orchestras and other musical ensembles. These are patterns cut in the air with the right hand (a baton is optional!). Here are the patterns that conductors use to show $\frac{2}{4}$ and $\frac{3}{4}$ meter:

EXAMPLE 2–11

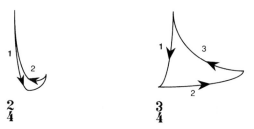

$$\frac{2}{4} \qquad \frac{3}{4}$$

Notice that in both of these patterns, and indeed in all conducting patterns, the first beat is indicated by a downward movement of the hand. This is called the **downbeat**. It is always the first and by far the strongest beat in the measure. In $\frac{2}{4}$ the downbeat is stronger, or more accented, than the **upbeat** (the beat signaled by an upward motion); in $\frac{3}{4}$ it is more accented than either the middle beat (2) or the upbeat (3). When listening to a piece of music, then, tap the beat with your foot, listen for the downbeat, and try to get your con-

feel the downbeat

ducting pattern synchronized with the music. If you hear only one weak beat between each strong beat, the music is in duple meter and you should be conducting in $\frac{2}{4}$ time. If you hear two weak beats between each downbeat, on the other hand, you are listening to a piece in triple meter and should be using the $\frac{3}{4}$ pattern. Try conducting *Yankee Doodle* and *America* in $\frac{2}{4}$ and $\frac{3}{4}$, respectively.

EXAMPLE 2–12

Yan - kee doo - dle	went to town	rid - ing on a	po - ny.
ONE two	**ONE** two	**ONE** two	**ONE** two

My coun- try	'tis of thee,	sweet land of	lib - er- ty	of thee I	sing.
ONE two three	**ONE** two three	**ONE** two three	**ONE** two three	**ONE** two three	**ONE** two three

One final observation about meters and conducting patterns: Almost all music that we hear, and especially dance music, has a clearly identifiable meter and a strong downbeat. But not all music *starts* with the downbeat. Often a piece will begin with an upbeat. An upbeat at the very beginning of a piece is called a pickup.

pickup to the downbeat

The **pickup** is usually only a note or two, but it gives a little momentum or extra push into the first downbeat, as can be seen in the following two patriotic songs.

EXAMPLE 2–13

Oh	beau- ti- ful	for	spa- cious	skies
two	**ONE** two	**ONE** two	**ONE** two	**ONE** two

Oh	say can you	see	by the	dawn's ear - ly	light
three	**ONE** two three	**ONE** two three	**ONE** two three	**ONE** two three	**ONE** two

To sum up: To identify whether the meter of a piece is duple ($\frac{2}{4}$) or triple ($\frac{3}{4}$), try using this simple three-step approach. First, tap your foot or hand with the beat. Second, identify where the downbeat is falling—where do you hear strong beats instead of weak beats? Third and finally, conduct with the music and decide if you hear one or two weak beats between each strong beat. If just one, then the piece is in duple meter; if two, then it is triple meter.

three steps to hearing meters

Turn now to the end of the chapter and complete Listening Exercise 2b. Then go on to Listening Exercise 3, which asks you to identify the meter of several musical works and gives you a chance to practice conducting in $\frac{2}{4}$ and $\frac{3}{4}$ time.

Syncopation

One of the ways to add variety and excitement to music is by the use of syncopation. In most music the **accent**, or musical stress, falls on the beat, with the downbeat getting the greatest accent of all. **Syncopation** places the accent either on a weak beat or between the beats. The note that is syncopated sounds accented because it is played louder or held longer than the surrounding notes. A good example of syncopation is found at the end of the first phrase of Stephen Foster's *Camptown Races*, where the "dah" of "doo-dah" is syncopated.

EXAMPLE 2–14

Syncopation gives an unexpected bounce or lift to the music and is a prominent feature in jazz. Indeed, part of the fun of playing jazz is to obscure the beat by means of syncopation and thereby to tease or tantalize the listener.

Tempo

Meter is the grouping of beats into regularly recurring units. Rhythm is the durational patterns (longs and shorts) superimposed above the meter. Tempo, finally, is the speed at which the beats occur. Obviously, the tempo of the beat can be fast or slow, but it usually falls somewhere in the neighborhood of 60 to 100 beats per minute. Tempo is indicated to the performer by means of tempo markings placed at the beginning of the piece. Because they were first used in Italy in the seventeenth century, at the beginning of the Baroque period in music, tempo markings are most often written in Italian. The following are a few of the most common tempo indications, arranged from slow to fast:

tempo: the speed of the beat

grave (grave)	very slow
largo (broad)	
lento (slow)	slow

tempo markings	*adagio* (slow)
	andante (moving) moderate
	andantino (slightly faster than *andante*)
	moderato (moderate)
	allegretto (moderately fast) fast
	allegro (fast)
	vivace (fast and lively) very fast
	presto (very fast)
	prestissimo (as fast as possible)

Naturally, general terms such as these allow for a good deal of interpretive freedom. Conductors like Leonard Bernstein (1918–1990), Arturo Toscanini (1867–1957), and Seiji Ozawa (b. 1935), for example, have had different notions of just how fast a movement of Beethoven marked *allegro* (fast) should really go. In addition, composers often call for fluctuations in tempo within a piece by placing commands such as *accelerando* (getting faster) and *ritardando* (getting slower) in the score. One particularly colorful term is *rubato* (robbed), meaning that the performer is given license to steal some additional time for the passage of music in question and thus to slow it down. Frequent changes in tempo make it more difficult for the listener to follow the beat, but they add much in the way of expression and feeling to the music.

MELODY

A **melody** is a series of notes arranged in order to form a recognizable unit. The more beautiful the melody, the more we are drawn to the music. When supported by its companions, rhythm and harmony, melody can produce an overwhelming emotional experience. Yet one of the wonders of music is that we are hard pressed to explain in precise terms why this is so. What is it about the shape of a melody, its balance and contour, that makes one so moving and another so very forgettable? The pursuit of this question, however, would carry us off into the realm of aesthetic theory. Instead, let us simply describe how melodies are put together so that we can more readily grasp them.

Pitch

Just as a grammatical sentence is made up of building blocks we call words, so a melody is composed of individual units called pitches. **Pitch** is the relative position, high or low, of a musical sound. When sound comes in regular vibrations, it produces a musical **tone**. If it occurs in irregular vibrations, then it is merely noise of the sort generated by a crashing plate or a barking dog. Musical tones are usually produced when a string or a column of air is set in motion on a musical instrument, and this motion, in turn, creates vibrating airwaves that reach the ear at equal time intervals. The faster a string vibrates, for example, the higher the pitch. Normally, humans will hear sounds produced in a range between a low of about 20 vibrations (or cycles) per second to a high of about 16,000. (Some animals can hear sounds twice this high.) In theory, pitch can occur anywhere on this wide band of sound—think of a fire siren starting low, rising, and then falling back down. But when making music, we take this broad spectrum of sound and divide it into individual steps or degrees of pitch. We then string these units together in time to produce a melody.

faster vibrations produce a higher pitch

EXAMPLE 2–15

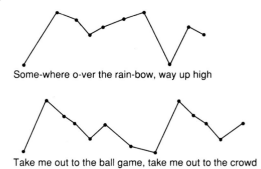

Some-where o-ver the rain-bow, way up high

Take me out to the ball game, take me out to the crowd

The Octave

One of the remarkable qualities of pitch is that, when singing or playing a succession of tones up or down, a performer often comes to a tone that sounds like an exact duplication of an earlier pitch, but at a higher or lower level. For a reason that will become clear shortly, the duplicating pitch is called an **octave**. Pitches an octave apart sound similar because the frequency of vibration of the higher pitch, or note, is precisely twice that of the lower. Middle C on the piano, for example, vibrates at 256 cycles per second, while the C an octave above does so at 512 cycles. When men and women sing a song or hymn together without harmony, they invariably sing at the octave; it sounds as if they are all singing the same notes, but, in fact, the men are an octave below the women. All musical cultures, Western and non-Western, make use of the principle of octave duplication in their melodies. But not all cultures agree as to how the octave should be divided, that is, how many notes there should be within an octave. In many traditional Chinese melodies, the octave is divided into five separate pitches. Some Arabic and Turkish melodies, however, make use of fourteen. Judging from our earliest written music, which dates back more than a thousand years, we in the West have always preferred melodies that were built on seven pitches within the octave. The eighth pitch duplicated, or doubled, the sound of the first, and thus it was called the octave.

octave duplications used in all musical cultures

dividing the octave

At first, the seven notes within the octave corresponded to the white keys of the keyboard. Eventually, five additional notes were inserted within the span of the octave, and these correspond to the black keys.

EXAMPLE 2–16

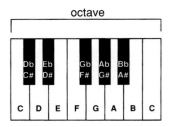

To get the sound of the octave in your ear, try singing *Over the Rainbow* and *Take Me Out to the Ball Game*. Both begin with a leap up an octave no matter on what pitch you choose to start.

Notating Melodies

The type of notation used for the two tunes in Ex. 2–15 is useful if you merely need to be reminded of how a melody goes, but it is not precise enough to allow a singer to produce the tune if he or she didn't know it already. When the melody goes up, how *far* up does it go? More precision for musical notation began to appear in the West as early as the eleventh century, when notes came to be situated on lines and spaces so that the exact distance between pitches could be judged immediately. This gridwork of lines and spaces came to be called a **staff**. The higher on the staff the note is placed, the higher the pitch.

EXAMPLE 2–17

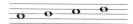

treble and bass clefs

The staff is always provided with a **clef sign** to indicate the range of pitch in which the melody is to be played or sung. One clef, called the **treble clef,** designates the upper range and is appropriate for high instruments like the trumpet and the violin, and a woman's voice. A second clef, called the **bass clef,** covers the lower range and is used for lower instruments like the trombone and the cello, and a man's voice.

EXAMPLE 2–18

For a single vocal part or a single instrument, a melody could easily be placed on either one of these two clefs. But for two-hand keyboard music with greater range, both clefs are used, one on top of the other. The performer looks at this combination of clefs, called the **great staff**, and relates the notes to the keys beneath the fingers. The space between the two clefs is filled in by a short, temporary line called a ledger line. On the keyboard it indicates middle C (the middle-most C key on the piano).

EXAMPLE 2–19

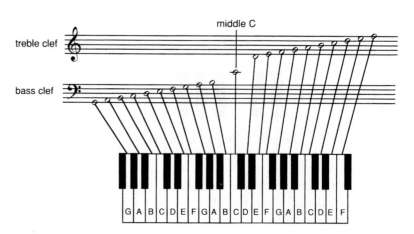

Each musical pitch can be referred to by a letter name, like C, as well as represented by a note placed on the great staff. Only seven letter names (A, B, C, D, E, F, and G) are used because, as we have said, melodies were originally made up of only seven pitches within each octave—corresponding to the seven white notes of the keyboard. When the pitch is duplicated at the octave, the letter name repeats (see Ex. 2–19). But gradually, the spaces between the white keys were divided and additional (black) keys inserted. This increased the number of pitches within the octave from seven to twelve. Since they were not originally part of the staff, the five additional pitches were not represented by a line or space, nor were they given a separate letter name. Instead, they came to be indicated by a symbol, either a sharp or a flat, applied to one of the existing notes. A **sharp** (♯) raises the note to the key immediately above, usually a black one, whereas a **flat** (♭) lowers it to the next key below, again usually a black one. A **natural** (♮), on the other hand, cancels either of the two previous signs. Here, as an example of musical notation on the great staff, is a well-known melody as it might be notated for a chorus of male and female voices, the women an octave higher than the men. To keep things simple, the melody is notated in equal whole notes (without rhythm).

names of the notes

sharps and flats

EXAMPLE 2–20

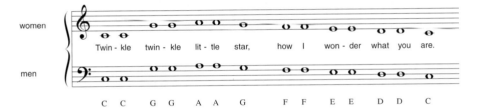

Tonality, Keys, and Scales

Melodies have a central pitch, called the **tonic**, around which they gravitate and on which they usually end. The organization of music around this central tone, the tonic, is called **tonality**. In the case of *Twinkle, Twinkle*, C is the tonic—the tune not only ends on C but happens to begin on C as well. A melody may, in fact, have C or D or F♯, or any other of the twelve notes within the octave, as the tonic. In addition, we say that *Twinkle, Twinkle* is written in the tonality, or key, of C major, meaning that it has the tonic C, but also that it makes use of a C major scale. A **key**, then, is a tonal center built on a tonic note and making use of a scale.

But what is a scale? A **scale** is an arrangement of pitches that ascends and descends in a fixed and unvarying pattern. Almost all Western melodies are written in one of two types of scales—one called major, the other called minor. To understand the difference between the major and minor scale, it's necessary to look at a keyboard for a moment (see Ex. 2–19). Notice that there are no black keys between B and C and between E and F. All the adjacent white notes of the keyboard are not the same distance apart. The difference, or distance, in sound between B and C is only half of that between C and D. B to C is the interval of a half step, while C to D is the interval of a whole step. The major and minor scales, in turn, are built on two distinctly different patterns of whole and half steps, each starting on a tonic note. The **major scale** has a succession of whole and half steps that proceeds 1–1–½–1–1–1–½. The **minor scale** goes

FIGURE 2–5

G Clef (1935) by Josef Albers (1888–1976).

1–½–1–1–½–1–1. Every scale uses only seven of the available twelve pitches within each octave; and once the octave is reached, the pattern can start over again. A major or minor scale may begin on any of the twelve notes within the octave, and thus there are twelve major and twelve minor scales and keys. Here are the notes of the major and minor scales as they start on C and then on A. Next time you pass by a piano, try playing these to get the sound of major and minor in your ear.

EXAMPLE 2–21

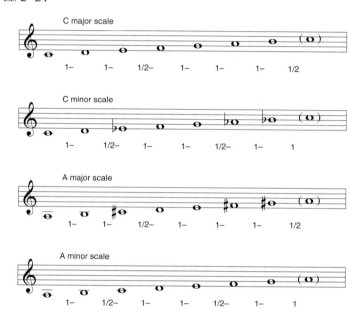

A major scale built on C uses only the white notes of the keyboard, as does a minor scale constructed on A. When begun on a note other than C (for the major scale) or A (for the minor scale), however, sharps and flats are needed so that the pattern of whole and half steps does not vary. For example, a major scale may begin on A and ascend up the octave; but to keep the major scale pattern intact, the notes C, F, and G must be sharped (see Ex. 2–21). Similarly, starting the minor scale pattern on C will require that E be lowered to E♭, A to A♭, and B to B♭ (see Ex. 2–21).

Composing a piece in A major would require writing out many sharps, just as one in C minor would require writing many flats. To avoid this labor, musicians have developed the custom of "preplacing" the sharps or flats at the beginning of the staff. These sharps or flats are then active throughout the entire piece. Preplaced sharps or flats are called a **key signature**.

major and minor scales

FIGURE 2–6

Contrasting Sounds (1924) by Wassily Kandinsky (1866–1944).

Musée Nationale de l'Arte Moderne, Paris

EXAMPLE 2–22

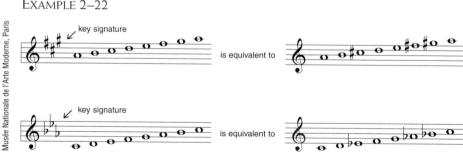

Key signatures indicate to the performer the key in which a piece is written; that is, they show what scale is about to be employed and what the tonic note is.

Modulation **Modulation** is the change from one key to another. Most short pieces—folk songs, hymns, and the like—don't modulate; they stay in one key. But longer pieces need to modulate or the listener is soon bored. Modulation gives a dynamic sense of movement to music. As the composer Arnold Schoenberg (1874–1951) said, "Modulation is like a change of scenery." The beginning listener will find modulations difficult to hear. You may not recognize precisely when they occur, but you will sense, however subconsciously, that the music is changing from one key to another.

changing keys

Hearing Major and Minor Scales are like colors on an artist's palette. A composer will choose what he or she believes is the right scale to achieve the desired musical mood or feeling for the composition. The differences in mood or color within each of the two principal melodic types, major and minor, are small and are not commonly agreed on even by professional musicians. Some say D major is a bright key, F major comfortable and restful, Db major dark and rich. But what may seem rich to one listener may sound bright to the next. Taste in music, as in the other arts, is a very personal matter.

One thing we can all agree on, however, is that a melody in a major key sounds decidedly different from one in a minor. Major melodies seem bright, cheery, optimistic, while minor ones are dark, somber, even sinister. Try singing the beginning of the following familiar major and minor songs to establish firmly in your mind's ear the difference between major and minor:

major and minor have different moods

EXAMPLE 2–23

Music theorists since the sixteenth century have noticed the distinctly different moods associated with major and minor. Positive emotions (joy, confidence, triumph, tranquility, love, etc.) have traditionally been expressed in major, while negative feelings (fear, anxiety, sorrow, despair, etc.) have usually been played out in minor. Major and minor scales are constructed according to two distinctly different patterns of whole and half steps (see Ex. 2–21), and this is why they affect us in different ways. The change from a major key to a minor one with the same tonic (C major to C minor, for example), or from minor to major (F minor to F major, for example) is called a change of **mode**. Lest there be any doubt that a change in mode can change how you feel about a melody, listen to the following familiar tunes (your instructor will play them for you). The mode in each has been changed from major to minor by inserting a flat into the scale near the tonic note (C). Notice here how all the happiness, joy, and sunshine have disappeared from these formerly major tunes. Such shifts create the subtle emotional language of music.

changing the mode

EXAMPLE 2–24

Joy to the world, the Lord is come

You are my sun - shine, my on - ly sun - shine

Hap- py birth - day to you

Now turn to Listening Exercise 4, which asks you to distinguish between melodies in the major and minor mode.

Diatonic Versus Chromatic Most of the melodies we know are what we call **diatonic** melodies, meaning that they are written in either the major or the minor scale and use only the seven notes of each, the so-called diatonic notes. A scale using all twelve notes within the octave, however, is called a **chromatic** scale. In a chromatic scale all twelve pitches are a half step apart.

chromatic scale

EXAMPLE 2–25

Chromatic scale

Chromatic (from the Greek *chroma*, "color") is a good word for this scale because the additional five pitches do indeed add color and richness to a melody. Here is a popular tune that begins by using a chromatic scale.

EXAMPLE 2–26

I'm dream - ing of a white Christ - mas

In general, chromatic melodies sound more intense, tight, and angular than diatonic ones.

Melodic Structure

Difficult as it is to say why some melodies are so pleasing and others so dull, all good melodies seem to have a few essential qualities: a strong tonic note, forward motion, a goal or climax, and ultimately a feeling of repose or completion. These qualities are all found in abundance in the *Ode to Joy* by Ludwig van Beethoven (1770–1827). Beethoven originally composed this music for the last movement of his Symphony No. 9 (1824), but in more recent times the melody has been used as a Christmas carol, a hymn for the United Nations, a movie score (*Die Hard*), and as background music in countless TV commercials. Here the melody is notated in the bass clef in D major, the key in which Beethoven composed it.

EXAMPLE 2–27

Beethoven's Ode to Joy

We can make a few general observations about Beethoven's melody: First, notice that it moves mainly by **step,** from one letter name of the scale to the next (D to E, for example), and rarely moves by **leap,** a jump of one or more letter names (D to F♯, or D to G, for example). Melodies that move predominantly by step are called **conjunct** melodies, while those that move mainly by leap are called **disjunct** ones. *Ode to Joy* may be the most conjunct melody ever written! The only leaps of any importance are the two at the end of phrase **c** (measure 12). Clearly, Beethoven wanted to keep this melody simple so that all the world could sing it.

a simple melody for all

Next, notice that there are, in fact, four melodic phrases here. A **phrase** in music functions much like a dependent phrase or clause within a grammatical sentence. It constitutes a dependent idea within a melody. Here four four-measure phrases form a complete sixteen-bar melody. Let's concentrate for a moment on the first two phrases. The opening phrase (**a**) begins on the third step of the D major scale, F♯, and ends on the second step, E. If you try to sing, hum, or whistle this first phrase, you will notice that when you get to the end ("Elysium"), the music doesn't sound complete or finished—it wants to go on. By the end of the second phrase (**b**), however, you arrive on the

FIGURE 2-7
A portrait of Ludwig van Beethoven painted in 1818–1819 by Ferdinand Schimon (1797–1852).

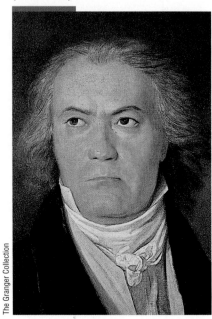

tonic note ("welcome") and now do have a feeling of arrival and completion. Many melodies begin this way: The initial phrase opens the melody and ends on some note *other* than the tonic; the second phrase answers this idea and returns the melody to the tonic. Two phrases that work in tandem this way are called **antecedent** and **consequent** phrases. Both end with a cadence. A **cadence** is the concluding part of a musical phrase. The cadence at the end of Beethoven's antecedent phrase does not sound final, and therefore is called a **half cadence**; the one at the end of his consequent phrase, because it ends on the tonic, does sound complete and is called a **full cadence**. A half cadence functions like a comma, a full cadence like a period.

Ode to Joy then pushes off in a new direction (**c**). The music gains momentum by means of a repeating rhythm in measures 10–11 and reaches a musical climax in measure 12 with the two leaps. The fourth and final phrase is an almost exact repeat of the second phrase (**b**), with the exception of one interesting detail (see * in Ex. 2–27). Beethoven brings the return of this phrase in one beat early—a bit of rhythmic syncopation*—thereby giving an unexpected lift to the melody.

The melodic structure of Beethoven's *Ode to Joy*—balanced groups of four-bar phrases arranged antecedent–consequent–extension–consequent—is found frequently in music, from the works of Haydn, Mozart, and Beethoven in the eighteenth and early nineteenth centuries to popular songs of nineteenth- and twentieth-century America. You may have been singing antecedent–consequent phrases and using full and half cadences all your life and not been aware of it. To prove the point, sing the following two well-known tunes:

The Saints Go Marching In (traditional)
"Oh when the saints, go marching in, oh when the saints go marching in"   (half cadence)
(antecedent phrase)
"Oh how I want to be in that number, when the saints go marching in."   (full cadence)
(consequent phrase)

Oh Suzanna (Stephen Foster)
"Oh I come from Alabama with my banjo on my knee"   (half cadence)
(antecedent phrase)
"I'm bound for Louisiana my true love for to see."   (full cadence)
(consequent phrase)

Now do Listening Exercise 5, which invites you to become more familiar with the melodic structure of Beethoven's famous *Ode to Joy*.

Hearing Melodies

Hearing melodies may be the single most important part of listening to music. Melodies contain the main musical ideas the composer wishes to communicate. Once a composer has hit on a good melody, he or she is likely to repeat or elaborate on it several times in the course of a composition. Beethoven, for example, brings back his *Ode to Joy* in various guises at least a half-dozen times in his Symphony No. 9. Indeed, by reintroducing a melody at certain important moments in a work, the composer reveals the form, or structure, of the musical creation. It is important, therefore, that the listener be able to seize on the melody, to remember it over a span of time, and to recognize its return, as if welcoming an old friend.

How do we improve our ability to hear melodies and recognize their return? The best way is perhaps not to try to take in an entire melody, or even a full phrase, at once. A melody can move by rapidly, and the beginning listener can expect to absorb only three to four seconds of it at a time. Instead of trying to grasp everything at once, grab hold of some small part of the melody. Find a distinctive rhythmic figure of three or four notes, or a salient melodic motive. A **motive** in music is a short, distinctive melodic figure that stands by itself. Concentrate on this one figure and lock it into your mind by asking: What is it doing? Does it drop down rapidly? If so, by a lot or just a little? Does it move up by steps? Does it repeat a note in some distinctive way? Does it end on the same pitch as it began? To do this it is helpful to visualize, even draw a picture of (see Ex. 2–15), the melodic motive that you seize on.

melodic motives

HARMONY

Melody provides a lyrical voice for music, rhythm gives vitality and definition to that voice, while harmony adds depth and richness to it, just as the dimension of depth in painting adds a rich backdrop to that art. Although melody can and sometimes does stand by itself, most often it is closely bound to, and, indeed, grows out of, the harmony. The two work gracefully in tandem, the harmony supporting and amplifying the melody. Sometimes, however, discord arises—as when a folksinger strumming a guitar fails to change the chord to make it agree with the melody—and the result can be startling. The melody and harmony now clash: They are out of harmony. The double sense of this last statement shows that the term **harmony** has several meanings. Broadly speaking, harmony means the peaceful cohabitation of diverse elements; the ancient Greeks, for example, spoke of the unheard harmony of the planets and of the soul. When applied specifically to music, harmony is said to be the sounds that provide a support and enrichment—an accompaniment—for melody. Finally, we often speak of harmony as if it was a specific musical event, as when we say the harmony changes, meaning that one chord in the accompaniment changes to another. Thus, we say that the cowboy ballad *The Streets of Laredo* is a harmonious piece, harmonized in the key of F major, and that the harmony changes fifteen times:

three meanings of harmony

EXAMPLE 2–28

Building Harmony

Chords are the building blocks of harmony. A **chord** is simply a group of two or more pitches that sound at the same time. When we learn to play guitar or jazz piano, we first learn mainly how to construct chords. The basic chord in music is the **triad**, so called because it consists of three pitches arranged in a very specific way. Here is a C major triad:

EXAMPLE 2–29

building triads

Note that it comprises the first, third, and fifth notes of the C major scale. The distance between each of these notes is called an **interval**. C to E, spanning three letter names (C,D,E) is the interval of a third. E to G, again spanning three letter names (E,F,G) is another third. Triads always consist of two intervals of a third placed one on top of the other. Here are triads built on every note of the C major scale:

EXAMPLE 2–30

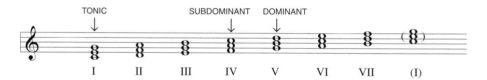

These triads provide all the basic chords necessary to harmonize a melody in C major.

Notice that each of the chords is given a Roman numeral, indicating on which note of the scale the triad is built, and that the triads built on I, IV, and V are called the tonic, subdominant, and dominant chords. We have already met the tonic note in our discussion of melody—it is the pitch around which a tune gravitates and on which it ends. Similarly, the tonic chord, or triad, is the "home" chord of the harmony. It is the most stable and the one toward which the other chords move. The **dominant** triad, always built on the fifth note of the scale, is next in importance. Note in *The Streets of Laredo* how most of the melody is harmonized simply by changing back and forth between tonic and dominant triads. Dominant triads are especially likely to move to tonic triads at the ends of musical phrases, where such a movement (V–I) helps create the strong effect of a full cadence*. The **subdominant** triad is built on the note below the dominant, and it frequently moves to the dominant, which, in turn, moves to the tonic (IV–V–I). A movement of chords in a purposeful fashion like this is called a **chord progression**. The separate chords in a chord progression pull one to the next, all gravitating toward the powerful tonic. The end of *The Streets of Laredo* is marked by a subdominant–dominant–tonic chord progression (IV–V–I), one that is heard frequently in music and, perhaps for that reason, gives a solid, reliable feeling to the harmony.

Why is it necessary for chords to change? The answer lies in the fact that the pitches of a melody continually change, sometimes moving through all the notes of the scale. But a single triadic chord can only be harmonious, or

FIGURE 2–8

The Harlem Boys' Choir. Some voices (usually the highest) sing the melody while others supply the harmony.

© AFP/CORBIS

consonant, with three notes of the scale. Chords must change to keep the harmony consonant with the melody. If they don't, dissonance results.

Finally, the notes of a triad need not always enter together but can be spaced out over time. Such a broken, or staggered, triad is called an **arpeggio.** Arpeggios can appear either as part of the melody or in the harmony that supports a melody. An arpeggio used in an accompaniment usually gives the listener the sense that the harmony has more substance than it really does. In Ex. 2–31, the beginning of *The Streets of Laredo* is harmonized with the triads spaced out as arpeggios (beneath the brackets). The supporting triads are the same as in Ex. 2–28, but now the accompaniment seems more active because one note of the triad is sounding on every beat:

EXAMPLE 2–31

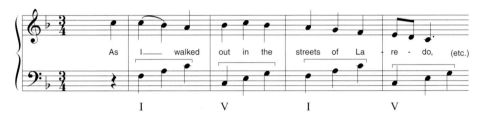

As I walked out in the streets of La - re - do, (etc.)

I   V   I   V

Consonance and Dissonance

You have undoubtedly noticed, when pressing the keys of the piano at one time or another, that some combinations of keys produce a harsh, jarring sound, while others are pleasing and harmonious. The former chords are characterized by **dissonance** (pitches sounding disagreeable and unstable) and the latter by **consonance** (pitches sounding agreeable and stable). Generally speaking, chords that contain pitches that are very close together, just a half or a whole step apart, sound dissonant. On the other hand, chords that involve a third, a somewhat larger interval, are usually consonant. Each of the triads built on the notes of the major scale (see Ex. 2–30), for example, contains two intervals of a third and therefore is consonant. Dissonant chords add a feeling of tension and anxiety to music; consonant ones produce a sense of rest and stability. Composers have traditionally used dissonant chords sparingly, like a hot spice. They prepare them carefully in a bed of consonance and then immediately resolve them—move them—back to a consonance. Our musical psyche demands this constant ebb and flow between the tension of dissonance and the stability of consonance.

Hearing the Harmony Change

Chords move from consonance to consonance, from consonance to dissonance, from dissonance to consonance, and sometimes, in modern music, from dissonance to dissonance. The rate of change may be rapid or slow, regular or irregular. In *The Streets of Laredo* (Ex. 2–28), the rate of harmonic change is moderately fast and regular. There are three beats for each chord and then a new chord appears, without exception, at the beginning of each group of three (each new measure).

FIGURE 2–9

Rouen Cathedral: Harmony in Blue and Gold. In his many paintings of Rouen Cathedral, Claude Monet (1840–1926) emphasized the harmonious relationships of different colors seen in changing light. It was during the Impressionist period (see Chapter 16) that painters began to borrow musical terms such as "harmony" and "symphony" to characterize their works.

FIGURE 2–10

Henri Matisse, *Violinist at the Window* (1918). In his writings on art, Matisse often spoke of the "consonance and dissonance of color."

Peter Willi/Bridgeman Art Library, London/NY

Composers can alter the rate at which new chords appear in order to achieve particular effects. A rapid rate of change communicates to the listener a feeling of movement and perhaps tension. A deceleration in the speed with which chords change from one to the next can convey a sense of slowing down and relaxation, even though the tempo of the piece (the real speed at which it is moving) remains the same. Handel (1685–1759) and Beethoven (1770–1827) were especially fond of slowing down the rate of harmonic change toward the end of a piece in order to give it a feeling of conclusion, to tell the listener that the piece, in fact, is at an end.

The first step to listening to harmony is to focus your attention on the bass, separating it from the higher melody line. Chords are often built upon the bass note, and a change in the bass from one pitch to another may signal a change in chord. Concentrating on the bass at first will not be easy. Most of us have always thought that listening to music is listening to melody. Certainly, hearing melody is crucial. But the bass is next in importance, and it rules supreme in a sort of subterranean world. It carries the chords and determines where the harmony is going, more so than the higher melody. Baroque music (1600–1750) usually has a clear, driving bass line, and hard rock music perhaps even more so. Next time you listen to a piece of rock, follow the bass guitar line instead of the melody and lyrics. See if you don't begin to sense when the chords are changing and when you have reached a chord that feels like the home key (the tonic triad). Listening Exercises 6 and 7 help you to focus on the bass and begin to recognize when the harmony changes from one chord to the next.

Listening Exercises

2a

Identification of Rhythm

In this exercise you are asked to recall and listen to rhythms that are already in your musical memory. Following are the opening text and rhythm of several well-known songs. Place the correct note values above the unnotated portion of the text in order to complete the rhythm for the entire phrase. For example:

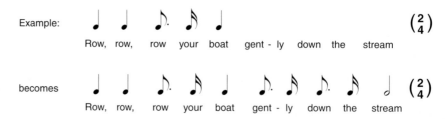

Example:

Row, row,   row your boat   gent - ly down the   stream $\binom{2}{4}$

becomes:

Row, row,   row your boat   gent - ly down the   stream $\binom{2}{4}$

(If you are unfamiliar with one or more of these tunes, feel free to substitute your own. Simply write out the text and then try to indicate the musical rhythm above it by writing in the note values.)

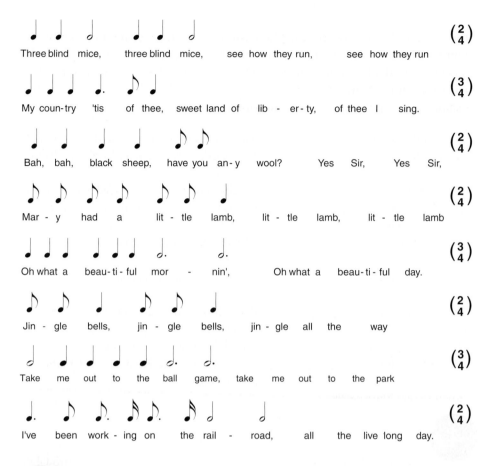

♩ ♩ ♩   ♩ ♩ ♩   (2/4)

Three blind mice,   three blind mice,   see how they run,   see how they run

♩ ♩ ♩ ♩. ♪ ♩   (3/4)

My coun-try 'tis   of thee,   sweet land of   lib - er-ty,   of thee I   sing.

♩ ♩ ♩ ♩ ♪ ♪   (2/4)

Bah, bah,   black sheep,   have you an-y   wool?   Yes Sir,   Yes Sir,

♪ ♪ ♪ ♪ ♪ ♪ ♩   (2/4)

Mar - y   had   a   lit - tle   lamb,   lit - tle   lamb,   lit - tle   lamb

♩ ♩ ♩ ♩ ♩ ♩ ♩. ♩.   (3/4)

Oh what a   beau-ti-ful mor - nin',   Oh what a   beau-ti-ful   day.

♪ ♪ ♩ ♪ ♪ ♩   (2/4)

Jin - gle   bells,   jin - gle   bells,   jin - gle all   the   way

♩ ♩ ♩ ♩ ♩ ♩. ♩.   (3/4)

Take   me   out   to   the   ball   game,   take   me   out   to   the   park

♩. ♪ ♪. ♪ ♪. ♪ ♩ ♩   (2/4)

I've   been work - ing on   the rail - road,   all   the live long   day.

2b

Now that you have read about meters and time signatures (pages 16–18), complete this exercise by inserting the bar lines and beats (1 2 or 1 2 3) for each of the preceding examples. The meter for each example is either $\frac{2}{4}$ or $\frac{3}{4}$, and each begins with a downbeat, not a pickup. For example:

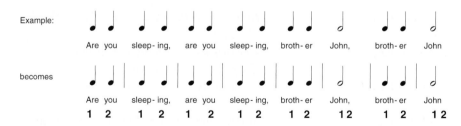

Example:

♩ ♩ ♩ ♩ ♩ ♩ ♩ ♩ ♩ ♩ ♩   ♩ ♩ ♩

Are you   sleep- ing,   are you   sleep- ing,   broth- er   John,   broth- er   John

becomes

♩ ♩ | ♩ ♩ | ♩ ♩ | ♩ ♩ | ♩ ♩ | ♩ | ♩ ♩ | ♩

Are you   sleep- ing,   are you   sleep- ing,   broth- er   John,   broth- er   John
1 2   **1 2**   **1 2**   **1 2**   **1 2**   **1 2**   **1 2**   **1 2**

3

Hearing Meters   Intro CD/5

On your Introduction to Listening CD, track 5, you have ten short musical excerpts, each played once. (You can replay each many times in rapid succession using the "reverse" control on your CD machine.) Identify the meter of each excerpt. To do this, you should listen for the beat, count 1–2 or 1–2–3, and get your conductor's beat pattern in synchrony with the music (downbeat of the hand with the downbeat of the music). If you have done it correctly, the completion of each full conductor's pattern will equal one measure. All the pieces are in duple ($\frac{2}{4}$) or triple ($\frac{3}{4}$) meter. Most begin with a downbeat, some with a pickup.[†] Write "duple" or "triple" in the following blanks. There are five examples in duple meter and five in triple.

1. (0:00) Meter _____ Mouret, *Rondeau* from *Suite de symphonies*[†]
2. (0:28) Meter _____ Musorgsky, *Pictures at an Exhibition, Polish Ox-Cart*
3. (0:55) Meter _____ Beethoven, *Variations on God Save the King*
4. (1:08) Meter _____ Handel, Hornpipe from *Water Music*
5. (1:51) Meter _____ Brahms, *Wiegenlied (Lullaby)*[†]
6. (2:15) Meter _____ Mozart, Symphony No. 40, 1st movement[†]
7. (2:35) Meter _____ Mozart, *A Little Night Music*, 3rd movement[†]
8. (3:00) Meter _____ Bach, Brandenburg Concerto No. 5, 1st movement
9. (3:24) Meter _____ Handel, Minuet from *Water Music*
10. (3:55) Meter _____ Clara Schumann, Romance for Piano and Violin

[†]Excerpt begins with a pickup.

Hearing Major and Minor   Intro CD/6

On your Introduction to Listening CD, track 6, you will find ten musical excerpts that will help you begin to differentiate a piece in a major key from one in a minor key. For most listeners, pieces in major are bright, cheerful, sometimes bland, whereas those in minor tend to be darker, more somber, sometimes exotic, even oriental, in sound. In the blanks below indicate whether each piece is in major or minor. Five are in major and five in minor.

1. (0:00) Key _____ Musorgsky, *Pictures at an Exhibition, Polish Ox-Cart*
2. (0:26) Key _____ Musorgsky, *Pictures at an Exhibition, Goldenberg and Schmuyle*
3. (1:05) Key _____ Musorgsky, *Pictures at an Exhibition, The Great Gate of Kiev*
4. (1:34) Key _____ Tchaikovsky, *Dance of the Reed Pipes* from *The Nutcracker*
5. (2:07) Key _____ Mouret, *Rondeau* from *Suite de symphonies*
6. (2:36) Key _____ Robert Schumann, *Scenes from Childhood, Of Foreign Lands and People*
7. (2:54) Key _____ Mozart, Overture to *Don Giovanni*
8. (3:39) Key _____ Handel, Minuet from *Water Music*
9. (4:10) Key _____ Vivaldi, Violin Concerto, "The Spring," 1st movement
10. (4:45) Key _____ Vivaldi, Violin Concerto, "The Spring," 1st movement

5

Hearing Melodic Structure
Ludwig van Beethoven, *Ode to Joy* from Symphony No. 9 (1824)

On your Introduction to Listening CD, track 7, you have an excerpt from the last movement of Beethoven's Symphony No. 9, in which his famous *Ode to Joy* can be heard. You are probably familiar with the tune already, but look at it again as it is given on page 27. Try to get the antecedent (**a**), consequent (**b**), and extension (**c**) phrases firmly in your ear. Now listen to the music on your CD. The melody is actually heard four times, first played softly by the low string instruments, then more loudly by the higher strings, then louder still by yet higher strings, and finally loudest of all by the trumpets and full orchestra.

Your task is to fill in the missing times in the listening chart below. Indicate the minute and second when each phrase is heard—by writing 1:23, for example. Notice that Beethoven actually repeats the extension (**c**) and consequent (**b**) phrases at the end of each of the four presentations of the melody. Many of the times of entry have been filled in to get you off to a solid start and keep you on track.

After you have filled in the blanks, go back and treat yourself to one final hearing in which you listen, unencumbered, to the growing power of Beethoven's melody.

Playing Number:	1	2	3	4
	Low strings (double basses)	Higher strings (2nd violins)	Higher strings (1st violins)	Trumpets with full orchestra
Antecedent	**a** 0:00	**a** 0:49	**a** 1:40	**a** 2:30
Consequent	**b** 0:09	**b** 0:58	3. **b** _____	7. **b** _____
Extension	**c** 0:17	**c** 1:07	4. **c** _____	8. **c** _____
Consequent	**b** 0:25	1. **b** _____	5. **b** _____	9. **b** _____
	(repeat)	(repeat)	(repeat)	(repeat)
Extension	**c** 0:33	**c** 1:23	**c** 2:13	**c** 3:03
Consequent	**b** 0:42	2. **b** _____	6. **b** _____	10. **b** _____

Hearing the Bass Line and the Harmony   Intro CD/8
Barbara Strozzi, *Voglio morire* (*I want to die*) (1651)
(for more on Barbara Strozzi and this aria, see page 112)

When we listen to music, most of us naturally concentrate on the highest-sounding part—that is usually where we find the melody or the tune. To hear harmony, however, we need to focus on the lowest-sounding line, the bass. The following example is drawn from an aria of Barbara Strozzi (1619–1677), a singer and composer living in Venice during the Baroque period (1600–1750). The aria is written for female voice, which sings the melody, and a low string instrument (an early cello), which plays the bass. Two other instruments (harpsichord and guitar) fill out the harmony by building chords upon the bass line. The bass is easy to hear because it constantly repeats. Focus now on the bass and answer the following questions:

1. The bass pattern
   a. descends by step   b. ascends by step
2. The bass pattern takes about four seconds to play. How many notes are there in the pattern?
   a. two notes   b. four notes   c. six notes
3. How many chords are there in the pattern? (same number as in question 1)
   a. two   b. four   c. six
4. At the beginning of the piece (between 0:00 and 0:18), the bass can be heard alone before the voice enters. How many complete presentations of the pattern occur before the voice enters?
   a. three presentations   b. five presentations   c. seven presentations
5. Now the voice enters and the pattern continues. Between 0:19 and 0:35, how many times is the pattern heard?
   a. three times   b. five times   c. seven times
6. Between 0:36 and 0:43 the bass pattern suddenly changes—a note is added to the bass pattern. Now how many notes are in the pattern?
   a. three notes   b. five notes   c. seven notes

STOP: Go back to the beginning and begin to listen again, now focusing on the length of time each bass note (and each chord) is held. Each bass note and each chord lasts for one measure or bar. The bass (cello) is playing on the downbeat of each new measure. The tempo (rate of the beat) is rather fast.

7. What is the meter of the piece?
   a. duple   b. triple
8. What is the rate of harmonic change? (If the notes of the bass have the same duration, then the harmony is changing at a regular rate; if they do not, then the harmony is changing at an irregular rate.)
   a. regular   b. irregular
   Continue on now with the rest of the aria.
9. From 0:44 to the end does the bass pattern ever change?
   a. yes   b. no
10. A melody, rhythm, or harmony that repeats over and over is called
    a. a crescendo   b. a pizzicato   c. an ostinato   d. a tempo

Hearing Chord Changes in the Harmony   Intro CD/9
Listening to Music Blues

For this listening exercise we have created a blues composition in which the chord changes are rather easy to hear. In our performance the left hand of the electric keyboard player holds one chord until it is time to move on to the next. Each time he stops holding and moves elsewhere, we have a new chord. Below, you are asked to fill in a time log for the chord changes in this repeating blues harmony. At numbers 1–9, record the minute and second that a new chord appears (write 1:10, for example). Several of the correct times are already filled in to make your task easier.

There are several traditional blues harmonies. The one employed here is an old standard that uses the repeating chord progression tonic (I), subdominant (IV), tonic (I), dominant (V), subdominant (IV), tonic (I) to carry the blues tune. There are three statements here of this blues chord progression, starting at 0:00, 0:25, and 0:50. The blues and its history are discussed in Chapter 18, but for now let's just concentrate on the harmony.

Statement one:

0:00	1. ____	2. ____	0:17	3. ____	0:22
I	IV	I	V	IV	I

Statement two:

0:25	4. ____	5. ____	0:42	6. ____	0:47
I	IV	I	V	IV	I

Statement three:

0:50	7. ____	8. ____	9. ____	1:08	1:11
I	IV	I	V	IV	I

Finally, is the rate of harmonic change here regular or irregular?
   a. regular   b. irregular

Key Words

arpeggio (31)	harmony (29)	octave (21)
bass clef (22)	key (23)	pickup (18)
beat (14)	key signature (24)	rhythm (14)
cadence (28)	major scale (23)	subdominant chord (30)
chord (30)	measure (16)	syncopation (19)
chord progression (30)	melody (20)	time signature (17)
chromatic (26)	meter (16)	tonality (23)
diatonic (26)	minor scale (23)	tonic (23)
dominant chord (30)	mode (26)	treble clef (22)
downbeat (18)	modulation (25)	triad (30)
great staff (22)	motive (29)	upbeat (18)

(Cultural Context box, "Melodies of the World," completes this chapter beginning on the next page.)

Melodies of the World

Indian Classical Music

In the preceding chapter we have seen how Western classical and popular music make use of major and minor scales, each with its own distinctive pattern of seven notes. We have also discussed how we in the West have, since the sixteenth century, generally associated the major mode with bright, happy feelings, and the minor mode with darker, gloomier, more apprehensive sentiments. But these are particularly Western constructs—the rest of the musical world often has its own, and very different, ways of making music.

In India a remarkably complex, yet subtle, type of melody marks the classical music of that country. Perhaps more than any other musical culture, Indian music relies exclusively on melody for musical expression. There are no contrapuntal lines and no harmony other than a constant drone on the tonic and dominant notes of the melody. For an Indian musician, chords are thought to create too much sound at once and thus detract from what is truly important: the expressive nuances of the melody and the intricate rhythmic patterns of the accompanying drummer.

India, of course, is a vast, populous land of many ethnic and religious groups, with Muslims strong in the north and Hindus dominating the south. Indian music, too, is divided somewhat along regional lines. What is called **Hindustani-style music** is heard in the north, while **Karnatak-style music** prevails in the south. Among the many differences between the two is the fact that Karnatak music is almost always sung, whereas Hindustani music frequently makes use of an instrument called the sitar. The highly flexible quality of Indian melody can best be heard on this string instrument.

The **sitar** is a large lute-like instrument with as many as twenty strings, some of which are used to play a melody, some simply to vibrate sympathetically with the melody strings, and some to provide a constant drone*. The strings are plucked by a plectrum, or pick, made of twisted wire, worn on the right index finger of the per-

former. As you can see from the illustration, the sitar is equipped with metal frets placed at right angles to the strings. The performer can not only set a pitch, by pushing the string against the fret, but also slightly alters the pitch by pulling the string sideways along the fret—something not done on our Western guitar, for example. At each end of the instrument is a large, semi-circular gourd that serves as a resonator to amplify the sound of the strings. A performance on the sitar is invariably accompanied by a **tabla**, a pair of tuned drums. The left-hand drum can produce almost any low pitch, depending on the amount of pressure the drummer applies. The right-hand drum is set to a fixed pitch, usually tonic or dominant, that is important in the sitar melody.

Every melody in Indian classical music makes use of a raga. Like our western scale, a **raga** is a basic pattern of pitches. But it is more. A raga expresses feeling—the mood of the piece. It has been called "the mystical expressive force" at the heart of every Indian composition. To the trained ear, *Raga Jogeshwari*, which we shall hear, has the mood of love and pathos. It makes use of six notes as the melody rises and falls. In this Indian raga then, the octave is divided into six pitches, not seven as in the Western major and minor scales.

EXAMPLE 2–32

Raga Jogeshwari sounds different to our ears because it employs a six-note scale. It also sounds "non-Western" because the performer "bends" the pitches by subtly pulling the strings of the sitar as the pitch is sounding. We in the West move along a scale from one specific pitch to the next. We have the notes, yet nothing in between. In much of the music of the world, however, great beauty is found between pitches. Small microtones (less than the smallest interval on our keyboard) give expressive power to the music. In the course of

Raga Jogeshwari the melody becomes increasingly saturated with melodic ornaments and gradations of pitch, all growing out of the basic six-note scale.

The performance of *Raga Jogeshwari* that you will hear is by Ravi Shankar, one of India's finest sitar players. Shankar personifies the ideal of Indian music in which composer and performer are one and the same person. Indeed, *Raga Jogeshwari* is his own creation. Yet each new performance of this raga results in a new composition because so much of the performance is improvised. For an Indian musician, composition, improvisation, and performance are three simultaneous manifestations of the urge for creative expression.

© Bettmann Archives/CORBIS

Ravi Shankar performing on the sitar. Shankar is the father of Grammy award-winning pop singer Norah Jones.

Listening Guide

WWW

	Raga Jogeshwari	6CD 6/12
	Gat II (Theme II)	
	(performed by Ravi Shankar, sitar, and Alla Rakha, tabla)	

0:00	Scale of raga played as quick arpeggio
0:08	Sitar presents theme three times against beat in the tabla
0:45	Alternation of the theme with free improvisations
1:17	Ascending and descending improvisations on the scale of the raga
2:11	A strong cadence for the tabla
2:40	More elaborate patterns repeated on successive degrees of the scale
4:18	Tempo increases
4:45	Strumming on the drone strings of the sitar
5:00	Sitar explores half steps that occur naturally in ascending version of the raga
5:50	Tabla mimics rhythmic patterns of the sitar

Jewish Klezmer Music

Every musical culture around the world makes use of the octave. Its two similar sounding pitches, one higher, the other lower, serve as poles at opposite ends of the scale. The number and arrangement of scalar pitches within the octave, however, varies greatly from culture to culture. As we have seen, Indian classical music sometimes has scales with only six pitches within the octave. Chinese and Indonesian music often make use of just five-note scales. Western classical and popular music divide the octave into seven pitches (the eighth duplicates the first, that's why the interval is called an "octave"). Moreover, we in the West have two specific and unvarying patterns for those seven-note scales: the major and minor mode (see page 23). Other cultures, however, use (continued on next page)

CULTURAL CONTEXT (continued)

different seven-note scale patterns, or modes, within the octave.

One such musical culture is that of klezmer music. **Klezmer music** is the traditional folk music of the Jews of Eastern Europe. It dates back to at least the seventeenth century and originated in countries such as Poland, Romania, Russia, Lithuania, and the Ukraine. Usually klezmer music is played by a small band, drawing on a variety of instruments including clarinet, trumpet, violin, accordion, and double bass, along with a singer. Some klezmer music is associated with Jewish religious rites, but most of it is heard at social events, particularly weddings. Although klezmer music, like the Jews themselves, was once threatened with extermination in Eastern Europe, it enjoyed a huge revival in the late twentieth century, particularly in Western Europe, Israel, and the United States. Klezmer music has managed to survive, and indeed flourish, by adapting elements of Western popular music, specifically rock, funk, and jazz.

The lively sounds of klezmer music can be clearly heard in *Fun Taschlich*, a tune associated with the High Holy Days. On the Jewish New Year (*Rosh Hashana*) Jews walk to the nearest sea, lake, or stream and symbolically wash away their sins by casting bread on the water. This ceremony is called *Taschlich. Fun Taschlich*

means "returning from the casting away of sin," for now it is time to dance and rejoice. This joyful tune is made up of three separate melodies (labeled **A**, **B**, and **C** on next page). Each is in duple meter and each is repeated to extend the dance. Most important, each phrase has its own particular scale pattern, or mode*. None of the three modes, however, exactly corresponds to our Western major or minor mode: melody **A** is similar, but not identical, to our D minor scale; melody **B** has much in common with our F major scale; while melody **C** approximates a mixture of our F and D minor scales. As you listen you will hear a decidedly exotic sound. It is the augmented second (three ½ steps or 1½ whole steps), an interval that occurs in much Eastern European and North African music, but not in our two Western scales. The most striking moments of *Fun Taschlich* come at the shift between the minor-like **A** melody and the major-like **B** tune. Finally, note that this Eastern European piece is a happy dance, yet it is written mainly in what sounds like our minor mode. While music in a minor key may sound sad to Western ears, to more Eastern ones it has happy connotations. Humans' emotional response to music is not conditioned by the physical properties of sound, but rather by each group's cultural traditions and musical habits.

Photograph by Michael Macione

The Klezmatics, a popular klezmer band, has been successful by blending traditional klezmer tunes with contemporary rock idioms.

Melody **A**
  Scale: D, E, F, G, A♭, B, C, D
  Pattern: 1, ½, 1, ½, 1½, ½, 1 steps

Melody **B**
  Scale: F, G, A, B♭, C, D, E♭, F
  Pattern: 1, 1, ½, 1, 1, ½, 1 steps

Melody **C**
  Scale: F, G, A♭, B, C, D, E♭, F
  Pattern: 1, ½, 1½, ½, 1, ½, 1 steps

KEY WORDS

Hindustani-style music   klezmer music
Karnatak-style music   sitar

EXAMPLE 2–33

Melody A

Melody B

Melody C

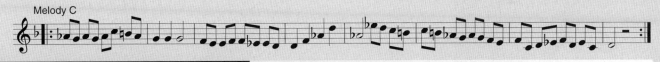

Listening Guide
WWW

Fun Taschlich   6CD 6/13
Traditional klezmer tune performed by the Klezmatics

0:00   Introduction: bass clarinet solo above North-African-like drum pattern
0:42   Melody **A** played by bass clarinet
1:06   Melody **A** played by electric violin alternating with muted trumpet and bass clarinet
1:21   Sudden mode shift of mode for melody **B** played by bass clarinet, supported by electric violin and muted trumpet
1:38   Melody **C** played by electric violin and muted trumpet
1:54   Melody **A** played by all melodic instruments
2:10   Melody **B** played by bass clarinet, supported by electric violin and muted trumpet
2:26   Melody **C** played by electric violin and muted trumpet
2:44   Free improvisation around notes of modes 1 and 3 (melodies **A** and **C**)
4:21   Melody **A** played by all melodic instruments
4:35   Melody **B** played by bass clarinet, supported by electric violin and muted trumpet
4:51   Melody **C** played by electric violin and muted trumpet
5:07   Fade out with opening motive

Chapter 3

SuperStock

Musical Color, Texture, and Form

E very musical composition is made up of a number of elements, just as every painting has a number of components to it. Color, texture, and form are important in both these arts. They are the broad, general qualities of a work that help give it its meaning and structure. Form in music is the general shape of a composition as perceived by the listener. It becomes apparent only gradually as the work progresses from beginning to end. Color and texture, on the other hand, are qualities that may be obvious to the listener immediately. We may be struck by a particular melody, not so much because of its pitches or rhythm, but because it is played on a brilliant-sounding instrument like the trumpet. Or we may be captivated by a musical climax, not because the melody at that point is particularly original, but because the full sound of a large orchestra is heard for the first time—the musical texture has gained impressive substance. Color and texture, then, are less musical ideas in themselves and more ways of expressing ideas.

COLOR

Simply said, **color** in music is the tone quality of any sound produced by a voice or an instrument. **Timbre** is another term for the tone quality of musical sound. Instruments produce sounds of different colors, or timbres, because they are constructed in different ways and of different materials. We need not go into the acoustical reasons why this is so—instinctively, we all recognize that the sound of a flute has a different tone quality from that of a trombone. Similarly, the voice of pop singer Britney Spears has a different timbre to it than that of opera star Renée Fleming (Fig. 3–2), even when the two produce the same pitches. Since the human voice was probably the first "instrument" to make music, let's start our investigation of musical color with it.

The Voice

The human voice is an instrument of a very special sort that naturally generates sound without the aid of any kind of mechanical contrivance. It is highly expressive, in part because it can produce an enormously wide range of sounds.

When we sing we force air up through our vocal cords (two folds of mucous membrane within the throat), causing them to vibrate. Men's vocal cords are longer and thicker than women's, and for that reason the sound of the mature male voice is lower. (This principle is also at work with the string instruments: the longer and thicker the string, the lower the pitch.) Voices are classified by range into four principal parts. The two women's vocal parts are the **soprano** and the **alto**, and the two men's parts the **tenor** and the **bass**. The soprano is the highest voice and the bass the lowest. When many voices join together, they form a **chorus**; the soprano, alto, tenor, and bass constitute the four standard choral parts. In addition, the area of pitch shared by the soprano and alto is sometimes designated as a separate vocal range called the **mezzo-soprano**, just as the notes adjoining the tenor and bass are said to be encompassed by the **baritone** voice.

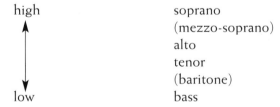

high | soprano
(mezzo-soprano)
alto
tenor
(baritone)
low | bass

The voice is capable of producing many different styles of singing: the raspy sound of a blues singer, the twang of the country balladeer, the gutsy belt of a Broadway songster, or the lyrical tones of an operatic soprano. We all try to sing, and we would like to sing well. How well we do, and what kind of sound we produce, depends on our training and our physical makeup—the lungs, vocal cords, throat, nose, and mouth are all involved in the production of vocal sound.

Musical Instruments

Musical instruments come in groups, or families. The symphony orchestra traditionally includes four such groups. The first is the string family, so called

FIGURE 3–1

In *The Fife* (1866), Edouard Manet uses unshaded patches of color and a few simple lines to create form.

FIGURE 3–2

Grammy award–winning soprano Renée Fleming is arguably America's current opera diva.

families of instruments

because these instruments produce sound by plucking or bowing a string. The second and third groups are the woodwind and brass families, both of which generate music by blowing air through a pipe or tube of one sort or another. The fourth group is the percussion family, which makes music—and sometimes just plain noise—usually by striking a suspended membrane (a drum), a block of wood, or a piece of metal with a stick of some kind. In addition, there is a fifth group of instruments, the keyboard instruments, which are not normally part of the symphony orchestra. The organ, harpsichord, and piano are the main keyboard instruments, and they make sound by means of keys and pipes (organ) or keys and strings (harpsichord and piano). The organ is usually played alone, while the piano is most often heard either by itself or as an accompaniment to another solo instrument.

Why does a composer choose a particular instrument to present a melody and not some other? In general, one instrument is chosen over another because of its capacity to express what the composer feels about the music that he or she intends to create. Invariably, the instrument with the tone color best able to portray the composer's feeling about a given musical line—and what the composer wishes to express to the listener—is the one selected. To be able to hear these subtle emotional shadings in music, it is important that we sharpen our awareness of the separate tone colors of the various instruments.

Strings Generally speaking, when we speak of string instruments we broadly include all instruments that produce sound by means of vibrating strings: the guitar, banjo, ukulele, and the harp, as well as the violin and its close relatives, the viola, cello, and double bass. But the guitar, banjo, ukulele, and harp usually produce their sound when plucked, whereas the violin and its relatives are normally played with a bow, not just plucked. Indeed, it is their use of a bow, along with their distinctive shape, that identifies the four members of the violin group. We traditionally associate these instruments with classical music. The guitar, banjo, ukulele, and harp, on the other hand, have their origins in folk music.

Violin group The violin group constituted the original core of the symphony orchestra when it was first formed during the Baroque era (1600–1750). In numbers of players, the violins, violas, cellos, and double basses still make up the largest part of any orchestra. A large symphony orchestra can easily include as many as a hundred members, at least sixty of whom play one of these four instruments.

The **violin** is chief among the string instruments. It is also the smallest—it has the shortest strings and therefore the highest pitch. Because of its high range and singing tone, it often is assigned the melody in orchestral and chamber music. The violins are usually divided into groups known as firsts and seconds. The seconds play a part slightly lower in pitch and subordinate in function to the firsts.

The sound of the violin is produced when a bow is pulled across one of four strings held tightly in place by tuning pegs at one end of the instrument and by a tailpiece at the other (Fig. 3–3). The strings are slightly elevated above the wooden body by means of a supporting bridge. Different sounds or pitches are produced when a finger of the left hand shortens, or "stops," a string by pressing it against the fingerboard—again, the shorter the string, the higher

FIGURE 3–3
Violinist Sarah Chang.

© Sheila Rock/ICM Artists, Ltd.

the pitch. Because each of the four strings can be stopped quickly in many different places, the violin possesses both great range and agility. The strings themselves are made either of animal gut or of metal wire. The singing tone of the violin, however, comes not so much from the strings as from the wooden body, known as the sound box, which amplifies and enriches the sound. The better the design, wood, glue, and varnish of the sound box, the better the tone. (For the sound of the violin, turn to Intro CD, track 10 at 0:00.)

The **viola** (Fig. 3–4) is about six inches longer than the violin and it produces a somewhat lower sound. If the violin is the string counterpart of the soprano voice, then the viola has its parallel in the alto voice. Its tone is darker, richer, and more somber than the brilliant violin. (For the sound of the viola, turn to Intro CD, track 10 at 1:37.)

You can easily spot the **cello** (violoncello) in the orchestra because the player sits with the instrument placed between the legs (Fig. 3–5). The pitch

FIGURE 3–4
Violist Uri Bashmet.

FIGURE 3–5
Cellist Yo-Yo Ma.

of the cello is well below that of the viola. It can provide a low bass sound as well as a singing melody. When played in its middle range by a skilled performer, the cello is capable of producing an indescribably rich, expressive tone. (For the sound of the cello, turn to Intro CD, track 10 at 2:10.)

The **double bass** (Fig. 3–6) gives weight and power to the bass line in the orchestra. Since at first it merely doubled the notes of the cello an octave* below, it was called the double bass. As you can see, the double bass is the largest, and hence lowest sounding, of the string instruments. Its job in the orchestra, and even in jazz bands, is to help set a firm base for the musical harmony. (For the sound of the double bass, turn to Intro CD, track 10, at 2:50.)

Special Effects. The members of the violin group all generate pitches in the same way: A bow is drawn across a tight string. This produces the traditional, penetrating string sound. In addition, a number of other effects can be created by using different playing techniques.

vibrato: By shaking the left hand as it stops the string, the performer can produce a sort of controlled wobble in the pitch. This adds richness to the tone of the string because, in fact, it creates a blend of two or more pitches. (For an example of a violin playing without vibrato and then with vibrato, turn to Intro CD, track 10 at 0:31 and at 0:51.)

FIGURE 3–6
Double-bass player Gary Karr.

pizzicato: Instead of bowing the strings, the performer plucks them. With this technique, the resulting sound has a sharp attack, but it dies away quickly. (For an example of pizzicato, turn to Intro CD, track 10 at 1:13.)

tremolo: The performer creates a musical "tremor" by rapidly repeating the same pitch with quick up and down strokes of the bow. Tremolo creates a feeling of heightened tension and excitement when played loudly, and a velvety, shimmering backdrop when performed quietly. (For an example of tremolo, turn to Intro CD, track 10 at 1:24.)

trill: The performer rapidly alternates between two distinctly separate but neighboring pitches. Most instruments, not only the strings, can play trills. (For an example of a trill, turn to Intro CD, track 10 at 1:30.)

mute: If a composer wants to dampen the penetrating tone of a string instrument, he or she can instruct the player to place a mute (a metal or rubber clamp) on the strings of the instrument.

Harp. Although originally a folk instrument, one found in virtually every musical culture, the **harp** (Fig. 3–7) is sometimes added to the modern symphony orchestra. Its role is to add color to the orchestral sound and sometimes to create special effects, the most striking of which is a rapid run up or down the strings called a **glissando.** (For the sound of the harp and an example of a glissando, turn to Intro CD, track 10 at 3:35 and 3:44.)

Listening Guide

WWW

Instruments of the Orchestra
Strings

Intro CD/10

0:00	Violin plays a major scale
0:13	Violin solo: Tchaikovsky
0:31	Violin plays without vibrato: Haydn
0:51	Violin plays with vibrato: Haydn
1:13	Violin plays pizzicato
1:24	Violin plays tremolo
1:30	Violin plays a trill
1:37	Viola plays a major scale
1:49	Viola solo: Haydn
2:10	Cello plays a major scale
2:30	Cello solo: Haydn
2:50	Double bass plays a major scale
3:13	Double bass solo: Haydn
3:35	Harp plays an arpeggio
3:44	Harp solo: Tchaikovsky

FIGURE 3-7

The harp's unique special effect is its glissando, a rapid run up and down the strings that seem to color the airwaves with sound.

SuperStock

Woodwinds The name "woodwind" was originally given to this family of instruments because they emit sound when air is blown through a wooden tube or pipe. The pipe has holes along its length, and the player covers or uncovers these to change the pitch. Nowadays, however, some of these woodwind instruments are made entirely of metal. Flutes, for example, are constructed of silver, and sometimes of gold or even platinum. As with the violin group, there are four principal woodwind instruments in every modern symphony orchestra: flute, oboe, clarinet, and bassoon. In addition, each of these has a close relative that is larger or smaller in size and that possesses a somewhat different timbre and range. The larger the instrument or length of pipe, the lower the sound.

The lovely, silvery tone of the **flute** is probably familiar to you. The instrument can be rich in the lower register and then light and airy on top. It is especially agile, capable of playing tones rapidly and moving quickly from one range to another. (For the sound of the flute, turn to Intro CD, track 11 at 0:00.)

The smaller cousin of the flute is the **piccolo.** ("Piccolo" comes from the Italian *flauto piccolo*, meaning "little flute".) It can produce higher notes than any other orchestral instrument. And though very small, its sound is so shrill that it can always be heard, even when the full orchestra is playing loudly. (For the sound of the piccolo, turn to Intro CD, track 11 at 0:38.)

The **clarinet** produces sound when the player blows against a single reed fitted to the mouthpiece. The tone of the clarinet is more mellow than that of the other woodwinds, especially in the lower register of the instrument. It also has the capacity to slide or glide smoothly between pitches, and this allows for a highly expressive style of playing. The flexibility and expressiveness of the instrument have made it a favorite with jazz musicians. (For the sound of the clarinet, turn to Intro CD, track 11 at 0:54.) A lower, larger version of the clarinet is the **bass clarinet.**

The **oboe** is equipped with a double reed—two reeds tied together with an air space in between. When the player blows into the instrument through the double reed, a nasal, slightly exotic sound is created. It is invariably the oboe that gives the pitch at the beginning of every symphony concert. Not only was the oboe the first nonstring instrument to be added to the orchestra, but it is a difficult instrument to tune. Better have the other instruments tune to it than to try to have it adjust to them. (For the sound of the oboe, turn to Intro CD, track 11 at 1:24.)

Related to the oboe is the **English horn.** Unfortunately, it is wrongly named, for the English horn is neither English nor a horn. It is simply a larger (hence lower-sounding) version of the oboe that originated on the continent of Europe. The English horn produces a dark, haunting sound, one that was especially favored by composers of the Romantic period (1820–1900). (For the sound of the English horn, turn to 6CD4/14 at 0:50.)

The **bassoon** functions among the woodwinds much as the cello does among the strings. It can serve as a bass instrument, adding weight to the lowest sound, or it can act as a soloist in its own right. When playing moderately fast or rapid passages as a solo instrument, it has a dry, almost comic tone. (For the sound of the bassoon, turn to Intro CD, track 11 at 1:54.)

There is also a double bassoon, usually called the **contrabassoon.** Its sound is deep and sluggish. Indeed, the contrabassoon can play notes lower than any other orchestral instrument.

The bassoon, contrabassoon, and English horn are all double-reed instruments, just like the oboe. Their tones, therefore, may sound more vibrant, even exotic, than those of the single-reed instruments like the clarinet and saxophone.

G. LeBlanc Corporation, Kenosha, WI

FIGURE 3–8

(from left to right) A flute, two clarinets, an oboe, and a bassoon. The flute, clarinet, and oboe are about the same length. The bassoon is nearly twice their size.

Strictly speaking, the single-reed **saxophone** is not a member of the symphony orchestra, though it can be added on occasion. Its sound can be mellow and expressive but also, if the player wishes, shrill and raucous. The expressiveness of the saxophone makes it a welcome member of most jazz ensembles, while the shrill, penetrating tone of the instrument is prized by rock musicians.

Listening Guide

Instruments of the Orchestra   Intro CD/11
Woodwinds

0:00	Flute plays a major scale
0:11	Flute solo: Debussy
0:38	Piccolo plays a major scale
0:47	Piccolo solo: Tchaikovsky
0:54	Clarinet plays a major scale
1:02	Clarinet solo: Berlioz
1:24	Oboe plays a major scale
1:33	Oboe solo: Tchaikovsky
1:54	Bassoon plays a major scale
2:05	Bassoon solo: Stravinsky

Listening Guide

Strings and Woodwinds   Intro CD/17
George Frideric Handel, Hornpipe from *Water Music*
(1717)

0:00	Strings alone
0:41	Woodwinds (piccolo, flute, oboe, and bassoon) with drums
1:19	Strings and woodwinds together with drums

A fuller discussion and a Listening Guide for this piece are given on page 157.

Brasses Like the woodwind and string groups of the orchestra, the brass family consists of four primary instruments: trumpet, trombone, French horn, and tuba. Brass players use no reeds but instead blow into their instruments through a cup-shaped **mouthpiece** (Fig. 3–10). By adjusting valves or moving a slide, the performer can make the length of pipe on the instrument longer or shorter, and hence the pitch lower or higher.

Everyone has heard the high, bright, cutting sound of the **trumpet.** Whether on a football field or in an orchestral hall, the trumpet is an excellent solo instrument because of its agility and penetrating tone. (For the sound of the trumpet, turn to Intro CD, track 12 at 0:00.) The trumpet sounds forth with special brilliance at the beginning of Musorgsky's *Pictures at an Exhibition* (Intro CD, track 1). When provided with a mute (a hollow plug placed in the bell of the instrument to dampen the sound), the trumpet can produce a softer tone that blends well with other instruments. (To hear a trumpet with mute, turn to Intro CD, track 12 at 0:22.)

Although distantly related to the trumpet, the **trombone** (Italian for "large trumpet") plays in the middle range of the brass family. Its sound is large and full. Most important, the trombone is the only brass instrument to generate sounds by moving a slide in and out, thereby producing higher or lower pitches. Needless to say, the trombone can easily slide from pitch to pitch, sometimes for comical effect. (For the sound of the trombone, turn to Intro CD, track 12 at 0:35.)

The **French horn** was the first brass instrument to join the orchestra, back in the seventeenth century. Its sound is rich and mellow, yet somewhat veiled or covered. The French horn was especially popular during the Romantic period (1820–1900) because the horn's traditional association with the hunt and with Alpine mountains suggested nature, a subject dear to the hearts of the Romantics. (For the sound of the French horn, turn to Intro CD, track 12 at 0:59.) It is easy to confuse the sound of the French horn with that of the trombone, because both are middle-range brass instruments and have a full, majestic tone. But the sound of the trombone is somewhat clearer and more focused, and its attack more direct than that of the French horn. (An immediate comparison of the trombone with the French horn can be had by playing Intro CD, track 12, first at 0:45 and then at 1:17.)

The **tuba** is the largest and lowest-sounding of the brass instruments. It produces a full, though sometimes muffled, tone in its lowest notes. Like the double bass of the violin group, the tuba is most often used for setting a base, or foundation, for the melody. (For the sound of the tuba, turn to Intro CD, track 12 at 1:39.) On occasion, the tuba itself is assigned a melodic line, as in Picture 4 of Musorgsky's *Pictures at an Exhibition* (Intro CD, track 2 at 0:00.) Here, the tuba demonstrates the melodious upper range of the instrument in a lengthy solo.

Martin Reichenthal

FIGURE 3–9
Members of the Canadian Brass, with the French horn player at the left and the tuba player at the right.

Yamaha Corp.

FIGURE 3–10
Mouthpieces for brass instruments.

Listening Guide

WWW

Instruments of the Orchestra
Brasses

Intro CD/12

0:00	Trumpet plays a major scale
0:09	Trumpet solo: Mouret
0:22	Trumpet solo with mute: Mouret
0:35	Trombone plays a major scale
0:45	Trombone solo: Copland
0:59	French horn plays a major scale
1:17	French horn solo: Copland
1:39	Tuba plays a major scale
2:00	Tuba solo: Copland

Percussion Percussion instruments are those that are struck in some way, either by hitting the head of a drum with a stick or by banging or scraping a piece of metal or wood in one fashion or another. Some percussion instruments, like the timpani (kettledrums), produce a specific pitch, while others

FIGURE 3-11
Timpanist Peter Kogan of the Minnesota Orchestra.

just generate noise without a recognizable musical tone. It is the job of the percussion instruments to sharpen the rhythmic contour of the music. They can also add color to the sounds of other instruments and, when they play loudly, can heighten the sense of climax in a piece. For example, much of the majesty to be heard in the climactic final tableau of Musorgsky's *Pictures at an Exhibition* (Intro CD, track 4 at 4:49) is created by the timpani, bass drum, and cymbals.

The **timpani** (Fig. 3-11) is the percussion instrument most often heard in classical music. Whether struck in single, detached strokes or hit rapidly to produce a thunderlike roll, the function of the timpani is to add depth, tension, and drama to the music. Timpani usually come in pairs, one instrument to play the tonic* note and the other to play the dominant*.

The rat-ta-tat-tat of the **snare drum**, the dull thud of the **bass drum**, and the crashing ring of the **cymbals** are sounds well known from marching bands and jazz ensembles, as well as the classical orchestra. None of these instruments produces a specific musical tone. (To hear all three in succession, turn to Intro CD, track 13 at 0:11.)

The xylophone, glockenspiel, and celesta, however, are three percussion instruments that do generate specific pitches. The **xylophone** (Fig. 3-12) is a set of wooden bars that, when struck by two hard mallets, produce a dry, wooden sound. The **glockenspiel** works the same way, but the bars are made of metal so that the tone is brighter and more ringing. The **celesta**, too, produces sound when hammers strike metal bars, but the hammers are activated by keys, as in a piano; the tone of the celesta is bright and tinkling—a delightful, "celestial" sound, as the name of the instrument suggests.

Listening Guide

WWW

Percussion   Intro CD/13

0:00	Timpani
0:11	Snare drum
0:19	Bass drum
0:31	Cymbal

Listening Guide

WWW

Brasses and Percussion with Full Orchestra   Intro CD/18
George Frideric Handel, Minuet from *Water Music*
(1717)

0:00	French horns play jaunty melody
0:13	Trumpets help complete the melody
0:29	Woodwinds and French horn play melody
0:41	Full orchestra repeats, with prominent timpani and snare drum
0:54	Woodwinds with French horn complete the melody
1:07	Full orchestra repeats, with prominent timpani and snare drum

A fuller discussion and a Listening Guide for this piece are given on page 156.

You have now been introduced to the principal instruments of the Western symphony orchestra. Go on to do Listening Exercises 8, 9, and 10. They are graduated in difficulty. First you are asked to identify one instrument, then two playing together, and finally three together.

The Symphony Orchestra The modern Western symphony orchestra is one of the largest and certainly the most colorful of all musical ensembles. It originated in the seventeenth century and has continually grown in size since then. When at full strength, the symphony orchestra can include upward of one hundred performers and nearly thirty different instruments, from the high piping of the piccolo down to the rumble of the contrabassoon. A typical seating plan for an orchestra is given in Fig. 3–13. To achieve the best balance of sound, strings are placed toward the front, and the more powerful brasses at the back. Other seating arrangements are also used, according to the special requirements of the composition to be performed.

Surprisingly, a separate conductor was not originally part of the orchestra. For the first 200 years of its existence (1600–1800), the symphony was led by one of the performers, either a keyboard player or the principal first violinist. By the time of Beethoven (1770–1827), however, the group had so grown in size that it was thought necessary to have someone stand before it and lead, not only to keep all the players together but also to help draw out

PhotoDisc

FIGURE 3–12

The xylophone is a fixed-pitch percussion instrument on which can be played a fully chromatic scale of several octaves.

ORCHESTRAL SEATING PLAN

FIGURE 3–13

Seating plan of a symphony orchestra.

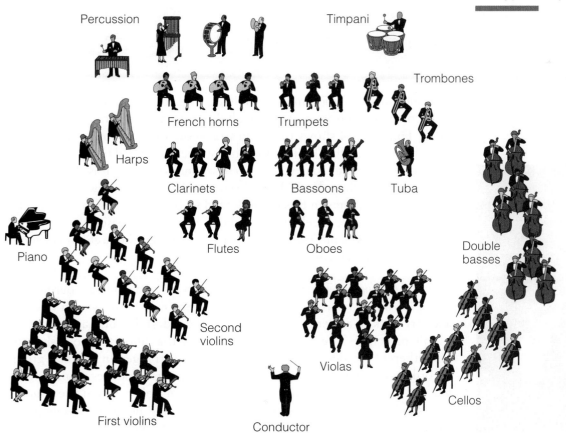

Percussion

Timpani

Trombones

French horns   Trumpets

Harps

Clarinets   Bassoons   Tuba

Piano

Flutes   Oboes   Double basses

Second violins

Violas

Cellos

First violins   Conductor

FIGURE 3–14

The orchestral score of an excerpt from Beethoven's Symphony No. 3 (1803), the "Eroica," with instruments listed.

FIGURE 3–15

Conductor Seiji Ozawa recently retired as leader of the Boston Symphony Orchestra, where he had served for twenty-five years. By watching the gestures of the conductor, the listener is often able to follow the principal themes as they are passed from player to player or section to section.

and elucidate the important musical lines. The conductor follows an **orchestral score**, a composite notation of all the instrumental parts for a particular piece. Figure 3–14 shows the orchestral score of a portion of Beethoven's Symphony No. 3, the "Eroica." Obviously, Beethoven had to put many, many notes on the page to achieve just a few seconds of music. It is the job of the conductor to follow the orchestral score and pick out any wrongly played pitches and rhythms in this complicated web of instrumental sounds. For this they must have excellent musical ears. That's one reason the great conductors, such as Seiji Ozawa (Fig. 3–15) are among the highly paid superstars of the musical world.

Keyboard Instruments The pipe organ, harpsichord, and piano are our most familiar keyboard instruments. The **pipe organ** (Fig. 3–16), which traces its ancestry back to ancient Greece, is by far the oldest. It works according to a simple principle: The player depresses a key that allows air to rush into a pipe, thereby producing sound. The pipes are arranged in separate groups according to their shape and material. Each group produces a full range of musical tones with one special tone quality or color. When the organist wants to bring a particular group of pipes into play, he or she simply pulls a switch, called a **stop**. The most colorful, forceful sound occurs when all the stops have been activated (thus the expression "pulling out all the stops"). The several keyboards of the organ make it possible to play several musical lines at once, each with its own timbre. There is even a keyboard for the feet! The largest fully functioning pipe organ in the world is in the Cadet Chapel of the United States Military Academy at West Point, New York. It has 270 stops and 18,408 pipes.

The **harpsichord** (Fig. 3–17) was known in northern Italy as early as 1400, but it reached its heyday during the Baroque era (1600–1750). It produces sound not by means of pipes but by strings. When a key is depressed, it drives a lever upward that, in turn, forces a pick to pluck a string. The plucking creates a bright, jangling sound. Some harpsichords are equipped with two keyboards so that the player can change from one group of strings to another, each with its particular tone color and volume of sound. The harpsichord has one important shortcoming, however: The lever mechanism does not allow the performer to control the force with which the string is plucked, so each string always sounds at the same volume. (For more on the harpsichord, see page 110.)

The **piano** (Fig. 3–18) was invented in Italy in 1709, in part to remove the dynamic limitations of the harpsichord. In a piano, strings are not plucked but hit by soft hammers. A lever mechanism makes it possible for the player to regulate how hard each string is struck, thus producing softs and louds (the original piano was called the *pianoforte*, the "soft-loud"). During the lifetime of Mozart (1756–1791), the piano replaced the harpsichord as the favorite domestic musical instrument. By the nineteenth century every aspiring household had to have a piano, whether as an instrument for real musical enjoyment or as a symbol of affluence.

If the organ's familiar home is the church, where it is heard in association with religious services, the versatile piano is found almost everywhere. With equal success it can accompany a school chorus or an opera singer; it can harmonize with a rock band when in the hands of an Elton John or a Billy Joel; or it can become a powerful, yet expressive, solo instrument when played by a master such as André Watts. The harpsichord, on the other hand, is used mainly to recreate the music of the time of Johann Sebastian Bach (1685–1750).

FIGURE 3–16

A pipe organ in the Chapel of St. Thomas Aquinas at the University of St. Thomas, Minnesota.

FIGURE 3–17

A two-manual harpsichord built by Pascal Taskin (Paris, 1770), preserved in the Yale University Collection of Musical Instruments, New Haven, Connecticut.

FIGURE 3–18

Pianist André Watts.

CULTURAL CONTEXT

An Orchestra from Bali, Indonesia

Indonesia is a Southeast Asian country with 250 million citizens, and thus the fourth most populous country on earth. Toward the center of this vast archipelago is the island of Bali, a place of swaying palm trees, fertile fields, and hundreds of small villages, each with its own vital and distinctive musical tradition. For the more than two million inhabitants of Bali, music is an integral part of their daily lives, for music is intimately bound up with religion and folklore. Hindu deities and local spirits must be honored daily in the temple and in the home. Larger ceremonies are invariably celebrated to the accompaniment of music performed by a gamelan.

A **gamelan** is a collection of as many as twenty-five musical instruments played together as an orchestra. The ensemble, however, sounds very unlike our Western orchestra, for the dominant family of the gamelan is not the strings, but percussion: **metallophones** (xylophone-like instruments with bronze keys struck by hammers, see Figure on page 55), tuned gongs, gong-chimes, cymbals, and drums, along with an occasional flute. So, too, the gamelan employs a different approach to generating musical lines. In the Western orchestra a single instrument is responsible for providing a melody or counter-melody, or creating a single instrumental color. In gamelan music, however, players of several instruments continually contribute bits of music which, when taken together, form a composite line of distinctive color. In the example that follows, notice how the parts are interlocking and mutually interdependent.

EXAMPLE 3–1

Baris is a traditional Balinese composition used to accompany a solo dance—one portraying a warrior-in-training. The dancer's taut, raised-up posture, darting eye-movements, and cautious forays around the stage create a tense and exciting mood. Every so often, the dancer initiates bolder, more aggressive turns and steps, which are interpreted as cues by the lead drummer. The gamelan responds to the gestures of the dancer with crashing chords and sudden breaks. In the recorded example, the many

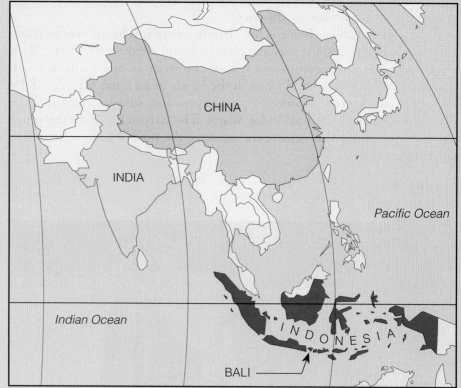

The subcontinent of Asia, Southeast Asia, and the Pacific rim.

Carto-Graphics

musical parts are demonstrated at a slow tempo. After a drum introduction, a set of three gongs creates an eight-beat rhythmic cycle. Thereafter the various metallophones* and drums enter one-by-one to present, or elaborate, the eight-note cycle four times; each four-cycle unit is separated from the preceding one by an "empty" cycle, one in which the gongs alone sound. The Listening Guide contains a bewildering variety of names for the Indonesian musical instruments. These terms are not important for our purposes. Nevertheless, the great number of instruments and the variety of their sounds show that the Balinese orchestra—though producing a completely different sound from our Western symphony orchestra—is every bit as complex and colorful.

KEY WORDS

Bali
gamelan
metallophone

Michael Tenzer

A Balinese gamelan with gongs (first row) and metallophones (second and third rows).

Listening Guide

WWW

Baris for Balinese Gamelan
Prepared by ethnomusicologist Michael Tenzer
Recorded July 1989 in Denpasar, Bali, with students of the Indonesian Arts Academy

6CD/14

0:00	Introduction to *kendang* (two-headed drums)
0:12	Full ensemble enters for introductory phrase
0:23	Gongs *kempur* (mid-range gong) and *kempli* (a muted, small gong) lay the foundation for the rhythmic cycle
0:42	*Ugal* (lead metallophone) plays the basic eight-note melody, one note per beat
1:00	Two *pemade* and two *kantilan* (metallophones) play the *ugal's* melody with repeated pitches
1:19	Two more *pemade* and *kantilan* play a complementary part
1:38	All *pemade* and *kantilan* plus the *ugal* play together
1:56	Two *calung* (metallophones) play a simplified version of the *ugal* melody
2:13	Two deep-tone *jegogan* (metallophones) play a further simplified version
2:32	Several *reyong* (tiny gongs) play a rhythmically more complex version of the melody
2:51	Other *reyong* gongs respond
3:10	Together, the whole *reyong* interlocks to create a swift variant of the *ugal* melody
3:28	The first *kendang* (two-headed drum) plays a rhythm composed to accompany the melody
3:48	The second *kendang* plays a complementary rhythm
4:04	The two *kendang* interlock
4:27	Conclusion: all instruments reenter in a growing wave of sound
4:52	A cue from the drums heralds a *ritardando* and a final cycle

Electronic Instruments In addition to natural musical instruments around the world—acoustical instruments, as they are called—machines that produce musical sounds by electronic means have been invented in the twentieth century. The electric keyboard synthesizer has recently gained great favor among rock and jazz musicians because of the variety of sounds it can create and the ease with which it can be moved from job to job. Contemporary rock groups such as Radiohead and Kraftwork, as well as "techno music" bands, are heavily dependent upon electronic instruments, synthesizers, and computers for their sound. These instruments and sound processing computers are discussed in Chapter 17.

Dynamics

In all music **dynamics** are the various levels of volume, loud and soft, at which sounds are produced. Dynamics work together with tone colors to affect the way we hear and react to musical sound. A high note in the clarinet has one quality—shrill and harsh—when played *fortissimo* (very loud) and quite another—vague and otherworldly—when played *pianissimo* (very soft). Following are the names of the most common musical dynamics. Since they were first used by composers working in Italy, these terms are traditionally written in Italian.

louds and softs

Term	Musical Symbol	Definition
fortissimo	*ff*	very loud
forte	*f*	loud
mezzo forte	*mf*	moderately loud
mezzo piano	*mp*	moderately soft
piano	*p*	soft
pianissimo	*pp*	very soft

Dynamics sometimes change abruptly, for special effects. Most common among these quick changes is the **sforzando,** a sudden, loud attack on one note or chord. A famous *sforzando* occurs in the second movement of Joseph Haydn's "Surprise" Symphony (1792), for example, in which the composer interrupts a soft melody with a thunderous crash on a single chord (Intro CD/23 at 0:33)—his intent was apparently to awaken those listeners who might have dozed off!

But changes in dynamics need not be sudden and abrupt. They can be gradual and extend over a long period of time. A gradual increase in the intensity of sound is called a crescendo, while a gradual decrease is called either a decrescendo or diminuendo.

Term	Musical Symbol	Definition
crescendo		growing louder
decrescendo		
or		growing softer
diminuendo		

Ludwig van Beethoven was a master at writing long crescendos. The transition to the last movement of his Symphony No. 5 comes upon the listener like a great tidal wave of sound (6CD3/4 at 5:00). An equally impressive crescendo, and then diminuendo, can be heard in Musorgsky's *Pictures at an Exhibition* (Intro CD/2 at 1:33), where the Polish ox-cart rumbles forward loudly and then disappears quietly in the distance.

TEXTURE

Texture in music is the density and disposition of the musical lines that make up a musical composition. To understand this better, picture in your mind a tapestry or some other type of woven material. The individual strands, or lines, can be dense or thin; colors can be bunched toward the center or spread out more or less evenly; the lines may have either a strong vertical or a horizontal thrust. Just as a weaver or painter can fabricate a particular texture—dense, heavy, light, or thin, with independent or interdependent strands—so, too, can the composer create similar effects with musical lines. Musorgsky's *Polish Ox-Cart* (Intro CD/2), from his *Pictures at an Exhibition*, begins with a thin texture of low sounds (tuba and double basses only). As the piece progresses, the strings and then the full orchestra join in, giving the music an impressive, dense texture. Finally, toward the end, the music returns to the thin, low sounds heard at the beginning.

Tate Gallery, London

FIGURE 3–19

Piet Mondrian's *Composition with Red, Yellow, and Blue* (1939–1942) has a rather thin texture with uneven linear spacing and occasional zones of dense color.

Monophonic, Polyphonic, and Homophonic Textures

There are three primary textures in music—monophonic, polyphonic, and homophonic—depending on the number of musical lines and the way they relate to one another. Often we call these lines, or parts, "voices" even though they may not actually be sung.

Monophony is the easiest to hear. As the name "one sounding" indicates, there is only a single line of music, with no accompaniment. When you sing by yourself, you are creating monophonic music. When a group of men (or women) sing the same pitches together—singing in unison*, as it is called—they produce monophonic texture. Even when men and women sing together at the octave*, the texture is still monophonic. Singing in unison and at the octave adds richness to the otherwise sparse sound of monophonic music.

As you may suppose from the name "many sounding," **polyphony** requires two or more lines in the musical fabric. In addition, the term "polyphonic" also implies that each of the lines will be autonomous and independent. They compete equally for the listener's attention. Usually, they move against one another, and when this happens they create what is called counterpoint. **Counterpoint** is simply the harmonious opposition of two or more independent musical lines. Because counterpoint presupposes polyphony, the terms "contrapuntal texture" and "polyphonic texture" are often used interchangeably.

FIGURE 3–20

Simultaneous Counter Composition (1929–1930), by Theo van Doesburg, comes very close to a musical definition of counterpoint: "the harmonious opposition of two or more independent [entities]."

The Museum of Modern Art, New York, The Sidney and Harriett Janis Collection. Photograph © 2000 The Museum of Modern Art, New York

types of counterpoint

What is more, there are two types of counterpoint: imitative and free. In imitative counterpoint the individual voices enter separately and the followers duplicate at least a part of what the first, or lead, voice had presented. If they copy exactly, note for note, what the first part plays or sings, then a **canon** results. Think of *Three Blind Mice, Are You Sleeping?*, or *Row, Row, Row Your Boat*, and remember how each voice enters in turn and then exactly imitates the first voice from beginning to end. These are all short canons, or rounds, a type of strict counterpoint popular since the Middle Ages. Among the more famous longer canons in music is the well-known canon of Johann Pachelbel (1653–1706) that goes on for several minutes. Example 3–2 shows the beginning of a brief canon for three voices:

canon

EXAMPLE 3–2

free counterpoint

Free counterpoint is counterpoint without any sort of imitation among the voices. The voices, or lines, may begin all together or begin separately, but they go their separate ways. Much jazz improvisation is done in free counterpoint.

Homophony means "same sounding." In this texture the voices, or lines, move to new pitches at roughly the same time. Homophony, then, differs from polyphony in that the strands are not independent but interdependent; they proceed in a tight, interlocking fashion. Usually, the lines form harmonious blocks of sound, called chords*, which support and draw attention to a higher voice that carries the melody. Hymns, Christmas carols, popular songs, and folk songs almost always have a homophonic texture because they consist of a simple melody with blocks of accompanying chords below. Melody plus accompaniment then—perhaps the most common musical arrangement—produces homophonic texture. As the arrows in Exs. 3–2 and 3–3 show, in polyphonic texture the musical fabric has lines with a strong linear (horizontal) thrust, whereas in homophonic texture the fabric is marked by lines that are more vertically conceived, as blocks of accompanying chords.

EXAMPLE 3–3

Of course, composers are not limited to just one of these three musical textures within any given work. They can change from one to another at will. By adding one or two independent lines, for example, a composer can slip easily from homophonic to polyphonic texture. As a rule, the longer the piece, the greater the number of changes in texture. But changes in texture can come in rapid succession in short pieces as well. George Frideric Handel (1685–1759) is perhaps best known as the composer of *Messiah*, a large work for chorus and orchestra usually performed just before Christmas. By far the most familiar number within *Messiah* is the "Hallelujah" chorus, for which the audience traditionally rises to its feet.[†] To get the sound of the various textures securely in your ear, listen to this famous chorus. Notice how rapidly and how smoothly the composer moves back and forth among homophonic, polyphonic, and monophonic textures. The following Listening Guide makes it clear where the changes come.

changing textures

Listening Guide

WWW

George Frideric Handel
"Hallelujah" chorus from *Messiah* (1741)

Intro CD/19

0:06	"Hallelujah! Hallelujah!"—homophony
0:25	"For the Lord God Omnipotent reigneth"—monophony
0:32	"Hallelujah! Hallelujah"—homophony
0:37	"For the Lord God Omnipotent reigneth"—monophony
0:44	"Hallelujah! Hallelujah!"—homophony
0:47	"For the Lord God Omnipotent reigneth" together with "Hallelujah"—polyphony
1:13	"The Kingdom of this world is become"—homophony
1:31	"And He shall reign for ever and ever"—polyphony
1:53	"King of Kings and Lord of Lords" together with "Hallelujah"—homophony
2:33	"And He shall reign for ever and ever"—polyphony
2:44	"King of Kings and Lord of Lords" together with "Hallelujah"—homophony
2:54	"And He shall reign for ever and ever"—polyphony
3:00	"King of Kings and Lord of Lords" together with "Hallelujah"—homophony

When you have finished, turn to Listening Exercise 11, which provides additional practice in hearing musical textures.

FORM

Form in art is the purposeful organization of the artist's materials. It is present in every medium of creative expression. In architecture, sculpture, and painting, for example, the formal design imposes a shape and a definition on physical space. In poetry the meter, the rhyme, and the stanza give a sense of logic and coherence to the sounds, ideas, and images. And in music the melody, harmony, rhythm, tone color, and texture can be arranged to create a sequence of events that the composer and listener find pleasing and convincing.

A composer needs formal principles to help in the process of selecting and arranging materials. Nothing is more frightening to an artist, as the composer Igor Stravinsky (1882–1971) remarked, than absolute freedom. How to begin? What to write now? What next? When and how to end? The selection

a composer needs a plan

[†]It seems that King George II (ruled 1727–1760) stood up at this point during a performance of *Messiah* in London. If the King stood, so did everyone else; hence the tradition of the audience standing.

of a musical form can help with these decisions by suggesting an overall shape as well as a set of operating procedures. Sometimes a composer will create a novel design because the subject matter at hand seems to demand it. Thus in his *Pictures at an Exhibition,* Modest Musorgsky fashions a long chain of musical pictures linked by a short refrain (the Promenade music). But more often a composer will fall back on a time-honored form. Using a traditional form does not tell the composer what to do at every step, but it does suggest plausible paths that might be taken—paths that other composers at other times have used and with which the listener is likely to be familiar.

From the listener's standpoint, an awareness of form is perhaps the most important tool he or she can employ while listening to music. If the composer needs help in setting a broad musical plan, the listener needs formal guideposts as a means of following what the composer is trying to communicate. The music rushes by quickly: What has happened? Where am I? What is about to come? These questions are invariably asked, consciously or unconsciously, when hearing a piece for the first time. By working through the discussion and diagrams that follow, you will acquire a mental picture of the most commonly used musical forms. You will more easily comprehend the material that you hear, and be comfortable with it, because you will have met these forms before and now know what to expect. You may also gain satisfaction from hearing the composer deviate from your expectations by treating the traditional time-honored form in some new and surprising fashion.

a listener needs to know the plan

Creating Formal Designs: Repetition, Contrast, and Variation

repetition

How are formal designs created in music? By means of repetition, contrast, and variation. **Repetition** establishes the most obvious formal units. When a distinctive melody returns, for example, it strikes the ear as an important event. Such repeating events set forth the outlines of a musical design in the same way that a steel framework outlines and holds together the materials of a building. Repetition is essential to music, perhaps because music is the most abstract of all the arts. Instead of creating tedium or boredom, each return helps to establish weight, balance, and symmetry. Because the musical material is familiar, repetition conveys to the listener a feeling of comfort and security.

contrast

Contrast, on the other hand, takes us away from the familiar and into the unknown. A quiet melody in the strings can suddenly be followed by an insistent theme blasting from the French horns, as happens, for example, in the third movement of Beethoven's well-known Symphony No. 5 (6CD3/4). Contrasting melodies, rhythms, textures, and moods can be used as a foil to familiar material, to provide variety, even conflict. In many aspects of our lives we have a need to balance comfort and security with novelty and excitement. In music this human necessity is given expression through the juxtaposition of the familiar and the unknown—through the interplay of repeating and contrasting musical units.

variation

Variation stands midway between repetition and contrast. The original melody returns, but it is altered in some way. For example, the tune may now be more complex, or new instruments may be added against it to create counterpoint. The listener has the satisfaction of hearing the familiar melody, yet is challenged to recognize in what way it has been changed.

Needless to say, memory plays an important role in hearing musical form. In architecture, painting, and sculpture, form is taken in all at once by a single glance. But in music, as to some extent in poetry and literature, formal relationships only become obvious over the course of time. Here our memory must put the pieces together and show us the relationships. For this to happen, we must be able to recognize an exact repetition, a varied repetition, and a contrasting musical event. To help in this process, musicians have developed a simple system to visualize forms by labeling musical units with letters. The first prominent musical idea is designated **A**. Subsequent contrasting sections are each labeled **B, C, D**, and so on. If the first or any other musical unit returns in varied form, then that variation is indicated by a superscript number: A^1, B^2, for example. Subdivisions of each large musical unit are shown by lowercase letters (**a, b**, etc.). How this works will become clear in the following examples.

the role of memory

Musical Forms

Most musical forms transcend musical epochs—they are not unique to any one period in the history of music. The following musical forms are universal as well as timeless.

Strophic Form This is the most familiar of all musical forms because our hymns, carols, folk tunes, and patriotic songs invariably make use of it. In **strophic form** the composer sets the words of the first stanza and then uses the same entire melody for all subsequent stanzas. A good example is the Welsh holiday carol *Deck the Halls*. Notice how the first phrase (**a**) of the musical unit (**A**), or stanza, is repeated.

hymns and carols

	a	Deck the halls with boughs of holly, fa, la, la, la, etc.
A	a	'Tis the season to be jolly, fa, la, la, la, la, etc.
	b	Don we now our gay apparel, fa, la, la, la, la, etc.
	a^1	Troll the ancient Yule-tide carol, fa, la, la, la, etc.

The basic musical unit, **A**, with the subdivisions **a, a, b, a^1**, is then heard four more times for each of the remaining stanzas, or strophes, of text. The overall form is thus:

A	A	A	A	A
a a b a^1	a a b a^1	a a b a^1	a a b a^1	a a b a^1

A famous example of strophic form can be heard in the well-known *Wiegenlied (Lullaby)* of Johannes Brahms. Here the same music is used for each of two strophes of text (for more on this piece, see page 325).

Listening Guide
Johannes Brahms
Lullaby (1868)

Intro CD/21

WWW

0:00	Piano introduction to first strophe
0:05	Strophe one
0:50	Piano introduction to second strophe
0:56	Strophe two

FIGURE 3-21

Louise Bourgeois' *Quarantania* (1941) displays six variations on a simple theme.

Theme and Variations If, in the preceding example, the music of the first stanza (**A**) is altered in some way each time it returns, then **theme and variations** form is present. Additions to the melody, new chords in the supporting accompaniment, and more density in the texture are the sort of changes that might occur. The return of the basic musical unit (**A**) provides a unifying element, while the changes add variety. Theme-and-variations form can be visualized in the following scheme:

Statement of theme	Variation 1	Variation 2	Variation 3	Variation 4
A	A^1	A^2	A^3	A^4

When Mozart was a young man he lived briefly in Paris, where he heard the French folk song, *Ah, vous dirai-je Maman*. We know it today as *Twinkle, Twinkle, Little Star*. Upon this charming tune (**A**) he later composed a set of variations for piano, the first three of which are described in the following Listening Guide (for more on this piece, see page 193).

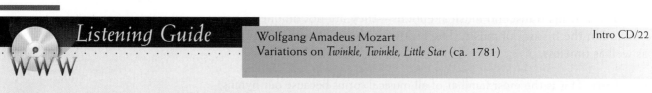

Listening Guide

Wolfgang Amadeus Mozart   Intro CD/22
Variations on *Twinkle, Twinkle, Little Star* (ca. 1781)

0:00	A	Tune played without ornamentation; melody above, harmony below
0:51	A^1	Variation 1: tune above decorated with florid, fast-moving figurations
1:45	A^2	Variation 2: tune above undecorated; florid, fast-moving figurations now in bass
2:36	A^3	Variation 3: tune above decorated with graceful arpeggios*

Binary Form As the name indicates, **binary form** consists of two contrasting units, **A** and **B**. In length and general shape, **A** and **B** are constructed so as to balance and complement each other. Variety is usually introduced in **B** by means of a dissimilar mood, key*, or melody. Sometimes in binary form, both **A** and **B** are immediately repeated, note for note. Musicians indicate exact repeats by means of the following sign: ‖: :‖. Thus, when binary form appears as ‖: A :‖: B :‖ it is performed **AABB**.

Joseph Haydn created a perfect example of binary form in music for the second movement of his Symphony No. 94. Here an eight-bar musical phrase (**A**) is balanced by a different but corresponding eight-bar phrase (**B**). First **A** and then **B** are repeated. Notice that the repeats involve slight alterations. In the repeat of **A**, Haydn adds a sudden *sforzando* to startle sleepy listeners. From this musical gesture the symphony derives its name: the "Surprise" Symphony. In the repeat of **B**, flutes are added to the melody to enrich it.

Listening Guide

Joseph Haydn   Intro CD/23
Symphony No. 94, The "Surprise" Symphony
Second movement, *Andante* (moving)

0:00	A presented by strings
0:17	A repeated with surprise *sforzando* at end
0:33	B presented by strings
0:50	B repeated with flutes added to the melody

With this charming binary-form melody now in place, Haydn proceeds to compose a set of variations upon it. The movement is discussed in full on page 195.

Ternary Form **Ternary form** in music is even more common than binary. It consists of three sections. The second is a contrasting unit, and the third is a repeat of the first—hence the formal pattern is **ABA**. As we will see later (page 183), ternary form has appeared at many different times in the history of music. It is an especially satisfying arrangement because it is simple yet rounded and complete. It, too, sometimes uses musical repeats, first of the **A** section, then of both **B** and **A** together (‖: A :‖‖: B A :‖).

Listen now to the *Dance of the Reed Pipes* from Peter Tchaikovsky's famous ballet *The Nutcracker*. The **A** section is bright and cheery because it makes use of the major mode as well as silvery flutes. However, **B** is dark and low, even ominous, owing to the minor mode and the insistent ostinato* in the bass. The return of **A** is shorted because the melody is not repeated.

Listening Guide
WWW

Peter Tchaikovsky
Dance of the Reed Pipes from *The Nutcracker* (1891)

Intro CD/24

0:00	Flutes play melody above low string pizzicato*	A
0:34	English horn and then clarinet add counterpoint	
0:49	Melody repeats with violins now adding counterpoint	
1:20	Change to minor mode: trumpets play melody above two-note bass ostinato*	B
1:35	Violins join melody	
1:53	Return to flute melody (with violin counterpoint) in major mode	A

Rondo Form **Rondo form** is almost as old as music itself. It uses a simple principle: A refrain alternates with contrasting music. Perhaps because of this simplicity, rondo form has been favored by musicians of every age—Medieval songsters, Classical symphonists such as Mozart and Haydn, and even contemporary rock stars like Elton John and Sting. Although the principle of a recurring refrain is a constant, composers have written rondos in several different formal patterns, including the following ones:

A B A B A   A B A C A   A B A C A B A

You may already be familiar with a rondo composed by Jean-Joseph Mouret (1682–1738), for it is used as the theme music for "Masterpiece Theatre" on PBS-TV. Mouret was a composer at the French court during the reign of Louis

Tate Gallery, London/Art Resource, New York

Cosy-Verlag, Salzburg

FIGURES 3–22 AND 3–23

(far left) The essence of binary form can be seen in Barbara Hepworth's *Two Figures (Menhirs)* (1964). Here the two units of sculpture are distinctly different, yet mutually harmonious. (left) Ternary form, or ABA form, can clearly be seen in the architecture of the cathedral of Salzburg, Austria, where Mozart and his father frequently performed.

FIGURE 3–24
The château of Chambord, France, has a formal design equivalent to **ABACABA** structure, a pattern often encountered in music in the rondo.

XV (1715–1774), and his well-known *Rondeau* typifies the ceremonial splendor of the royal household during the Baroque era (1600–1750). Here the refrain (**A**), played by full orchestra with brilliant trumpets and drums, alternates with two contrasting ideas (**B** and **C**) to form a neatly symmetrical pattern. The divisions between sections are clearly audible because each unit is played by a distinctive group of instruments. As you listen to Mouret's rondo, perhaps you will agree that a simple, effective formal principle is at work here.

Listening Guide

WWW

Jean-Joseph Mouret   Intro CD/25
Rondeau from *Suite de symphonies* (1729)

0:00	**A**	Refrain played by full orchestra, including trumpets and drums, and then repeated (at 0:12)
0:24	**B**	Quieter contrasting section played by organ
0:37	**A**	Refrain returns but without repeat
0:50	**C**	New contrasting section played by organ
1:21	**A**	Refrain returns and is repeated (at 1:33)

Although these examples of musical form are all short, they clearly show that an internal logic and cohesiveness is at work in each piece. More complex musical forms, of course, do exist, and these give rise to longer, more complex compositions. Sonata–allegro form and fugal form are the principal ones. These we will discuss when we come to the music of the Baroque and Classical periods. In addition, there are also free musical forms, such as the fantasy and the prelude, which give free reign to the composer's imagination without tight formal restraints. These, too, we will meet in good time.

Listening Exercises

8

Hearing the Instruments of the Orchestra   Intro CD/14
Identifying a Single Instrument

By listening to Intro CD, tracks 10–13, you have heard all of the principal instruments of the Western symphony orchestra. Now it is time to test your ability to identify these instruments. Intro CD, track 14 contains excerpts of performances of ten solo instruments. Write the name of the correct instrument in the blank by choosing one from the right-hand column.

1. 0:00 _____
2. 0:25 _____
3. 0:42 _____
4. 0:59 _____
5. 1:22 _____
6. 1:44 _____
7. 1:56 _____
8. 2:15 _____
9. 2:33 _____
10. 2:49 _____

trombone (Ravel)
double bass (Beethoven)
cello (Saint-Saëns)
flute (Tchaikovsky)
French horn (Brahms)
violin (Tchaikovsky)
bassoon (Rimsky-Korsakov)
tuba (Berlioz)
oboe (Tchaikovsky)
clarinet (Rimsky-Korsakov)

9

Hearing the Instruments of the Orchestra   Intro CD/15
Identifying Two Instruments

Now things get more difficult. Can you identify two instruments playing at once, and which is playing in a higher range? To keep you on track, a few instruments have been filled in. Choose from among the following instruments for the remaining blanks below: violin, viola, cello, double bass, flute (heard twice), clarinet, oboe (heard twice), bassoon, trumpet, and French horn.

	First Instrument	Second Instrument	Higher Instrument
0:00 Brahms:	French horn	1. _____	2. _____
0:40 Mahler:	3. _____	4. _____	5. _____
1:08 Lully:	6. _____	clarinet	7. _____
1:29 Bach:	8. _____	bassoon	9. _____
1:44 Bach:	10. _____	11. _____	12. _____
2:00 Telemann:	13. _____	viola	14. _____
2:27 Bartok:	15. _____	16. _____	17. _____
2:52 Bach:	18. _____	19. _____	20. _____

10

Hearing the Instruments of the Orchestra   Intro CD/16
Identifying Three Instruments

Ready for the ultimate test? Now you are asked to identify three instruments. Choose from among the following instruments for the blanks below: violin, viola, cello, flute (twice), clarinet, bassoon, trumpet (twice), trombone, French horn, and tuba.

	First Instrument	Second Instrument	Third Intrument
0:00 Lully:	1. _____	bassoon	2. _____
0:20 Tchaikovsky:	3. _____	French horn	4. _____
0:40 Tchaikovsky:	5. _____	6. _____	7. _____
1:00 Beethoven:	8. _____	9. _____	10. _____
1:34 Bach:	11. _____	French horn	12. _____

Finally, identify the highest and lowest sounding of the three instruments in the first four examples.

	Highest	Lowest
0:00 Lully:	13. _____	14. _____
0:20 Tchaikovsky:	15. _____	16. _____
0:40 Tchaikovsky:	17. _____	18. _____
1:00 Beethoven:	19. _____	20. _____

11

Hearing Musical Textures   Intro CD/20

This exercise asks you to become familiar with the three basic textures of music: monophonic, polyphonic, and homophonic. On your Intro CD, track 20, you have ten excerpts that exemplify these various textures. Monophonic texture, you will find, is easy to hear because it has only one line of music. More difficult is to differentiate between polyphonic texture and homophonic texture. Polyphonic texture embodies many active, independent lines. Homophonic texture, on the other hand, usually uses blocks of chords that accompany and support a single melody. Identify the texture of each of the excerpts by writing an M, P, or H in the appropriate blank.

1. (0:00) _____ Musorgsky, *Promenade* from *Pictures at an Exhibition*
2. (0:11) _____ Musorgsky, *Promenade* from *Pictures at an Exhibition*
3. (0:21) _____ Bach, *The Art of Fugue*, Contrapuntus IX
4. (1:07) _____ Musorgsky, *Goldenberg and Schmuyle* from *Pictures at an Exhibition*
5. (1:32) _____ Dvořák, Symphony No. 9, "From the New World," *Largo*
6. (2:05) _____ Bach, Organ Fugue in G minor
7. (2:58) _____ Louis Armstrong, *Willie the Weeper*
8. (3:22) _____ Josquin Desprez, *Ave Maria*
9. (3:49) _____ Debussy, *Prelude to The Afternoon of a Faun*
10. (4:14) _____ Tchaikovsky, *The 1812 Overture*

Key Words

binary form (62)	*piano* (56)	timbre (43)
canon (58)	pizzicato (45)	tremolo (45)
color (43)	polyphony (57)	trill (46)
counterpoint (57)	rondo form (63)	vibrato (45)
dynamics (56)	*sforzando* (56)	‖:‖ (indication to
forte (56)	strophic form (61)	performer to repeat
glissando (46)	ternary form (63)	the music) (62)
homophony (58)	texture (57)	
monophony (57)	theme and	
orchestral score (52)	variations (62)	

Hearing Musical Styles

WHAT IS MUSICAL STYLE?

One of the challenges of listening to music is to evaluate what we hear. Consciously or not, we do this every day. When we turn on the radio, for example, we often meet an unknown work for the first time. Intuitively we try to make an educated guess as to the genre and period of the music, and perhaps the composer. Is it rap or reggae, Romantic or Baroque, Bach or Beethoven? In regard to classical music, identifying the type and period of a composition, and even the composer, is the first step toward true musical enjoyment. This recognition is mainly an exercise in hearing musical style. But what is musical style? Style in music is the distinctive sound produced by the interaction of the elements of music: melody, rhythm, harmony, color, texture, and form. The special manner of presentation of all of these elements creates a style. Every composer, like every creative artist, has a personal style, one that makes his or her work different from that of all other artists. Take a work by Mozart (1756–1791), for example. A trained listener will recognize it as a piece from the Classical period (1750–1820) because of its generally symmetrical melodies, light texture, and dynamic ebb and flow. A truly experienced ear will identify Mozart as the composer, perhaps by recognizing the sudden shifts to minor keys, the intensely chromatic melodies, or the colorful writing for bassoon or clarinet—all hallmarks of Mozart's personal musical style.

Each period in the history of music has a musical style, too. That is to say, the music of one epoch will possess qualities common to much other music of that same time. A common set of musical practices and procedures is at work. Many motets* from the Renaissance (1475–1600) exhibit short bursts of imitative counterpoint sung by voices alone without instrumental accompaniment. A symphony* from the Romantic period (1820–1900), on the other hand, will typically exhibit long, non-imitative melodies, chromatic* harmonies, languid rhythms, and uniformly dense orchestral textures.

Historical periods, in some ways, mirror the ages of humankind. We cannot identify the precise moment in which an infant becomes a child or the child the adult. Similarly, musical styles do not change overnight; they evolve and overlap. Composers can stand midway between periods. For example, Guillaume Dufay (ca. 1400–1474) is a composer of the Middle Ages in his use of texture, but of the Renaissance in regard to his harmonies. Ludwig van Beethoven (1770–1827) straddles the Classical and Romantic periods, being somewhat conservative in his choice of harmonies but radically progressive in his use of form and rhythm. Despite such contradictions, historians of music, like historians of art, find it useful to discuss style in terms of historical periods. This makes it possible to conceptualize and speak about these arts in a more convenient way. Here are the stylistic periods that are discussed in the following chapters:

listening according to style

STYLES

Portions of the East Wing of the National Gallery of Art in Washington, designed by I. M. Pei, stand in contrast to the United States Capitol in the background. Pei's building, with its flat surfaces and unadorned geometric shapes, is representative of the modern style in architecture, while the Capitol reflects the neoclassical style of the eighteenth century.

National Gallery of Art, Washington/Photo: Dennis Brack/Black Star

Middle Ages: 400–1475   Classical: 1750–1820
Renaissance: 1475–1600   Romantic: 1820–1900
Early Baroque: 1600–1710   Impressionist: 1880–1920
Late Baroque: 1710–1750   Twentieth Century: 1900–present

CHECKLIST OF MUSICAL STYLE BY PERIODS

Middle Ages: 400–1475

Representative composers: Hildegard of Bingen, Leoninus, Perotinus, Machaut, Countess of Dia, Dufay, Binchois

Principal genres: Gregorian chant, polyphonic Mass, *troubadour* and *trouvère* songs, secular polyphonic chanson, instrumental dance

Melody:	Moves mostly by step within a narrow range; uses diatonic and not chromatic notes of the scale
Harmony:	Most surviving medieval music is monophonic Gregorian chant or monophonic *troubadour* and *trouvère* songs—hence there is no harmony
	Medieval polyphony (Mass, motet, and chanson) has dissonant phrases ending with open, hollow-sounding chords
Rhythm:	Gregorian chant as well as *troubadour* and *trouvère* songs sung mainly in notes of equal value without clearly marked rhythms; medieval polyphony is composed mostly in triple meter and uses repeating rhythmic patterns
Color:	Mainly vocal sounds (choir or soloists); little instrumental music survives
Texture:	Mostly monophonic—Gregorian chant as well as *troubadour* and *trouvère* songs are monophonic melodies
	Medieval polyphony (two, three, or four independent lines) is mainly contrapuntal
Form:	Strophic form of *troubadour* and *trouvère* songs; ternary form of the Kyrie; rondo form of the French *rondeau*

Renaissance: 1475–1600

Representative composers: Desprez, Palestrina, Byrd, Lasso, Weelkes, Dowland

Principal genres: sacred Mass and motet, secular chanson and madrigal, instrumental dance

Melody:	Mainly stepwise motion within a moderately narrow range; still mainly diatonic, but some intense chromaticism found in madrigals from end of period
Harmony:	More careful use of dissonance than in the Middle Ages as the triad, a consonant chord, becomes the basic building block of harmony
Rhythm:	Duple meter is now as common as triple meter; rhythm in sacred vocal music (Mass and motet) is relaxed and without strong downbeats; rhythm in secular vocal music (chanson and madrigal) and in instrumental dances is usually lively and catchy, with frequent use of syncopation
Color:	Although more music for instruments alone has survived, the predominant sound remains that of unaccompanied vocal music, whether for soloists or for choir

Texture: Contrapuntal, polyphonic texture for four or five vocal lines is heard throughout Mass, motet, and madrigal, though occasional passages of chordal homophonic texture are inserted for variety

Form: Strict musical forms are not often used; most Masses, motets, madrigals, chansons, and instrumental dances are through-composed—have no musical repetitions and hence no standard formal plan

Early Baroque: 1600–1710

Melody: Less stepwise movement, larger leaps, wider range, and more chromaticism reflect influence of virtuosic solo singing; melodic patterns idiomatic to particular musical instruments emerge; introduction of melodic sequence

Harmony: Stable, diatonic chords played by *basso continuo* support melody; clearly defined chord progressions begin to develop; tonality reduced to major and minor keys

Rhythm: Relaxed, flexible rhythms of the Renaissance transformed into regularly repeating, driving rhythms

Color: Musical timbre becomes enormously varied as traditional instruments are perfected (e.g., harpsichord, violin, and oboe) and new combinations of voices and instruments are explored; symphony orchestra begins to take shape; sudden shifts in dynamics (terraced dynamics) reflect dramatic quality of Baroque music

Texture: Chordal, homophonic texture predominates; top and bottom lines are the strongest as *basso continuo* creates a powerful bass to support the melody above

Form: Arias and instrumental works often make use of *basso ostinato* procedure; ritornello form emerges in the concerto grosso; binary form regulates most movements of the sonata and orchestral suite

Representative composers: Gabrieli, Monteverdi, Barbara Strozzi, Purcell, Corelli, Vivaldi

Principal genres: polychoral motet, cantata, opera, sonata, concerto grosso, solo concerto, orchestral suite

Late Baroque: 1710–1750

Melody: Grows longer, more expansive, and more asymmetrical; idiomatic instrumental style influences vocal melodies

Harmony: Functional chord progressions govern harmonic movement—harmony moves purposefully from one chord to the next; *basso continuo* continues to provide strong bass

Rhythm: Exciting, driving, energized rhythms propel music forward with vigor; "walking" bass creates feeling of rhythmic regularity

Color: Instruments reign supreme; instrumental sounds, especially of violin, harpsichord, and organ, set musical tone for the era; one tone color used throughout a movement or large section of movement

Texture: Homophonic texture remains important, but polyphonic texture reemerges because of growing importance of the contrapuntal fugue

Form: Binary form in sonatas and orchestral suites; *da capo* aria (ternary) form in arias; fugal procedure used in fugue

Representative composers: Bach, Handel, Telemann, Vivaldi

Principal genres: cantata, opera, oratorio, sonata, orchestral suite, concerto grosso, prelude, and fugue

Classical: 1750–1820

Representative composers: Mozart, Haydn, Beethoven, Schubert

Principal genres: symphony, sonata, string quartet, solo concerto, opera

Melody:	Short, balanced phrases create tuneful melodies; melody more influenced by vocal than instrumental style; frequent cadences produce light, airy feeling
Harmony:	The rate at which chords change (harmonic rhythm) varies dramatically, creating a dynamic flux and flow; simple chordal harmonies made more active by "Alberti" bass
Rhythm:	Departs from regular, driving patterns of Baroque era to become more stop-and-go; greater rhythmic variety within a single movement
Color:	Orchestra grows larger; woodwind section of two flutes, oboes, clarinets, and bassoons becomes typical; piano replaces harpsichord as principal keyboard instrument
Texture:	Mostly homophonic; thin bass and middle range, hence light and transparent; passages in contrapuntal style appear sparingly and mainly for contrast
Form:	A few standard forms regulate much of Classical music: sonata–allegro, theme and variations, rondo, ternary (for minuets and trios), and double exposition (for solo concerto)

Romantic: 1820–1900

Representative composers: Beethoven, Schubert, Berlioz, Mendelssohn, Robert Schumann, Clara Schumann, Chopin, Liszt, Verdi, Wagner, Bizet, Brahms, Dvořák, Tchaikovsky, Musorgsky, Mahler, Puccini

Principal genres: symphony, program symphony, symphonic poem, concert overture, opera, *Lied*, orchestral *Lied*, solo concerto, character piece for piano, ballet music

Melody:	Long, singable lines with powerful climaxes and chromatic inflections for expressiveness
Harmony:	Greater use of chromaticism makes the harmony richer and more colorful; sudden shifts to remote chords for expressive purposes; more dissonance to convey feeling of anxiety and longing
Rhythm:	Rhythms are flexible, often languid, and therefore meter is sometimes not clearly articulated; tempo can fluctuate greatly (tempo *rubato*); tempo can slow to a crawl to allow for "the grand gesture"
Color:	The orchestra becomes enormous, reaching upward of one hundred performers: trombone, tuba, contrabassoon, piccolo, and English horn added to the ensemble; experiments with new playing techniques for special effects; dynamics vary widely to create different levels of expression; piano becomes larger and more powerful
Texture:	Predominantly homophonic but dense and rich because of larger orchestra; sustaining pedal on the piano also adds to density
Form:	No new forms created, rather traditional forms (strophic, sonata–allegro, and theme and variations, for example) used and extended in length; traditional forms also applied to new genres such as *Lied*, symphonic poem, and orchestral *Lied*

Impressionist: 1880–1920

Representative composers: Debussy, Ravel, Fauré

Melody:	Varies from short dabs of sound to long, free-flowing lines; melodies are rarely tuneful or singable; they often twist and turn rapidly in undulating patterns; chromatic scale, whole-tone

scale, and pentatonic scale often replace usual major and minor scales

Harmony: Primarily homophonic; triad is extended to form seventh chords and ninth chords, and these frequently move in parallel motion

Rhythm: Usually free and flexible with irregular accents, making it sometimes difficult to determine the meter; rhythmic ostinatos used to give feeling of stasis rather than movement

Color: More emphasis on woodwinds and brasses and less on the violins as primary carriers of melody; more soloistic writing to show that the color of the instrument is as important as the melody line it plays

Texture: Can vary from thin and airy to heavy and dense; sustaining pedal of the piano often used to create a wash of sound; glissandos run quickly from low to high or high to low

Form: Traditional forms involving clear-cut repetitions rarely used; composers try to develop a form unique and particular to each new musical work

Principal genres: symphonic poem, string quartet, orchestral *Lied*, opera, character piece for piano

Twentieth Century: 1900–present

Melody: Wide-ranging disjunct lines, often chromatic and dissonant, angularity accentuated by use of octave displacement

Harmony: Highly dissonant; dissonance no longer must move to consonance but may move to another dissonance; sometimes two conflicting, but equal, tonal centers sound simultaneously (polytonality); sometimes there is no audible tonal center (atonality)

Rhythm: Vigorous, energetic rhythms; conflicting simultaneous meters (polymeters) and rhythms (polyrhythms) make for temporal complexity

Color: Color becomes an agent of form and beauty in and by itself; composers seek new sounds from traditional, acoustical instruments, from electronic instruments and computers, and from noises in the environment

Texture: As varied and individual as the men and women composing music

Form: A range of extremes: sonata–allegro, rondo, theme and variations benefit from a Neo-classical revival; twelve-tone procedure allows for an almost mathematical formal control; yet chance music permits random happenings and noises from the environment to shape a musical work; the forms and processes of classical music, jazz, and pop music begin to influence one another in exciting new ways.

Representative composers: Stravinsky, Schoenberg, Berg, Webern, Bartók, Varèse, Ives, Cage, Prokofiev, Shostakovich, Copland, Zwilich, Adams, Tavener, Bernstein, Gershwin

Principal genres: symphony, solo concerto, string quartet, opera, ballet music, electronic music, chance music, Broadway musical, film music

Chapter 4

Bibliothèque nationale, Paris

Medieval Music

Historians use the term "Middle Ages" as a catchall phrase to refer to the thousand years of history between the fall of the Roman Empire (late 400s) and the age of reawakening and discovery, exemplified by the voyages of Christopher Columbus (late 1400s). It was a period of triumphs and tragedies, of soaring cathedrals and murderous plagues, of sublime spirituality and abject poverty, of knightly chivalry and barbarous warfare. Seen from our modern perspective, the medieval period appears as a vast chronological expanse dotted by occasional outposts of dazzling architecture, stunning stained glass, and equally compelling poetry, painting, and music.

MUSIC IN THE MONASTERY

There were many kinds of music in the Middle Ages: songs for the knights as they rode into battle, songs for the men in the fields and the women around the hearth, songs and dances for the nobles in their castles, and chants for the priests as they celebrated the Christian service in the monasteries and cathedrals. Unfortunately, most of this music, and virtually all of it emanating from the common folk, is now lost because it was never written down. Only the music of the Church is preserved in any significant amount, because at that time only the men of the Church, and to a lesser degree the nuns, were educated. Even the nobility was more or less illiterate. The reading and copying of texts was the private preserve of the rural monasteries and, somewhat later, the urban cathedrals. The monks were encouraged to read and write as a means of becoming more familiar with the scriptures, and it was they who devised a system to notate and copy music. In this way, the music of the Church could be spread to other monastic communities and taught to succeeding generations of novices.

Life was rigorous in a medieval monastery. The founder of the principal monastic order, St. Benedict (died ca. 547), prescribed a code of conduct, or rule, for his followers. The Benedictines rose at about four o'clock in the morning for the night office (matins), at which they sang psalms and read scripture. After a break "for the necessities of nature" the brethren returned at daybreak to sing another service in praise of the Lord. The high point of the church day was the Mass, celebrated about nine o'clock in the morning; it commemorated Christ's suffering on the cross through the ritual act of communion (see page 78). Between these religious services the monks dispersed to farm and otherwise attend to their lands. They worked to feed their bodies, and they prayed and sang to save their souls, day after day, year after year.

life in the monastery

GREGORIAN CHANT

The music sung daily at the eight monastic hours of prayer and at Mass was what we today call Gregorian chant, named in honor of Pope Gregory the Great (540?–604). Ironically, Gregory wrote little, if any, of this music. Being more a church administrator than a musician, he merely decreed that certain chants should be sung on certain days of the liturgical year. Melodies for the Christian service had, of course, existed since the time of the Apostles, a very few perhaps taken directly from the Jewish Temple. What we now call **Gregorian chant** (also called **plainsong**) is really a large body of unaccompanied vocal music, setting sacred Latin texts, written for the Western (Roman Catholic) Church over the course of fifteen centuries. Churchmen and churchwomen composed chant from the time of the earliest Fathers to the Council of Trent (1545–1563), which brought sweeping reforms to the Church of Rome.

chant composed for fifteen centuries

Gregorian chant is like no other music. It has a timeless, otherworldly quality that arises, no doubt, because Gregorian chant has neither meter nor regular rhythms. True, some notes are longer or shorter than others, but they do not recur in obvious patterns that would allow us to clap our hands or tap our feet. This is music intended to encourage pious reflection, not dancing. It is free of tension and drama. All voices sing together in unison*. Thus all Gregorian chant is considered monophony*, or music for one line. There is no instrumental accompaniment, nor, as a rule, are men's and women's voices mixed when performing chant. Finally, Gregorian chant has a uniform, monochromatic sound. Any contrasts that occur are of the mildest sort. Sometimes a soloist will alternate with a full choir, for example. Occasionally, a passage of **syllabic singing** (only one or two notes for each syllable of text) will give way to **melismatic singing** (many notes sung to just one syllable), as in Ex. 4–1, from Hildegard of Bingen's O *Greenest Branch.*

FIGURE 4–1

A twelfth-century illumination depicting Hildegard of Bingen receiving divine inspiration, perhaps a vision or a chant, directly from the heavens. To the right, her secretary, the monk Volmar, peeks in on her in amazement.

FIGURE 4–2

(upper frame) A vision of Hildegard revealing how a fantastic winged figure of God the Father, the Son, and the Mystical Lamb killed the serpent Satan with a blazing sword. (lower frame) Hildegard (center) receives the vision and reports it to her secretary (left). This manuscript dates from the twelfth century.

EXAMPLE 4–1

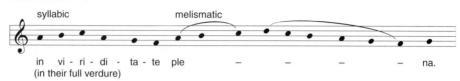

in vi - ri - di - ta - te ple — — — — na.
(in their full verdure)

syllabic   melismatic

The overall effect of Gregorian chant is thus one of endless peace and serenity. Through chant, the receptive listener can gradually disengage from the anxieties and tensions of the present world.

THE GREGORIAN CHANT OF HILDEGARD OF BINGEN (1098–1179)

We know the names of only a few of the composers of Gregorian chant. And what we know of their lives suggests that they thought of themselves not so much as creators or composers, but as conduits for the voice of God—vessels through which the divine message might be brought to those here on earth. One of the most remarkable contributors to the repertoire of Gregorian chant was Abbess Hildegard of Bingen (1098–1179), from whose pen we have received seventy-seven chants (Fig. 4–1). Hildegard was the tenth child of noble parents who gave her to the Church as a tithe (a donation of a tenth of one's worldly income). She was educated by Benedictine nuns and then, at the age of fifty-two, founded her own convent near the small town of Bingen, in Germany, on the west bank of the Rhine River. In the course of time, Hildegard manifested her extraordinary intellect and imagination as a playwright, poet, musician, naturalist, pharmacologist, and visionary. Popes and kings sought her advice. Though never officially canonized by the Roman Church, Hildegard is nonetheless widely regarded as a saint.

From an early age, Hildegard possessed unusual spiritual gifts. During moments that we might recognize as severe migraine attacks, she heard a voice and saw visions accompanied by great flashes of light: a serpent-like Satan devouring the petals of a scarlet rose, or the blood of Christ streaming in the heavens, for example (Fig. 4–2). These images she transformed into poetry and set to music as liturgical chant—Gregorian chant. Her mystical song to the Virgin Mary, *O viridissima virga* (*O Greenest Branch*, Ex. 4–2), vividly depicts Mary as the most verdant branch of the tree of Jesse, through whom the heat of the sun radiates like the aroma of balm. The joyful Mary brings new life to all flora and fauna of the earth.

Hildegard's *O Greenest Branch* possesses many qualities typical of Gregorian chant. It gravitates around a tonal center—here, the pitch G. Notice in the first stanza (Ex. 4–2) how the music starts on G, works up a fifth to the pitch D and then down an octave to the D below, finally returning to the initial G. Notice also how *O Greenest Branch* is a predominantly stepwise melody, one without large leaps. It also avoids chromatic* twists—added sharps and flats—that might make the chant more difficult to perform. This was, after all, choral music to be sung by the full community of musically unsophisticated monks or nuns, so it had to be simple and direct. In the case of *O Greenest Branch*, we have a chant intended to be sung at Mass. (It is a Sequentia, the sixth musical portion of the Mass—see page 79.) Finally, *O*

Greenest Branch was conceived without rhythm or meter. The notes are generally of one basic value, something close to our eighth note in length. The unaccompanied, monophonic line and the absence of rhythmic drive allow a restful, contemplative mood to develop. The music is meant to float unfettered as it bears the transcendent spirit aloft.

EXAMPLE 4–2: Hildegard of Bingen, *O Greenest Branch*

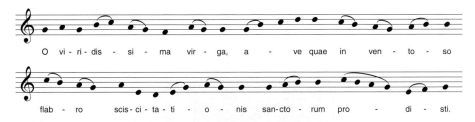

O vi - ri - dis - si - ma vir - ga, a - ve quae in ven - to - so

flab - ro scis - ci - ta - ti - o - nis san-cto - rum pro - di - sti.

Listening Guide
WWW

Hildegard of Bingen
Gregorian chant, *O Greenest Branch* (ca. 1150)

6CD 1/1;
2CD 1/1

Texture: monophonic

Stanza 1

0:00   O viridissima virga, ave
quae in ventoso flabro sciscitationis
sanctorum prodisti.

Hail, o greenest branch
who sprang forth in the airy breeze
of the prayers of the saints.

Stanza 2

0:27   Cum venit tempus,
quod tu floruisti,
in ramis tuis,
ave, ave sit tibi,
quia calor solis in te sudavit
sicut odor balsami.

So the time has come that
you flourished
in your boughs,
hail, hail to you,
because the heat of the sun radiated
in you like the aroma of balm.

Stanza 3

1:01   Nam in te floruit pulcher flos
qui odorem dedit omnibus aromatibus
quae arida erant.

For in you bloomed the beautiful
flower which scented all parched
perfumes.

Stanza 4

1:28   Et illa apparuerunt omnia
in viriditate plena.

And all things have been manifested
in their full verdure.

Stanza 5

1:46   Unde celi dederunt rorem super gramen
et omnis terra leta facta est,
quoniam viscera ipsius frumentum protulerunt
et quoniam volucres celi nidos in ipsa habuerunt.

Whence the skies set down dew on the
pasture, and all the earth was made
more joyful because her womb produced
grain, and because the birds of Heaven
built their nests in her.

Stanza 6

2:27   Deinde facta est esca hominibus
et gaudium magnum epulantium;
inde, o suavis virgo,
in te non deficit ullum gaudium.

Then the harvest was made ready for
Man, and a great rejoicing of
banqueters, because in you,
o sweet Virgin, no joy is lacking.

Stanza 7

2:59   Hec omnia Eva contempsit.
Nunc autem laus sit altissimo.

All these things Eve rejected.
Now let there be praise to you in the Highest.

(Listening Exercise 12)

Chant at the Top of the Charts

In recent years, Gregorian chant has become all the rage. The excitement began in 1994 with the release, appropriately enough by Angel Records, of the CD *Chant*, which sold one million copies within the first two months of its appearance. That success spawned sequels, leading to the present *Chant IV* (Angel 56373). Much of the popularity of Gregorian chant can be attributed to the fact that it has stylistic traits in common with New Age Music. Both project smooth, uniform, rhythmically fluid sounds that are decidedly non-assertive and nonconfrontational.

Hildegard, too, has been popularized as something of a New Age mystic. She is a fixture on the World Wide Web, where you can study her chants in the original notation, find translations of her poetry, view spectacular medieval depictions of her visions, and order the latest CD. The year 1998 marked the nine-hundredth anniversary of Hildegard's birth and, right on cue, a half-dozen new Hildegard CDs appeared, as well as a lengthy video and a shorter video clip for MTV. On one recent CD entitled *Vision* (Angel 55246), Hildegard's chants are accompanied by synthesizer and rock guitar. Could the visionary nun have foreseen that the intensely spiritual would become the overtly commercial?

MUSIC IN THE CATHEDRAL

If the monastery was primarily a rural establishment, one of solitude and spiritual contemplation, the cathedral was an urban institution. Every cathedral served as the "home church" of a bishop, the spiritual leader of the people, and only in a city could a bishop minister effectively to a flock of any size. During the twelfth and thirteenth centuries, the population of the urban centers of Europe—Milan, Paris, and London, among others—grew significantly, owing to a healthy revival of trade and commerce. Much of the commercial wealth that flowed to the cities was channeled toward the construction of splendid new churches that served not only as houses of worship but also as civic auditoriums. So substantial was this building campaign that the period 1150–1350 is often called "the Age of the Cathedrals." In these years, the great urban cathedrals of England, Spain, France, Italy, and Germany rose above the city skyline; many of them are still visible today. Most were constructed in what we call the Gothic style, with pointed arches, high ceiling vaults, supporting buttresses, and richly colored stained glass.

the age of cathedrals

Gothic architecture began in France and radiated in all directions to foreign lands, even to the Christian-held territories of the Near East. In a similar way, France was the wellspring of other intellectual and artistic developments at this time. Paris, which by the end of the thirteenth century counted eighty thousand inhabitants, had become the leading university town in Europe for the study of the arts and theology. Young clerical scholars from distant countries flocked to the Parisian schools, and when they returned to their native lands they took with them the teachings of philosophers like Peter Abelard (1079–1142) and Thomas Aquinas (1225?–1274) as well as the music they had heard at the cathedral of Notre Dame (Our Lady) of Paris (Fig. 4–3).

Paris, an intellectual center

Notre Dame of Paris

Notre Dame of Paris was begun in the 1160s, yet was not completed until more than a hundred years later. Throughout this period the cathedral was blessed with a succession of churchmen who were not only theologians and philosophers but poets and musicians as well. Foremost among these were Master Leoninus (fl. 1169–1201) and Master Perotinus, called the Great (fl. 1198–1236). Leoninus wrote a great book of religious music (*Magnus liber organi*) to adorn the Gregorian chant sung at Notre Dame on high feasts. Perotinus revised the book of Leoninus and also composed many additional pieces of his own.

What is new about this Gothic church music is that it is written in polyphony* (two or more voices, or lines, sounding simultaneously) and not merely monophonic (one-voice) Gregorian chant. In truth, earlier church musicians had attempted to enhance the sound of the plainsong of the Church by adding another voice to it, but these efforts often required the new voice to move in exact parallel motion, usually at the interval of a fourth, a fifth, or an octave, with the preexisting chant. Leoninus, however, seized the opportunity to create an autonomous second voice, one that did not merely duplicate and amplify the plainsong but that complemented and graced it. Indeed, the added voice became the center of attention. In this musical development, we see an early instance of a creative spirit breaking free of the constraints of the ancient authority of the Church.

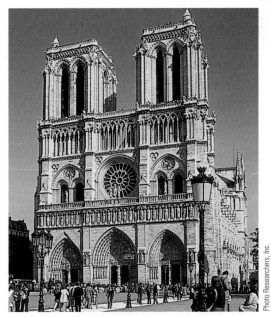

FIGURE 4–3

The Cathedral of Notre Dame of Paris, begun ca. 1160, was one of the first to be built in the new Gothic style of architecture. The polyphony of Master Leoninus and Master Perotinus was composed as the building was being constructed.

LEONINUS: ORGANUM *VIDERUNT OMNES*

The expressive freedom Leoninus imparted to the new voice can be seen in his setting of the Gregorian chant *Viderunt omnes* for Mass on Christmas Day. By adding his own musical line above the chant, Leoninus created a two-voice **organum**, the name given to early church polyphony. The old chant is strung out in the lower voice and Leoninus's newly created line is on top. Soloists were assigned to the organum. Yet they sang in this new polyphonic style only for the first two words of the chant, "Viderunt omnes," which become much longer because of the addition of the new voice. Thereafter, the full clerical choir entered to continue and complete the remaining music in monophonic Gregorian chant. Try listening to this piece twice, first as it is given in the nearby Listening Guide, which shows the Gregorian chant in full below and a graphic indication of Leoninus's added part above. Then listen again, now trying to follow both lines of the organum as they appear in an original thirteenth-century manuscript from Paris (Fig. 4–4). As you can see in the manuscript, Leoninus's newly created upper voice undulates and even cascades in a virtuosic way as the lower voice holds the chant in long notes. Only at the beginning of the word "omnes" is any sort of rhythmic precision introduced. At this time medieval musical notation could indicate pitches accurately, but was only beginning to deal with matters of rhythm. What Leoninus has fashioned here is a rather free, rhapsodic hymn in praise of the Christ child. Imagine how these new sounds struck the ear of the citizen of medieval Paris as the notes rebounded around the bare stone walls of the vast, newly constructed cathedral of Notre Dame.

FIGURE 4–4

A thirteenth-century manuscript preserving Leoninus's organum for Christmas, *Viderunt omnes*. Here, eleven four-line staves are shown. Leoninus's newly created voice is notated on each of the odd-numbered staves while the slower-moving Gregorian chant appears below it on each of the even-numbered staves.

Listening Guide

WWW

Master Leoninus
Organum with Gregorian chant, *Viderunt omnes*
(ca. 1180)

6CD 1/2

Texture: polyphonic, then monophonic

0:00 Leoninus' added line   1:21

Chant

Vi- de- runt o - - - mnes fi - nes ter - rae

sa- lu - ta - re De - - i no- stri: ju- bi- la- te De -

- o o - - mnis ter - ra.

All the ends of the earth have seen the salvation of our God: Sing joyfully to God, all the earth.

0:00   Polyphonic organum sung by soloists
1:21   Monophonic chant sung by choir

FIGURE 4–5

Interior of the cathedral of Reims looking from floor to ceiling. The pillars carry the eye up to the ribbed vaults of the roof, creating a feeling of great upward movement, just as the Mass of Machaut, with four superimposed voices, has a new sense of verticality.

Craig Wright, New Haven

Notre Dame of Reims

Notre Dame of Paris was not the only important cathedral devoted to Our Lady in northern Europe. The city of Reims, one hundred miles east of Paris in the Champagne region, was graced with a monument equally large and impressive (Fig. 4–5). In the fourteenth century it, too, benefited from the service of a poetically and musically talented churchman, Guillaume de Machaut (1300?–1377). Judging by his nearly 150 surviving works, Machaut was the most important composer of the fourteenth century. And he was equally esteemed as a narrative and lyric poet. Today, historians of literature place him on a pedestal with his slightly younger English counterpart, Geoffrey Chaucer (1340?–1400), author of the *Canterbury Tales*. Indeed, Chaucer knew and borrowed heavily from the poetic works of Machaut.

MACHAUT: *MASS OF OUR LADY*

Machaut's *Messe de Nostre Dame (Mass of Our Lady)* is deservedly the best-known work in the entire repertoire of medieval music. It is impressive for its length and novel way it applies music to the texts of the **Mass**—the central and most important service of the Roman Catholic Church. Before Machaut's time, composers writing polyphony for the Mass had set only one or two sections of what is called the **Proper of the Mass** (chants whose texts changed to suit the feast day in question). Leoninus's *Viderunt omnes*, for example, is a setting of the Gradual (see box) of the Proper of the Mass for Christmas Day. Machaut, on the other hand, chose to set all of the chants of the **Ordinary of the Mass** (chants with unvarying texts that were sung virtually every day),

Musical Portions of the Mass

PROPER OF THE MASS	ORDINARY OF THE MASS
1. Introit (an introductory chant for the entry of the celebrating clergy)	
	2. Kyrie (a petition for mercy)
	3. Gloria (a hymn of praise to the Lord)
4. Gradual (a reflective chant)	
5. Alleluia or Tract (a chant of thanksgiving or penance)	
6. Sequentia (a chant commenting on the text of the Alleluia)	
	7. Credo (a profession of faith)
8. Offertory (a chant for the offering)	
	9. Sanctus (an acclamation to the Lord)
	10. Agnus Dei (a petition for mercy and eternal peace)
11. Communion (a chant accompanying communion)	

and he united, or linked, these together by placing a distinctive musical motive, a descending scale, in each of the five movements. Setting the Ordinary of the Mass had the obvious practical advantage that the composition could be heard more than on just one feast day of the church year. Machaut's *Mass of Our Lady*, for example, could be sung any time a Mass in honor of the Virgin Mary was celebrated. The box at the top of this page lists the musical portions of the Mass and the order in which they are sung.

Although Machaut's innovation—creating a unified setting of the Ordinary of the Mass—was not embraced immediately by all composers in all regions, by the early fifteenth century his idea had come to be adopted universally in the West. Henceforth, to write a polyphonic Mass for the Church meant that a composer would set the five texts of the Ordinary (Kyrie, Gloria, Credo, Sanctus, and Agnus Dei) and find some way to bind or shape them musically into an integrated unit. This is true not only for later masters like Bach, Mozart, Beethoven, and Schubert, but also for more modern composers like Igor Stravinsky, whose Mass of 1948, by his own admission, owes much to the model of Machaut.

Ordinary of the Mass

The *Kyrie* of Machaut's *Mass of Our Lady* is a threefold petition for mercy (*Kyrie eleison* means "Lord have mercy upon us"). As in the previous example by Leoninus, it is built on a preexisting Gregorian chant that is held in longer notes than the surrounding material. Because the men who sang the chant sustained it in long notes, they came to be called the "tenors" (from the Latin *tenere*, "to hold"). Around them Machaut added not one new line but three, thereby creating four-voice polyphony. The two voices added above the tenor came to be called the *superius* and the *contratenor altus*, whence we get our terms "soprano" and "alto." The voice added below the tenor was called the *contratenor bassus*, whence our term "bass" (for more on the four standard voice parts, see page 43). By writing for four voices and spreading these over a range of two and a half octaves, Machaut was able to create truly sonorous

names of the voice parts

Music at the Forefront of Science

During the Middle Ages—indeed since the time of Plato—music was viewed not as an art but as a science. It was studied in the schools and universities along with geometry, astronomy, and arithmetic in a curriculum called the *quadrivium*. These four subjects were deemed the core sciences because each could be precisely measured. The musical interval of the octave, for example, could be demonstrated by means of two strings the lengths of which were in a 2:1 proportion; a fifth could be produced by strings with a ratio of 3:2, and so on. A separate curriculum, called the *trivium* (grammar, logic, and rhetoric), was devoted to the study of language and philosophy. These subjects together constituted the seven liberal arts. Such English phrases as Bachelor of Arts and Master of Arts recall this ancient formulation.

The Middle Ages gave to Western society a gift that accounts for the near total domination of the West today in matters of science and technology: rigorous quantification. During the late Middle Ages most important modes of human experience—the measurement of time, the calculation of the value of goods and services, the mapping of the surface of the earth, even the visual layout of a painting—came to be measured in proportional units. Around 1320 pipe organs and mechanical clocks appear in the naves of churches—shining examples of the new technology wrought by measurement. Measurement also was applied to music by means of a system of notation that regulated the two primary components of this art: sound and time (see Fig. 4–6). Pitch was determined by setting symbols higher or lower on a grid of horizontal lines. Time was controlled by giving different shapes (note shapes) to those symbols so as to indicate precise durations. The larger notes were exact multiples of smaller ones, just as whole, quarter, and half notes are today. Thus by 1350, the heyday of Machaut, all the elements of modern musical notation were essentially in place. The components of music were precisely measured and manipulated far earlier than those in other areas of human activity. The musical staff was the West's first graph.

FIGURE 4–6

A poem by Machaut, a miniature portrait of the composer at work, and a poem by him set to music. The position of the notes on the vertical axis gives the pitch; the shape of the notes on the horizontal axis indicates their duration.

choral polyphony. In the *Kyrie* of his Mass, Machaut intended his four-voice polyphony to alternate with the sections of monophonic Gregorian chant.

When you listen to Machaut's *Kyrie* for the first time, you will be struck by its dark, dissonant sound. The dark quality is present because only male voices are employed here. Only men and choirboys were allowed to sing in medieval cathedrals. Men in falsetto voice (see page 98) or boys sang the soprano and alto parts. Sacred singing by women was confined to nunneries (for more on this point, see pages 82 and 99). As to the dissonant, biting sound, it is caused by the fact that Machaut makes use of many unusual dissonances, ones later forbidden in Western polyphonic music by music theorists. In stark contrast to these dissonances, each section of polyphony ends with an open, somewhat hollow-sounding consonant chord. These chords use only the intervals of a fifth and an octave. Such open, hollow final chords sound especially rich in buildings with very resonant, or "lively," acoustics of the sort universally found in medieval cathedrals.

Listening Guide

WWW

Guillaume de Machaut
Kyrie of the *Mass of Our Lady* (ca. 1360)

6CD 1/3

Form: ternary
Texture: polyphonic and monophonic

0:00	Kyrie eleison (polyphony)	Lord have mercy upon us
1:00	Kyrie eleison (Gregorian chant)	Lord have mercy upon us
1:22	Kyrie eleison (polyphony)	Lord have mercy upon us
2:22	Christe eleison (Gregorian chant)	Christ have mercy upon us
2:41	Christe eleison (polyphony)	Christ have mercy upon us
3:35	Christe eleison (Gregorian chant)	Christ have mercy upon us
3:56	Kyrie eleison (polyphony)	Lord have mercy upon us
4:40	Kyrie eleison (Gregorian chant)	Lord have mercy upon us
4:59	Kyrie eleison (polyphony)	Lord have mercy upon us

MUSIC AT THE COURT

Outside the walls of cathedral there was yet another musical world, one of popular song and dance centered at the court. Indeed, the court embraced forms of public entertainment not permitted by church authorities. Itinerant actors, jugglers, jesters, and animal acts all provided welcome diversions. Minstrels wandered from castle to castle, bringing the latest tunes, along with bits of news and gossip. Churchmen, too, sojourned at court. Guillaume de Machaut, for example, enjoyed a double career as cleric and courtier. He composed liturgical music for the cathedral of Reims, yet at various times in his life was employed by the king of Bohemia, the king of Navarre, and the duke of Berry. While it may seem strange that a clergyman like Machaut was active in worldly affairs at court, during the Middle Ages learned churchmen were much in demand for their ability to read and write. And because of their skill with letters and their knowledge of musical notation gained in the church, clerics were inevitably drawn to the poetry and music of the courtly song. Indeed, most of the polyphonic love songs emanating from the court in the late Middle Ages were written by ordained priests.

churchmen active at the court

The court first emerged as a center for the patronage of the arts during the years 1150–1400. The fourteenth century in particular witnessed a general decline in the authority of the Church, epitomized by the "Babylonian captivity" (1309–1377), during which the popes, driven from Rome, lived as exiles in France. Kings, dukes, counts, and lesser nobles now assumed responsibility for the defense of the land as well as for affairs of commerce and justice. The aristocratic court became a small, independent city-state. To enhance the ruler's prestige and show that he or she was a person of refinement and sensibility, the noble often engaged bands of trumpeters to herald an arrival, instrumentalists to provide dance music for the festivals of the court, and singers and poets to create lyric verse. Some poems were meant to be recited, others sung.

decline of the Church; rise of the court

FIGURE 4–7

A thirteenth-century Spanish miniature showing a medieval fiddle (the rebec) on the left and a lute on the right. Both instruments were brought into Spain by the Arabs and then carried northward into the lands of the *troubadours* and *trouvères*.

ARXIV MAS

Troubadours and Trouvères

Southern France was the center of this new courtly art, though it extended into northern Spain and Italy as well. The poet-musicians who flourished there went by the name of **troubadour** (for men) and **trobairitz** (for women). Both terms derived from the verb **trobar**, which meant "to find" in the vernacular tongue of medieval southern France. Thus the *troubadours* and *trobairitz* were finders or inventors of new modes of verbal and vocal expression. Their art was devoted mainly to the creation of songs of love that extolled the courtly ideals of faith and devotion, whether to the ideal lady, to the just seigneur, or to the knight crusading in the Holy Land. Their songs were not in the Latin of the Church, but in the vernacular tongue: medieval Italian, Catalan, and Provençal (medieval French of the South). The origins of the *troubadours* were equally varied. Some were sons of bakers and drapers, others were members of the nobility, many were clerics living outside the Church, and not a few were women.

In the Middle Ages, and later during the Renaissance (1475–1600), women were not allowed to sing in church, except in convents, owing to the early injunction of the Apostle Paul ("A woman must be silent in the church"). But at court, women often appeared as reciters of poetry, singers, and performers on the so-called *bas* (soft) instruments like the harp, lute, rebec (medieval fiddle), and flute (Fig. 4–7). Moreover, *trobairitz* were not merely performers, but creators in their own right. One such composer was Beatriz, Countess of Dia (Fig. 4–8), who lived in southern France during the middle of the twelfth century. She was married to Count William of Poitiers but fell in love with a fellow *troubadour*, Raimbaut d'Orange (1146–1173). Her song *A chantar m'er* (*I Must Sing*) laments her failure in love, despite her self-proclaimed charms. It is composed of five strophes, or stanzas, each with seven lines of text and seven musical phrases. The seven-phrase melody, which owes much to the music of the Church in its stepwise movement and strong tonal feeling, displays a clear musical form, **ABABCDB** (the use of letters to indicate musical form is explained on page 61). Also in common with the chant of the Church, this *troubadour* song, as true of most, has no clearly articulated meter and rhythm, but is sung in notes of more or less equal length.

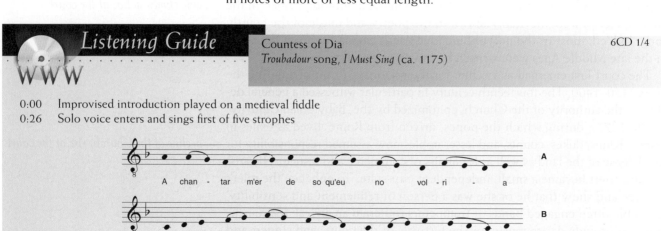

Listening Guide

Countess of Dia
Troubadour song, I Must Sing (ca. 1175)

6CD 1/4

WWW

0:00   Improvised introduction played on a medieval fiddle
0:26   Solo voice enters and sings first of five strophes

A chan - tar m'er   de   so qu'eu   no   vol - ri - a   **A**

Tant me ran - cur   de   lui   cui sui   a - mi - a   **B**

(Continued on next page)

A Car eu l'am mais que nul-ha ren que si - a

B Vas lui no'm val mer - ces ni cor - te - zi - a

C Ni ma bel - tatz ni mos pretz ni mos sens

D Qu'a - tres - si'm sui en - ga - nad' e tra - hi - a

B Com de-gr'es - ser s'eu fos de - sa - vi - nens.

(I must sing of that which I'd rather not,
So bitter do I feel toward him
Whom I love more than anything.
But with him kindness and courtliness get me nowhere,
Neither my beauty, nor my worth, nor my intelligence.
In this way am I cheated and betrayed,
Just as I would be if I were ugly.)

Gradually, the musical traditions created by the *troubadours* were carried to the north of France, where such composer-performers came to be called **trouvères,** and even to Germany, where they were called **Minnesingers.** Around 1300, some of the *trouvères* began to mix the traditions of the *troubadours* with the learned vocal polyphony coming from the Church. Soon churchmen such as Guillaume de Machaut (see page 78) adopted the musical forms and poetic style of the *trouvères* to fashion a new genre of music, the polyphonic **chanson** (French for "song"). The chanson is simply a love song, normally in French, for two, three, or four voices. At its best, the chanson is a small jewel of poignant lyricism.

Music at the Court of Burgundy

During the late Middle Ages the Court of Burgundy (flourished 1364–1477) was the envy of all courts in Western Europe. Its army was the most powerful, its arts the most beautiful, and its fashions the most *à la mode.* Moreover, the Burgundian treasury was the richest, primarily because the dukes of Burgundy controlled not only the territory of Burgundy in eastern France but also parts of northern France as well as most of modern-day Belgium and Holland. Among the musicians of Burgundy (Fig. 4–9) were Gilles Binchois (1400?–1460) and Guillaume Dufay (1397?–1474) both of whom excelled at writing chansons. Although they were both ordained priests, they moved easily between ecclesiastical and courtly circles.

FIGURE 4–8

Beatriz Countess of Dia as depicted in a manuscript of *troubadour and trouvère* poetry.

FIGURE 4–9

Guillaume Dufay and Gilles Binchois as depicted in a manuscript copied ca. 1440. Dufay stands next to a small organ, the quintessential instrument of the church, while Binchois holds a harp, one of the principal instruments of the court.

Bibliothèque nationale, Paris

Indeed, political affairs then united church and court. In 1453 the West suffered a stunning blow when the Muslim Turks captured the ancient Christian city of Constantinople (today Istanbul, Turkey). To Western eyes the capital of the Eastern Church had fallen into the hands of the infidels. Pope Nicholas V called upon the rulers of the West to mount a holy war, but only Duke Philip the Good of Burgundy responded enthusiastically.

In February 1454 Duke Philip summoned the knights of his lands to the town of Lille in northern France. There he staged what has come to be called the Feast of the Pheasant—a rally for the crusade that became, in truth, the greatest party of the fifteenth century. The court banquet hall was organized around three large tables. On one was a mock church "in which was a sounding bell and four singers who sang and played on organs when their turn came." Another table supported a huge pastry, so formed that it could house "twenty-eight living persons playing on divers instruments." At a third table "three children and a tenor sang a very sweet chanson, and when they had finished a shepherd played on a bagpipe in a most novel fashion." Finally, an elephant (symbol of the East) was led into the hall and upon its back was a small castle. Inside the castle a man disguised as a woman to represent the figure of the Holy Mother Church sang a lament over the fall of Constantinople. To create a high feminine sound the man sang in what is called **falsetto** voice, one generated by resonating not in the chest but in the head.

Guillaume Dufay composed a four-voice *Lamentatio sanctae matris Ecclesiae Constantinopolitanae (Lament of the Holy Mother Church of Constantinople)*. Here the Virgin Mary (soprano voice) pleads in French for divine aid: "O most merciful fountain of all hope." Below, the voice of the nation of Israel (tenor voice) chants a passage in Latin from the Lamentation of Jeremiah (I:2): "All her friends have dealt treacherously with her." Instruments fill in the alto and bass lines. Just as Israel of the Old Testament was once endangered, so now the Latin Church of the West is threatened. In Dufay's *Lament* the worlds of art and politics, church and court, become inextricably twined. So too are different types of medieval music, for here the soprano sings a newly composed chanson, while the tenor intones an ancient Gregorian chant.

Listening Guide

WWW

Guillaume Dufay   6CD 1/5
Lament of the Holy Mother Church of Constantinople (1453)

Part I

0:00	Duet: Virgin Mary (soprano), supported by instrument, pleads for divine assistance	O tres piteulx de tout espoir fontaine, Pere du filz dont suis mere esploree,	O most merciful fountain of all hope, Father of the son of whom I am the despairing mother,
		Plaindre me viens a ta court souveraine. De ta puissance et de nature humaine,	I come to your sovereign court, To appeal to your power and human kindness
		Qui ont souffert telle durte villaine A mon filz, qui tant m'a hounouree.	For those who have done such villainy To my son, who has done me such honor.
0:24	Bass instrument enters		
0:26	Israel (tenor) laments her fate	Omnes amici ejus spreverunt eam. Non est qui consoletur eam Ex omnibus caris ejus.	All her friends have deserted her. Among all those dear to her There are none to console her.

(Continued on next page)

Part II			
1:26	Trio: Virgin Mary (soprano) supported by two instruments, continues her lament and petition	Dont suis de bien et de joye separee,	Thus I am separated from goodness and joy
		Sans qui vivant veulle entendre mes plains.	And not a living soul will heed my pleas.
		A toy, seul dieu, du forfait me complains,	To you, sole God, I bring my complaint,
		Du gref tourment et douloureulx oultrage,	Of grievous suffering and pain
		Que voy souffrir au plus bel des humains,	That the finest of men suffers
		Sans nul confort de tout humain lignage.	Without humans offering any comfort.
1:55	Israel (tenor) laments her fate	(same text as above)	(same text as above)

(Listening exercise 13 asks you to focus in greater detail on the voices and supporting instruments.)

MEDIEVAL MUSICAL INSTRUMENTS

In the late Middle Ages the principal musical instrument of the monastery and cathedral was the pipe organ. Indeed, the organ was the only instrument admitted by church authorities. At court, however, a variety of instrumental sounds could be heard. Instruments were divided into two groups according to the amount of volume they produced. The first group was called the *hauts* (loud) instruments and included trumpet, **sackbut** (forerunner of the trombone), and **shawm** (ancestor of the oboe), as well as the drums. Later, in the Renaissance, a **cornetto**, a curved wooden instrument sounding something like a cross between a trumpet and a clarinet joined the *hauts* instruments. The second group was called the *bas* (soft) instruments and included flute, recorder, fiddle, psaltery, harp, and lute. Dancing was an inevitable part of courtly recreation, and for this a standard "dance band" of *hauts* instruments was required: two or three shawms, a sackbut, and perhaps a cornetto and a drum (Figs. 4–10 and 4–11). The sackbut played the dance tune in long notes while the shawms

FIGURES 4–10 AND 4–11

(below) Dance scene at a wedding at a French court in the mid-fifteenth century. The musicians, who play shawms and a sackbut, are placed on high in a balcony. (lower left) A later scene, ca. 1600, showing musicians in a procession as painted by Denis van Alsloot. The instruments are, from right to left, a sackbut, two shawms, a cornetto, another shawm, and an early bassoon.

Bibliothèque Nationale, Paris

© Museo del Prado, Madrid

or other instruments wove ornamental lines, much like a contemporary jazz quartet in which a piano and saxophone improvise above the fundamental bass notes provided by the double bass or the guitar. The late fifteenth-century tune entitled *La Spagna* (*The Spanish Tune*) is typical of the dance melodies played at the court of Burgundy during the waning years of the Middle Ages.

Listening Guide

Anonymous	6CD 1/6
Instrumental Dance Tune, *The Spanish Tune* (ca. 1470)	
Set for three instruments by Heinrich Isaac ca. 1490	

Texture: Polyphonic

0:00	Sackbut plays tune in long notes in the bass while shawm provides counterpoint above
0:05	Cornetto enters to add another line of counterpoint above the tune
1:04	Repeat of the previous music

Listening Exercises

12

Hildegard of Bingen   6CD 1/1; 2CD 1/1
Gregorian chant, *O Greenest Branch* (ca. 1150)

O Greenest Branch was intended to be sung as part of the Mass by male or female clerics, alternating a soloist with a full choir. First listen to this chant to determine which stanzas are sung by a soloist and which by a choir. Next to each stanza, write "soloist" or "choir," as appropriate.

Stanza 1 _____	Stanza 5 _____
Stanza 2 _____	Stanza 6 _____
Stanza 3 _____	Stanza 7 _____
Stanza 4 _____	

Now go on to answer the following, more general, questions:

8. How would you describe the musical texture of this chant?
   a. monophonic   b. homophonic   c. polyphonic
9. Melismatic singing occurs in this chant
   a. more at the end of each stanza than at the beginning.
   b. more at the beginning of each stanza than at the end.
10. Does an organ accompany the female voices on this recording? _____

13

Guillaume Dufay   6 CD 1/5
Lament of the Holy Mother Church of Constantinople (1453)

In music we speak of four standard voice parts, or musical lines, which proceed in range from top to bottom: soprano, alto, tenor, and bass. Each may be actually sung, or simply played by an instrument. On this recording of

Guillaume Dufay's *Lament* the soprano is sung, the alto is played on a late-medieval double-reed instrument called the *kortholt* (predecessor of the bassoon), the tenor is sung, while the bass is played by a *sackbut* (ancestor of the modern trombone). Moreover, in this performance a male falsettist sings in the range of the soprano voice, just as was the case at the famous Feast of the Pheasant. The challenge here is to recognize the different sound qualities and levels of activity of the four "voices" (two voices and two instruments).

1. (0:00–0:23) At the beginning, which two parts are sounding?
   a. soprano and kortholt   b. kortholt and tenor   c. tenor and sackbut
2. (0:24–0:28) Which part enters first, the sackbut or the tenor?
   a. sackbut   b. tenor
3. (0:42–0:52) Which part is silent during this passage?
   a. soprano   b. kortholt   c. tenor   d. sackbut
4. (1:18–1:25) Here there is a very clear cadence* (end of a musical phrase). Which is true?
   a. all four voices are sounding
   b. only three are sounding
   c. only two are sounding
5. (1:26–1:54) Which part is silent during this passage?
   a. soprano   b. kortholt   c. tenor   d. sackbut
6. (2:11–2:21) Which part is silent during this passage?
   a. soprano   b. kortholt   c. tenor   d. sackbut

Review

7. The sackbut was a member of which family of instruments (see page 85)?
   a. *hauts* instruments   b. *bas* instruments
8. Which of the four voice parts is named, not for its range, but for the function it serves (see page 79)?
   a. soprano   b. alto   c. tenor   d. bass
9. When sung by itself, Gregorian chant creates which type of texture?
   a. monophonic   b. polyphonic   c. homophonic
10. When chant is joined to other highly independent musical lines, as is true in Dufay's *Lament*, which texture is created?
    a. monophonic   b. polyphonic   c. homophonic

Key Words

bas instruments (85)	*Minnesinger* (83)	sackbut (85)
chanson (83)	Ordinary of the	shawm (85)
cornetto (85)	Mass (78)	syllabic singing (73)
falsetto voice (84)	organum (77)	*trivium* (80)
Gregorian chant (73)	plainsong (73)	*trobairitz* (82)
hauts instruments (85)	Proper of the	*troubadour* (82)
Mass (78)	Mass (78)	*trouvère* (82)
melismatic	*quadrivium* (80)	
singing (73)		

For a checklist of musical style in the Middle Ages, see page 68.

(Cultural Context box, "An Islamic Call to Worship," follows on pages 88 and 89.)

CULTURAL CONTEXT

An Islamic Call to Worship

During the Middle Ages, Western Europe was Christian in matters of religion. The center of the Western Latin (Catholic) Church was Rome. Much of Eastern Europe and western Asian lands, including what is now called Russia and the Ukraine, gradually came to profess the faith of the Eastern Orthodox Church, which was centered in Constantinople (renamed Istanbul [Turkey] in 1930). Lands to the south of Constantinople were under the control of Arab Muslims. The fall of Constantinople in 1453, as bewailed in Guillaume Dufay's *Lament* (see page 84), represented a milestone that marked the spreading power of the Muslims in the near East. Tensions and hostilities between followers of the Eastern Orthodox Church (Christians) and the brotherhood of Islam (Muslims) continue to play out even today in the countries of Serbia, Bosnia, Macedonia, and the region of Chechnia in Russia.

Islam is the name that all Muslims give to their religion. It is based on the teachings of the prophet Mohammed (570?–632), born in Mecca [Saudi Arabia]. The revelations of Mohammed, believed to have been sent from Allah (God) to the prophet in the year 610,

A mosque with ascending minaret in Cairo, Egypt.

© Jose Fuste Raga/CORBIS

are collected in the **Koran**. Written in Arabic but translated into many languages, the Koran provides Muslims with direction in religious and civic duties, just as the Torah and the New Testament guide Jews and Christians, respectively.

Within a century of the death of the prophet Mohammed (632), Islam had spread around North Africa to Spain and, following the silk trade route, as far east as China. The most populous Islamic countries today, moving roughly west to east, are Egypt, Saudi Arabia, Turkey, Iraq, Iran, Afghanistan, Pakistan, (northern) India, and Indonesia. Of the great world religions today, Islam ranks second in number of adherents, as the following approximate numbers suggest: Christians (2.1 billion), Muslims (1.2 billion), Hindus (0.9 billion), and Buddhists and Chinese folk religionists (0.8 billion).

Every devout Muslim is required to worship God five times each day: just before sunrise, at noon, before sunset, just after sunset, and just after the day has closed. (In medieval monasteries in the West, Benedictine monks and nuns gathered daily for eight hours of prayer plus Mass.) Muslims may pray alone or in a house of worship called a **mosque**. On Friday, the Muslim holy day, the noon service is set for the full community in the mosque. Men pray in rows and women in rows behind them or in a separate area of the mosque. The service consists of exclamations and the recital of parts of the Koran, accompanied by prostrations of the body. No matter where in the world Muslim worshippers may be, they face in the direction of Mecca as they pray.

Christians around the world have historically summoned the faithful to the church by means of bells. Muslims, however, call the faithful to each of the five times of prayer by chanting from the tall tower of the mosque, called the **minaret** (see Figure). The call to worship is named the **Adhan**. In large cities the voice of a single cantor is linked by loudspeakers, and thus he chants the Adhan in synchronized fashion around the city. In nearly all Islamic countries, no matter what the native language, the call to worship is sung in Arabic, and the text (see Listening Guide following) is always the same. The melody, however, can vary according to the style of singing of the cantor.

The cantor, or principal singer, of the mosque is called the **muezzin**. Some muezzins know the entire Koran by memory and the more famous of them have recorded it (all 6,236 verses) on CDs. Among these is muezzin Wahid Zafer of Pakistan. On the recording discussed below, the voice of Wahid Zafer can be heard calling all Muslims to worship, just as it still can be heard today live above the houses and mosques of Islamabad, Pakistan.

Islamic chant compared to Gregorian chant: Although it would be unwise to draw too much from a single example, Islamic and Gregorian chant can be instructively compared. Both are monophonic* in texture, and both avoid regular rhythms or meters. Because of this, both musics also have a floating, undulating quality to them. Here the word *arabesque* (meaning Arab-like) can correctly be used, for the Muslim melody, like Gregorian chant, seems to twist and turn to form elaborate patterns.

There is, however, one distinctive quality of the Adhan sung by Wahid Zafer, and this characteristic marks much of non-Western music: The performer slides between pitches. In fact, much of the musical interest and beauty of this call to worship derives from what the performer is doing between pitches, not what he does on them. By way of comparison, Gregorian chant—indeed almost all Western music—moves from one discrete pitch to the next, carefully avoiding all intermediate sounds.

Finally, it is quite possible, even likely, that when Gregorian chant was created during the Middle Ages it sounded much like Islamic music—it too, most probably, originally involved singing between pitches. In the course of time we in the West, influenced by fixed-pitched instruments such as the organ and the piano, have eliminated from our melodies the microtonal sounds between pitches. Thus, a comparison with music of other cultures reveals how our distinctly Western musical practices have evolved over the centuries, and how they are different from those of the rest of the world.

KEY WORDS

Adhan	mosque
Koran	muezzin
minaret	

Listening Guide

Adhan (Islamic Call to Worship)   6CD 6/15
A Timeless Islamic Chant sung by Wahid Zafer

WWW

0:00	Phrase **a**: chant rises from first note to fifth degree of scale.	Allahu Akbar. God is great.
0:20	Phrase **a** repeats with slight variation	God is great.
0:38	Phrase **b**: syllabic chant gives way to more melismatic singing in higher range	I testify that there is no God but Allah.
1:17	Phrase **b**: repeated with slight variation	I testify that Mohammed is his prophet.
1:55	Phrase **c**: voice rises to higher level concludes with a repeating turn figure	Come to Prayer. Come to Prayer.
2:30	Phrase **c** repeats	Come to Salvation. Come to Salvation.
3:05	Phrase **a** returns	God is great.
3:23	End of phrase **b** returns	There is no God but Allah.

Chapter 5

Fratelli Alinari/SuperStock

Renaissance

"Renaissance" means rebirth or reawakening. As a historical designation, the term was first used in the nineteenth century to characterize a great flowering of intellectual and artistic activity that occurred first in Italy and then in France, Germany, England, and the Low Countries during the years 1350–1600. In music the term is more narrowly applied to musical developments in those countries between the years 1475 and 1600. Although the Renaissance did not represent a radical split with an earlier period of darkness and ignorance, as has sometimes been assumed, it was, nonetheless, a time in which new ideas and new attitudes sprang forth and flourished in a hospitable Italian climate. As the Florentine philosopher Marsilio Ficino said in the eventful year 1492:

> If then we are to call any age golden, it is beyond doubt that age which brings forth golden talents in different places. That such is true of this our age he who wishes to consider the illustrious discoveries of this century will hardly doubt. For this century, like a golden age, has restored to light the liberal arts, which were almost extinct: grammar, poetry, rhetoric, painting, sculpture, architecture, and music, the ancient singing of songs to the Orphic lyre.

The thinkers of the Renaissance wished to invigorate the liberal arts, not by looking to an uncertain future, but by returning to a glorious past. They were convinced that a better society could be built by studying the accumulated wisdom of the ancient Greeks and Romans. The cradle of the Renaissance was, of course, Italy, because so many classical texts still survived there

Music Becomes a Fine Art

Music enjoyed a new, higher estimation in public consciousness during the Renaissance because it was now less a science, more an art. Recall that during the Middle Ages music had been grouped with three other mathematical disciplines (arithmetic, geometry, and astronomy) to form a core curriculum called the *quadrivium* (see page 80). These subjects, along with the *trivium* of grammar, logic, and rhetoric, constituted the seven liberal arts. But now a new appreciation of the so-called mechanical arts led to a wholesale reshuffling of categories. Leonardo da Vinci himself argued that painting should be added to these seven disciplines, indeed placed at their head. So, too, poetry should join her sisters, though sculpture, because it was wrought by hard manual labor, should not. By the end of the sixteenth century, academies of painting and of music had replaced the medieval craft guilds. The expressive disciplines of poetry, painting, music, and architecture were now separated into a category of "fine arts," a worthy complement to the liberal arts and the sciences.

and because the ruins of the mighty Roman Empire were everywhere to be seen. But for musicians in Italy and elsewhere, the process of reviving things classical—singing songs to the Orphic lyre—was less obvious and immediate, for almost no music from classical antiquity survived for them to imitate, and what little there was could not be deciphered. Hence, for musicians, rebirth meant not copying earlier musical styles but adopting the attitudes about music that the ancients had possessed. This was done, in part, by writing books about music—on melody, harmony, counterpoint, and rhythm—in which the author adopted the format and terminology of ancient Greek music theory and aesthetics.

The ancient Greek writers, especially Homer and Plato, had spoken of the great emotional power of music. Their stories told how music had calmed the agitated spirit or made brave the warrior. The musicians of the Renaissance eagerly embraced this notion that music could sway the emotions, even the behavior, of the listener. To heighten the emotional intensity of music, they selected a mode (major, minor, or one of several others then in use) and a musical style that would amply suit the meaning of the text they wished to set. A hymn would be set in one style, a lament in another, a love song in yet a third. The belief in the persuasive power of music and the capacity of music to intensify the meaning of the text were two primary articles of faith held by musicians of the Renaissance. The practical result was music in a great variety of styles and wide range of moods. In this way music mirrored the visual arts of the Renaissance, which now likewise allowed for a great range of emotional expression. Compare, for example, the peaceful serenity of Raphael's *The Holy Family* (Fig. 5–1) with the anguished expressiveness in Mathias Grünewald's altarpiece for the parish church at Issenheim (Fig. 5–2).

Alte Pinakothek, Munich

Bridgeman Art Library, London/NY

FIGURES 5–1 AND 5–2
(above) *The Holy Family* painted by Raphael in 1505–1506. Notice the human expression and the near-complete absence of medieval religious symbolism, as well as the highly formalistic composition of the painting; the figures form successively larger triangles and are balanced on either side by groups of angels. (left) The expressive grief of the Virgin, St. John, and Mary Magdalene mark this portion of an altarpiece painted by Mathias Grünewald 1510–1515.

FIGURE 5-3
Michelangelo's giant statue of David
(1501–1504) expresses the heroic nobility
of man in near-perfect form. Like Leonardo
da Vinci, Michelangelo made a careful
study of human anatomy.

Bridgeman Art Library, London/NY

artists becoming forceful personalities

Attending the rebirth of the arts and letters of classical antiquity was a renewed interest in humankind itself. We have come to call this enthusiastic self-interest humanism. Simply said, **humanism** is the belief that people have the capacity to shape their world, to create many things good and beautiful; that they are something more than a mere conduit for gifts descending from heaven. Even the human form, in all its physical fullness, has aesthetic value (Fig. 5–3). This attitude, with its emphasis on self-esteem and human worth, differs markedly from the prevailing view in the Middle Ages, when the individual was seen as a covered, almost faceless object in a great, divine pageant. The culture of the Middle Ages was fostered by the Church; it emphasized the group and submission to the almighty within a cloistered setting. The culture of the Renaissance, on the other hand, with its focus on personal achievement, looked outward and indulged its passion for travel, adventure, and discovery.

New meaning and value were given to what artists produced in the Renaissance, as well as to the artists themselves. By the end of the fifteenth century, the system of the medieval guilds, which regulated the type of work an artist might accept, began to break down. Now an artist might take any commission he wished. He became the intimate friend of leading citizens, and his idiosyncracies were tolerated. No longer was he merely a craftsman who manipulated materials; he was a discoverer, an inventor, a visionary—in a word, an artist! Consequently, the work of art itself came to be viewed, not as the handiwork of the Lord, but as the visible record of an individual's creative genius.

This new attitude about art and about the artist affected the way in which society viewed the composer and the way in which the listener appreciated the composer's work. In the Middle Ages most compositions were preserved anonymously in manuscripts, but, from the fifteenth century on, the name of the creator was usually placed at the head of each piece. One composer even went so far as to insert his own name in a setting of a liturgical text in honor of the Virgin, a novel act of self-aggrandizement. (In a similar way the artists Raphael, Botticelli, and Michelangelo painted their own faces into various religious frescoes they created [Fig. 5–4].) Composers also gained an increased awareness of the monetary value of their art. This can be seen not only in the high salaries they commanded at court but also in the astute way in which they played one patron off against another to gain additional economic benefits. Painters, too, found that money primed the pump of creativity. The prolific Michelangelo left an estate worth some $10 million in terms of money today.

Society's view about art and music had changed. No longer was music merely the subject of scholastic theorizing; it could be a source of enjoyment and fun. Music in the Renaissance was composed by proud artists who aimed to give pleasure. Their music conversed, not with eternity but with the listener. It was judged good or bad only to the degree that it pleased fellow human beings. Music, like the other arts, could now be freely evaluated in the secular world for its quality, and composers ranked according to their greatness. Artistic judgment, appreciation, and criticism enter Western thought for the first time in the humanistic Renaissance.

Bridgeman Art Library, London/NY

FIGURE 5–4

The School of Athens (1505) by Raphael reflects the Renaissance attitude toward the arts in three ways: the Roman arches, antique dress, and classical sculptures reintegrate into the art of the Renaissance motifs from ancient Greece and Rome. The subject matter, which places the seven liberal arts in the context of Plato's school in ancient Athens, likewise is drawn from classical antiquity. Finally, by depicting key figures in the likeness of himself, of Leonardo da Vinci, and of Michelangelo (front left center, wearing the boots of a sculptor), Raphael suggests that the fine arts of painting and sculpture are worthy companions of the traditional seven liberal arts.

JOSQUIN DESPREZ (CA. 1455–1521) AND THE RENAISSANCE MOTET

FIGURE 5–5

The only surviving portrait of Josquin Desprez.

© The British Library, London

Josquin Lebloitte dit Desprez was one of the greatest composers of the Renaissance or, indeed, of any age (Fig. 5–5). He was born somewhere near the present border between France and Belgium about 1455, and died in the same region in 1521. Yet, like so many musicians of northern France, he was attracted to Italy for reasons of professional and monetary gain. Between ca. 1484 and 1504 he worked successively as a singer at the chapel of the duke of Milan, in the chapel of a cardinal in Rome, in the Sistine Chapel of the pope, and finally in the chapel of the duke of Ferrara. Several contemporary accounts, as well as his frequent movement from one employer to another, suggest that he possessed a temperamental, egotistical spirit typical of many artists of the Renaissance: He composed only when he, not his patron, wished; he demanded a salary twice that of composers only slightly less gifted; and he would break into a rage when singers tried to tamper with the notes he had written. Yet Josquin's contemporaries and immediate successors recognized his genius.

Castiglione (*The Book of the Courtier*, 1528) and Rabelais (*Pantagruel*, 1535) praised him. He was the favorite of Martin Luther, who said, "Josquin is master of the notes, which must express what he desires; other composers can do only what the notes dictate." Florentine humanist Cosimo Bartoli compared him to the great Michelangelo (1475–1564), who decorated the ceiling of the Sistine Chapel where Josquin had once sung (Fig. 5–6). As he said:

> Josquin may be said to have been a prodigy of nature, as our Michelangelo Buonarroti has been in architecture, painting, and sculpture; for, as there has not thus far been anybody who in his compositions approaches Josquin, so Michelangelo, among all those who have been active in these arts, is still alone and without a peer; both Josquin and Michelangelo have opened the eyes of all those who delight in these arts or are to delight in them in the future.

Fratelli Alinari/SuperStock

FIGURE 5–6

Interior of the Sistine Chapel. The high altar and Michelangelo's *Last Judgment* are at the far end, the balcony for the singers, including Josquin Desprez, at the lower right. The congregants could stand and listen from the near side of the screen.

Josquin composed in all of the musical genres of his day, but he excelled in writing motets. Composers had written motets in different forms and styles since the thirteenth century and continued to do so into the nineteenth century. The **motet** in the Renaissance can be defined as a composition for a choir, setting a Latin text on a sacred subject, and intended to be sung in a church or chapel, or at home in private devotion. While composers of the Renaissance continued to set the text of the Ordinary of the Mass*, they turned increasingly to the motet because its texts were more vivid and expressive. Most motet texts were drawn from the Old Testament of the Bible—from Psalms or Lamentations, for example. A vivid text cried out for an equally vivid musical setting, and the composer happily obliged. Josquin composed about twenty polyphonic Masses but nearly seventy motets.

Most motets in the Renaissance, as well as most Masses for the church, were sung **a cappella** (literally, "in the chapel"), meaning that they were performed by voices alone, without any instrumental accompaniment. (Instruments other than the organ were generally not allowed in churches during the Middle Ages and the Renaissance.) This, in part, accounts for the often serene quality of the sound of Renaissance sacred music. Indeed, the Renaissance has been called "the golden age of *a cappella* singing."

vocal music without instruments

Josquin's motet *Ave Maria* was written about 1485 when the composer was in Milan, Italy, in the service of the duke of Milan. It was composed in honor of the Virgin Mary, and employs the standard four voice parts: soprano, alto, tenor, and bass. As the motet unfolds, the listener hears the voices enter in succession with the same musical motive. This process is called **imitation**, a procedure whereby one or more voices duplicate in turn the notes of a melody:

EXAMPLE 5–1

Josquin will also sometimes have one pair of voices imitate another, the tenor and bass, for example, imitating what the alto and soprano have just sung:

EXAMPLE 5–2

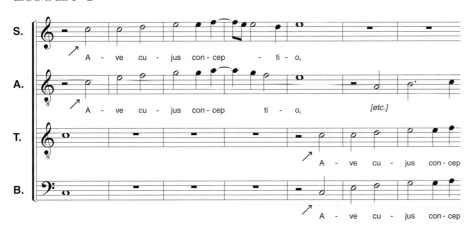

In imitative writing the voices all have a chance to present equally the melodic material and thus are all of equal importance. Moreover, because the voices all enter independently, imitative writing invariably produces counterpoint*—independent voices working with and against one another in a harmonious fashion. In Josquin's *Ave Maria*, sections in imitative counterpoint (polyphony*) alternate with passages of chordal writing (homophony*) in order to achieve musical variety. Josquin and his contemporaries favored imitative writing because the quality of balance and proportion that could be achieved by four equal voices was harmonious with the notion of balance and symmetry much prized in the visual arts during the Renaissance.

varying textures

As to the overall structure of Josquin's *Ave Maria*, it is organized in something akin to the way a humanistic orator would construct a persuasive speech or address. It begins with an introductory salutation to the Virgin sung in imitation. Thereafter, a key word, "Ave" ("Hail"), sparks a series of salutes to the Virgin, each making reference to one of her principal feast days during the church year (Conception, Nativity, Annunciation, Purification, and Assumption). At the end of this series of hails comes a final exclamation, "O mother of God, be mindful of me. Amen." These last words are set in a striking succession of imposing chords, with each syllable of text getting its own chord. The chordal, homophonic treatment allows this final text to stand out with absolute clarity. In this way is fulfilled the basic principle of musical humanism: Text and music must work together to persuade and move the listener. Here they must persuade the Virgin Mary as well, for she is asked to intercede on behalf of the needy soul at the hour of death.

Listening Guide

WWW

Josquin Desprez
Motet, *Ave Maria* (ca. 1485)

6CD 1/7;
2CD 1/2

Time	Description	Latin	English
0:00	All four voices present each two-word phrase in turn	Ave Maria, gratia plena, Dominus tecum, virgo serena.	Hail Mary, full of grace. The Lord be with you, serene Virgin.
0:46	Soprano and alto are imitated by tenor and bass; then all four voices work to a peak on "laetitia" ("joy")	Ave cujus conceptio, Solemni plena gaudio, Coelestia, terrestria, Nova replet laetitia.	Hail to you whose conception, With solemn rejoicing, Fills heaven and earth With new joy.
1:20	Imitation in pairs; soprano and alto answered by tenor and bass	Ave cujus nativitas Nostra fuit solemnitas, Ut lucifer lux oriens, Verum solem praeveniens.	Hail to you whose birth Was to be our solemnity, As the rising morning star Anticipates the true sun.
1:58	More imitation by pairs of voices; soprano and alto followed by tenor and bass	Ave pia humilitas, Sine viro foecunditas, Cujus annuntiatio, Nostra fuit salvatio.	Hail pious humility, Fruitful without man, Whose annunciation Was to be our salvation.
2:26	Chordal writing; meter changes from duple to triple	Ave vera virginitas, Immaculata castitas, Cujus purificatio Nostra fuit purgatio.	Hail true virginity, Immaculate chastity, Whose purification Was to be our purgation.
3:03	Return to duple meter; soprano and alto imitated by tenor and bass	Ave praeclara omnibus Angelicis virtutibus, Cujus fuit assumptio Nostra glorificatio.	Hail shining example Of all angelic virtues, Whose assumption Was to be our glorification.
3:58	Strict chordal writing; clear presentation of the text	O Mater Dei, Memento mei. Amen.	O Mother of God, Be mindful of me. Amen.

(Listening Exercise 14)

THE COUNTER-REFORMATION AND PALESTRINA (1525–1594)

On October 31, 1517, an obscure Augustinian monk named Martin Luther nailed to the door of the castle church at Wittenberg, Germany, ninety-five complaints against the Roman Catholic Church—his famous ninety-five theses. With this defiant act Luther began what has come to be called the Protestant Reformation. Luther and his fellow reformers sought to bring an end to corruption within the Roman Catholic Church: the opulence and worldliness of the papacy, the selling of indulgences (forgiveness of sin in exchange for money), and the abuse of power in church appointments (one pope rewarded the fifteen-year-old keeper of his pet monkey by making him a cardinal). By the time the Protestant Reformation had run its course, most of Germany,

Protestant Reformation

Switzerland, the Low Countries, and all of England, as well as parts of France, Austria, Bohemia, Poland, and Hungary, had gone over to the Protestant cause. The established Roman Catholic Church was shaken to its very foundations.

In response to the Protestant Reformation, the Church of Rome began to clean its own house. The cleansing applied not only to matters of spirituality and church administration but also to art, liturgy, and music. Nudity in religious paintings, musical instruments within the church, pop tunes and jazzy rhythms in the midst of polyphonic Masses, and married church singers—all were now deemed inappropriate to a truly pious environment.

The movement that fostered this counter reform and promoted a more conservative and austere art within the established Church is called the **Counter-Reformation.** Its spirit was institutionalized in the **Council of Trent** (1545–1563), a congress of bishops and cardinals held at the small town of Trent in the Italian Alps. Although the assembled prelates debated many aspects of reform within the Church of Rome, the liturgy and its music occupied much of their time. What bothered the Catholic reformers most about the church music of the day was that the incessant entry of voices in musical imitation caused an overlapping of lines that obscured the text—excessively dense counterpoint was burying the sacred word of the Lord. As one well-placed bishop said derisively:

the Counter-Reformation

> In our times they [composers] have put all their industry and effort into the writing of imitative passages, so that while one voice says "Sanctus," another says "Sabaoth," still another says "Gloria tua," with howling, bellowing, and stammering, so that they more nearly resemble cats in January than flowers in May.

Initially, the assembled prelates considered banning music altogether from the service or limiting it to just the old, monophonic Gregorian chant. But the timely appearance of a few sacred compositions by Giovanni Pierluigi da Palestrina (1525–1594), among them his *Mass for Pope Marcellus* (1562), demonstrated to the council representatives that sacred polyphony for four, five, or six voices could still be written in a clear, dignified manner. For his role in maintaining a place for composed polyphony within the established Church, Palestrina came to be called "the savior of church music."

Palestrina was born in the small town of that name outside Rome, and spent almost his entire professional life as a singer and composer at various churches in and around the Vatican: St. Peter's Basilica, St. John Lateran, St. Mary Major, and the **Sistine Chapel** (Fig. 5–6), the pope's private chapel within his Vatican apartments. Although Paul IV, one of the more zealous of the reforming popes, dismissed him from the Sistine Chapel in 1555 because he was a married layman not conforming to the rule of celibacy, Palestrina returned to papal employment at St. Peter's in 1571, holding the titles *maestro di cappella* (master of the chapel) and ultimately *maestro compositore* (master composer).

The *Sanctus* of Palestrina's *Missa Aeterna Christi munera* (*Mass: Eternal Gifts of Christ*) epitomizes the musical spirit of the Counter-Reformation that then radiated from Rome. (Remember, a *Sanctus* is the fourth of five parts of the Ordinary of the Mass* that composers traditionally set to music; see page 79.) Palestrina's *Sanctus* unfolds slowly and deliberately with long notes gradually giving way to shorter, faster-moving ones, but without catchy rhythms or a strong beat. As is true for Gregorian chant*, the melodic lines move mainly in stepwise fashion, avoiding large leaps and chromatic turns. The sober mood is created in part by the careful use of imitative counterpoint. Each phrase of text

FIGURE 5–7
A portrait of Giovanni Palestrina. Palestrina was the first important composer of the Church to have been a layman rather than a member of the clergy.

Male Choirs

Notice on our recording of Palestrina's *Sanctus* that the soprano part is performed by men singing in head voice, or what is called **falsetto** voice. This is a historically authentic manner of performance. Following an early decree of the Apostle Paul, women in the Middle Ages and Renaissance were not allowed to sing in the Roman Church, except in convents. Similarly, women were not allowed to appear in public in theatrical productions, tragic or comic, in territories under strict church control. Thus, most polyphonic church choirs in the Renaissance were exclusively male, the soprano part being performed by either choirboys or by adult men singing in *falsetto*. Beginning in 1565, however, **castratos** (castrated males) were introduced into the papal chapel, mainly as a money-saving measure. A single castrato could produce as much volume as two falsettists or three or four boys. Castrati were renowned for their power and their great lung capacity, which allowed them to execute unusually long phrases in a single breath. Surprisingly, castrati sopranos remained a hallmark of the papal chapel until 1903, when they were officially banned by Pope Pius X.

All-male choir with choirboys for the soprano part as depicted in a sixteenth-century Italian fresco.

is assigned its own motive*, which appears, in turn, in each voice. A motive used in this fashion is called a **point of imitation**. Palestrina's *Sanctus* has four points of imitation (see examples in the following Listening Guide). The first enters in the order soprano, alto, tenor, bass, and the music works to a cadence*. While the soprano and bass conclude the cadence, the alto and tenor begin the second point of imitation. Soon this section cadences in the soprano and alto as the bass and tenor enter with the third point. Palestrina was a master at sewing a cadence to the beginning of a new point of imitation. The listener experiences not only a sense of satisfaction on arrival at the cadence, but also a feeling of ongoing progress as the new point pushes forward. As you listen to the *Sanctus*, follow the diagram in the Listening Guide and see if you can hear when the voices are cadencing and when a new point of imitation begins.

Listening Guide

Giovanni Pierluigi da Palestrina   6CD 1/8
Sanctus of the Mass: Eternal Gifts of Christ (1590)

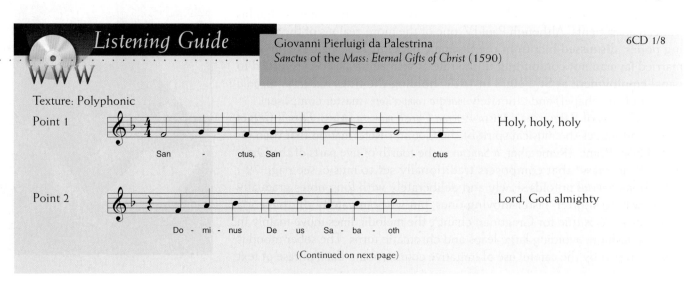

Texture: Polyphonic

Point 1   San - ctus, San - ctus   Holy, holy, holy

Point 2   Do - mi - nus De - us Sa - ba - oth   Lord, God almighty

(Continued on next page)

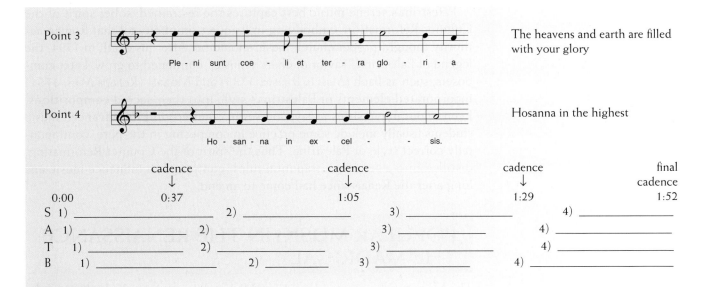

Point 3   Ple - ni sunt coe - li et ter - ra glo - ri - a   The heavens and earth are filled with your glory

Point 4   Ho - san - na in ex - cel - sis.   Hosanna in the highest

	cadence ↓		cadence ↓		cadence ↓		final cadence
0:00	0:37		1:05		1:29			1:52
S 1) _____	2) _____		3) _____				4) _____	
A 1) _____	2) _____		3) _____			4) _____		
T 1) _____	2) _____		3) _____			4) _____		
B 1) _____		2) _____	3) _____		4) _____			

Female Choirs in Convents

Although public church choirs in the Middle Ages and Renaissance were all-male ensembles, there was still much opportunity for women to make music. They did so as singers and performers in secular genres, such as the chanson* and madrigal*, at court and in the home. In convents, too, women formed female performing forces, yet always under the watchful eye of an outside father superior. Behind cloistered walls, the sisters sang not only Gregorian chant but also the latest polyphonic Masses and motets of Palestrina and Orlando di Lasso (ca. 1530–1594). They, too, had old manuscripts of plainsong*, and this monophonic chant

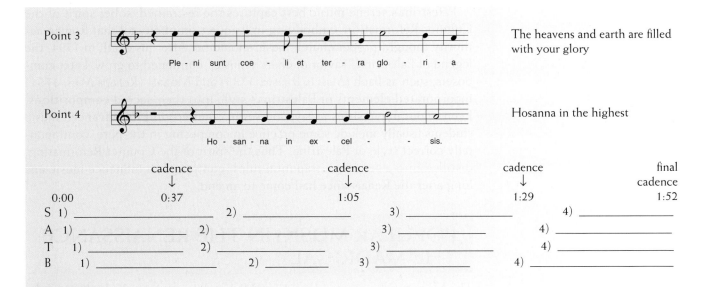

Nuns in the choir stalls of their convent singing a religious service, from a fifteenth-century English manuscript.

they transposed into their own, higher vocal range. When it came to singing polyphony, the normally male parts of tenor and bass were played on an organ while the sisters sang alto and soprano. Thus organs and organists were of primary importance in convents. Yet, because almost all music teachers in this period were males, cloistered women were separated from proper tutors. When a nun tried to circumvent the rules of strict segregation by gender, painful consequences might result, as Sister Angela Serafina, nun and principal musician at the monastery of San Appolinare in Milan, learned in 1571:

> Suor Angela Serafina is to be without her veil [i.e. with a bare shaven head] for three months. She is relieved of the organist's duties, nor may she return to this position for six years. The large harpsichord is not to be kept in her room, but somewhere else in the house; nor can she play it or any other keyboard, nor sing polyphony for three years. And every Wednesday for six months she is to eat on the floor of the refectory, and ask forgiveness for the disturbance she caused, for the scandal of having fed the [male] organist inside the convent. (from Robert L. Kendrick, *Celestial Sirens*)

So extreme a punishment for such a seemingly minor offence! Yet here we see the tension inherent in the very thought that women might make music in the Catholic Church during the austere Counter-Reformation.

Palestrina's serene music best captures the restrained, sober spirit of the Counter-Reformation, embodying in its quiet simplicity all that Roman authority thought proper church music should be. After his death in 1594, the legend of Palestrina, "savior of church music," continued to grow. Later composers, such as Bach (*Mass in B minor*, 1733) and Mozart (*Requiem Mass*, 1791) incorporated elements of Palestrina's style into their sacred compositions. Even in our universities today, courses in counterpoint for advanced music students usually include some practice in composing in the pure, contrapuntally correct style of Palestrina. Thus the spirit of the Counter-Reformation, distilled into a set of contrapuntal rules, continued to influence musicians long after the Renaissance had come to an end.

POPULAR MUSIC IN THE RENAISSANCE: THE MADRIGAL

The Masses and motets of Josquin and Palestrina represent the high art of the Renaissance—the learned music of the church. But there was popular music as well. Indeed, the sixteenth century witnessed an increase in commerce and trade, and with it came a growing middle class. This group was made up of tradesmen, merchants, bankers, lawyers, physicians, and civil servants. Though it constituted only about 6 percent of the population, the middle class was important because it was concentrated in the cities, the traditional centers of learning and the arts. Naturally the urban middle class had different, more popular musical tastes than did the high churchmen and the nobles.

rise of the middle class

In truth, there had always been popular music for the less exalted members of society. Dance music and popular songs, for example, are indigenous to all classes in all societies. Yet we know much less about popular music than we do about the music of the church and the aristocratic court. The reason for this is simple: Popular music was usually not written down and only rarely survived in written form. It was most often improvised on the spot, created on the spur of the moment by musicians who had learned their art orally from master teachers rather than by studying written manuscripts. Like many jazz artists, blues singers, and rock musicians of today, they performed without benefit of written musical notation. Most people in the Middle Ages could not read at all, and certainly not complicated music manuscripts. Written music was traditionally the private preserve of a wealthy, educated elite.

unwritten music

All of this changed, however, with Johann Gutenberg's invention of printing by moveable type around 1460. Printing revolutionized the world of information in the late fifteenth century no less than did the computer during the late twentieth century. Hundreds of copies could be quickly produced once the type of a book had been set. By 1500, 30,000 individual works had been published, most in printing shops in Venice and Rome. The first printed book of music appeared in Venice in 1501, and to this important event can be traced the origins of the "music business" of today. The standard "press run" for a printed book of music was usually 500 copies. Mass production drastically reduced the cost of each book, putting notated music within the reach of the banker, merchant, and shopkeeper as well as the bishop and prince. What is more, the new consumers lured to the market by a lower-cost product wanted a more immediately accessible sort of entertainment. They wanted music they could learn to sing and play at home—music in a simpler, more

music printing

chordal, more tuneful style. Henceforth public taste shaped musical style, at least the style of music sold commercially for recreation and entertainment.

About 1530 a new genre of music, the madrigal, arose in Italy as a direct result of this demand for a new, more popular kind of music. The **madrigal** was a piece for several solo voices (usually four or five) that set a poem, most often about love, written in some vernacular (non-Latin) tongue (Fig. 5–8). At times imitative and contrapuntal, at other times chordal and homophonic, the music of the madrigal seeks to mirror the meaning of the poetry at any given moment. What mattered was the vivid imagery of the text. Within a few short bars the emotional range of a madrigal might move from the airy heights of a starry night to the depths of a lover's despair.

Nowhere in all of music does sound so artfully depict, even mimic, text as in the sixteenth-century madrigal. Each individual phrase, sometimes each word of an extravagant text, will receive its own musical painting. Thus, when the madrigal text says "chase after" or "follow quickly," the music becomes fast and one voice chases after another in musical imitation. Should the text say "arise, awake" or "clouds in showers descending," the music will ascend or descend. For words such as "pain," "anguish," "death," and "cruel fate," invariably the madrigal composer will employ a twisting chromatic* scale or a biting dissonance*. The practice of depicting the text in music, be it subtly, overtly, or even jokingly as a musical pun, is called **word painting**. Word painting became all the rage with madrigal composers in Italy and England. Even today such musical clichés as sighs and dissonances for "harsh" words are called **madrigalisms**.

The madrigal was born in Italy, but popular favor soon carried it over the Alps to Germany, Denmark, the Low Countries, and England. The first madrigals to be printed in England appeared in a publication of 1588 called *Musica transalpina (Music from across the Alps)*, a collection of more than fifty madrigals, mainly by Italian composers, with the texts translated into English. Soon English composers—all contemporaries of William Shakespeare (1564–1616)—were writing their own madrigals to new English poems. One of the best of the English madrigalists was Thomas Weelkes (1576–1623), an organist who spent most of his career in rural Chichester but ended his days in London, an honorary Gentleman of the Royal Chapel.

In 1601 Weelkes and twenty-three other English composers each contributed a madrigal to a collection entitled *The Triumphs of Oriana*, an album of music compiled in honor of the Virgin Queen Elizabeth (1533–1603). (Oriana, a legendary British princess and maiden, was widely used as the poetic nickname of Queen Elizabeth.) Thomas Weelkes's contribution to *The Triumphs of Oriana* was the six-voice madrigal *As Vesta Was from Latmos Hill Descending*. Its text, likely fashioned by Weelkes himself, is a rather confused mixture of images from classical mythology: The Roman goddess Vesta, descending the Greek mountain of Latmos, spies Oriana (Elizabeth) ascending the hill; the nymphs and shepherds attending the goddess Diana desert her to sing the praises of Oriana. The sole virtue of this verse is that it provides frequent opportunity for word painting in music. The music descends, ascends, runs, mingles imitatively, and offers "mirthful tunes" to the maiden Queen as the text commands. Would the mirror on the wall have deemed the Queen "the fairest of them all" (Fig. 5–9)? Perhaps not. Yet Weelkes saw fit to end his madrigal with imitative cries of "Long live fair Oriana"—an exceptional example of art doing duty as political flattery in Elizabethan England.

FIGURE 5–8

Singers of a four-part madrigal during the middle of the sixteenth century. Women were very much a part of this secular, nonreligious music-making.

the madrigal

FIGURE 5–9

Queen Elizabeth I of England (1533–1603) painted by an anonymous artist.

madrigal as social pastime

The madrigal was a truly social art, one both men and women could enjoy (see Fig. 5–8). It was meant to be sung, usually with just one singer on a part, though a lute or a harpsichord might sometimes provide a background accompaniment. Most madrigals were not difficult to perform, for above all else they were intended to provide recreation for cultivated amateurs. Skill in singing such pieces was thought to be a necessary social grace for members of the upwardly mobile middle class. Thus, more than a thousand collections of madrigals, each containing approximately twenty pieces, were printed in Europe before 1620. If the madrigal was popular, this was because it was fun to sing. Vocal lines were written within a comfortable range, melodies were often triadic, rhythms were catchy, and the music full of puns. When Vesta descends the mountain, so too her music moves downward in a descending scale; when Oriana (Queen Elizabeth) ascends, her music, in turn, scales the staff; when Diana, the goddess of virginity, is all alone—you guessed it, we hear a solo voice! With sport like this to be had, no wonder the popularity of the madrigal endured beyond the Renaissance. Even today there are countless madrigal groups and societies that, to recall the evocative words of Shakespeare, "sing sounds and sweet airs, that give delight, and hurt not" (*The Tempest*).

Listening Guide

Thomas Weelkes
Madrigal, *As Vesta Was from Latmos Hill Descending* (1601)

6CD 1/9;
2CD 1/3

WWW

0:00   As Vesta was from Latmos Hill descending,
       [Opening homophonic chords give way to falling pitches on "descending"]

0:13   She spied a maiden Queen the same ascending,
       [Imitation falls, then rises on the word "ascending"]

0:36   Attended on by all the shepherds' swain;
       [Simple repeating notes suggest simple, country swains]

0:52   To whom Diana's darlings came running down amain,
       [All voices come "running down amain"]

1:17   First two by two, then three by three together,
       [Two voices exemplify "two by two," then three "three by three"]

1:28   Leaving their goddess all alone, hasted thither;
       [Solo voice highlights "all alone"]

1:41   And mingling with the shepherds of her train,
       [Imitative entries suggest "mingling"]

1:48   With mirthful tunes her presence did entertain.
       [Light, rapid singing produces "mirthful tunes"]

2:03   Then sang the shepherds and nymphs of Diana:
       [Stark chords announce the final acclamation:]

2:15   Long live fair Oriana.
       [Long life to the Queen is declaimed endlessly]

(Listening Exercise 15)

England was the last major country in Europe to experience a cultural reawakening. The Renaissance arrived there late, around 1550, but blazed brightly, lasting into the seventeenth century. Queen Elizabeth died in 1603, Shakespeare in 1616, and the composer Thomas Weelkes in 1623. Their passing marked the end of a glorious English Renaissance, as well as the Renaissance generally.

Listening Exercises

14

Josquin Desprez   6CD 1/7;
Motet   2CD 1/2
Ave Maria (ca. 1485)

Ave Maria by Josquin Desprez is a fine example of a motet using imitative counterpoint, a texture that dominated the musical style of sacred motets and Masses during the Renaissance. As you work through this exercise, you will become more familiar with how the voices unfold in this imitative, polyphonic texture. On this modern recording women sing the soprano part.

1. (0:00) What is the order in which the voices enter?
   a. soprano, bass, tenor, alto
   b. soprano, alto, tenor, bass
   c. bass, tenor, alto, soprano
2. (1:05–1:14) What is the general direction of the music during the phrase "Coelestia, terrestria" ("heaven and earth")?
   a. rises from "heaven" to "earth"
   b. falls from "heaven" to "earth"
3. (1:18) Which voice sings the final "laetitia" ("joy")?
   a. soprano   b. male alto   c. bass
4. (2:26) The meter changes here. Which is correct?
   a. It changes from triple to duple.
   b. It changes from duple to triple.
5. (2:57) Which voice ends this section (on the word "purgatio")?
   a. soprano   b. male alto   c. bass
6. (3:58) Is this final, chordal section written in homophony or polyphony (counterpoint)?
   a. homophony   b. polyphony
7. (4:23) On the last word ("Amen"), do the voices change pitches on the two syllables ("A" and "men"), or do they repeat the pitches?
   a. change pitches   b. repeat the pitches
8. Which is true throughout this motet?
   a. In the imitative sections the tenor and bass always enter before the soprano and alto.
   b. In the imitative sections the soprano and alto always enter before the tenor and bass.
9. Do instruments accompany the voices in this performance?
   a. yes   b. no

10. What do we call the style of performance referred to in Question 9?
    a. imitative   b. chordal   c. *a cappella*   d. a cabaletta

Thomas Weelkes   6CD 1/9;
Madrigal   2CD 1/3
As Vesta Was from Latmos Hill Descending (1601)

So striking is the depiction of the text through music in the madrigal of the Renaissance that these instances of musical word painting are called "madrigalisms." Often the music depicts the text by its motion (up, down, or stationary) or by its texture (polyphonic, homophonic, or monophonic). At these moments the word painting is so obvious as to be amusing, and that makes several of the following questions rather easy to answer.

1. (0:00–0:13) The text sets the scene of this madrigal at the top of Latmos Hill, a mountain in Greek mythology. At the beginning we hear sounds that are
   a. generally high with female voices predominating
   b. generally low with male voices predominating
2. (0:00–0:34) Which is true about the direction of the music for the words "descending" and "ascending"?
   a. It descends for "descending" and ascends for "ascending."
   b. It ascends for "descending" and descends for "ascending."
   c. There is no clear direction and word painting is not present.
3. (0:36–0:47) Which is true about the music for the words "attended on"?
   a. It ascends.
   b. It descends.
   c. The singers mostly repeat the same pitches, so the music sounds static.
4. (0:58–1:13) Here the music seems to go faster because the performers sing shorter notes so as to depict the word "running." What is the direction of the music?
   a. It goes up to suggest "running up."
   b. It goes down to suggest "running down."
5. (1:28–1:33) What is the texture of the music at the words "Leaving their goddess"?
   a. imitative polyphony   b. homophony   c. monophony
6. (1:34–1:37) What is the texture of the music at the words "all alone"?
   a. imitative polyphony   b. homophony   c. monophony
7. (2:03–2:10) What is the texture at the words "Then sang the shepherds"?
   a. imitative polyphony   b. homophony   c. monophony
8. (2:15–3:09) What is the texture at the words "Long live fair Oriana"?
   a. imitative polyphony   b. homophony   c. monophony
9. (2:20–end) When the bass enters with a presentation of "Long live fair Oriana," what is the nature of the musical line?
   a. The bass sings long, steady notes to emphasize the word "long."
   b. The bass sings rapid notes, joining the many acclamations of the upper voices.

10. Which statement correctly describes the forces used in the performance of this madrigal?
    a. There is one voice and one instrument on each part.
    b. The performance is *a cappella* with two voices on each part.
    c. The performance is *a cappella* with one voice on each part.

Key Words

a cappella (94)	*falsetto* voice (98)	motet (94)
castrato (98)	humanism (92)	point of imitation (98)
Council of Trent (97)	imitation (94)	Sistine Chapel (97)
Counter-Reformation (97)	madrigal (101)	word painting (101)
	madrigalism (101)	

For a checklist of musical style in the Renaissance, see page 68.

Scala/Art Resource, NY

Early Baroque Music

Music historians agree, with unusual unanimity, that Baroque music first appeared in northern Italy in the early seventeenth century. To be sure, around 1600 certain qualities of the Italian madrigal—virtuosic solo singing, for example—came to be cultivated with unusual intensity. Soon the older equal-voiced polyphony of the Renaissance was superseded by an exuberant new style. Eventually, this new style was given a new name: Baroque.

   "Baroque" is the term used to describe the art, architecture, dance, and music of the period 1600–1750. It is taken from the Portuguese word *barroco*, meaning a pearl of irregular shape then used in jewelry and fine decoration. Critics applied the term "Baroque" to indicate a rough, bold instrumental sound in music and excessive ornamentation in the visual arts. To the philosopher Jean-Jacques Rousseau (1712–1778), "A baroque music is that in which the harmony is confused, charged with modulations and dissonances, the melody is harsh and little natural, the intonation difficult, and the movement constrained." Thus, originally, "Baroque" had a pejorative meaning. It signified distortion, excess, and extravagance. Only during the twentieth century, with a new-found appreciation of the painting of Peter Paul Rubens

Scala/Art Resource, NY

Archiv fur Kunst und Geschichte, Berlin

(1577–1640), the sculpture of Gian Lorenzo Bernini (1598–1680), and the music of Antonio Vivaldi (1678–1741), among others, has the term "Baroque" come to assume a positive meaning in Western cultural history.

Baroque art and architecture have several distinctive characteristics. These qualities are observable in the music of the period as well. What strikes us most when we encounter a monument of Baroque planning, such as the basilica of St. Peter in Rome or the palace of Versailles outside of Paris, is that everything is constructed on a massive scale. The plazas, gardens, fountains, colonnades, and buildings are all of the grandest design. Similarly, human forms, as presented in the painting and sculpture of the time, are larger than life. Look at the ninety-foot-high baldachin inside St. Peter's and imagine how it dwarfs the priest at the altar below (Fig. 6–1). Outside the basilica a circle of colonnades forms a courtyard large enough to encompass several football fields (Fig. 6–2). Or consider the French king's palace of Versailles, constructed during the reign of Louis XIV (1643–1715), so monumental in scope that it formed a small independent city, home to several thousand court functionaries (Fig. 6–3).

The music composed for performance in such vast expanses was also grandiose. Instrumental groups approaching the size of the modern orchestra came into being, and choral works for twenty-four, forty-eight, and even fifty-three separate vocal parts were written. Mostly intended for spacious churches, these compositions for multiple choruses with instrumental accompaniment have come to epitomize the grand or colossal Baroque.

Once the exteriors of these large Baroque palaces and churches were built, the artists of the time went to the opposite extreme, filling the long lines with an overabundance of small, decorative details. It is as if monumental space had created a vacuum into which the artist rushed with a certain nervous energy. The large painting entitled *The Lion Hunt* by Peter Paul Rubens (1577–1640), for example, has the spatial proportions of colossal Baroque art (Fig. 6–4). The figures are larger than life. Bodies twist and turn to suggest enormous energy and effort. The principal colors (black, white, and red) are not modulated but strongly contrasting. The painting is at once monumental yet cluttered. When filling the interior of a church the sculptor

FIGURES 6–1 AND 6–2

(left) The high altar at St. Peter's Basilica, Rome, with baldachin by Gian Lorenzo Bernini. Standing more than ninety feet high, this canopy is marked by twisted columns and curving shapes, color, and movement, all typical of Baroque art. (above) St. Peter's Square, designed by Bernini in the mid-seventeenth century. The expanse is so colossal it seems to swallow people, cars, and buses.

FIGURE 6–3

The chapel of the palace of Versailles (1699–1710) exalts the power of the French monarch as much as it does the Lord. Note the organ at the far end.

Musée National des Chateaux de Versailles

Bayerische Staatsbemaldesammlungen, Munich, Alte Pinakothek

Chorherrenstift St. Florian, Austria

FIGURE 6–4 AND 6–5

(above) *The Lion Hunt* (1621) by Peter Paul Rubens. Like much of Rubens' art, this canvas is both colorful and large, measuring ten by thirteen feet. The large field, moreover, is filled with a swirl of activity. (right) Church of the monastery of St. Florian, Austria (1686–1708). The powerful pillars and arches set a strong structural framework, while the painted ceiling and heavily foliated capitals provide decoration and warmth.

or carver employed decorative scrolls, floral capitals, and multiple layers of adornment to complete and add warmth to a large expanse (Fig. 6–5).

Similarly, when expressed in the music of the Baroque era, this love of busy detail within large-scale compositions took the form of vigorous, pulsating rhythms with strong, regular beats and many smaller subdivisions. It also was expressed by the use of musical ornaments, whether for instruments such as the violin or harpsichord (see page 110) or for voice. Notice, in Fig. 6–6, the abundance of ornaments and figural patterns in just a few bars of music for violin by Arcangelo Corelli (1653–1713). Such ornaments were equally popular with the singers of the early Baroque era, when the cult of the vocal virtuoso first began to emerge.

We observed in the music of the Renaissance (1475–1600) a growing awareness of the capacity of this art to sway, or affect, the emotions. This belief in the powers of music to move the listener intensified in the Baroque period. Musical moods now came to be called the "affections," and it was the task of

Yale University Music Library

FIGURE 6–6

Arcangelo Corelli's sonata for violin and *basso continuo,* Opus 5, No. 1. The bass provides the structural support, while the violin adds elaborate decoration above.

the composer to fashion a musical language that could vividly express many and varied emotions. Composers of early Baroque opera, in particular, aimed to convey impassioned speech through music. They believed that music could express love and joy, as well as jealousy and hate.

Painters and sculptors, too, sought to increase emotional expression, which they did by means of exaggeration and distortion. The new emotionalism in Baroque art can easily be seen by comparing the *David* of Gian Lorenzo Bernini (1598–1680), with its fierce visage and twisted body (Fig. 6–7), with Michelangelo's serenely balanced treatment of the same subject done about a hundred years earlier (see page 92). Moreover, the spirit of the Baroque age required of both artist and composer that the emotional "units" they created be large, or long-lasting, and clearly defined. Baroque music does not change hurriedly from one mood to another, as was the practice, for example, in the Renaissance madrigal, where the musical feeling changed to reflect the meaning of each new phrase or word (see page 101). Instead, in the newer Baroque style each piece or each large section of a piece carried a single mood or affection throughout—joy, jealousy, resignation, agony, triumph, and others. What is perhaps unique about Baroque music and Baroque art in general is not only its intense expression but also the clear-cut way in which one emotion, color, or spatial unit is kept separate and distinct from the next.

FIGURE 6–7

Gian Lorenzo Bernini's *David* (1623) displays a vitality and restless energy of the sort that can be heard in the music of the Baroque era. Compare Michelangelo's serenely balanced treatment of the same subject from the Renaissance (see Fig. 5–3).

CHARACTERISTICS OF BAROQUE MUSIC

The 150 years encompassed by the Baroque era (1600–1750) witnessed significant changes in musical style, from the straightforward homophony of Giovanni Gabrieli (ca. 1557–1612) to the complex polyphony of Johann Sebastian Bach (1685–1750). It also saw the introduction of many new musical forms and genres, which we discuss later in this chapter and the next: the sonata, suite, concerto, cantata, opera, oratorio, and fugue. Yet despite such stylistic evolution and formal innovation, there was one musical element that remained constant throughout the Baroque—the *basso continuo*, or "thorough bass," as it was called in seventeenth-century England.

The *Basso Continuo*

The **basso continuo** was a small ensemble of at least two instrumentalists who provided a foundation, or "continuous bass," for the melody or melodies above. One performer played an instrument that could produce chords, usually the organ or harpsichord, but sometimes even a large lute or guitar. The other played a low-sounding instrument, like the cello, the cellolike *viola da gamba* (Fig. 6–8) or the bassoon, which played the bass line. By having the harpsichord, for example, generate the basic chords of the piece, a composition acquired a solid harmonic foundation. At the same time, the bass instrument always doubled the lowest note played by the left hand of the harpsichordist, thereby giving the bass line new and greater power.

a bass and harmonic foundation

The additional weight that the *basso continuo* lent to the bass reflected the fact that the music of the early Baroque period had assumed a new structure. In the Mass and motet of the Renaissance, the voices spin out a web of imitative counterpoint, and the character and importance of each of the lines is equal:

The Harpsichord

The **harpsichord** has been called the workhorse of the Baroque era because it served both as the main instrument for accompaniment and as a solo instrument in its own right (see Figs. 3–17 and 6–8). In this sense the harpsichord functioned much like the piano would later in the Classical and Romantic periods, as an accompanying and a solo instrument. The sound of the harpsichord is produced by depressing a key that pushes up a quill or (nowadays) a plastic "pick" to pluck a taut wire string. This abrupt plucking of wire is what creates the tinkling sound of the instrument. Unlike the piano, in which a complicated mechanism permits different levels of finger pressure to achieve a wide range of dynamics, the harpsichord cannot produce a louder or softer sound, because the plucking mechanism transmits a constant level of force to the string. There are, therefore, no subtle gradations of sound on the harpsichord. When greater volume is needed, an additional full set of strings is brought into play to double the sound, and all the music thereafter will be loud until this set of strings is disengaged. Thus, the harpsichord typifies the way in which sound was produced in the Baroque period. There are no gradual swells and decreases, but only abrupt changes in the amount or volume of sound. The harpsichord was invented in the late Middle Ages, reached the peak of its popularity in the Baroque era, and went out of fashion in the time of Mozart (1756–1791), replaced by the more flexible, responsive, and potentially powerful piano.

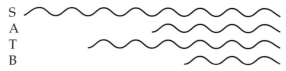

In early Baroque music, however, the voices are no longer equal. Rather, there is a polarity of force directed toward the top and bottom:

S
A
T
B

FIGURE 6–8

Basso continuo and violin. This continuo consists of a harpsichord and a large string instrument, the **viola da gamba,** or **bass viol.** The viol had six strings and frets (as on a guitar), and produced a slightly darker, less brilliant sound than members of the violin family. The gambist playing here is Eva Linfield.

Barrie-Kent Photographers

The soprano carries the melody; the bass provides a strong harmonic support. In between, the middle voices often do little more than fill out the texture. If Renaissance music is conceived polyphonically and horizontally, line by line, that of the early Baroque period is organized homophonically and vertically, chord by chord. The *basso continuo* helps establish a strong bass and ensures that the fundamentally chordal structure of the music holds tight.

The sound of the *basso continuo* (or simply continuo in English) pervaded almost all Baroque music. When a solo violinist or flutist played a sonata, or when a singer performed a recitative or aria (see page 117), the continuo was there; thus, three performers were involved, a principal and an accompanying cast of two (see Fig. 6–8). As we shall see, the continuo also held together soloists and orchestra in the Baroque concerto, just as it unified multiple choirs in polychoral motets for the church. For church music it was the organ—the traditional instrument of the church—that played the keyboard continuo, while in virtually all other music that chord-supplying function was provided by the harpsichord. Indeed, it is the continual tinkling of the harpsichord, in step with the bass sounds of a cello, *viola da gamba*, or bassoon, that signals to the listener that the music being played comes from the Baroque era.

Because the *basso continuo* is basic to nearly all Baroque music, every listener should be familiar with its sound. In the recording of the aria by Barbara Strozzi presented below, the continuo is supplied by a harpsichord, guitar, and *viola da gamba*. The continuo group is clearly audible because it sounds by itself at the beginning, in the middle, and at the end. Moreover, the bass line consists of the same four descending notes (C, B, A, G) played again and again. Above it a soprano sings a lament in the new expressive vocal style of the Baroque, *Voglio morire* (*I want to die*). As we shall see (page 121), it is common for composers in the Baroque era to set a repeating bass beneath a ravishing vocal lament. For the moment, however, concentrate on the sound of the *basso continuo*, ignoring, if you can, the seductive tones of the voice.

the sound of the basso continuo

Listening Guide

Barbara Strozzi
Aria, *I want to die* (1651): Part I

Intro CD/8

0:00	*Basso continuo* plays descending four-note pattern
0:19	Soprano enters as the *basso continuo* proceeds
0:41	Four-note bass pattern extended to accommodate a cadence*
0:45	*Basso continuo* alone
0:50	Soprano enters as the *basso continuo* proceeds
1:29	*Basso continuo* plays descending pattern and then adds a final cadence

Voglio, voglio morire,	I want to die,
più tosto ch'il mio mal venga a scoprire;	rather than have my pain discovered;
ò, disgrazia fatale,	oh, fatal misfortune,
quanto più miran gl'occhi il suo bel volto	the more my eyes admire his beautiful face
più tien la bocca il mio desir sepolto.	the more my mouth keeps hidden my desire.

For a discussion of the life of Barbara Strozzi, see the boxed essay on page 112. For a Listening Exercise for this aria, see page 35.

Baroque Musical Elements

Baroque music, as we have seen, is marked by spaciousness and grandeur, by passionate expression, and by the urge to create special effects. It is held together by a chordal framework and a strong bass line, both generated by the *basso continuo*. These are qualities to be heard in all Baroque music. In the music of the early Baroque in particular, the artistic expression of emotions became increasingly exaggerated and exalted in tone. Later, in the eighteenth century, some of the more excessive qualities of early Baroque music would be smoothed out and regularized by Bach and Handel (see Chapter 7). For the moment, let us analyze early Baroque music in terms of the most basic musical elements: melody, harmony, rhythm, and dynamics.

exaggerated sounds

MELODY

In the Renaissance, melody was more or less all of one type. It was a direct, uncomplicated line that could be performed by either a voice or an instrument. Now, in early Baroque music, beginning about 1600, two different

Barbara Strozzi: *Professional Composer*

Until the twentieth century, women who earned a living as professional composers were rare. Although women composed art music in every period in the history of Western music, their numbers were historically small. In the Middle Ages, for example, a few *trobairitz* wrote chansons; but to a woman, they were all members of the lesser nobility and thus not financially dependent upon the success of their creations. So, too, a few women composed during the late Renaissance and early Baroque, but they were mainly cloistered nuns who wrote for the Church and received their sustenance from it. The reason for the absence of independent women composers in the Baroque era is simple: musical performance within the home was thought to be an appropriate activity for ladies, so long as it was done with modesty; but musical performance outside the home was not deemed proper, and even the best female opera singers of the day were viewed with suspicion. As to musical composition, it was considered a remunerative profession, the fruits of which were exhibited in public. As a rule women did not engage in income-earning professions or trades. Given this tradition, the career of Barbara Strozzi is all the more remarkable. She was not only that rare creature, the woman composer, but she was also the first to support herself from the commissions she received from her compositions.

Barbara Strozzi (1619–1677) was a native of Venice, the illegitimate daughter of a merchant and his domestic servant. Like many prominent Venetians at this time, her father, Giulio Strozzi, was a man both of business and of letters. Giulio fostered his daughter's musical talent by providing her with lessons in musical composition, texts for her pieces, and even a regular audience to hear them. Given this encouragement, Barbara Strozzi began to compose and eventually created more than a hundred works, an impressive number for a composer of either sex. Three-quarters of Strozzi's music is scored for solo soprano and *basso continuo*. Many of these works she herself undoubtedly sang as vocal chamber music in Venice, for numerous commentators praised her fine voice. (For an example of Barbara Strozzi's compositional style, listen to her aria *I want to die* discussed on page 111.)

When Giulio Strozzi died in 1652 Barbara was left both destitute and desperate—she had four children but was unmarried. Over the course of the next six years she published six collections of arias, approximately one a year. Each of these publications she dedicated to a member of the high nobility, and, according to custom, the dedicatee paid for the honor. Barbara Strozzi may have been unique as a professional woman composer but she was not exempt from the economic realities of the day. Throughout the Baroque era composers earned far more from the fees received by dedicating a work to a wealthy patron than they did from royalties generated by sales of the music itself.

A portrait of Barbara Strozzi painted in the 1630s by Bernardo Strozzi, perhaps a relative.
Gemäldegalerie Alter Meister, Dresden

melodic styles begin to develop: a dramatic, virtuosic style in singing and, by contrast, a more mechanical, repetitious style in instrumental music. Despite the increasing virtuosity of vocal music, attention is no longer focused exclusively on the voice. Throughout the Baroque era there is a new emphasis on writing melodies specifically for instruments such as the harpsichord and violin. These new melodies are idiomatic in that they are well suited to the technical demands of these instruments.

melodic sequence

Early in the Baroque period a new melodic technique called sequence was applied to melody. A **melodic sequence** is the repetition of a musical motive at successively higher or lower degrees of the scale. Example 6–1 shows a sequence, indeed an exceptionally long sequence, from the music of the early Baroque composer Claudio Monteverdi (1567–1643). Notice how the initial motive is repeated seven times, each time one step lower than before.

EXAMPLE 6–1

The melodic sequence first appears extensively in the music of the Baroque era and continues to be a standard melodic procedure into the twentieth century.

HARMONY

Baroque harmonies are chordally conceived and tightly bound to the *basso continuo*. As the seventeenth century progresses, harmonies unfold more and more in familiar patterns as standard harmonic progressions; in other words, chord progressions* begin to emerge. The shortest and most frequent of these is the V–I (dominant–tonic) cadence (see page 30). The advent of standard harmonic progressions like the V–I cadence gives added direction and cohesion to the music.

chord progressions

Attending this development is the growing importance—and eventual total domination—of the major and minor system of keys. These two scale patterns, major and minor, replaced the dozen or so scales (or "modes," as they were called) used during the Renaissance and before. Moreover, as music was reduced to just two qualities of sound, the listener could more easily focus on the distinct properties of each. Composers could play the dark minor off against the bright major, or vice versa, to create the emotional effects so important in Baroque music.

major and minor keys

RHYTHM

Rhythm in Baroque music is characterized by uniformity. Just as a single mood, or affect, is carried from the beginning to the end of a piece, so the rhythmic patterns heard at the beginning will surface again and again, right to the end. This tendency toward rhythmic uniformity and rhythmic drive becomes more and more pronounced as the Baroque era proceeds. It culminates in the rhythmically propulsive music of J. S. Bach.

uniform rhythms

DYNAMICS

Baroque music, like Baroque art, is organized in units of distinctly different, yet independent, moods and colors. Dynamics do not change gradually from one section or piece to the next. Rather, a single dynamic range, whether loud or soft, will hold fast until abruptly replaced by another. This phenomenon of shifting the volume of sound suddenly and dramatically from one level to another is called **terraced dynamics**. Changing dynamics in this fashion, especially when combined with equally abrupt changes in orchestration and shifts to major or minor tonality, helps create the clearly sectionalized sound of Baroque music. The first composer in the history of music to place dynamic marks, such as *piano* and *forte*, in the score was Giovanni Gabrieli (ca. 1557–1611), who spent his entire career in Venice.

THE VENETIAN POLYCHORAL MOTET

Venice, the Queen of the Seas, was—and remains—a city of canals, arching bridges, and exotic palaces. Reaching its zenith of economic power in the fifteenth century, Venice owed its success partly to its truly republican form of government and partly to its strategic location at the head of the Adriatic Sea, which made it a natural center of trade (Fig. 6–9). By 1581 its population had reached ninety thousand. The focus of civic and spiritual life in Venice was the palace of the doge (or mayor) and the adjoining basilica of St. Mark, with its

FIGURE 6–9

A map of present-day Italy showing Mantua, Venice, Florence, and Rome, each an important city for the cultivation of music during the early Baroque period.

Precision Graphics

FIGURE 6–10

Piazza San Marco painted by Gentile Bellini, ca. 1500. St. Mark's was the focal point of all religious and civic activities in Venice. Processions such as these concluded with a performance of religious music inside the church.

spacious piazza in front (Fig. 6–10). St. Mark's, which preserves the remains of the Evangelist Mark beneath the high altar, has an architectural plan unique among the major churches of the West. It is built in the form of an equal-sided Greek cross, probably because in its early history Venice was under the political and artistic domination of the Byzantine Empire.

Beginning in the mid-sixteenth century, musicians exploited the unusual architectural plan of St. Mark's by composing motets for it for two, three, or four choirs. At first these separate ensembles were placed in the two singers' galleries on opposite sides of the main aisle (Fig. 6–11). Later they were also stationed in the other elevated galleries that adjoined the central dome. By situating groups of musicians in these separate, elevated lofts—or loggias, as they are called—composers were able to create new sonic effects that astonished the listeners seated or standing below. To a visitor to St. Mark's in the early seventeenth century, the novelty of the musical environment must have been as striking as the twentieth-century change from monophonic to multiphonic surround sound.

Giovanni Gabrieli (ca. 1557–1612)

The composer who made the most of the opportunities afforded by the architecture of St. Mark's was Giovanni Gabrieli, a native of Venice and organist at the church. Gabrieli wrote little secular music and few Masses for the church. Instead, he directed his creative energy toward the composition of ceremonial motets for the semi-religious occasions of state that culminated beneath the domes of St. Mark's. Each of these special ceremonies included a triumphant procession during which the Doge and the various religious confraternities of Venice filed into St. Mark's (see Fig. 6–10). Gabrieli composed

FIGURE 6–11

Interior of the basilica of St. Mark, with a view of the upper galleries, where musicians often performed polychoral motets such as those by Giovanni Gabrieli.

his polychoral motet *In ecclesiis* (*In the Churches*) for such an occasion. It is written for three separate choirs: the first musical group consists of a quartet of vocal soloists; the second is a vocal chorus; and the third is an ensemble of six instruments: a violin, two trombones, and three cornettos (see Fig. 4–11). Accompanying all three groups is the *basso continuo*, here supplied by an organ. Because St. Mark's has an exceptionally lively, indeed muddy, acoustical environment—it takes more than five seconds for sounds to die out—Gabrieli had ample reason to adapt his music to the architecture of the church. He writes short melodies, simple harmonies, and snappy rhythms. He also repeats the text frequently so it can be clearly heard.

Giovanni Gabrieli was the first composer in the history of music to indicate in the score a dynamic level at which the music was to be played (either *piano* or *forte*). He was also the first to prescribe specific instruments—here violin, trombone, and cornetto. The instruments (choir 3) have their own timbre, one distinct from the voices. They also tend to play short bursts of music with strong attacks. The solo voices (choir 1), on the other hand, sometimes sing long notes or lengthy, difficult melismas*. Notice that the role of the chorus (choir 2) is simple: It regularly inserts a chordal refrain on the word "Alleluja." Thus from beginning to end, different blocks of sound are suddenly added or subtracted to create high drama. If Palestrina's music of the late Renaissance is uniformly serene from start to finish (see page 97), Gabrieli's Baroque music is full of ever-varying textures, colors, and dynamic levels. Individual choirs can be contrasted for dramatic effect, or they can be combined, as occurs at the end of *In ecclesiis*, to produce the impressive volume of the colossal Baroque. Renaissance cool has given way to Baroque opulence.

specific dynamics and instruments

Listening Guide

WWW

Giovanni Gabrieli
Motet, *In the Churches* (1612)

6CD 1/10

Time	Description	Latin	English
0:00	Soprano soloist of Choir 1 plus organ *basso continuo*	In ecclesiis, benedicite Domino	In the churches, bless the Lord
0:18	Choir 2 and soprano echo, rising rapid notes on third and final time	Alleluja	
0:35	Tenor soloist of Choir 1 plus continuo; peaks on "anima mea" ("my soul")	In omni loco dominationis, benedic anima mea Dominum	In every holy place, may my soul bless the Lord
1:19	Choir 2 and tenor echo	Alleluja	
1:33	An instrumental interlude; begins solemnly but changes to lively dotted rhythms, ends with descending melodic sequence	Choir 3	
2:03	Alto and tenor of Choir 1 sing duet accompanied by the instrumental ensemble and continuo	In Deo salutari meo, et gloria mea	In God is my salvation and my glory
2:45	Duet continues; notes become more rapid and rise in a melodic sequence	Deus, auxilium meum et spes mea in Deo est	Lord, my help and my hope is in God
3:29	Choir 2 with alto and tenor echos	Alleluja	
3:44	Soprano and bass duet with imitation and echos	Deus noster, te invocamus, te laudamus, te adoramus	Our Lord, we call to you, we praise you, we adore you
4:31	Duet continues; change to lively triple meter on "vivifica nos" ("revivify us")	Libera nos, salva nos, vivifica nos	Deliver us, save us, revivify us

(Continued on next page)

5:02	Choir 2 with soprano and bass echo	Alleluja	
5:19	Rich-sounding chords for all three choirs on "Deus," followed by long notes in the bass	Deus, adjutor noster in aeternum (repeated)	Lord, our judge forever
6:39	Choirs 2 and 3 with echoes by Choir 1 (soloists); third statement of "Alleluja" repeated; strong final cadence added	Alleluja	

(Listening Exercise 16)

EARLY BAROQUE OPERA

Given the popularity of opera today—and the fact that there had been opera in China and Japan since the thirteenth century—it is surprising that this genre of music emerged comparatively late in the history of Western European culture. Not until around 1600 did opera appear, and its native soil was Italy.

Opera literally means "work": The word was first employed in the Italian phrase *opera drammatica in musica* (a dramatic work set to music). In opera, then, the lines of the actors and actresses are not merely spoken, but sung. In this way music heightens the emotional intensity of the action on the stage. Rejecting the notion that the emotions of an individual could be best expressed by a group of singers, opera stressed solo singing at the expense of the polyphonic choir. Choral singing might be a useful way to convey the abstract religious thoughts of the multitudes, but to communicate raw human emotion, the individual appeal of a soloist was needed. Thus from its very beginnings opera possessed three qualities that remain true today: (1) all parts of the drama are sung, mainly by soloists; (2) the major roles go to the best singers; and (3) the costs are enormous because of lavish costumes and sets, and the fees paid to virtuoso singers—star singers quickly became the highest paid musicians of the early Baroque, as they are today.

new emphasis on solo singing

The origins of opera can be found in the progressive thinking of musicians and intellectuals in a few northern Italian cities such as Florence, Mantua, and Venice (see Fig. 6–9). Pursuing a humanistic goal of the late Renaissance, they aimed to recapture the expressive power of ancient Greek music, as reported by Plato and others. Florence, in particular, was home to several musically gifted intellectuals, including Vincenzo Galilei (1533–1591), the father of the famous astronomer Galileo Galilei (1564–1642). These music lovers formed an aristocratic society called the Florentine *camerata* (academy) to promote their new ideals. They recognized that the power of classical drama owed much to the fact that every line was sung, not spoken. All that was needed to recreate the style of ancient Greek drama, they theorized, was to compose simple recitations sung to the plainest of accompaniments. From these developments emerged the first full-fledged opera, Claudio Monteverdi's *Orfeo*.

FIGURE 6–12

Portrait of Claudio Monteverdi by Bernardo Strozzi (1581–1644). Strozzi also painted the singer and composer Barbara Strozzi (see page 112).

Tiroler Landesmuseum Ferdinandeum, Innsbruck

Claudio Monteverdi (1567–1643)

Claudio Monteverdi was a musical genius who could manifest his enormous talents equally well in a madrigal, a motet, or an opera (Fig. 6–12). He was born in the northern Italian town of Cremona in 1567 and moved to the larger city of Mantua (see Fig. 6–9) about 1590 to serve Duke Vincenzo

Gonzaga as a singer and as a player of string instruments. In 1601 he was appointed director of music, and in this capacity composed two operas for the court, *Orfeo* (1607) and *Arianna* (1608). But the duke failed to pay Monteverdi what he had promised. "I have never in my life suffered greater humiliation of the spirit than when I had to go and beg the treasurer for what was mine," said the composer some years later. Thus disenchanted with Mantua, Monteverdi accepted the much-coveted position of *maestro di cappella* at St. Mark's in Venice, which fell vacant on the death of Giovanni Gabrieli in 1612. Although called to Venice ostensibly to write church music, Monteverdi nevertheless continued to compose opera as well. Among his important later works in this genre are *The Return of Ulysses* (1640) and *The Coronation of Poppea* (1642). He died in Venice in 1643 after thirty years of faithful service.

FIGURE 6–13

The beginning of the third act of Monteverdi's *Orfeo* (1607), from the original print of the opera. The vocal part of Orfeo is on the staff above, the slower-moving bass line of the *basso continuo* is below.

Monteverdi's first operatic masterpiece—indeed the first important opera in the history of Western music—is his *Orfeo* (Fig. 6–13). Every composer of opera must begin by setting to music a dramatic text, called the **libretto.** Because the aim of early opera was to reproduce the style of ancient Greek drama, it was only natural that Monteverdi's libretto was drawn from a tale found in classical Greek mythology. Our hero is Orfeo (Orpheus), the son of Apollo, the Greek god of the sun and of music. (Indeed, the very word "music" comes from the muses that attend Apollo.) Orfeo, himself a demi-god, finds love in the form of the beautiful earthling Euridice. No sooner are they married but she is fatally bitten by a serpent and carried off to Hades (the realm of the dead). Orfeo mourns her death and vows to descend into the Underworld to rescue her and restore his love to earthly life. This he nearly accomplishes by exploiting his divine musical powers, for Orfeo can make trees sway, calm savage beasts, and even overcome the demonic forces of Hades with the beauty of his song. The theme of *Orfeo*, then, is the divine power of music.

Monteverdi's Orfeo

To convey a feeling of heightened passions, Monteverdi and other composers of early opera developed a new, more expressive and flexible style of solo singing for the stage called **stile rappresentativo** ("the representational style"). Sometimes requiring rapid declamation on a single pitch, and at other times wide-ranging vocal flourishes, *stile rappresentativo* permitted the singer to move almost imperceptibly from one mood to another. Monteverdi himself said: "I am aware that contrasts are what stir our souls, and that such stirring is the aim of all good music." In the hands of Monteverdi and later composers, *stile rappresentativo* would soon be transformed into two different and contrasting types of vocal writing, recitative and aria.

Recitative, from the Italian word *recitativo* ("something recited"), is musically heightened speech. In opera recitative is usually used to tell the audience what has happened. Because recitative attempts to mirror the natural stresses of oral delivery, it is often made up of rapidly repeating notes followed by one or two long notes at the ends of phrases, as in the following recitative from Act II of *Orfeo*:

recitative

EXAMPLE 6–2

A l'a-ma - ra no-vel-la Ras-sem-bra l'in-fe-li - ceun mu-to sas-so
(At the bitter news the unhappy one resembled a mute stone)

Recitative in Baroque opera is accompanied only by the *basso continuo* playing simple chords. Such a sparsely accompanied recitative is called **secco recitative,** from the Italian for "dry." (By the nineteenth century, recitative will be accompanied by the full orchestra and will be called *accompagnato.*) A good example of *secco* recitative can be heard at the beginning of the vocal excerpt from Act II of *Orfeo* discussed later in the Listening Guide.

aria If a recitative relates action, an aria expresses feeling. An **aria,** Italian for "song" or "ayre," is more passionate, more expansive, and more tuneful than a recitative. It also tends to have a clear meter and more regular rhythms. Finally, arias are usually sung with a less rapid-fire delivery and more in the way of vocal melisma* (one vowel luxuriously spread out over many notes) as can be seen, for example, in Orfeo's aria "Powerful spirit."

EXAMPLE 6–3

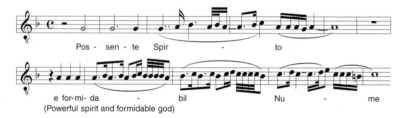

Pos-sen-te Spir - to

e for-mi-da - bil Nu - me
(Powerful spirit and formidable god)

Bibliothèque et Musée de l'Opera, Paris

FIGURE 6–14
Orfeo charms the guardians of Hades with his lyre. A detail from a painting by Nicolas Poussin (1594–1665).

Similarly, while the text of a recitative is normally written in blank verse, that of an aria is usually composed in rhyming lines organized in stanzas (strophes). The text of Orfeo's aria "Powerful spirit" consists of five three-line stanzas, each with a rhyme scheme "a-b-a." Moreover, the music for each stanza starts and ends in the same key (G minor). Tonally and textually, then, an aria constitutes a self-contained, independent musical unit. Operatic arias are nearly always accompanied not merely by the *basso continuo,* but also by part or all of the orchestra. Monteverdi gives special prominence to the violins and the cornettos in "Powerful spirit" to show how music can charm and delight even the guardians of Hades (Fig. 6–14).

Recitative and aria are the two main structural units and styles of singing in Baroque opera and in opera in general. In addition, there is a third structural unit called the arioso. An **arioso** is a passage of vocal music sung in a manner halfway between aria and recitative. Its style is actually more faithful to the original concept of *stile rappresentativo* than either aria or recitative. An arioso is more declamatory than an aria but has fewer quickly repeating notes than a recitative. The lament that Orfeo sings on learning of the death of Euridice, "Thou art dead," is a classic example of an arioso and *stile rappresentativo* singing as well.

Like all operas, *Orfeo* begins with an introductory piece for instruments alone, here called a toccata. The term **toccata** (literally "a touched thing") refers to an instrumental piece, for keyboard or other instruments, requiring great technical dexterity of the performers. It is, in other words, an instrumental showpiece.

Here the trumpet races up and down the scale while many of the lower parts rapidly articulate repeating pitches. Monteverdi instructs that the toccata be sounded three times. Brief though it may be, this toccata is sufficiently long to suggest the richness and variety of instrumental sounds available to a composer in the early Baroque period. Its theatrical function, of course, is to call the audience to attention, to signal that the action is about to begin.

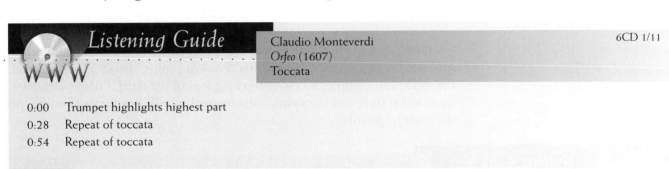

		6CD 1/11
Listening Guide	Claudio Monteverdi *Orfeo* (1607) Toccata	

0:00	Trumpet highlights highest part	
0:28	Repeat of toccata	
0:54	Repeat of toccata	

Although Monteverdi divided his *Orfeo* into five short acts, this two-hour opera was originally performed at Mantua without intermission. The first dramatic high point occurs midway through Act II, when the hero learns that his new bride, Euridice, has been claimed by the Underworld. In a heartfelt arioso, "Thou art dead," Orfeo laments his loss and vows to enter Hades to reclaim his treasure. Listen especially to the poignant conclusion in which Orfeo, by means of an ascending chromatic vocal line, bids farewell to earth, sky, and sun, and thus begins his journey to the land of the dead.

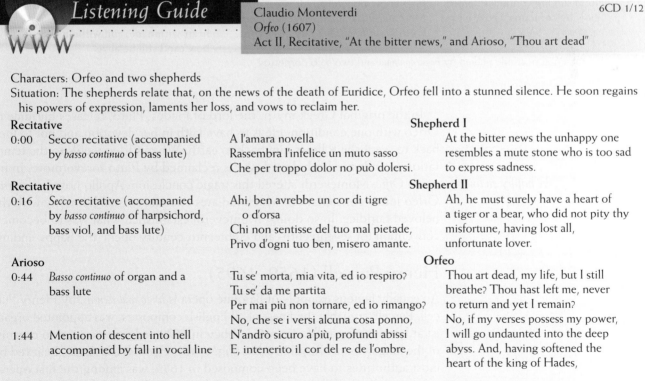

		6CD 1/12
Listening Guide	Claudio Monteverdi *Orfeo* (1607) Act II, Recitative, "At the bitter news," and Arioso, "Thou art dead"	

Characters: Orfeo and two shepherds
Situation: The shepherds relate that, on the news of the death of Euridice, Orfeo fell into a stunned silence. He soon regains his powers of expression, laments her loss, and vows to reclaim her.

Recitative

			Shepherd I
0:00	Secco recitative (accompanied by *basso continuo* of bass lute)	A l'amara novella Rassembra l'infelice un muto sasso Che per troppo dolor no può dolersi.	At the bitter news the unhappy one resembles a mute stone who is too sad to express sadness.

Recitative

			Shepherd II
0:16	*Secco* recitative (accompanied by *basso continuo* of harpsichord, bass viol, and bass lute)	Ahi, ben avrebbe un cor di tigre o d'orsa Chi non sentisse del tuo mal pietade, Privo d'ogni tuo ben, misero amante.	Ah, he must surely have a heart of a tiger or a bear, who did not pity thy misfortune, having lost all, unfortunate lover.

Arioso

			Orfeo
0:44	*Basso continuo* of organ and a bass lute	Tu se' morta, mia vita, ed io respiro? Tu se' da me partita Per mai più non tornare, ed io rimango? No, che se i versi alcuna cosa ponno, N'andrò sicuro a'più, profundi abissi E, intenerito il cor del re de l'ombre,	Thou art dead, my life, but I still breathe? Thou hast left me, never to return and yet I remain? No, if my verses possess my power, I will go undaunted into the deep abyss. And, having softened the heart of the king of Hades,
1:44	Mention of descent into hell accompanied by fall in vocal line		

(Continued on next page)

2:03	Vision of Euridice climbing to heaven causes flourish in high register	Meco trarrotti a reveder le stelle; O, se ciò negherammi empio destino, Rimarrò teco in compagnia di morte.	I will transport thee to again see the stars. And, if cruel destiny works against me, I will remain with thee in the company of death.
2:32	Growing conviction portrayed by chromatic ascent in vocal line	Addio terra, addio, cielo e sole, addio.	Farewell earth, farewell heaven and sun, farewell!

Having descended to the shores of Hades, Orfeo now invokes all his musical powers to gain entry. In the aria "Powerful spirit," he addresses Charon, the spirit who controls access to the kingdom of the dead. Orfeo's elaborate, florid vocal style and the exotic instrumental sounds he creates soon disarm the frightful guard.

Listening Guide

Claudio Monteverdi
Orfeo (1607)
Act III, Aria, "Powerful spirit" (strophes 1 and 2 only)

6CD 1/13

Characters: Orfeo and Charon
Situation: Orfeo pleads through his music that Charon grant passage into Hades

Aria (strophe 1)   **Orfeo**

0:00	Florid singing, joined by violin flourishes, above a *basso continuo*	Possente spirto e formidabil nume, Senza cui far passagio a l'altra riva Alma da corpo sciolta in van presume	Powerful spirit and formidable god, without whom no soul, deprived of body, may presume to pass to Hades's shore.
1:35	Instrumental postlude played by *basso continuo* and two solo violins		

Aria (strophe 2)   **Orfeo**

1:57	Florid singing continues, joined now by cornettos, above a *basso continuo*	Non viv'io, no, che poi di vita è priva Mia cara sposa, il cor non è più meco, E senza cor com'esser può ch'io viva?	I live no longer, since now my dear spouse is deprived of life, I have no heart within me, and without a heart how can I still be alive?
3:07	Instrumental postlude played by *basso continuo* and two solo cornettos		

the happy ending

In the original Greek myth, the lord of Hades, Pluto, releases Euridice to Orfeo with one condition: He is to have faith in her devotion and not to look back to see if she follows him back to earth. When Orfeo yields to the temptation to embrace his beloved, she is reclaimed by Pluto forevermore. In his opera *Orfeo*, Monteverdi altered this tragic conclusion: Apollo now transforms Orfeo into a constellation, which radiates eternal spiritual harmony with the beloved Euridice. In so doing, Monteverdi established what was to become a convention for seventeenth- and eighteenth-century opera, the happy ending.

Henry Purcell (1659–1695)

An equally famous example of Baroque opera is *Dido and Aeneas*, by Henry Purcell. Purcell, arguably the finest of all English composers, was appointed organist at London's great Westminster Abbey in 1679 and was elevated to organist of the king's Chapel Royal in 1682 (Fig. 6–15). His *Dido and Aeneas*, believed by most authorities to have been composed in 1689, was among the first operas written in the English language. Yet it was apparently created not for the king's court, but for a private girls' boarding school in the London suburb of Chelsea.

The students evidently served as the singers of the chorus, while professionals from London sang the principal roles. The libretto* of the opera, one appropriate for a school curriculum steeped in classical Latin, is drawn from Virgil's *Aeneid.* The Trojan hero Aeneas, fleeing his conquered homeland, sails west to found the city of Rome, but is blown off course and onto the shores of Carthage, where the widowed Dido rules as queen. No sooner does the proud queen surrender herself to the soldier of fortune than the gods command him to depart for Italy and fulfill his divine destiny—to found the city of Rome. Betrayed and alone, Dido vents her feelings in an exceptionally beautiful aria, "When I am laid in earth," and then expires. In Virgil's original story Dido stabs herself with the sword of Aeneas (Fig. 6–16). Here in Purcell's opera she dies of a broken heart: pain is poison enough.

Dido's final aria is introduced by a brief bit of recitative, "Thy hand, Belinda." As recitative goes, this is one of the more expressive examples of what is at heart a declamatory, businesslike style. As her voice twists chromatically downward through an entire octave, we feel the pain of the abandoned Dido. By the end, she has slumped into the arms of her servant Belinda.

FIGURE 6–15

Henry Purcell by an anonymous painter.

EXAMPLE 6–4

The aria that follows is constructed of two beautifully shaped musical phrases that carry the following two lines of text:

"When I am laid in earth, may my wrongs create
no trouble in thy breast.
Remember me, but ah! forget my fate."

Each of the lines is repeated, as are many individual words and pairs of words within them. Repetition of text is typical of an aria but not a recitative. It is one means by which the composer depicts emotion—the heroine can vocalize but cannot clearly articulate her feelings in complete sentences. The listener cares less about the syntax and more that the text and music together are emotionally charged. No fewer than six times does Dido plead with Belinda, and with us, to remember her. And, indeed, we do remember, for this plaintive aria is one of the most moving in all of opera.

Purcell constructs his aria "When I am laid in earth" on a *basso ostinato.* The term **basso ostinato** is an extension of the Italian word *ostinato* (meaning "obstinate," "stubborn," or "pig-headed") and refers to the fact that a phrase in the bass, whether just a few notes or several measures, repeats over and over. English composers of the seventeenth century called the *basso ostinato* the **ground bass** because the repeating bass provided a solid foundation on which an entire composition could be built, or grounded. The repeated bass pattern may be only a few notes or

FIGURE 6–16

A detail from the painting *The Death of Dido* by Guercino (1599–1666). The servant Belinda bends over the dying Dido, who has fallen on her formidable sword.

several measures in length. *Basso ostinato* is a common feature of Baroque music, often used to symbolize grief. Indeed, we have already met a clear example of a *basso ostinato* supporting a lament in Barbara Strozzi's aria *Let me die* (see page 111).

The ostinato, or ground bass, Purcell composed for Dido's lament is five measures long and is heard eleven times. It consists of two sections (see the Listening Guide): a chromatic descent over the interval of a fourth (G, F♯, F, E, E♭, D) and a two-measure cadence returning to the tonic G (B♭, C, D, G). The aria begins with one statement of this ostinato pattern played by low string instruments alone. When Dido enters she sings her phrase "When I am laid in earth, may my wrongs create no trouble in thy breast" above two statements of the ostinato. This music and text together are then repeated. The second and last phrase, "Remember me, but ah! forget my fate," is also stated and then repeated. At the end of the repeat of this final line, the singer breaks off, as if unable to articulate her grief further. But the strings press on, carrying Dido's highly charged emotion across two final statements of the ostinato.

a lament above a basso ostinato

Henry Purcell
Dido and Aeneas (1689)
Aria, "When I am laid in earth"

6CD 1/14;
2CD 1/4

Characters: Dido, queen of Carthage; Belinda, her servant
Situation: Having been deserted by her lover, Aeneas, Dido sings
  farewell to Belinda (and to all) before dying of a broken heart.

BRIEF RECITATIVE

0:00   Continuo played by large lute and cello

Thy hand, Belinda! Darkness shades me; on thy bosom let me rest. More I would—but Death invades me: Death is now a welcome guest.

ARIA (0:58)

(Continued on next page)

0:58	*basso ostinato* alone in cellos and double basses
1:10	*basso ostinato* with voice and strings
1:27	*basso ostinato* repeats beneath voice
1:44	*basso ostinato* repeats beneath voice
2:02	*basso ostinato* repeats beneath voice
2:19	*basso ostinato* repeats beneath voice
2:37	*basso ostinato* repeats beneath voice
2:53	*basso ostinato* repeats beneath voice
3:10	*basso ostinato* repeats beneath voice
3:29	*basso ostinato* alone with strings
3:46	*basso ostinato* alone with strings

(Listening Exercise 17)

When I am laid in earth, may my wrongs create no trouble in thy breast. Remember me, but ah! forget my fate.

Elton John and Basso Ostinato

For an up-to-date example of ostinato bass, we can look at a modern aria-lament by a more recent English composer, Elton John. Although not built exclusively on an ostinato figure, John's song *Sorry Seems to Be the Hardest Word* (*Live in Australia*, MCA2-8022) nonetheless has one striking affinity to the aria by Purcell—it, too, makes use of a *basso ostinato*, incorporating a chromatically descending fourth as a way of setting a very, very sad text. The ostinato pattern begins on G, with a chromatically descending fourth followed by a one-measure cadence.

It's sad (so sad), it's a sad, sad situation
Bass
G   F♯   F   E
          And it's getting more and more absurd
          E♭   D   F♯GAD
                 (cadence)

This *basso ostinato*, and a slightly varied form of it, is then repeated several times for this and other lines of text. Compare Elton John's bass line with Purcell's *basso ostinato* (see page 122) and note that both laments are set in the key of G minor. Was the pop artist, who studied at the Royal Academy of Music in London, inspired by the famous aria of his well-coiffured countryman (see Fig. 6–15)?

Elton John (Sir Reginald Dwight).

THE RISE OF INSTRUMENTAL MUSIC: SONATA AND CONCERTO GROSSO

Composers of the Baroque period were the first to think of instrumental music as different from vocal music. Earlier, during the Renaissance, a musical line could either be sung by the voice or played on an instrument, according to the wishes of the performer. Baroque composers not only started to differentiate between a vocal style of writing and an instrumental one but they also began to assign specific musical lines to specific instruments, according to *idiomatic writing*

their natural strengths and weaknesses. The brasses, for example, were often given short figures with dotted rhythms, which maximized their capacity for sharp attacks (see, for example, Monteverdi's *Toccata*, page 119). Brasses would not, however, be asked to run up and down the chromatic scale, because of the difficulties in pitch they would encounter. Fast scales were most often given over to the more agile violins. Thus here, in the Baroque era, the practice of writing music idiomatic (well-suited) for the instruments first appears.

virtuosity

Not only did Baroque composers begin to write idiomatically for the instruments, they also began to demand of the performer virtuosity—the ability to play technically difficult passages rapidly and surely. Many of the most renowned composers of the Baroque era, including Corelli (1653–1713), Vivaldi (1678–1741), and Bach (1685–1750), were themselves virtuosos on a particular instrument. Naturally, their passion for instrumental music led to the creation of new instrumental forms, like the fugue (see page 141), and new genres, such as the sonata and concerto.

The Baroque Sonata

A **sonata** is a type of chamber music to be played on an instrument. The term was first used in Venice around 1600 to indicate a composition intended specifically to be played or sounded, as opposed to one that was to be sung. Hence, a sonata is "something sounded" in distinction to a cantata (see page 146), which is "something sung."

chamber sonata

Usually, a sonata consisted of a collection of short pieces, each of which is called a **movement**. In the Baroque era these collections of movements were of two types. One, called the **sonata da camera** (chamber sonata), was made up of a series of dancelike movements that had the name and character of a particular dance. A typical chamber sonata might consist of an allemand, sarabande, gavotte, and gigue—all dances. (For more on Baroque dances, see page 154.) The second type of sonata was called the **sonata da chiesa** (church sonata), and its movements were designated only by a tempo marking such as *grave, vivace, adagio,* or *allegro* (grave, fast and lively, slow, fast)—it was thought inappropriate to have the movements of a piece destined for the church associated with secular dances. Indeed, as the names *sonata da camera* and *sonata da chiesa* indicate, the church sonata was intended to provide background music for religious services, while the chamber sonata, with its links to the dance, was usually heard at court or in the private homes of the well-to-do.

church sonata

A sonata might be written for a solo keyboard instrument like the harpsichord. Or it might be composed for a solo melody instrument like the violin, in which case three performers would be involved—the violinist and two persons playing the continuo (Fig. 6–8). But whether for solo keyboard or solo melody instrument plus continuo, the work was called a **solo sonata**. Similarly, many Baroque sonatas were written for two melody instruments, two violins or violin and oboe, for example, plus continuo. Such a force was called a **trio sonata** because the composer wrote only three musical lines, even though four performers were involved—two soloists and two players on the *basso continuo*.

Arcangelo Corelli (1653–1713)

The composer-virtuoso who made the Baroque solo and trio sonata internationally popular was Arcangelo Corelli. Corelli was born in 1653 near Bologna, Italy, then an important center for violin instruction and perfor-

The Baroque Violin

The most important string instrument in the Baroque period was the violin. The term derives from the Italian "violino" ("little viol"), from which English-speakers gradually dropped the final "o" to create "violin." Unlike the viol (see Fig. 6–8), the violin has no frets and only four strings. At first the violin was something of a "low-class" instrument used to accompany dancing in inns and taverns. But the violin had two special virtues: First, it produced a more powerful, penetrating sound than had the earlier viol; and second, it was more versatile and expressive. Of all the instruments, the violin comes closest to the sound of the human voice in its agility, flexibility, and expressiveness. It can play a gentle lullaby with great tenderness, just as it can a loud fanfare with splendor. By 1650 the violin had become the string instrument of preference for the opera, the solo and trio sonata, and the concerto.

The center of violin making during the Baroque era was, and remains today, Cremona, Italy. Cremonese makers were able to assure that one violin was almost identical in shape to the next because they worked from wooden molds, and because one craftsman passed his secrets on to the next, generation after generation. The best of the violin makers was Antonio Stradivari (1644–1737), who produced nearly a thousand violins, violas, cellos, and guitars. In fact, Stradivari was still making violins in his last year, at the age of ninety-two. Today good Stradivari violins sell for about $2 million each at auction houses in London and New York. Some of these violins have provocative names such as "The Messiah" and "Lady Blunt." Over the centuries murder and intrigue have been associated with these rare instruments, as represented in the music-murder-mystery film *The Red Violin.*

The front of a Stradivari violin.
Bridgeman Art Library, London/NY

mance. By 1675 he had moved to Rome, where he remained for the duration of his life as a teacher, composer, and performer on the violin (Fig. 6–17). Although Corelli's musical output was small, consisting only of five sets of sonatas and one of concertos, his works were widely admired. Such diverse composers as Johann Sebastian Bach in Leipzig, François Couperin (1668–1733) in Paris, and Henry Purcell in London either borrowed his melodies directly or more generally studied and absorbed his style.

The most remarkable aspect of Corelli's music is its harmony. It sounds modern to our ears. That is to say, we have heard so much classical and popular music that we have come to possess an almost subconscious sense of how a succession of chords, or harmonic progression, should sound. Corelli was the first in a long line of composers to establish that harmonic norm. He was the first to write fully functional harmony; in other words, in his sonatas each chord has a specific function or role in the succession of chords. Not only does the individual chord constitute an important sound in itself, but it also prepares or leads toward the next, thereby helping to form a tightly linked chain of chords. They sound purposeful, well directed. The most basic link in the chain is the V–I (dominant–tonic) cadence (see page 30). In addition, Corelli will often construct a bass line that moves upward chromatically by half step. This chromatic, stepwise motion pulls up and into the next higher note, increasing the sense of direction and cohesiveness we feel in Corelli's music.

TRIO SONATA IN C MAJOR, OPUS 4, NO. 1 (1694)
The Trio Sonata in C major, Opus 4, No. 1, is a chamber sonata written by Corelli in 1694 for two violins and *basso continuo*, here played by a harpsichord

FIGURE 6–17

Arcangelo Corelli looks placid enough in this late seventeenth-century portrait. But when playing the violin, according to a contemporary, "his eyes turn red as fire, his face becomes distorted, and his eyeballs roll as if in agony."

Staatliche Schlösser and Gärten Berlin, Schloss Charlottenburg and cello. Corelli called this sonata Opus 4, No. 1. (Composers frequently use **opus**, the Latin word meaning "work," to enumerate and identify their compositions; this was Corelli's fourth publication.) This chamber sonata is in four movements, the second and fourth of which are dance movements in binary form* (**AB**), the most common musical form for Baroque dances.

a four-movement chamber sonata

The opening *preludio* (prelude) gives the players a chance to warm up as well as establishes the general musical mood of the sonata. Note that the prelude makes use of what is called a **walking bass**, a bass that moves at a moderate, steady pace, mostly in equal note values and often stepwise up or down the scale:

EXAMPLE 6–5

The second movement, a dance called the *corrente* (from the Italian *correre*, "to run") is rather fast and in triple meter. Here the first violin engages in a rapid dialogue with the cello. The second violin is scarcely audible as it helps fill in the chords, literally playing "second fiddle" to the first violin. The short *adagio* ("slow" movement) merely serves as a bridge that links the *corrente* with the final movement—the brisk, duple meter *allemanda* (literally, "the German dance"). This last movement, too, has a walking bass, but the tempo is so fast (presto) that it sounds more like a running or a sprinting bass. Of course, the dances of this chamber sonata were not actually danced; they were stylized abstractions intended only to be listened to—just as one would listen, but not dance, to a minuet by Beethoven or a waltz by Chopin.

Listening Guide

Arcangelo Corelli
Trio Sonata in C major, Opus 4, No. 1 (1694)

6CD 1/15

Ensemble: two violins, cello, and harpsichord

PRELUDE
0:00 "Walking bass" descends stepwise below dotted rhythms in violins
0:28 Cadence
0:32 Bass now moves twice as fast
0:41 Bass returns to original slow pace

CORRENTE
1:17 First violin and cello lead lively dance in triple meter
1:34 Repeat of **A**
1:49 **B** section begins with sequences in cello and violins
2:10 Rhythmic syncopation signals arrival of final cadence
2:19 Repeat of **B** including syncopation (2:40)

ADAGIO
2:53 Stationary chords in violins; only the cello moves in a purposeful fashion
4:05 Cadential chords prepare way to next movement

ALLEMANDA
4:25 Two violins move together above a racing bass
4:46 Repeat of **A** and pause
5:07 **B** section begins with sudden shift to minor key
5:23 Moves back to tonic major key for final cadence
5:27 Repeat of **B** including final shift back to major (5:43)

The Baroque Concerto

The concerto was to the Baroque era what the symphony would later become to the Classical period: the most popular and important genre of instrumental music. A Baroque concerto emphasized abrupt contrasts within a unity of mood, just as striking change between the zones of light and darkness often characterizes a Baroque painting (see, for example, Fig. 6–4).

A **concerto** (from the Latin *concertare*, "to strive together") is a musical composition marked by a friendly contest or competition between a soloist and an orchestra. When only one soloist confronts the orchestra, the work is a **solo concerto**. When more than one is present and they function as a unit, the piece is a **concerto grosso**. The soloists in a concerto grosso constitute a subgroup called the **concertino** ("little concert"), and the full orchestra is called the **tutti** ("all" or "everybody"). A typical concerto grosso had a concertino of two or four violins and continuo. The soloists were not highly paid masters imported from afar, but rather the regular first-chair players who, when they were not serving as soloists, joined with the tutti to play the orchestral string parts. The contrast in sound between the heavy tutti and the lighter, more virtuosic concertino is the most distinctive feature of the concerto grosso.

concerto grosso

As written by Vivaldi, Bach, and Handel, the solo concerto and the concerto grosso usually had three movements: fast, slow, fast. The serious first movement is composed in a carefully worked-out structure called ritornello form (see page 129); the second movement is invariably more lyrical and tender; while the third movement, though usually using ritornello form, tends to be lighter, more dancelike, sometimes even rustic in mood. Both the solo concerto and the concerto grosso originated in Italy toward the end of the seventeenth century. Solo concertos for violin, flute, recorder, oboe, trumpet, and harpsichord were especially popular. The vogue of the concerto grosso peaked about 1730 and then all but came to an end about the time of the death of Bach (1750). But the solo concerto continued to be cultivated during the Classical and Romantic periods, becoming increasingly a showcase in which a single soloist could display his or her technical mastery of an instrument.

FIGURE 6–18

Portrait of a violinist and composer believed by some to be the musician Antonio Vivaldi.

Antonio Vivaldi (1678–1741)

No composer was more influential, and certainly none more prolific, in the creation of the Baroque concerto than Antonio Vivaldi (Fig. 6–18). Vivaldi, like Gabrieli, a native of Venice, was the son of a barber and part-time musician at the church of St. Mark (see Figs. 6–10 and 6–11). Young Vivaldi's proximity to St. Mark's naturally brought him into contact with the clergy. Although he became a skilled performer on the violin, he also entered Holy Orders, ultimately becoming a priest. Vivaldi's life, however, was by no means confined to the realm of the spirit: He concertized on the violin throughout Europe; he wrote and produced nearly fifty operas, which brought him a great deal of money; and for fifteen years he lived with an Italian opera star. The worldly pursuits of *il prete rosso* (the red-haired priest) eventually provoked a response from the authorities of the Roman Church. In 1737 Vivaldi was forbidden to practice his musical artistry in papally controlled lands. This ban affected his income as well as his creativity. He died poor and obscure in 1741 in Vienna, where he had gone in search of a post at the imperial court.

Civico Museo Bibliografico Musicale, Bologna

music in an orphanage for girls

From 1703 until 1740 Vivaldi worked in Venice at the *Ospedale della Pietà* (Hospice of Mercy), first as a violinist and music teacher and then as its musical director. The Hospice of Mercy was an orphanage for the care and education of young women. It was one of four such charitable institutions in Venice that accepted abandoned, mostly illegitimate girls, who, as several reports state, "otherwise would have been thrown in the canals." By 1700, music had been made to serve an important role in the religious and social life of the orphanage. Each Sunday afternoon its orchestra of young women offered public performances for the well-to-do of Venice (see boxed essay). Also attending these concerts were foreign visitors—Venice was already a tourist city—among them a French diplomat, who wrote in 1739:

> These girls are educated at the expense of the state, and they are trained solely with the purpose of excelling in music. That is why they sing like angels and play violin, flute, organ, oboe, cello, and bassoon; in short, no instrument is so big as to frighten them. They are kept like nuns in a convent. All they do is perform concerts, always in groups of about forty girls. I swear to you that there is nothing as pleasant as seeing a young and pretty nun, dressed in white, with a little pomegranate bouquet over her ears, conducting the orchestra with all the gracefulness and incredible precision one can imagine.

VIOLIN CONCERTO IN E MAJOR, OPUS 8, NO. 1, "THE SPRING" (EARLY 1700s)

During the early 1700s Vivaldi composed literally hundreds of solo concertos for the all-female orchestras of the Hospice of Mercy in Venice. In 1725 he

The Hospice of Mercy: Convent and Concert Hall

In the early eighteenth century there were approximately four hundred girls and young women residents at the Hospice of Mercy in Venice. All received not only religious instruction but also training in academic disciplines and domestic crafts (cooking, embroidery, lace-making, cotton-spinning, health care, and music). Those who showed a special talent for music were placed within a core of forty young musicians, a prestigious group given special privileges and a distinctive red habit. Each day these young women studied or practiced for as much as four hours, and their musical education included tutelage in singing, ear-training, and counterpoint, as well as instruction on at least two musical instruments. To guide them, music teachers, such as Antonio Vivaldi, were hired from out-

Women musicians perform behind a grill at an eighteenth-century Venetian orphanage.
Photo Costa

side the walls of the convent. The level of performance at the Hospice of Mercy was thought to be the highest in Venice, higher than at the opera.

When performing publicly in the chapel of the orphanage, the members of the girls' musical corps stood on high in a special gallery, a musicians' loft, and played to the outside world through a grill. Like disembodied voices, their sounds could be heard, but their faces not fully seen. Each Sunday and religious holiday they performed the musical parts of the Mass, and purely instrumental concertos as well. After individual pieces, the audience applauded. On Sunday afternoons the all-female orchestra played publicly in a different room from 4 to 6 P.M. What had begun as religious music in a convent had become a public concert series.

gathered twelve of the more colorful of these together and published them under the title "Opus 8." (As we have seen, composers frequently use the term "opus," the Latin noun meaning "work," to enumerate and identify their compositions at the time of publication; this set of concertos was thus Vivaldi's eighth published work.) In addition, he called the first four of these solo concertos **The Seasons**. What Vivaldi meant by this was that each of the four concertos in turn represents the feelings, sounds, and sights of one of the four seasons of the year, beginning with spring. So that there be no ambiguity as to what sensations and events the music represents at any given moment, Vivaldi first composed a poem (an "illustrative sonnet" he called it) about each season. Then he placed each line of the poem at the appropriate point in the music where that particular event or feeling was to be expressed, even specifying at one point that the violins are to sound "like barking dogs." In so doing, Vivaldi created a landmark in what is called program music—music that plays out a story or a series of events or moods (for more on program music, see page 252).

It is fitting that *The Seasons* begins with the bright, optimistic sounds of spring (Fig. 6–19). In fact, "The Spring" Concerto for solo violin and small orchestra is Vivaldi's best known work. The fast first movement of this three-movement concerto is composed in **ritornello** form, a form that Vivaldi was the first to popularize. The Italian word *ritornello* means "return" or "refrain." In ritornello form, all or part of the one main theme—the ritornello—returns again and again, invariably played by the tutti, or full orchestra. Between the tutti's statements of the ritornello, the soloist inserts fragments and extensions of this ritornello theme in virtuosic fashion. Much of the excitement of a Baroque concerto comes from the tension between the reaffirming ritornello played by the tutti and the fanciful free-flights of the soloist.

The jaunty ritornello theme of the first movement of "The Spring" Concerto has two complementary parts, the second of which returns more often than the first. Between appearances of the ritornello, Vivaldi inserts the music that represents his feelings about spring. He creates the songbirds of May by asking the violins to play rapidly and staccato* in a high register. Similarly, he depicts the sudden arrival of thunder and lightning by means of a tremolo* and shooting scales, then returns to the cheerful song of the birds. Thereafter, in the slow second movement, a vision of a flower-strewn meadow is conveyed by an expansive, tender melody in the violin. Finally, during the fast finale, a sustained droning in the lower strings invokes "the festive sounds of country bagpipes." The full text of Vivaldi's "program" for the first movement of "The Spring" Concerto is given in the Listening Guide.

The Frick Collection, New York

FIGURE 6–19

The musician Vivaldi, the poet John Milton (1608–1674), and the painter François Boucher (1703–1770) were among the many artists of the seventeenth and eighteenth centuries to expound on the activities and feelings of the four seasons. Boucher's *The Four Seasons: Spring* captures the freshness and amorous possibilities of springtime.

"The Spring" Concerto

Listening Guide

Antonio Vivaldi
Violin Concerto in E major, Opus 8, No. 1 ("The Spring";
early 1700s) First movement, *Allegro* (fast)

Meter: duple
Texture: mainly homophonic

0:00	Ritornello part 1 played by tutti	
0:07	Ritornello part 1 repeated by tutti *pianissimo*	
0:14	Ritornello part 2 played by tutti	
0:22	Ritornello part 2 repeated by tutti *pianissimo*	

0:30	Solo violin (aided by two violins from tutti) chirp on high	"Spring with all its festiveness has arrived And the birds salute it with happy song"
1:05	Ritornello part 2 played by tutti	
1:13	Tutti softly plays running sixteenth notes	"And the brooks, kissed by the breezes, Meanwhile flow with sweet murmurings"
1:36	Ritornello part 2 played by tutti	
1:45	Tutti plays tremolo and violins shoot up the scale	"Dark clouds cover the sky Announced by bolts of lightning and thunder"
1:51	Solo violin plays agitated, broken triads while tutti continues with tremolos below	
2:11	Ritornello part 2 played by tutti	
2:19	Solo violin chirps on high, adding an ascending chromatic scale and trill	"But when all has returned to quiet The birds commence to sing once again their enchanted song"
2:37	Ritornello part 1, slightly varied, played by tutti	
2:48	Solo violin plays rising sixteenth notes	
3:03	Ritornello part 2 played by tutti	

(Listening Exercise 18)

art music becomes classical pops

Vivaldi composed more than 450 concertos and thus is known as "the father of the concerto." Widely admired as both a performer and composer in his day, within a few years of his death he was largely forgotten, a victim of rapidly changing musical tastes. Not until the revival of Baroque music in the 1950s were his scores resurrected from obscure libraries and dusty archives. Now his music is loved for its freshness and vigor, its exuberance and daring. Today it can be heard in television commercials, in film scores, and as background music in Starbucks. More than 200 professional recordings have been made of *The Seasons* alone. So often is "The Spring" Concerto played that it has passed from the realm of art music into that of "classical pops."

Listening Exercises

Giovanni Gabrieli   6CD 1/10
Motet, *In the Churches* (1612)

The text of this motet is given below. First listen to the motet following the
text, then answer the questions that follow:

In ecclesiis, benedicite Domino	In the churches, bless the Lord
Alleluja	
In omni loco dominationis, benedic	In every holy place, may my soul
anima mea Dominum	bless the Lord
Alleluja	
In Deo salutari meo, et gloria mea	In God is my salvation and my
	glory
Deus, auxilium meum et spes mea in	Lord, my help and my hope is in
Deo est	God
Alleluja	
Deus noster, te invocamus, te laudamus,	Our Lord, we call to you, we praise
te adoramus	you, we adore you
Libera nos, salva nos, vivifica nos	Deliver us, save us, revivify us
Alleluja	
Deus, adjutor noster in aeternum	Lord, our judge forever
Alleluja	

1. (0:00 and 0:09) Which keyboard instrument plays in the *basso continuo?*
   a. harpsichord   b. clavichord   c. organ
2. (0:18–0:32) In this "Alleluja" which is true?
   a. A homophonic chorus echoes a soloist, and then they sing together.
   b. A soloist echoes a homophonic chorus, and then they sing together.
3. At the very beginning of the "Alleluia," the music has a dance-like quality created in part by the meter. The meter here (0:18–0:24) is
   a. duple   b. triple
4. (0:34–1:08) In this tenor solo the words "in omni loco," "dominationis,"
   and "benedic" are each *repeated:*
   a. once   b. twice   c. three times
5. (1:34–2:02) Which family of musical instruments dominates during the
   instrumental interlude?
   a. strings   b. woodwinds   c. brasses   d. percussion
6. (2:03–3:29) Which of the following statements is true about this section?
   a. Throughout only two voices sing, accompanied by brasses.
   b. Four voices sing, each in turn; they are accompanied first by strings,
   then by brasses.
7. (3:45–4:07) What happens at the beginning of this section ("Deus nos-
   ter, te invocamus")?
   a. Tenor sings first and soprano answers.
   b. Soprano sings first and tenor answers.
8. (5:20–5:31 and 5:50–6:00) What kind of musical texture does Gabrieli
   use so as to emphasize the word "Deus"?
   a. monophonic   b. homophonic   c. polyphonic

9. (7:10) The motet ends with what kind of chord (does it sound bright or dark and gloomy)?
   a. major   b. minor
10. Finally, is *In the Churches* an example of an *a cappella* motet?
    a. yes   b. no

Henry Purcell   6CD 1/14; 2CD 1/4
Recitative, "Thy hand, Belinda" and aria,
"When I am laid in earth" from *Dido and Aeneas* (1689)

Your selection begins with about a minute of recitative (see page 121). Notice how Dido's deflated spirits are reflected in the music: She gradually sinks down from the C above middle C to middle C itself, touching the chromatic notes of the scale along the way. Next comes the aria, "When I am laid in earth." The opening is easy to recognize because it starts with a chromatically descending ostinato bass.

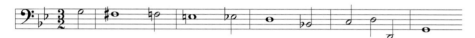

1. (0:00–0:57) Is the recitative "Thy hand, Belinda" an example of *secco* recitative (accompanied only by *basso continuo*) or *accompagnato* recitative (accompanied by full orchestra including strings and woodwinds)?
   a. *secco* recitative   b. *accompagnato* recitative
2. Purcell's *basso ostinato* pattern is somewhat unusual because it is
   a. four measures long   b. five measures long   c. six measures long
3. (0:58–1:09) How many statements of the *basso ostinato* are heard before the voice enters?
   a. one   b. two   c. three
4. (1:10–1:43) How many statements of the *basso ostinato* are heard during the first presentation of the text "When I am laid in earth, may my wrongs create, no trouble in thy breast"?
   a. one   b. two   c. three
5. (1:44–2:18) How many statements of the *basso ostinato* are heard during the second statement of the text "When I am laid in earth, may my wrongs create, no trouble in thy breast"?
   a. one   b. two   c. three
6. (2:17–2:53) How many statements of the *basso ostinato* are heard during the first presentation of the text "Remember me, but ah! forget my fate"?
   a. one   b. two   c. three
7. (2:53–3:28) During the second presentation of this text, does the soprano sing the vocal line with greater extremes of dynamics than during the first presentation (2:19–2:53) of this text?
   a. First presentation is more extreme (more softs and louds).
   b. Second presentation is more extreme (more softs and louds).
8. In the final two statements of the ground bass, what is the general direction of the melody, as might be appropriate for a long lament?
   a. up by step   b. up by leap   c. down by step   d. down by leap
9. What is the mode of this aria, as might be appropriate for a lament?
   a. major   b. minor

10. Which is true about this lament?

a. It unfolds in a very slow tempo (as appropriate for a lament) in duple meter.

b. It unfolds in a very slow tempo (as appropriate for a lament) in triple meter.

Antonio Vivaldi   6CD 1/16; 2CD 1/5
Violin Concerto in E major, Opus 8, No. 1
("The Spring"; early 1700s)

Listen once again to the opening movement of Vivaldi's "The Spring" Concerto, and answer the following questions regarding instrumentation, rhythm, tonality, and structure.

1. Vivaldi was a virtuoso on this instrument and it dominates the sound of this concerto.

a. harpsichord   b. organ   c. cello   d. violin

2. How would you describe the rhythms of this movement?

a. languid with no clear sense of a downbeat

b. energetic with regularly repeating patterns

3. (0:00–0:29) How would you describe the activity of the bass during the opening presentation of the ritornello theme?

a. It repeats one pitch and moves only at the end of each phrase.

b. It moves quickly up the scale and then repeats one pitch.

c. It moves slowly and continually down the scale.

4. (0:30–1:05) Does the *basso continuo* play during this solo section?

a. yes   b. no

5. (1:51–2:11) How many violins play during this solo section?

a. one   b. two   c. three

6. (2:11–2:18) When the ritornello reappears, in what mode is it?

a. major   b. minor

7. (2:19–2:37) During this passage and beyond, what does the cello do?

a. It plays a pedal point* (holds one bass note).

b. It rises by step.

c. It falls by step.

8. (3:11–3:23) At the very end of the movement, one of the two parts of the ritornello theme is repeated quietly (*piano*). Which part is it?

a. part 1   b. part 2

9. Which of the following is true about "The Spring" Concerto?

a. It has neither a *basso ostinato* nor a *basso continuo*.

b. It has a *basso ostinato* but no *basso continuo*.

c. It has a *basso continuo* but no *basso ostinato*.

d. It has both a *basso continuo* and a *basso ostinato*.

10. Finally, how did Vivaldi communicate his "program" to his listeners?

a. A narrator read the program as the music played.

b. A conductor held up cue cards.

c. The composer wrote onomatopoeic music that mimicked in sound the words of his own poem.

Key Words

aria (118)	melodic sequence (112)	*sonata da camera* (124)
arioso (118)	movement (124)	*sonata da chiesa* (124)
Barbara Strozzi (112)	opera (116)	*stile rappresentativo* (117)
basso continuo (109)	opus (126)	terraced dynamics (113)
basso ostinato (ground bass) (121)	recitative (117)	toccata (118)
	ritornello (129)	trio sonata (124)
concertino (127)	*The Seasons* (129)	tutti (127)
concerto grosso (127)	*secco* recitative (118)	*viola da gamba* (bass viol) (110)
harpsichord (110)	solo concerto (127)	
libretto (117)	solo sonata (124)	walking bass (126)

For a checklist of musical style in the early Baroque period, see page 69.

Giraudon/Art Resource, NY

Late Baroque Music:
Bach and Handel

The music of the late Baroque era (1710–1750), represented by the two great figures Johann Sebastian Bach and George Frideric Handel, stands as a high-water mark in Western musical culture. In this period were created such masterpieces as Bach's Brandenburg Concerto No. 5 and Handel's *Messiah.* These are large, grandiose works distinguished, at various moments, by great dramatic power, broad gestures, complex counterpoint, and opulent instrumental color. At the same time they convey to the listener a sense of technical mastery—that Bach and Handel could compose with grace and skill in a variety of musical forms, techniques, and styles—building on the innovations of previous Baroque composers.

Earlier in the Baroque era, in the early 1600s, the desire for passionate expression had led to far-reaching stylistic innovations, such as the *basso continuo** and the recitative*. Claudio Monteverdi (1567–1643) helped create an entirely new category of music, namely, opera*. Other new genres—the sonata*, the solo concerto*, and the concerto grosso*—emerged during the second half of the seventeenth century. But the opera, the sonata, and the concerto of the early Baroque era show all the signs of an art in its adolescence. They possess a certain awkwardness and instability, no matter how exciting, vital, and brash they may sound.

The late Baroque, by contrast, is not a period of musical innovation, but one of refinement. Bach and his contemporaries did not, in the main, invent new forms, styles, techniques, or genres, but rather gave greater weight, length, and polish to those established by their musical forebears. Arcangelo Corelli (1653–1713), for example, had introduced functional harmony in his sonatas, but Bach and Handel smoothed away the occasional jarring chord and made the harmony work so as to expand small musical units into larger, more compelling works of art. Bach and Handel approached the craft of composition with unbounded self-confidence. Their music has a sense of rightness, solidity, and maturity about it. Each time we choose to listen to one of their compositions, we offer further witness to their success in bringing a hundred years of musical development to a glorious culmination.

a period of refinement

THE THEATRICAL QUALITY OF BAROQUE ART

A striking feature of much Baroque art is its theatrical quality. Drama in the arts is created by conflict, by forces that move in opposition, and yet, at the same time, are so positioned as to project a satisfying wholeness. In late Baroque music the competing musical units are generally lengthy and unchanging in mood. Large, clearly defined blocks of sound are placed in opposition.

By the early 1700s, Bach and Handel could make music theatrical by drawing on many opposing styles, textures, colors, and performing groups. For example, a chorus could be set against instruments, a soloist against a full orchestra, an aria against a recitative, and a homophonic passage against a polyphonic one. Nonetheless, these large-scale forces compete within boundaries carefully defined by musical form. In Handel's *Messiah*, for example, ternary form* controls the flow of several arias, whereas strict fugal procedure regulates parts of the "Hallelujah" chorus. This same theatrical equilibrium is apparent in the visual arts of the late Baroque, as can be seen, for example, in Giambattista Tiepolo's *The Triumph of Nobility and Virtue over Ignorance* (Fig. 7–1). Here, two large-scale units contrast in position (high and low) and color (white and black). Yet the artist creates a grand spatial harmony because the two units have approximately the same mass and because intersecting diagonal lines within each unit pull with equal force. There is energy, movement, spectacle, and grandeur—theatricality—yet there is formal control. These are important qualities of late Baroque art, widely expressed in music as well as painting.

Baroque art: energy, movement, spectacle, and grandeur

ASPECTS OF LATE BAROQUE MUSICAL STYLE

Treatment of Musical Elements

During the years 1710–1750, Bach, Handel, and their contemporaries continued to develop the distinctive elements of musical style that appeared in the early Baroque era (see pages 109–113), now amplifying and extending

The Norton Simon Museum, Pasadena

FIGURE 7–1

*The Triumph of Nobility and Virtue over
Ignorance* (ca. 1740) by Giambattista
Tiepolo (1692–1770) offers a splendid
example of late Baroque theatricality, with
its grand gestures, vivid colors, and distinctly
separate, yet balanced, zones of action.

them. In brief, melodies became longer, rhythms more driving, harmonies
more purposeful, and textures more contrapuntal.

MELODY

Melody in late Baroque music is governed by the principle of continuing development. An initial motive or theme is set forth and then continually expanded, or spun out, over an ever-lengthening line. Such a melody tends to
be long and ornate. Often the notes are propelled forward by melodic sequence*, the repetition of a motive or phrase on successively higher or lower
degrees of the scale. Sequence helps the melody fly higher and farther and
postpones the time when it must arrive at a cadence, as is the case in this example from Handel's *Messiah:*

melodic sequence

EXAMPLE 7–1

ex - alt - ed,

The exuberant quality of late Baroque melody, however, makes it more impressive than memorable; that is, it is hard to sing or hum, even after repeated hearings. This is due, in part, to the fact that the phrases are frequently not short, narrow, and symmetrical, but rather long, expansive, and
irregular. They are also often instrumental in nature, meaning that melodic
patterns that can easily be played on instruments are frequently transferred
to the voice, where they can be difficult to sing. Bach, for example, often
wrote difficult vocal lines that are instrumental in character.

RHYTHM

driving rhythms

Rhythm is the most distinctive and exciting element of late Baroque music. If a concerto by Bach or Handel seems to chug along with an irrepressible optimism and vitality, it is because of the almost unstoppable quality of the rhythm. A piece will begin with one prominent rhythmic idea, and it or a complementary one will continue energetically to the very end of the movement. In this context, meter is firmly established by regular accents and a steady beat. Indeed, meter is more easily recognized in late Baroque music than in the music of any other period. Usually, one or two prominent instruments, often those assigned the bass line, play a regular rhythmic pattern that sets a strong beat. This clear, regular beat, in turn, makes the meter immediately audible. The strong beat and powerful bass are elements of late Baroque music that make it appealing to modern listeners. In these it has a certain affinity to contemporary rock and jazz.

HARMONY

forceful chord progressions

The pull of forceful chord progressions and the use of only major and minor keys were qualities of harmony found earlier, in the music of Corelli (see page 125). They continue to be embodied in the music of the late Baroque era. So, too, does the *basso continuo* (see page 110), consisting of a small ensemble: usually a keyboard and a bass instrument that gives added weight to the bass and generates chords, thereby providing the harmonic support for the melody above. What chords the keyboard player is to construct are suggested to him or her by means of a **figured bass**—a numerical shorthand placed in the music that tells the player which unwritten notes to fill in above the written bass note. (Figured bass is similar in intent to the numerical code found in "fake books" used by modern jazz pianists that indicates which chords to play beneath the written melody.)

EXAMPLE 7–2

figured bass

 becomes

regular harmonic change

What is new in the harmony of the late Baroque is the regularity with which it moves. Specifically, chords appear at regular intervals and produce a constant rate of harmonic change. Chord changes may occur every beat, every other beat, or just once in each measure, but usually the rate of change is stable. Regular harmonic change and repetitious rhythms are what give the music of this period its sense of relentless, unstoppable movement.

TEXTURE: THE RETURN OF COUNTERPOINT

We have seen that imitative counterpoint with independent polyphonic lines dominated the church music of the Renaissance and that, partly as a reaction to this, composers of the early Baroque era began to avoid counterpoint. In the late Baroque period, however, they returned to contrapuntal writing, in part to add richness to the middle range of what was otherwise a top–bottom (soprano–bass) dominated texture. German composers were particularly fond of counterpoint, perhaps because of their traditional love of the organ, an instrument with several keyboards and thus well suited to playing many musical lines at once. The gradual reintegration of counterpoint into the fabric of Baroque music culminates in the rigorously contrapuntal vocal and instrumental music of Bach.

The Late Baroque Orchestra

The beginnings of the modern symphony orchestra can be traced to the late Baroque period. By 1700 the following four developments had occurred within the ensembles of Western Europe: (1) the violins had replaced the softer viols as the dominant string instrument; (2) the string family had come to be the core of the orchestra; (3) brasses and woodwinds added color to the basic string sound; and (4) some parts, especially the strings, could be doubled or tripled—two or three players might play the same musical line.

strings are the core of the orchestra

STRINGS

The core of the orchestra was formed by the violins, violas, cellos, and double basses (which doubled the cello line an octave below). They played, almost nonstop, from beginning to end of every orchestral piece. The melody, of course, was carried by the highest part, the violin, which was prized for its penetrating sound.

WOODWINDS

During the seventeenth century, the blaring, double-reed shawm* of the Middle Ages had been transformed into a more refined instrument, the oboe. Similarly, its lower cousin the double-reed bassoon had evolved from the Renaissance korthold*. In addition, there were two types of Baroque flutes, the recorder and the transverse flute, both made of wood. Because of limitations in tuning, recorders usually played when the music was written in keys with flats, while transverse flutes played in keys with sharps. In the eighteenth century, wind players were expected to master at least two instruments. Obviously, they couldn't play both at the same time, so a composer would score his piece for either oboes or flutes, for example.

BRASSES

The trumpet, which had formerly been used alone (or with drums) as a purely ceremonial or military instrument, was now welcomed into the orchestra for its bright sound, replacing the duller wooden cornetto (see Fig. 4–11). At the same time the horn left the hunting field and watchtower and took a place in the ensemble. Again, one player usually performed on both

FIGURE 7–2

Detail of an orchestra playing for a Baroque opera, as seen in Pietro Domenico Olivero's *Interior of the Teatro Regio*, Turin (1740). From left to right are a bassoon, two French horns, a cello, a double bass, a harpsichord, and then violins, violas, and oboes.

Museo Civico di Torino, Italy

trumpet and horn, so when the trumpets played the horns did not, and vice versa. The trombone, which had evolved from the medieval sackbut*, was limited to accompanying sacred vocal music in the church and did not join the orchestra until the nineteenth century.

PERCUSSION

Percussion instruments are rare in Baroque music. Only the timpani*, or kettledrums*, were used and then only in festive pieces such as Handel's Water Music. Generally, the timpany parts were not written out; rather, the performer would simply beat the rhythmic articulation, military style, where it was deemed necessary.

BASSO CONTINUO

The *basso continuo* continued to be an essential part of the Baroque orchestra, setting a firm bass and holding the harmonies together. It consisted of a harpsichord (or organ in church) and cello, perhaps with a bassoon or double bass playing as well.

holds the orchestra together

Many concertos, overtures, and dance suites of the late Baroque period were written for an orchestra of just string instruments and *basso continuo*. Pieces for especially festive occasions, however, would normally include a greater number of instruments for greater brilliance. Yet never were all possible instruments heard at once, even in the largest orchestral scores. As mentioned, if the trumpets played, there were usually no horns; if there were oboes, then there were no flutes, and vice versa. Hence, by modern standards the late Baroque orchestra was at best a mid-size group. Rarely did it include more than twenty-five players, about fifteen of whom belonged to the nucleus of strings.

a mid-size group

JOHANN SEBASTIAN BACH (1685–1750)

In the creations of Johann Sebastian Bach (Fig. 7–3), the music of the Baroque reaches its greatest glory. Bach was born to a musical dynasty, though one originally of common standing. For nearly two hundred years members of the Bach family served as musicians in small towns in Thuringia, a province in central Germany. Johann Sebastian was merely the most talented of the ubiquitous musical Bachs, though he himself had four sons who achieved international fame. Although he received an excellent formal education in the humanities, as a musician Bach was largely self-taught. To learn his craft he studied, copied, and arranged the compositions of Corelli, Vivaldi, Pachelbel, and even Palestrina. He also learned to play the organ, in part by emulating others, once traveling two hundred miles each way on foot to hear a great performer. Bach's first position of importance was in the town of Weimar, Germany, where he served as organist to the court beginning in 1708. It was here that he wrote many of his finest works for organ. Soon Bach became the most renowned virtuoso of the organ in Germany, and his improvisations on that instrument became legendary.

the center of an illustrious musical family

Of all the instruments, the organ is the most adept at playing polyphonic counterpoint. Most organs have at least two separate keyboards for the hands, in addition to one placed on the floor, which the performer plays with the feet (see Fig. 3–16). This gives the instrument the capacity to play several lines simultaneously. More important, each of these keyboards can be set to engage a different group (rank) of pipes, each with its own color, and thus the ear can more readily hear the individual musical lines. For these reasons the organ is the instrument *par excellence* for playing fugues.

Fugue

Bach was the master of counterpoint, and it is rich, complex counterpoint that lies at the heart of the fugue. A fugue is a contrapuntal form and procedure that flourished during the late Baroque era. The word "fugue" itself comes from the Latin *fuga*, meaning "flight." Within a fugue one voice presents a theme and then "flies away" as another voice enters with the same theme. The theme in a fugue is called the **subject**. At the outset each voice presents the subject in turn, and this successive presentation is called the **exposition** of the fugue. As the voices enter, they do not imitate or pursue each other exactly—this would produce a canon* (see page 58). Rather, passages of exact imitation are interrupted by sections of free writing in which the voices more or less go their own ways. These freer sections, where the subject is not heard in its entirety, are called **episodes**. Episodes and further presentations of the subject alternate throughout the remainder of the fugue.

Fugues have been written for two to as many as thirty-two voices, but usually the norm is three, four, or five. These may be actual voices in a chorus or choir, or they may be simply lines or parts played by a group of instruments, or even by a solo instrument like the piano, organ, or guitar, which has the capacity to play several "voices" simultaneously. Thus, a formal definition of a **fugue** might be as follows: a composition for three, four, or five parts played or sung by voices or instruments, which begins with a presentation of a subject in imitation in each part (exposition), continues with modulating passages of free counterpoint (episodes) and further appearances of the subject, and ends with a strong affirmation of the tonic key. Fortunately, the fugue is easier to hear than to describe: The unfolding and recurrence of one subject makes it easy to follow.

ORGAN FUGUE IN G MINOR (ca. 1710)

Bach has left us nearly one hundred keyboard fugues, about a third of these for organ. The organ was Bach's favorite instrument, and in his day he was known more as a performer and improviser on it than as a composer. Bach's G minor organ fugue was composed rather early in his career, sometime between 1708 and 1717, when he was in Weimar. It is written for four voices, which we will refer to as soprano, alto, tenor, and bass, and it begins with the subject appearing first in the soprano:

EXAMPLE 7–3

As fugue subjects go, this is a rather long one, but it is typical of the way Baroque composers liked to "spin out" their melodies. It sounds very solid in tonality. That's because the subject is built clearly around the notes of the G minor triad (G, B♭, D), not only in the first measure but on the strong beats

The Collection of William H. Scheide, Princeton, NJ

FIGURE 7–3

The only authentic portrait of Johann Sebastian Bach, painted by Elias Gottlob Haussmann in 1746. Bach holds in his hand a six-voice canon*, or round, which he created to symbolize his skill as a musical craftsman.

fugues often for organ

FIGURE 7–4

The organ presently in the choir loft of St. Thomas's Church, Leipzig. It was from this loft that Bach played and conducted.

St. Thomas's Church, Leipzig

of the final measures as well. The subject also conveys a sense of gathering momentum. It starts moderately with quarter notes, and then seems to gain speed as eighth notes and finally sixteenth notes are introduced. This, too, is typical of fugue subjects. After the soprano gives forth the subject, it is then presented, in turn, by the alto, the tenor, and the bass. The voices need not appear in any particular order; here Bach just decided to have them enter in succession from top to bottom.

Once Bach has each voice present the subject and join the polyphonic complex, his exposition is at an end. Now a short passage of free counterpoint follows—the first episode—which makes use of just bits and pieces of the subject. Then the subject returns, but in a highly unusual way: It begins in the tenor, but continues and ends in the soprano (see † in the following Listening Guide). Thereafter, Bach's G minor fugue unfolds in the usual alternation of episodes and statements of the subject. The episodes sound unsettled and convey a sense of movement. They modulate from one key to another. The subject, on the other hand, doesn't modulate. It is *in* a key, here the tonic, G minor, or the dominant, D minor, or some other closely related key. This tension between unsettled music (the episode) and stationary music (the subject) is what creates the exciting, dynamic quality of the fugue. Ultimately, Bach modulates back to the tonic key, G minor, for one final statement of the subject in the bass, and the fugue is ended. Note that, although this fugue is in a minor key, Bach puts the final chord in major. This is common in Baroque music, composers preferring the brighter, perhaps more optimistic, sound of major in the final chord.

follow the subject

To hear this fugue by Bach, and all others as well, the listener is urged to proceed in the following manner. First, get the subject locked securely in your ear. When the fugue begins, follow the subject as it appears in rapid succession in each voice in the exposition. Next, differentiate the episodes from the subject as the fugue continues to unfold; if you don't clearly hear the subject, then you are in an episode. Finally, recognize that the home key has been reached when the subject enters in strong fashion for the last time. Because fugues are full of reciprocating, almost mathematical relationships (Fig. 7–5), they have traditionally appealed to listeners with scientific interests. Fugues are music for the eye and the mind, as much as for the ear and the heart.

Listening Guide

Johann Sebastian Bach
Organ Fugue in G minor (ca. 1710)

6CD 1/17;
2CD 1/6

Texture: polyphonic

(The time log has been intentionally omitted here. You are asked to provide your own as part of Listening Exercise 19.)

(continued on next page)

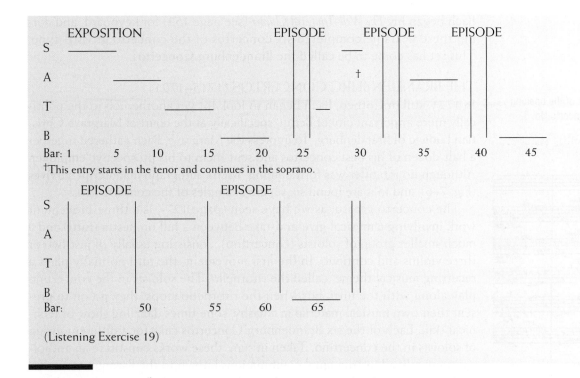

EXPOSITION   EPISODE   EPISODE   EPISODE

S

A   †

T

B

Bar: 1   5   10   15   20   25   30   35   40   45

†This entry starts in the tenor and continues in the soprano.

EPISODE   EPISODE

S

A

T

B

Bar: 50   55   60   65

(Listening Exercise 19)

Öffentliches Kunstmuseum, Basel

FIGURE 7–5

Fugue (1925) by Josef Albers. Albers'
design suggests the "constructivist"
quality of the fugue, one full of repeating
and reciprocal relationships. The black-
and-white units seem to allude to subject
and episode, respectively.

Bach's Orchestral Music

After nine years as organist in Weimar, Bach, then a young man with a wife
and four children, determined to improve his station in life. In 1717 he audi-
tioned for the position of music director at the court of Cöthen, Germany,
and was awarded the post. When he returned to Weimar to collect his family and possessions, the duke of Weimar had Bach thrown in jail for a month;
the duke was displeased that his church organist had "jumped ship." (Composers before the era of Beethoven were little more than indentured servants
who needed to obtain a release from one employer before entering the service of another.) When freed from jail, Bach fled to Cöthen, where he remained for six years (1717–1723).

At Cöthen, Bach turned his attention from organ music for the church to
instrumental music for the court. It was here that he wrote the bulk of his orchestral scores, including more than a dozen solo concertos. The prince of
Cöthen had assembled something of an "all-star" orchestra, drawing many
top players from the larger city of Berlin. He also ordered a large two-
keyboard harpsichord from Berlin and sent Bach to fetch it. About this time

Bach began his *The Well-Tempered Clavier* (see page 152) for keyboard, and during these years he completed six concertos of the concerto grosso* type. This set has come to be called the Brandenburg Concertos.

THE BRANDENBURG CONCERTOS (1715–1721)

In 1721, still in Cöthen, Bach began to look for yet another job in the politically more important city of Berlin, specifically at the court of Margrave Christian Ludwig of Brandenburg. To impress the Margrave, Bach gathered together a half-dozen of his best concertos and sent them to his prospective employer. Although no job offer was forthcoming, Bach's autograph manuscript survives (Fig. 7–6), and in it are found six superb examples of the concerto grosso.

The concerto grosso, as we have seen (page 127), is a three-movement work involving a musical give-and-take between a full orchestra (tutti) and a much smaller group of soloists (concertino), consisting usually of just two or three violins and continuo. In the first movement, the tutti normally plays a recurring musical theme, called the ritornello. The soloists in the concertino play along with the tutti; but when the ritornello stops, they go on to present their own musical material in a flashy, sometimes dazzling show of technical skill. Each of the six Brandenburg Concertos calls for a different group of soloists in the concertino. Taken in sum, these works constitute an anthology of nearly all instrumental combinations known to the Baroque era.

Bach's aim in the Brandenburg Concertos was to show his ability to write challenging music for any and all instruments. A listener cannot fail to be impressed by the brilliant writing for the harpsichord in Concerto No. 5, for example. Here the full orchestra (tutti) is pitted against a concertino consisting of solo violin, flute, and, most important, harpsichord. In principle, the tutti plays the ritornello, and the soloists play motives derived from it. In practice, however, the separation between ritornello and concertino is not as distinct with Bach as it had been in the earlier concertos of Vivaldi (see page 129). In Bach's more refined treatment of ritornello form, the line between the large (loud) ensemble and the small (soft) group of soloists is less obvious. Notice here that Bach's ritornello (see Listening Guide) possesses many characteristics of Baroque melody: It is idiomatic to the violin (having many repeated notes); it is lengthy and somewhat asymmetrical (spinning out over many measures); and it possesses a driving rhythm that propels the music forward. While the sound of the violins dominates the ritornello, soon the solo harpsichord takes center stage. In fact, this work might fairly be called the first

FIGURE 7–6
The autograph manuscript of the opening of Bach's Brandenburg Concerto No. 5.

Berlin, Deutsches Staadsbibliothek

ritornello form

FIGURE 7–7
The Hall of Mirrors at the court of Cöthen, Germany, the hall in which most of Bach's orchestral music was performed while he resided in that town.

harpsichord concerto: In earlier concertos the harpsichord had appeared only as part of the *basso continuo**, not as a solo instrument. Toward the end of the movement all other instruments fall silent, leaving the harpsichord to sound alone in a lengthy section full of brilliant scales and arpeggios. Such a showy passage for soloist alone toward the end of a movement in a concerto is called a **cadenza**. One can easily imagine the great virtuoso Bach performing Brandenburg Concerto No. 5 in the Hall of Mirrors at Cöthen (Fig. 7–7 on preceding page), the principal concert hall of the court. Here, seated at the large harpsichord he had brought from Berlin, Bach would have dazzled patron and fellow performers alike with his bravura playing.

culminates in a cadenza

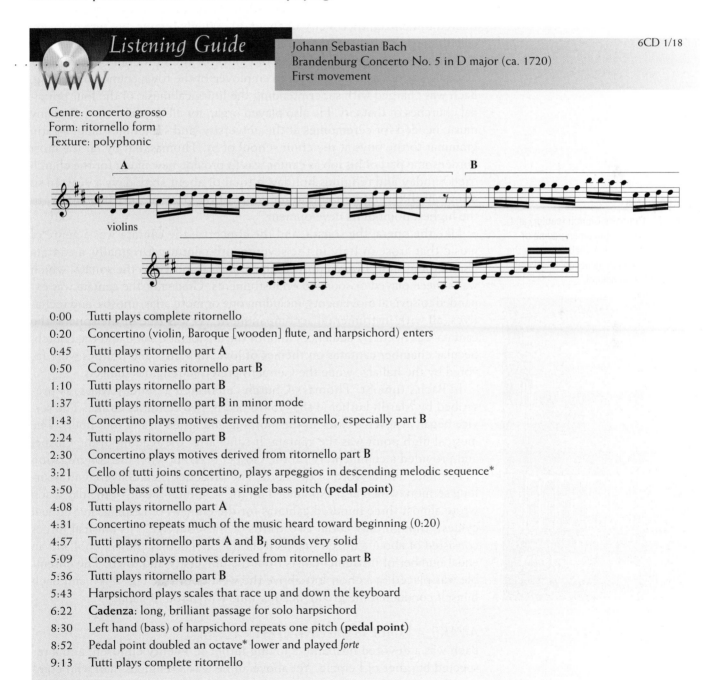

Listening Guide

WWW

Johann Sebastian Bach
Brandenburg Concerto No. 5 in D major (ca. 1720)
First movement

6CD 1/18

Genre: concerto grosso
Form: ritornello form
Texture: polyphonic

0:00	Tutti plays complete ritornello
0:20	Concertino (violin, Baroque [wooden] flute, and harpsichord) enters
0:45	Tutti plays ritornello part **A**
0:50	Concertino varies ritornello part **B**
1:10	Tutti plays ritornello part **B**
1:37	Tutti plays ritornello part **B** in minor mode
1:43	Concertino plays motives derived from ritornello, especially part **B**
2:24	Tutti plays ritornello part **B**
2:30	Concertino plays motives derived from ritornello part **B**
3:21	Cello of tutti joins concertino, plays arpeggios in descending melodic sequence*
3:50	Double bass of tutti repeats a single bass pitch (**pedal point**)
4:08	Tutti plays ritornello part **A**
4:31	Concertino repeats much of the music heard toward beginning (0:20)
4:57	Tutti plays ritornello parts **A** and **B**; sounds very solid
5:09	Concertino plays motives derived from ritornello part **B**
5:36	Tutti plays ritornello part **B**
5:43	Harpsichord plays scales that race up and down the keyboard
6:22	**Cadenza**: long, brilliant passage for solo harpsichord
8:30	Left hand (bass) of harpsichord repeats one pitch (**pedal point**)
8:52	Pedal point doubled an octave* lower and played *forte*
9:13	Tutti plays complete ritornello

The fingers of the harpsichordist get a much-deserved rest in the slow-moving second movement of Brandenburg Concerto No. 5. Now an elegiac mood envelops the music as the violin and flute engage in a quiet dialogue. The fast finale is dominated by fugal writing, a style in which Bach excelled above all other composers.

The Cantata

In 1723 Bach moved yet again, this time to assume the coveted position of cantor of St. Thomas's Church and choir school in Leipzig, Germany (Fig. 7–8), a post he retained until his death in 1750. He seems to have been attracted to Leipzig, then a city of about 30,000 inhabitants, because of its excellent university where his sons might enroll at no cost.

Although prestigious, the post of cantor of the Lutheran church of St. Thomas was not an easy one. As an employee of the town council of Leipzig, Bach was charged with superintending the liturgical music of the four principal churches of that city. He also played organ for all funerals, composed any music needed for ceremonies at the university, and sometimes taught Latin grammar to the boys at the choir school of St. Thomas. But by far the most burdensome part of his job as cantor was to provide new music for the church each Sunday and religious holiday, a total of about sixty days a year. In so doing, Bach brought an important genre of religious music, the cantata, to the highest point of its development.

Like the opera, the sonata, and the concerto, the **cantata** was a genre of music that arose in Italy in the seventeenth century. Originally, a cantata ("something sung") was simply a sung aria, as opposed to the sonata, which was a piece played or sounded on instruments. Gradually, the cantata was expanded to several movements, including one or more arias, ariosos, and recitatives, all with instrumental accompaniment. As was true of the sonata, the cantata was heard by audiences in both the aristocratic salon and the church. Secular chamber cantatas on themes of love, morality, and politics were favored by the Italians, while the Germans preferred religious subjects.

In Bach's time St. Thomas's Church celebrated a Sunday Mass, as prescribed by Martin Luther (1483–1546) nearly two centuries earlier. The service began at seven o'clock in the morning and lasted nearly four hours. The musical high point was the cantata. It came after the reading of the Gospel and provided a commentary on the Gospel text, allowing the congregation to meditate on the word of the Lord. The preacher then delivered an hour-long sermon, which also expounded on the scriptural theme of the day. Bach wrote almost three hundred cantatas for the citizens of Leipzig (five annual cycles), though only about two-thirds of these survive. His musical forces consisted of about a dozen singers from the St. Thomas choir school and an equal number of instrumentalists from the university and town. The ensemble was placed in a choir loft above the west door (see Fig. 7–4), and Bach himself conducted the group, beating time with a roll of paper.

AWAKE, A VOICE IS CALLING (1731)

Bach was a devoted husband, a loving father to twenty children, and a respected burgher of Leipzig. Yet above all he was a religious man who composed not only for self-expression but also for the greater glory of God. His

FIGURE 7–8

Leipzig, St. Thomas's Church (center) and choir school (left) from an engraving of 1723, the year in which Bach moved to the city. Bach's large family occupied several floors of the choir school.

Bach-Archiv, Leipzig

What Did Mrs. Bach Do?

Actually, there were two Mrs. Bachs. The first, Maria Barbara, died suddenly in 1720, leaving the composer with four young children. The second, Anna Magdalena, he married in 1722, and she would bear him thirteen more. Anna Magdalena Bach was a professional singer, earning about as much as her new husband at the court of Cöthen. But when the family moved to Leipzig and the St. Thomas Church, Anna Magdalena curtailed her professional activities. Women did not perform publicly in the Lutheran church at this time; the difficult soprano lines in Bach's religious works were sung by choirboys. Consequently, Anna Magdalena put her musical skills to work as an employee and manager of what might be called "Bach Inc."

For almost every Sunday throughout the year, J. S. Bach was required to produce a new cantata, about twenty to twenty-five minutes of new music, week after week, year after year. Writing the music was only part of the high-pressure task. Rehearsals had to be set and music learned by the next Sunday. But composing and rehearsing paled in comparison to the amount of time needed to copy all the parts—these were the days be-fore photocopy machines and software programs to notate music. Each of the approximately twelve independent lines of the full score had to be copied, entirely by hand, for each new cantata, along with sufficient copies (parts) for all the singers and players. For this, Bach turned to the members of his household, namely his wife and children (both sons and daughters) as well as the nephews, and other fee-paying private students who resided in the cantor's quarters at the St. Thomas School (see Fig. 7–8). In 1731, the year he composed cantata *Awake, a Voice Is Calling*, the roof was taken off the building and two more stories added to accommodate the Bach family and its "music industry."

When Bach died in 1750, he left his most valuable assets (his musical scores) to his eldest sons. The performing parts to many of his cantatas, however, he left to his wife with the expectation that she would rent or sell them in the course of time—her old-age pension in the days before social security. In the end, however, the income from these cantata manuscripts did not prove sufficient, and Anna Magdalena Bach finished her days on 27 February 1760 as a ward of the city of Leipzig.

---

cantata *Awake, a Voice Is Calling* reveals his abiding faith in the religious traditions of his German Lutheran community. It was written in 1731 for a service on a Sunday immediately before the beginning of Advent (four Sundays before Christmas). The text of the cantata announces the coming of a bridegroom toward his hopeful bride. Christ is the groom. A group of ten Virgins, whose story is recounted in the Gospel of St. Matthew (25:1–13), symbolizes the bride and the entire community. Here is the Gospel of Matthew as it was read to the congregation at St. Thomas's Church immediately before Bach's cantata was performed:

> Then shall the kingdom of heaven be likened unto ten virgins, which took their lamps, and went forth to meet the bridegroom. And five of them were wise, and five were foolish. They that were foolish took their lamps, but took no oil with them. . . . And at midnight there was a cry made, Behold, the bridegroom cometh; go ye out to meet him. Then all those virgins arose, and trimmed their lamps. And the foolish said unto the wise, Give us of your oil; for our lamps are gone out. But the wise answered, saying, Not so; lest there be not enough for us and you: but go ye rather to them that sell, and buy for yourselves. And while they went to buy, the bridegroom came; and they that were ready went in with him to the marriage: and the door was shut . . . . Watch therefore, for ye know neither the day nor the hour wherein the Son of man cometh.

The message to every good Lutheran of Leipzig was clear: Get your spiritual house in order so as to receive the coming Christ. Thus Bach's cantatas were

FIGURE 7–9

Looking across the parishioner's pews and toward the high altar at St. Thomas's Church, Leipzig, as it was in the mid-nineteenth century. The pulpit for the sermon is at the right. In Bach's day nearly 2,500 people would crowd into the church.

St. Thomas's Church, Leipzig

not intended as concert pieces but religious instruction for his community—sermons in music.

The cantata *Awake, a Voice Is Calling* is made up of a succession of seven independent movements. Those for chorus provide a structural framework, coming at the beginning, the middle, and the end. They make use of the three stanzas of text of a sixteenth-century Lutheran hymn, *Awake, a Voice Is Calling*, from which this cantata derives its name. The text of the recitatives and arias, on the other hand, is a patchwork of biblical quotations cobbled together by a contemporary of Bach's. Thus the chorus sings the verses of the traditional hymn while the soloists present the biblical excerpts in the recitatives and arias. Notice how the structure of the cantata creates a formal symmetry: recitative–aria pairs surround the central choral movement, and are preceded and followed in turn by a chorus.

the chorale cantata

Movement:

1	2	3	4	5	6	7
Chorus	Recitative	Aria (duet)	Chorus	Recitative	Aria (duet)	Chorus
1st stanza			2nd stanza			3rd stanza

Awake, a Voice Is Calling is a chorale cantata, meaning that the work is built around a chorale. A **chorale** is a well-known spiritual melody or religious folksong of the German Protestant (Lutheran) church, what other denominations would simply call a hymn. In this case the chorale had been written in 1597 and had been widely used in the Lutheran church before Bach took it up. The structure of *Awake, a Voice Is Calling* is typical of chorale melodies (see upcoming Listening Guide). It begins with three phrases that emphasize, in turn, the tonic, the dominant, and again the tonic of the key E♭ major. These are stated and repeated. Thereafter come four shorter phrases (4–7) that allow for tonal contrast. Finally, a concluding phrase, which is nothing other than a repeat of phrase three, rounds off the melody. The form of this chorale is thus A(1,2,3) A(1,2,3) B(4–7,3). And the chorale is just the starting point for Bach's complex structure!

Of the seven movements of the cantata *Awake, a Voice Is Calling*, the most remarkable is the first, a gigantic chorale fantasy that displays a polyphonic mastery exceptional even for Bach. Here Bach creates a multidimensional spectacle surrounding the coming of Christ. First the orchestra announces Christ's arrival by means of a three-part ritornello* that conveys a sense of growing anticipation. Part **a** of the ritornello, with its dotted rhythm, suggests a steady march; part **b**, with its strong downbeat and then syncopations, imparts a tugging urgency; part **c**, with its rapid sixteenth notes, implies an unrestrained race toward the object of desire. Now the chorale melody enters, high in the sopranos, the voice of tradition, perhaps the voice of God. In long, steady notes placed squarely on downbeats it calls the people to prepare themselves to receive God's Son. Beneath this the voices of the people—the altos, tenors, and basses—scurry in rapid counterpoint, excited by the call to meet their savior. Lowest of all is the bass of the *basso continuo*. It plods along, sometimes in a dotted pattern, sometimes in rapid eighth notes,

FIGURE 7–10

Like the opening chorus of Bach's cantata, *Awake, a Voice Is Calling*, Tiepolo's *Vision of St. Clement* projects three distinct levels of activity: the Trinity on high, two angels in the middle, and Pope Clement I, Christ's vicar on earth, at the bottom.

but mostly in regularly recurring quarter notes falling on the beat. In sum, the opening movement of *Awake, a Voice Is Calling* is the musical equivalent of a great religious painting in which the canvas is energized by several super-imposed levels of activity (see Fig. 7–10 on preceding page). The enormous complexity of a movement such as this shows why musicians, then and now, view Bach as the greatest contrapuntalist who ever lived.

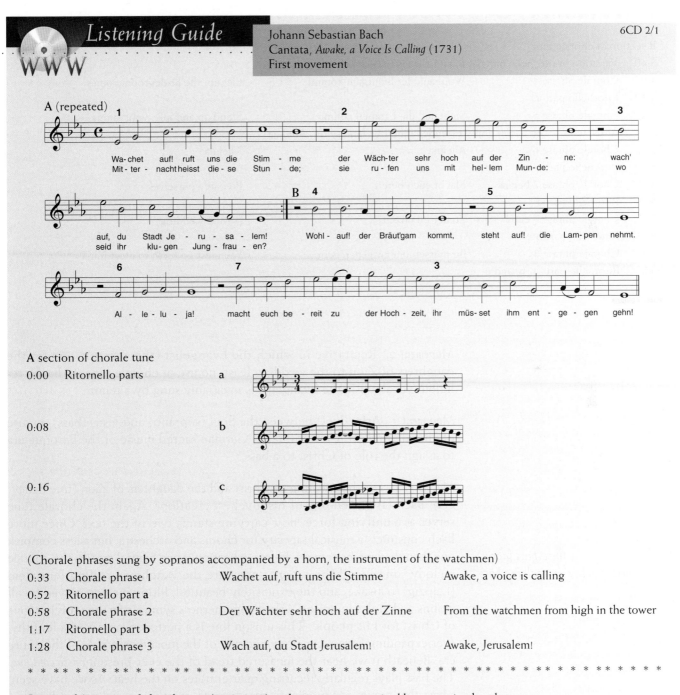

Listening Guide

Johann Sebastian Bach
Cantata, *Awake, a Voice Is Calling* (1731)
First movement

6CD 2/1

A section of chorale tune

0:00	Ritornello parts	a
0:08		b
0:16		c

(Chorale phrases sung by sopranos accompanied by a horn, the instrument of the watchmen)

0:33	Chorale phrase 1	Wachet auf, ruft uns die Stimme	Awake, a voice is calling
0:52	Ritornello part **a**		
0:58	Chorale phrase 2	Der Wächter sehr hoch auf der Zinne	From the watchmen from high in the tower
1:17	Ritornello part **b**		
1:28	Chorale phrase 3	Wach auf, du Stadt Jerusalem!	Awake, Jerusalem!

* *

Repeat of **A** section of chorale tune (0:00–1:49) with new text as required by repeat in chorale tune

(continued on next page)

1:50	Ritornello parts **a**, **b**, and **c**		
2:22	Chorale phrase 1	Mitternacht heisst diese Stunde	Midnight is the hour
2:41	Ritornello part **a**		
2:48	Chorale phrase 2	Sie rufen uns mit hellem Munde	They call us with a clarion voice
3:07	Ritornello part **b**		
3:18	Chorale phrase 3	Wo seid ihr klugen Jungfrauen?	Where are the Wise Virgins?

* *

B section of chorale tune

3:40	Variation of ritornello parts **a**, **b**, and **c** leads to new keys		
4:05	Chorale phrase 4	Wohl auf, der Bräutgam kommt	Get up, the Bridegroom comes
4:19	Ritornello part **a**		
4:27	Chorale phrase 5	Steht auf, die Lampen nehmt	Stand up and take your lamps
4:44	Altos, tenors, and basses enjoy extended imitative fantasy on "Alleluja"		
5:18	Chorale phrase 6	Alleluja	Alleluia
5:30	Ritornello part **a**		
5:40	Chorale phrase 7 begins	Macht euch bereit	Prepare yourselves
5:50	Ritornello part **a**		
5:57	Chorale phrase 7 ends	Zu der Hochzeit	For the wedding
6:11	Ritornello part **b**		
6:17	Chorale phrase 3	Ihr müsset ihm entgegen gehn!	You must go forth to meet him!
6:38	Ritornello parts **a**, **b**, and **c**		

Movement 2. Recitative in which the Evangelist (the narrator) invites the daughters of Zion to the wedding feast; no use of chorale tune. In Bach's religious vocal music the Evangelist is invariably sung by a tenor.

Movement 3. Aria (duet) between the Soul (soprano) and Jesus (bass); no use of chorale tune. It is traditional in German sacred music of the Baroque era to assign the role of Christ to a bass.

a three-part fabric: melody, chorale, walking bass

Movement 4. For this meeting of Christ and the daughters of Zion (true believers), Bach fashioned one of his loveliest creations. Again the chorale tune serves as a unifying force, now carrying stanza two of the text. Once more Bach constructs a musical tapestry for chorus and orchestra, but a less complex one than the first movement. Here we hear only two central motifs: the chorale melody sung by all the tenors—they are the watchmen calling Jerusalem (Leipzig) to awake; and the exquisitely beautiful, lilting melody played by all violins and violas in unison—their togetherness symbolizes the unifying love of Christ for His people. This unison line is a perfect example of a lengthy, ever-expanding Baroque melody and one of the most memorable of the entire era. Beneath it we hear the measured tread of the ever-present *basso continuo*. The bass plays regularly recurring quarter notes on the beat. As we have seen, a bass that moves at a moderate, steady pace, mostly in equal note values and often stepwise up or down the scale, is called a walking bass*. The walking bass in this movement enhances the meaning of the text, underscoring the

steady approach of the Lord. This movement was one of Bach's own favorites
and the only cantata movement that he published—all the rest of his Leipzig
cantata music was left in handwritten scores at the time of his death.

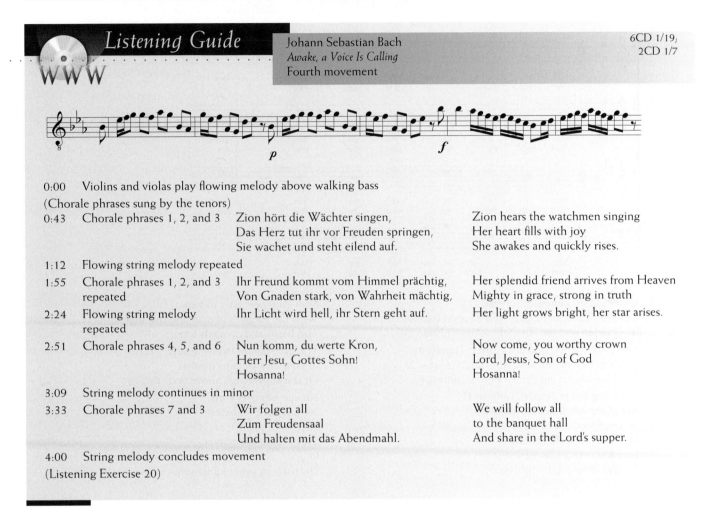

Listening Guide

WWW

Johann Sebastian Bach
Awake, a Voice Is Calling
Fourth movement

6CD 1/19;
2CD 1/7

0:00	Violins and violas play flowing melody above walking bass		
(Chorale phrases sung by the tenors)			
0:43	Chorale phrases 1, 2, and 3	Zion hört die Wächter singen, Das Herz tut ihr vor Freuden springen, Sie wachet und steht eilend auf.	Zion hears the watchmen singing Her heart fills with joy She awakes and quickly rises.
1:12	Flowing string melody repeated		
1:55	Chorale phrases 1, 2, and 3 repeated	Ihr Freund kommt vom Himmel prächtig, Von Gnaden stark, von Wahrheit mächtig,	Her splendid friend arrives from Heaven Mighty in grace, strong in truth
2:24	Flowing string melody repeated	Ihr Licht wird hell, ihr Stern geht auf.	Her light grows bright, her star arises.
2:51	Chorale phrases 4, 5, and 6	Nun komm, du werte Kron, Herr Jesu, Gottes Sohn! Hosanna!	Now come, you worthy crown Lord, Jesus, Son of God Hosanna!
3:09	String melody continues in minor		
3:33	Chorale phrases 7 and 3	Wir folgen all Zum Freudensaal Und halten mit das Abendmahl.	We will follow all to the banquet hall And share in the Lord's supper.
4:00	String melody concludes movement		
(Listening Exercise 20)			

Movement 5. Recitative for Christ (bass); no use of chorale tune. Christ invites the anguished Soul to find comfort in Him.

Movement 6. Aria (duet) for bass and soprano; no use of chorale tune. This is
a strict *da capo* aria (see page 159) in which Christ and the Soul sing a passionate love duet. A religious man who did not compose operas, Bach most
closely approaches the world of the theater in this beautiful duet.

Movement 7. Bach's cantatas usually end with a simple four-voice homophonic
setting of the last stanza of the chorale. He always places the chorale tune in
the soprano part, harmonizing and supporting it with the other three voices
below. The instruments of the orchestra have no line of their own and merely
double the four vocal parts. But more important, the members of the congregation join in the singing of the chorale melody. At that moment all of the
spiritual energy of Leipzig was concentrated into this one emphatic declaration of belief. The coming Christ reveals to all believers a vision of life in
the celestial kingdom.

the community sings the chorale

0:00	Gloria sei dir gesungen (phrase 1)	May Glory be sung to you
	Mit Menschen und englischen Zungen (phrase 2)	With the tongues of man and the angels
	Mit Harfen und mit Zimbeln schon. (phrase 3)	And harps and cymbals too.
0:38	Von zwölf Perlen sind die Pforten, (phrase 1)	The gates are of twelve pearls,
	An deiner Stadt, wir sind Konsorten (phrase 2)	In your city we are consorts
	Der Engel hoch um deiner Thron. (phrase 3)	Of the angels high above your throne.
1:16	Kein Aug hat je gespürt, (phrase 4)	No eye has ever seen,
	Kein Ohr hat je gehört (phrase 5)	No ear has ever heard
	Solche Freude. (phrase 6)	Such joy.
	Des sind wir froh, (phrase 7)	Let us therefore rejoice,
	Io, io!	Io, io!
	Ewig in dulci jubilo. (phrase 3)	Eternally in sweet jubilation.

In the last decade of his life Bach gradually withdrew from the world to dwell in the contrapuntal realm of his own mind. He finished the best-known of his large-scale, contrapuntal projects, *The Well-Tempered Clavier* (1720–1742), a "clavier" simply being Bach's word for keyboard. It consists of two sets of twenty-four preludes and fugues. The **prelude** is a short preparatory piece that sets a mood and serves as a technical warm-up for the player before the fugue. In both sets of twenty-four there is one prelude and fugue in each of the major and minor keys: the first pair in C major, the next in C minor, the next in C♯ major, then C♯ minor, and so on. Through this arrangement Bach showed that it was possible to write a piece—in this case a prelude and fugue—in every key, something that had not been done in a systematic fashion up to that time. Today every serious pianist around the world "cuts his teeth" on what is affectionately known as the "WTC."

The Well-Tempered Clavier

The Art of Fugue

Bach's last project was the *The Art of Fugue* (1742–1750), an encyclopedic treatment of all known contrapuntal procedures set forth in nineteen canons and fugues. The final fugue, one in which Bach combines four related subjects,

Bach's Bones

When Bach died in 1750 the music of "the old wig," as one of his sons irreverently referred to him, was soon forgotten. His style was thought to be too old-fashioned, with its heavy reliance on traditional chorale tunes and dense counterpoint. Bach was buried in a distant parish church. Not until nearly a hundred years after his death did the citizens of Leipzig come to discover that they had once had in their midst a genius—perhaps the greatest composer of all time! A statue of Bach was then placed before St. Thomas's Church, and a stained glass window with the composer's likeness was set within the church. Most strange of all, in 1895 Bach's corpse was unearthed. His skull was examined to see if it was unusually large (it was not), and his skeleton photographed. Ultimately Bach's bones were reinterred, but now at the high altar of St. Thomas's Church. A patron saint of music had been created. Today thousands of pilgrims come each year to this shrine to pay homage to the great man and hear his music.

Bach's bones.

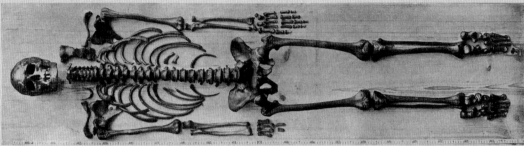

"Gesammtansicht des Bach-Skeletts" In: W. His, Anatomische Forschungen über Johann Sebastian Bach's Gebeine und Antlitz Š Leipzig: S. Hirzel, 1895.

was broken off by his death in 1750. *The Art of Fugue* was thus Bach's valedictory statement of a musical form he brought to supreme mastery. It remains a fitting testimony to this composer's stylistic integrity, grand design, and superhuman craftsmanship.

GEORGE FRIDERIC HANDEL (1685–1759)

The careers of Bach and Handel could hardly have been more different. While Bach spent his life confined to towns in central Germany, his cosmopolitan countryman Handel traveled the world—from Rome, to Venice, to Hamburg, to Amsterdam, to London, to Dublin. If Bach was most at home conducting chorale cantatas and playing organ fugues from the church choir loft, Handel was a man of the public theater, a denizen of the orchestra pit, by training and temperament a composer of opera. And if Bach fell into virtual obscurity at the end of his life, retreating into a world of esoteric counterpoint, Handel's stature only grew larger on the international stage. He became the most famous composer in Europe and a treasured national institution in England.

a musician of the world

George Frideric Handel (as he styled himself after becoming a naturalized English citizen) was born in the town of Halle, Germany, in 1685, and died in London in 1759 (Fig. 7–11). Although his father had decreed a program of study in law, the young Handel managed to cultivate his intense interest in music, sometimes secretly in the attic. At the age of eighteen he got his first taste of opera in the city of Hamburg, where he had gone to take a job as violinist in the public opera theater. But since the musical world around 1700 was dominated by things Italian, he, too, set off for Italy to learn his trade and broaden his horizons. He moved between Florence and Venice, for which cities he wrote operas, and Rome, where he composed mainly secular cantatas. In 1710 Handel returned to North Germany to accept the post of chapel master to the elector of Hanover, but on the condition that he be given an immediate leave of absence to visit London. Although he made one additional voyage back to his employer in Hanover in 1711 and many subsequent visits to the Continent, Handel conveniently forgot about his obligation to the Hanoverian court. London became the site of his musical activity and the place where he won fame and fortune.

After four years in Italy, London must have seemed a cultural backwater to Handel. Many of the streets were unpaved, the buildings were black with the soot of coal fires, and there was none of the art and architecture that graced Venice, Florence, or Rome. But there was opportunity. As the eighteenth-century saying went, "In France and Italy there is something to learn, but in London there is something to earn."

Handel soon found employment in the homes of the aristocracy and became the music tutor to the English royal family. As fate would have it, his continental employer, the elector of Hanover, became King George I of England in 1714, when the Hanoverians acceded to the throne on the extinction of the Stuart line. Fortunately for Handel, the new king bore his truant musician no grudge, and he was called on frequently to compose festival music to entertain the court or mark its progress. For these events Handel produced such works as *Water Music* (1717), *Music for the Royal Fireworks* (1749), and *Coronation Service* (1727), parts of which have been used at the coronation of every English monarch since its first hearing.

Handel and the Orchestral Dance Suite

WATER MUSIC (1717)

Aside from *Messiah*, Handel's most beloved composition is his *Water Music*. Handel's *Water Music* belongs to a genre of composition called a dance suite, a term derived from the French word *suite* (a succession of pieces). The **dance suite** is a collection of dances, usually varying from four to seven, all in one key and for one group of instruments, be it full orchestra, trio, or solo. *Water Music*, in fact, is a collection of three suites for orchestra that were performed one after the other. The listeners did not dance the music of Handel's suites; these were stylized, abstract dances. But it was the job of the composer to bring each one to life, to make it recognizable to the audience by incorporating the salient elements of rhythm and style of each particular dance. Among the dances that Handel popularized in his orchestral suites are the following.

Allemande. A stately dance in $\frac{4}{4}$ meter with gracefully interweaving lines.

Courante. A lively dance in $\frac{6}{4}$ with a pickup* and frequent changes of metrical accent.

Saraband. A slow, elegant dance in $\frac{3}{4}$ with a strong accent on the second beat.

FIGURE 7–11

Thomas Hudson's 1749 portrait of Handel with the score of *Messiah* visible beneath the composer's left hand. Handel had a quick temper, could swear in four languages, and liked to eat.

Staats-und-Universitätsbibliothek, Hamburg

the dance suite

Giraudon/Art Resource, NY

FIGURE 7–12
View of London, St. Paul's Cathedral, and the Thames River by Canaletto (1697–1768). Note the large barges. Crafts such as these could have easily accommodated the fifty musicians reported to have played behind the king as he moved upstream in 1717, listening to Handel's *Water Music*.

Minuet. A moderate dance in $\frac{3}{4}$ usually followed by another, shorter dance in the same style called the trio (see page 184).

Hornpipe. An energetic dance, derived from the country jig, in either $\frac{3}{2}$ or $\frac{2}{4}$ time.

Gigue. A fast dance in $\frac{6}{8}$ or $\frac{12}{8}$ with a constant eighth-note pulse that produces a galloplike effect.

But no matter what the rhythm or style of the dance, the form of each dance movement in the Baroque era was invariably the same: binary form* (see page 62). Binary form, of course, is a musical form with only two sections, **A** and **B**, each of which may be repeated. Normally **A** takes the movement from tonic to dominant, while **B** brings it back home to the tonic. Some dance movements are followed by a second, complementary dance, as the minuet is followed by a trio. In such cases the first dance should be repeated after the second.

The English royal family has historically had a problem with its image, sometimes giving concerts of popular music to win favor with the public, as Queen Elizabeth II did recently at Buckingham Palace. Handel's *Water Music* was created for another royally sponsored bit of image-building. In 1717 King George I, a direct ancestor of the present queen, was an unpopular monarch. He refused to speak a word of English, preferring his native German. He fought with his son, the Prince of Wales, and banned him from court. His subjects thought George dimwitted, "an honest blockhead," as one contemporary put it.

To improve his standing in the eyes of his subjects the king's ministers planned a program of public entertainments, including an evening of music on the River Thames for the lords of Parliament and the lesser people of London (Fig. 7–12). Thus on July 17, 1717, the King and his court left London,

Water Music: *music to polish the royal image*

accompanied by a small navy of boats, and progressed up the Thames to the strains of Handel's orchestral music. An eyewitness describes this nautical parade in detail:

> About eight in the evening the King repaired to his barge, into which were admitted the Duchess of Bolton, Countess Godolphin, Madam de Kilmansech (the king's mistress), Mrs. Were and the Earl of Orkney, the Gentleman of the Bedchamber in Waiting. Next to the King's barge was that of the musicians, about 50 in number, who played on all kinds of instruments, to wit trumpets, horns, hautboys [oboes], bassoons, German flutes, French flutes [recorders], violins and basses; but there were no singers. The music had been composed specially by the famous Handel, a native of Halle [Germany], and His Majesty's principal Court Composer. His Majesty so greatly approved of the music that he caused it to be repeated three times in all, although each performance lasted an hour—namely twice before and once after supper. The evening weather was all that could be desired for the festivity, the number of barges and above all of boats filled with people desirous of hearing the music was beyond counting.

Water Music heard on the Thames River

So broad are Handel's musical gestures and so brilliant his orchestral effects that even the "blockhead" king was enchanted by the fifty musicians playing *Water Music* on the neighboring barge. What makes the dance movements of *Water Music* so easy to comprehend is their formal clarity. Notice in the Minuet how Handel asks the French horns and trumpets first to announce both the **A** and **B** sections before passing this material on to the woodwinds and then to the full orchestra.

Listening Guide

WWW

George Frideric Handel
Water Music (1717)
Minuet and Trio

Intro CD/18

Genre: dance suite
Form: ternary

Minuet (triple meter, major key)
0:00   French horns introduce part **A**

0:12   Trumpets introduce part **B**

0:29   Winds and continuo play **A**
0:42   Full orchestra repeats **A**
0:55   Winds and continuo play **B**
1:08   Full orchestra repeats **B**

Trio (triple meter, minor key)
1:28   Strings and continuo play part **C**
1:43   Strings and continuo play part **D**

Minuet
2:19   Full orchestra plays **A**
2:31   Full orchestra plays **B**

The jaunty triple-meter Hornpipe is very brief, the complete dance requiring only forty seconds. For such a short piece to have an effect, Handel directed that it be played three times, first by strings and continuo, then by woodwinds and continuo, and finally by both strings and woodwinds together, along with continuo. The Minuet and the Hornpipe are just two of the twenty dances that make up Handel's *Water Music.*

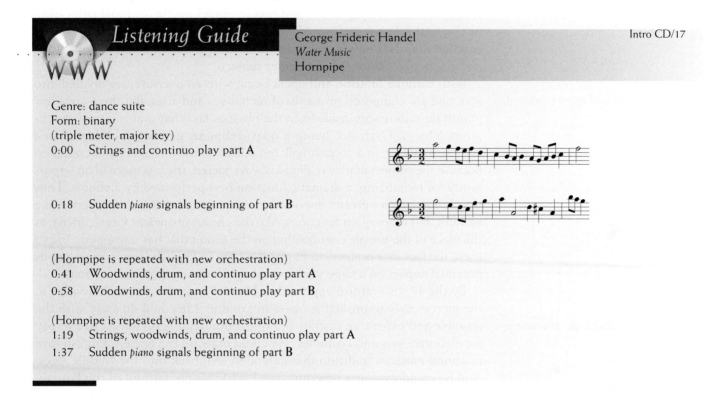

Listening Guide

WWW

George Frideric Handel
Water Music
Hornpipe

Intro CD/17

Genre: dance suite
Form: binary
(triple meter, major key)
0:00   Strings and continuo play part **A**

0:18   Sudden *piano* signals beginning of part **B**

(Hornpipe is repeated with new orchestration)
0:41   Woodwinds, drum, and continuo play part **A**
0:58   Woodwinds, drum, and continuo play part **B**

(Hornpipe is repeated with new orchestration)
1:19   Strings, woodwinds, drum, and continuo play part **A**
1:37   Sudden *piano* signals beginning of part **B**

Handel and the Oratorio

Handel moved to London in 1710, not for the chance to entertain the royal family, and certainly not for the climate or cuisine, but to make money by composing opera. With the rare exception of a work such as Purcell's *Dido and Aeneas* (see page 121), there was no English opera at this time. Instead, spoken plays with occasional musical interludes dominated the London stage. Handel intended to fill this void by importing Italian opera, which was then enormously popular on the Continent. Guaranteed a healthy share of the profits from the operas he produced, Handel rented the theater, composed the music, engaged high-paid soloists from Italy, led the rehearsals, and conducted the finished product from the harpsichord in the orchestra pit. From 1710 until 1728 he had great artistic and some financial success, producing two dozen examples of Italian **opera seria** (literally, serious, as opposed to comic, opera). *Opera seria* tended to portray historical or mythological subjects—high-born characters—and their stiff, formalized emotions. Foremost among Handel's was *Giulio Cesare* (*Julius Caesar;* 1724), a recasting of the story of Caesar's conquest of the army of Egypt and its queen, Cleopatra. But opera is a notoriously risky business, and in 1728 the company Handel had founded went

Handel as composer of opera seria

bankrupt, a victim of the exorbitant fees paid the star singers and competition from other, upstart operatic companies. Handel continued to write opera into the 1730s, but he increasingly turned his attention to a musical genre similar in construction to opera, oratorio.

An **oratorio** is literally "something sung in an oratory," an oratory being a hall or chapel used specifically for prayer and sometimes prayer with music. Thus, the oratorio as it first appeared in seventeenth-century Italy was an extended musical setting of a sacred text intended for the spiritual edification of the faithful and performed in a special hall or chapel. By the time it reached Handel's hands, however, the oratorio had become in most ways nothing but an opera with a religious subject.

oratorio and opera compared

Both Baroque oratorio and opera begin with an overture, are divided into acts, and are composed primarily of recitatives and arias. But there are a few important differences, aside from the obvious fact that oratorio treats a religious subject. Oratorio, being a quasi-religious genre, is performed in a church, a theater, or a concert hall, but makes no use of staging and costumes. Because the subject matter is almost always sacred, there is more of an opportunity for moralizing, a dramatic function best performed by a chorus. Thus the chorus assumes greater importance in an oratorio. It sometimes serves as a narrator, but more often functions, like the chorus in ancient Greek drama, as the voice of the people commenting on the action that has transpired. Add to these the fact that oratorio in England is sung in English (not Italian), and its potential impact on a large segment of English society becomes obvious.

advantages of oratorio

By the 1730s oratorio appeared to Handel as an attractive alternative to the increasingly unprofitable opera in London. He could do away with the irascible and expensive castrati and prima donnas. He no longer had to pay for elaborate sets and costumes. He could draw on the ancient English love of choral music, a tradition that extended well back into the Middle Ages. And he could exploit a new, untapped market—the faithful of the Puritan, Methodist, and growing evangelical sects in England who had viewed the pleasures of foreign opera with distrust and even contempt.

MESSIAH (1741)

Beginning in 1732 and continuing over a twenty-year period, Handel wrote upward of twenty oratorios. The most famous of these is his *Messiah*, composed in the astonishingly short period of three-and-a-half weeks during the summer of 1741. It was first performed in Dublin, Ireland, the following April as part of a charity benefit, with Handel conducting. Having heard the dress rehearsal, the local press waxed enthusiastic about the new oratorio, saying that it "far surpasses anything of that Nature, which has been performed in this or any other Kingdom." Such a large crowd was expected for the work of the famous Handel that ladies were urged not to wear hoopskirts, and gentlemen admonished to leave their swords at home. In this way could an audience of 700 be squeezed into a hall possessing only 600 seats.

Messiah premiere in Dublin

Buoyed by his artistic and financial success in Dublin, Handel took *Messiah* back to London, made minor alterations, and performed it in Covent Garden Theater. In 1750 he again offered *Messiah*, this time in the chapel of the Foundling Hospital for orphans in London (Fig. 7–13), and again there was much popular acclaim for Handel as well as profit for charity. This was the first time one of his oratorios was sung in a religious setting rather than a theater or a concert hall. The annual repetition of *Messiah* in the Foundling Hospital chapel during Handel's lifetime and long after did much to convince the public that his oratorios were essentially religious music to be performed in church.

In a general way, *Messiah* tells the story of the life of Christ. It is divided into three parts (instead of three acts): (I) the prophecy of His coming and His Incarnation; (II) His Passion and Resurrection, and the triumph of the Gospel; and (III) reflections on the Christian victory over death. In *Messiah* dramatic confrontation is replaced by a mood of lyrical meditation and, ultimately, exaltation. The music consists of fifty-three numbers: Nineteen are for chorus, sixteen are solo arias, sixteen are recitatives, and two are purely instrumental pieces.

There are many beautiful and stirring arias in *Messiah*, including "Every valley shall be exalted," "O thou that tellest good tidings to Zion," and "Rejoice greatly, O daughter of Zion." Significantly, "Rejoice greatly, O daughter of Zion" is on the same topic as Bach's cantata, *Awake, a Voice Is Calling* (see page 146): It tells of the joy felt by all true believers, here personified by the daughter of Zion, at the coming of the Messiah.

Handel composed "Rejoice greatly, O daughter of Zion" in the form of a modified *da capo* aria. A **da capo aria** has two musical sections, **A** and **B**, with the second usually contrasting in key and mood. When the singer reaches the end of part **B**, he or she is instructed by the words "da capo" to "take it from the top" and thus repeat **A**, note for note. What results is **ABA**, another example of ternary form* in music. Composers such as Handel and Bach sometimes change **A** when it returns so as to achieve variety. A modified *da capo* aria (**ABA'**) is thus created. When such a modification is effected, it usually allows the soloist to build to a final climax by means of embellishment and vocal virtuosity. At the end of "Rejoice greatly, O daughter of Zion," for example, what was a relatively easy passage of simple stepwise motion at the end of **A** is transformed into a more difficult, and dramatic, series of leaps of octaves and sevenths in **A'**.

FIGURE 7-13
The chapel of the Foundling Hospital, London, where *Messiah* was performed annually for the benefit of the orphans. Handel himself designed and donated the organ seen at the back of the hall.

da capo *aria*

EXAMPLE 7-4

be-hold, thy King cometh un - to thee   be-hold, thy King cometh un - to thee, be-hold, thy King

Examples of *da capo* form and modified *da capo* form abound in arias in both oratorio and opera of the late Baroque era. Indeed, the line of distinction between these two Baroque musical genres, between the sacred oratorio and the profane opera, was a thin one. Although the text of "Rejoice greatly, O daughter of Zion" comes from scripture (Zechariah 9:9–10), the daredevil style of singing has its origins in the more worldly opera house.

Listening Guide

George Frideric Handel
Aria, "Rejoice greatly, O daughter of Zion" from
Messiah (1741)

6CD 2/3

Genre: oratorio
Form: *da capo* (ternary)

A

0:00   Orchestral ritornello for violins and continuo

0:17   Soprano enters   Rejoice greatly, O daughter of Zion, shout,

0:40   Soprano spins out long melisma at repeat of "rejoice"   O daughter of Jerusalem,

re - joice, _____

1:02   Soprano assumes longer notes and more stately quality   Behold, thy King cometh unto thee.

B

1:32   Sudden shift to minor key; calm, steady pace of eighth   He is the righteous Saviour,
       notes emphasizes the peace to be spoken by Jesus   And he shall speak peace unto the heathen.

2:30   Ritard and broadening signal end of part **B**

A′

2:40   Return to major key (tonic) and original fast tempo   Rejoice greatly, O daughter of Zion, (etc.)

2:44   Soprano returns with varied version of **A**   Behold, thy King cometh unto thee.

3:45   Soprano sings more difficult and dramatic conclusion
       (see Example 7–4)

Handel's choruses

Despite the bravura quality of the arias, the true glory of *Messiah* is to be found in its choruses. Handel was arguably the finest composer for chorus who ever lived. As a world traveler with an unsurpassed ear, he had absorbed the German tradition of the fugue and the Lutheran chorale; he knew the Venetian polychoral style of Gabrieli (see page 115) and the powerful English church anthems* (extended motets) of Henry Purcell; and, of course, he had a flair for the dramatic, gained from a lifetime in the theater.

Nowhere is Handel's choral mastery more evident than in the justly famous "Hallelujah" chorus that concludes Part II of *Messiah*. Here a variety of choral styles are displayed in quick succession: chordal, unison, chorale, fugal, and fugal and chordal together. The opening word "Hallelujah" recurs throughout as a powerful refrain, yet each new phrase of text generates its own distinct musical idea. The vivid phrases speak directly to the listener, making the audience feel like a participant in the drama. So moved was King George II when he first heard the great opening chords, as the story goes, that he rose to his feet in admiration, thereby establishing the tradition of the audience standing for the "Hallelujah" chorus—for no one sat while the king stood. Indeed, this movement would serve well as a royal coronation march, though in *Messiah*, of course, it is Christ the King who is being crowned.

"Hallelujah" chorus

Listening Guide

George Frideric Handel
"Hallelujah" chorus from *Messiah* (1741)

0:00   Brief string introduction

0:06   Chorus enters with two salient
motives:

Hal - le - lu - jah,   Hal - le - lu - jah,

Hal - le - lu - jah,   Hal - le - lu - jah,

0:16   Five more chordal exclamations of the
"Hallelujah" motive, but at a higher
pitch level

0:25   Chorus sings new theme in unison
answered by chordal cries of
"Hallelujah"

For the Lord God om-ni - po-tent reign-eth,

0:35   Music repeated but at a lower pitch

0:47   Fuguelike imitation begins with subject   "For the Lord God omnipotent reigneth"

1:13   Quiet and then loud; set in chorale style   "The kingdom of this world is become the Kingdom of our Lord . . ."

1:31   New fuguelike section begins with
entry in bass

and he shall   reign for ev - er and   ev - er,

1:53   Altos and then sopranos begin long ascent   "King of Kings and Lord of Lords"
in long notes

2:33   Basses and sopranos reenter with   "And he shall reign for ever and ever"

2:44   Tenors and basses sing in long notes   "King of Kings and Lord of Lords"

3:00   Incessant major tonic chord   "King of Kings"

3:26   Broad final cadence   "Hallelujah"

(Listening Exercise 21)

The "Hallelujah" chorus is a strikingly effective work mainly because the large choral force creates a sense of heavenly power and strength. In fact, however, Handel's chorus for the original Dublin *Messiah* was much smaller than those used today. It included about four singers on the alto, tenor, and bass parts and six choirboys singing the soprano (Fig. 7–14). The orchestra was equally slight. For the Foundling Hospital performances of the 1750s, however, the orchestra grew to thirty-five players. Then, in the course of the next hundred years, the chorus progressively swelled to as many as four thousand with a balancing orchestra of five hundred in what were billed as "Festivals of the People" in honor of Handel.

And just as there was a continual increase in the performing forces for his *Messiah*, so too Handel's fortune and reputation grew. Toward the end of his life he occupied a squire's house in the center of London, bought paintings, including a large and "indeed excellent" Rembrandt, and, on his death, left an enormous estate of nearly twenty thousand pounds, as the newspapers of

Handel's fame grows

Yale Center for British Art, Paul Mellon Collection

FIGURES 7–14 AND 7–15

(right) Eighteenth-century London was a place of biting satire. Here, in William Hogarth's *The Oratorio Singer* (1732), the chorus of an oratorio is the object of parody. But there is an element of truth here: the chorus for the first performance of *Messiah,* for example, numbered about sixteen males, with choirboys (front row) taking the soprano part. Women, however, sang soprano and alto for the vocal solos. (below) Handel's funeral monument at Westminster Abbey. The composer holds the aria "I know that my Redeemer liveth" from *Messiah.* When Handel was buried, the gravedigger left room to cram in another body immediately adjacent. That space was later filled by the corpse of Charles Dickens.

Bridgeman Art Library, London/NY

the day were quick to report. More than three thousand persons attended his funeral in Westminster Abbey on April 20, 1759, and a sculpture of the composer holding an aria from *Messiah* was erected above his grave and is still visible today (Fig. 7–15). As a memento of Handel's music, *Messiah* was an apt choice, for it is still performed each year at Christmas and Easter by countless amateur and professional groups throughout the world.

Listening Exercises

19

Johann Sebastian Bach   6CD 1/17; 2CD 1/6
Organ Fugue in G minor (ca. 1710)

The following diagram is essentially the same as that found on page 142. It charts the flow of the music as Bach's Organ Fugue in G minor unfolds from the straightforward exposition, through the increasingly lengthy episodes, to the final statement of the subject in the bass. Your task is to differentiate statements of the subject from the episodes—can you hear when the subject is being played or not? The first statement of the subject appears at 0:00, so your first question is easy. For the other eight statements of the subject, however, you may find yourself more challenged. Indicate the correct time that all nine statements of the subject of the fugue occur by choosing "a" or "b" below. You are not asked to indicate the times at which the episodes begin, but see if you can sense that the subject is no longer present and that modulations are occurring.

EXPOSITION   EPISODE   EPISODE   EPISODE

S1. 0:00

A   2._____   †   6._____

T   3._____   5. __

B   4._____   7._____

†This entry starts in the tenor and continues in the soprano.

EPISODE   EPISODE

S   8._____

A

T

B   9. _____

1. a. 0:00 or b. 0:05   6. a. 1:56 or b. 2:04
2. a. 0:15 or b. 0:19   7. a. 2:25 or b. 2:33
3. a. 0:37 or b. 0:42   8. a. 3:00 or b. 3:09
4. a. 0:59 or b. 1:06   9. a. 3:39 or b. 3:48
5. a. 1:20 or b. 1:28
10. Finally, which of the four parts is played by the pedals of the organ?
    a. soprano   b. alto   c. tenor   d. bass

Johann Sebastian Bach   6CD 1/19; 2CD 1/7
Cantata, *Awake, a Voice Is Calling* (1731)
Fourth movement

The most famous portion of cantata *Awake, a Voice Is Calling* is the middle (fourth) movement in which Bach assigns the violins a lovely counter melody to sound against the chorale tune. The following exercise asks you to concentrate mainly on the relationship between the three musical lines that are clearly audible throughout this beautiful work: bass, chorale tune, and violin counter melody.

1. (0:00–0:42) How many musical lines or parts do you hear at the beginning of the movement?
    a. one   b. two   c. three
2. (0:00–0:34) A bass that plods along in equal note values moving in predominantly conjunct* motion (stepwise motion) is called
    a. an ostinato bass   b. a pedal point   c. a walking bass

(0:00–0:42) The meter of the movement is duple, indeed $\frac{4}{4}$. There are four quarter notes in each measure. You can hear the beat by focusing on the bass.

At the beginning (0:00–0:34) the double basses play nothing but quarter notes; that is to say, they are playing the beat.

3. (0:00–0:01) Does the melody begin with a pickup* before the double basses enter with the first downbeat? (Do you hear a bit of violin sound before the basses enter?)
   a. The melody begins with a pickup in the violins.
   b. The melody does not begin with a pickup in the violins.

4. (0:00–0:40) Count and conduct the music. Your beat should be marching in sync with the bass. How many **full** measures of music do you hear before the voices enter?
   a. four b. eight c. twelve

5. (0:43) When the chorale tune enters it is sung
   a. in four-part harmony
   b. in unison by the sopranos
   c. in unison by the tenors

6. (0:43–1:13) Bach sets the chorale tune in notes that are
   a. longer (hence sound slower) than those of the strings
   b. shorter (hence sound faster) than those of the strings

7. (0:43–1:13) Throughout this section, which is true?
   a. The chorale tune is at the top of the texture, strings in the middle, double basses at the bottom.
   b. The chorale tune is in the middle of the texture, strings at the top, double basses at the bottom.
   c. The chorale tune is at the bottom of the texture, strings at the top, double basses in the middle.

8. (1:10–1:18) Which is true of the conclusion of section **A** of the movement?
   a. The strings begin to repeat their flowing melody before the voices conclude their phrase of the chorale tune.
   b. The voices conclude their phrase of the chorale tune and then the strings begin to repeat their flowing melody.

(1:12–2:50) Repeat of section **A** of the movement. Check your answers to questions 1–8.

9. (3:17–3:32) Which is true about this section?
   a. It is in a major key and the chorale tune is present in the sopranos.
   b. It is in a minor key and the chorale tune is not sung during this passage.

10. At any time throughout this movement is the three-line texture (bass, choral tune, violin counter melody) increased by the addition of woodwinds and brasses?
    a. Yes, woodwinds and brasses are added at the end for extra weight. Bach likes the big, dramatic event.
    b. No, Bach never uses more than a three-line texture in this movement. Once he decides on a texture, he prosecutes it rigorously to the end.

21

George Frideric Handel   Intro CD/19
"Hallelujah" chorus from *Messiah* (1741)

As a man of the theater, Handel was the master of the dramatic gesture. Sometimes, as we shall see, he would even insert a "thundering silence" for special effect. This exercise asks you to hear the frequent changes of texture in the "Hallelujah" chorus. It is by means of striking textural changes that Handel creates the grand effects of this classical favorite.

1. How many musical lines are prominent during the instrumental introduction?
   a. one: basses (cellos and double basses)
   b. two: violins and basses (cellos and double basses)
   c. three: oboes, violins, and basses (cellos and double basses)

2. In what kind of musical texture do the voices sing when they enter with "Hallelujah"?
   a. homophony b. polyphony c. monophony

3. (0:25–0:31; "For the Lord God omnipotent reigneth") As the chorus sings in unison, do the violins double (play the same line as) the voices?
   a. yes b. no

4. Unison singing and playing creates what kind of texture?
   a. monophonic b. polyphonic c. homophonic

5. (0:48–1:12; "For the Lord God omnipotent reigneth") Now we have a passage of imitative, contrapuntal writing in which a subject is presented in succession in the voices. In what order do the voices enter with this subject?
   a. soprano, alto, male voices
   b. soprano, male voices, alto
   c. alto, male voices, soprano

6. (1:32–1:52; "And he shall reign for ever and ever") Again, Handel offers another passage of imitative writing, with a new subject. In what order do the voices enter?
   a. bass, alto, tenor, soprano
   b. bass, tenor, soprano, alto
   c. bass, soprano, alto, tenor
   d. bass, tenor, alto, soprano

7. Polyphonic passages such as this (1:32–1:52) most closely approximate the style and musical texture found in
   a. a fugue b. a chorale tune c. a Gregorian chant

8. (2:06–2:30) What are the sopranos doing here on "King of Kings and Lord of Lords"?
   a. rising in an arpeggio
   b. rising by leap
   c. rising by step

9. (3:22–3:24) In a brilliant stroke Handel sets off and highlights the final statement of "Hallelujah" (and the final cadence) by inserting a new kind of texture. Which is correct?
   a. He inserts a homophonic brass fanfare.
   b. He inserts the texture of silence.

10. What is it that creates the drama and grandeur in this choral movement?
    a. the skillful use of a variety of textures and styles
    b. a very clear setting of the English text (music reflecting the natural stresses in the words)
    c. the concentration of all voices and instruments on a few, simple musical gestures
    d. all of the above

Key Words

The Art of Fugue (152)	episode (141)	pedal point (145)
cadenza (145)	exposition (141)	prelude (152)
cantata (146)	figured bass (138)	subject (141)
chorale (148)	fugue (141)	*The Well-Tempered*
da capo aria (159)	*opera seria* (157)	*Clavier* (152)
dance suite (154)	oratorio (158)	

For a checklist of musical style of the late Baroque period, see page 69.

Bridgeman Art Library, London/NY

Classical Ideals: The World of Haydn and Mozart

"Classical" as a musical term has two separate, though related, meanings. We use the word "classical" to signify the "serious" or "art" music of the West as distinguished from folk music, popular music, jazz, and the traditional music of various ethnic cultures. We call this music "classical" because there is something about the excellence of its form and style that makes it enduring, just as a finely crafted watch or a vintage automobile may be said to be a "classic" because it has a timeless beauty. Yet in the same breath we may refer to "Classical" music (now with a capital C), and by this we mean the music of a specific historical period, 1750–1820, a period of the great works of Haydn and Mozart and the early masterpieces of Beethoven. The creations of these artists have become so identified in the public mind with musical proportion, balance, and formal correctness—with standards of musical excellence—that this comparatively brief period has given its name to all music of lasting aesthetic worth.

"Classical" derives from the Latin *classicus*, meaning "something of the first rank or highest quality." To the men and women of the eighteenth century, no art, architecture, philosophy, or political institutions were more admirable, virtuous, and worthy of emulation than those of ancient Greece and Rome. Other periods in Western history also have been inspired by classical antiquity—the Renaissance heavily, the early Baroque less so, and the twentieth century to some degree—but no period more than the eighteenth century. This was the time of the discovery of the ruins of Pompeii (1748), of the publication of Winkelmann's *History of Ancient Art* (1764) and Gibbon's *Decline and Fall of the Roman Empire* (1788).

It was also the period in which young English aristocrats made the "grand tour" of Italy and carted back to their country estates Roman statues, columns, and parts of entire villas. Classical architecture, with its formal control of space, geometric shapes, balance, and symmetrical design, became the only style thought worthy for domestic and state buildings of consequence. European palaces, opera houses, theaters, and country homes all made use of it. Thomas Jefferson also traveled to Italy in these years while American ambassador to France, and later brought Classical design to this country. Our nation's capitol, many state capitols, and countless other governmental and university buildings abound with the well-proportioned columns, porticos, and rotundas of the Classical style.

FIGURES 8–1 AND 8–2

(top) The second-century Pantheon in Rome. (bottom) The library of the University of Virginia, designed by Thomas Jefferson in the late eighteenth century. Jefferson had visited Rome and studied the ancient ruins while ambassador to France (1784–1789). The portico, with columns and triangular pediment, and the central rotunda are all elements of Classical style in architecture.

Editoriale Museum, Rome

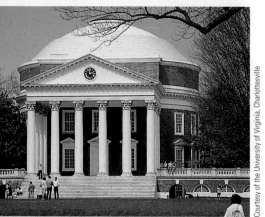

Courtesy of the University of Virginia, Charlottesville

THE ENLIGHTENMENT

The Classical era in music, art, and architecture coincides with the period in philosophy and letters called the Enlightenment. During the Enlightenment, also referred to as the Age of Reason, thinkers gave free rein to the pursuit of truth and the discovery of natural laws. This is the era that saw the rise of a natural religion called Deism, the belief that a Creator made the world, set it in motion, and has left it alone ever since. This is also the age of such scientific advances as the discovery of electricity and the invention of the steam engine. The first *Encyclopedia Britannica* appeared in 1771 and the French *Encyclopédie* between 1751 and 1772, a twenty-four volume set whose authors discarded traditional religious convictions and superstitions in favor of more rational scientific, philosophical, and political beliefs. In France the encyclopedists Voltaire (1694–1778) and Rousseau (1712–1778) espoused the principles of social justice, equality, religious tolerance, and freedom of speech. These Enlightenment ideals subsequently became fundamental to all democratic governments and were enshrined in our American constitution.

Needless to say, the notion that all persons are created equal and should enjoy full political freedom put the thinkers of the Enlightenment on a collision course with the defenders of the existing social order. The old political structure had been built on the superstitions of the church, the privileges of the nobility, and the divine right of kings. Voltaire attacked the habits and prerogatives of both clergy and aristocracy, and championed middle-class virtues: honesty, common sense, and hard work. The extravagant gestures, sword, and wig of the frivolous courtier were an easy target for his pen. A more natural appearance, one appropriate to a tradesman, merchant, or manufacturer, now became the paradigm. Spurred on by economic self-interest and the principles of the philosophers, an increasingly numerous and self-confident middle class in France and America rebelled against the monarchy and its supporters. The Age of Reason gave way to a newer Age of Revolution.

MUSIC AND SOCIAL CHANGE: COMIC OPERA

Music was affected by these profound social changes, and in some ways it helped to precipitate them. A new form of opera, comic opera, proved to be a powerful vehicle for social reform. Opera in the Baroque period had been dominated by *opera seria** (see page 157). It was beautiful, grandiose, some-what stiff, and expensive to mount. Portraying the deeds of mythological gods and goddesses, and historical emperors and kings, it was the quintes-sential opera of the aristocracy. By contrast, the new **comic opera**, called **opera buffa** in Italy, was the opera of the middle class. It made use of every-day characters and situations; it employed spoken dialogues and simple songs in place of recitatives and *da capo** arias; and it was liberally spiced with sight gags, slapstick comedy, and bawdy humor. The librettos, such as they were, either poked fun at the nobility for its pomposity and incompe-tence or criticized it for being heartless.

Like seditious pamphlets, comic operas appeared in every country; among them were John Gay's *The Beggar's Opera* (1728) in England, Giovanni Per-golesi's *La serva padrona* (*The Maid Made Master*, 1733) in Italy, and Jean-Jacques Rousseau's *Le devin du village* (*The Village Soothsayer*, 1752) in France. And com-posers of greater stature were seduced by the charms of this middle-class en-tertainment. Mozart, who was treated poorly by the nobility throughout his short life, set one libretto in which a barber outsmarts a count and holds him up to public ridicule, *Le nozze di Figaro* (*The Marriage of Figaro*, 1786) (Fig. 8–4), and another, *Don Giovanni* (1787), in which the villain is a leading nobleman of the town. The play that served as the basis for Mozart's *Figaro* was initially banned by French King Louis XVI. By the time of the French Revolution (1789), comic opera, a rebellious upstart, had nearly driven the established *opera seria* off the eighteenth-century stage.

PUBLIC CONCERTS

The social changes of the eighteenth century, in turn, affected who listened to music. In an earlier day a citizen might only hear sacred vocal music in a church or a bit of instrumental music at court, if he or she happened to be

FIGURE 8–3
Thomas Jefferson, by the French sculptor Houdon, done in 1789, the year of the French Revolution.

FIGURE 8–4
"Cherubino is discovered by the Count," an illustration of a scene in Pierre Beaumar-chais's play *The Marriage of Figaro* (1784). The play was revolutionary because it depicted the servants to be more clever and more honest than their master. Mozart's comic opera of the same name, written in 1786, is based on the play. Both playwright and composer had to dance quickly to stay one step ahead of the censors.

FIGURE 8–5

A performance at the Burgtheater in Vienna in 1785. The nobility occupied the front-most seats on the floor, but the area behind (to the left of) the partition was open to all. So, too, in the galleries, the aristocracy bought boxes low and close to the stage, while commoners occupied higher rungs as well as the standing room in the fourth gallery. Ticket prices depended, then as now, on proximity to the performers.

lucky enough to be an invited guest. But by mid-century the bookkeeper, physician, cloth merchant, and stock trader collectively had enough disposable income to organize and patronize their own concerts. In Leipzig, for example, the merchants got together to form the *Gewandhaus* ("Clothiers' House") concerts, which were held in the great hall of that guild; this *Gewandhaus* orchestra is still active today. Entrepreneurs in London offered concerts in the Vauxhall Gardens, where music could be heard inside in the orchestra room and outside as well. In Vienna, the Burgtheater (City Theater) opened in 1759 to paying customers of whatever class, as long as they were properly clothed and properly behaved. Although the nobility still occupied the best seats (Fig. 8–5), opening the doors to the general public fostered a leveling between classes with respect to the fine arts.

In Paris, then a city of 500,000, one could attend, as a citizen of the day said, "the best concerts every day with complete freedom." The most successful Parisian concert series was the *Concert spirituel* (founded in 1725), which was advertised to the public by means of flyers distributed in the streets. To make its offerings accessible to several strata of society, it also instituted a two-tiered system of prices (four *livres* for boxes and two *livres* for the pit). Women were almost as numerous as men in the audience. By 1798 children under fifteen were admitted half-price. Thus we can trace to the middle of the eighteenth century the tradition of middle-class citizens attending public performances in return for an admission fee. The institution of "concerts" as we know them, with a broadly-based listening audience, dates from this time. Classical music was becoming public entertainment.

THE ADVENT OF THE PIANO

The newly affluent middle class wished not only to listen to music but also to play it. Most of this music making was centered in the home and around an instrument that first entered public consciousness in the Classical period: the piano. Invented in Italy about 1700, the piano gradually replaced the harpsichord as the keyboard instrument of preference (Fig. 8–6)—and with good reason, for the piano could play at more than one dynamic level (hence the original name **pianoforte**, "soft-loud"). Compared with the harpsichord, the piano could produce gradual dynamic changes, more subtle contrasts, and—ultimately—more power.

Those who played this new domestic instrument were mostly amateurs, and the great majority of these were women. A smattering of French, an eye for needlepoint, and some skill at the piano—these were signs of status and gentility that rendered a young woman suitable for marriage. This social skill, in turn, required a simpler, more homophonic style of keyboard music, one that would presumably not tax the technical limitations of the female performer. The spirit of democracy may have been in the air, but this was still very much a sexist age. It was assumed that ladies would not wish, as one publication said, "to bother their pretty little heads with counterpoint and harmony," but would be content with a tuneful melody and a few rudimentary chords to flesh it out. Collections such as *Keyboard Pieces for Ladies* (1768) were directed at these new musical consumers.

piano music for women

CLASSICAL SIMPLICITY AND BALANCE

Painting of the late eighteenth century is often called Neoclassical, because it draws heavily on the themes and styles of classical antiquity. Many of the major artists of the day—among them American Benjamin West (1738–1820), Frenchman Jacques Louis David (1748–1825), and Englishwoman Angelica Kauffman (1741–1807) (Fig. 8–7)—traveled to Rome between 1760 and 1790 to study the architecture, mosaics, and sculpture that remained in the Roman forum and elsewhere around the city. They incorporated in their works not only the style and ornament of Roman dress but also the clarity, simplicity, and formal balance inherent in ancient classical design.

Angelica Kauffman's painting *The Artist [Angelica Kauffman] in the Character of Design Listening to the Inspiration of Poetry* (see Fig. 8–7) shows a pair of balanced figures in Roman costume, Design on the left and Poetry on the right. Poetry is crowned with the laurel wreath of the Roman poet laureate. In addition, each figure holds a symbol of her art, Design a drawing board and Poetry a Greek lyre. To their left are a pair of Greek columns, which similarly invoke a feeling of antiquity and at the same time balance the female pair. Nowhere to be seen are secondary figures who might clamor for the viewer's attention. Our eyes focus solely on Design and Poetry. The simplicity, balance, and static quality of the painting creates a feeling of calm, serenity, and repose.

These same features are to be found in the aria "Voi che sapetc" ("You ladies who know") from Mozart's comic opera *The Marriage of Figaro* (1786). Here our ears concentrate exclusively on the melody. It consists of a succession of short phrases, almost all of them four measures in length. The opening provides a very clear example of a couplet of four-bar phrases arranged as an antecedent–consequent* pair.

EXAMPLE 8–1

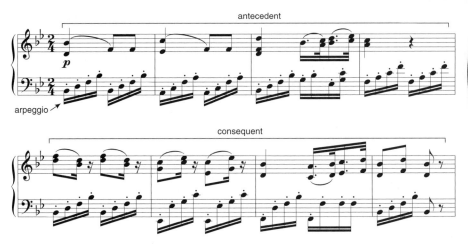

Subsequent phrases are also usually grouped in pairs. The simple chordal harmony (spaced out beneath as arpeggios*) supports, but in no way competes with, the lyrical top line. In fact, the heavy Baroque *basso continuo** has been entirely eliminated. Toward the end, the opening phrase returns to round off the whole. The text of the aria is a succession of couplets arranged to form seven stanzas. When the opening music returns at the end, so does the first stanza of

Vienna, Kunsthistorisches Museum

FIGURE 8–6

Marie Antoinette, in 1770 at the age of fifteen, seated at an early piano. In 1774 this Austrian princess became queen of France, but in 1793 she was beheaded at the height of French Revolution.

FIGURE 8–7

Angelica Kauffman's *The Artist in the Character of Design Listening to the Inspiration of Poetry* (1782).

The Iveagh Bequest, Kenwood, London

text. All is clarity, balance, and simplicity. Yet somehow, from the simplest of materials, the genius of Mozart creates a musical object of sublime beauty. The aria "You ladies who know" is the essence of classical perfection.

Listening Guide

WWW

Wolfgang Amadeus Mozart
Aria, "You ladies who know"
from the comic opera *The Marriage of Figaro* (1786)

6CD 2/4

Characters: Cherubino (see Fig. 8–4), an infatuated youth, and Suzanna, the older, wiser betrothed of Figaro. [Because Cherubino is a young adolescent, Mozart wrote the part for a high (soprano) voice. It is traditionally sung by a woman dressed as a boy.]
Situation: Cherubino (a soprano), sings to Suzanna of the pains and pleasures of love.

Time	Description	Italian	English
0:00	Orchestral introduction with antecedent–consequent phrases		
0:17	Voice enters with the antecedent phrase, inserts a new four-bar phrase, and then moves on to the consequent phrase	Voi che sapete che cosa è amor, donne, vedete s'io l'ho nel cor.	You ladies who know the nature of love, see if I have it within my heart.
0:42	A succession of paired phrases	Quello ch'io provo vi ridirò; è per me nuovo, capir non so. Sento un affetto pien di desir,	What I experience I will explain; it's so new to me I don't understand it. I have a feeling full of desire,
1:08	Charming major on "delightful" turns to anguished minor on "tormenting"	ch'ora è diletto, ch'ora è martir. Gelo, e poi sento l'alma avvampar, e in un momento torno a gelar. Ricero un bene fuori di me, non so chi'l tiene, non so cos'è.	sometimes delightful, sometimes tormenting. At first I freeze, and then my spirit burns, and then in a moment I turn to ice. I seek a treasure outside myself, I don't know who holds it, I don't even know what it is.
1:50	Rising repetitions insistently suggest "sighing and groaning"	Sospiro e gemo senza voler, palpito e tremo senza saper. Non trovo pace notte, nè dì ma pur mi piace languir così.	I sigh and groan without wanting to, I shake and tremble and know not why. I find no peace night or day, yet it only pleases me to languish so.
2:10	Peace is restored with return of opening phrase	Voi che sapete che cosa è amor, donne, vedete s'io l'ho nel cor.	You ladies who know the nature of love, see if I have it within my heart.

VIENNA: A CITY OF MUSIC

During the second half of the eighteenth century, Vienna rose to prominence as a place hospitable to the growth of music in the new Classical style. Indeed, Vienna became so important as a center of musical composition that the late eighteenth century is often called the age of the Viennese Classical style. The

city owed its importance to a for-
tuitous location. As the capital city
of the old Holy Roman Empire,
Vienna was the administrative
center for portions of modern-day
Germany, Croatia, Bosnia, Serbia,
Slovakia, The Czech Republic,
Hungary, and Italy, in addition
to all of Austria, and thus was
a cultural crossroads for Central
Europe (Fig. 8–8). Musicians such
as Christoph Gluck (1714–1787)
from Bohemia (The Czech Republic), Antonio Salieri (1750–1825)
from northern Italy, Franz Joseph
Haydn (1732–1809) from Rohrau
in lower Austria, Wolfgang Amadeus Mozart (1756–1791) from
Salzburg in upper Austria, and
Ludwig van Beethoven (1770–
1827) from the German Rhineland
gravitated toward Vienna for its
rich musical life. There were the-

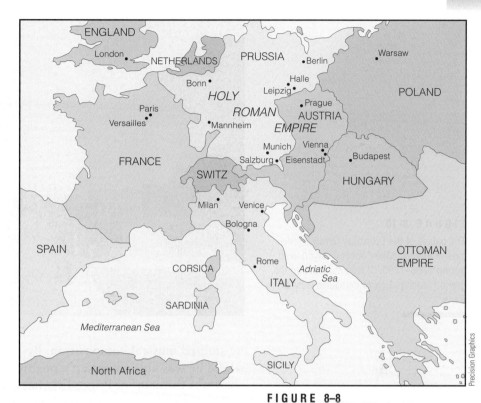

Precision Graphics

FIGURE 8–8

A map of eighteenth-century Europe
showing the Holy Roman Empire and
the principal musical cities, including
Vienna, Austria.

aters for German and Italian opera, concerts in the streets on fine summer
nights, and ballroom dances where as many as four thousand persons might
sway to a minuet, a contradance, or even a waltz by Mozart or Beethoven. In a
city of nearly 200,000 inhabitants (the fourth largest in Europe behind London, Paris, and Naples), there were estimated to be 300 piano teachers. "There
cannot be many cities in which musical amateurism is as widespread as it is
here. Everybody plays, everybody takes music lessons," reported a journal of
the day. And the musical allure of Vienna continued into the nineteenth century. In addition to native-born Franz Schubert (1797–1828), outsiders such as
Anton Bruckner (1824–1896), Johannes Brahms (1833–1897), and Gustav
Mahler (1860–1911) spent many of their most productive years there. Even
today Vienna remains the capital of a nation (Austria) that spends nearly as
much money on its state opera as it does on national defense.

FIGURE 8–9

Portrait of Joseph Haydn (ca. 1762–1763)
wearing a wig and the blue livery of the
Esterházy court.

FRANZ JOSEPH HAYDN (1732–1809)

Thus, it was only natural that Franz Joseph Haydn, the son of a wheelwright
from Rohrau in lower (eastern) Austria, should be sent to the capital to nur-
ture his obvious musical talent. Haydn was born in 1732, and by the age of
eight his pleasing voice had caught the attention of local church authorities.
Soon he was singing among the choirboys at the cathedral of St. Stephen in
Vienna. After nearly ten years of service his voice broke and he was abruptly
dismissed. For most of the 1750s Haydn eked out a meager living as a freelance musician—"miserable breadwinning" he called it: He gave keyboard
lessons, accompanied singers, and sang or played violin or organ at three
churches each Sunday, moving quickly from one to the next. All the while

With the kind permission of Professor Daniel Heartz

FIGURE 8–10

The palace of the Esterházy family southeast of Vienna, where Joseph Haydn lived during 1766–1790. It was modeled on the grand French palace of Versailles west of Paris.

he studied musical composition. By 1761 he had progressed to the point where he was able to obtain a position as composer and leader of the orchestra at the court of Prince Esterházy (Fig. 8–10).

the Esterházy as patrons

The Esterházy were a noble Hungarian family with extensive landholdings southeast of Vienna and a passionate interest in music. As did many wealthy aristocrats of the time, Prince Nikolaus Esterházy (1714–1790) maintained an orchestra, a chapel for singing religious music, and a theater for opera. When Haydn was first engaged he was required to sign a contract of employment, one that suggests the subservient place of the composer in eighteenth-century society:

> [He] and all the musicians shall appear in uniform, and the said Joseph Haydn shall take care that he and all the members of the orchestra follow the instructions given, and appear in white stocking, white linen, powdered, and with either a pigtail or a tiewig. . . .
>
> The said [Haydn] shall be under obligation to compose such music as his Serene Highness may command, and neither to communicate such compositions to any other person, nor to allow them to be copied, but he shall retain them for the absolute use of his Highness, and not compose for any other person without the knowledge and permission of his Highness.

Thus, not only did Haydn lead the life of a liveried servant at court, dressing like the other domestics, but he also was prohibited from circulating his music without the express permission of his patron. But Nikolaus Esterházy was a benign ruler, and Haydn's symphonies, quartets, and sonatas came to be known not only in Vienna but also in foreign capitals. In the 1770s they surfaced in Amsterdam, London, and Paris in "pirated" editions. Since there was no international copyright in those years, a publisher might simply print a work from a copyist's score without the composer's knowledge or consent. When Haydn signed another contract with Prince Nikolaus in 1779, there was no such "exclusive use" provision, and he began to sell his works to various publishers, sometimes consigning the same piece to two or three at the same time!

composing before the time of copyright

For a period of nearly thirty years Haydn served Nikolaus Esterházy, writing symphonies and divertimentos* for evening entertainment, operas for the court theater (see Fig. 10–3), and string trios in which the prince himself might participate. When Nikolaus died in 1790, the Esterházy orchestra was dismissed in favor of a smaller, military band. Haydn retained his title as court composer as well as his full salary, but he was now free to travel as he wished. After settling briefly in Vienna, he journeyed to London where he had been engaged at a substantial fee to compose and conduct. From this commission resulted the twelve **London Symphonies,** which were first performed in the Hanover Square Rooms (see Fig. 9–6), a large public concert hall built in part with capital supplied by Johann Christian Bach, old Bach's youngest son. Haydn stayed in London during 1791–1792 and returned again for the concert season 1794–1795. He was presented to the king and queen, received the honorary degree of doctor of music at Oxford, and was generally accorded the status of a visiting celebrity, as a letter written within a fortnight of his arrival attests:

Haydn in London

> Everyone wants to know me. I had to dine out six times up to now, and if I wanted, I could have an invitation every day; but first I must consider my health and second my work. Except for the nobility, I admit no callers 'til 2 o'clock in the afternoon.

After Haydn returned home to Vienna for good in the summer of 1795, he wrote mainly Masses for chorus and orchestra and two oratorios, *The Creation* (1798) and *The Seasons* (1801)—it seems that he had been deeply impressed by the performances of Handel's oratorios he had heard while in England. He died the following spring, on May 31, 1809, just two weeks after the besieging armies of Napoleon had conquered Vienna.

Haydn's long life, commitment to duty, and unflagging industry resulted in an impressive number of musical compositions: 104 symphonies, about 70 string quartets, nearly a dozen operas, 52 piano sonatas, 15 Masses, and 2 oratorios. He began composing before the death of Bach (1750) and did not put down his pen until about the time Beethoven set to work on his Fifth Symphony (1808). Thus, Haydn not only witnessed but, more than any other composer, helped to create the mature Classical style.

Haydn's works

Despite his accomplishments, Haydn did not rebel against the modest station assigned to him in traditional eighteenth-century society: "I have associated with emperors, kings, and many great people," he said, "and I have heard many flattering things from them, but I would not live in familiar relations with such persons; I prefer to be close to people of my own standing." And though keenly aware of his own musical gifts, he was quick to recognize talent in others, especially Mozart: "Friends often flatter me that I have some genius, but he [Mozart] stood far above me."

WOLFGANG AMADEUS MOZART (1756–1791)

Indeed who, except possibly Bach, can match the diversity, breadth of expression, and perfect formal control present in the best works of Mozart? (Fig. 8–11). Wolfgang Amadeus Mozart was born in the mountain town of Salzburg, Austria, in 1756. His father, Leopold, was a violinist in the orchestra of the archbishop of Salzburg, and his older sister, Nannerl, was also a talented performer. Leopold was quick to recognize the musical gifts of his son, who by the

FIGURE 8–11

An unfinished portrait of Mozart painted by his brother-in-law Joseph Lange during 1789–1790.

Mozart Museum, Salzburg

age of six was playing the piano, violin, and organ as well as composing. The Mozart family coached off to Vienna, where the children displayed their musical wares before Empress Maria Theresa (1717–1780). They then embarked on a three-year tour of Northern Europe that included extended stops in Munich, Brussels, Paris, London, Amsterdam, and Geneva (Fig. 8–12). In London, Wolfgang sat on the knee of Johann Christian Bach (1735–1782) and improvised a fugue. And here, at the age of eight, he heard his first two symphonies performed. Eventually, the Mozarts made their way back to Salzburg. But in 1768 they were off again to Vienna, where the now twelve-year-old Wolfgang staged a production of his first opera, *Bastien und Bastienne*, in the home of the famous Dr. Franz Anton Mesmer (1733–1815), the inventor of the theory of animal magnetism (hence, "to mesmerize"). The next year father and son visited the major cities of Italy, including Rome, where, on 8 July 1770, the pope dubbed Wolfgang a Knight of the Golden Spur (Fig. 8–13). Although the aim of this globe-trotting was to acquire fame and fortune, the result was that Mozart, unlike Haydn, was exposed at an early age to a wealth of musical styles—French Baroque, English choral, German polyphonic, and Italian vocal. His extraordinarily keen ear absorbed them all, and ultimately they increased the breadth and substance of his music.

A period of relative stability followed: For much of the 1770s Mozart resided in Salzburg, where he served as violinist and composer to the archbishop. But the reigning archbishop, Colloredo, was a stern, miserly man who had little sympathy for Mozart, genius or not (the composer referred to him as the "Archboobie"). Mozart was given a place in the orchestra, a small salary, and his board. Like the musicians at the court of Esterházy, those at Salzburg ate with the cooks and valets. For a Knight of the Golden Spur who had played for kings and queens across Europe, this was humble fare indeed, and Mozart chafed under this system of aristocratic patronage. After several unpleasant scenes in the spring of 1781, the twenty-five-year-old composer cut himself free of the archbishop and determined to make a living as a freelance musician in Vienna.

Mozart chose Vienna partly because of the city's rich musical life and partly because it was a comfortable distance from his overbearing father. In a letter to his sister written in the spring of 1782, Wolfgang spells out his daily regimen in the Austrian capital.

> My hair is always done by six o'clock in the morning and by seven I am fully dressed. I then compose until nine. From nine to one I give lessons. Then I lunch, unless I am invited to some house where they lunch at two or even three o'clock. . . . I can never work before five or six o'clock in the evening, and even then I am often prevented by a concert. If I am not prevented, I compose until nine. Then I go to my dear Constanze.

FIGURES 8-12 AND 8-13

(top) The child Mozart at the keyboard, with his sister Nannerl and his father Leopold, in Paris in 1764 during their three-year tour of Europe. (bottom) Young Mozart proudly wearing the collar of a Knight of the Order of the Golden Spur, an honor conferred upon him for his musical skills by Pope Clement XIV in July 1770.

Bridgeman Art Library, London/NY

Civico Museo Bibliografico Musicale, Bologna

What's a Genius? Was Mozart a Musical Genius?

The notion of "genius" likely involves at least two types of special qualities. Some people are clearly creative geniuses. They have the capacity to think "outside the box"—to formulate intellectual constructs or works of art that are original, compelling, and visionary so as to make some extraordinary contribution to human civilization. So measured, the poet Shakespeare, the painter Michelangelo, and the scientist Isaac Newton would clearly qualify as geniuses. Other persons are what might be designated cognitive geniuses. They have the ability to process or manipulate information with incredible facility. Those who can do large sums in their heads, who have photographic memories, or who have absolute musical pitch can be called cognitive geniuses. By any criteria, Mozart was both a creative and a cognitive genius.

Although Mozart may not have been the most precocious child composer in the history of music—that honor would have to go to Schubert or Mendelssohn—once he reached the age of twenty-two, he tossed off one masterpiece after another with frightening frequency. Moreover, Mozart's prodigious cognitive skills are legendary. As a child he could identify the notes played in any chord, judge the pitch of an instrument within an eighth of a tone, or pick out a wrong note in a musical score while crawling on his back across a table. At the age of fourteen he heard a motet sung in the Sistine Chapel in Rome and wrote it down by memory, note for

note. This motet was about two minutes long and in several voices. How much music can we remember on first hearing—four or five seconds of the melody? Obviously Mozart could store and process a great deal of music in his mind's ear. And not just music but other sounds as well! Mozart was a superb mimic and he learned to speak several foreign languages almost upon first hearing. Little wonder that the great German poet Goethe (1749–1832) referred to him as "the human incarnation of a divine force of creation."

But with the gifts of genius came disorders of personality—geniuses are rarely "normal." Mozart fidgeted constantly with both hands and feet, and his mouth filled the air with childish jokes and puns. Until the age of ten or so, he was terrified by the sound of the trumpet, and out-of-tune instruments brought physical pain to his ears (was he mildly autistic?). Mozart's numerous apartments in Vienna were messy, indeed chaotic. He often both ate and composed in bed. Never did he attend a school or receive a systematic education beyond the art of music, though his letters reveal him to be highly intelligent. Mozart owned few books and read fewer. His almost sole interest, indeed obsession, was music. When possessed by this muse, he became oblivious of the growing chaos around him. Ironically, his inner world of music, judging from the works he created, was all balance, order, and perfection.

Against the advice of his father, Wolfgang married his "dear Constanze" (Weber) in the summer of 1782 (Fig. 8–14). But, alas, she was as romantic and impractical as he, though less given to streaks of hard work. In addition to his composing, teaching, and performing, Mozart now found time to study the music of Bach and Handel, play chamber music with his friend Joseph Haydn, and join the Freemasons. Although still very much a practicing Catholic, he was attracted to this fraternity of the Enlightenment because of its belief in tolerance and universal brotherhood. His opera *Die Zauberflöte* (*The Magic Flute*, 1791) is viewed by many as a hymn in praise of masonic ideals.

The years 1785–1787 witnessed the peak of Mozart's success and the creation of many of his greatest works. He had a full complement of pupils, played several concerts a week, and enjoyed lucrative commissions as a composer. Piano concertos, string quartets, and symphonies flowed from his pen, as well as his two greatest Italian operas, *The Marriage of Figaro* and *Don Giovanni*. But *Don Giovanni*, a huge success when first performed in Prague in 1787, was little appreciated when mounted in Vienna in the spring of 1788. "The opera is divine, perhaps even more beautiful than *Figaro*," declared Emperor Joseph II, "but no food for

FIGURE 8–14

St. Stephen's Cathedral, Vienna, where Mozart was married in 1782 and where his funeral was held in 1791.

Museum der Stadt Wien, Vienna

the teeth of my Viennese." Mozart's music was no longer in vogue. His pupils began to dwindle and the elite failed to subscribe to his concerts. His style was thought to be too dense, too intense, too dissonant. One publisher warned him: "Write in a more popular style or else I cannot print or pay for more of your music."

Mozart's last year

Although now in declining health, Mozart was still capable of creating the greatest sort of masterpieces. In his last year (1791) he composed a superb clarinet concerto and the German comic opera *The Magic Flute*, and began work on a Requiem Mass, one he was never to finish. Mozart died on December 5, 1791, at the age of thirty-five. The precise reason for his death has never been determined, though kidney failure made worse by needless blood-letting was the most likely cause. No single event in the history of music was more tragic than the premature loss of Mozart. What he would have given to the world had he enjoyed the long life of a Bach or a Haydn!

CLASSICAL STYLE IN MUSIC

Even for a music lover of many years' experience, it is sometimes difficult to distinguish the sound of Haydn from that of Mozart or, similarly, to differentiate late Haydn or Mozart from early Beethoven. This easy confusion points up the fact that music in the Classical period is more homogeneous in style than in any other period in the history of music—pieces in the same genre but by different composers tend to sound like one another. Clearly, there was then a consensus among creative musicians as to what music was supposed to sound like, an ideal tacitly agreed upon, not only by Haydn, Mozart, and Beethoven in Vienna but also by lesser composers working in Milan, Paris, London, and elsewhere. The Viennese Classical style embodied universal principles in an age that greatly valued universal ideals.

classical balance and symmetry

Much has been written about the Classical style in music: its quiet grace, noble simplicity, purity, and serenity. It is certainly "classical" in the sense that extreme emphasis is placed on formal clarity, order, and balance. Compared with the relentless, grandiose, sometimes pompous sound of the Baroque, Classical music is lighter in tone, more natural, yet less predictable. It is even capable of humor and surprise, as when Mozart again and again leads up to, but carefully avoids, a cadence, or when Haydn explodes with a thunderous chord in the midst of a sea of quiet. But what is it in precise musical terms that creates this feeling of levity and grace, of clarity and balance, in Classical music?

MELODY

antecedent and consequent phrases

Perhaps the first thing that strikes the listener about the music of Haydn or Mozart is that the theme is often tuneful, catchy, even singable. Not only are melodies simple and short but also the phrases tend to be organized in antecedent–consequent*, or question–answer, pairs. Indeed, antecedent–consequent phrases in significant number appear for the first time in the history of music in the Classical period. The melody usually progresses by playing out these short phrases in symmetrical groups of two, three, four, eight, twelve, or sixteen bars. The brevity of the phrase and frequent cadences allow for ample light and air to penetrate the melodic line.

Below is the theme from the second movement of Mozart's Piano Concerto in C major (1785). It is composed of two three-bar phrases—an antecedent and a consequent phrase. The melody is light and airy, yet perfectly balanced. It is also singable and quite memorable—indeed, it has been turned into a popular movie theme (the "love song" from *Elvira Madigan*). Compare this with the long, asymmetrical melodies of the Baroque that were often instrumental in character (see page 137).

EXAMPLE 8–2

HARMONY

After about 1750 all music assumed a more homophonic, less polyphonic character. The new tuneful melody was supported by a simple harmony. In the preceding example only two chords, tonic and dominant, support Mozart's lovely melody. The bass still generates the harmony, but it does not always move in the regular, constant fashion typified by the Baroque walking bass*. Rather, the bass might sit on the bottom of one chord for several beats, even several measures, then move rapidly, and then stop again. Thus, the rate at which chords change—the harmonic rhythm as it is called—is much more fluid and flexible with Classical composers.

flexible harmonic rhythm

To avoid a feeling of inactivity when the harmony is static, Classical composers invented new accompanying patterns. Sometimes, as in Ex. 8–2, they simply repeat the accompanying chord in a uniform triplet rhythm. More common is the pattern called the **Alberti bass**, named after the minor Italian keyboard composer Domenico Alberti (1710–1740) who popularized this figure. Instead of playing the pitches of a chord all together, the performer spreads them out to provide a continual stream of sound. Mozart used an Alberti bass at the beginning of his famous C major piano sonata (1788):

EXAMPLE 8–3

Alberti bass

The Alberti pattern serves essentially the same function as the modern "boogie-woogie" bass. It provides a feeling of harmonic activity for those moments when, in fact, the harmony is stationary.

RHYTHM

Rhythm, too, is more flexible in the hands of Haydn and Mozart. It animates the stop-and-go character of their melodies and harmonies. Rapid motion

Mozart and Amadeus

Perhaps you have seen the extraordinary film *Amadeus* (1985), based on a play by Peter Schaffer, and wondered if the Mozart portrayed there bore any relation to the real Mozart. The answer is, in a few ways, yes; in most ways, no. To be sure, Mozart's lifestyle was chaotic, he had expensive tastes, and he was often downright silly in his behavior. Yet there is no hint of drunkenness in the contemporary documents; he had an excellent, if erratic income; and his childish behavior, according to his brother-in-law Joseph Lange, was the way in which he released excess tension built up during concentrated periods of creative activity. Mozart did not die poor. Indeed, his income from two major operas in 1791 and the famous Requiem Mass made his last year one of his most lucrative. Nor was he abandoned to suffer a pauper's funeral. He received the same sort of burial (placed in a common grave) as eighty-five percent of the upper-middle-class in Vienna at that time. Nor, finally, was Mozart poisoned by his principal rival in Vienna, the composer Antonio Salieri (1750–1825). Salieri, court composer to Emperor Joseph II and his two successors, was a universally respected, if not supremely gifted, musician who later went on to become, at

various times, the teacher of Beethoven, Schubert, Liszt, and even one of Mozart's two sons. Salieri may have been a mediocre composer, but he was no murderer.

A scene from Amadeus. *Mozart did, in fact, keep a billiard table in his bedroom.*

may be followed by repose and then further quick movement, but there is little of the driving, perpetual motion of Baroque musical rhythm.

TEXTURE

Musical texture was also transformed in the latter half of the eighteenth century, mainly because composers began to concentrate less on writing dense counterpoint than on creating charming melodies. No longer are independent polyphonic lines superimposed, layer upon layer, as in a fugue of Bach or a polyphonic chorus of Handel. The lessening of counterpoint, then, made for a lighter, more transparent sound, especially in the middle range of the texture. Mozart, after a study of Bach and Handel in the early 1780s, infused his symphonies, quartets, and concertos with greater polyphonic content, but this seems to have caused the pleasure-loving Viennese to think his music too dense!

The Classical Orchestra

The development of the orchestra during the Classical period is discussed in connection with the creation of the Classical symphony in Chapter 10 (page 206). For the moment, suffice it to say that during the late eighteenth century the orchestra grows in size as a direct response to the larger audience that crowded into the new public concert halls. The strings still constitute the core of the orchestra, but the woodwinds—oboes, flutes, bassoons, and the new clarinets—gain increased autonomy. They no longer merely double or echo the violins and the bass line as they had during the Baroque era. Henceforth, they enter and depart, seemingly at will, now to play a theme as a solo, now to thicken momentarily the musical texture or to add a dash of instrumental color.

FIGURE 8–15

The composer Antonio Salieri (1750–1825). History has unfairly portrayed him as Mozart's nemesis.

The Dramatic Quality of Classical Music

What is perhaps most revolutionary in the music of Haydn, Mozart, and their younger contemporary, Beethoven, is its capacity for rapid change and endless fluctuation. Recall that in earlier times a work by Purcell, Corelli, Vivaldi, or Bach would establish one "affect," or mood, to be rigidly maintained from beginning to end—the rhythm, melody, and harmony all progressing in a continuous, uninterrupted flow. Such a uniform approach to expression is part of the "single-mindedness" of Baroque art. Now, with Haydn, Mozart, and the young Beethoven, the mood or character of a piece may change radically within a few short phrases. An energetic theme in rapid notes may be followed by a second one that is slow, lyrical, and tender. Similarly, textures may change quickly from light and airy to dense and more contrapuntal so as to create tension and excitement. For the first time composers began to call for crescendos and diminuendos, a gradual increase or lessening of the dynamic level, so that the volume of sound might continually fluctuate. When skilled orchestras made use of this technique, audiences were fascinated and rose to their feet. Keyboard players, too, now took up the crescendo and diminuendo, assuming that the new multidynamic piano was at hand in place of the old, less flexible harpsichord. These rapid changes in mood, texture, color, and dynamics give to Classical music a new sense of urgency and drama. The listener feels a constant flux and flow, not unlike the continual swings of mood we all experience.

frequent changes of mood

crescendos and diminuendos

Classical Forms

How did composers of the Classical period reconcile their desire to express changing moods, colors, and textures with the Classical principles of grace, order, and balance? They did so, in a word, by means of form. All of the elements of expression—themes, harmonic relationships, colors, textures, dynamics—are precisely positioned within the boundaries of strict musical form. Limits are set as to where the changing or conflicting elements may be placed, how intense they may be, and how long they may last. By placing the musical events, or sections, in a carefully regulated order, the composer achieves grace, balance, and proportion. As one critic observed in 1777: "A knowledge of the proper ordering of sections is essential to any friend of music who wishes to be a conoisseur and who desires to derive pleasure from the workings of this art." Indeed, so important is form in Classical music that the subject requires a chapter unto itself.

form controls the unfolding of musical events

Key Words

Alberti bass (179)
Antonio Salieri (180)
comic opera (169)
London
   Symphonies (175)

Nikolaus
   Esterházy (174)
opera buffa (169)
pianoforte (170)

Salzburg (175)
The Magic Flute (177)
*The Marriage
   of Figaro* (169)

A checklist of musical style in the Classical era is given on page 70.

Chapter 9

Museum der Stadt Wien

Classical Forms

To understand and appreciate Classical music, it is especially important to understand musical form. For in the Classical period, more so than any other, a small number of forms—ternary, sonata–allegro, rondo, and theme and variations—regulated nearly all music. Indeed, there are few compositions written during the years 1750–1820 that are not shaped according to one of these. At the same time, it is important to realize that none of these forms was unique to the Classical period. Ternary form can be found in the earliest examples of Gregorian chant* as well as in all *da capo** arias of the Baroque era (1600–1750). The rondo had its origins in the popular dances and songs of the Middle Ages, though its repetitive structure has made it attractive to such diverse musicians as Mozart, Beethoven, Elton John, and Sting. And theme and variations, as both a musical and a literary process, is at once ancient and eternal. Only sonata–allegro form actually came into being in the Classical period. It dominated musical structure during the time of Mozart and Haydn, but it also remained a potent force in the works of most composers of the Romantic era (1820–1900) and in the creations of some twentieth-century musicians as well. Thus, the forms discussed in this chapter should be thought of not as belonging to the Classical period alone, but in the broader meaning of the term "classical." With the single exception of the more recent sonata–allegro form, they are all timeless and universal.

FIGURE 9–1

A ball at the Redoutensaal in the emperor's palace in Vienna, ca. 1800. Mozart, Haydn, and, later, Beethoven composed minuets and "German dances" for these events, which sometimes attracted nearly 4,000 fee-paying dancers. The orchestra can be seen in the gallery at the left.

TERNARY FORM

Ternary structure (**ABA**) is a form often encountered in the history of music. Yet the simple principle of presentation, contrast, and return was especially favored by Classical composers for its simplicity and directness. Everyone is familiar with the tune *Twinkle, Twinkle, Little Star* (also the tune of *Bah, Bah, Black Sheep*, and *A, B, C, D, E, F, G*). Less well known is the fact that it began life as a French folk song, *Ah, vous dirai-je, Maman (Ah, Let Me Tell You, Mama)*. Wolfgang Amadeus Mozart (1756–1791) came to know the melody when he toured France as a youth, and he wrote it down in a keyboard version. Here is his setting of it:

EXAMPLE 9–1

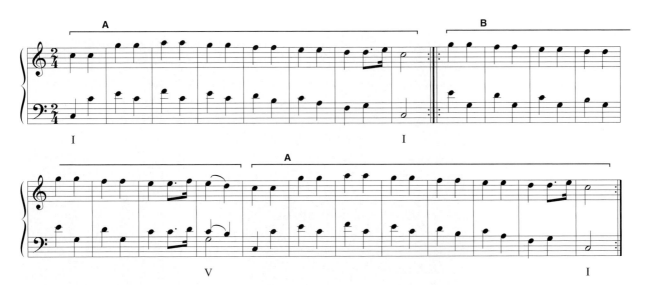

Notice that both units (**A** and **BA**) are repeated. Observe also that **A** is in the tonic, **B** emphasizes a contrasting key (here the dominant), and the returning **A** is again in the tonic. If a piece in ternary form is in a minor key, the contrasting **B** section will usually be in what is called the **relative major**.[†] Needless to say, most pieces in ternary form are more complex than *Twinkle, Twinkle*. Most have more contrast of melody, key, and/or mood between the **B** section and the surrounding units of **A**.[††]

Minuet and Trio

The most common use of ternary form in the Classical period is found in the minuet and trio. Strictly speaking, the **minuet** is not a form, but rather a genre of dance implying an elegant musical style, stately tempo, and constant triple meter. It first appeared at the French royal court early in the reign of King Louis XIV (1643–1715). Most minuets in the Baroque era were in binary form (**AB**). But by 1770 the minuet was usually composed in ternary form and grouped with a second minuet possessing a much lighter texture. Because this second minuet had originally been played by only three instruments, it was called the **trio**, a name that persisted into the nineteenth century, no matter how many instrumental lines were required in this second minuet. Once the trio was finished, convention dictated that there be a return to the first minuet, now performed without repeats. Since the trio also was composed in ternary form, an **ABA** pattern was heard three times in succession. (In the following, the **ABA** structure of the trio is represented by **CDC**, to distinguish it from the minuet.) And, since the trio was different from the surrounding minuet, the entire movement minuet–trio–minuet formed an **ABA** arrangement.

minuet: an elegant dance

A (minuet)	B (trio)	A (minuet)
‖: A :‖‖: BA :‖	‖: C :‖‖: DC :‖	ABA

[†]Relative keys are keys that share the same key signature, E♭ major and C minor (both with three flats), for example.

[††]Note for instructors: on the designation "ternary form" for this and other pieces, see the Preface in the front of this book.

CORBIS/Bettmann

FIGURE 9–2

Couples in the late eighteenth century dancing the stately minuet. In some areas of Europe at this time women were forbidden to dance the minuet because it was thought to involve excessive body contact!

Mozart's *Eine kleine Nachtmusik* (*A Little Night Music*), written in the summer of 1787, is among his most popular works. It is a **serenade**, a light, multi-movement piece for strings alone or small orchestra, one intended for public entertainment and often performed outdoors. Although we do not know the precise occasion for which Mozart composed it, we might well imagine *A Little Night Music* providing the musical backdrop for a torch-lit party in a formal Viennese garden. The *Menuetto* appears as the third of four movements in this serenade, and is a model of grace and concision.

Mozart's A Little Night Music

EXAMPLE 9–2

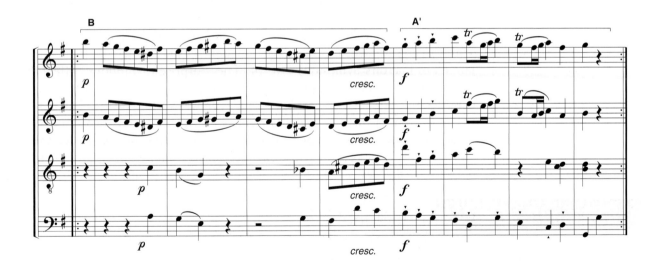

As you can see, the **B** section is only four measures long, and the return to **A** does not reproduce the full eight bars of the original but only the last four—thus, this pattern might be viewed as **ABA'**. In the trio that follows, a lighter texture is created as the first violin plays a solo melody quietly above a soft accompaniment in the lower strings. The **D** section of the trio is distinguished by a *forte* stepwise run up and down the scale, and then the quiet melody of **C** returns to complete the ternary form. Finally, the minuet appears once again, but now without repeats.

formal symmetry

Listening Guide

Wolfgang Amadeus Mozart
Serenade, *A Little Night Music* (1787)
Third movement, Minuet and Trio

6CD 2/6;
2CD 1/9

Form: ternary

MINUET		Form	Number of bars
0:00	Strong violin melody with active bass	A	8
0:10	Repeat of A		
0:20	Softer violin scales	B	4
0:26	Return of violin melody	A'	4
0:30	Repeat of B and A'		
TRIO			
0:41	Soft, stepwise melody in violins	C	8
0:52	Repeat of C		
1:03	Louder violins	D	4
1:09	Return of soft stepwise melody	C	8
1:20	Repeat of D and C		
MINUET			
1:37	Return of A	A	8
1:48	Return of B	B	4
1:54	Return of violin melody A'	A'	4

We have said that Classical music is symmetrical and proportional. Note here how both minuet and trio are balanced by a return of the opening music (**A** and **C**) and how all the sections are either four or eight bars in length.

If Mozart's *Menuetto* represents the minuet in its most succinct form, the minuet of Haydn's Symphony No. 94 (The "Surprise" Symphony) offers a more typically symphonic presentation of this ternary design. The form is considerably extended, in part because Haydn was writing for a full orchestra rather than a small string ensemble as in Mozart's serenade. (It is axiomatic in music that the larger the performing force, the more extended the musical form.) But keeping the model of Mozart's simple ternary minuet in our ears, we can easily follow Haydn's more expansive formal plan.

Listening Guide

Franz Joseph Haydn
Symphony No. 94, The "Surprise" Symphony (1791)
Third movement, Minuet and Trio

6CD 2/7

Form: ternary

MINUET	[	] = repeats		Form
0:00		Rollicking dance in triple meter begins		A
0:19		Repeat of A		
0:40	[1:33]	Imitation and lighter texture		B
0:50	[1:43]	Strong harmonic movement		
0:58	[1:51]	Bass sits on dominant note		
1:05	[1:59]	Return of A		A'

(Continued on next page)

1:13	[2:07]	Pause on dominant chord	
1:23	[2:17]	Gentle rocking over tonic pedal point*	
TRIO			
2:27		Light descending scales for violins and bassoon	C
2:37		Repeat of **C**	
2:46	[3:08]	Two-voice counterpoint for 1st and 2nd violins	D
2:58	[3:21]	Bassoon reentry signals return of **C**	C
MINUET			
3:30		Return to minuet	A
3:51		Return of **B**	B
4:16		Return of **A**	A'

SONATA–ALLEGRO FORM

Sonata–allegro form is at once the most complex and most satisfying of musical forms. It is also the only form to originate during the Classical period (1750–1820). We must keep in mind, however, the distinction between the general term "sonata" and the more specific term "sonata–allegro form"—that is, between the multimovement composition called the sonata and the single-movement form called sonata–allegro.

Recall that in the Baroque period a multimovement work was often called a sonata, either a solo sonata or a trio sonata. These consisted of a succession of binary-form movements that often proceeded slow–fast–slow–fast (see page 124). By the early Classical period, however, the usual arrangement of movements for a sonata had become fast–slow–minuet–fast, or occasionally just fast–slow–fast. When played by a solo instrument like the piano, this group of movements is called a solo sonata. When this same sort of three- or four-movement composition is written for string quartet or quintet, it is called simply a string quartet or quintet. And when intended for a full symphonic orchestra, it is called a symphony.

Yet no matter what the performing force, the form of each of these movements can be one of several different types. As we have seen, if there are four movements the third is usually a minuet with trio. The second and fourth movements might be, for example, in rondo form or theme and variations form (both discussed later in the chapter). The fast first movement, however, is almost invariably written in what is called **sonata–allegro form**. Thus, the term "sonata–allegro" derives from the fact that sonata–allegro form was usually applied to the fast (allegro) first movement. Slow second movements and fast finales sometimes make use of sonata–allegro form as well. To show at least two typical arrangements, here are the movements and forms of Mozart's *A Little Night Music* and Haydn's Symphony No. 94:

"sonata" contrasted with "sonata–allegro form"

Mozart, *A Little Night Music* (1787)

Fast	Slow	Minuet and Trio	Fast
(sonata–allegro)	(rondo)	(ternary)	(rondo)

Haydn, Symphony No. 94 (1791)

Fast	Slow	Minuet and Trio	Fast
(sonata–allegro)	(theme and variations)	(ternary)	(sonata–allegro)

a dramatic form

Sonata–allegro form came into being around 1750 as a means of incorporating more drama and conflict into a single movement of music. Like a great play, a movement in sonata–allegro form has the potential for dramatic presentation, conflict, and resolution. The form provides a stage on which the musical drama can play out in any number of individual ways. Sonata–allegro form would continue to serve composers into the Romantic period and beyond. Almost all first movements of symphonies and string quartets are written in sonata-allegro form. Thus, every serious listener of classical music should have it committed to memory.

The Shape of Sonata–Allegro Form

To get a sense of what might happen in a typical first movement of a sonata, string quartet, symphony, or serenade, look at the diagram appearing below. As with all models of this sort, this one is an ideal, an abstraction of what commonly occurs in sonata–allegro form. It is not a blueprint for any composition. Composers have exhibited countless individual solutions to the task of writing in this and every other form. Yet such a model can be of great use to the listener because it gives a clear picture of what we might expect to hear. Ultimately, once we have embraced the form and are familiar with its workings, we will take as much delight in having our musical expectations foiled or delayed as in having them fulfilled.

SONATA-ALLEGRO FORM

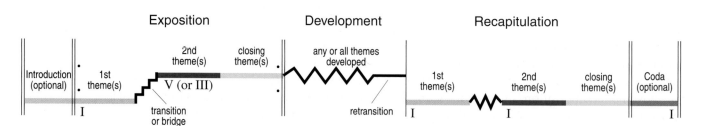

In its broad outline, sonata–allegro form looks much like ternary form. It consists of an **ABA** plan, with the **B** section providing contrast in mood, key, and thematic treatment. The initial **A** in sonata–allegro form is called the exposition, the **B** the development, and the return to **A** the recapitulation. In the early Classical period the exposition (**A**) and the development and recapitulation (**BA**) were each repeated, as in ternary form. But Haydn and Mozart eventually dropped the repeat of the development and recapitulation, and composers of the Romantic period gradually dispensed with the repeat of the exposition. Let's take each of these sections in turn and see what we are likely to hear.

EXPOSITION

The purpose of the **exposition** is to present, or expose, the main thematic material of the movement, just as the exposition of a fugue exposes the subject.

First theme The exposition begins with a first theme, or group of themes, and can be anywhere from four to forty measures or more in length. If not easily singable, the first theme is at least distinctive, memorable enough so that later returns and references to it will be recognized and enjoyed by the listener. The first theme is always in the tonic key (I).

presentation

Transition The aim of the **transition,** or **bridge** as it is sometimes called, is to carry the music from the tonic to the dominant (from tonic to relative major if the movement is in a minor key) and prepare for the arrival of the second theme. The transition is usually made up of rapidly moving figural patterns—running scales, arpeggios*, and the like—which are frequently put forth as melodic sequences*. In order to effect the tonic-dominant (I–V) modulation, the bass becomes active and generates quick chord changes. This lively harmonic movement may subside if the transition ends with a solid cadence.

Second theme Not only does a new melody usually appear at this point, but it enters in the fresh context of a new key, the dominant or, less frequently, the relative major. The second theme often contrasts in mood with the first: If the first is rapid and assertive, the second may be more languid and lyrical. Because a clear-cut theme holds center stage here, the accompanying harmonic material is stable, not modulatory. The listener's attention is focused on melody, not on harmonic movement.

Closing theme The second theme usually gives way to a closing theme, one that is normally light and carefree in style. It often ends in a harmonically simple way, merely rocking back and forth between dominant and tonic chords. The static harmony and repeated full cadences* signal the conclusion of the exposition. The piece has stopped moving forward, and therefore the exposition is at an end. Tradition requires that the exposition now be repeated note for note.

DEVELOPMENT

As the name indicates, the **development** is a section in which there is a further working out, or developing, of the thematic material presented in the exposition. Both the first and the second theme may be manipulated, and occasionally even the closing theme is exploited as well. A theme may be elaborated on and expanded, or, just as often, it may be taken apart, reduced to just a few notes to be tossed around from instrument to instrument. One typical technique is for the composer to show the contrapuntal possibilities lurking within a theme by using it as the subject of a brief fugue*. (A fugue within a movement of a sonata is called a **fugato.**) Like the transition, the development tends to have unstable harmonies. The use of melodic sequence* is plentiful, and this encourages rapid modulation from one key, or tonal center, to another. Only toward the end of the development, in the area called the **retransition,** does tonal stability return, often in the form of a pedal point* on the dominant note. When the dominant chord (V) finally gives way to the tonic (I), the recapitulation begins.

confrontation

RECAPITULATION

After the turmoil of the development, the listener greets the return of the first theme and the tonic key of the exposition with welcome relief. Though the **recapitulation** is not an exact, note-for-note repetition of the exposition, it nonetheless presents the same musical events in the same order, reaffirming

resolution

FIGURE 9-3
A portrait of the young Mozart at the keyboard painted in 1770 during his first trip to Italy.

optional elements

FIGURE 9-4
The Mozart family (1781) with Wolfgang and his sister playing four-hands at the keyboard, his father with violin, and a portrait of his deceased mother on the wall.

the logic and integrity of the original. The only change that regularly occurs in this restatement is the rewriting of the transition, or bridge. Because the movement must end in the tonic, the bridge must not modulate to the dominant (or relative major) as before but stay at home in the tonic key. Thus, the recapitulation imparts to the listener not only a feeling of return to familiar surroundings but also an increased sense of harmonic stability, as all themes are now heard in the tonic key.

The following two elements are optional to sonata–allegro form.

INTRODUCTION

About half the mature symphonies of Haydn and Mozart have brief introductions before the exposition begins. These are, without exception, slow and stately and usually filled with ominous or puzzling chords designed to set the listener wondering what sort of musical excursion he or she is about to undertake. That the introduction is not part of the exposition is shown by the fact that it is never repeated.

CODA

As the name **coda** (Italian for "tail") indicates, this is a section added to the end of the sonata–allegro movement. It may be just a few bars long, as is most often the case with Mozart, or it may, in the hands of Beethoven, for example, expand into an independent section, one equal in size to the development. The melodic material is usually no more than a short motive extracted from the first theme or sometimes from the closing theme, or it may be a newly created motive. But whatever the source, normally this motive is sounded again and again in conjunction with repeating dominant–tonic chords, or merely the tonic chord alone played over and over, all intended to create a grand effect and announce to the listener that the movement is at an end. Again, thematic repetition at the same pitch level and static harmony are two ways a composer can signal the end of a section or the end of a piece. The more of this that goes on, the greater the feeling of conclusion.

Hearing Sonata–Allegro Form

Given its central place in the music of Mozart and Haydn, and later in Beethoven, Schubert, Brahms, and Mahler, among others, sonata–allegro is perhaps the most important of all musical forms. But it is also the most complex and the most difficult for the listener to follow. A sonata–allegro movement tends to be long, lasting anywhere from a minimum of four minutes in a simple piece of the Classical period to twenty minutes or more in a full-blown movement of the Romantic era. Moreover, it embodies many kinds of musical events and many styles of writing—thematic and transitional, for example. And finally, sonata–allegro form does not merely involve one theme but several, and all of these have to be remembered and their development followed.

How does one get the better of this musical beast? First of all, be sure you have memorized the diagram of sonata–allegro form given on page 188. This will help you know what to expect, what you are likely to hear. Next, sharpen your ability to grasp and remember melodies, or at least the beginnings of melodies. If necessary, return to Chapter 2 and practice some melodic graphing (see page 21). And finally, think carefully about the four principal styles of writing found in sonata–allegro form. Each has its own distinct character. A thematic section has clearly recognizable themes or melodies, sometimes even singable tunes. The transition is full of melodic movement, sequences, and rapid chord changes. The development is also disjunct, agitated, contrapuntal, and harmonically active, but it makes use of a recognizable theme, albeit extended or cut up into small pieces. And a concluding passage, whether at the end of the exposition, in the retransition at the end of the development, or in the coda at the end of the movement, tends to repeat motives or cadential phrases over and over above a static harmony. Each of these four styles has a specific function within sonata–allegro form: to state, to move, to develop, or to conclude. The composer employs a rhetoric of music, just as the orator practices a rhetoric of speech. Much of your success in hearing sonata–allegro form will come from your ability to recognize each of these four functional types of music. With this by way of preparation, let's listen to a movement in sonata–allegro form.

four functional styles within sonata–allegro form

For this we once again turn to the familiar sound of Mozart's *A Little Night Music.* The first movement (*Allegro*) of this four-movement serenade offers a concise, graceful example of sonata–allegro principle. Yet even a straightforward sonata–allegro-form movement such as this requires the listener's full attention. The following Listening Guide is not typical of this book. It is unusually lengthy so as to lead you through the difficult process of hearing sonata–allegro form. First read the description in the center column, then listen to the music, stopping where indicated to rehear each of the principal sections of the form.

Likely this movement, one of the favorites in the classical repertoire, will sound like an old friend. Its sophisticated, elegant sounds have been used as background music in countless radio and TV commercials to suggest that the product is classically elegant.

Listening Guide
WWW

| Wolfgang Amadeus Mozart
A Little Night Music (1787)
First movement, *Allegro* (fast) | 6CD 2/5;
2CD 1/8 |

Form: sonata–allegro

FIRST THEME GROUP [ ] = repeats

| 0:00 | [1:37] | The movement opens aggressively with a leaping, fanfarelike motive. It then moves on to a more confined, pressing melody with sixteenth notes agitating beneath, and ends with a relaxed, stepwise descent down the G major scale, which is repeated with light ornamentation. |

STOP: LISTEN TO THE FIRST THEME GROUP AGAIN

TRANSITION

| 0:30 | [2:08] | This starts with two quick turns and then races up the scale in repeating sixteenth notes. The bass is at first static, but when it finally moves it does so with great urgency, pushing the modulation along until a cadence. The stage is then cleared by a brief pause, allowing the listener an "unobstructed view" of the new theme that is about to enter. | 0:30 Rapid scales
0:40 Bass moves
0:45 Cadence and pause |

(Continued on next page)

STOP: LISTEN TO THE TRANSITION AGAIN

SECOND THEME

0:48   [2:26]   With its *piano* dynamic level and separating rests, the second theme sounds soft and delicate. It is soon overtaken by a light, somewhat humorous closing theme.

STOP: LISTEN TO THE SECOND THEME AGAIN

CLOSING THEME

1:01   [2:39]   The light quality of this melody is produced by its repeating note and the simple rocking of dominant-to-tonic harmony below. Toward the end of it more substance is added when the music turns *forte*, and good counterpoint is inserted in the bass. The bass closing theme is then repeated, and a few cadential chords are tacked on to bring the exposition to an end.

1:09   Loud; counterpoint in bass
1:14   Closing theme repeated
1:33   Cadential chords

STOP: LISTEN TO THE CLOSING SECTION AGAIN

1:37–3:14   The exposition is now repeated.

DEVELOPMENT

3:15   Just about anything can happen in a development, so the listener had best be on guard. Mozart begins with the fanfarelike first theme again in unison, as if this were yet another statement of the exposition! But abruptly the theme is altered and the tonal center slides up to a new key. Now the closing theme is heard, but soon it, too, begins to slide tonally, down through several keys that sound increasingly remote and bizarre. From this arises a unison scale (all parts move up stepwise together) in a dark-sounding minor key. The dominant note is held, first on top in the violins and then in the bass (3:48). This is the retransition. The mode changes from dark minor to bright major, and the first theme returns with force in the tonic key, signaling the beginning of the recapitulation.

3:15 First theme developed
3:20 Quick modulation
3:25 Closing theme developed
3:32 More modulations
3:41 Rising scale in unison
3:48 Retransition: held note (dominant) in violins and then bass

STOP: LISTEN TO THE DEVELOPMENT AGAIN

RECAPITULATION

3:52   It is this "double return" of both the tonic key and the first theme that makes the arrival of this and all recapitulations so satisfying. We expect the recapitulation to more or less duplicate the exposition, and this one holds true to form. The only change comes, as usual, in the transition, or bridge, where the modulation to the dominant is simply omitted—there's no need to modulate to the dominant since tradition demands that the second theme and the closing theme appear in the tonic.

3:52 Loud return of first theme
4:23 Transition much abbreviated
4:38 Second theme
4:51 Closing theme
5:05 Closing theme repeated
5:23 Cadential chords

CODA

5:26   After the cadential chords that ended the exposition are heard again, a brief coda begins. It makes use of a fanfare motive that strongly resembles that of the opening theme, but this one is supported below by a pounding tonic chord that drives home the feeling that the movement has come to an appropriate end.

What we have just heard is an example of sonata–allegro form in miniature. Rarely has this design been produced in less time, or space, and almost never as artfully. But sonata–allegro is a dynamic, flexible form, one that can serve equally well as an appropriate vessel for a large symphonic movement, a dramatic overture to an opera, or a Romantic tone poem*. We will meet it again in several later compositions. Listening Exercise 22 presents another, even more dramatic, unfolding of sonata–allegro form: the overture to Mozart's tragic-comic opera *Don Giovanni*.

THEME AND VARIATIONS

After the complexity of sonata–allegro form, a movement in theme and variations form seems relatively simple and straightforward. This is partly because just one theme is used and that theme is subjected to only one sort of compositional treatment: variation. For theme and variations to be effective, the theme itself must be easy to grasp and clearly stated at the outset. As the Enlightenment philosopher Jean-Jacques Rousseau said in his *Dictionnaire de musique* (1768): "Through all the embroidery, one must always be able to recognize the essence of the melody."

To that end composers of the Classical period and beyond often chose themes that were already well-known to the listener: folk songs, popular tunes, and favorite arias and marches from successful operas, for example. Patriotic songs have always seemed especially apt for musical variation. Those so treated include *God Preserve Franz the Emperor* (Haydn), *God Save the King* (Beethoven), *Rule Britannia* (Beethoven), and later *Yankee Doodle* (Vieuxtemps) and *America* (Ives). Such tunes are popular, in part, because they are simple, and this, too, is an advantage for the composer. Melodies that are spare and uncluttered can more easily be dressed in new musical clothing. The essence of theme and variations, then, is to present a simple, direct melody and restate it again and again, each time musically varying or disguising the theme in some novel fashion.

simple tunes are favored

How is variation of a theme brought about? It is done one of two ways: either by merely ornamenting the theme, overlaying it with figural patterns, or, what produces a more radical transformation, by altering the shape of the theme—changing its rhythmic, harmonic, or melodic profile in some way. In the two examples that follow, one by Mozart and one by Haydn, the specific techniques of ornamentation and alteration of a melody will become apparent. You will be challenged to retain a familiar tune in your ear as the composer embellishes or transforms it.

changing the context or changing the tune

Mozart: Variations on
Twinkle, Twinkle, Little Star (ca. 1781)

In the Classical period it was common for a composer-pianist to improvise in concert a set of variations on a well-known tune, perhaps one called out from the audience. Contemporary reports tell us that Mozart was especially skilled in this art of spontaneous variation. In the early 1780s Mozart wrote down a set of such improvised variations built on the French folk song *Ah, vous dirai-je, Maman*, which we know as *Twinkle, Twinkle, Little Star*. With a tune as well known as this, it is easy to follow the melody as it is increasingly ornamented and transformed in the course of twelve variations. (Only the first eight bars of the theme are given here; for the complete melody, see page 183; the music through the first three variations can be heard on Intro CD/22.)

EXAMPLE 9–3a: *Twinkle, Twinkle, Little Star,* Basic Theme (0:00)

Variation 1 ornaments the theme and almost buries it beneath an avalanche of sixteenth notes. Would you know that *Twinkle, Twinkle* lurks herein (see the asterisks) if you did not have the tune securely in your ear?

EXAMPLE 9–3b: Variation 1 (0:51)

In variation 2 the rushing sixteenth notes are transferred to the bass, so that the theme surfaces again rather clearly in the upper voice.

EXAMPLE 9–3c: Variation 2 (1:45)

In variation 3, triplets* appear in the right hand, and only the general contour of the melody is audible. Thus, the melody here is transformed.

EXAMPLE 9–3d: Variation 3 (2:36)

After the same technique has been applied to the bass (variation 4), a thematic alteration again occurs in variation 5. Here the rhythm of the melody is "jazzed up" by placing part of it off the beat, in syncopated fashion.

EXAMPLE 9–3e: Variation 5

Of the remaining seven variations, some change the tune to minor, others add Bach-like counterpoint against it, while the final variation presents this duple-meter folk tune reworked into a triple-meter waltz! Yet throughout all of Mozart's magical embroidery, the theme remains clearly audible, so well ingrained is *Twinkle, Twinkle* in our musical memory.

Haydn: Symphony No. 94 (The "Surprise" Symphony) 1792, Second movement

Joseph Haydn (1732–1809) was the first composer to take theme and variations form and use it for a movement inside a symphony. To be sure, Haydn was an innovative composer—he could "surprise" or "shock" as no other composer of the Classical period. In his "Surprise" Symphony the shock comes in the form of a sudden *fortissimo* chord inserted, as we shall see, in the second movement in the middle of an otherwise serene theme. When Haydn's Symphony No. 94 was first heard in London in 1792, the audience cheered this second movement and demanded its immediate repetition (Fig. 9–6). Ever since, this surprising movement has been Haydn's most celebrated composition.

The famous opening melody of the second movement (*Andante*) is written in binary form (**AB**), and to this simple sixteen-bar theme Haydn then adds four variations. Notice how the beginning of the theme is shaped by laying out in succession the notes of a tonic triad (I) and then a dominant chord (V) in C major (see the first example in the Listening Guide). The triadic nature

Mozarteum, Salzburg

FIGURE 9–5

The autograph manuscript of Mozart's variations on *Twinkle, Twinkle, Little Star* (ca. 1781), beginning with the theme and first three variations. Notice how the texture is very thin at the beginning, but becomes thicker as ornamentation is added to the theme in the variations.

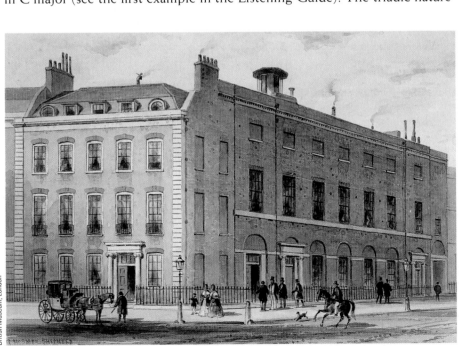

British Museum, London

FIGURE 9–6

The Hanover Square Rooms in London, the hall in which Haydn's "Surprise" Symphony was first performed in 1792. Designed for an audience of 800 to 900, nearly 1,500 crowded in for the performances of these London Symphonies*.

of the tune accounts for its folksong-like quality and makes it easy to remember during the variations that follow. These first eight bars (**A**) are stated and then repeated quietly. And just when all is ending peacefully, the full orchestra comes crashing in with a *fortissimo* chord, as if to shock the drowsy listener back to attention. What better way to show off the latent dynamic power of the larger Classical orchestra? The surprise *fortissimo* chord is a dominant chord that leads into the **B** section of the theme (second example in the Listening Guide), another eight-bar phrase, which is also repeated but with added flute and oboe accompaniment. With the simple yet highly attractive binary theme now in place, Haydn proceeds to compose four variations on it, adding a superb coda at the end.

a surprising chord

Listening Guide

Joseph Haydn
Symphony No. 94, The "Surprise" Symphony (1791)
Second movement, *Andante* (moving)

Intro CD/23

Form: theme and variations

THEME

0:00   First part (**A**) of the theme
0:16   A repeated softly with second violins adding chords to the accompaniment, then *fortissimo* chord

0:33   Second part (**B**) of the theme
0:49   B repeated with flute and oboe added

VARIATION 1

1:06   A played by second violins while first violins and flute add
         counterpoint above
1:22   A repeated
1:39   B with counterpoint continuing above in first violins and flutes
1:55   B repeated

VARIATION 2

2:11   A played loud and in minor key, shift (2:19) to rich major chord
2:27   A repeated
         (Variation of **B** omitted)
2:43   Full orchestra develops A in minor key
3:11   First violins alone, playing in unison

VARIATION 3

3:20   A ornamented rapidly by oboe
3:34   A repeated; melody in strings with oboe and flute ornamenting above
3:50   B now in strings with oboe and flute ornamenting above
4:05   B repeated

(Continued on next page)

VARIATION 4

4:23   A loud, in full orchestra, with violins playing running scales

4:38   A repeated with theme rhythmically varied

4:55   B varied further by the violins

5:11   B repeated loudly by full orchestra

5:27   Transition to coda, pause (5:35)

CODA

5:40   Reminiscences of theme in its original form

After listening to this movement by Haydn, you can now understand that hearing theme and variations form requires listening to discrete units of music. Each block (variation) is marked by some new treatment of the theme. In the Classical period all the units are usually the same size, that is, the same number of measures. The variations become progressively more complicated as more ornamentation and transformation are applied, but each unit remains the same length (like links of sausage!). The addition of a coda after the last variation gives extra weight to the end, so that the listener feels the set of variations has reached an appropriate conclusion. If such extra bars were not appended, the audience would be left hanging, expecting yet another variation to begin.

RONDO FORM

Of all the musical forms, rondo is perhaps the easiest to hear because a single, unvaried theme (the refrain) returns again and again. Rondo form is also one of the oldest musical forms; the rondo (originally called rondeau) existed as a sung-dance in the Middle Ages and as the ritornello* form in the Baroque concerto grosso* (see page 129). Often in rondo form the refrain (**A**) is set against contrasting material (**B**, **C**, or **D**) to create a symmetrical pattern such as **ABABA**, **ABACABA**, or even **ABACADA**. The rondo of the Classical period, however, is not merely a collection of short sections linked back to back, as is usually true of the Baroque rondo (see page 64). Classical composers such as Haydn and Mozart took the principle of rondo form and infused it with the musical processes found in the transitions and development section of sonata–allegro form. They thereby created a more elastic, flexible environment in which the refrain (**A**) and, more often, the contrasting sections (**B**, **C**, or **D**) might develop and expand dramatically.

FIGURE 9–7

A portrait of Joseph Haydn at work. His left hand is trying an idea at the keyboard while his right is ready to write it down. Haydn said about his compositional process: "I sat down at the keyboard and began to improvise. Once I had seized upon an idea, my whole effort was to develop and sustain it."

Mozart: Horn Concerto in E♭ major (1786), K. 495, Third movement

In his short lifetime Mozart wrote an enormous amount of music, more than 650 compositions. To help us keep track of them, a musicologist in the nineteenth century, Ludwig von Köchel, published a list of Mozart's works in approximate chronological order, and still today we identify Mozart's compositions by a **Köchel (K) number.** This is especially handy in the case of Mozart's concertos for the French horn, as he wrote four of them, three in E♭. How else

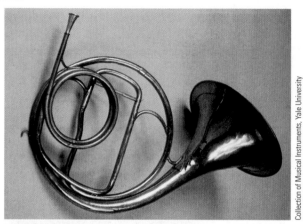

FIGURE 9–8

A natural French horn of the late eighteenth century, the sort of horn that would have been used in the Classical orchestras of Mozart, Haydn, and Beethoven.

could we differentiate them without a number? Thus, the concerto in E♭ written in Vienna in 1786 is identified as K. 495.

The fact that Mozart wrote three of his four horn concertos in E♭ major tells us something about the French horn in the Classical era. It was a "natural" horn (one without valves or keys) and it was set to play only in a few tonal centers, usually in keys with flats (Fig. 9–8). Because the French horn then had no valves or mechanical keys, it had difficulty playing a fully chromatic scale in tune. For that reason, composers wrote for the horn what it could play easily: repeated notes, as well as triads* spun out as arpeggios*.

Mozart conceived all four of his horn concertos with one performer in mind, Joseph Leutgeb (1732–1811). Mozart had grown up with Leutgeb in Salzburg and counted him among his best friends, one at whom he could poke fun. Thus the inscription to the first horn concerto in E♭ (K. 417) reads: "Wolfgang Amadé Mozart has taken pity on Leutgeb, ass, ox, and fool." All four horn concertos by Mozart end with a movement in rondo form. The horn had something of a light-hearted, playful sound in Mozart's day, one particularly suited for the light-hearted, playful quality of the Classical rondo.

Listening Guide

Wolfgang Amadeus Mozart
Horn Concerto in E♭ major (1786) K. 495
Third movement, Rondo

6CD 2/8;
2CD 1/10

Form: rondo

0:00	A played by French horn	A (refrain)
0:08	A repeated by orchestra	
0:15	B part 1: triad spun out as arpeggios	
0:35	B part 2: circling arpeggios	B
0:45	B part 3: rising arpeggio	
0:56	Transition back to A	A
1:03	A played by French horn	
1:11	A repeated by orchestra	
1:18	C new theme played in a minor key	
1:34	Rising melodic sequence is then balanced by	C
1:46	Falling melodic sequence	
1:55	A played by French horn	A
2:02	A repeated by orchestra	
2:10	B part 1 developed	
2:26	B part 2 developed	B
2:35	B part 3 ends with *fortissimo*	
2:54	A played by horn	A
3:00	Orchestra begins to repeat A but then launches into	
3:02	Coda: reminiscences of A and descending arpeggios	**Coda**

(Listening Exercise 23)

A Rondo By Sting

While the rondo may have enjoyed its greatest favor in the sphere of art music during the Baroque and Classical periods, it has continued to live on in the realm of folk and popular song, undoubtedly because the refrain–digression pattern has such universal appeal. Traditional ballads such as *Tom Dooley* make use of it, and so do more recent pop songs by artists such as Arlo Guthrie in *City of New Orleans*. Sting's *Every Breath You Take* produces a rondo pattern (**ABACABA**) that in its symmetrical, indeed palindromic, shape would do any Classical composer proud. Indeed, this song has now been around for about twenty years and has become something of a classic itself, most recently reborn as the title song of the album *Every Breath You Take: The Classics* (A & M Records). The song has also crossed over into the classical-pop repertoire, having been recorded recently by the Royal Philharmonic Orchestra of London. Finally, in 2002, it crossed back, becoming hip-hop in the hands of Sean "Puffy" Combs.

Every breath you take	Every single day	
Every move you make	Every word you say	
Every bond you break	Every game you play	A
Every step you take	Every night you stay	
I'll be watching you.	I'll be watching you.	

O can't you see, you belong to me
How my poor heart aches, with every step you take.   B

Every move you make
Every vow you break
Every smile you fake   A
Every claim you stake
I'll be watching you.

Since you've gone I've been lost without a trace
I dream at night I can only see your face
I look around but it's you I can't replace   C
I feel so cold and I long for your embrace
I keep crying baby please.

Instrumental interlude (no text) to **A** music,   A

O can't you see, you belong to me . . . (etc.)   B

Every move you make . . . (etc.)   A

Coda (fade out)

Sting (Gordon Sumner)

Photofest

The general mood of this movement by Mozart is typical of the lively rondo, which tends to be lighter and more jovial in spirit than does a movement in sonata–allegro form. Classical composers most often used rondo form as the final movement (finale) of a sonata, quartet, or symphony. The tuneful refrain and easily grasped digressions produce a carefree ending intended to leave the audience, if not euphoric, at least in a pleasant state of mind.

FORM, MOOD, AND THE LISTENER'S EXPECTATIONS

The audience of the late eighteenth century brought to the concert hall certain expectations, not only about the structure but also about the mood of the music that was to be performed. Listeners had a notion of what the form, tempo, and general character would be of each movement of a sonata, quartet, or symphony. For the Classical period we might summarize these as follows:

Movement:	1	2	3	4
Tempo:	Fast	Slow	Lively	Fast
Form:	Sonata–allegro	Large ternary, theme and variations, or rondo	Minuet and trio in ternary form	Sonata–allegro, theme and variations, or rondo
Mood:	Serious and substantive despite fast tempo	Lyrical and tender	Usually light and elegant, sometimes spirited	Bright, light-hearted, sometimes humorous

lasting influence of the Classical model

Ludwig van Beethoven (1770–1827) and later composers of the Romantic period (1820–1900) modified somewhat this conventional format—the third movement, for example, was often treated as a boisterous scherzo (see page 210) rather than as an elegant minuet, and the finale became a more serious, weighty conclusion, with the result that the lighthearted rondo fell out of fashion. Yet the Classical model was well established in the mind of the listener. For, unlike previous periods in the history of music, succeeding generations did not forget the music of Haydn, Mozart, and their contemporaries. Their sonatas, quartets, and symphonies enjoyed undiminished favor with the listening public, and the formal designs they created or popularized have remained, with a few exceptions, the norm for the concert hall down to the present day.

Listening Exercises

Wolfgang Amadeus Mozart   6CD 2/12
Overture to the opera *Don Giovanni* (1787)

As is typical of overtures in the Classical period, the one Mozart wrote to precede his opera *Don Giovanni* (1787) is composed in sonata–allegro form. (The opera itself is discussed at length in the following chapter.) Mozart begins his overture with a slow introduction that incorporates many of the musical motives he will later use within the opera. This ominous beginning is written in D minor, which brightens to D major at the start of the exposition. Since this is an overture and not a symphony, there is no repetition of the exposition.

In the exercise that follows, the sections of the exposition are identified for you so that you become familiar with the main thematic material of this piece. Then, beginning with the development and continuing through the recapitulation and brief coda, you are asked a series of questions that follow the unfolding of sonata form.

0:00   Introduction commences with slow, sinister chords that give way to twisting chromaticism, and, finally, writhing scales.

1:56   Exposition begins fast but quietly in major key with **first theme** in the strings.

2:15   Cadential pattern brings first theme group to a close.
2:20   **Transition** starts with scalar theme presented in melodic sequence*.

2:30   Continues with unstable chords that build tension.
2:35   Transition ends with strong cadence.
2:41   **Second theme** marked by scalar descent and then "birdlike fluttering" in woodwinds.

3:00   Light **closing theme**.

3:10   Static, cadential harmony signals end of exposition.

Questions:

1. 3:20   Which theme is used here at the beginning of the development?
   a. first theme   b. second theme   c. closing theme
2. 3:31   This same theme is now heard in the woodwinds in which guise?
   a. in overlapping imitation   b. as a chorale   c. as a cadence
3. 3:40   Which theme enters?
   a. first theme   b. second theme   c. closing theme
4. 3:54   Which theme now returns?
   a. first theme   b. second theme   c. closing theme
5. 4:20–4:26   Retransition: In this section, is the harmony active or static? [Listen to the double basses and timpani. Are they moving to different pitches [active harmony] or just repeating one note [static harmony]?)
   a. active harmony   b. static harmony
6. 4:27   Now the recapitulation begins. With which theme does it commence?
   a. first theme   b. second theme   c. closing theme
7. 4:49   Which material is returning here?
   a. first theme   b. transition   c. second theme
8. 5:08   Which material is returning here?
   a. first theme   b. transition   c. second theme
9. 5:29   Which material is returning here?
   a. transition   b. second theme   c. closing theme
10. 5:45   A brief coda begins here. A reminiscence of which theme is heard as the main melodic material (5:46–5:52)?
    a. first theme   b. second theme   c. closing theme

N.B. There are no *forte* cadential chords to produce a "big bang" ending for this overture. Rather, Mozart writes an orchestral fadeout designed to co-incide with the raising of the curtain and to lead into the music of the first scene of the opera.

23

Wolfgang Amadeus Mozart   6CD 2/8; 2CD 1/10
Horn concerto in E♭ major (1786) K. 495
Third movement, Rondo

The key to hearing rondo form is to recognize the refrain and know when it has returned. By using simple "melodic graphs," it is possible to differentiate thematic material and thereby more easily identify the refrain. Below are three melodic graphs that represent the beginnings of three themes in this movement.

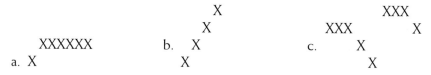

1. (0:00) Which melodic graph most closely approximates the beginning of the refrain, "a," "b," or "c"?
2. (0:00) Listen carefully to the beginning again. Which is true?
   a. The French horn plays entirely by itself at the beginning.
   b. The French horn is accompanied quietly by the strings.
3. (0:08–0:14) When the orchestra repeats the refrain, does the French horn play?
   a. yes   b. no
4. (0:15–0:20) Which melodic graph most closely approximates the beginning of this contrasting section, "a," "b," or "c"?
5. (1:03) Which melodic graph most closely approximates the returning refrain, "a," "b," or "c"?
6. (1:18) Which melodic graph most closely approximates the beginning of this contrasting section, "a," "b," or "c"?
7. (1:18–1:30) This contrasting C section is mainly in
   a. a major key   b. a minor key

Finally:
8. How many times in all does the French horn play the refrain in this movement in rondo form?
   a. three times   b. four times   c. five times   d. six times
9. Which is true regarding the tonality of this movement?
   a. The refrain is always in a happy-sounding major key.
   b. The contrasting B section is always in a sad-sounding minor key.
   c. The contrasting C section is in a happy-sounding major key.
   d. All of the above.
10. Judging from this movement and your experience with sonata–allegro form as well as theme-and-variations form, which is true?

a. In sonata–allegro form there are many themes and often no one theme predominates.
b. In theme-and-variations form there is usually only one theme but it is continually ornamented and altered.
c. In rondo form only one theme predominates and it usually appears unaltered.
d. All of the above.

Key Words

coda (190)
development (189)
exposition (188)
fugato (189)
Köchel (K) number (197)

minuet (184)
recapitulation (189)
relative major (184)
retransition (189)
serenade (185)

sonata–allegro form (187)
transition (bridge) (189)
trio (184)

A checklist of musical style in the Classical period is given on page 70.

Chapter
10

Mozart Memorial Collection, Prague

Classical Genres

I n music the general term "genre" refers to that special quality of musical style, performing medium, and even place of performance that we associate with one class or type of music. The string quartet is a genre of music just as is the country music ballad, the blues, the military march, and even the rap song. When we listen to a piece of music, we come armed with expectations as to how it will sound, how long it will last, and how we should behave. We may even go to a special place, an opera house or a bar, and dress a certain way—in tuxedo and earrings or black leather jacket and nose rings, for example. It all depends on the genre of music we expect to hear. In simplest terms, then, a musical genre is a general type of music.

In the age of Mozart there were four genres of painting: historical paintings, portraits, scenes of everyday life, and still-lifes. Similarly, there were five main genres of secular art music in the Classical period: the symphony, string quartet, sonata, concerto, and opera. Though performed by different forces and usually in different places, the same sort of audience might attend each. One of these genres, the opera, was taken over from the Baroque era and, though modified by Classical composers, retained its fundamental structure. Two others, the sonata and concerto, had also existed during the Baroque

period, but were so changed by Haydn, Mozart, and their contemporaries that they were now tantamount to new genres.
And still two others, the symphony and the string quartet, had
no immediate ancestors in the Baroque era but were created
wholly new during the Classical period.

THE SYMPHONY

During the Classical era the symphony sprang forth to become
the preeminent musical genre. The fact that Haydn composed
so many (104) and Mozart an even more astonishing number
(41), given his short life, shows that the symphony had become, and would remain, the genre through which an aspiring
composer might test his mettle and start on the road to international fame.

The symphony traces its origins to the late seventeenth-
century Italian opera overture called the **sinfonia** ("a harmonious sounding together"). Around 1700 the typical Italian *sinfonia* was a one-movement instrumental work in three sections,
fast–slow–fast. Soon Italian musicians and foreigners alike took the *sinfonia* out
of the opera house and expanded it into three separate and distinct movements. A fourth movement, the minuet, was inserted by composers north of
the Alps beginning in the 1740s. Thus, by mid-century the symphony had
emerged as an independent genre and assumed its familiar four-movement format, fast–slow–minuet–fast.

The public favor the symphony came to enjoy was tied directly to certain
revolutionary social changes that swept Europe during the Enlightenment.
Not the least of these, as we have seen, was the impressive growth of public
concerts (see page 169). The center of musical life in such cities as London,
Paris, and, to a lesser degree, Vienna gradually shifted from the aristocratic
court to the newly constructed or refurbished public concert hall. Larger audiences and greater financial gain for the composer could be had at public concerts like those mounted in the Hanover Square Rooms in London (see Fig.
9–6) or the Burgtheater in Vienna (Figs. 10–1 and 10–2), where commoner
and aristocrat met on more-or-less equal footing. Although some members of

Museum der Stadt Wien

FIGURE 10–1

The Burgtheater in Vienna, where many
symphonies, concertos, and operas by
Mozart were first heard. This colored
engraving dates from the early nineteenth
century.

Museum der Stadt Wien

FIGURE 10–2

The interior of the Burgtheater, which
could accommodate an audience of about
700. Not only were works of Mozart and
Haydn performed here but Beethoven also
made his Viennese debut in this theater on
March 29, 1795, at a benefit concert for
Mozart's widow. For another interior view,
see Fig. 8–5.

symphonies for public concerts

the nobility, notably the elector at Mannheim and the Esterházy princes, were important patrons of the early symphony, the genre ultimately flourished in an upper-middle-class pay-per-ticket environment. All but a few of Haydn's last twenty symphonies were composed for public performance in Paris and London, and Mozart wrote no symphonies for a court patron during the last ten years of his life. His G minor symphony was apparently first performed in a casino (see Fig. 10–4)—that's where the people were and that's where the money was to be found. Henceforth, the listening public, and not the aristocratic prince, provided the principal support for the symphony and for the instrumental ensemble that performed it, the symphony orchestra.

The Classical Orchestra

Naturally, as the place of performance of the symphony moved from the private salon to the public auditorium, the size of the audience and the size of the concert hall increased. The orchestra of Haydn's patron, Prince Nikolaus Esterházy, was never larger than twenty-five, and the audience at court was often only the prince and his staff (Fig. 10–3). But when Haydn went to London to appear before the public in 1791, his "London Symphonies" were performed in the Hanover Square Rooms (see Fig. 9–6), which accommodated between eight hundred and nine hundred persons. Indeed, for one of his public concerts in the spring of 1792, nearly 1,500 eager patrons crowded in. To fill these larger halls with sound, a larger orchestra was needed. Mozart mentions an orchestra of at least eighty players, including forty violins, ten violas, eight cellos, and ten double basses, for a public concert in the Burgtheater in Vienna in 1781 (see Fig. 10–2). And although this ensemble was unusually large, orchestras of fifty or sixty players for public performance were not uncommon in Paris and London by the end of the century.

The heart of the Classical orchestra, as had been true of the earlier Baroque orchestra, was the string section: the ensemble of violins, violas, cellos, and double basses. But not only were there now more instruments in the group, the violin was modestly different as well. To produce a larger, more penetrating tone, metal strings, which could be strung to greater tension, began to replace those of animal gut. The winds were also increased in number so as to be heard in the midst of the large string sound. Now, instead of just one flute or one bassoon, there were usually pairs. And a new woodwind was introduced, the clarinet. Mozart was particularly delighted when he first heard the clarinet used as an orchestral instrument during a visit to the Mannheim court in 1778. "Ah, if only we had clarinets too! You cannot imagine the glorious effect of a symphony with flutes, oboes, and clarinets," he wrote to his father back in provincial Salzburg. All of these woodwinds added tone, color, and variety to what had been a string-dominated sound. By the 1780s, then, the full Classical orchestra consisted of strings, two

FIGURE 10–3

A watercolor of 1775 shows Haydn leading the orchestra at the court of the Esterházy princes during a performance of a comic opera. The composer is seated at the keyboard, surrounded by the cellos. The higher strings and woodwinds are seated in two rows at the desk.

Bridgeman Art Library, London/NY

oboes, two flutes, two clarinets, two bassoons, two horns, and, for especially festive symphonies, two trumpets and timpani. Compared to the Baroque orchestra, its sound was larger, more colorful, and more flexible.

Mozart: Symphony No. 40 in G minor (1788) K. 550

Mozart's celebrated symphony in G minor requires all of the full instrumental sound and disciplined playing the late eighteenth-century orchestra could muster. This is not a festive composition (hence no trumpets and drums), but rather an intensely brooding work that suggests tragedy and feverish despair. While we might be tempted to associate the minor key and despondent mood with a specific event in Mozart's life, apparently no such causal relationship exists. This was one of three symphonies, his last three, that Mozart produced in the incredibly short span of six weeks during the summer of 1788, and the other two are sunny, optimistic works. Rather than responding to a particular disappointment, it is more likely that Mozart invoked the tragic muse in this G minor symphony by drawing on a lifetime of disappointments and a premonition—as his letters attest—of an early death.

an intensely brooding work

FIRST MOVEMENT (*MOLTO ALLEGRO*)

Exposition Although Mozart begins his G minor symphony with a textbook example of Classical phrase structure (four-bar antecedent, four-bar consequent phrases), an unusual sense of urgency is created by the repeating, insistent eighth-note figure at the beginning. This urgent motive is immediately grasped by the listener and becomes the most memorable theme of the work. Imbedded in the motive is a falling half step* (here "E♭" to "D"), an interval used throughout the history of music to denote pain and suffering.

EXAMPLE 10–1

What is not so quickly seized, but yet contributes equally to the sense of urgency, is the accelerating rate of harmonic change. At the outset chords are set beneath the melody at an interval of one chord every four measures, then one every two bars, then one every measure, then two chords per measure, and finally four. Thus, the harmony, or harmonic rhythm, is moving sixteen times faster at the end of this section than at the start. This is how Mozart creates the drive and urgency we all feel yet may be unable to explain. After this quickening start, the first theme begins once again, but soon veers off its previous course and into the transition. Transitions are filled with motion, especially running scales, and this one is no exception. What is unusual is that a motive is inserted, one so distinctive we might call it a transition theme (see the example in the following Listening Guide). As if to reciprocate for an extra theme here, Mozart dispenses with one toward the end of the exposition, at the point where we would expect a closing theme to appear. Instead, as closing material he makes use of the persistent motive and rhythm from the beginning of the first theme, and this rather nicely rounds off the exposition. Finally, a single,

accelerating harmonic rhythm

isolated chord is heard, one that leads back to a repeat of the exposition, or, second time through, launches into the development.

Development In the development Mozart employs only the first theme (and then only the first four bars), but subjects it to a variety of musical treatments. First he carries it through several distantly related keys, next shapes it into a fugue subject for use in a fugato*, then sets it as a descending melodic sequence, and finally inverts the direction of the half-step* motive.

manipulation of the motive

The retransition* is suddenly interrupted by *sforzandi* (loud attacks). But soon a dominant pedal point* is heard in the bassoons, and above it the flute and clarinets begin to cascade down to the tonic pitch. This use of colorful, solo woodwinds in the retransition is a hallmark of Mozart's symphonic style.

Recapitulation As expected, the recapitulation offers the themes in the same order in which they appeared in the exposition. But now the transition theme, which Mozart has left untouched since its initial appearance, receives extended treatment, creating something akin to a second development section as it pushes through one new key after another, only to end up back in the original tonic minor. When the lyrical second theme finally reappears, it has a more somber, plaintive mood now that it is in minor. Because the repeating figure of the first theme rounds off the recapitulation by way of a closing theme, only the briefest coda is needed to end this passionate, haunting movement.

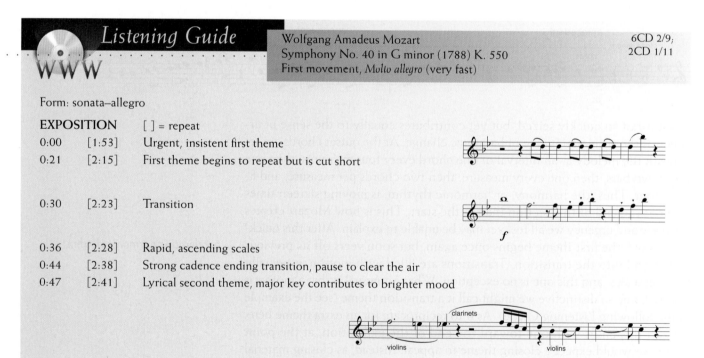

Listening Guide

WWW

Wolfgang Amadeus Mozart
Symphony No. 40 in G minor (1788) K. 550
First movement, *Molto allegro* (very fast)

6CD 2/9;
2CD 1/11

Form: sonata–allegro

EXPOSITION   [ ] = repeat
0:00   [1:53]   Urgent, insistent first theme
0:21   [2:15]   First theme begins to repeat but is cut short

0:30   [2:23]   Transition

0:36   [2:28]   Rapid, ascending scales
0:44   [2:38]   Strong cadence ending transition, pause to clear the air
0:47   [2:41]   Lyrical second theme, major key contributes to brighter mood

(Continued on next page)

| 0:56 | [2:50] | Second theme repeated with new orchestration |
| 1:09 | [3:02] | Crescendo leading to closing material (taken from first theme); abrupt stop |

DEVELOPMENT

3:49		First theme modulates through several distant keys
4:01		First theme used as fugue subject in a fugato in basses and then violins
4:23		First theme reduced to just opening motive
4:43		*Sforzandi* (loud attacks) give way to retransition*
4:52		Retransition: dominant pedal point* in bassoons with cascading flute and clarinets above

RECAPITULATION

4:59		First theme returns
5:19		First theme begins to repeat but cut off by transition
5:27		Transition theme returns but is greatly extended
5:55		Rapid, ascending scales
6:04		Cadence and pause
6:07		Second theme now in (tonic) minor
6:17		Second theme repeated with new orchestration
6:30		Return of crescendo leading to closing material (taken from first theme)

CODA

| 7:11 | | Begins with rising chromatic scale |
| 7:18 | | Opening motive returns, then three final chords |

(Listening Exercise 24)

SECOND MOVEMENT (*ANDANTE*)

After the feverish excitement of the opening movement, the slow, lyrical *Andante* comes as a welcome change of pace. What makes this movement exceptionally beautiful is the extraordinary interplay between the light and dark colors of the woodwinds against the constant tone of the strings. If there is no thematic contrast and confrontation here, there is, nonetheless, heartfelt expression brought about by Mozart's masterful use of orchestral color.

THIRD MOVEMENT (*MINUETTO: ALLEGRETTO*)

We expect the aristocratic minuet to provide elegant, graceful dance music. But much to our surprise, Mozart returns to the intense, somber mood of the opening movement. This he does, in part, by choosing to write in the tonic minor key—a rare minuet in minor.

FOURTH MOVEMENT (*ALLEGRO ASSAI*)

The finale starts with an ascending rocket that explodes in a rapid, *forte* flourish—and only carefully rehearsed string playing can bring off the brilliant effect of this opening gesture. The contrasting second theme of this sonata–allegro form movement is typically Mozartean in its grace and charm, a proper foil to the explosive opening melody. Midway through the development musical compression takes hold: There is no retransition, only a pregnant pause before the recapitulation; the return dispenses with the repeats built into the first theme; and a coda is omitted. This musical foreshortening at the end produces the same psychological effect experienced at the very beginning of the symphony—a feeling of urgency and acceleration.

FIGURE 10–4

The New Market in Vienna, as painted in 1759. The building on the right housed the city casino, and it was here that Mozart's G minor symphony was first performed in 1788. Even today famous musicians, such as Luciano Pavarotti, still perform in casinos. That's where the money is!

Kunsthistorisches Museum, Vienna

THE STRING QUARTET

The symphony is the ideal genre for the public concert hall, for it aims to please a large listening public. The string quartet, on the other hand, is a genre of music that typifies **chamber music**—music for the small concert hall, for the private chamber, or, often, for just the enjoyment of the performers themselves. Unlike the symphony, which might have a dozen violinists joining on the first violin line, the **string quartet** has only one player per part: one first violinist, one second violinist, one violist, and one cellist (Fig. 10–5). Moreover, there is no conductor. All performers function equally and communicate directly among themselves. No wonder the German poet Johann Wolfgang von Goethe (1749–1832) compared the string quartet to a conversation among four intelligent people. All chamber music, whether for string quartet, solo piano or violin, wind quintet, or even a string octet, employs just one player on a part. Of these chamber media, the string quartet is historically the most important.

chamber music: one player per part

In the Baroque era the favored ensemble for chamber music was the trio sonata*, a group of two melody instruments, usually violins, and a *basso continuo**, which set the harmonies from below. As the bottom-heavy music of the Baroque era gave way to the lighter, top-heavy melodies of the early Classical period, the trio sonata ceded pride of place in the 1750s to the string quartet. The *basso continuo* gradually disappears and a new type of bass line emerges, a more melodically active one played by an agile cello alone. Moreover, the middle of the texture is given greater substance by assigning a lively role to the viola, the instrument playing immediately above the cello.

Joseph Haydn created this new style of chamber music and thus is known as "the father of the string quartet." In his mature quartets, the spectrum of sound from top to bottom is covered evenly by four instruments that participate more or less equally in a give and take of theme and motive. But the string quartet, of course, is not only a performing force but it is also a genre of music involving four movements. As with most Classical quartets, Haydn's usually have the following succession of movements: fast–slow–minuet–fast. Moreover, in a set of quartets he wrote in 1772, Haydn dubbed each minuet a **scherzo** (Italian for "joke"), suggesting the high-spirited style of playing intended for this movement and the string quartet in general.

It was the chance to play string quartets together that gave rise to a lasting friendship between Haydn and Mozart. During the summer of 1784 and winter of 1785, the two men met in Vienna, sometimes at the home of an aristocrat, sometimes in Mozart's own apartment. Haydn played first violin, Mozart viola, in their quartet. As a result of this experience, Mozart was inspired to dedicate

FIGURE 10–5

A representation of a string quartet at the end of the eighteenth century. The string quartet was at first an ensemble for playing chamber music in the home. Not until 1804 did a string quartet appear in a public concert in Vienna, and not until 1814 in Paris.

Mozart Memorial Collection, Prague

a set of his best works in this genre to the older master, which he published in 1785 (Fig. 10–6). Yet in this convivial, domestic music-making, Haydn and Mozart merely joined in the fashion of the day. For whether in Vienna, Paris, or London, aristocrats and members of the well-to-do middle class were encouraged to play quartets with friends as well as to engage professional musicians to entertain their guests.

Haydn: Opus 76, No. 3, The "Emperor" Quartet (1797)

Haydn's "Emperor" Quartet, written in Vienna during the summer of 1797, is counted among the best works of the string quartet genre. It is known as the "Emperor" because it makes liberal use of *The Emperor's Hymn*, a melody that Haydn composed in response to the military and political events of his day.

In 1796 the armies of Napoleon invaded the Austrian Empire and this, in turn, ignited a firestorm of patriotism in Vienna, the Austrian capital. But the Austrians were at a musical disadvantage: The French now had the *Marseillaise*, the English had their *God Save the King*, but the Austrians had no national anthem. To this end, the ministers of state approached Haydn, who quickly fashioned one to the text "Gott erhalte Franz den Kaiser" ("God preserve Franz the Emperor") in honor of the reigning Austrian Emperor Franz II (Fig. 10–7). Called *The Emperor's Hymn*, it was first sung in theaters throughout the Austrian realm on the Emperor's birthday, 12 February 1797. Later that year, Haydn took the tune and worked it into a string quartet.

In truth, when Haydn fashioned string quartet Opus 76, No. 3, he made use of his imperial hymn mainly in the slow, second movement, where it serves as the basis of a theme-and-variations set. The theme (see the example in the following Listening Guide) is first presented by the first violin, and harmonized in simple chords. Four variations follow. In these all four instruments are given equal opportunity to hold forth with the tune. Example 10–2 shows how in the Classical string quartet the melodic profile of each of the lines is pretty much the same, a far cry from the melody–walking-bass* polarity that typified the earlier Baroque trio sonata.

Private Collection

FIGURES 10–6 AND 10–7

(above) Title page of six string quartets by Mozart dedicated to Haydn (1785). Mozart offers them to Hadyn as "six children," asking Haydn to be their "father, guide, and friend." (below) Franz II (1765–1835), last Holy Roman Emperor, first Emperor of Austria. Haydn composed *The Emperor's Hymn* in his honor.

Historisches Museum der Stadt Wien

EXAMPLE 10–2

Had Haydn been writing for a symphony orchestra, he could not have composed his bass line in this fashion. For the lowest string instrument in the orchestra is the low double bass, which plays an octave below the cello and in that range produces a resonant, yet slightly muddled sound. But the more flexible fingering and singing tone of the cello make it possible for even the lowest instrument of the string quartet to participate as an equal partner. What the quartet gives up by way of depth and richness of sound, it gains in increased motivic interaction and in a more transparent texture.

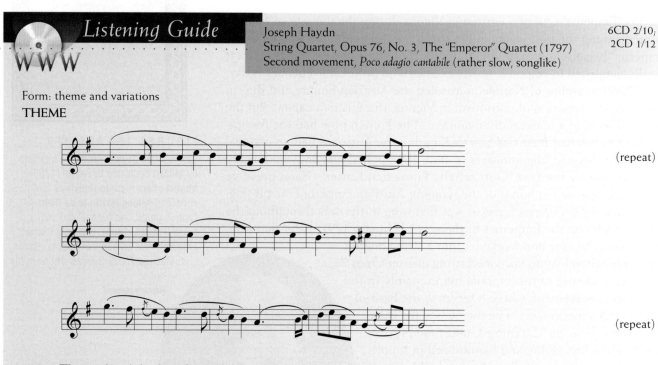

Listening Guide

WWW

Joseph Haydn
String Quartet, Opus 76, No. 3, The "Emperor" Quartet (1797)
Second movement, *Poco adagio cantabile* (rather slow, songlike)

6CD 2/10;
2CD 1/12

Form: theme and variations
THEME

(repeat)

(repeat)

0:00   Theme played slowly in first violin; lower three parts provide chordal accompaniment

VARIATION 1

1:29   Theme in second violin while first violin ornaments above it

VARIATION 2

2:46   Theme in cello while other three instruments provide counterpoint against it

VARIATION 3

4:13   Theme in viola; other three instruments only gradually enter

VARIATION 4

5:38   Theme returns to first violin, but now the accompaniment is more contrapuntal than chordal

(Listening Exercise 25)

The popularity of *The Emperor Hymn* did not end with the defeat of Napoleon in 1815 or the death of Emperor Franz II in 1835. So alluring is Haydn's melody that, with altered text, it became a Protestant hymn, as well as the national anthem of Austria [1853] and Germany [1950]. It was also Haydn's own favorite piece and he played a piano arrangement of it daily. In fact, *The Emperor's Hymn* was the last music Haydn played before he died in the early hours of May 31, 1809.

THE SONATA

The **sonata** was another important genre of chamber music that flourished during the Classical period. No longer was it a succession of four or five dance movements, as was usually the case during the Baroque era (see page 124). Now the sonata was a work in three movements (fast–slow–fast), each of which might make use of one or another of the forms favored by Classical composers: sonata–allegro, ternary, rondo, or theme and variations.

The sonata came to enjoy great popularity during the Classical period. According to publishers' inventories from the end of the eighteenth century, more sonatas were printed than any other type of music. The explanation for this sudden vogue is tied to the equally sudden favor experienced by the piano. Indeed, the word "sonata" has become so closely associated with the piano that unless otherwise qualified as "violin sonata," "cello sonata," or the like, we usually assume that "sonata" refers to a three-movement work for piano.

the piano sonata

Who played this flood of new sonatas for the piano? Amateur musicians, mostly women, who practiced and performed for polite society in the comfort of their own homes. As we have seen (page 170), in Mozart's time the ability to play the piano, to do fancy needlework, and to utter a few selected words of French were thought by male-dominated society all that was necessary to be a cultured young lady. To teach the musical handicraft, instructors were needed. Mozart, Haydn, and Beethoven all served as piano teachers in fashionable circles early in their careers. The piano sonatas they composed for their numerous pupils were not intended to be played in the public concert halls. Sonatas were to provide students with material that they might practice to develop technique and that they might play as musical entertainment in the home. Even among the splendid thirty-two piano sonatas that Beethoven composed, only one was ever performed at a public concert in Vienna during his lifetime.

piano sonatas for women

(An example of a Classical piano sonata by Beethoven, his *Pathétique* Sonata, is found on 6CD 3/1 and 2CD 1/13. It is discussed in detail on page 230.)

THE CONCERTO

With the genre of the concerto we leave the salon or private chamber and return once again to the public concert hall. For the Classical concerto is a large-scale, three-movement work for instrumental soloist and orchestra, and thus of the same grandiose magnitude as the symphony itself. And while the symphony might provide the greatest musical substance at a concert, more often than not the audience was lured to the hall by the prospect of hearing a virtuoso performer play a concerto. Audiences then as now had a special fascination with personal virtuosity and all the daring and excitement that a stunning technical display might bring. The soloist in such concertos was a single performer whose place in the musical firmament was that of a star. Gone was the Baroque tradition of the concerto grosso*, which pitted an orchestra (tutti*) against a *group* of soloists (the concertino*). From now on the concerto was a **solo concerto**, usually for piano, but sometimes for violin, cello, or wind instrument.

solo concerto offers technical display

FIGURE 10–8

One of the few surviving tickets to a concert mounted by Mozart in Vienna. These were sold in advance, not from a ticket agency, but from Mozart's own apartment!

Development of the solo concerto for piano had begun with the two sons of Johann Sebastian Bach: Carl Philipp Emanuel Bach (1714–1788), living in Berlin, and Johann Christian Bach (1735–1782), resident in London. The London Bach, as he was called, experimented with the piano concerto in connection with a series of public concerts he gave both in London and Paris during the 1760s and 1770s. But no one did more to bring the form and style of the piano concerto to maturity than Wolfgang Amadeus Mozart. The piano concerto was a form of public theater and no composer was ever more at home in the theater than Mozart.

Mozart wrote twenty-seven piano concertos, more than any other important composer. He did so mainly because his economic livelihood depended on it, especially after he took up residence in Vienna as a freelance musician in 1781. Most of his masterpieces in this genre were composed so that Mozart himself might showcase his talents at public concerts that he alone had organized, for to attract attention in this period a composer not only had to write the music but also had to serve as performer, concert manager, and ticket seller all in one (Fig. 10–8). It was up to Mozart to rent the hall (see Figs. 10–1 and 10–2), hire the orchestra, solicit an audience, and offer his paying public a collection of his newest creations. A musical journal for March 22, 1783, reports one of Mozart's more successful ventures of this sort:

Mozart plays two concertos before the emperor

> Today the celebrated Chevalier Mozart gave a musical concert for his own benefit at the Burgtheater in which pieces of his own music, which was already very popular, were performed. The concert was honored by the presence of an extraordinarily large audience and the two new concertos and other fantasies which Mr. Mozart played on the Forte Piano were received with the loudest approval. Our Monarch [Emperor Joseph II], who contrary to his custom honored the entire concert with his presence, joined in the applause of the public so heartily that one can think of no similar example. The proceeds of the concert are estimated at sixteen hundred gulden.

With a take such as this, Mozart could, at least for a time, indulge his expensive tastes.

Mozart: Piano Concerto No. 17 in G major (1784), K. 453

We derive our term "concerto" from the Italian word "concertare." It means above all else "to strive together," but it also resonates with the sense of "to struggle against." Thus the solo concerto requires two separate forces (orchestra and soloist) to collaborate, but also pits them against each other. Of all the solo instruments, the piano, with its capacity for melody, for speed of execution, and full, clear sound, is perhaps most up to the task of competing with an orchestra in a spirited give-and-take of musical material. If the orchestra comes forward with a rich, full sound or varied instrumental color, the piano can counter with a line of tender expression, a virtuosic run, or a passage of *fortissimo* chords.

a contest between piano and orchestra

When Mozart played concertos in Vienna, he usually had his own piano carried to the hall (Fig. 10–9). Although Mozart's piano was small by the standards of today, during the performance of a concerto the lid was sometimes removed to permit the sound to project more freely. Most often Mozart wrote piano concertos to show off his own talents, but he also composed several for

Barbara Ployer: Concert Pianist

I n 1781 Mozart broke from his patron, the Archbishop of Salzburg, to establish himself as a freelance musician in Vienna. To earn a living, he took on a small number of piano students whom he visited daily for their lessons. Most of these were young women, and for the more talented of them he composed piano sonatas and concertos. Among the best was Barbara Ployer (1765–1811), the daughter of an old and wealthy acquaintance from Salzburg. It was for Fraulein Ployer "who paid me handsomely" that Mozart composed his Concerto No. 17 in G. When it came time to perform the work publicly in June 1784, Ployer did so at a concert organized in the town of Döbling outside of Vienna. For this premier, Mozart brought along the well-known composer Giovanni Paisiello (1740–1816) to show off both his pupil and concerto. The next year Ployer was described as "a marvelous pianist." She also studied musical composition with Mozart, and some alternative cadenzas* for his concertos are thought to be from her hand.

A young woman performs a keyboard concerto in 1777.

Engraving by Johann Rudolf Holzhalb, 1777.
Reproduced with the kind permission of Oxford University Press.

his students. He created this piano concerto in G, for example, for the nineteen-year-old Barbara Ployer (see boxed essay).

FIRST MOVEMENT (ALLEGRO)

As with all of Mozart's concertos, this one is in three movements (there is never a minuet or scherzo in a concerto). And, as is invariably the case, the first movement is written in sonata–allegro form. However, here it is modified to meet the special demands and opportunities of the concerto. What results is **double exposition form,** an extension of sonata–allegro form in which the orchestra plays one exposition and the soloist then plays another. First, the orchestra presents the first, second, and closing themes, all in the tonic key. Next, the soloist enters and, with orchestral assistance, offers the piano's version of the same material, but modulating to the dominant in the transition. Then a surprise in the middle of the transition: A new lyrical theme sounds forth in the piano alone. This is another feature of the Classical concerto—a melody held back, or saved, for presentation by the soloist. Toward the end of this second exposition a part of the first theme returns, a throwback to the ritornello* principle of the old Baroque concerto grosso.

The development focuses more on harmonies than themes, as the piano leads the orchestra through a succession of striking chord changes. The recapitulation compresses the two expositions into one, presenting the themes in the same order as before but now all in the tonic key. Finally, toward the end of the movement the orchestra suddenly stops its forward motion and comes to rest on a single chord. Using this chord as a springboard, the pianist plunges headlong into a flight of virtuosic fancy, the **cadenza.** Now playing alone, the performer mixes rapid runs, arpeggios, and snippets of previously heard themes into a fantasy-like improvisation. Although Mozart wrote down these cadenzas, when he performed them the notated score was merely a stimulus to his

FIGURE 10–9

Mozart's piano, preserved in the house of his birth in Salzburg, Austria. The keyboard spans only five octaves and the black-and-white color scheme of the keys is reversed, both typical features of the late eighteenth-century piano. Mozart purchased the instrument in 1784, the year after he composed his G major piano concerto.

imagination, just as in our own century a talented jazz musician might depart from a musical sketch to improvise an extended solo. After a minute or so of this razzle-dazzle, the pianist plays a trill* in the right hand to signal the orchestra that it is time for it to reenter the competition. From here to the end the orchestra holds forth, making use of the closing theme. There is much to follow in the Listening Guide for this movement in double exposition form, but the glorious music of Mozart will amply reward the attentive listener.

Listening Guide

Wolfgang Amadeus Mozart
Piano Concerto No. 17 in G major (1784), K. 453
First movement, *Allegro* (fast)

6CD 2/11

Form: double exposition sonata–allegro

EXPOSITION 1 (orchestra)

0:00   Strings present elegant first theme, part **a**

0:29   *Forte:* Full orchestra presents first theme part **b**

0:39   Transition: running scales, agitation, then calm cadence

1:02   Strings and then woodwinds play quiet, plaintive second theme

1:27   Bold harmonic shift momentarily sends music off course

1:43   Strings quietly present closing theme part **a**

2:03   Full orchestra loudly plays closing theme part **b**

EXPOSITION 2 (piano and orchestra)

2:15   Piano ornaments first theme part **a**
       with Alberti bass* accompaniment

2:48   Woodwinds and then full orchestra play first theme part **b**

2:59   Transition begins with piano playing runs and then arpeggios

3:16   Piano, solo, injects a graceful new theme

3:44   Transition continues as piano plays falling arpeggios

4:07   Piano plays second theme, then woodwinds take it over

(Continued on next page)

4:32 Piano plays passage of rapid figuration, scales, and arpeggios

5:03 Full orchestra brings back first theme part **b**

5:15 Full orchestra plays closing theme part **b**

DEVELOPMENT

5:26 Bold harmonic shift, then piano plays arpeggios in midst of continually shifting harmonies

6:14 Piano develops turning motive from "new" theme in minor key

6:28 French horns play pedal point* signalling retransition* back to recapitulation

RECAPITULATION

6:43 Strings play first theme part **a**

7:09 Full orchestra plays first theme part **b**

7:20 Transition begins with runs in the violins

7:35 Piano gradually leads up to "new" theme

8:10 Transition continues through minor keys

8:32 Piano plays second theme, then woodwinds take it over

8:58 Piano plays scales, then arpeggios, and then a trill

9:23 Bold harmonic shift

9:33 Full orchestra plays loud, syncopated chords, then holds a chord

9:42 **Cadenza** for piano alone: references to first theme, second theme, and "new" theme; ends with trill signalling orchestra to recommence playing

11:00 Full orchestra plays closing theme parts **a** and **b**

11:27 Final cadential chords

SECOND MOVEMENT (*ANDANTE*)

Mozart saved some of his most heart-wrenching music for the slow, middle movements of his piano concertos. In this typical andante (gently moving movement) in **aba'** form, the expressive dialogue is mainly between the piano and the woodwinds. As one commentator has said about this movement: "The mingling of serenity and sadness is more marked; the lights are higher, the shadows deeper."

THIRD MOVEMENT (*ALLEGRETTO*)

This movement demonstrates perhaps better than any other the delightful "tug-of-war" that can exist between soloist and orchestra in a concerto. In form it is a simple theme and variations. The theme, however, may have an unusual origin. It was apparently given to Mozart by a bird, a pet starling the composer purchased in the spring 1784. When he bought the bird, Mozart entered into his expense book its cost as well as a seventeen-note, four-measure tune it could mimic—the first seventeen notes of the theme of this finale.

Mozart's bird

EXAMPLE 10–3

In truth, it is not certain whether Mozart had taught this tune to the bird, or if the bird already knew it. At the least, it suggests that in the Classical period, even birds could be made to think in balanced, four-bar phrases!

OPERA

features of opera

Opera is drama, yes, but drama propelled by music. In the Classical period, opera maintained the broad features passed on to it from the Baroque era. It still began with an overture, was divided into two or three acts, and made use of a succession of arias and recitatives along with an occasional choral number. Also, needless to say, it still was performed in a theater, one large enough to accommodate both an orchestra and elaborate stage sets.

Yet, while the genre of opera retained its overall shape, it nonetheless underwent important internal changes during the second half of the eighteenth century. Italian comic opera *(opera buffa)*, a powerful voice for social change in the Enlightenment (see page 169), came to dominate the stage and gradually replace the serious opera *(opera seria)* of the Baroque period. The statuelike gods and goddesses, emperors and queens, of the older style have departed, replaced by more natural, realistic characters drawn from everyday life. Gone, too, are the rigid sectional divisions between aria, recitative, and chorus that segregate one emotion from another. Baroque opera posed magnificently; Classical opera moves gracefully. Although aria and recitative were still differentiated, in Classical opera they now flow more easily one to another. The mood of the music changes rapidly to reflect the up-and-down emotions of the characters. The more fluid Classical style is better suited to comic situations that invariably involve a quick give-and-take between characters.

easy flow of comic opera

Comic opera also brought a new element into the opera house, the **vocal ensemble**. While recitatives are still used to narrate action and arias to express emotion, now a variety of emotions can be expressed simultaneously by means of a vocal trio, quartet, or even sextet of soloists. One character might sing of her love, another of his fear, another of her outrage, while a fourth pokes fun at the other three. Vocal ensembles are especially favored at the ends of acts. No longer does the curtain fall after a solo "exit aria" from a famous leading lady, but after a vocal ensemble including the principals— another manifestation of the more democratic spirit, and better dramatic sense, of the late eighteenth century.

Mozart: master of the vocal ensemble

The master of Classical opera, and of the vocal ensemble in particular, is Wolfgang Amadeus Mozart. While Haydn wrote more than a dozen operas and conducted others (see Fig. 10–3), he lacked Mozart's instinct for what would work in the theater and what would not. Nor did he have Mozart's uncanny ability to depict and differentiate characters through music. With its lightning-quick changes in mood and color, and juxtaposition of themes of different character, Mozart's music is inherently theatrical and perfectly suited to the genre of opera.

Mozart wrote Italian *opera seria* of the old Baroque sort as well as German comic opera, which was called *Singspiel*. Like a Broadway musical, a **Singspiel** is made up of spoken dialogue (instead of recitative) and songs. Mozart's best work of this type is *Die Zauberflöte* (*The Magic Flute*, 1791). But Mozart also wrote operas more in the tradition of Italian comic opera. These include his masterpieces *Le nozze di Figaro* (*The Marriage of Figaro*, 1786), *Don Giovanni* (1787), and *Così fan tutte* (*Thus Do They All*, 1790), all three with text (libretto) by Lorenzo da Ponte.

Mozart: *Don Giovanni* (1787), K. 527

Don Giovanni has been called not only Mozart's greatest opera but also the greatest opera ever written. The story tells the tale of a wicked philanderer, a Don Juan, who seduces and murders his way across Europe before being pursued and finally dragged down to hell by the ghost of a man whom he has killed. Since the seducer and mocker of public law and morality is a nobleman, *Don Giovanni* is implicitly critical of the aristocracy, and Mozart and da Ponte danced quickly to stay one step ahead of the imperial censor before production. Mozart's opera was first performed on October 29, 1787, in Prague, Czech Republic, a city in which his music was especially popular. As fate would have it, the most notorious Don Juan of the eighteenth century, Giacomo Casanova (1725–1798), was in the audience that first night in Prague. It turns out that he had had a small hand in helping his friend da Ponte shape the libretto.

an opera critical of the nobility

The overture to *Don Giovanni*, as we have seen (6CD 2/12; Listening Exercise 22), is a fine example of sonata–allegro form. It begins with a slow introduction that incorporates several themes or motives important later in the opera. Just as an author postpones writing a preface until after a book is finished, so a composer saves the overture for the end of the creative process. In this way the overture can not only prefigure important themes in the opera but also characterize the overall tone of the work. Mozart, as was his custom, postponed much of the writing of *Don Giovanni* to the last minute, and the overture was not completed until the night before the premiere, the copyist's ink still wet on the pages as the music was handed to the orchestra.

overture

As the last strains of the overture die away, the curtain rises on the comic figure Leporello, Don Giovanni's faithful, though reluctant, servant. He has been keeping a nocturnal vigil outside the house of Donna Anna while his master is at work inside. Grumbling as he paces back and forth, Leporello sings about how he would gladly trade places with the fortunate aristocrat ("I would like to play the gentleman"; 6CD 2/13). Immediately, we see Mozart working to establish the musical character of Leporello: He sets this opening aria in F major, a traditional key for the pastoral in music, showing that Leporello is a rustic fellow; he gives him a narrow vocal range, yet no fancy chromaticism; and he has him sing quick repeated notes, almost as if he were stuttering. This last technique, called "patter song," is a stock device used to depict low-caste, inarticulate characters in comic opera.

character depiction through music

As Leporello concludes his complaint, the masked Don Giovanni rushes on stage, chased by the virtuous Donna Anna. Here the strings rush up the scale and the music modulates up a fourth (at 1:32) to signify that we are now dealing with the highborn. It seems that the Don has been checked in his advances toward Donna Anna, and the affronted lady wants him captured and unmasked. While the gentleman and lady carry on a musical tug-of-war in long notes above, the cowering Leporello patters away fearfully below. This excellent example of a vocal ensemble* makes clear the conflicting emotions of each party.

Now the cast of characters in the ensemble changes as Donna Anna runs to get help and her father enters to challenge Don Giovanni. The listener senses that this bodes ill—there is an ominous tremolo* in the strings, and the music

Lorenzo da Ponte: Librettist to Mozart

Mozart's principal librettist during the 1780s was Lorenzo da Ponte, whose own life was more unbelievable than the theatrical characters he created. Born in northern Italy of Jewish parents, he received his only formal education in a Catholic seminary. He became a teacher of Italian and Latin literature and then an ordained priest, but was banned from his native Venice for his libertine, democratic thinking and sexual escapades. Having made his way to Vienna in 1781, he was introduced to Emperor Joseph II by the imperial court composer Antonio Salieri (see page 180). Da Ponte became the official court librettist ("Poet to the Imperial Theaters"), and both Salieri and Mozart made use of his talents. But when Joseph died in 1790 and Mozart the following year, da Ponte's fortunes in Vienna declined. After passing time with another famous Venetian adventurer, Giacomo Casanova (1725–1798), da Ponte made his way to London, where he opened a bookstore. But he was soon charged with shady financial dealings, so in 1805 da Ponte stole away from London for America, one step ahead of his creditors. After a brief stop in New York, he established himself in Sunbury, Pennsylvania, as a trader, distiller, and occasional gunrunner during the War of 1812. Eventually, he gave this up and returned to New York, becoming the first professor of Italian literature at Columbia University in 1825. The high point of his final years came in May 1826, when he helped bring *Don Giovanni* to the stage in New York, the first opera by Mozart to be performed in America.

Lorenzo da Ponte (1749–1838).
The Granger Collection, New York

shifts from major to minor mode (2:50). Our fear is immediately confirmed as the Don, first refusing to duel, draws his sword and attacks the aging Commandant. In the brief exchange of steel, Mozart depicts the rising tension by means of ascending chromatic scales and tight, tense chords (3:32). At the very moment Don Giovanni's sword pierces the Commandant, the action stops and the orchestra holds on a painful **diminished chord** (3:44)—a chord made up of all minor thirds. Mozart then clears the air of discord with a simple texture and accompaniment as Don Giovanni and Leporello gaze in horror on the dying Commandant. The listener can feel the Commandant expire, his life sinking away through the slow descent of a chromatic scale (4:52). In its intensity and compression, the opening scene of *Don Giovanni* has no equal outside of Shakespeare's *King Lear*.

a duel set to music

Listening Guide

Wolfgang Amadeus Mozart
Opera, *Don Giovanni* (1787), K. 527
Act I, Scene 1

6CD 2/13

Characters: Don Giovanni, a rakish lord; Leporello, his servant; Donna Anna, a virtuous noblewoman; the Commandant, her father, a retired military man

ARIA

Leporello

| 0:00 | The pacing Leporello grumbles as he awaits his master Don Giovanni | Notte e giorno faticar, per chi nulla sa gradi, piova e il vento sopportar, mangiar male e mal dormir. | On the go from morn 'til night for one who shows no appreciation, sustaining wind and rain, without proper food or sleep. |

(Continued on next page)

	Voglio far il gentilumo	I would like to play the gentleman
	e non volgio più servir . . .	and no more a servant be . . .
	(Leporello continues in this vein)	

1:32 Violins rush up the scale and music
modulates upward as Don Giovanni
and Donna Anna rush in

ENSEMBLE (TRIO)

1:38 Donna Anna tries to hold and unmask
Don Giovanni while Leporello cowers
on the side

Donna Anna

| Non sperar, se non m'uccidi, | Do not hope you can escape |
| ch'io ti lasci fuggir mai'. | unless you kill me. |

Don Giovanni

| Donna folle, indarno gridi, | Crazy lady, you scream in vain, |
| chi son io tu non saprai. | you will never know who I am. |

Leporello

| Che tumulto, oh ciel, che gridi | What a racket, heavens, what screams, |
| il padron in nuovi guai. | my master in a new scrape. |

Donna Anna

| Gente! Servi! Al traditore! | Everyone! Help! Catch the traitor! |
| Scellerato! | Scoundrel! |

Don Giovanni

| Taci et trema al mio furore! | Shut up and get out of my way! |
| Sconsigliata! | Fool! |

Leporello

| Sta a veder che il malandrino | We will see if this malefactor |
| mi fara recipitar. . . . | will be the ruin of me. . . . |

(The trio continues in this manner with liberal repeats of text and music.)

2:50 String tremolo and shift from major to
minor as the Commandant enters

ENSEMBLE (TRIO)

The Commandant comes forward to
fight; Don Giovanni first refuses, then
duels; Leporello tries to flee

Commandant

| Lasciala, indegno! | Let her go, villain! |
| Battiti meco! | Fight with me! |

Don Giovanni

| Va! non mi degno | Away, I wouldn't deign |
| di pugnar teco! | to fight with you! |

Commandant

| Così pretendi | So you think |
| da me fuggir! | you can get away thus? |

Leporello (aside)

| Potessi almeno | If I could only |
| di qua partir! | get out of here. |

Don Giovanni

| Misero! attendi | You old fool! Get ready then, |
| se vuoi morir! | if you wish to die! |

3:32 Musical duel (running scales and
tense diminished chords)

3:44 Climax on intense chord (the
Commandant falls mortally wounded),
then a pause

(Continued on next page)

ENSEMBLE (TRIO)

3:50   Don Giovanni and Leporello look
       on the dying Commandant; the "ticking"
       sound in the strings freezes time

Ah, soccorso! son tradito.
L'assassino m'ha ferito,
e dal seno palpitante
sento l'anima partir.

Commandant
Ah, I'm wounded, betrayed
The assassin has run me through,
and from my heaving breast
I feel my soul depart.

Don Giovanni
Ah, gia cade il sciagurato,
affannoso e agonizzante,
gia del seno palpitante
Veggo l'anima partir.

Ah, already the old fool falls,
gasping and writhing in pain,
and from his heaving breast
I can see his soul depart.

Leporello
Qual misfatto! qual eccesso!
Entro il sen dallo spavento
palpitar il cor mi sento.
Io non so che far, che dir.

What a horrible thing, how stupid!
I can feel within my breast
my heart pounding from fear.
I don't know what to say or do.

4:52   A slow, chromatic descent as the last
       breath seeps out of the Commandant

FIGURE 10–10

Don Giovanni (Thomas Hampson) and
Zerlina (Marie McLaughlin) sing the duet
"Là ci darem la mano" from *Don Giovanni*.
It has been called "the most perfect duet of
seduction imaginable."

When we next meet the unrepentant Don Giovanni, he is in pursuit of the country girl Zerlina. She is the betrothed of another peasant, Masetto, and the two are to be married the next day. Don Giovanni quickly dismisses Masetto and turns his charm on the naive Zerlina. First he tries verbal persuasion carried off in *secco* recitative* (the harpsichord is still used to accompany *secco* recitatives in Classical opera, a vestige of the older Baroque practice). Zerlina, he says, is too lovely for a country bumpkin like Masetto. Her beauty demands a higher state: She will become his wife.

This preliminary discussion in *secco* recitative now gives way to more passionate expression in the form of a charming duet, "Là ci darem la mano" ("Give me your hand, oh fairest") (Fig. 10–10). Don Giovanni begins with a seductive melody (**A**) cast squarely in the Classical mold of two four-bar phrases. Zerlina repeats and extends this, but is still singing alone and untouched. The Don becomes more insistent in a new phrase (**B**), and Zerlina, in turn, becomes flustered, as her quick sixteenth notes reveal. The initial melody (**A**) returns but is now sung together by the two principals, their voices intertwining—musical union accompanies the act of physical touching that occurs on stage. Finally, as if to further affirm this coupling through music, a concluding section (**C**) is added in which the two characters skip off, arm in arm ("Let's go, my treasure"), their voices linked together, mainly in parallel-moving thirds to show unity of feeling and purpose. These are the means by which a skilled composer like Mozart can underscore, through music, the drama unfolding on the stage.

Listening Guide

Wolfgang Amadeus Mozart
Opera, *Don Giovanni* (1787)
Act I, Scene 7

6CD 2/14

Characters: Don Giovanni and the peasant girl Zerlina

Situation: Don Giovanni tries, and apparently succeeds, in the seduction of Zerlina.

RECITATIVE

Don Giovanni

0:00 Alfin siam liberati, Zerlinetta gentil,
da quel sioccone.
Che ne dite, mio ben,
sò far pulito?

At last, gentle Zerlina,
we are free of that clown.
And say, my love, didn't
I handle it well?

Zerlina

Signore, è mio marito . . .

Sir, he is my fiance.

Don Giovanni

Chi? Colui?

Vi par che un onest'uomo,
un nobil cavalier, qual io mi vanto,
possa soffrir che quel visetto d'oro,
quel viso inzuccherato
da un bifolcaccio vil sia strapazzato?

Who? Him?

Do you think that an honorable
man, a noble cavalier as I
believe I am, could let such a
golden face, such a sweet
beauty, be profaned by that
clumsy oaf?

Zerlina

Ma, signor, io gli diedi
parola di sposarlo.

But sir, I have already given
my word to marry him.

Don Giovanni

Tal parola non vale un zero.
Voi non siete fatta per esser paesana;
un altra sorte vi procuran quegli
occhi bricconcelli, quei labretti si
belli, quelle dituccia candide e
odorose, par me toccar giuncata e
fiutar rose.

Such a promise counts for
nothing. You were not made
to be a peasant girl, a higher
fate is in store for those
roguish eyes, those beautiful
lips, those milky, perfumed
hands, so soft to touch,
scented with roses.

Zerlina

Ah! . . . Non vorrei . . .

Ah! . . . I do not wish . . .

Don Giovanni

Che non vorreste?

What don't you wish?

Zerlina

Alfine ingannata restar.
Io sò che raro colle donne voi
altri cavalieri siete onesti e sinceri.

In the end to be deceived.
I know that rarely with
women are you noblemen
honest and sincere.

Don Giovanni

Eh, un'impostura della gente plebea!
La nobiltà ha dipinta negli occhi
l'onestà. Orsù, non perdiam tempo;
in questo istante io ti voglio sponsar.

A vile slander of the low
classes. Nobility can be
seen in honest eyes. Now
let's not waste time. I
will marry you immediately.

Zerlina

Voi?

You?

(Continued on next page)

Don Giovanni

Certo, io. Quell casinetto è mio.
Soli saremo, e là, gioiello mio,
ci sposeremo.

Certainly I. That villa
over there is mine. We
will be alone, and there, my
little jewel, we will be married.

ARIA (DUET)

A

1:45

Don Giovanni

Là ci da-rem la ma-no, là mi di-rai di sì.

Là ci darem la mano,
là mi dirai di sì.
Vedi, non è lontano:
partiam, ben mio, da qui.

Give me your hand, oh fairest,
whisper a gentle "yes."
See, it's not far,
let's go, my love.

Zerlina

2:03 Vorrei, e non vorrei,
mi trema un poco il cor;
felice, è ver, sarei,
ma può burlarmi ancor.

I'd like to but yet I would not.
My heart will not be still.
Tis true I would be happy,
yet he may deceive me still.

B

Don Giovanni

Vie - ni, mio bel di - let - to!

2:26 Vieni, mio bel diletto!

Come with me, my pretty!

Zerlina

Mi fa pietà Masetto!

May Masetto take pity!

Don Giovanni

Io cangierò tua sorte!

I will change your fate!

Zerlina

Presto, non son più forte.

Quick then, I can no longer resist.

A'

2:51 Repeat of first eight lines, but with Don Giovanni's and Zerlina's parts moving closer together

B'

3:14 Repeat of next four lines

C

3:42 Change of meter to dancelike $\frac{6}{8}$ as the principals skip off together

Together

(Zerlina)
An - diam, an-diam, mio be-ne, a ri-sto-rar le pe-ne d'un' in - no - cen-te a - mor!

(Don Giovanni)
An - diam, an-diam, mio be-ne, a ri-sto-rar le pe-ne d'un' in - no - cen-te a - mor!

Andiam, andiam mio bene,
a ristorar le pene
d'un innocente amor!

Let's go, let's go, my treasure,
to soothe the pangs
of innocent love.

Ultimately, in the duet "Give me your hand, oh fairest," Don Giovanni persuades Zerlina to extend her hand and the prospect of a good deal more. The tune, perhaps the most memorable of the opera, became a popular favorite in the nineteenth century. No less so *Don Giovanni*. From the moment of its first performance in Prague, Mozart's tragic-comic opera has enjoyed enormous favor with all who are moved by alluring melodies and passionate drama. *Don Giovanni* is one of those rare instances in the fine arts of a work that has immediate popular appeal, yet is universally judged to be a masterpiece of the highest order.

a popular masterpiece

Listening Exercises

Wolfgang Amadeus Mozart   6CD 2/9; 2CD 1/11
Symphony No. 40 in G minor (1788), K. 550
First movement, *Molto allegro* (very fast)

Mozart's Symphony No. 40 in G minor has been discussed in detail (page 207), as has the development of the symphony orchestra in the Classical period. The following questions focus on the various instruments and instrumental families of the orchestra as they work within the framework of sonata–allegro form. This is not a festive symphony, so there are no trumpets and drums. Mozart is writing for French horns, woodwinds, and strings. How does he use these instrumental forces to achieve his musical aims?

0:00–0:29   First theme
  1. Which instruments are playing the melody here?
     a. violins   b. cellos   c. double basses
  2. At what time do the woodwinds finally enter?
     a. 0:05   b. 0:15   c. 0:25
0:30–0:45   Transition
  3. (0:37–0:45) Which statement is true regarding the function of the French horns in this, and most, Classical symphonies?
     a. They add to the "background" resonance of the orchestra by repeating one or two pitches.
     b. They stand out by playing independent solo melodies as in a French horn concerto.
0:47–1:04   Second theme
  4. Which is true?
     a. The strings and woodwinds participate about equally in the presentation of the theme.
     b. The strings dominate this second theme area, and the woodwinds are scarcely heard.
1:22–1:32   Echoes of the first theme provide a closing.
  5. Which woodwind instrument plays a main motive of the first theme?
     a. flute   b. French horn   c. bassoon
1:53–3:45   Repeat of exposition

3:49–4:28   Development section, first of two parts
6. Which family of instruments dominates this contrapuntal working out of the first theme?
    a. woodwinds   b. brasses   c. strings

4:52–4:58   Retransition at the end of the development
7. Which family of instruments can be heard cascading downward during this retransition?
    a. woodwinds   b. brasses   c. strings

4:59–5:26   Beginning of recapitulation (compare with 0:00–0:29 of the exposition)
8. Which of the following is true?
    a. Mozart has radically changed the orchestration. The woodwinds come in first with the theme, and the strings come in later.
    b. The orchestration here at the beginning of the recapitulation is mostly the same as that at the beginning of the movement (strings followed by later woodwind entry).

5:27–6:05   Transition
9. Which family of instruments dominates this extended transition?
    a. woodwinds   b. brasses   c. strings

6:07–6:25   Second theme
6:48   Echoes of first theme provide a quick, driving end
10. Which of the following is true generally about this movement?
    a. The violins introduce all themes, the woodwinds add color and counterpoint, and the brasses play sustaining pitches in the background.
    b. The woodwinds introduce all themes, the violins add color and counterpoint, and the brasses play sustaining pitches in the background.
    c. The brasses introduce all themes, the woodwinds add color and counterpoint, and the violins play sustaining pitches in the background.

Joseph Haydn   6CD 2/10; 2CD 1/12
Opus 76, No. 3, The "Emperor" Quartet (1797)
Second movement, *Poco adagio cantabile* (rather slow, songlike)

The string quartet is a type of chamber music, and its musical style is different from that of the symphony. Here we have a quartet by the aging Haydn in which the slow movement is composed in the form of theme and variations. Go back and have another look at the melody that constitutes the theme (page 212) and then answer the following questions.

1. First of all, how many performers are playing on each of the four parts that comprise a string quartet?
    a. one   b. two   c. three   d. four
2. 0:00–1:26   **Theme**
Listen to the theme. Why does it sound so secure and firm—an appropriate musical vehicle to represent a national identity?
    a. Because all the notes are the same length.
    b. Because the theme starts low and ends high.
    c. Because each phrase is the same length and each ends on a dominant or a tonic note.

1:28–2:44   **Variation 1**

3. The second violin has the theme while the first violin rapidly ornaments above. Do the viola and cello (the lowest two instruments) play at all during this variation?

    a. yes   b. no

2:46–4:12   **Variation 2**

4. The cello has the theme in this variation. Would you say the instrument is playing in the higher or the lower part of its range? (Listen especially to the last section of the melody.)

    a. higher   b. lower

4:14–5:36   **Variation 3**

5. The viola has the melody but is gradually joined by the other instruments. Which instrument is the last to enter in this variation?

    a. first violin   b. second violin   c. cello

6. The style of writing in this variation is

    a. homophonic (chordal)   b. polyphonic (contrapuntal)

5:38–7:08   **Variation 4**

7. The theme now returns to the first violin. When the violin repeats the first phrase of the melody, it does so

    a. at the same pitch level   b. an octave higher   c. an octave lower

7:09–end   **A brief coda**

8. What does the cello do for much of the coda (7:09–7:38)?

    a. plays an arpeggio

    b. repeats a melodic sequence*

    c. sustains a pedal point*

9. In what way does Haydn conclude the movement?

    a. He has the players execute a "fadeout" by means of a ritard* and diminuendo*.

    b. He has the players accelerate for a *fortissimo* climax.

10. A general question about this movement: Which of the following is true?

    a. In this set of theme and variations, Haydn radically transforms the theme while keeping its context pretty much intact.

    b. In this set of theme and variations, Haydn keeps the theme pretty much intact and changes, or varies, the context in which it appears.

Key Words

cadenza (215)	Lorenzo da Ponte	solo concerto (213)
chamber music (210)	(220)	sonata (213)
diminished chord (220)	scherzo (210)	string quartet (210)
double exposition form	*sinfonia* (205)	*The Emperor's Hymn* (211)
(215)	*Singspiel* (218)	vocal ensemble (218)

A checklist of musical style in the Classical period is given on page 70.

Chapter

11

British Library, London, Collection Stefan Zweig

The Bridge to Romanticism: Ludwig van Beethoven

No composer is more revered than Ludwig van Beethoven (1770–1827), no music more loved than his. Indeed, when one conjures up the image of a classical composer, most likely it is the figure of Beethoven that comes to mind—the angry, defiant, disheveled Beethoven. Is it not the bust of Beethoven, rather than the elegant Mozart or the stalwart Bach, that sits atop Snoopy's piano in the comic strip *Peanuts*? Is it not Beethoven who is the namesake of nearly a dozen popular kids' films (*Beethoven*, *Beethoven's 2nd*, and *Beethoven Lives Upstairs*, for example)? Is it not his music to *Ode to Joy* that serves as the TV jingle "Movies, movies, movies, movies, movies, movies, moooo-vies"? Such observations are not mere trivialities. Beethoven is deeply ingrained in our popular culture. For many, Beethoven personifies the idea of "the musician as artist"; for some, he is the consummate "artist as hero."

   In his day Beethoven was seen as both mad genius and popular hero. Oblivious to the world, he walked about Vienna humming and scribbling music in a notebook. When he died in March 1827, 20,000 people turned out for the funeral. Schools were closed, and the army mobilized to control the crowd.

   Today Beethoven's music continues to enjoy popular favor. Statistics show that his symphonies, sonatas, and quartets are performed in concert halls and heard on radio more than those of any other classical composer. These works are tender but powerful, carefully controlled but exploding with energy. And just as Beethoven the composer struggled to overcome personal adversity—his growing deafness—so his music imparts a feeling of struggle and ultimate victory. It has a sense of rightness, even morality, about it. It elevates and inspires the listener, and for that reason it has an immediate and universal appeal.

Beethoven's life spanned the last quarter of the eighteenth century and the first quarter of the nineteenth. For the most part his music belongs to the tradition of the Viennese Classical masters. He composed predominantly in the Classical genres of symphony, piano sonata, concerto, string quartet, and opera; and he wrote within the Classical forms of sonata–allegro, rondo, and theme and variations. Yet even in the compositions of his youth, there is unmistakably a new spirit at work in his music, one that foreshadows the musical style of the Romantic period (1820–1900). An intense, lyrical expression is heard in his slow movements, while his allegros abound with striking themes, pounding rhythms, and startling dynamic contrasts. He stays within the bounds of Classical forms, yet he pushes their confines to the breaking point, so great is his urge for personal expression. Though a pupil of Haydn and a lifelong admirer of Mozart, he nonetheless elevated music to new heights of eloquence and dramatic power. For this reason he can rightly be called the prophet of Romantic music.

THE EARLY YEARS (1770–1802)

Like Bach and Mozart before him, Beethoven came from a family of musicians. His father and grandfather were performers at the court of the Elector at Bonn, Germany, a small town on the Rhine River where Beethoven was born on December 17, 1770. Seeing great musical talent in his young son, Beethoven's father, a violent, alcoholic man, forcibly made him practice at the keyboard at all hours, day and night. Soon he tried to exploit his son as a child prodigy, a second Mozart, telling the world the diminutive boy was a year or two younger than he actually was. At the age of seventeen Beethoven was packed off to faraway Vienna to study with Mozart himself. But no sooner had he arrived and played for the master than his mother became seriously ill, and he was forced to return to Bonn. Five years later, in 1792, Beethoven finally went to Vienna for good. As one of his benefactors said, "You are going to Vienna in fulfillment of your long-frustrated wishes . . . you will receive the spirit of Mozart from the hands of Haydn."

Mozart had died since Beethoven's last visit, so he now took up the study of musical composition with Haydn. But alas the aging Haydn and the youthful, impetuous Beethoven were not compatible. So when Haydn set off for his second sojourn in London in 1794 (see page 175), Beethoven began to work with other teachers, including a certain Johann Albrechtsberger (1736–1809), with whom he studied fugue, and the ever-present Antonio Salieri (1750–1825; see page 180), who taught him the Italian vocal style. At the same time Beethoven tried to make himself acceptable to polite society in Vienna: He bought new clothes, located a wigmaker, and found someone who could give him dancing lessons.

Historisches Museum der Stadt Wein

FIGURE 11–1
Beethoven, neat. A somewhat glamorized portrait of Beethoven painted ca. 1804. In reality he had a pockmarked face and was usually unshaven. Beethoven's fingers, as the portrait suggests, were short and stubby, but nevertheless he developed a prodigious technique on the piano.

Beethoven's teachers

Beethoven, the piano virtuoso

Beethoven and the aristrocracy

Beethoven's aim was to gain an entrée into the homes of the wealthy of the Austrian capital. And this he soon did, not because of his skill as a composer, and less because of his woeful social graces, but because of his phenomenal talent as a pianist. His playing was louder, more violent, more forceful, yet more expressive than the aristocrats of the salons had ever heard. He possessed an extraordinary technique—even if he did hit occasional wrong notes—and this he put to good use, especially in his fanciful improvisations. As a contemporary witness observed: "He knew how to produce such an impression on every listener that frequently there was not a single dry eye, while many broke out into loud sobs, for there was a certain magic in his expression."

The aristocracy was captivated. One patron put a string quartet at his disposal, another made it possible for Beethoven to experiment with a small orchestra, and all showered him with gifts. He acquired well-to-do pupils; he sold his compositions ("I state my price and they pay," he said with pride in 1801); and he requested and eventually received an annuity from three noblemen so that he could work undisturbed. The text of this arrangement includes the following lines:

> It is recognized that only a person who is as free as possible from all cares can consecrate himself to his craft. He can only produce these great and sublime works which ennoble Art if they form his sole pursuit, to the exclusion of all unnecessary obligations. The undersigned have therefore taken the decision to ensure that Herr Ludwig van Beethoven's situation shall not be embarrassed by his most necessary requirements, nor shall his powerful genius be hampered.

What a contrast between Beethoven's contract and the one signed by Haydn four decades earlier (see page 174)! Music is no longer merely a craft and the composer a servant. It is now an exalted Art, and the great creator a Genius who must be protected and nurtured—this is a new notion of the value of music, one of the Romantic age. And Beethoven did his best to encourage a belief in the exalted mission of the composer as artist. He would not stand at the beck and call of a master. When one patron demanded that he play for a visiting French general, Beethoven stormed out of the salon and responded by letter: "Prince, what you are, you are through the accident of birth. What I am, I am through my own efforts. There have been many princes and there will be thousands more. But there is only one Beethoven!"

Piano Sonata, Opus 13, The *Pathétique* Sonata (1799)

The bold originality in Beethoven's music can be heard in one of his most celebrated compositions, the *Pathétique* Sonata. A sonata*, as we have seen, is a multi-movement work for solo instrument or solo instrument with keyboard accompaniment. That Beethoven himself supplied the title *Pathétique* ("Plaintive") for this solo piano sonata suggests the passion and pathos he felt within this work. It has great drama and intensity, mainly because it deals in extremes. There are extremes of dynamics (from *fortissimo* to *pianissimo*), of tempo (from very fast to very slow), and of range (from very high to very low). It also requires of the pianist more technical skill and stamina than any piano sonata of Mozart or Haydn. Beethoven himself frequently performed the *Pathétique* in the homes and palaces of the Viennese aristocracy.

FIGURE 11–2

Beethoven, messy. A fanciful, yet in many ways accurate, depiction of Beethoven in the midst of creative chaos. The illustrator has assembled many objects from Beethoven's daily life: his ear-trumpet, used in a vain attempt to correct his growing deafness; the bowl of porridge about to spill onto the keyboard; and the broken strings protruding from the back of his Graf piano. When composing, Beethoven was famously given to cursing, howling, and pounding on the piano.

British Library, London, Collection Stefan Zweig

FIRST MOVEMENT

Contemporaries recount how Beethoven the pianist played with "superhuman" speed and force, and how he banged so hard on one occasion that he broke six strings. The crashing C minor chord that opens the *Pathétique* Sonata suggests Beethoven's sometimes violent approach to the instrument. After this startling opening gesture, Beethoven the dramatist continues by juxtaposing music of wildly differing moods: the *sforzando* chord is immediately followed by quiet lyricism, only to be interrupted by another chordal thunderbolt. This slow introduction probably is a written-out version of the sort of improvisation at the piano that gained Beethoven great fame in Vienna. The introduction leads to a racing first theme that rises impetuously in the right hand. The sense of anxiety the listener feels is amplified by the bass, where the left hand of the pianist plays broken octaves (the alternation of two tones an octave apart) reminiscent of the rumble of distant thunder.

crashing chords and quiet lyricism

EXAMPLE 11–1

The remainder of the movement now plays out as a match between the impetuous, racing themes and the stormy chords. There is much passion and intensity here, yet there is also Classical formal control. The crashing chords come back at the beginning of both the development and coda in this sonata–allegro form movement. Thus the chords set firm formal boundaries and thereby prevent the racing theme from flying out of control. Beethoven's music often conveys a sense of struggle: Classical forms gave Beethoven something to struggle against.

Ludwig van Beethoven
Piano Sonata, Opus 13, the *Pathétique* Sonata (1799)
First movement, *Grave; Allegro di molto e con brio*
(grave; very fast and with gusto)

6CD 3/1;
2CD 1/13

Form: sonata–allegro

INTRODUCTION

0:00	Crashing chords alternate with softer, more lyrical chords
0:46	Softer chords continually cut off by crashing chords below
1:10	Melody builds to a climax and then rapid descent

EXPOSITION [ ] = repeats

| 1:41 [3:14] | Rising agitated melody in right hand against broken octaves in left (first theme) |

(Continued on next page)

1:59 [3:34]   Transition with modulation to new key, thinner texture

2:11 [3:44]   Bass, followed by treble, initiates a "call and response" (second theme)

2:39 [4:12]   Right and left hands race in opposite directions (closing theme, part 1)

2:58 [4:31]   Rapid scales in right hand above simple chords in left (closing theme, part 2)

3:04 [4:37]   Reminiscence of first theme

[3:14–4:47]   Repeat of exposition

DEVELOPMENT

4:48   Crashing chords and softer chords from introduction

5:32   First theme extended and varied

6:09   Rapid twisting descent played by right hand leads to

RECAPITULATION

6:15   Rising agitated melody in right hand (first theme)

6:25   Transition

6:35   Call and response between bass and treble (second theme)

6:59   Hands move rapidly in opposite directions (closing theme, part 1)

7:18   Scale runs in right hand (closing theme, part 2)

7:24   Reminiscence of first theme

CODA

7:35   Recall of chords from the introduction

8:14   Reminiscence of first theme leads to a drive to the final cadence

(Listening Exercise 26)

SECOND MOVEMENT

Eyewitnesses who heard Beethoven at the piano remarked on the "legato" quality of his playing, and contrasted it with Mozart's lighter, more staccato style. Beethoven himself said in 1796 that "one can sing on the piano, so long as one has feeling." We can hear Beethoven sing through the legato melodic line that dominates the slow second movement of the *Pathétique* Sonata. Indeed, the expression mark he gave to the movement is *cantabile* ("songful"). The singing quality of the melody seems to have appealed to pop star Billy Joel, who borrowed this theme for the refrain of his song "This Night" on the album *Innocent Man* (SONY ASIN:B00000DCHG).

THIRD MOVEMENT

A comparison of the second and third movements of the *Pathétique* Sonata will show that musical form does not determine musical mood. Although both the *Adagio* and the fast finale are in rondo form, the first is a lyrical hymn and the latter a passionate, but slightly comical, chase. The finale has hints of the crashing chords and stark contrasts of the first movement, but the earlier violence and impetuosity have been softened into a mood of impassioned playfulness.

The eighteenth-century piano sonata had been essentially private music of a modest sort—music a composer-teacher like Mozart or Haydn would write for a talented amateur pupil to be played in the home. Beethoven took the modest, private piano sonata and infused it with the technical bravura of the public stage. The louder sound, wider range, and greater length of Beethoven's thirty-two piano sonatas made them appropriate for the increasingly large concert halls—and pianos—of the nineteenth century. Beginning in the Romantic period the piano sonatas of Beethoven became a staple of the professional pianist's repertoire, and so they remain today.

from salon to concert hall

Beethoven Becomes Deaf

Beethoven cut a strange, eccentric figure as he wandered the streets of Vienna, sometimes humming, sometimes mumbling, and sometimes jotting on a music paper. Adding to the difficulties of his somewhat unstable personality was the fact that he was gradually going deaf—a serious handicap for any person, but a tragic condition for a musician. Can you imagine a blind painter? In fact, there have been many composers in the history of music who were blind, among them Francesco Landini (†1397), Ray Charles, and Stevie Wonder, but only one who was deaf: Beethoven.

Beethoven first complained about his hearing and a ringing in his ears in the late 1790s, and he suffered considerable anguish and depression. His growing deafness perhaps least affected his work as a composer—good musicians can hear with an "inner ear" and do not need actual sound. But it caused him to retreat from society even more, and it all but ended his career as a performer, since he could no longer gauge how hard to press the piano keys. By late 1802 Beethoven recognized that he would suffer a gradual, though ultimately total, loss of hearing. In despair he wrote his last will and testament (see boxed essay). Yet he emerged from this period of crisis with a renewed conviction to do great things. His music had sustained him: "I would have ended my life—it was only *my art* that held me back," he said. He would now "seize Fate by the throat."

growing deafness

THE "HEROIC" PERIOD (1803–1813)

It was in this resurgent, defiant mood that Beethoven entered what we call his "heroic" period of composition (1803–1813). His works became longer, more assertive, and full of grand gestures. Simple, often triadic, themes predominate, and these are repeated, sometime incessantly, as the music swells to majestic proportions. When these themes are played *forte* and given over to the brass instruments, a heroic, triumphant sound results.

Beethoven wrote nine symphonies in all, six of them during his "heroic" period. These symphonies are few in number in part because they are so much longer and more complex than those of Mozart or Haydn. They set the standard for the epic symphony of the nineteenth century. Most noteworthy are the "Eroica" (Third), the famous Fifth Symphony, the Sixth (called the "Pastoral" because it tries to evoke the ambiance of the Austrian countryside), the Seventh, and the monumental Ninth. In these, Beethoven introduces new orchestral colors by bringing new instruments into the symphony orchestra: the trombone (Symphony Nos. 5, 6, and 9), the contrabassoon (Symphony Nos. 5 and 9), the piccolo (Symphony Nos. 5, 6, and 9), and even the human voice (Symphony No. 9).

Beethoven's symphonies

Beethoven's Confession: The Heiligenstadt Testament

Beethoven was a physically powerful, proud, egotistical man who suffered no fools and had few doubts about his own worth as a musician. The loss of his hearing, which began in 1798, was a near fatal blow. It not only jeopardized his profession but also caused him to withdraw increasingly from society, creating the image of Beethoven the loner, the outcast, the misanthrope. The Heiligenstadt Testament is a lengthy, confessional statement that Beethoven, having finally decided against suicide, wrote in the fall of 1802. It is a remarkable document—part last will and testament, part artistic manifesto. The name "Heiligenstadt" derives from the fact that Beethoven penned it in the village of that name, just to the north of Vienna, where he had gone in 1802 for a "cure" for his deafness. The following extract offers an insight into Beethoven's anguished state of mind:

Oh my fellow men who consider me an unfriendly, hostile, peevish man or even misanthropic, how greatly you wrong me. For you do not know the secret reason why I appear to be so to you. . . . Though endowed with a passionate and lively temperament and even fond of the distractions offered by society, I was soon obliged to withdraw and live in solitude. . . . I could not bring myself to say to people: "Speak up, shout, for I am deaf." Alas, how could I possibly mention the loss *of a sense* which in me should be more perfectly developed than in other people, a sense which at one time I possessed in the greatest perfection, even to a degree few in my profession possess or have ever possessed. . . . But how humiliated I have felt if somebody standing beside me heard the sound of a flute in the distance and *I heard nothing!* Such experiences made me despair. I would have ended my life—it was only *my art* that held me back.

Symphony No. 3 in E♭ major ("Eroica," 1803)

As its title suggests, Beethoven's "Eroica" Symphony epitomizes the grandiose, heroic style. More than any single orchestral work, it changed the historical direction of the symphony. Its length, some forty-five minutes, is nearly twice that of a symphony by his teacher Haydn. It assaults the ear with startling rhythmic effects and chord changes that were shocking to early-nineteenth-century listeners. The slow movement is a funeral march, while the finale not merely ends the symphony but provides a culmination of all that has preceded. Most novel for Beethoven, the work has biographical content, for the hero of the "Eroica" Symphony, at least originally, was Napoleon Bonaparte.

Austria and the German states were at war with France during the early years of the nineteenth century. Yet German-speaking Beethoven was much taken with the enemy's revolutionary call for liberty, equality, and fraternity. Napoleon Bonaparte became his hero, and the composer dedicated his third symphony to him, writing on the title page "intitolata Bonaparte." But when news that Napoleon had declared himself emperor reached Beethoven, he flew into a rage saying "Now he, too, will trample on all the rights of man and indulge his ambition." Taking up a knife, he scratched so violently to erase the name Bonaparte from the title page that he left a hole in the paper (Fig. 11–3). When the work was published, Napoleon's name had been removed in favor of the more general title, "Heroic Symphony: To Celebrate the Memory of a Fallen Hero" (Fig. 11–4).

FIGURE 11–3

The title page of the autograph of Beethoven's "Eroica" Symphony: *Sinfonia grande intitolata Bonaparte.* Note the hole where Beethoven took a knife and scratched out the name "Bonaparte."

Gesellschaft der Musikfreunde, Vienna

Symphony No. 5 in C minor (1808)

At the center of Beethoven's symphonic output stands his remarkable Symphony No. 5. Its novelty rests in the way the composer conveys a sense of psychological progression over the course of four movements. An imaginative listener might feel the following sequence of events: (1) a fateful encounter with elemental forces, (2) a period of quiet soul-searching, followed by (3) a further wrestling with the elements, and, finally, (4) a triumphant victory over the forces of Fate. Beethoven himself is said to have remarked with regard to the famous opening motive of the symphony: "There Fate knocks at the door!"

The rhythm of the opening—perhaps the best-known moment in all of classical music—animates the entire symphony. Not only does it dominate the opening *Allegro* but it reappears in varied form in the three later movements as well, binding the symphony into a unified whole.

EXAMPLE 11–2

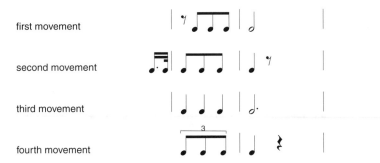

CORBIS/Burstein Collection

FIGURE 11–4

As a young officer, Napoleon Bonaparte seized control of the government of France in 1799. He established a new form of republican government that emphasized the revolutionary ideals of liberty, equality, and humanity. After Napoleon elevated himself to emperor in 1804, Beethoven changed the title of his Symphony No. 3 from "Bonaparte" to "Eroica." The portrait by Jacques-Louis David shows the newly crowned Napoleon in full imperial regalia. Liberator had become oppressor.

FIRST MOVEMENT

At the very outset the listener is jolted to attention, forced to sit up and take notice by a sudden explosion of sound. And what an odd beginning to a symphony—a blast of three short notes and a long one, followed by the same three shorts and a long, all now a step lower. The movement can't quite get going. It starts and stops, then seems to lurch forward and gather momentum. And where is the theme or melody? This three-shorts-and-a-long pattern is more a motive or musical cell than a melody. Yet it is striking by virtue of its power and compactness. As the movement unfolds, the actual pitches of the motive prove to be of secondary importance. Beethoven is obsessed here with rhythm. He wants to demonstrate the enormous latent force that lurks within even the simplest rhythmic cell just waiting to be unleashed by a composer who understands the secrets of rhythmic energy.

To control the sometimes violent forces that will emerge, the musical processes unfold within the traditional confines of sonata–allegro form. The basic four-note motive provides all the musical material for the first theme area:

EXAMPLE 11–3

There is a brief transition played by a solo French horn. It is only six notes long and is formed simply by adding two notes to the end of the basic four-note motive. As expected, the transition moves the tonality from the tonic (C minor) to the relative major* (E♭ major):

EXAMPLE 11–4

a famous musical motive

The second theme seems to offer a moment of escape from the rush of the motive, but even here the pattern of three shorts and a long is heard underneath in the low strings:

EXAMPLE 11–5

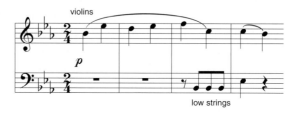

The closing theme, too, is none other than the motive once again, now presented in a somewhat different guise:

EXAMPLE 11–6

With the development, the opening motive returns and assumes all, if not more than all, of the force it had at the beginning. It soon takes on different melodic forms, as it is tossed back and forth between instruments, though the rhythmic shape remains constant:

EXAMPLE 11–7

manipulation of the motive

As the motive rises, so does the musical tension. A powerful rhythmic climax ensues and then gives way to a brief imitative passage. Soon Beethoven reduces the six-note motive of the transition down to merely two notes, and then just one, as he passes these around *pianissimo* between the strings and the winds:

EXAMPLE 11–8

Beethoven was a master of the process of thematic condensation—stripping away all extraneous material to get to the core of a musical idea. Here in this mysterious *pianissimo* passage he holds up the irreducible minimum of his motive: a single note. In the midst of this quiet, the original four-note motive tries to reassert itself *fortissimo*, yet at first cannot do so. Its explosive force, however, cannot be held back. A thunderous return of the opening chords signals the beginning of the recapitulation.

Although the recapitulation offers a repeat of the events of the exposition, Beethoven has one surprise in store. No sooner has the motive regained its momentum than an oboe interjects a tender, languid, and wholly unexpected solo. Though a deviation from the usual path of sonata–allegro form, this brief oboe cadenza* allows for a momentary release of excess energy. The recapitulation then resumes its expected course.

a surprise oboe solo

What is not expected is the enormous coda that follows. It is even longer than the exposition! A new form of the motive appears and it, too, is subjected to development. In fact, what Beethoven does here is write a second development section, so great is his urge to exploit the latent power of this one simple musical idea.

a coda longer than the exposition

Listening Guide
WWW

Ludwig van Beethoven
Symphony No. 5 in C minor (1808)
First movement, *Allegro con brio* (fast with gusto)

6CD 3/2;
2CD 1/14

Form: sonata–allegro

EXPOSITION [ ] = repeats

0:00	[1:23]	Two statements of the motive
0:06	[1:29]	Motive builds momentum in a crescendo working up to climax and three chords, the last of which is held
0:23	[1:46]	Another crescendo begins as motive is piled upon itself in imitative counterpoint
0:40	[2:04]	Loud climax on two chords
0:43	[2:06]	Short transition played by solo French horn
0:45	[2:09]	Quiet second theme in new major key (relative major)
0:58	[2:22]	Crescendo
1:04	[2:27]	Loud string passage prepares arrival of closing theme
1:13	[2:36]	Closing theme

[1:23–2:44] Repeat of exposition

DEVELOPMENT

2:46	Motive played *fortissimo* by horn and strings and then passed back and forth between woodwinds and strings
3:07	Another crescendo or "Beethovenian swell"
3:13	Rhythmic climax in which motive is pounded incessantly
3:20	Short passage of imitative counterpoint using transition motive
3:30	Two notes of transition motive passed back and forth

(Continued on next page)

3:40	One note passed back and forth between winds and strings; gets quiet
3:50	Basic four-note motive tries to reassert itself loudly
3:54	More *pianissimo* one-note alternation between winds and strings
3:58	Motive reenters insistently

RECAPITULATION

4:04	Return of motive
4:10	Motive gathers momentum and cadences with three chords
4:20	Unexpected oboe solo
4:36	Motive returns and moves hurriedly to a climax
4:56	Transition now played by bassoon instead of horn
4:59	Quiet second theme with timpani now playing rhythm of motive
5:15	Crescendo leading to closing theme
5:32	Closing theme

CODA

5:40	Motive pounded *fortissimo* on one note, then again a step higher
5:53	Imitative counterpoint
6:07	Rising quarter notes form new four-note pattern
6:19	New four-note pattern alternates between strings and woodwinds
6:39	Pounding on a single note, then motive as at beginning
6:53	Succession of I–V–I chords brings movement to abrupt end

(Listening Exercise 27)

FIGURE 11–5

Original autograph of Beethoven at work on the second movement of his Symphony No. 5. The many corrections in different-colored inks and red pencil suggest the turmoil and constant evolution involved in Beethoven's creative process.

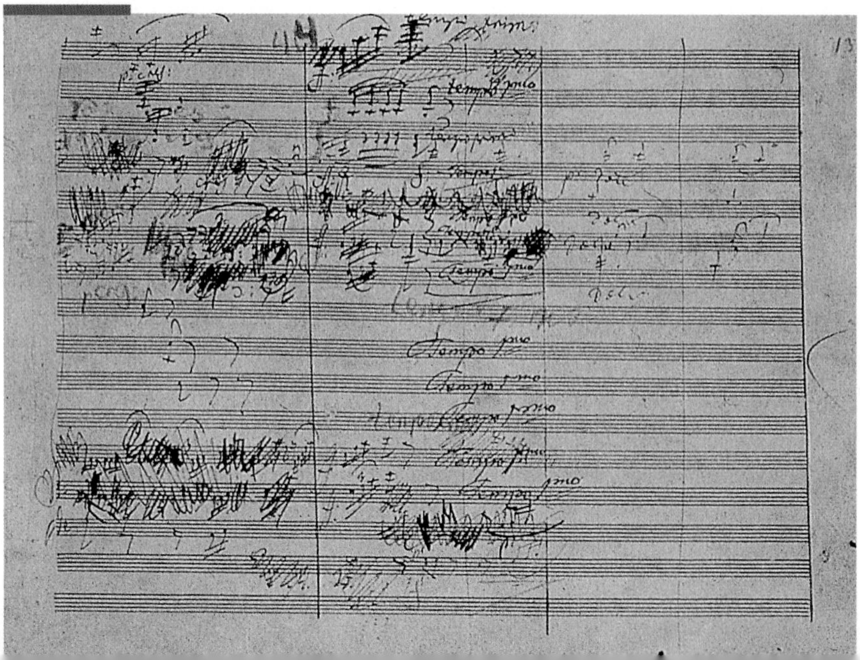

Deutsche Staats, Berlin

SECOND MOVEMENT

After the pounding we have been subjected to in the explosive first movement, the calm, noble *Andante* comes as a welcome change of pace. The key is now major (A♭), the mood serene, and the melody expansive—instead of beginning with a four-note motive, the opening theme here runs on for twenty-two measures. The musical form is also a familiar one: theme and variations (see pages 193–97). But this is not the simple, easily audible theme and variations of Haydn. There are two themes, and the first one has three parts. Not only do the variations become more complex as the movement progresses, but also, beginning with variation 2, Beethoven shuffles the order in which the themes and parts of themes appear. In this way Beethoven challenges the listener to pay attention to what he has composed.

Listening Guide

Ludwig van Beethoven
Symphony No. 5 in C minor (1808)
Second movement, *Andante con moto* (progressing with movement)

6CD 3/3

Form: theme and variations

THEMES

0:00   Violas and cellos play beginning of theme 1

0:24   Woodwinds play middle of theme 1

0:38   Violins play end of theme 1

0:54   Clarinets, bassoons, and violins play theme 2

1:16   Brasses play theme 2 in fanfare style
1:34   Mysterious *pianissimo*

VARIATION 1

2:01   Violas and cellos vary beginning of theme 1 by adding sixteenth notes

2:24   Woodwinds play middle of theme 1
2:34   Strings play end of theme 1
2:53   Clarinets, bassoons, and violins play theme 2
3:14   Brasses return with fanfare (theme 2)
3:32   More of the mysterious *pianissimo*

VARIATION 2

4:00   Violas and cellos overlay beginning of theme 1
        with rapidly moving ornamentation

4:36   Pounding repeated chords with theme below in cellos and basses
4:53   Rising scales lead to a fermata (hold)
5:12   Woodwinds play fragments of beginning of theme 1
5:54   Fanfare (theme 2) now returns in full orchestra
6:43   Woodwinds play beginning of theme 1 detached and in a minor key

(Continued on next page)

VARIATION 3

7:23   Violins play beginning of theme 1 *fortissimo*

7:48   Woodwinds play middle of theme 1

7:58   Strings play end of theme 1

CODA

8:12   Tempo quickens as bassoons play reminiscence of beginning of theme 1

8:28   Violins play reminiscence of theme 2

8:37   Woodwinds play middle of theme 1

8:48   Strings play end of theme 1

9:09   Ends with repetitions of the rhythm of the very first measure of the movement

THIRD MOVEMENT

In the Classical period the third movement of a symphony or quartet was usually a graceful minuet and trio (see page 184). Haydn and his pupil Beethoven wanted to infuse this third movement generally with more life and energy, so they often wrote a faster, more rollicking piece and called it a scherzo*, meaning "joke." There is nothing really humorous about the mysterious and sometimes threatening sound of the scherzo of Beethoven's Symphony No. 5, yet it is certainly far removed from the elegant world of the courtly minuet.

The formal plan of Beethoven's scherzo, **ABA'**, is taken over from the ternary form of the minuet, as is the triple meter heard here. The scherzo, **A**, is in the tonic key of C minor, while the trio, **B**, is in C major. This conflict, or juxtaposition, of major and minor, of dark and light, is just one of several confrontations that is resolved in the course of this four-movement symphony.

FIGURE 11–6

Interior of the Theater-an-der-Wien, Vienna, where Beethoven's Symphony No. 5 received its premiere on December 22, 1808. This all-Beethoven concert lasted four hours, from 6:30 until 10:30 P.M., and presented eight new works, including his Symphony No. 5. During the performance of the symphony the orchestra sometimes halted because of the difficulties in playing Beethoven's radically new music.

Museum der Stadt Wien

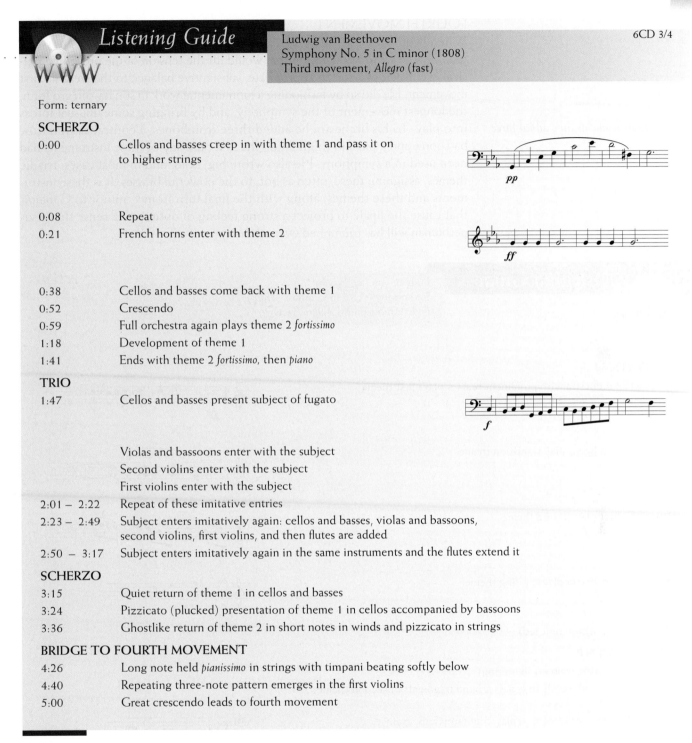

Listening Guide

WWW

Ludwig van Beethoven
Symphony No. 5 in C minor (1808)
Third movement, *Allegro* (fast)

6CD 3/4

Form: ternary

SCHERZO

0:00	Cellos and basses creep in with theme 1 and pass it on to higher strings	
0:08	Repeat	
0:21	French horns enter with theme 2	
0:38	Cellos and basses come back with theme 1	
0:52	Crescendo	
0:59	Full orchestra again plays theme 2 *fortissimo*	
1:18	Development of theme 1	
1:41	Ends with theme 2 *fortissimo*, then *piano*	

TRIO

1:47	Cellos and basses present subject of fugato
	Violas and bassoons enter with the subject
	Second violins enter with the subject
	First violins enter with the subject
2:01 – 2:22	Repeat of these imitative entries
2:23 – 2:49	Subject enters imitatively again: cellos and basses, violas and bassoons, second violins, first violins, and then flutes are added
2:50 – 3:17	Subject enters imitatively again in the same instruments and the flutes extend it

SCHERZO

3:15	Quiet return of theme 1 in cellos and basses
3:24	Pizzicato (plucked) presentation of theme 1 in cellos accompanied by bassoons
3:36	Ghostlike return of theme 2 in short notes in winds and pizzicato in strings

BRIDGE TO FOURTH MOVEMENT

4:26	Long note held *pianissimo* in strings with timpani beating softly below
4:40	Repeating three-note pattern emerges in the first violins
5:00	Great crescendo leads to fourth movement

Now, a stroke of genius on Beethoven's part: He links the third and fourth movements by means of a musical bridge. Holding a single pitch as quietly as possible, the violins create an eerie sound, while the timpani beats menacingly in the background. A three-note motive grows from the violins and is repeated over and over as a wave of sound begins to swell from the orchestra. With enormous force the wave finally crashes down, and from it emerges the triumphant beginning of the fourth movement—one of the most thrilling moments in all of music.

a bridge to the finale

FOURTH MOVEMENT

When Beethoven arrived at the finale, he was faced with a nearly impossible task: how to write a conclusion that would lift the tension of the preceding musical events yet provide an appropriate, substantive balance to the weighty first movement. He did so by fashioning a monumental work in sonata–allegro form, the longest movement of the symphony, and by bringing some unusual forces into play. To his orchestra he added three trombones, a contrabassoon (low bassoon), and a piccolo (high flute), the first time any of these instruments had been used in a symphony. He also wrote big, bold, and in most cases, triadic themes, assigning these, often as not, to the powerful brasses. It is these instruments and these themes, along with the final turn from C minor to C major, that cause the finale to project a strong feeling of optimism, a sense that a superhuman will has triumphed over adversity.

new instruments give added force

Listening Guide

Ludwig van Beethoven
Symphony No. 5 in C minor (1808)
Fourth movement, *Allegro* (fast)

6CD 3/5

Form: sonata–allegro

EXPOSITION

0:00   Full orchestra with prominent brasses plays first theme

0:36   French horns play transition theme

1:04   Strings play second theme

1:33   Full orchestra plays closing theme

(Repeat of exposition omitted)

DEVELOPMENT

2:06   Loud string tremolo (fluttering)

2:11   Strings and woodwinds pass around fragments of second theme in different keys

2:36   Double basses begin to play countermelody against the second theme

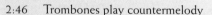

2:46   Trombones play countermelody

3:13   Woodwinds and brasses play countermelody above dominant pedal point in cellos and basses

3:30   Climax and pause on dominant triad

3:48   Ghostlike theme from the scherzo with four-note rhythm

(Continued on next page)

RECAPITULATION

4:17   Full orchestra plays first theme *fortissimo*
4:54   French horns bring in transition theme
5:26   Strings play second theme
5:54   Woodwinds play closing theme

CODA

6:26   Violins play second theme
6:37   Brasses and woodwinds play countermelody from development
6:50   V–I, V–I chords sound like final cadence
6:59   Bassoons, French horns, flutes, clarinets, and then piccolo continue
       with transition theme
7:27   Trill high in piccolo
7:50   Tempo changes to *presto* (very fast)
8:14   Brasses recall first theme but now twice as fast
8:21   V–I, V–I cadence followed by pounding tonic chord

Beethoven's Symphony No. 5 reveals his genius in a paradox: From minimal material (the basic cell) he derives maximum sonority. Climaxes are achieved by incessantly repeating the cell-like motive. Long crescendos swell like tidal waves of sound. Wildly different moods are accommodated within a single movement. In the quiet string music of the *Andante* (second movement), for example, we are never far from a heroic brass fanfare. Everywhere there is a feeling of raw, elemental power pushed forward by the newly enlarged orchestra. Beethoven was the first to recognize that massive sound could be a potent psychological weapon. No wonder that during World War II (1939–1945) both sides, Fascist as well as Allied, used the music of this symphony to symbolize "Victory."[†]

THE FINAL YEARS (1814–1827)

By 1814 Beethoven had become totally deaf and had withdrawn almost completely from society. His music, too, took on a more remote, inaccessible quality, placing heavy demands on both performer and audience. In these late works Beethoven requires the listener to connect musical ideas over long spans of time, to follow the variation of a theme when that variation has become quite remote from the original theme itself. Most of these late works are piano sonatas and string quartets—intimate, introspective chamber music. But two pieces, the Mass in D (*Missa solemnis*, 1823) and the Symphony No. 9 (1824), are large-scale compositions for full orchestra and chorus. In these works for larger forces, Beethoven seems again to wish to communicate directly to a broad spectrum of humanity.

Beethoven's Symphony No. 9, his last, was the first work in the history of this genre to include a chorus. It is as if the composer's need for expression in his final symphonic work was so great that the instruments of the orchestra alone were no longer sufficient. Something more was necessary: text and voices. And so they enter in the finale of this four-movement work. The text,

[†]In Morse code, short–short–short–long is the letter "V," as in "Victory."

FIGURE 11–7

Beethoven walking in the rain, as sketched in Vienna ca. 1823. The composer cut an odd figure. He would repeatedly stop to record an idea in his music sketchbook as he hummed or howled in an off-key voice. In 1821, Beethoven was mistakenly arrested as a tramp.

Original lost

An die Freude (Ode to Joy), was written by the German poet Friedrich von Schiller in 1786. It is a hymn, in the spirit of the French Revolution, in honor of universal brotherhood, a theme that had been important to Beethoven since his earliest years. Beethoven set Schiller's text to a melody that has become well known to all of us as his *Ode to Joy*. (In recent times the tune has been popularized in several TV commercials, a movie score, as a Christmas song, and, more appropriately, as an anthem for the United Nations.) Beethoven intentionally constructed a melody that is folk-song-like, simple and conjunct*, so that we can all sing it—a fitting musical companion to a text extolling the commonality of humankind. (For a detailed discussion of the structure of the melody, see page 27).

EXAMPLE 11–9; INTRO CD, TRACK 7

Ode to Joy

In the last great movement of his last great symphony, Beethoven's *Ode to Joy* serves as the theme for a magnificent set of variations. (The theme and three variations can be heard on the Intro CD, track 7.) For twenty-five minutes the music marches toward a grandiose climax. Beethoven pushes the voices to sing louder and louder, higher and higher, faster than they can enunciate the text. The instrumentalists, too, are driven by the *presto* tempo to go so quickly they can scarcely play the notes. All performers strain to exceed the limits of their physical abilities and accomplish the impossible. The sound is not so much beautiful as it is overwhelming, for the chorus and orchestra speak with one exalted voice. Their message is Beethoven's message: Art will unify all humanity.

a message for humanity

EPILOGUE: BEETHOVEN AND THE NINETEENTH CENTURY

The figure of Beethoven towered over all the arts during the nineteenth century. He had shown how personal expression might expand the confines of Classical form with astonishingly powerful results. He had given music "the grand gesture," stunning effects like the crashing introduction of the *Pathétique* Sonata or the gigantic crescendo leading to the finale of the Fifth Symphony. He had shown that pure sound—sound divorced from musical idea—could be glorious in and of itself. At once he had made music both grandiose and intensely lyrical. His works became the standard against which later composers of the Romantic era measured their worth. The cover of this book shows poet, novelist, playwright, performer, and composer all turning in reverence toward the bust of Beethoven. Beethoven, larger than life, gazes down from Olympian heights, a monument to all that is noble and sublime in art.

British Library, London, Collection Stefan Zweig

FIGURE 11–8

A drawing of the deceased Beethoven sketched on the morning of March 28, 1827, the day after the composer's death. It was made by Josef Danhauser, the same artist who painted the group portrait that appears on the cover of this book.

Listening Exercises

26

Ludwig van Beethoven 6CD 3/1; 2CD 1/13
Piano Sonata, Opus 13, the *Pathétique* Sonata (1799)
First movement, *Grave; Allegro di molto e con brio*
(grave; very fast and with gusto)

0:00–1:40

1. The introduction imparts an unsettled, uncertain feeling to the mind of the listener. What, specifically, does Beethoven do to create this feeling? Which answer is *not* correct?
   a. starts with happy major chords and moves to sad minor ones
   b. contrasts slow chords with racing descents
   c. contrasts high and low ranges of the piano
   d. puts very loud and very soft sounds in close proximity
2. (1:36–1:39) The end of the introduction is marked by a long descent. Which hand of the pianist plays this descent?
   a. right hand   b. left hand

1:41–3:13 Exposition

3. (1:33–1:53) The descent gives way to the first theme (1:41) and the tempo changes. Which statement is true?
   a. A fast tempo gives way to a slower one.
   b. A fast tempo gives way to an even faster one.
   c. *Grave* (grave) gives way to *allegro con brio* (fast with gusto).
4. A rumbling broken-octave bass had accompanied the agitated first theme (1:41–1:58). Now here in the transition, (1:59–2:09) can these menacing broken octaves still be heard in the bass?
   a. yes   b. no
5. (2:11–2:38) What about now during the second theme. Are the broken octaves still present?
   a. yes   b. no
6. (2:39–2:56) Here, in the first part of the closing theme, the right hand drives rapidly to the top range of the piano while the left hand dives deep into the bass. Is this one long, twenty-second passage of music, or two presentations (statement and repeat) of a shorter, ten-second passage?
   a. one long passage of music   b. two presentations of a shorter passage

7. (3:07–3:13) The final cadence at the very end of the exposition is marked by a thick texture. How is this created?

a. The left hand alternates chords in the top and middle ranges while the right plays ascending broken chords.

b. The right hand alternates chords in the top and middle ranges while the left plays descending broken octaves.

3:14–4:47 Now comes the repeat of the exposition. As you listen, check your answers to questions 4–7.

4:48–6:14 Development

8. (5:15–5:40) The development begins with a return to the chords of the introduction and then proceeds with the first theme. Which statement is true about the tempo in this passage?

a. The music accelerates and then becomes progressively slower.

b. The music gets progressively slower, almost stopping, and then suddenly becomes fast.

c. The music proceeds at a moderate pace and then suddenly becomes fast.

9. (6:09–6:14) Does the left hand (bass) rest during the rapid twisting descent at the end of the development? In other words, is this a solo for the right hand?

a. yes   b. no

6:15–7:34 Recapitulation

7:35–8:24 Coda

10. (8:18–8:24) How does this movement end?

a. with the closing theme

b. with a soft fadeout

c. with the crashing chords of the introduction

Ludwig van Beethoven   6CD 3/2; 2CD 1/14
Symphony No. 5 (1808) in C minor
First movement, *Allegro con brio* (fast with gusto)

There is perhaps no more famous single movement in classical music than the first movement of Beethoven's Symphony No. 5. The following questions refer to places that correspond to the major formal divisions of the movement. They are designed to show how Beethoven honored, and sometimes broke with, the usual Classical treatment of sonata–allegro form.

1. (0:00–0:30) Which instruments carry the motive and its immediate repetitions?

a. strings   b. woodwinds   c. brasses   d. percussion

(0:41–0:44) French horn plays short transition

2. (0:45–0:51) When the quiet, brief second theme enters it is played three times in succession by three different instruments. In what order do these instruments present the theme?

a. clarinet, violins, flute

b. violins, clarinet, flute

c. flute, clarinet, violins

3. Normally in a sonata–allegro form movement in a minor key the second theme first appears in the major mode. Does Beethoven honor the tradition? Is the second theme in major or minor?

a. major   b. minor

4. (1:13–1:28) In this passage we have the closing theme and final chords of the exposition, and then the return to the beginning, which commences the repeat of the exposition. What happens to the mode in this passage from the end of the exposition back to the beginning?
   a. The major mode shifts back to minor.
   b. The minor mode shifts back to major.

1:23–2:44 Repeat of the exposition. Check your answers to questions 1–3.

2:46–3:59 Development

5. (2:46–2:49) When the solo French horn announces the beginning of the development, it does so with material taken from
   a. the motive   b. the second theme

6. (3:58–4:08) At the end of the development the orchestra insistently repeats the motive, and then the recapitulation begins. Beethoven helps announce the recapitulation by using a dynamic level that is
   a. *pianissimo*   b. *piano*   c. *fortissimo*

7. (4:20–4:36) An oboe suddenly interrupts the recapitulation. Was this lyrical solo heard in the exposition?
   a. yes   b. no

8. (4:56–5:08) In the recapitulation, Beethoven reorchestrates and rewrites the transition and second theme. The brief transition, which was played by a solo French horn in the exposition, is now given over to a solo bassoon. Then the short second theme is played four times and this passage, too, is reorchestrated. Which sequence of instruments correctly represents the orchestration applied to the four statements of the second theme?
   a. flutes, clarinet, violins, clarinet
   b. violins, flutes, violins, flutes
   c. clarinet, violins, flutes, clarinet

9. (4:59–5:08) If Beethoven's treatment of sonata–allegro form holds true to the form, he will bring the second theme back in the minor mode. Does the second theme, in fact, come back in minor?
   a. yes   b. no

10. In this movement, Beethoven expands considerably the traditional treatment of sonata–allegro form. Which of the following is *not* a way he carries out this expansion?
    a. He provides an introduction that is longer than the coda.
    b. He provides a coda that is longer than the exposition.
    c. He provides a development section that is almost as long as the exposition.
    d. He adds an unexpected oboe solo at the beginning of the recapitulation.

Key Words

"Eroica" Symphony (234)
Heilingenstadt Testament (234)
"heroic" period (233)
Ode to Joy (244)
Pathétique Sonata (230)

Chapter 12

Private Collection

The Romantic Spirit
(1820—1900)

The mature music of Beethoven, with its powerful crescendos, pounding chords, grand gestures, and larger, more colorful orchestra, announces the arrival of the Romantic era in music. The transition from musical Classicism to Romanticism in the early nineteenth century coincides with similar stylistic changes in the poetry, literature, and painting of the period. In all the arts revolutionary sentiments were in the air: a new desire for liberty, self-expression, bold action, passionate feeling, and a love of nature. And just as the impatient Beethoven finally cast off the wig and powdered hair of the eighteenth century, so now all artists gradually cast aside the formal constraints of the old Classical style.

REVOLUTIONARY SENTIMENT AND ROMANTIC CREATIVITY

Romanticism is often defined as a revolt against the Classical adherence to reason, rules, forms, and traditions. Whereas artists of the eighteenth century sought to achieve unity, order, proportion, and a balance of form and content, those of the nineteenth century strove for self-expression, to communicate with passion no matter what sort of imbalance, contradiction, or formal inconsistency might result. If Classical architecture, painting, and music drew its inspiration from the monuments of ancient Greece and Rome, Romantic literature, poetry, painting, and music found creative encouragement in the newly proclaimed liberty of man and in the wonders of nature. The Romantic artist exalted instinctive feelings, human and natural, above all else. These were not the feelings of the masses that Beethoven addressed in his Ninth Symphony, however, but individual, personal, private feelings. Music and her sister arts now withdrew from Beethoven's vision of humanity. They became more intensely expressive yet highly personal and introspective.

If there was a single feeling or sentiment that pervaded the Romantic era it was love. Indeed, love, or "romance," is at the very heart of the word "Romantic." The loves of Romeo and Juliet and of Tristan and Isolde, for example, captured the imagination of the Romantic century. These were ardent tales in which desire, anguish, longing, and despair were felt far more powerfully than any enjoyment or happiness in love. The endless pursuit of love, the search for the unattainable, became an obsession that, when expressed as music, produced the sounds of longing and of yearning heard in so much of Romantic music.

Yet love was only one of many emotions felt strongly by the Romantics. Despair, revenge, pride, frenzy, and heavenly exaltation were a few of the others they communicated in their music and poetry. Classical music had exhibited only a modest range of emotional expression. Romantic music, on the other hand, was marked by wide swings of mood, just as some composers, namely Berlioz, Liszt, and Wagner, indulged in wild, even bizarre, behavior. Just how the range of expression was broadened in Romantic music can be seen in the "expression marks" that came into being at this time: *espressivo* (expressively), *dolente* (sadly), *presto furioso* (fast and furiously), *con forza e passione* (with force and passion), *misterioso* (mysteriously), and *maestoso* (majestically). Although these are directives to the performer explaining how a passage is to be played, they also reveal what the composer felt about the music.

Feelings about nature also received unprecedented attention with the Romantics. Nature came to be seen as the source of ultimate truth, of certainty and perfection, a reflection of God and His Eternal Mind. Romantic painters, like J. M. W. Turner (1775–1851) and Caspar David Friedrich (1774–1840), stood in awe of nature's powerful, mysterious forces (Fig. 12–1). The English Romantic poets John Keats (1795–1821), William Wordsworth (1770–1850), and Lord Byron (1778–1824) communed with her verdant woods, dissolving mists, and tender twilights.

Musicians, too, paid homage to nature. "I perform most faithfully the duties that Humanity, God, and Nature enjoin upon me," said Beethoven in 1821. He sought to capture nature's lyrical song, spacious majesty, and destructive fury in his "Pastoral" Symphony (Symphony No. 6), the first of these Romantic nature pieces. Schubert's "Trout" Quintet, Liszt's *Lake of Wallenstadt*, Schumann's *Forest Scenes*, and Strauss's "Alpine" Symphony are just a few of the musical works that continue the tradition.

Bridgeman Art Library, London/NY

FIGURE 12–1

A Traveler Looking over a Sea of Fog (ca. 1818). The themes of travel, solitude, oblivion, and endless time are explored in this early Romantic painting by Caspar David Friedrich. The artist is not interested in the subject (hence the backward pose) but only in suggesting that humans should contemplate the mysterious power of nature.

music and nature

Lord Byron's Childe Harold's Pilgrimage

The English poet George Gordon, Lord Byron (1788–1824), was the epitome of the Romantic hero: dashing, passionate, self-absorbed, idealistic, and guilt-ridden (he had had an affair with his half-sister). "He is mad, bad, and dangerous to know," said one of his lovers. Byron climbed the Swiss Alps, swam the Hellespont (separating Europe from Asia Minor), and died, at age thirty-six, fighting for Greek independence from Turkish rule. His *Childe Harold's Pilgrimage*, part autobiography and part poetic travelogue, is the fruit of his travels around Europe and Asia Minor between 1809 and 1817. Typical of the Romantics, Byron found creative stimulus in all that was foreign and in the delights of nature. He condenses into poetic verse what he saw, heard, and felt.

There is a pleasure in the pathless woods;
There is a rapture on the lonely shore;
There is society, where none intrudes,
By the deep sea, and music is its roar:
I love not man the less, but Nature more.

(*Childe Harold's Pilgrimage; canto iv, stanza 178; 1817*)

National Portrait Gallery, London

A portrait of the English poet Lord Byron in the dress of an Albanian adventurer. Another portrait of Byron can faintly be seen hanging on the wall in the painting on the cover of this book.

Associated with this desire to be at one with nature was a passion for travel, what the Germans call a *Wanderlust*. Far-off places and people stirred the imagination of the Romantics. The German composer Felix Mendelssohn (1809–1847) journeyed to Italy, to Scotland, and to the Hebrides Islands to find inspiration for his symphonies and overtures. The English poet Byron sailed to Greece and Turkey and infused his art with a sense of travel and adventure (see boxed essay).

MUSIC AND NATIONALISM

Byron had gone to Greece to foment a revolution—to help the Greeks break free from the empire of the Ottoman Turks. The struggle of the Greeks was symptomatic of the desire of many of Europe's people to throw off the rule of foreign powers or oppressive monarchs. In the 1830s, Poland fought (unsuccessfully) for freedom from Russia, Belgium broke free from the Dutch, and Italy, long controlled by the Austrian Empire and by Spain, began its *wars of independence* long march toward liberation and national unity. In 1830, and again in 1848, Paris rebelled against a repressive king. The uprising of 1848 sparked similar revolts in many cities throughout German- and Italian-speaking lands. The composer Hector Berlioz took to the streets of Paris, rifle in hand, during the insurgence of 1830. Richard Wagner led, and then fled, the unsuccessful revolt in Dresden in 1849. Verdi's name was an acronym for the Italian liberation movement (see page 300). In 1861, Italy finally achieved full unification, with Rome as its capital. Ten years later a German Empire, under the political leadership of Chancellor Otto von Bismarck (1815–1898), was formally recognized. Pride in a national culture and character was likewise felt by smaller groups, such as the Czechs, Hungarians, Poles, and Finns, each of which was trying to free itself from more powerful countries such as Germany, Austria, and Russia.

Not surprisingly, patriotism was accompanied by musical **nationalism**. A flood of national anthems, native dances, military marches, protest songs, and victory symphonies gave musical voice to the rising tide of nationalism. The *Marseillaise*, *The Star Spangled Banner*, and the Italian national anthem (*Italian Brothers, Italy Has Arisen*) were all products of revolution and patriotic fervor. We have the early Romantics to thank for the ever-popular marching bands and the mass singing of patriotic songs that mark our national holidays today.

Culture—and especially music—was the proudest expression of national spirit. National identity was fostered by incorporating native elements into the "high art" forms of classical music, poetry, literature, and painting. National color in music was communicated by means of indigenous folk elements—folk songs, native scales and dance rhythms, and local instrumental sounds.

Giraudon/Art Resource, NY

FIGURE 12–2

Eugène Delacroix's *Liberty Leading the People* was inspired by the Parisian Revolution of 1830. The allegorical figure Liberty leads an urban worker, a middle-class merchant, and a pistol-toting street urchin. The composer Berlioz participated in and wrote music to commemorate those killed in this revolt. His version of *La Marseillaise* is now the official French national anthem.

Earlier we met a staunch proponent of musical nationalism, the composer Modest Musorgsky (see page 6). Musorgsky was one of "The Russian Five," a group of composers dedicated to creating purely Russian art. In 1859 he declared: "I have been a [European] cosmopolitan, but now there's been some sort of regeneration. Everything Russian is becoming dear to me." Musorgsky's musical nationalism sounds forth in the opening *Promenade* (Intro CD/1) of his *Pictures at an Exhibition* (1874). The tempo is marked "Fast but resolute, in the Russian manner"; the meter is irregular, as in a folk dance, mixing groups of five beats with those of six; and the melody is built on a folk-influenced scale, called a **pentatonic scale**, which uses only five notes instead of the usual Western scale of seven, here B♭, C, D, F, and G:

Russian music by a Russian nationalist

EXAMPLE 12–1

(For other examples of musical nationalism, turn to the Russian *The 1812 Overture* of Tchaikovsky and the Polish mazurka of Frédéric Chopin, which are discussed on pages 330 and 288, respectively).

MUSIC AND THE LITERARY IMAGINATION: THE ART SONG

Romantic fantasy

If nationalism offered hope for the future, imagination brought escape from the present. Fantasy, dreams, even nightmares were the stuff of creative inspiration for the Romantics. Composers gave free reign to their musical imaginations in countless pieces called "fantasies" and "romances," while writers explored the dark side of human nature. In 1818 Mary Shelley (1797–1851) published her *Frankenstein,* and in 1831 Victor Hugo (1802–1885) gave to his readers *The Hunchback of Notre Dame,* both showing empathy for the deformed and the grotesque. In music, as we shall see, magic bullets (in Weber's *The Magic Bullet,* 1821), an evil elf king (in Schubert's *Erlking,* 1815), and a witches' black mass (in Berlioz's *Symphonie fantastique,* 1830) demonstrate the allure of the supernatural. For the nineteenth century, these works—with their appropriately spooky music—served the same emotional purposes as our modern horror films.

music and literature

Word and tone were never more closely allied than during the Romantic era, as parallel developments in music and literature attest. The poets viewed music as the truest and most pure of all the arts. Composers, in turn, found resonant chords in the poetry of Byron, Goethe, and above all, Shakespeare. They transformed the poetry and plays of these writers into songs, symphonic poems, overtures, and operas. Now for the first time Shakespeare became widely read on the Continent, in part because of the publication of an authoritative German translation of his work in 1801. Berlioz, Mendelssohn, Verdi, Tchaikovsky, and Dvořák were just a few of the many nineteenth-century musicians who tried to capture in sound the spirit of one or more of the Bard's great plays.

the art song: poetry and music

The strong bond between music and poetry fashioned by the Romantics gave rise to a new musical genre, the art song. Simply said, an **art song** is a piece for solo voice and piano accompaniment with high artistic aspirations. Of course, there had been songs of artistic merit for voice and accompanying instrument since the Middle Ages. But the early nineteenth century saw a frenzy of poetic activity. The English Romantic poets Wordsworth, Keats, Shelley, and Byron burst on the scene in the early 1800s, and they had their counterparts in Germany in the person of the great Goethe and the gifted Heinrich Heine (1797–1856). Literally thousands of odes, sonnets, ballads, and romances poured from their pens. Swept up in this new-found enthusiasm for poetry, composers set many of these texts for voice and piano, believing that music could intensify poetic sentiments by expressing things that words alone could not. Because the art song was cultivated mainly in German-speaking lands, the genre is also called the *Lied,* German for song. In the next chapter we will explore the works of the master of the *Lied,* Franz Schubert.

PROGRAM MUSIC

The great innovation in nineteenth-century music was program music. True, there had been isolated examples of program music earlier in the history of music, in Vivaldi's *The Seasons,* for example (see page 129). But the Romantics took as an article of deep faith that music could be more than just sound. They believed that the musical and literary muses were inseparably bound.

Program music is a piece of instrumental music, usually for symphony orchestra, that seeks to recreate in sound the events and emotions portrayed in some extramusical source: a story, a play, a historical event, or even a painting. The theory of program music rests on the obvious fact that specific kinds of music can evoke particular feelings and associations. A lyrical melody may recall memories of love, harshly dissonant chords may create a sense of conflict, rapidly flowing notes may produce a vision of a mountain stream, distant trumpet calls may suggest the imminent arrival of a hero. By stringing together such musical gestures in a convincing sequence, a composer might tell a story through music. Program music is fully harmonious with the strongly literary spirit of the nineteenth century.

Some Romantic composers, notably Johannes Brahms (1833–1897) and Anton Bruckner (1824–1896), resisted the allure of program music and continued to write what came to be called **absolute music**—symphonies, sonatas, quartets, and other instrumental music without extramusical or programmatic references. But most composers succumbed to the temptation to make their instrumental works take on an overtly narrative character. The programmatic influence crept into established genres like the symphony and overture. It also gave rise to an entirely new genre, the symphonic poem. The principal kinds of nineteenth-century program music can be defined as follows:

Program symphony: A symphony with the usual three, four, or five movements, but now the individual movements together tell or depict a succession of specific events or scenes drawn from some extramusical work or story. Examples include Berlioz's *Symphonie fantastique* (1830) and Liszt's "Faust" Symphony (1857).

Symphonic poem (also called the **tone poem**): A one-movement work for orchestra that gives musical expression to the emotions and events associated with a story, play, political occurrence, personal experience, or encounter with nature. It is usually a lengthy piece composed in any one of several forms including sonata–allegro, theme and variations, and rondo. Examples include Liszt's *Les Préludes* (1854), Modest Musorgsky's *Night on Bald Mountain* (1867), Tchaikovsky's *Romeo and Juliet* (1869), and Richard Strauss's *Don Juan* (1888).

Overture (to an opera or a play): A one-movement work, usually in sonata–allegro form, which foretells in music the essential dramatic events that will follow in an opera or a play. Many overtures, because of unusual color or special effects, became popular with the listening public and came to be performed by themselves. Examples include Rossini's Overture to his opera *William Tell* (1829) and Mendelssohn's Overture to Shakespeare's play *A Midsummer Night's Dream* (1826).

Concert overture: Similar to the overture but *not* designed to precede an opera or play; thus, an independent one-movement work of programmatic content originally intended for the concert hall. Examples include Mendelssohn's *Hebrides Overture* (1830) and Tchaikovsky's *The 1812 Overture* (1880). In fact, there is little difference between the symphonic poem and the concert overture. Both are one-movement programmatic works intended for the concert hall.

Incidental music: Music to be inserted between the acts or during important scenes of a play to add an extra dimension to the drama. Examples include

FIGURE 12–3

The Balcony Scene of Romeo and Juliet (1845) by Eugène Delacroix typifies the nineteenth-century fascination with Shakespeare. Berlioz sought to capture the spirit of the play in a five-movement program symphony *Roméo et Juliette*, 1839); Tchaikovsky tried to do so in a one-movement symphonic poem (*Romeo and Juliet*, 1869).

types of program music

Mendelssohn's incidental music to Shakespeare's *A Midsummer Night's Dream* (1843) and Edvard Grieg's music to Henrik Ibsen's play *Peer Gynt* (1875).

About 1850 Franz Liszt, a leading advocate of program music, said that an explicit program gave the composer "a means by which to protect the listener against a wrong poetical interpretation and to direct his attention to the poetical idea of the whole." Soon we will hear and discuss three imaginative examples of program music: Berlioz's *Symphonie fantastique* (a program symphony), Mendelssohn's overture to *A Midsummer Night's Dream* (an overture to a play), and Tchaikovsky's *The 1812 Overture* (a concert overture). You will be able to decide whether the presence of a program is useful, allowing you to make sense of the music more easily, or harmful, restricting your creative imagination as you listen.

THE MUSICIAN AS ARTIST, MUSIC AS ART

With the nineteenth century came the idea that music was something more than mere entertainment and the composer more than a mere mortal. Bach had been a municipal civil servant, devoted and dutiful, to the town of Leipzig. Haydn and Mozart served, and were treated, as domestics in the homes of the great lords of Europe. But Beethoven began to break the chains of submission. He was the first to demand, and receive, the respect and admiration due a great creative spirit. Ultimately, Franz Liszt and Richard Wagner, as much through their literary works as through their musical compositions, caused the public to view the artist as a sort of demigod, a prophet able to inspire the audience through the creation of music that was morally uplifting as well as beautiful. "To the artist is entrusted the upbringing of mankind," said Liszt. Never was the position of the creative musician loftier than in the mid-nineteenth century.

the artist as prophet to the world

Just as the musician changed from servant to artist, so the music he or she produced changed from passing amusement to work of art. Classical music had been created for the immediate gratification of patron and audience, with little thought given to its lasting value. With the mature Beethoven and the early Romantics, this attitude began to change. Symphonies, quartets, and piano sonatas sprang to life, not to give immediate pleasure to a listener, but to gratify a deep-seated creative urge within the composer. They became extensions of the artist's inner personality. These works might not be understood by the creator's contemporaries, as was true of the late piano sonatas of Beethoven and the orchestral works of Hector Berlioz, for example, but they would be understood by posterity, by future generations of listeners. The idea of "art for art's sake"—art free of all functional concerns—was born of the Romantic spirit.

art for art's sake

The new exalted position of the composer and his work of art soon brought a more serious tone to the concert hall. Before 1800 a concert was as much a social event as a musical experience. People talked, drank, ate, played cards, flirted, and wandered about. Dogs ran freely on the ground floor and armed guards roamed the theater to maintain a minimum of order. When people turned to the music, they were loud and demonstrative. They hummed along with and tapped the beat to the music they liked. If a performance went well, people applauded, not only at the ends of the pieces but also between movements. Sometimes they demanded an immediate encore, sometimes they hissed their disapproval.

Around 1840, however, a sudden hush came over the concert hall. With the revered figure of the Romantic artist-composer now before them, the members of the audience sat in respectful silence. A listener not distracted socially became a listener engaged emotionally. More was expected of the audience, partly because symphonies and sonatas were longer and more complex. But the audience, in turn, expected more from the music: not just entertainment but an emotionally satisfying encounter that would leave the attentive person exhausted yet somehow purified and uplifted by the artistic experience. The cover of this book, a painting of 1840, suggests how the Romantic imagination wrapped the art of music in a sacred aura. We see a temple of art: the artists are the congregants; Liszt (center) is the high priest; the piano is the altar; Beethoven is the god.

the concert hall becomes silent

Romantic Ideals and Today's Concert Hall

Romanticism has kept its grip on the Western imagination. Belief in the artist as hero, reverence toward the work of art as an object of moral inspiration, and the expectations of silence and even formal dress at a concert—these are all attitudes that developed in the early Romantic period. What is more, the notion that a particular group of pieces should get a repeated hearing gains currency at this time. Prior to 1800 almost all music was disposable music: It was written for the enjoyment of the moment and then was no longer in vogue. But the generation following Beethoven began to see his best symphonies, concertos, and quartets, as well as those of Mozart and Haydn, as worthy of continued performance and preservation. These and the best works of succeeding generations came to constitute a "canon" of music—a body of music possessing attributes of unity, expression, and form that should be continually revisited. Such masterpieces, as they were correctly viewed, came to form the core of today's concert repertoire. Thus what we think about the composer, how we view the work of art, what we can expect to hear at a concert, and even how we behave during the performance are not ideals, with us since time immemorial, but are paradigms created during a special period in history. In many respects, the attitudes about art and music that arose in the early nineteenth century still govern our thinking today.

a core repertoire for the concert hall

THE STYLE OF ROMANTIC MUSIC

The Romantic spirit rebelled against Classical ideals in ways that allow us to generalize these two artistic movements as pairs of opposites: rational against irrational, intellect opposed to heart, conformity versus originality, and the masses in contradistinction to the individual. Yet in purely musical terms, the works of the Romantic composers represent not so much a revolution against Classical ideals as an evolution that goes beyond them. The Classical genres of the symphony, concerto, string quartet, piano sonata, and opera remained fashionable, though somewhat altered in appearance, throughout the nineteenth century. The symphony now grows in length, embodying the widest possible range of expression, while the concerto becomes increasingly virtuosic, as a heroic soloist does battle against an orchestral mass. The Romantics introduced no new musical forms and only two new genres: the art song* and the symphonic poem*. Instead, Romantic composers took the musical materials received from Haydn, Mozart, and young Beethoven and made

greater length, greater virtuosity

them more intensely expressive, more personal, more colorful, and in some cases, more bizarre.

Romantic Melody

the popular quality of Romantic melody

The Romantic period witnessed the apotheosis of melody. Melodies become broad, powerful streams of sound intended to sweep the listener away. They go beyond the neat symmetrical units of two plus two, four plus four, inherent in the Classical style. They become longer, rhythmically more flexible, and more irregular in shape. At the same time, Romantic melodies continue a trend that developed in the late eighteenth century in which themes became vocal in conception, more singable. Countless melodies of Schubert, Chopin, and Tchaikovsky have been turned into popular songs and movie themes—Romantic music is perfectly suited for the romance of film—because these melodies are so profoundly expressive. They sigh and lament. They grow and become ecstatic. They start haltingly and then build to a grandiose climax, sublime and triumphant. Example 12–2 is a melody by Hector Berlioz, the principal theme of his *Symphonie fantastique* (1830). Notice that it is long and rhythmically rather free, with many syncopations* that cross the bar lines and obscure the downbeats*. Observe, too, that by means of an ascending melodic sequence (see brackets) the melody climbs inexorably upward to a lofty climax, from where it gradually relaxes back down to the tonic note.

EXAMPLE 12–2

Colorful Harmony

chromatic harmony

Part of the emotional intensity of Romantic music is generated by a new, more colorful harmony. Classical music had, in the main, made use of chords built only on the seven notes of the major or minor scale—the so-called diatonic* notes of the scale (see page 26). Romantic composers went farther by constructing chords on the five additional notes within the full twelve-note chromatic scale—the so-called chromatic* notes. This gave more colors to their harmonic palette. It also gave fluency to the sound, as chords and inner voices glide smoothly to notes only a half step away. Using chromatic chords similarly made it easier for the composer to modulate to distant keys, to carry the music tonally away to some far-off, exotic land of six flats or seven sharps.

The rich, lush sounds of the Romantics are also created by setting up novel relationships between chords. In the Baroque and Classical periods, harmony often moved along in chord progressions in which the roots of the chords were an interval of a fifth apart. Now chords only a third apart are frequently set in close proximity, and these can require radically different key signatures*—a harmony with three sharps might be followed immediately by one with six flats, for example. The striking sound that results from these unusual relationships is appropriate for music that seeks to express a wider range of feeling.

bold chord changes

Finally, much of the sound of pain and anguish that we hear in Romantic music comes about because of a greater use of dissonance. Dissonant notes are not only more numerous, but they are held for longer periods of time as well. Since dissonance always wants to move, or resolve, to consonance, the delay of the resolution produces a feeling of anxiety, longing, and searching, all sentiments appropriate for music that often deals with the subject of love.

dissonance longs for consonance

All three of these qualities of Romantic harmony—bold chordal shifts, chromaticism, and dissonance-consonance movement—can be heard in Frédéric Chopin's Nocturne in C♯ minor (1835). Neither you nor the author can take in all the music given in the following three examples simply by looking at them. (To hear them, turn to 6CD 4/4 and 2CD 2/3.) We can, however, visualize here some of the music's inner workings—first the bold harmonic shift from a chord with four sharps to one with four flats, then the chromaticism, and finally the movement of dissonance to consonance. In this way we may begin to understand, when hearing the rich, sensuous sound of Romantic music, how it is created.

EXAMPLE 12–3: bold harmony heard at 2:11

EXAMPLE 12–4: chromaticism heard at 2:51

EXAMPLE 12–5: dissonance resolves to consonance at 4:20

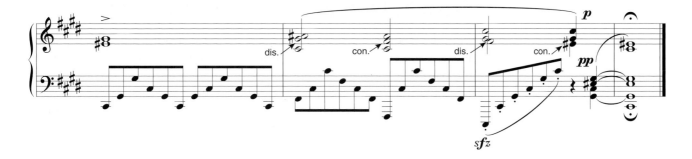

Romantic Tempo: *Rubato*

a flexible tempo

In keeping with an age that glorified personal freedom and tolerated eccentric behavior, tempo in music was cut loose from the restraints of a regular beat. The watchword here was *rubato* (literally "robbed"), an expression mark for the performer written into the score by the composer. A performer playing tempo **rubato** stole some time here and gave it back there, moving faster or slower so as to effect an intensely personal performance. The free approach to tempo was often reinforced by fluctuating dynamic levels—ritards were done with diminuendos* and accelerations with crescendos*—as a way of explaining, even exaggerating, the flow of the music. Whatever excesses might result, could be excused under license of artistic freedom.

Romantic Forms: Monumental and Miniature

colossal symphonies

The musical forms that had earlier served Haydn and Mozart continued to satisfy the needs of the nineteenth-century composer. Sonata–allegro form, in particular, remained useful because its flexible format could accommodate any number of individual solutions. What developed, then, was not a rush to invent new forms but a trend to extend the existing ones. As composers laid out broad, sweeping melodies, indulged in gigantic crescendos, and reveled in the luxurious sound of the enlarged orchestra, the length of individual movements increased dramatically. Mozart's G minor symphony (1788) lasts about twenty minutes, depending on the tempo of the performance. But Berlioz's *Symphonie fantastique* (1830) takes nearly fifty-five minutes, and Mahler's Symphony No. 2 (1894) nearly an hour and a half. Perhaps the longest of all musical works is Richard Wagner's four-opera *Ring* cycle (1853–1876), which continues some seventeen hours during the course of four evenings. In these extended visions the Romantic composer seems to be saying along with the poet: "Romanticism is beauty without bounds—the beautiful infinite."

small-scale character pieces

Yet, paradoxically, Romantic composers were fascinated by miniature forms as well. In brief works of a scant minute or two, they tried to capture the essence of one single mood, sentiment, or emotion. Such a miniature was called a **character piece**. It was usually written for the piano and often made use of simple binary (**AB**) or ternary (**ABA**) form. Because the character piece passes by in a twinkling of an eye, it was sometimes given a whimsical title, such as bagatelle (a trifle), humoresque, arabesque, musical moment, caprice, romance, intermezzo, or impromptu. Schubert, Schumann, Chopin, Liszt, Brahms, and Tchaikovsky all enjoyed creating these musical miniatures, perhaps as antidotes to their lengthy symphonies and concertos.

EXPRESSIVE TONE COLORS, GREATER SIZE, GREATER VOLUME

From the listener's perspective, perhaps the most striking aspect of Romantic music is the color and sheer volume of the sound. Sometimes all thematic and harmonic movement stops and nothing but pure sound carries the moment. During the nineteenth century the orchestra became larger and more varied, the piano bigger and more powerful. Composers demanded, and received, musical forces equal to the task of expressing the extremes of emotion, changing moods, and extravagant gestures of the Romantic spirit.

The Romantic Orchestra

The Industrial Revolution brought with it mechanical innovations that made the instruments of the symphony orchestra essentially what they are today. The wood of the flute was replaced by silver, and the instrument was supplied with a new fingering mechanism that added to its agility and made it easier to play in tune. Similarly, the trumpet and French horn were provided with valves that improved technical facility and accuracy of pitch in all keys (Figs. 12–4 and 12–5). These brass instruments were now capable of playing intricate, chromatic melodies as well as providing the traditional backdrop of sonic support for the rest of the orchestra. The French horn, in particular, became an object of special affection during the Romantic period. Its rich, dark tone and its traditional association with the hunt— and by extension nature—made it the Romantic instrument par excellence. Composers often called on a solo horn when they wished to express something mysterious or distant.

Besides improvements to existing instruments, several new instruments were added to the symphony orchestra during the nineteenth century. We have seen how Beethoven brought the piccolo (a high flute), the trombone, and the contrabassoon (a bass bassoon) into the orchestra in his famous Symphony No. 5 (1808). In 1830 Hector Berlioz went even farther, requiring an ophicleide* (an early form of the tuba), an English horn* (a low-pitched oboe), a cornet*, and two harps in his *Symphonie fantastique*. Berlioz, the embodiment of the Romantic spirit, had a typically grandiose notion of what the ideal symphony orchestra should contain. He wanted no fewer than 467 instrumentalists including 120 violins, 40 violas, 45 cellos, 35 double basses, and 30 harps. Needless to say, such a gigantic instrumental force was never assembled, but Berlioz's utopian vision indicates the direction in which Romantic composers were headed. By the second half of the nineteenth century, orchestras with nearly a hundred players were not uncommon. Compare the instruments and their number required for a typical eighteenth-century performance of Mozart's G minor symphony with the symphony orchestra called on to play Berlioz's *Symphonie fantastique* and that required for Gustav Mahler's Symphony No. 1 (see box following). Our ears today have been desensitized by an over-exposure to electronically amplified sound to the point that we can hardly imagine the overwhelming impact that a large symphony orchestra had on concertgoers in the nineteenth century.

Victoria & Albert Museum, London/Art Resource, NY

FIGURE 12–4

A large orchestra depicted at Covent Garden Theater, London, in 1846. The conductor stands toward the middle, baton in hand, with strings to his right and woodwinds, brass, and percussion to his left. It was typical in this period to put all or part of the orchestra on risers to allow the sound to project more fully.

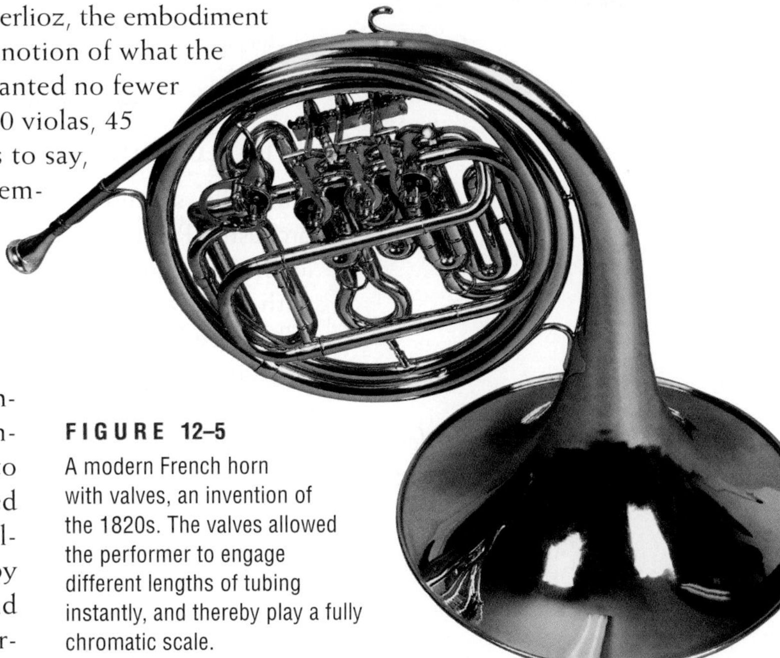

FIGURE 12–5

A modern French horn with valves, an invention of the 1820s. The valves allowed the performer to engage different lengths of tubing instantly, and thereby play a fully chromatic scale.

CORBIS

The Growth of the Symphony Orchestra

Mozart (1788) Symphony in G minor	Berlioz (1830) *Symphonie fantastique*	Mahler (1889) Symphony No. 1
1 flute	1 piccolo	3 piccolos
2 oboes	2 flutes	4 flutes
2 clarinets	2 oboes	4 oboes
2 bassoons	1 English horn	1 English horn
2 French horns	2 B♭ clarinets	4 B♭ clarinets
1st violins (8)†	1 E♭ clarinet	2 E♭ clarinets
2nd violins (8)	4 bassoons	1 bass clarinet
violas (4)	4 French horns	3 bassoons
cellos (4)	2 trumpets	1 contrabassoon
double basses (3)	2 cornets	7 French horns
	3 trombones	5 trumpets
Total: 36	2 ophicleides (tubas)	4 trombones
	1st violins (15)†	1 tuba
	2nd violins (14)	1st violins (20)†
	violas (8)	2nd violins (18)
	cellos (12)	violas (14)
	double basses (8)	cellos (12)
	2 harps	double basses (8)
	timpani	1 harp
	bass drum	timpani (2 players)
	snare drum	bass drum
	cymbals and bells	triangle, cymbals
		tam-tam
	Total: 89	
		Total: 115

Bibliothèque Nationale

A satirical engraving suggesting the public's impression of Berlioz conducting his vastly enlarged symphony orchestra.

†Number of string players estimated according to standards of the period.

The Conductor

a leader needed for the ever-larger orchestra

Naturally, someone was needed to coordinate the efforts of the enlarged orchestra. Previously, in the days of Bach and Mozart, the orchestra had been led from within, either by the keyboard player of the *basso continuo** gesturing with his head and hands or by the chief violinist directing with his bow. When Beethoven played and conducted his piano concertos, he did so seated at his instrument. When he led one of his symphonies, especially toward the end of his life, he stood before the orchestra, back to the audience, waving his hands. In 1820 the composer Louis Spohr became the first to use a wooden baton to lead the orchestra. Other objects were used as well, including a rolled-up piece of paper (Fig. 12–6), a violin bow, and sometimes even a handkerchief. As symphony orchestras became larger and symphonic scores more complex, every orchestral ensemble needed a leader to keep it from falling apart during performance. In the course of the nineteenth century this leader evolved from a mere time-beater into an interpreter, sometimes a dictator, of the musical score. The modern conductor had arrived.

The Piano

During the nineteenth century the piano became what the computer is today, something of a home entertainment center. Every middle-class household had to have one, as well as the software to make it work. The software was then the **piano transcription**—a reduction for piano solo of some larger orchestral or operatic work. Surprisingly, most often not one person but two people played the piano transcription, both seated at a single instrument; the transcription was made for four hands to include as much of the original score as possible. In this way, symphonies of Beethoven and Berlioz were condensed for piano as were whole operas of Bellini and Wagner, for example. Attending a concert in the nineteenth century was a rare treat. Music lovers in Brussels, Baltimore, or Birmingham might never have the chance to hear a "live" performance of a Beethoven symphony, but they might come to know it at home by means of a piano transcription by Liszt, for example. Before the age of electronically reproduced sound, the general listening public came to know the major works of the great composers by means of these piano transcriptions.

That the piano could provide a good approximation of the symphony orchestra suggests that it, too, grew considerably in size during the early 1800s. Here also the new technology of the Industrial Revolution was decisive. Although still surrounded by a wooden shell, the internal wooden frame was replaced by a cast-iron one that allowed for greater tension on the strings. This necessitated thicker steel strings which, in turn, greatly increased the volume of sound. The pianist could bang away and no strings would break. To soften the blow, hammers were covered with felt, which made the instrument "sing" with a mellow tone, in contrast to the "ping" of the pianos of Mozart's day. The range of the instrument was extended both high and low, expanding from the five-octave piano of the 1790s to a seven-octave instrument by the 1840s. By mid-century, all pianos were equipped with at least two pedals: a **sustaining pedal** (right), which enabled some strings to continue to sound while others were being struck; and a **soft pedal** (left), which allowed the instrument to play at a softer dynamic by shifting the position of the keyboard. Finally, in the 1850s, the Steinway Company of New York began **cross-stringing** the piano, a

The Bettmann Archive

FIGURE 12–6

Silhouette of composer Karl Maria von Weber conducting with a rolled sheet of music so as to highlight the movement of his hand.

Sterling and Francine Clark Art Institute

FIGURE 12–7

A Steinway grand piano of 1883 painted and decorated to be an object of visual as well as sonic delight. Needless to say, this instrument is far larger and more powerful than the one Mozart had at his disposal (see Fig. 10–9).

practice whereby the strings of the lowest keys ride up over those of the middle register, thereby producing a richer, more homogenous sound. By the mid-nineteenth century, all the essential features of the modern piano were in place: The basic design of the piano has not changed in 150 years.

The Virtuoso

Appropriate for an era that glorified the individual, the nineteenth century was the age of the solo virtuoso. Of course, there had been instrumental virtuosos before—Bach on the organ, Mozart on the piano, to name just two—but now enormous energy was expended by many musicians to raise their performing skills to an unprecedented height. Pianists and violinists in particular practiced long hours just on technical exercises—arpeggios, tremolos, trills, and scales played in thirds, sixths, and octaves—to develop wizardlike hand speed on their instrument. Naturally, some of what they played for the public was lacking in musical substance, tasteless show pieces designed to appeal immediately to the large audiences that packed the ever-larger concert halls. Pianists developed tricks of playing to make it appear they had more hands than two (see Fig. 13–20). Franz Liszt (1811–1886) sometimes played at the keyboard with a lighted cigar between his fingers. The Italian Niccolò Paganini (1782–1840) secretly tuned the four strings of his violin in ways that would allow him to negotiate with ease extraordinarily difficult passages. If one of his strings broke, he could play with just three; if three broke, he could continue apace with just one. As the composer Debussy later remarked, "The attraction of the virtuoso is like that of the circus performer, there's always the hope that something disastrous will happen." The daredevil quality of the music can be seen in Example 12–6, which looks something like a roller coaster. Fortunately, as we shall see, some of these performing daredevils were also gifted composers.

EXAMPLE 12–6: Paganini, Caprice, Opus 1, No. 5

CORBIS

FIGURE 12–8 AND 12–9

(above) Niccolò Paganini. (above right) *Paganini and the Witches*, a lithograph by an unknown artist. Paganini's extraordinary powers on the violin led some to believe that he had acquired them in a deal with the devil. The highest string of his violin was said to be made of the intestine of his mistress, whom he had murdered with his own hands. None of this was true, and Paganini undertook several libel suits to reclaim his honor.

Listening Exercise

28

Comparing Orchestral Works of the
Classical and Romantic Periods

The transition from the Classical to the early Romantic period witnessed an enormous change in musical style. To appreciate the extent of this musical transformation, let us compare two orchestral works: the first movement of Mozart's Symphony No. 40 in G minor (1788) (6CD 2/9 and 2CD 1/11) and the finale of Hector Berlioz's *Symphonie fantastique* (1830) (6CD 3/9 and 2CD 2/1). Listen to the first four minutes of each work and answer the following questions indicating "a" for Mozart or "b" for Berlioz. If you need help, consult the Listening Guides given on pages 208 and 278.

1. Which composer begins with a clear-cut pair of four-bar antecedent-consequent phrases? _____
2. Which composer begins with pure musical atmosphere, much as in a score for a modern-day motion picture? _____
3. Which composer exhibits greater "mood swings," in which the music oscillates between louds and softs, high pitches and low pitches? _____
4. Which composer maintains a constant tempo throughout (to which you can easily set and maintain a conducting pattern)? _____
5. Which composer requires a large, colorful orchestra? _____
6. Which composer requires the violins to present all themes at first appearance? _____
7. Which composer designates a brass instrument and a percussion instrument play the melody? _____
8. Which composer is more resolute, in that he moves purposefully and without delay from one section to the next? _____
9. Which composer has written an example of program music? _____
10. Which composer has written an example of absolute music? _____

Key Words

absolute music (253)	overture (253)	*rubato* (258)
art song (252)	pentatonic scale (251)	soft pedal (261)
character piece (258)	piano transcription	sustaining pedal (261)
concert overture (253)	(261)	symphonic poem
cross stringing (261)	program music (253)	(253)
incidental music (253)	program	tone poem (253)
nationalism (251)	symphony (253)	

Chapter 13

Bridgeman Art Library, London/NY

The Early Romantics

The decade 1803–1813 was perhaps the most auspicious in the history of music. In this short span of time were born the composers Hector Berlioz (1803), Felix Mendelssohn (1809), Frédéric Chopin (1810), Robert Schumann (1810), Franz Liszt (1811), Giuseppe Verdi (1813), and Richard Wagner (1813). Add to this the shining figure of Franz Schubert (born 1797) and this brilliant galaxy of musical geniuses is complete. We call them Romantics because they were part of, indeed they created, the Romantic movement in music. But with the possible exception of Mendelssohn, they were very unconventional people. Their lives typify all that we have come to associate with the Romantic spirit: self-expression, passion, excess, the love of nature and literature, as well as a certain selfishness, irresponsibility, and even a bit of lunacy. Not only did they create great art, but life, and how they lived it, also became an art.

THE LIED

One of the hallmarks of the Romantic era, as we have seen, was a quickening interest in literature, and especially poetry. The enormous outpouring of the Romantic poets was matched by the creative enthusiasm of the Romantic composers, who set hundreds of ballads, odes, and romances to music. In so doing they created a new genre of music called the art song* (see page 252)—a song for solo voice and piano accompaniment with high artistic aspirations. Because the art song was cultivated most intensely in German-speaking lands, it is usually called the **Lied** (plural **Lieder**), German for "song." Although Beethoven, Schumann, Brahms, and Mahler all wrote *Lieder*, none had greater success with this genre than Franz Schubert. His special talent was to fashion music that captures both the spirit and the detail of the text, creating a sensitive mood painting in which the voice, and especially the piano accompaniment express every nuance of the poem. Schubert said, "When one has a good poem the music comes easily, melodies just flow, so that composing is a real joy."

FIGURE 13–1
Franz Schubert.

Franz Schubert (1797–1828)

Franz Schubert was born in Vienna in 1797 (Fig. 13–1). Among the great Viennese masters—Haydn, Mozart, Beethoven, Schubert, Brahms, and Mahler—only he was native-born to the city. Schubert's father was a schoolteacher, and the son, too, was groomed for that profession. Yet the boy's obvious musical talent made it imperative that he also have music lessons, so his father taught him to play the violin and his older brother, the piano. At the age of eleven Schubert was admitted as a choirboy in the emperor's chapel (the group today is called the Vienna Choirboys). Proximity to the royal palace brought young Schubert into contact with Antonio Salieri, erstwhile rival of Mozart and still imperial court composer (see page 180). He began to study composition with Salieri in 1810. Soon Schubert was composing his own musical works at an astonishing rate.

After his voice changed in 1812, young Franz left the court chapel and enrolled in a teacher's college. He had been spared compulsory military service because he was below the minimum height of five feet and his sight was so poor he was compelled to wear the spectacles now familiar from his portraits (Fig. 13-1). By 1815 he had become a teacher at his father's primary school. But he found teaching demanding and tedious and so, after three unpleasant years, Schubert quit his "day job" to give himself over wholly to music.

"You lucky fellow; I really envy you! You live a life of sweet, precious freedom, can give free rein to your musical genius, can express your thoughts in any way you like." This was Schubert's brother's view of the composer's newfound freedom. But as many Romantics would find, the reality was harsher than the ideal. Aside from some small income he earned from the sale of a few songs, he lacked a means of support. Schubert, unlike Beethoven, kept no company with aristocrats and thus received no patronage from them. Instead, he lived a Bohemian life, helped along by the generosity of his friends, with whom he often lodged when he was broke. His mornings were consumed passionately composing music; his afternoons were passed in cafés discussing literature and politics; and his evenings were often spent playing his songs and dances before friends and admirers.

a Bohemian life

While Schubert was coming to his artistic maturity, the era of the great aristocratic salon was drawing to an end. Its place, as a focus for artistic expression, was taken by the middle-class parlor or living room. Here in less pretentious surroundings, groups of men and women with a common interest in music, the novel, drama, or poetry would meet to read and hear all that was new in these arts. The gatherings at which Schubert appeared, and at

FIGURE 13–2

A Schubertiade in progress. The singers Josephine Fröhlich and Johann Vogl surround Schubert at the piano, while other devotees listen. From a pencil drawing of Georg Waldmüller of 1827.

FIGURE 13–3

The ballad of the *Erlking* depicted by Schubert's close friend Moritz von Schwind. The artist had heard Schubert perform the *Lied* at many Schubertiades.

which only his compositions were played, were called **Schubertiades** by his friends. It was in small, purely private assemblies such as these (Fig. 13-2), not in large public concerts, that most of his best songs were first performed.

In 1822 disaster befell the composer: He contracted syphilis, a venereal disease tantamount to a death sentence before the discovery of antibiotics. His lyrical Symphony in B minor of that fateful year was left incomplete. (Appropriately called the Unfinished Symphony, it can be heard as background music in the Tom Cruise film *Minority Report*.) Yet during the years that remained before his premature death in 1828 Schubert created some of his greatest works: the song cycles *Die schöne Müllerin* (*The Pretty Maid of the Mill*, 1823) and *Winterreise* (*Winter Journey*, 1827), the "Wanderer" Fantasy for piano (1822), and the great C major Symphony (1828). When Beethoven died in 1827, Schubert served as one of the torchbearers at the funeral. The next year, he too was dead, the youngest of the great composers. The epitaph for his tombstone reads: "The art of music here entombed a rich treasure, but even fairer hopes."

In his brief life of thirty-one years, Franz Schubert wrote eight symphonies, fifteen string quartets, twenty-one piano sonatas, seven Masses for chorus and orchestra, and four operas—a sizable *oeuvre* by any standards. Yet in his day Schubert was known almost exclusively as a writer of *Lieder*. Indeed, he composed more than six hundred works of this genre, many of them minor masterpieces. In a few cases, Schubert chose to set several texts together in a series. In so doing he created what is called a **song cycle**—a tightly structured group of individual songs that tell a story or treat a single theme. *The Pretty Maid of the Mill* (twenty songs) and *Winter Journey* (twenty-four songs), both of which relate the sad consequences of unrequited love, are Schubert's two great song cycles.

ERLKING (1815)

To gain an idea of Schubert's extraordinary musical talent, we need only listen to his song *Erlkönig* (*Erlking*), written when he was just seventeen. The text itself is a ballad—a dramatic story told in alternating narrative verse and dialogue—from the pen of the famous poet Goethe. It relates the tale of the evil King of the Elves and his quest for the soul of a young boy, for legend had it that whosoever was touched by the King of the Elves would die. According to the account of one of Schubert's friends, the composer was reading a book of Goethe's poetry, pacing back and forth in his room. Suddenly, he sprang to the piano and, as fast as he could write, set the entire ballad to music. From there Schubert and his friend hastened to the composer's college to play it for a few kindred spirits. In his lifetime *Erlking* became Schubert's best-known song, one of the few that brought him any money.

The opening line of the poem sets the sinister nocturnal scene: "Who rides so late through night and wind?" With his feverish son cradled in his arms, a father rides at breakneck speed to an inn to save the child. Schubert captures both the general sense of terror in the scene and the detail of the galloping horse; he creates an accompanying figure in the piano that pounds on relentlessly just as fast as the pianist can make it go:

EXAMPLE 13–1

The specter of death, the Erlking, beckons gently to the boy. He does so in seductively sweet tones, in a melody with the gentle lilt and folksy accompaniment of a popular tune:

EXAMPLE 13–2

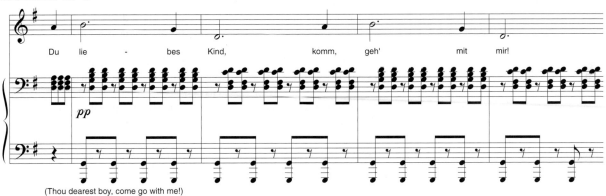

(Thou dearest boy, come go with me!)

The frightened boy cries out to his father in an agitated, then chromatic, line:

EXAMPLE 13–3

(Dear father, my father, say, did'st thou not hear the Erlking whisper promises in my ear?)

This cry is heard again and again in the course of the song, each time at a successively higher pitch and with increasingly dissonant harmonies. In this way the music mirrors the growing terror of the boy. The father tries to calm him and does so in low tones that are steady, stable, and repetitive. Thus, each of the three characters of the story is portrayed with a specific musical quality.

This is musical characterization at its finest: The melody and accompaniment not only support the text but also intensify and enrich it. Suddenly, the end is reached. The hand of the Erlking (Death) has touched his victim. The accompaniment figure is abruptly choked off as the narrator announces in increasingly somber (minor) tones: "But in his arms, his child was dead!"

Listening Guide	Franz Schubert	6CD 3/6;
WWW	*Lied, Erlking* (1815)	2CD 1/15

Form: through composed

0:00   Introduction by piano accompaniment;
       pounding triplets in the right hand and an
       ominous minor motive in the left

Narrator

0:23		Wer reitet so spät	Who rides so late
		durch Nacht und Wind?	through night so wild?
		Es ist der Vater	A loving father
		mit seinem Kind.	with his child.
		Er hat den Knaben	He clasps his boy close
		wohl in dem Arm,	with his arm,
		er fasst ihn sicher,	He holds him tightly
		er hält ihn warm.	and keeps him warm.

Father

0:56		"Mein Sohn, was birgst	"My son, what makes you hide
		du so bang dein Gesicht?"	your face in fear?"

Son

1:05	With agitated leaps	"Siehst, Vater, du	"Father don't you see
		den Erlkönig nicht?	the Erlking—
		Den Erlenkönig	the Erlking
		mit Kron' und Schweif?"	with crown and shroud?"

Father

1:20	In low, calming tones	"Mein Sohn, es ist ein	"My son, it's only some streak
		Nebelstreif."	of mist."

Erlking

1:30	With a seductive melody	"Du liebes Kind,	"You dear child,
	in major key	komm, geh' mit mir!	come along with me!
		gar schöne Spiele	I'll play some very fine games
		spiel' ich mit dir;	with you;
		manch' bunte Blumen	where varied blossoms
		sing an dem Strand,	sing on meadows fair
		meine Mutter hat manch'	and my mother has golden
		gülden Gewand."	garments to wear."

Son

1:55	Tension depicted by	"Mein Vater, mein Vater	"My father, my father,
	tight chromatic movement	und hörest du nicht,	do you not hear
	in voice	was Erlenkönig mir	how the Erlking whispers
		leise verspricht?"	promises in my ear?"

Father

2:07	In low, steady pitches	"Sei ruhig, bleibe ruhig,	"Be calm, stay calm,
		mein Kind,	my child,
		in düren Blättern	Through wither'd leaves
		säuselt der Wind."	the wind blows wild."

(Continued on next page)

2:18	With a happy, lilting tune in major key	"Willst, feiner Knabe, du mit mir geh'n? Meine Töchter sollen dich warten schön, meine Töchter führen den nächtlichen Reih'n, und wiegen und tanzen und singen dich ein."	**Erlking** "My handsome young lad, will you come with me? My beauteous daughters wait for you, With them you would join in the dance every night, and they will rock and dance and sing you to sleep."
2:36	Same intense chromatic notes as before, but now a step higher; minor key	"Mein Vater, mein Vater und siehst du nicht dort Erlkönigs Töchter am düstern Ort?"	**Son** "My Father, my father, don't you see at all the Erlking's daughters over there in the dusk?"
2:48	Low register, but more leaps (agitation) than before	"Mein Sohn, mein Sohn, ich seh' es genau, es scheinen die alten Weiden so grau."	**Father** "My son, my son, the form you there see, is only the aging gray willow tree."
3:06	His music is no longer seductive but now threatening and in minor key	"Ich liebe dich, mich reizt deine schöne Gestalt; und bist du nicht willig, so brauch' ich Gewalt."	**Erlking** "I love you, I'm charmed by your fine appearance; And if you're not willing, I'll seize you by force!"
3:18	Piercing cries in highest range	"Mein Vater, mein Vater jetzt fasst er mich an! Erlkönig hat mir ein Leids gethan!"	**Son** "My father, my father, now he's got me, the Erlking has seized me by his trick."
3:32	With a rising and then falling line	Dem Vater grauset's; er reitet geschwind, er hält in den Armen das ächzende Kind. Erreicht den Hof mit Müh und Noth:	**Narrator** The father shudders, he rides headlong, holding the groaning child in his arms. He reaches the inn with toil and dread,
3:47	Piano slows and then stops, recitative	in seinen Armen das Kind war todt!	but in his arms, his child was dead!

(Listening Exercise 29)

Tension in Schubert's *Erlking* rises continually from the beginning to the very end. As the story is told, the music, too, continually unfolds without repetition. Compositions made up of ever-changing music are called **through composed**. *Erlking* is thus a through-composed *Lied*. For texts that do not tell a story or project a series of changing moods, however, **strophic form** is often preferred. Here a single poetic mood is maintained from one stanza, or strophe, of the text to the next. Accordingly, the same music is repeated, again and again, for each strophe, as in a hymn or a folk song. Schubert used strophic form, for example, when setting a prayer found in Sir Walter Scott's *The Lady of the Lake*. The result was his immortal *Ave Maria* (1825), a song in which the music for each of three strophes is identical, note for note.

through-composed and strophic forms

THE TROUT (1817)

Schubert's *Die Forelle* (*The Trout*) shows how both the Romantic poet and the musician were attracted to the charms of nature. Picture a fresh mountain stream where a trout darts happily about. Schubert captures this vision with a lively tune and a bubbling accompaniment figure in the piano—whether a spinning wheel, a rippling stream, or a galloping horse, Schubert knew better than anyone how to create the musical equivalent of such graphic details. The poem is composed of three eight-line stanzas, each with the rhyme scheme ABABCDCD. The first sets the scene of the crystal-clear stream, the second introduces a fisherman on the opposite bank, and the third tells how the invader tricks and catches the trout. Each strophe is set to the same music, with one exception. At the beginning of the third stanza, where the fisherman tricks the trout by muddying the stream, the bubbling accompaniment figure is replaced momentarily by a swirling effect using minor chords. Such a change within the basic strophic form produces **modified strophic form**. It allows the composer to highlight a particular detail without disturbing the overall structure of strophic form.

modified strophic form

Unlike the dramatic *Erlking* of Goethe, the lyrical text of *The Trout* (by one Daniel Schubart) is in no way exceptional as a poem. What is remarkable is the way that Schubert can make even the most ordinary verse into a song of extraordinary beauty.

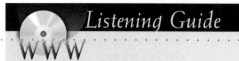

Listening Guide

Franz Schubert
Lied, The Trout (1817)

6CD 3/7

Form: modified strophic

0:00   Piano introduces the rippling accompaniment figure in bright major key

(Continued on next page)

0:07	First strophe	In einem Bächlein helle, Da schoss in froher Eil' Die launische Forelle Vorüber wie ein Pfeil. Ich stand an dem Gestade Und sah in süsser Ruh' Des muntern Fischleins Bade Im klaren Bächlein zu.	A streamlet clear and sunny With ripples all about, Was once the bath for pretty For gentle little trout. On shore I stood observing With exquisite delight, The happy little creature It was a lovely sight.
0:39	Second strophe: exact repeat of music of first strophe	Ein Fischer mit der Rute Wohl an dem Ufer stand Und sah's mit kaltem Blute, Wie sich das Fischlein wand. Solang dem Wasser Helle, So dacht ich, nicht gebricht, So fängt er die Forelle Mit seiner Angel nicht.	A fisher with his angle Stood on yonder shore Trying to entangle The fish from water's floor. I thought if clear the water Still races all about, He'd never, never capture My lovely, little trout.
1:13	Third strophe: minor replaces major; chords replace rippling figure; return to major tonality and rippling figure	Doch endlich ward dem Diebe Die Zeit zu lang. Er macht Das Bächlein tückisch trübe, Und eh' ich es gedacht. So zuckte seine Rute, Das Fischlein zappelt dran, Und ich mit regem Blute Sah die Betrog'ne an.	Yet the robber had no patience To while away the time He made the brook all muddy Ere I sensed the crime. His line went inward reeling My little fish so sweet, Then saw I with raging feeling The cheated and the cheat.

THE "TROUT" QUINTET (1819)

In the summer of 1819, two years after he wrote his song *The Trout,* Schubert decided to vacation in the hills west of Vienna, to enjoy the stunning beauty of the Austrian countryside. There an amateur cellist asked the composer to arrange for string quartet his charming song about a fish. Schubert accepted the challenge but changed the medium of performance. He decided to add a fifth instrument, a piano, to the ensemble (making it a piano quintet) and to replace the usual second violin of the quartet with a double bass. This would give added weight to the bass line and allow the piano to roam with little competition in the upper register. Having selected his instrumental forces, he then composed a five-movement piano quintet, the "Trout" Quintet, perhaps the most lyrical of all works of chamber music.

The fourth movement of Schubert's "Trout" Quintet makes prominent use of the lovely tune of the *Lied* and does so in the form of a theme and six variations. The two phrases of the melody (**A** and **B**) are stated and immediately repeated within each variation, though the repeat of **B** extends only to the last four bars (**B'**). Each instrument has its turn to present the melody—the piano does so in variation 1, the viola in variation 2, and the double bass, cello, and violin in variations 3, 5, and 6, respectively. Variations 4 and 5 take us away from the bright tonic key of D major, to D minor and B♭ major, but variation 6 returns us to the tonic major.

a theme and six variations

Schubert was fond of making use of the melodies of his songs in his instrumental chamber music. The "Trout" Quintet shows that he was not merely a songsmith but could also compose instrumental music with the sort of lyricism, fluidity, and grace that even Mozart might have envied.

Listening Guide

WWW

Franz Schubert
Piano Quintet in A major, the "Trout" Quintet (1819)
Fourth movement, *Andantino* (gently moving)

6CD 3/8

Form: theme and variations

0:00	**THEME** (in D major)	Strings play the theme quietly; both phrases of the melody (**A** and **B**) are repeated (**A** exactly, **B** as **B′**)
1:03	**VARIATION 1**	Piano finally enters and decorates theme with trills; violin flutters against the theme adding trills in high range
2:02	**VARIATION 2**	Viola has the theme; violin plays countermelody of stepwise scales above; piano echoes phrases of the theme
3:04	**VARIATION 3**	Double bass has the theme; piano plays virtuosic passage-work against the melody
3:56	**VARIATION 4**	Sudden shift to minor; *fortissimo* then *piano* chords followed by quiet dialogue between piano and violin; growing lyricism in cello, viola, and violin
4:55	**VARIATION 5**	Cello plays theme with only thin accompaniment; the repeat of phrase **B** is rewritten and extended by a dialogue between cello and violin
6:32	**VARIATION 6**	Violin has theme as piano plays accompaniment figure from song; cello has theme as violin plays this accompaniment figure; music fades out as figure is passed around to other instruments

PROGRAM MUSIC†

descriptive music

More than any other period, the nineteenth century was a time in which composers sought and received inspiration from sources outside music. An encounter with nature, the impressions of a voyage, a disappointment in love, a popular legend, or an entire play might provide a story, a scene, or an idea that could be described in music. Of course, music could not actually tell a tale. Yet it did have its own expressive figures of speech. By using different colors, moods, and sound effects, composers could suggest a particular sequence of events to a sensitive listener. To this end they wrote overtures*, concert overtures*, incidental music*, symphonic poems*, and program symphonies*, which taken together constitute a sizable part of the repertoire of Romantic music. Two of the best composers of this sort of descriptive music were Hector Berlioz and Felix Mendelssohn.

†Nineteenth-century program music is discussed more fully on pages 252–54.

Hector Berlioz (1803–1869)

Hector Berlioz was one of the most original figures in the history of music (Fig. 13–4). He was born in 1803 near the mountain city of Grenoble, France, the son of a local doctor. As a youth Berlioz studied mainly the sciences and ancient Roman literature. Although local tutors taught him to play the flute and guitar, he had no systematic training in music theory or composition and little exposure to the music of the great masters. Among the major composers of the nineteenth century, he was the only one without fluency at the keyboard. He never studied piano, and could do no more than bang out a few chords; yet he would become one of the greatest orchestrators of all time.

At the age of seventeen Berlioz was sent off to Paris to study medicine, his father's profession. For two years he pursued a program in the physical sciences, earning a degree in 1821. But Berlioz found the dissecting table repulsive and the allure of the opera house and concert halls irresistible. After a period of soul searching, and the inevitable falling out with his parents over the choice of a career, he vowed to become "no doctor or apothecary but a great composer."

His dismayed father immediately cut off his living stipend, leaving young Berlioz to ponder how he might support himself while studying composition at the Paris Conservatory (the French national school of music). Other composers had relied on teaching as a means to earn a regular income: Mozart, Haydn, Beethoven, Chopin, and Liszt, for example, all gave piano lessons as young men. But what could Berlioz teach? He had no particular skill on any instrument. So he turned to music criticism, writing reviews and articles for literary journals. Berlioz was the first composer to earn a livelihood as a music critic, and criticism, not the sale of his music, remained his primary source of income for the rest of his life.

Perhaps it was inevitable that Berlioz turned to writing about music, for literature was, and would remain, a powerful force in his life and art. As a boy his father had taught him to read Virgil's *Aeneid* in the original Latin; later he would use episodes from this classical epic to form the libretto of an opera called *Les Troyens* (*The Trojans*, 1858). As a young man he read Lord Byron's *Childe Harold's Pilgrimage* (see page 250) and Goethe's *Faust*, works that inspired his concerto for viola called *Harold in Italy* (1834) and his dramatic symphony *The Damnation of Faust* (1846). But of all literary influences, none was greater than that of Shakespeare. As we have seen (page 252), Shakespeare burst upon the consciousness of continental Europe for the first time early in the nineteenth century. For Berlioz the experience was shattering: "Shakespeare, coming upon me unawares, struck me like a thunderbolt. The lightning flash of that discovery revealed to me at a stroke the whole heaven of art." Berlioz devoured the Bard's plays and gave musical expression to four: *The Tempest*, *King Lear*, *Hamlet*, and *Romeo and Juliet*. For *Romeo and Juliet*, for example, he created a five-movement program symphony*, *Roméo et Juliette* (1839), in which a chorus and solo voices intermittently paraphrase Shakespeare's own words. The common denominator in the art of Shakespeare and Berlioz is range of expression. Just as no dramatist before Shakespeare had portrayed the full spectrum of human emotions on the stage, so no composer before Berlioz undertook to create the widest range of moods through sound.

To depict wild swings of mood in music, Berlioz called for enormous orchestral and choral forces—hundreds and hundreds of performers. He also

FIGURE 13–4
Hector Berlioz at the age of twenty-nine.

Berlioz and Shakespeare

FIGURE 13-5

A caricature of Berlioz conducting in mid-nineteenth-century Paris, in what became known as "monster concerts" because of the huge forces the composer required. Berlioz would have liked several hundred performers for the premiere of his *Symphonie fantastique* in 1830, but the printed program suggests he had to settle for about one hundred.

Berlioz in love

idée fixe: *a recurring melody*

experimented with new instruments: the **ophicleide** (an early form of the tuba), the **English horn** (a low oboe), the harp (an ancient instrument now brought into the symphony orchestra for the first time), the **cornet** (a brass instrument with valves, borrowed from the military band), and even the newly invented saxophone. His approach to musical form was also iconoclastic; he rarely wrote in strict sonata–allegro form or theme and variations, for example. His French compatriots found his compositions "bizarre" and "monstrous" and thought him something of a madman. Increasingly, he crisscrossed Europe to conduct his works before foreigners, who more readily appreciated his unique new sounds. To London, Bonn, Vienna, Prague, Leipzig, and even Moscow he went to introduce such works as *Symphonie fantastique*, *Damnation of Faust*, *Roméo et Juliette*, and *The Trojans*. He died in Paris in 1869, isolated and embittered. The little recognition he received in his native France came "too late," as he said, to help his career or self-esteem.

SYMPHONIE FANTASTIQUE (1830)

Berlioz's most celebrated work, then and now, is his *Symphonie fantastique*, perhaps the single most influential composition of the entire nineteenth century. Its form and orchestration are revolutionary. But what is more, it tells in music a vivid story and, as such, is the first complete program symphony. The story surrounding the creation of the descriptive program of the work is as fascinating as the program itself.

In 1827 a troupe of English actors came to Paris to present Shakespeare's *Hamlet* and *Romeo and Juliet*. Berlioz, of course, had read some of Shakespeare's plays in a French translation, but was eager to see these works performed on stage. Though he understood little English, he was overwhelmed by what he saw. The human insights, touching beauty, and onstage action in Shakespeare's work far surpassed the virtues found in traditional French theater. Not only was Berlioz smitten by Shakespeare, but he also fell in love with the leading lady who played Ophelia to Hamlet and Juliet to Romeo, one Harriet Smithson (Fig. 13–6). Like a lovesick adolescent Berlioz swooned at her sight and wrote such violently passionate letters that the frightened starlet refused to meet the student composer. Eventually, his ardor cooled—for a time he even became engaged to someone else. But the experience of an all-consuming love, the despair of rejection, and the vision of darkness and possible death furnished the stimulus—and story line—for an unusually imaginative symphony.

Berlioz wrote the *Symphonie fantastique*, not in the usual four movements of a symphony, but in five, an arrangement that may have been inspired by Shakespeare's use of a five-act format. Movements 1 and 5 balance each other in length and substance, as do 2 and 4, leaving the leisurely third movement as the center of the work. But symmetry is not the only element holding the symphony together. Berlioz creates a single melody that reappears as a unifying force, movement after movement, a total of eight times during the symphony. Earlier, Beethoven had experimented with thematic recall and transformation in his fifth and ninth symphonies. But Berlioz takes this technique one step farther by recalling the melody constantly and by associating it with an object, his beloved. The vision of his loved one, and her attending melody, become an obsession. Berlioz called this musical fixation his **idée fixe** ("fixed idea"). As his feelings about the beloved change from movement to movement, so the *idée fixe* is transformed. The composer alters the pitches slightly and assigns different instruments to play it, each adding its own tone color and feeling. To make sure the listener knows what these feelings are, Berlioz prepared a written program to be read as the music is performed. It tells the story of unrequited love, attempted suicide, imaginary murder, and hellish revenge.

First Movement: Reveries, Passions

> Program: A young musician . . . sees for the first time a woman who embodies all the charms of the ideal being he has imagined in his dreams. . . . The subject of the first movement is the passage from this state of melancholy reverie, interrupted by a few moments of joy, to that of delirious passion, with movements of fury, jealousy, and its return to tenderness, tears, and religious consolation.

A slow introduction ("this state of melancholy reverie") prepares the way for the first vision of the beloved, carried forward by the first appearance of the main theme, the *idée fixe*. (The entire melody is given earlier in Ex. 12–2.)

EXAMPLE 13–4

The movement unfolds in sonata–allegro form. The "recapitulation," however, does not so much repeat the *idée fixe* as it does transform the melody to reflect the artist's feelings of sorrow and tenderness.

Second Movement: A Ball

> The artist finds himself . . . in the midst of the tumult of a party.

A lilting waltz now begins, but it is interrupted by the unexpected appearance of the *idée fixe*, the rhythm changed to accommodate the triple meter of the waltz. Four harps add a graceful accompaniment when the waltz returns, and, toward the end, there is even a lovely solo for cornet. The sequence of waltz–*idée fixe*–waltz creates, once again, ternary form.

Third Movement: Scene in the Country

> Finding himself one evening in the country, the artist hears in the distance two shepherds piping. . . . He reflects upon his isolation and hopes that soon he will no longer be alone.

The dialogue between the shepherds is presented by an English horn and an oboe, the latter played offstage to give the effect of a distant response. The unexpected appearance of the *idée fixe* in the woodwinds suggests that the artist has hopes of winning his beloved. But has she falsely encouraged him? The shepherd's tune recurs, but the oboe doesn't respond. To the lonely petition of the English horn, we now hear only the empty rumble of distant thunder in the timpani. The call for love goes unanswered.

Fourth Movement: March to the Scaffold

> Having realized that his love goes unrecognized, the artist poisons himself with opium. The dose of the narcotic, too weak to kill him, plunges him into a sleep accompanied by the most horrible visions. He dreams that he has killed the one he loved, that he is condemned, led to the scaffold, and now witnesses his own execution.

Yale Center for British Art, Paul Mellon Collection

FIGURE 13–6

The actress Harriet Smithson became an obsession for Berlioz and the source of inspiration for his *Symphonie fantastique*. Eventually Berlioz did meet and marry Smithson. Today they lie side by side in the cemetery of Montmartre in Paris.

idée fixe *transformed*

reappearances of the idée fixe

Bridgeman Art Library, London/NY

FIGURE 13–7

Witches' Sabbath by Francisco de Goya (1746–1828) bears the same title as the finale of Berlioz's *Symphonie fantastique*. Both create images of the bizarre and macabre so dear to the hearts of Romantic artists.

This drug-induced nightmare centers on the march to the scaffold where the artist is to be executed. The steady beat of the low strings and the muffled bass drum sound the steps of the procession. Near the end the image of the beloved returns in the clarinet, only to be suddenly cut off by a *fortissimo* crash by the full orchestra. The guillotine has fallen.

Fifth Movement: Dream of the Witches' Sabbath

> He sees himself at the witches' sabbath surrounded by a troop of frightful shadows, sorcerers, and monsters of all sorts, gathered for his funeral. Strange noises, groans, bursts of laughter, distant cries echoed by others. The beloved melody returns again, but it has lost its noble, modest character and is now only base, trivial, and grotesque. An outburst of joy at her arrival; she joins in the devilish orgy.

In this monstrous finale Berlioz creates his personal vision of hell (Fig. 13–7). A crowd of witches and other ghouls is summoned to dance around the corpse of the artist on its way to the inferno. Weird sounds are produced by the strings, using mutes, and by the high woodwinds and French horn, playing glissandos*. A piercing clarinet enters with a burlesque parody of the *idée fixe* as Harriet Smithson, now in the frightful garb of a wicked old hag, comes on stage.

EXAMPLE 13–5

She is greeted by a joyous *fortissimo* outburst by the full assembly as all proceed to dance to the now perverted *idée fixe*. Suddenly, the music becomes ominously quiet and, in one of the most strikingly original moments in all of music, great Gothic church bells are heard. Against this solemn backdrop sounds the burial hymn of the medieval Church, the **Dies irae**, played by ophicleides (tubas) and bassoons. (Recently, the *Dies irae* has been used to signal doom and gloom in three "horror" films: *Nightmare before Christmas, Sleeping with the Enemy,* and *The Shining*.)

EXAMPLE 13–6

[Di - es i - rae di - es il - la sol - vet   sae - clum in fa - vil - la]
[Day of anger, day of wrath, on which the ages will be changed to ash]

Dies irae: a chant from the medieval Church

a mockery of the Church

Not only is the orchestration sensational, the musical symbolism is sacrilegious. Just as the painter Goya parodies the Catholic Mass in his *Witches' Sabbath*—making babies serve as communion wafers (Fig. 13–7), so Berlioz creates a mockery of one of the most venerable Gregorian chants of the Catholic Church. First the *Dies irae* is played by the horns twice as fast (a process called rhythmic **diminution**). Then the sacred tune is transformed into a jazzed-up dance tune played by a shrill, high clarinet, the entire scene now becoming a blasphemous black mass.

EXAMPLE 13–7

clarinet

f

As the ceremony proceeds, the witches begin to dance. But they do so in a strange way: They enter one by one and create a fugato*, a fugal passage within a symphonic movement. What is a learned fugue doing here in the middle of hell? Presumably because, having just mocked the ancient music of the Catholic Church, Berlioz now decides to ridicule the musical establishment and its strictest form, the academic fugue. But beyond this, the regular entry of more and more voices, or dancing witches, creates the effect of a growing tumult around the corpse of the artist.

a parody of the fugue

EXAMPLE 13–8

cellos and double basses

sfz

A climax is reached as the theme, or subject, of the witches, played by the strings, as well as the *Dies irae* melody, played by the brasses and woodwinds, sound together, though in different keys, a bizarre example of **double counterpoint**. Stranger still is the sound that follows, for Berlioz instructs the violins to play **col legno** ("with the wood")—to strike the strings, not with the usual front of the bow, but with the wooden back, creating a noise something akin to the crackling or burning of hellfire.

col legno: *a strange effect*

The Real End of the Program

In Berlioz's programmatic *Symphonie fantastique*, art imitates life—he constructs a musical narrative to mirror events (real and imagined) in his young life. But how did the story of Berlioz and his beloved Harriet Smithson really end? In truth, Berlioz did meet and marry Harriet, but the two lived miserably together ever after. Harriet died in 1854 and was buried in a small graveyard in Paris. In 1864, that cemetery was to be closed and the remains of all the deceased transferred to a new, larger burial ground. It fell to widower Berlioz to remove Harriet's corpse to the new cemetery, as he recounts in his memoirs:

One dark, gloomy morning I set forth alone for the sad spot. A municipal officer was waiting, to be present at the disinterment. The grave had already been opened, and on my arrival

The Parisian painter Eugène Delacroix's depiction of the graveyard scene in Hamlet *(1829).*
The Louvre, Paris, © R.M.N.

the gravedigger jumped in. The coffin was still entire, though it had been ten years underground; the lid alone was injured by the damp. The man, instead of lifting it out, tore away the rotten lid, which cracked with a hideous noise, and brought the contents of the coffin to light. He then bent down, took up the crowned, decayed head of the poor *Ophelia*—and laid it in a new coffin awaiting it at the edge of the grave. Then, bending down a second time, he lifted with difficulty the headless trunk and limbs—a blackish mass to which the shroud still adhered, resembling a heap of pitch in a damp sack. I remember the dull sound . . . and the odor. (Hector Berlioz, *Memoirs*)

Berlioz had begun by playing Romeo to Harriet's Juliet, and ended by playing Hamlet to her Ophelia. He cast his music, and his life, in terms of Shakespearean drama.

To the audience that first heard the *Symphonie fantastique* on December 5, 1830, all of this must have seemed incomprehensible: new instruments, novel playing effects, simultaneous melodies in different keys, and a form that is not traditional, like sonata–allegro or rondo, but grows out of the events in a soap-opera-like program. But it all works. Here is a rare example in the history of ideas in which a creator thinks "outside the box" of conventional art; yet he does so in a way that produces a wholly integrated, unified, and ultimately satisfying work. The separate effects may be revolutionary and momentarily shocking, but they are consistent and logical among themselves when subsumed in the total artistic concept. Had Berlioz never written another note of music, he would be justly famous for this single masterpiece of Romantic invention.

music "outside the box"

Listening Guide

Hector Berlioz
Symphonie fantastique (1830)
Fifth movement, Dream of the Witches' Sabbath

6CD 3/9;
2CD 2/1

0:00	"Strange noises, groans, bursts of laughter, distant cries" high and low
1:28	Grotesquely transformed *idée fixe* in shrill clarinet
1:36	Joyful, *fortissimo* outburst by full orchestra welcoming the now ugly beloved
1:46	Witches begin to dance to the newly grotesque *idée fixe*; bassoons add raucous counterpoint (1:55)
2:39	Sinister transition
2:59	Funeral bells sound
3:26	*Dies irae* heard in tubas and bassoons
3:48	French horns and trombones play *Dies irae* twice as fast (diminution)
3:58	Woodwinds pervert *Dies irae* chant
4:04	*Dies irae*, its diminution, and its perversion continue
4:30	Tubas and bassoons play *Dies irae* with bass drum reverberation
5:04	Introduction to witches' dance; crescendo
5:21	Witches' dance (fugato) begins with four entries of the subject
5:47	Fugal episode
6:06	Three more entries of the subject
6:22	More strange sounds and cries (transition out of fugato)
7:04	Fragments of the *Dies irae*
7:21	Witches' dance (fugue subject) grows to a rapid climax, then *fortissimo* syncopation (7:49)
8:06	Witches' dance and *Dies irae* combined; trumpets now added
8:35	Violins use wooden back of bow (*col legno**) to produce a crackling sound
8:56	*Fortissimo* chords
9:13	Fleeting recall of *Dies irae*
9:30	More chords with a striking harmonic shift
9:36	Final cadential fanfare

(Listening Exercise 30)

Felix Mendelssohn (1809–1847)

Berlioz was a child of the Romantic age: He tried suicide at least twice, ran around Italy with a gang of bandits in imitation of Lord Byron, and married an image, an ideal of a woman, with disastrous consequences. Felix Mendelssohn was an altogether different personality, anything but the stereotype of the rebellious, self-absorbed, struggling artist.

Mendelssohn was born in 1809 into a prosperous, indeed wealthy, Jewish family. His father was a banker, and his grandfather, Moses Mendelssohn (1726–1786), was a noted philosopher. At the family home in Berlin young Felix had every advantage: He studied languages, literature, and philosophy with private tutors, as well as painting, dancing, riding, and even gymnastics. In 1816 Mendelssohn's parents had their four children baptized Christians, partly so they might enjoy full legal equality and move freely in all social circles. Indeed, their home became a gathering place for artists and intellectuals of all sorts: the poet Heine, the philosopher Hegel, and the geographer Humboldt (discoverer of the Humboldt current) were all frequent guests. Because Felix had shown extraordinary musical talent, he was not only given piano lessons but also provided with a small orchestra on Sunday afternoons to try out his youthful compositions. At the age of sixteen he composed a masterpiece, his octet for strings. The next year (1826) witnessed an equally astonishing work, the Overture to *A Midsummer Night's Dream*. As a composer Mendelssohn was even more precocious than either Mozart or Schubert.

Taking advantage of his privileged station in life, Mendelssohn spent the years 1829–1835 traveling across Europe to discover its natural beauty and to meet the great artists of the day. He walked across most of Switzerland, sketching and painting as he went. He met Goethe in Weimar, Berlioz in Rome, Liszt, Chopin, and the painter Delacroix (see Fig. 13–14) in Paris, and the novelist Sir Walter Scott outside Edinburgh. The itinerant years ended in the spring of 1835 when he was appointed musical director of the Gewandhaus Orchestra in Leipzig, Germany.

Founded in 1781 by the merchants of Leipzig, the **Gewandhaus Orchestra** ("Clothiers' House" Orchestra) played in the guild hall of that trade association (Figs. 13–9 and 13–10). Mendelssohn recruited better players, increased their salaries, established a pension fund for the orchestra, and conducted as a musical interpreter, not just as a mere time-beater. By so doing he soon made the Gewandhaus Orchestra one of the finest in Europe, a position it has continued to hold to the present day. Mendelssohn was director of this ensemble for a dozen years, from 1835 until 1847, when he died prematurely by stroke at the age of thirty-eight.

During his tenure in Leipzig, Felix Mendelssohn changed the very purpose of the symphony orchestra. He established the modern notion that a symphony exists not only to promote contemporary music but also to preserve a past repertoire of musical masterpieces. In 1829 he mounted the first performance in almost a hundred years of Bach's great *St. Matthew Passion*, thereby bringing the long-forgotten Bach to the public's attention. ("And to think that it should be a Jew who gives back to the world the greatest of Christian works," he said at the time.) So, too, he programmed the works of other composers of historical interest: Handel, Haydn, and Mozart. The idea spread. From this time forward a concert by a symphony orchestra served not only as a forum for new or recent works but also as a museum for the old.

FIGURE 13–8

Felix Mendelssohn in 1829 at the age of twenty.

FIGURE 13–9

Exterior of the Gewandhaus in Leipzig, Germany, as depicted by Felix Mendelssohn. In addition to being a musician and composer and speaking four languages fluently, Mendelssohn was a gifted painter, his preferred medium being watercolor.

FIGURE 13–10

A concert in progress, ca. 1840, in the Gewandhaus, the hall where Mendelssohn, Liszt, Berlioz, and Clara and Robert Schumann frequently performed.

Given the fact that Mendelssohn revived the music of the eighteenth-century masters, it is not surprising that his own compositions are the most conservative, the most "classical," of the great Romantic composers. His harmonies are colorful but not revolutionary; his orchestration distinctive but not shocking—a light, dancing string sound is his hallmark; and his use of form is traditional, as seen in his heavy reliance on sonata–allegro form. Never does he indulge in startling outbursts of sound. The classical ideals of unity, grace, and formal balance predominate.

What then makes Mendelssohn a musical Romantic? Program music. Nature, travel, and literature provided stimuli for many of his creations. A trip to Italy in 1830–31 gave rise to his "Italian" Symphony, just as a lengthy sojourn in Scotland a year earlier had planted the seeds for the "Scottish" Symphony. On this same northern voyage he visited the windswept Hebrides Islands and soon captured the spirit of the churning sea and rocky coast in his *Hebrides Overture* (1830). Mendelssohn commented on the difficulty he faced when trying to harness a raging ocean within the confines of sonata–allegro form: "The whole development section smells more of counterpoint than of blubber, gulls, and salted cod."

As to literary influences, he heard the voices of Goethe and Shakespeare most clearly. To Goethe's *Faust* the composer owed the inspiration for the *Scherzo* of his early Octet (1825) and several later orchestral works. And to Shakespeare, of course, can be traced the genesis of the music for *A Midsummer Night's Dream*.

OVERTURE TO *A MIDSUMMER NIGHT'S DREAM* (1826)

Mendelssohn began to compose, or "to dream *A Midsummer Night's Dream*," as he says, during July 1826, when he was an impressionable youth of seventeen. His aim was to transform the romantic fantasy of Shakespeare's play into an independent concert overture (a piece for the concert hall, not the theater). Some years later, in 1843, he was commissioned by the king of Prussia to create incidental music (music to be heard during an actual performance) for a production of the play planned for Berlin. Among these incidental pieces is his famous *Wedding March*—originally written to accompany the marriage of the characters Theseus and Hippolyta, but now traditionally played at weddings as the recessional march.

recreating Shakespeare's play in music

To enter fully into the enchanted world of Mendelssohn's Overture to *A Midsummer Night's Dream*, we must know something of the play—the program—that inspired it. The drama begins in an imaginary city called Athens, where the ruler, Duke Theseus, is about to marry Hippolyta, queen of the Amazons. Nearby is an enchanted forest ruled by Oberon, king of the elves, and his estranged queen, Titania. Into this magical grove come Lysander and Hermia, another pair of would-be lovers. Then enters a group of common craftsmen, led by the blockheaded Bottom, who have come to prepare for the royal wedding. Finally, the hunting party of Theseus and Hippolyta joins the woodland scene. Confusion reigns as an agent of fairy king Oberon, the spirit Puck, administers a love potion to the wrong parties; fairy queen Titania falls in love with the clownish Bottom, who is made to wear the head of an ass. Eventually, all is set right and the nobles and gentry return to the court of Athens. The events in the enchanted forest had been no more real than a midsummer night's dream.

Mendelssohn's Overture closely follows the play. Separate and distinctly different musical colors and styles make the various characters clearly identifiable and the events easy to follow. At the same time, the music unfolds in sonata–allegro form. There is a slow four-chord introduction, a first theme (the dancing fairy music), a transition (royal music of the court of Athens), a second theme (the lovers' music), and a closing theme group (the craftsmen's music and the hunting calls). The fairies dominate the development section, and in the coda (or epilogue) they have the last word, just as in Shakespeare's play. Mendelssohn's own thoughts best describe the ending: "After everything has been satisfactorily settled and the principal players have joyfully left the stage, the elves follow them, bless the house, and disappear with the dawn. So ends the play, and my overture too."

Tate Gallery/Art Resource

FIGURE 13–11

Oberon, Titania, and Puck with Fairies Dancing by the English artist and poet William Blake (1757–1827).

Listening Guide

Felix Mendelssohn
Overture to *A Midsummer Night's Dream* (1826)

6CD 3/10

WWW

Form: sonata–allegro

	Program:	*Musical Events:*
EXPOSITION		
0:00	Introduction to enchantment	Four sustained chords in the winds (introduction)
0:20	Fairies' music	Rapid, light, staccato notes in violins (first theme)
1:04	Duke Theseus and his court	Full orchestra *fortissimo* (transition)
1:34		Fairies' music mixes into transition
2:08	Lovers' music	Quiet melody in woodwinds and strings grows more passionate (second theme)
3:00	Bottom's music	Raucous motive sounds like braying of a donkey (closing theme, part 1)
3:22	Hunting calls of regal party	Fanfares in brasses and woodwinds (closing theme, part 2)

(Continued on next page)

DEVELOPMENT

3:46	Fairies' music developed	Music of the fairies (first theme) worked out in different keys
4:22	French horn blasts	
4:52	Fairies' music extended	String pizzicato and string tremolo
5:27	Lysander and Hermia sleep	Ritard, soft string sound, music seems to come to a stop

RECAPITULATION

5:52	Return to enchantment	Four introductory chords return
6:14	Fairies' music	Dancing fairies' music returns (first theme), but transition is eliminated
6:58	Lovers' music	Lyrical melody in woodwinds and strings (second theme) as before
7:47	Bottom's music	Again raucous *fortissimo* music of the ass (closing theme, part 1)
8:52	Royal hunting party	Fanfares (closing theme, part 2) serve as ending to recapitulation

CODA

| 9:16 | Epilogue by fairy Puck | Light, quick music of the fairies; toward the end Duke Theseus and the four opening chords are recalled |

THE PIANISTS

By the 1840s the piano had evolved into essentially the instrument we know today (see also page 261). Its thundering power, rapid action, singing tone, and wide range of expression made it the most popular instrument of the Romantic period. No self-respecting middle-class home could be without one. No education was thought complete without lessons at it. Spurred by the extraordinary vogue of the instrument, a host of virtuoso performers set upon the concert halls of Europe with fingers blazing. What they played was often more a display of digital fireworks—rapid octaves, racing chromatic scales, thundering chords—than of musical substance. Happily, however, several of the greatest piano virtuosos of the nineteenth century were also gifted composers. While these artists sometimes wrote songs, symphonies, or concertos, the piano—and piano style—was at the heart of their creative process.

vogue of the piano

Robert Schumann (1810–1856)

In many ways Robert Schumann's life was a failure, indeed a tragedy. Sent to university at Heidelberg to study law, he attended not a single class—he had no more affinity for law than Berlioz had for medicine. With his mother's grudging consent, Schumann moved on to Leipzig to study piano, determined to become a virtuoso. But after two years of lessons with the eminent Friedrich Wieck (1785–1873), all he had to show for his labors was a permanently damaged right hand. His career as a virtuoso now frustrated, composition and music criticism became the focus of his creative energies. During the 1830s he produced a remarkable series of works for solo piano, mostly sonatas, variations, and collections of character pieces*. He also founded and served as editor for the new musical periodical, the *Neue Zeitschrift für Musik* (*New Journal of*

law student, pianist, then composer

Music). Schumann became the apostle for new music within the German Romantic movement, championing the works of such "radical" composers as Berlioz, Chopin, Mendelssohn, Liszt, and the young Johannes Brahms.

While studying piano in the Leipzig home of Friedrich Wieck, Schumann met, and soon fell in love with, Wieck's beautiful and talented daughter, Clara. They were married in 1840, over the violent objections of her father. The year of their union was one of feverish creation for Robert; from his pen flowed more than 125 *Lieder**, mostly love songs, for voice and piano. These include several now-famous song cycles* such as *Dichterliebe (Poet's Love)* and *Frauenliebe und -leben (Women in Love and Life)*, individual songs of which are the equal in quality to the works of the great Franz Schubert in this genre. Clara now encouraged him to extend himself beyond art songs and character pieces for piano, and into orchestral and chamber music. But in these larger forms he had only mixed success. His piano concerto (1845) and piano quintet (1842) are supreme accomplishments, but his four symphonies are not uniformly compelling. At heart Schumann was a miniaturist whose creativity was inextricably bound to the keyboard. And unlike his idol Beethoven, who composed on sketchbooks as he walked through forest and field, Schumann was unable to generate music except at the piano. Touch and sensation were intrinsic to his creative process.

Life between the Schumanns was marked by symbiotic artistry and personal agony. Husband and wife read poetry together, and each made suggestions on the other's musical compositions. But from his earliest years Robert Schumann had been afflicted with what psychiatrists now call bipolar disorder (likely exacerbated by doses of arsenic he had taken as a young man to cure a case of syphilis). His moods swung from nervous euphoria to suicidal depression. Naturally, this disease affected his creativity, both for good and for ill. In some years he produced a torrent of music, in others virtually nothing. As time progressed, Schumann's condition grew more extreme. He began to hear voices, both heavenly and hellish, and one morning, pursued by demons within, he jumped off a bridge into the Rhine river. Nearby fishermen pulled him to safety, but from that point on, by his own request, he was confined to an asylum, where he died of dementia in 1856. In his final, tragic years, his creative output dwindled to nothing.

FIGURE 13–12
Robert and Clara Schumann in 1850, from an engraving constructed from an early photograph.

SCENES FROM CHILDHOOD (1838)

To hear Schumann in a sunny, optimistic mood, let us turn to a group of thirteen miniature keyboard pieces he called *Kinderszenen (Scenes from Childhood)*. Schumann created this set in 1838 to satisfy the growing demand for piano music appropriate for the middle-class parlor. Yet despite the title, these are not pieces intended for children. Rather they are musical recollections of events and sensations from childhood—"reminiscences of a grown-up for grown-ups," the composer said. Each of the thirteen works in the set has its own suggestive title, such as *By the Fireside*, *Catch-as-Catch-Can*, or *Bogeyman's Coming*. Each invites the listener to enter the very private world of the imagination, to make one's own retrospective associations with the sounds. And each is a perfect example of the Romantic character piece*—a short work conveying a single character or mood in which that feeling is distilled to its very essence. In their musical form, the scenes are quite uncomplicated, usually in simple ternary structure (**ABA**). What is remarkable is the way in which a vision or sensation is instantly created and then, just as quickly, vanishes.

thirteen character pieces

The first of the scenes, *Von fremden Ländern und Menschen (Of Foreign Lands and People)*, may allude to a child's bright eyes seeing far-off places. Another, *Träumerei (Dreaming)*, suggests a child engrossed in a world of dreams. *Dreaming*, incidentally, was the character piece the great pianist Vladimir Horowitz (1904–1989) traditionally played as the last of his encores.

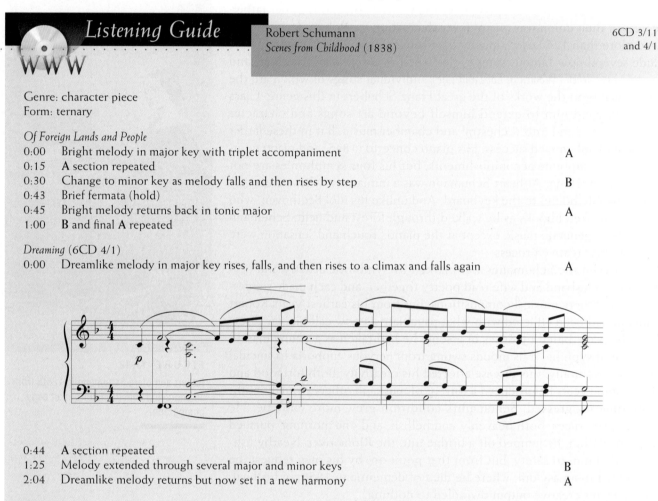

| | *Listening Guide* | Robert Schumann | 6CD 3/11 |
| | | *Scenes from Childhood* (1838) | and 4/1 |

Genre: character piece
Form: ternary

Of Foreign Lands and People

0:00	Bright melody in major key with triplet accompaniment	A
0:15	A section repeated	
0:30	Change to minor key as melody falls and then rises by step	B
0:43	Brief fermata (hold)	
0:45	Bright melody returns back in tonic major	A
1:00	B and final A repeated	

Dreaming (6CD 4/1)

| 0:00 | Dreamlike melody in major key rises, falls, and then rises to a climax and falls again | A |

0:44	A section repeated	
1:25	Melody extended through several major and minor keys	B
2:04	Dreamlike melody returns but now set in a new harmony	A

Clara Wieck Schumann (1819–1896)

a child prodigy

Unlike her husband, Robert, a gifted composer but failed performer, Clara Wieck Schumann was one of the great piano virtuosos of the nineteenth century (Fig. 13–13). A child prodigy, she made her debut at the age of eleven in the Gewandhaus (see Figs. 13–9 and 13–10) in Leipzig, Germany, the city of her birth. She then undertook a concert tour of Europe during which she impressed and befriended Mendelssohn, Berlioz, Chopin, and Liszt. In Austria, the Emperor named her "Royal and Imperial Chamber Virtuosa"—the first time that official title had been given to a Protestant, a teenager, or a woman. Unofficially, she became in time Europe's "Queen of the Piano."

When she married Robert Schumann in 1840, Clara Wieck was much better known on the international stage than he. Nevertheless, she put aside her own career to play the roles of wife and mother to the eight children she

Where Were the Women?

You may have noticed that female composers are poorly represented in this book. We have seen the works of some, Hildegard of Bingen (page 74) and Barbara Strozzi (page 112), for example, and we will meet those of Ellen Taaffe Zwilich later (page 390). But in general, although women have been actively engaged as performers of secular music since the Middle Ages, only rarely, until the twentieth century, did they become composers. While the causes of this condition are numerous, one factor stands out above all others: People then had no faith in the capacity, or the propriety, of female creativity. Although a young lady might learn to play the piano in a show of domestic refinement, a woman's function in society was defined as nurturer of children (preferably male) and handmaiden of husband. Fanny Mendelssohn Hensel (1805–1847), the gifted sister of Felix Mendelssohn, was fifteen and considering music as a profession when she received the following directive in a letter from her father: "What you wrote to me about your musical occupations, and in comparison to those of Felix, was rightly thought and expressed. But though music will perhaps become his profession, for you it can and must only be an ornament, never the core of your existence. . . . You must become more steady and collected, and prepare yourself for your real calling, the only calling for a young woman— the state of a housewife."

With no encouragement to become a creative force outside the home, little wonder that self-doubt arose among women of talent. As Clara Schumann wrote in her diary in 1839: "I once believed that I possessed creative talent, but I have given up this idea; a woman must not desire to compose. There has never yet been one able to do it. Should I expect to be that one?"

Composing a symphony or a string quartet is a complex process requiring years of schooling in harmony, counterpoint, and instrumentation. Women did not have access to such formal training in composition. For example, the Paris Conservatory was founded in 1793 but did not admit women into the classes in advanced music theory and composition until almost a century later. Women might study piano, but according to a decree of the 1820s they were to enter and leave by a separate door. (Similarly, women painters were not admitted to the state-sponsored Academy of Fine Arts in Paris until 1897. Even then they were barred from nude anatomy classes, instruction crucial to the figural arts, because their presence was thought "morally inappropriate.") Only in those exceptional cases in which a daughter received an intense musical education at home, as did Fanny Mendelssohn and Clara Schumann, did a woman have a fighting chance to become a musical creator.

Fanny Mendelssohn in 1829.
Culver Pictures

soon bore him (one died in infancy). Her compositions became few and far between, her public performances limited to an occasional tour. But when Robert Schumann was institutionalized in 1854 Clara was compelled by economic necessity again to pursue the concert circuit. There were annual tours to England and more than one to Russia. She continued to concertize until the age of seventy, having become a legend in her own time. A review from London in 1884 is typical:

a legendary pianist and composer

> We think we are correct in saying that no pianist ever before retained so powerful a hold upon the public mind for so long a period . . . . Though for years Madame Schumann has been acknowledged unequal as an exponent of [Robert] Schumann's music, yet one always hears from her wonderful interpretations of Bach, Mozart, and Beethoven. By her modesty, prudence, and talents she has gradually achieved a veritable triumph.

FIGURE 13–13

Clara Schumann at the piano with the young violinist Joseph Joachim in 1854. Schumann was something akin to a musical mother to Joachim and dedicated her Romances for violin and piano to him.

Robert-Schumann-Haus, Zwickau

Romance for Piano and Violin, Opus 22, No. 3 (1853)

Not only was Clara Schumann a piano virtuoso but she was also a gifted composer, as her Romance for Piano and Violin, No. 3, of 1853 demonstrates. A **romance** is a brief instrumental work, usually in a slow tempo, that conveys a single, intensely lyrical mood. It, too, belongs to that genre of music called the character piece* (see page 258). Clara Schumann wrote numerous romances for piano alone. And even in this set of three for piano with violin, it is the pianist who does most of the work, creating a rich chromatic texture, providing the harmony, and sometimes supplying the melody as well. What is of interest in this romance is the composer's unflagging industry and integrity. There are two themes, **a** (heard four times) and **b** (heard twice). Where a lesser composer might have relied on simple repeats, Clara Schumann continually varies the surrounding musical context each time the themes reappear. Here beauty is created through the subtle way in which the two themes continually take on new expressive meaning in an ever-changing sea of harmonic color.

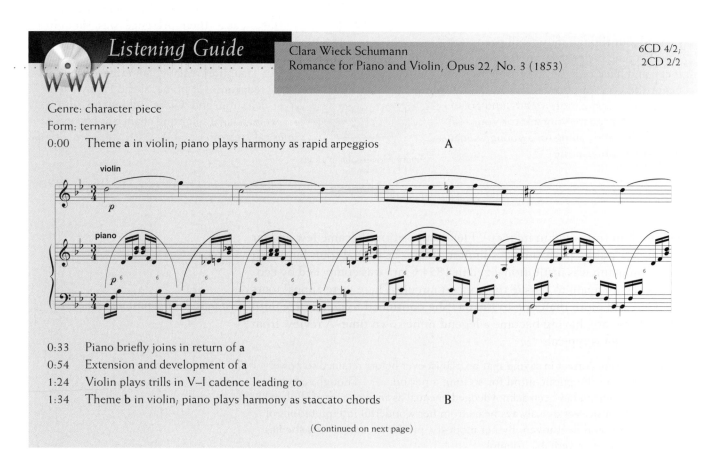

Listening Guide

www

Clara Wieck Schumann
Romance for Piano and Violin, Opus 22, No. 3 (1853)

6CD 4/2;
2CD 2/2

Genre: character piece
Form: ternary

0:00	Theme **a** in violin; piano plays harmony as rapid arpeggios	A

violin

piano

0:33	Piano briefly joins in return of **a**
0:54	Extension and development of **a**
1:24	Violin plays trills in V–I cadence leading to
1:34	Theme **b** in violin; piano plays harmony as staccato chords	B

(Continued on next page)

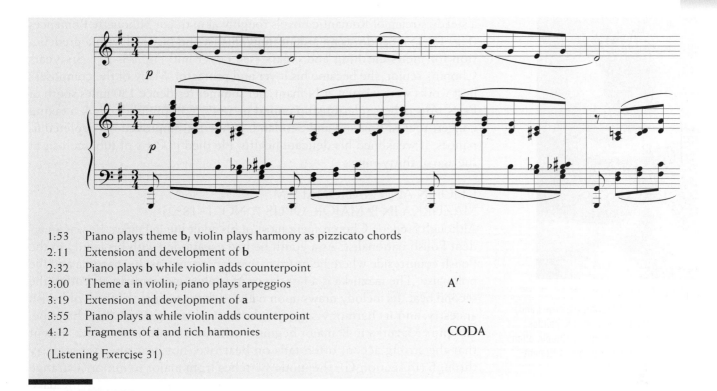

1:53   Piano plays theme **b**; violin plays harmony as pizzicato chords
2:11   Extension and development of **b**
2:32   Piano plays **b** while violin adds counterpoint
3:00   Theme **a** in violin; piano plays arpeggios   A′
3:19   Extension and development of **a**
3:55   Piano plays **a** while violin adds counterpoint
4:12   Fragments of **a** and rich harmonies   CODA

(Listening Exercise 31)

Frédéric Chopin (1810–1849)

In the compositions of Frédéric Chopin, the piano and its music have their most perfect union. This "poet of the piano," as he was called, was born near Warsaw, Poland, of a French father and a Polish mother. The father taught at an elite secondary school for the sons of Polish nobility, and it was there that Frédéric not only gained an excellent general education but acquired aristocratic friends and tastes as well. He then moved on to the newly founded Warsaw Conservatory, where, between 1826 and 1829, he concentrated on the study of piano and composition. It was during this period that he composed his first major work, a brilliant set of variations for piano and orchestra on Mozart's duet "Là ci darem la mano" ("Give me your hand") from *Don Giovanni* (on the duet, see page 224). Warsaw was now thought to be too small, too provincial, for a young man of his musical talents. So in 1830 he departed to seek his fortune in Vienna and Paris. The next year Poland's fight for freedom was crushed by Russian troops, and Chopin never returned to his homeland.

After an unsuccessful year in Vienna, the twenty-one-year-old Chopin arrived in Paris in September 1831. His inaugural concerts caught Parisians' fancy, and his imaginative playing soon became the stuff of legends. But Chopin was not cut out for the life of the public virtuoso. He was introverted, physically slight, and somewhat sickly. Consequently, he chose to play at private *musicales* (musical evenings) in the homes of the aristocracy and to give lessons for a fee only the very rich could afford. "I have been introduced all around the highest circles," he said within a year of his arrival. "I hobnob with ambassadors, princes, and ministers. I can't imagine what miracle is responsible for all this since I really haven't done anything to bring it about."

In October 1836 Chopin was introduced to Baroness Aurore Dudevant (1803–1876), a writer who under the pen name of George Sand poured forth

FIGURE 13–14

A superbly Romantic portrait of Chopin by Eugène Delacroix. It was originally painted with Chopin next to George Sand (see Fig 13–15). But in 1870 a vandal slashed the double portrait, thereby (unintentionally) creating two canvases.

The Louvre, Paris, © R.M.N.

FIGURE 13-15
Novelist Aurore Dudevant (George Sand) by Eugène Delacroix. Both the painter Delacroix and the composer Chopin often stayed at her summer estate in Nohant in the south of France.

a steady stream of Romantic novels roughly akin to our Silhouette Romances (Fig. 13–15). Sand was an ardent individualist and bisexual with a predeliction for men's clothing and cigars (see cover and Fig. 13–15). Six years Chopin's senior, she became his lover and protector. Many of the composer's best works were written at Nohant, her summer residence 150 miles south of Paris. After their relationship ended in 1847, Chopin undertook a taxing concert tour of England and Scotland. While this improved his depleted finances, it weakened his delicate health. He died in Paris of tuberculosis at the age of thirty-nine.

CHOPIN AND NATIONALISM: MAZURKA IN B♭ MAJOR, OPUS 7, NO. 1 (1832)

Although Frédéric Chopin spent most of his adult life in France, he was an ardent Polish nationalist. As a youth he had vacationed with his family in the Polish countryside where he heard native dances such as the mazurka and the polonaise. The **mazurka** is a fast dance in triple meter with an accent on the second beat. Its melody draws upon native folk tunes, some of them of Jewish ancestry, and its harmony suggests the static droning of a village bagpipe. Chopin's Mazurka in B♭ major begins much like a triple meter waltz, except that the strong accent often falls on beat two, not beat one. Yet midway through (in section **C**), the mode switches from major to minor, a strange scale sounds in the melody, and a drone appears in the accompanying bass. We have been transported from the world of the Parisian salon to a Polish village, from the familiar to the foreign. Chopin was something of a national hero in Poland, and his music was embraced as a way of preserving a national heritage. In Chopin's day these mazurkas were experienced as music or as dance: the Parisians listened, the Poles danced.

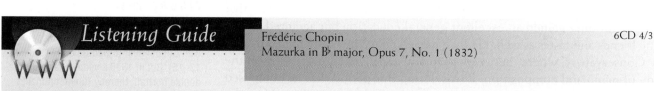

Listening Guide

Frédéric Chopin
Mazurka in B♭ major, Opus 7, No. 1 (1832)

6CD 4/3

WWW

Form: **ABACA** (with repeats)
0:00 Rapid dance with triple-meter accompaniment and accent on beat two (**A**)
0:16 Repeat of **A**
0:34 Lyrical interlude (**B**)
0:47 Return to **A**
1:03 Repeat of **B** and **A**
1:31 Exotic melody supported by constantly repeating (drone) bass (**C**)

1:46 Return to **A**
2:03 Repeat of **C** and **A**

Chopin was something of a rarity as a composer because each and every one of his works is either written for the piano alone or features the piano in some way, as in the case of his two piano concertos and twenty art songs* (in Polish). His works for piano alone include—in addition to his mazurkas and polonaises—three piano sonatas, a set of twenty-four preludes (brief character pieces, one in each of the major and minor keys), twenty-four etudes* (technical studies), and twenty-one nocturnes. Far better than the other genres, the dream-like nocturnes exhibit the essence of Romantic piano music.

NOCTURNE IN C♯ MINOR, OPUS 27, NO. 1 (1835)

A **nocturne** (night piece) is a slow, dreamy type of piano music that came into favor in the 1820s and 1830s. It suggests moonlit nights, romantic longing, and a certain painful melancholy, all evoked through bittersweet melodies and softly strumming harmonies. To set a nocturnal mood in his Nocturne in C♯ minor, Chopin begins with a tonic C♯ minor chord spun out as arpeggio in the bass, like a harp strumming in the moonlight. The melody (**A**) enters in minor but immediately turns to major, by means of an added sharp. As the opening melody repeats again and again in the course of the work, so too the harmony shifts expressively, bending back and forth from minor to major, from dark to light. This twisting of mode is one way that the composer creates intensity of feeling.

dreamy piano music

EXAMPLE 13–9

Soon the opening melody breaks off and a more passionate, agitated mood takes hold. A new theme (**B**) enters and the tempo increases. The bass now begins a long and mostly chromatic ascent. Here Chopin joins a long list of composers who have employed rising chromaticism to create a feeling of anxiety and rising tension.

EXAMPLE 13–10

A climax is reached at the peak of this line, emphasized by a remarkable chord change—a chord with four sharps is immediately followed by one with four flats (see Example 12–3). Juxtaposing chords from radically foreign keys is a means by which Chopin creates his bold harmonic shifts and rich

FIGURE 13-16
Following the lead of musicians, Romantic painters began to call their dreamy night scenes "nocturnes." James Whistler, *Nocturne in Black and Gold* (1874).

Detroit Institute of Art

harmonic colorings. Now another new melody (**C**) enters, which eventually gives way to **A** by means of a descending recitative-like passage.

The return to **A** is especially rich and satisfying as the harp-like accompaniment and plaintive melody seem to rise from the depths of the fading bass. Chopin's simple formal plan is now clear: statement-digression-return, each section with its own evocative atmosphere. The "lyrical expressive" (**A**) gives way to the "passionately anxious" (**B** and **C**), which yields to the initial lyricism (**A**). The returning **A** is extended by means of an exquisite little coda. At the very end, a painful dissonance sounds and then resolves to consonance (4:29–4:34), as the fears of the nocturnal world dissolve within a heavenly major realm. As the German poet Heine said of Chopin: "He hails from the land of Mozart, Raphael, and Goethe. His true home is in the realm of Poetry."

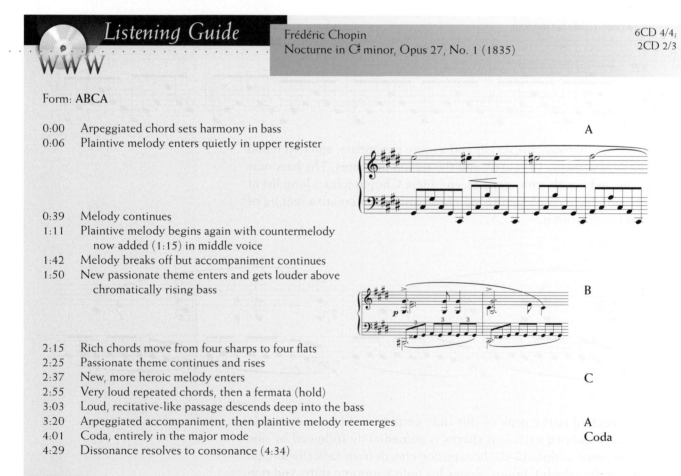

Listening Guide

WWW

Frédéric Chopin
Nocturne in C♯ minor, Opus 27, No. 1 (1835)

6CD 4/4;
2CD 2/3

Form: **ABCA**

0:00	Arpeggiated chord sets harmony in bass	
0:06	Plaintive melody enters quietly in upper register	**A**
0:39	Melody continues	
1:11	Plaintive melody begins again with countermelody now added (1:15) in middle voice	
1:42	Melody breaks off but accompaniment continues	
1:50	New passionate theme enters and gets louder above chromatically rising bass	**B**
2:15	Rich chords move from four sharps to four flats	
2:25	Passionate theme continues and rises	
2:37	New, more heroic melody enters	**C**
2:55	Very loud repeated chords, then a fermata (hold)	
3:03	Loud, recitative-like passage descends deep into the bass	
3:20	Arpeggiated accompaniment, then plaintive melody reemerges	**A**
4:01	Coda, entirely in the major mode	**Coda**
4:29	Dissonance resolves to consonance (4:34)	

Franz Liszt (1811–1886)

Franz Liszt was not merely a musician, he was a phenomenon, perhaps the most flamboyant artistic personality of the entire nineteenth century. Handsome, supremely talented, and equally self-confident, he strutted across the stage as the musical sex symbol of the Romantic era (Fig. 13–17). But he could also play the piano, and like no other.

Franz Liszt was born in Hungary of German-speaking parents. In 1822 his ambitious father took him to Vienna and finally to Paris to be the next child prodigy, the latest musical *wunderkind.* But when his father died suddenly of typhoid fever, the boy's career began to languish. He gave piano lessons, became something of a religious fanatic, and tried to enter a Parisian seminary in hopes of becoming a priest.

But on April 20, 1832, Liszt experienced an event that changed the course of his life—he attended a concert given by the great violin virtuoso Niccolò Paganini (see page 262). "What a man, what a violin, what an artist! O God, what pain and suffering, what torment in those four strings." Liszt vowed to bring Paganini's technical virtuosity to the piano, and he did. Practicing four to five hours a day—unusual dedication for a prodigy—he taught himself to play on the piano what had never been played before: tremolos, leaps, double trills, glissandos, simultaneous octaves in both hands, all at breathtaking speed. When he returned to the stage for his own concerts, he overwhelmed the audience. He had become the greatest pianist of that era, indeed of all time.

Then, in 1833, Liszt's life took another unexpected turn. He met the Countess Marie d'Agoult (see cover and Fig. 13–18) and decided to give up the life of the performing artist in exchange for domestic security. Although she was already married and the mother of two children, she and Liszt eloped, first to Switzerland and then to Italy. Residing in these countries for four years, the couple had three children of their own. (Their youngest daughter would become the wife of Richard Wagner; see Fig. 14–9, page 307.)

Beginning in 1839, and continuing until 1847, Liszt once more took to the road as a touring virtuoso. He played more than a thousand concerts: from Ireland to Turkey, from Sweden to Spain, from Portugal to Russia. Everywhere he went the handsome pianist was greeted with the sort of mass hysteria today reserved for rock stars. Audiences of three thousand crowded into the larger halls. Women tried to rip off his silk scarf and white gloves. They fought for a lock of his hair. **Lisztomania** swept across Europe.

Despite their obvious sensationalism, Liszt's concerts in the 1840s established the format of our modern-day piano **recital.** He was the first to play entire programs from memory (not reading from music). He was the first to place the piano parallel with the line of the stage so that neither his back nor full face, but rather his extraordinary side profile, was visible to the audience. He was the first to perform on the stage alone—up to that point concerts traditionally had included numerous performers on the program. At first these solo appearances were called "soliloquies," then "recitals," suggesting they were something akin to personal dramatic recitations. As Liszt modestly said in his adopted French, *"Le concert, c'est moi!"*

But Liszt was a complex person with many personalities. He thought of himself not only as a showman-pianist, but also as a serious composer. So in 1847 he suddenly quit the lucrative concert circuit and settled in Weimar,

FIGURE 13–17

A lithograph of the twenty-one-year-old Franz Liszt made in Paris in 1832.

FIGURE 13–18

Countess Marie d'Agoult in 1843. She was a novelist in her own right, and some of the tracts on music that appeared under Liszt's name were probably penned by her. Like many female writers of the day, including George Sand and George Eliot, she wrote under a masculine *nom de plume,* Daniel Stern.

FIGURE 13–19

Lisztomania, as depicted in 1842. A recital by Liszt was likely to create the sort of sensation that a concert by a rock star might generate today. Women fought for a lock of his hair, a broken string from his piano, or a shred of his velvet gloves.

FIGURE 13–20

The aged Liszt, still dazzling audiences and destroying pianos. As a critic of the day said of his slash and burn technique: "He is as much a piano slayer as a piano player."

Germany, to serve the ducal court as music director and composer-in-residence. Here he concentrated on writing orchestral music. All together he composed a dozen symphonic poems*, as well as two program symphonies*, and three piano concertos. In his instrumental music Liszt developed the process of "thematic transformation," in which a single main theme and its offshoots dominate an entire movement or all the movements of a work. In this he was carrying forward Berlioz's use of an *idée fixe* (see page 274).

In 1861 the unpredictable Liszt surprised the world again: He moved to Rome, entered the lower Holy Orders of the Roman Church, and took up residence in the Vatican! "Abbé Liszt," as the composer now styled himself, had replaced Don Juan. While in Rome Liszt wrote the bulk of his sixty religious works, including two oratorios. He died at the age of seventy-five in Bayreuth, Germany, where he had gone to hear the latest opera of his son-in-law, Richard Wagner.

Despite Liszt's interest in religious music and programmatic works for orchestra, he is known today primarily as the creator of sensational piano music. If Chopin composed in a way that made the piano sound its best, Liszt wrote in a style that made him sound best at the piano. He had large hands and unusually long fingers with no "webbing" between them (Fig. 13–20). This allowed him to make wide stretches with comparative ease. He could play a melody in octaves when others could play only the single notes of the line. If others could execute a passage in octaves, Liszt could dash it off in more impressive-sounding tenths (octave plus third). So he wrote daredevil music of this sort. His *Hungarian Rhapsodies* and numerous fantasies are among the most difficult pieces ever written for piano. Today only the most skilled virtuosos attempt them.

How did performers build sufficient technique to tackle the difficult showpieces by Liszt? They did so practicing a genre of music called the "etude." An **etude** is a short, one-movement composition designed to improve one or more aspects of a performer's technique (faster scales, more rapid note repetition, surer leaps, and so on). Before 1840 dozens of composers had published books of technical exercises that became the cornerstone of piano instruction for the burgeoning middle class. Chopin and Liszt took this development one step further. They added beautifully crafted melodies and unusual textures to what had been merely mind-numbing finger work, thereby demonstrating that an etude might require artistry as well as discipline. Liszt wrote twenty-three etudes in all. He called the first eighteen of these "transcendental etudes," meaning that these pieces required transcendent, indeed superhuman, technical skill. The last five he labeled "concert etudes," suggesting that they were appropriate not only for practice but also for public performance. Ironically, all of Liszt's etudes are useless to the average pianist—these pieces are so difficult that the performer must already be a virtuoso to play them! As Robert Schumann said of the *Grand Transcendental Etudes:* "They are studies in storm and dread designed to be performed by, at most, ten or twelve players in the world."

CONCERT ETUDE NO. 3, *UN SOSPIRO* (*A SIGH*) (1848)

Liszt often gave his etudes poetic titles to suggest that they were more than mere technical exercises. Indeed, *Un sospiro* (*A Sigh*) begins with a soft, enchanting melody worthy of an evocative nocturne*. But this etude also builds technique. By practicing it again and again the performer gains the ability to play the following: (1) rapid arpeggios in both hands, (2) cross-handed passages that divide the notes of the melody between the two hands, and (3) diatonic* and chromatic* scales in parallel sixths at the fastest possible tempo. So expansive is Liszt's piano music that he was often forced to notate it on three staves. The Listening Guide shows the beginning of *A Sigh* with the required crossing of hands indicated by the letters L (left) and R (right). By alternating hands across the full range of the keyboard, Liszt gives the impression of having three or four independent lines (and hands!) operating at once. Yet within this digital display glows a melody of exceptional radiance. The challenge to the performer is to make the melody shine while negotiating the dangers of the accompaniment—to be both artist and wizard.

Liszt's "four-hand" trick

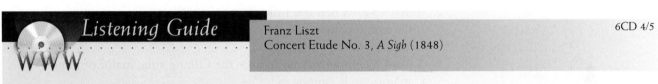

Listening Guide	Franz Liszt	6CD 4/5
WWW	Concert Etude No. 3, *A Sigh* (1848)	

Form: theme and variations (theme remains unchanged, context is varied)

0:00	Arpeggios shared by both hands
0:08	Melody part 1 emerges from arpeggios
0:30	Melody part 2 still within arpeggios
0:48	Melody part 1 now played in broken octaves
1:07	Melody part 2 now played in broken octaves
1:23	Melody part 3 emerges in the bass, then in treble
1:45	Trill in octaves played by right hand
1:51	Melody part 3 played by left hand in bass
2:01	Melody part 2 played by left hand in bass in sixths
2:11	Rapid descent of chromatic* scale played in sixths
2:28	Melody part 3 played in thirds in treble and set to new harmonies
2:42	Bold chord changes
3:08	Rapid descent and rise of diatonic* scale played in sixths
3:17	Melody part 1 in middle voice surrounded by arpeggios
3:40	Melody part 2 in middle voice surrounded by arpeggios
4:04	Melody part 3 in thirds in treble and set to new harmonies
4:17	Coda: bold chord changes interspersed with arpeggios and reminiscences of melody

Listening Exercises

29

Franz Schubert   6CD 3/6; 2CD 1/15
Lied, Erlking (1815)

Schubert was a master at bringing to life the essential characters and sentiments of the poetry he set to music. This exercise suggests how he used two very basic musical elements, a shift in mode and a change in the accompaniment, to intensify Goethe's dramatic ballad *Erlking*.

1. (0:00–0:22) The opening section has rapidly repeating notes in the right hand of the accompanist and an ominous motive below in the left. Is it written in the major mode or the minor mode?
   a. major   b. minor
2. (1:30–1:52) When the Erlking enters, is the ominous motive still heard in the accompaniment?
   a. yes   b. no
3. (1:30–1:52) In which mode does the Erlking sing, major or minor?
   a. major   b. minor
4. (1:55–2:06) As the son returns to speak, what happens in the piano accompaniment?
   a. Rapidly repeating notes return in the accompanist's left hand and the mode shifts from minor to major.
   b. Rapidly repeating notes return in the accompanist's right hand and the mode shifts from major to minor.
5. (2:18–2:34) For the second appearance of the Erlking, which is true?
   a. The rapidly repeating notes in the right hand continue and the mode is minor.
   b. Arpeggios replace the rapidly repeating notes in the right hand and the mode is major.
6. (3:06–3:17) For the third and final appearance of the Erlking, which is true?
   a. The accompaniment pattern changes to arpeggios in the right hand and the mode remains a happy major throughout.
   b. The repeating notes in the right hand continue and toward the end the mode changes abruptly from major to minor.
7. (3:47–3:58) How does Schubert tell us that the galloping horse has arrived at the inn?
   a. The piano accompaniment gradually retards and then comes to a stop.
   b. The piano accompaniment stops abruptly.
8. (4:06–4:11) How does Schubert emphatically emphasize that the child has died and that there will be no happy ending?
   a. He writes an abrupt V–I cadence in a major key.
   b. He writes an abrupt V–I cadence in a minor key.
9. Excluding the narrator, how many characters are portrayed in Schubert's *Erlking?*
   a. one   b. two   c. three
10. How many voices actually sing the *Lied?*
    a. one   b. two   c. three   d. four

30 . . . .

Hector Berlioz   6CD 3/9; 2CD 2/1
Symphonie fantastique (1830)
Fifth movement, Dream of the Witches' Sabbath

Imagine that you were among the audience in Paris on December 5, 1830, when Berlioz's *Symphonie fantastique* was first performed. If you had been a dedicated concertgoer up to that time, you might have heard one or two of the latest symphonies of Beethoven. This would have been the extent of your exposure to "radical" new music. How would you have reacted? Of course, it is now impossible to gauge the impact of Berlioz's progressive gestures—our ears have become accustomed to them in the music of other, later composers. The following set of questions asks you to focus on a few special aspects of orchestration and form in this astonishingly new work.

1. (0:00–0:09) The opening sounds eerie because the high strings are divided into many parts and are playing with a special string technique. What is this technique called?
   a. ostinato   b. pizzicato   c. tremolo

2. (0:19–0:23) Now another string technique is employed by the upper strings. Which is it?
   a. ostinato   b. pizzicato   c. tremolo

3. (1:28–1:36) The *idée fixe* returns, now transformed. The passage sounds weird because of the unusual orchestration Berlioz employs. What characterizes it?
   a. *idée fixe* in high clarinet against pounding bass drum
   b. *idée fixe* in oboe against pounding timpani

4. (3:26–3:47) Among the instruments that introduce the *Dies irae* is one that Berlioz introduced into the symphony orchestra. Which is it?
   a. piccolo   b. tuba   c. cornet   d. high clarinet

5. (3:48–3:58) The French horns now play the *Dies irae* melody twice as fast as before. This sort of reduction in duration in music is called?
   a. augmentation   b. diminution   c. contraction   d. discount

6. (4:30–4:47) In this passage the *Dies irae* continues in the low brasses against a pounding sound produced by the bass drum. Which of the following is true?
   a. The bass drum is playing on the downbeat while the low brasses syncopate against it.
   b. The low brasses are playing the melody on the downbeat while the bass drum syncopates against it.

7. (5:21–5:47) Now the fugato begins. Its structure is made clear, in part, because the composer cuts off the subject each time so as to announce the next entry. He does this by means of a burst of syncopated chords in the brasses. How many times does this occur?
   a. twice   b. three times   c. four times

8. (7:04–7:18) Which instruments play a reminiscence of the *Dies irae* chant?
   a. cellos and double basses   b. bells   c. tubas

9. (8:06–8:27) Now the *Dies irae* and the witches' dance (fugue subject) are heard simultaneously. How are they orchestrated?

a. *Dies irae* in violins, witches' dance in trumpets
b. *Dies irae* in trumpets, witches' dance in violins
10. (8:35–8:48) As the strings produce the crackling sound by playing *col legno* (with the wood of the bow and not the horsehair), a melody is heard in the woodwinds. Which is it?
a. the witches' dance (fugue subject)
b. the *idée fixe*
c. the *Dies irae* chant

31 ·

Clara Wieck Schumann   6CD 4/2; 2CD 2/2
Romance for Piano and Violin, Opus 22, No. 3 (1853)

Clara Schumann's Romance consists of a lovely melody with two parts (**a** and **b**), played mostly by the violin, and an accompaniment, furnished mainly by the piano. The piano usually plays the accompaniment as arpeggios, but sometimes plays chords. Occasionally, moreover, the roles of the instruments are reversed, with the piano now not only providing the accompaniment but also playing the melody, while the violin either joins in the accompaniment or sets a counterpoint against the melody. Four different ways in which the musical material is allocated to the piano are identified here as A, B, C, and D. Indicate which musical arrangement governs at the important musical moments listed below.

A. Piano plays accompaniment only as chords (violin has the melody).
B. Piano plays accompaniment only as arpeggios (violin has the melody).
C. Piano plays melody and its own accompaniment as chords.
D. Piano plays melody and its own accompaniment as arpeggios.

1. 0:00 _____   5. 2:32 _____   9. 3:55 _____
2. 1:34 _____   6. 2:47 _____ 10. 4:12 _____
3. 1:53 _____   7. 3:00 _____
4. 2:11 _____   8. 3:34 _____

Key Words

col legno (277)	Gewandhaus	nocturne (289)
cornet (274)	Orchestra (279)	ophicleide (274)
Dies irae (276)	Harriet Smithson (274)	recital (291)
diminution (276)	*idée fixe* (274)	romance (286)
double counterpoint	*Lied* (265)	Schubertiade (266)
(277)	Lisztomania (291)	song cycle (266)
English horn (274)	mazurka (288)	strophic form (269)
etude (292)	modified strophic	through composed
George Sand (288)	form (270)	(269)

A checklist of musical style in the Romantic period is given on page 70.

Museo Teatrale alla Scala, Milan

Chapter 14

Romantic Opera

The nineteenth century is often called the "golden age of opera." It is the century of Rossini, Bellini, Verdi, Wagner, Bizet, and Puccini. True, there had been great opera composers before them—Monteverdi and Mozart, to name two. But the nineteenth century saw the creation of much of the "core" repertoire of today. Presently, about two-thirds of the productions of the leading operatic companies—the Metropolitan Opera in New York and La Scala in Milan, for example—are works created during the years 1820–1900. Like the cinema in our time, Romantic opera offered a seemingly ever-grander trip to an imaginary world.

Italy, of course, is the home of opera. The Italian language, with its evenly spaced, open vowels, is perfectly suited for singing, and the people of Italy seem to have an innate love of melody. The first operas were created, beginning around 1600, for the cities of Florence, Rome, Venice, and Mantua (see page 116). For nearly two centuries Italian opera dominated the international stage. When Handel wrote operas for London in the 1720s, for example, he composed Italian operas, as did Mozart when he created musical theater for the courts of Germany and Austria in the 1770s and 1780s. With the onset of the nineteenth century, however, other people, driven by an emerging sense of national pride, developed idiomatic opera in their native tongues. Although Italian opera remained the dominant style, it now had to share the stage, not only with traditional French opera but also with the newer forms of Russian, Czech, and especially German opera.

FIGURE 14-1
Gioachino Rossini.

Edizioni Bolis, Bergamo, Museo Teatrale alla Scala, Milan

ROMANTIC OPERA IN ITALY

During the early decades of the nineteenth century, the primacy of Italian opera was maintained almost single-handedly by Gioachino Rossini (1792–1868). Surprising as it may seem today, Rossini was the most popular composer in Europe during the 1820s, far exceeding in celebrity Beethoven and Schubert. He owed his public favor not only to the charm of his music but also to the fact that the genre of music within which he chose to work— opera—was then the most popular form of public musical entertainment, much more so than the symphony or string quartet, for example. Rossini continued, and indeed brought to a glorious close, the eighteenth-century tradition of comic opera, or *opera buffa* (see page 169). Catchy, oft-repeating melodies, vivacious rhythms, and rollicking crescendos were his trademarks. His best-known comic opera, *The Barber of Seville*, has never disappeared from the operatic stage since it first appeared in 1816. Even casual music lovers know a little of this enduring work in the form of the "Figaro, Figaro, Figaro" call from the opening aria for the resourceful barber, Figaro. Rossini could also write in a more serious style, as exemplified in his last opera, *William Tell* (1829). This stormy drama, too, has achieved a measure of popular immortality, the overture providing the theme music for the radio and film character of the Lone Ranger.

Italian *Bel Canto* Opera

Whereas German operatic composers would come to emphasize the dramatic power and instrumental color of the orchestra, Italians after Rossini increasingly focused all of their energies on the solo voice and on melody—on the art of beautiful singing, or **bel canto**. The two most gifted of the early creators of *bel canto* opera were Gaetano Donizetti (1797–1848) and Vincenzo Bellini (1801–1835). In their works there is little orchestral color and almost no counterpoint. The orchestra merely provides a simple harmonic support for the soaring, sometimes divinely beautiful, lines of the voice. Look at the opening of the famous aria "Casta diva" from Bellini's *Norma* (1831), in which the heroine sings a prayer to a distant moon goddess. Here the orchestra functions like a giant guitar. Simple chords are fleshed out as arpeggios by the strings while an even simpler bass line is plucked below. All of the musical interest is in the rapturous sound of the human voice. One Italian newspaper of the day declared "In the theatrical arts it is said that three things are required: action, action, action; likewise, three things are demanded for music: voice, voice, voice."

importance of the voice

EXAMPLE 14–1

(Chaste goddess, who does bathe in silver light these hallowed, ancient trees)

Not surprisingly, by placing such importance on the voices of the leading singers, *bel canto* opera fostered a star system among the cast. Usually, it was the lyric soprano—heroine and **prima donna** (first lady)—who held the most exalted position in the operatic firmament. By the 1880s, she would also be called a **diva**, which, as in the aria "Casta diva," means "goddess." Indeed, the goddess of the beautiful female voice would rule Italian opera right through the nineteenth century, from the early *bel canto* operas of Donizetti and Bellini through the mature works of Giuseppe Verdi (1813–1901) and Giacomo Puccini (1858–1924).

cult of the diva

Giuseppe Verdi (1813–1901)

The name Giuseppe Verdi is virtually synonymous with Italian opera. For six decades, from the time of *Nabucco* in 1842 until *Falstaff* in 1893, he had almost no rival for the affections of the opera-loving public in Italy and elsewhere throughout Europe. Even today the best-loved of the twenty-six operas of Verdi are more readily available—in opera houses, in TV productions, and on videotape and DVD—than those of any other composer.

Verdi was born near Busseto in northern Italy in 1813, the son of a tavern keeper. He was apparently no musical prodigy, for at the age of eighteen he was rejected for admission to the Conservatory of Music in Milan because he was already too old and his piano technique faulty. But Verdi stayed on in Milan to study composition. He returned to Busseto in 1835 to serve as the town's bandmaster, and then four years later went back to Milan to earn his livelihood as a composer.

To be a composer in nineteenth-century Italy was to be a composer of opera. Verdi's first, *Oberto*, was produced at the famous La Scala Opera House in Milan (Fig. 14–3) in 1839, and it achieved a modicum of success. But his *Nabucco* of 1842 was a popular triumph, receiving an unprecedented fifty-seven performances at La Scala in that year alone. Through subsequent productions in other theaters, Verdi's name was quickly carried throughout Italy, Europe, and both North and South America. His career was launched.

The text, or libretto*, of *Nabucco*, as well as most of Verdi's other operas of the 1840s, was covertly political. It concerns the suppression of a people (in this case the Jews) by a cruel foreign power (the Babylonians). By analogy, Verdi thus called attention to the plight of the Italian people, who were

FIGURE 14–2

A photograph of Giuseppe Verdi on an early published score of his opera *La traviata.*

Museo Teatrale alla Scala, Milan

FIGURE 14–3
La Scala Opera House about 1830. Verdi's
first four and last two operas had their
premieres at La Scala, then and now the
foremost opera house in Italy.

then ruled in large measure by the Austrians. Verdi had become a spirited Italian patriot. Normally, we do not think of music as expressing political ideas, but because opera was an important part of Italian mass culture, it could suborn political revolution. Verdi's soloists and choruses (the voice of the people) sang such fiery words as "You may have the universe, so long as I keep Italy" and "Long live Italy! A sacred pact binds all her sons." Partly through such patriotic music and partly by accident, Verdi became a leader in the **Risorgimento**, the movement for a united Italy free of foreign domination. By handy coincidence, the letters of the composer's last name produced an acronym for **V**ittorio **E**manuele **R**e **d**'**I**talia (King Victor Emanuel being the people's choice for the throne of a united Kingdom of Italy). Thus, cries of "Viva, Verdi!" echoed throughout Italy in hopes of unification. In 1861, after that goal had been largely achieved, Verdi was elected to the country's first parliament, and later, in 1874, to its senate.

But in the late 1840s the drive for Italian independence was far from complete. Indeed, the liberal Revolution of 1848 failed to oust the Austrians from Milan, and Verdi for a time became disillusioned with politics. He now turned his attention to domestic themes and more personal drama, producing a trio of works without which no modern opera house could function: *Rigoletto* (1851), *La traviata* (1853), and *Il trovatore* (1853). For most of the early-to-mid-1850s, Verdi lived away from the area of Milan, residing in Paris or traveling throughout Europe to oversee the production of his increasingly numerous works. He called these years of toil and intense productivity "my years as a galley slave."

On his return to his homeland in 1857, the pace of Verdi's opera production slackened. He composed only when the subject was of interest or the fee so substantial he couldn't refuse. *La forza del destino* (*The Force of Destiny*, 1861) was written for St. Petersburg for the enormous commission of 60,000 francs; *Don Carlo* (1867) was composed for Paris for an equally large amount; and *Aïda* (1871), written for Cairo shortly after the opening of the Suez Canal, for the astonishing sum of 150,000 francs. Verdi had become more than a little wealthy, and he retired to his estate in northern Italy to lead the life of a country squire—or so he thought.

later operas

But like a performer who feels he owes the audience more, or has something more to prove to himself, Verdi returned to the theater for two final encores: *Otello* (1887) and *Falstaff* (1893), both exceptionally well-crafted operas based on dramas of Shakespeare. The latter work was written when the composer was on the threshold of eighty, a feat without parallel in music history or the annals of the dramatic stage. He died peacefully at his country home in 1901, a much-respected national institution.

VERDI'S DRAMATURGY AND MUSICAL STYLE

When the curtain goes up on a Verdi opera, the listener will find elements of dramaturgy—how the drama is put together—and musical style that are unique to this composer. For Giuseppe Verdi conflict was at the root of every emotion, and he expressed conflict, whether personal or national, by juxtaposing self-contained, yet clearly contrasting, units of music. A rousing march, a patriotic chorus, a passionate recitative, and a lyrical aria follow one after the other in quick succession. The composer aims not at musical and dramatic subtlety but rather at banner headlines of emotion. The emotional states of the characters are so clearly drawn, sometimes overdrawn, that the drama comes perilously close to melodrama—excessively sentimental or sensational. But it is never dull. There is action, passion, and intensity. "I am capable of setting a letter, even a newspaper, to music," Verdi said in 1854, "but the one thing the public will not tolerate in the theater is boredom."

banner headlines of emotion

How does Verdi generate this feeling of intense passion and nonstop action? He does so by creating a new kind of recitative and a new style of aria. Verdi continues to use the former to narrate the action and the latter to express feeling. But now the old *secco* recitative, with mere keyboard accompaniment, gives way to orchestrally accompanied recitative (**recitativo accompagnato**). This allows the action to flow smoothly from orchestrally accompanied aria to orchestrally accompanied recitative and back without a jarring change of texture. As to the aria, Verdi brings to it a new intensity. Yes, he is a composer squarely in the tradition of Italian *bel canto* opera. He, too, focuses all attention on the solo voice and on a lyrical, beautiful vocal line. Indeed, no composer had a greater gift for writing simple, memorable melodies that the audience could whistle on the way out of the theater. Yet Verdi also adds intensity and passion to these arias by pushing the singers to the utmost of their range. The tenor is asked to sing up to the B above middle C, the soprano two octaves and more above middle C. The thrilling moments in which the hero (the tenor) or the heroine (the soprano) go right to the top are literally the high points of any Verdi opera.

LA TRAVIATA (1853)

We may measure the high intensity and passion in Verdi's operas by listening to a portion of his *La traviata* (1853). *La traviata* literally means "The Woman Gone Astray." It tells the story of the sickly Violetta Valery, a courtesan, or "kept woman," who resists and then succumbs to the love of a new suitor, the young Alfredo Germont. For a while the couple retires from Paris to lead a quiet life in the country. But without explanation Violetta deserts Alfredo, in truth so that her former life will not bring disgrace on his respectable family. The hot-tempered Alfredo now publicly insults Violetta, fights a duel with her new "protector," and is banished from France. When the nature of Violetta's sacrifice is revealed, Alfredo rushes back to Paris. But it is too late. She is dying of tuberculosis—her fate is dictated by an operatic convention that requires the heroine to sing one last show-stopping aria and then expire.

Verdi first heard this sentimental tale, one that pits passionate love against middle-class morality, when in Paris during the winter of 1852. There he and his mistress, the singer Giuseppina Strepponi (Fig. 14–4), were captivated by a new play of Alexandre Dumas the younger entitled *The Lady of the Camellias*, now known to English audiences simply as *Camille*. The main character of

Christiane Issartel

FIGURE 14–5

Marie Duplessis. The end of her brief scandalous life is the subject of Giuseppe Verdi's opera *La traviata*. So notorious had she become by the time of her death at the age of twenty-three that Charles Dickens said: "You would have thought her passing was a question of the death of a hero or a Joan of Arc."

the drama, Violetta Valery, was modeled after a real-life figure, Marie Duplessis (Fig. 14–5), who had been the mistress of playwright Dumas and, briefly, of composer Franz Liszt as well. Like many in this period, she, too, died young of tuberculosis, at the age of twenty-three. Verdi's compassion toward this heroine probably was sparked by the fact that his mistress, too, was held in general disrepute at this time, having by then given birth to four illegitimate children.

We join *La traviata* toward the end of the first act. A gala party is in progress in a fashionable Parisian salon, and here the dashing Alfredo has finally managed to cut Violetta away from the crowd to profess to her his love. He does so in the aria "Un dì felice" ("One Happy Day"), which is lovely, yet somber in tone. The seriousness of Alfredo's intent is underscored by the slow, square, even plodding accompaniment in the orchestra. When Violetta enters she is supported by the same accompaniment, but the mood of the aria is radically changed to one that is light and carefree. Witness how Verdi's direct musical characterization works: Alfredo's slow melody with a hint of minor is replaced by Violetta's flighty sound of high, rapidly moving notes. Eventually, the two join together: he below, somberly proclaiming the mysteries of love; she above, making light of them. What started as a solo aria has become a duet, the voices and hands of the principals now intertwined. Once again, music enhances drama by replicating in its own language the action on stage.

Listening Guide

WWW

Giuseppe Verdi
La traviata (1853)
Act I, Scene 4

6CD 4/6

Characters: Alfredo, a young man of good standing; Violetta, a kept woman leading a wanton life in Paris
Situation: A party in a Parisian salon around 1850; Alfredo professes his love to Violetta, who at first rejects him.

Aria		**Alfredo (tenor)**	
0:00		Un dì felice, eterea,	One happy day,
		Mi balaneste innante,	you appeared to me.
		E da quel dì tremante	And from this day, trembling,
		Vissi d'ignoto amor.	I have lived in that
		Di quell'amor ch'è palpito	unspoken love, in that love
		Dell'universo intero,	which animates the world,
	Shift to minor	Misterioso, altero,	mysterious, proud, pain
		Croce e delizia al cor.	and delight to the heart.
		Violetta (soprano)	
1:22	Violetta changes aria to lighter mood	Ah, se ciò è ver, fuggitemi.	If that's true, leave me.
	through faster tempo and shorter notes	Solo amistade io v'offro;	Only friendship I offer you.
		Amar non so, nè soffro	I don't know how to love
		Un così eroico amore.	or suffer such a heroic love.
		Io sono franca, ingenua;	I'm being honest and sincere.
		Altra cercar dovete;	You must find another.
		Non arduo troverete	It won't be difficult.
		Dimenticarmi allor.	Just leave me.
(Duet)		**Alfredo**	
1:46	Alfredo and Violetta together	Oh amore!	Oh love!
	in rapturous duet	Misterioso, altero,	mysterious, proud, pain
		Croce e delizia al cor.	and delight to the heart.

(Continued on next page)

| 2:48 | Exuberant vocal flourishes for both | Non arduo troverete
Dimenticarmi allor.
"Ah" | **Violetta**
It won't be difficult.
Just leave me.
"Ah" |

Alfredo kisses Violetta's hand and departs, leaving her alone on stage to ponder her future. She reveals, in a slow strophic aria, "Ah fors'è lui" ("Ah, perhaps he's the one"), that Alfredo may be the lover she has long desired. But then abruptly Violetta rejects the whole idea as impossible. Forget love, she says in an impassioned accompanied recitative*, "Folly! Folly! What sort of crazy dream is this!" Recitative leads naturally to aria, and here follows "Sempre libera" ("Always free"), one of the great show-arias for soprano voice. It gives Violetta a chance to declare forcefully her resolve to remain free of love's entanglements. This aria, too, helps define through music the character of the heroine—the extraordinary, carefree flourishes on the word "pleasure," for example, reinforce her "live-for-the-moment" approach to life. Violetta's declaration of independence is momentarily broken by the distant voice of Alfredo, who again expresses his feelings about the mysterious powers of love. This, too, Violetta brushes aside as she emphatically repeats her pledge to always be free.

Verdi has moved quickly from slow aria, to recitative, to fast-concluding aria. Such a three-movement unit is a dramatic convention of Italian opera called a **scena** (a scenic plan made up of diverse movements). So, too, the fast aria at the end of the scena has a name, "cabaletta." A **cabaletta** is a fast-concluding aria in which the increased speed of the music allows one or more soloists to race off stage at the end of a scene or act. Here Violetta, vowing to remain free, dashes off as the curtain falls to end Act I. Needless to say, our heroine does not remain free—she falls fatally in love with Alfredo, as Acts II and III reveal. Listen now to the final scene of Act I of Verdi's *La traviata*. You will have the pleasure of hearing two of the greatest voices of the twentieth century, Joan Sutherland (soprano) and Luciano Pavarotti (tenor) (Fig. 14-6).

FIGURE 14-6

The great Australian soprano Joan Sutherland singing the role of Violetta, and tenor Luciano Pavarotti as Alfredo, in Verdi's *La traviata*.

Beth Bergman

Listening Guide

WWW

Giuseppe Verdi
La traviata (1853)
Act I, Scene 6

6CD 4/7;
6CD 4/8;
2CD 2/4

Characters: Violetta and Alfredo (outside her window)
Situation: Violetta at first believes Alfredo to be the passionate love she has long sought, but then rejects this notion, vowing to remain free.

Aria

First strophe

0:00	Soprano sings first phrase	Ah, fors'è lui che l'anima Solinga ne' tumulti	Ah, perhaps he's the one whom my lonely heart
0:33	First phrase repeated	Godea sovente pingere De' suoi colori occulti.	delighted often to paint with vague, mysterious colors.
0:56	Voice rises up in melodic sequence	Lui, che modesto e vigile All'egre sogli ascese, E nuova febbre accese Destandomi all'amor!	He who, so modest and attentive during my illness, waited and with youthful fervor aroused me again to love!

(Continued on next page)

Time	Description	Italian	English
1:24	Return of Alfredo's major-key refrain from previous aria	A quell'amor ch'è palpito Dell'universo intero, Misterioso altero, Croce e delizia al cor.	To that love which animates the universe, mysterious, proud, pain and delight to the heart.

Second strophe

Time	Description	Italian	English
2:26	Return of first phrase	A me, fanciulla, un candido E trepido desire, Quest'effgiò dolcissimo Signor dell'avvenire.	To me, a girl, this was an innocent, anxious desire, this sweet vision, lord of things to come.
2:51	First phrase repeated		
3:15	Voice rises up in melodic sequence	Quando ne' cieli il raggio Di sua beltà vedea E tuta me pascea Di quel divino error.	When in the heavens I saw rays of his beauty I fed myself completely on that divine error.
3:42	Return of Alfredo's major-key refrain from previous aria	Sentia che amore è il palpito Dell'universo intero, Misterioso altero, Croce e delizia al cor.	I felt that love which animates the universe, mysterious, proud, pain and delight to the heart.
4:16	Highly ornamental final cadence with lengthy trill		

6CD 4/8; 2CD 2/4

Recitative

Time	Description	Italian	English
			Violetta
0:00	Accompanied by orchestra	Follie! Follie! delirio vano è questo! Povera donna, sola, abbandonata, in questo populoso deserto che appellano Parigi. Che spero or più? Che far degg'io?	Folly! Folly! What sort of crazy dream is this! Poor woman, alone, adandoned in this populated desert that they call Paris. What hope have I? What can I do?
0:49	Flights of vocal fancy as she thinks of pleasure	Gioir! Di voluttà ne' vortici perir! Gioir!	Pleasure! Perish in a whirl of indulgence! Pleasure!
1:05	Introduction to cabaletta		

Cabaletta

Time	Description	Italian	English
			Violetta
1:16		Sempre libera degg'io Folleggiare di gioia in gioia, Vo' che scorra il viver mio Pei sentieri del piacer. Nasca il giorno, o il giorno muoia, Sempre lieta ne' ritrovi, A diletti sempre nuovi Dee volare il mio pensier.	Always free I must remain to reel from pleasure to pleasure, running my life along the paths of joy. From dawn to dusk I'm always happy finding new delights that make my spirit soar.
			Alfredo
2:01	Echoes of his previous aria	Amor è palpito dell'universo, misterioso, altero, croce e delizia al cor.	Love that animates the world, mysterious, proud, pain and delight to the heart.
			Violetta
2:48	Extravagant flourishes	Follie! Follie! Gioir! Gioir!	Folly! Folly! Pleasure! Pleasure!

Cabaletta returns

Time	Description	Italian	English
3:17	this time even more brilliant in its showy, superficial style	Sempre libera . . .	Always free . . .

(Listening Exercise 32)

ROMANTIC OPERA IN GERMANY

Before 1820 opera was mainly an Italian affair. It was first created in Italy around 1600 and then, during the next two hundred years, was exported to all parts of Europe and eventually to North and South America. But German opera, by comparison, was rather weak and provincial. Before 1820 the only German opera heard outside German-speaking lands was Mozart's *Die Za-uberflöte* (*The Magic Flute*, 1791), which owed its widespread appeal to the glories of Mozart's music rather than any fondness for the somewhat primitive conventions of German opera.

What passed as native opera in German-speaking lands went by the name of *Singspiel*. A **Singspiel** ("singing play") is a musical comedy or light musical drama that has, by sheer coincidence, many elements in common with our present-day Broadway musical: plenty of topical humor, tuneful solo songs, energetic choral numbers, and spoken dialogue instead of sung recitative. Mozart, in *The Magic Flute* (1791), and Beethoven, in his only opera, *Fidelio* (1805), each wrote a *Singspiel* in which he tried to bring greater seriousness and unity to the genre. A somewhat younger contemporary of Beethoven, Karl Maria von Weber (1786–1826), likewise attempted to develop a tradition of serious German opera distinct from the Italian style. His *The Magic Bullet* (1821) makes use of German folk songs, or folklike melodies, as well as a libretto that delights in the supernatural. The German passion for horror subjects and supernatural tales in the Romantic period can be seen in other works, such as Heinrich Marschner's *The Vampire* (1828) and Richard Wagner's *The Flying Dutchman* (1843).

a Singspiel *has much in common with a Broadway musical*

Richard Wagner (1813–1883)

The composer who realized the German dream of a truly national opera was the titanic figure Richard Wagner (Fig. 14–7). Wagner's theories and his art have made him both the object of almost religious adoration and, at the same time, the most detested composer in the history of music. In fact, he was not merely a composer but also a politician, philosopher, propagandist, and bully for his particular vision of dramatic music. For Wagner, opera was the most perfect form of artistic expression and the composer a religious prophet who could reveal a musical kingdom to his congregation, namely, the listening audience. Wagner's music is, indeed, often inspiring. It contains moments of grandeur unmatched by any other composer. His influence on the musical style of other composing musicians at the end of the nineteenth century was enormous. Yet his reception by the musical public at large, then and now, has been divided. Some listeners are immediately converted to adoring Wagnerites at the first sound of the heroic themes and powerful orchestral climaxes. Others are left cold, believing the music long-winded and the operatic plots devoid of realistic human drama.

Who was this controversial artist who has stirred such mixed feelings within the musical public for more than a century? Richard Wagner was born into a theatrical family in Leipzig, Germany, in 1813. His first passion was not music but poetry, drama, and the theater. Only in his late teens, when he began to immerse himself in the music of Beethoven, did he begin to consider music as a profession. He made piano transcriptions* of the orchestral music of

FIGURE 14–7
Richard Wagner in a photograph of 1871.

mixed opinions about Wagner

Beethoven, and took lessons in composition from the cantor of Leipzig's St. Thomas's Church, Bach's church (see page 147). After a succession of jobs as an opera director in several small German towns, Wagner and his young family moved to Paris in 1839 in hopes of seeing his first opera produced there. Instead of meeting acclaim in Paris, as had Liszt and Chopin before him, Wagner was greeted by thundering indifference. No one could be persuaded to produce his work. Reduced to poverty, he spent a brief sojourn in a Parisian prison for nonpayment of debts.

early career

When Wagner's big break came it was not in Paris but in his native Germany, in the city of Dresden. His opera *Rienzi* was given a hearing there in October 1842 and generated such an enthusiastic response that the composer was offered the post of opera director for the king of Saxony in this important city. During the next six years he created three additional German Romantic operas for the Dresden stage: *The Flying Dutchman* (1844), *Tannhäuser* (1845), and *Lohengrin* (1848). In the aftermath of the political revolution that swept much of Europe in 1848, Wagner was forced to flee Dresden, though in truth he took flight as much to avoid his creditors as to escape any repressive government.

Wagner found a safe haven in Switzerland, which was to be his home, on and off, for the next dozen years. Exiled now from the major opera houses in Germany, he began to imagine a complex of music dramas on a vast and unprecedented scale. What he ultimately created was *Der Ring des Nibelungen* (*The Ring of the Nibelung*), a set of four operas intended to be performed during the course of four successive evenings. *Das Rheingold*, the first, lasts 2½ hours; *Die Walküre* and *Siegfried* each run nearly 4½ hours; while the finale, *Götterdämmerung* (*Twilight of the Gods*), goes on for no less than 5½ hours.

the Ring *cycle*

Wagner was almost the only composer in the history of music who wrote not only the music for his operas but also the librettos. For his four-part *Ring* cycle he fashioned a single continuous epic by drawing upon tales from German mythology. The scene is set in the smoky mists of primeval time, in a land of gods, river nymphs, dwarfs, giants, dragons, and sword-wielding heroes. In many ways Wagner's *Ring of the Nibelung* is similar to J. R. R. Tolkien's best-selling trilogy *The Lord of the Rings* (film version, 2001, 2002, 2003). Both are multi-part sagas based on Nordic mythology, both are overrun with fantastic creatures (goblins, wizards, and dragons), and both revolve around a much-coveted ring, a magical source by which to rule the world.

plot of the Ring

But Wagner viewed his *Ring* cycle not as a timeless fairy tale but rather as a timely allegory exploring the themes of power, greed, honor, bravery, and race in nineteenth-century German society. At that moment bravery, power, and national identity were themes with special resonance in Germany, which was then in the process of becoming a unified nation. The German philosopher Friedrich Nietzsche (1844–1900), for a time a friend and confidant of Wagner, modeled his superhero, or superman, on Wagner's heroic character Siegfried in the *Ring*. In the twentieth century, Adolph Hitler exploited Wagnerian symbolism to foster the notion of a superior German race, building, for example, a Siegfried Line on the Western Front during World War II.

an allegory of events in German history

Needless to say, publishers and producers were at first reluctant to print or mount the operas of Wagner's *Ring*, given their massive scope and fantastic subject matter. They would, however, pay well for the rights to more traditional works by him. So in the midst of his labors on the *Ring* cycle, the always penurious Wagner interrupted the project for a period of years to create *Tristan und Isolde* (1865) and *Die Meistersinger von Nürnberg* (*The Mastersingers of Nuremberg*, 1868). But these, too, were long and not easy to produce. The bulky scores piled up on his desk.

In 1864 Wagner was rescued from his plight by King Ludwig II of Bavaria, who paid off his debts, gave him an annual allowance, encouraged him to complete the *Ring* tetralogy, and helped him to build a special theater where his giant operas could be mounted according to the composer's own specifications (Fig. 14–8). This opera house, or Festival Theater as Wagner called it, was constructed at Bayreuth, a small town between Munich and Leipzig in southern Germany. The first "Bayreuth Festival" took place in August 1876 with three successive performances of the entire *Ring* cycle. Wagner's last opera, *Parsifal*, premiered there as well, in 1882. Following Wagner's death the next year, his remains were interred on the grounds of the Wagner villa in Bayreuth. To this day the theater at Bayreuth continues to stage the music dramas of Wagner—and only Wagner. Each summer thousands of opera lovers make the pilgrimage to this theatrical shrine to one of art's most determined, and ruthless, visionaries.

FIGURE 14–8

Bayreuth Festival Theater, an opera house built especially to produce the music dramas of Richard Wagner—and only Wagner.

Richard Wagner Museum, Bayreuth

Wagner's "Music Dramas"

With minor exceptions, Richard Wagner wrote music, not for the concert hall (symphonies, concertos, and the like) but only for the theater (operas). He did not call these works operas, however, but "music dramas." A **music drama** for Wagner was a musical work for the stage in which all the arts—poetry, music, acting, mime, dance, and scenic design—function as a harmonious ensemble. Such an artistic union Wagner referred to as a **Gesamtkunstwerk** ("total art work"). Thus combined, the unified force of the arts would generate more realistic drama. No longer would the dramatic action grind to a halt in order to spotlight the vocal flourishes of a soloist, as often happened in Italian opera.

Indeed, Wagner's music drama differs from conventional Italian opera in several important ways. First, Wagner did away with the traditional "numbers" opera—a string of separate units such as aria, recitative, duet, and the like. Instead, he wrote a seamless flow of undifferentiated solo singing and declamation, what is called "endless melody." Second, he removed ensemble singing almost entirely; duets, trios, choruses, and full-cast finales became rare in the extreme. Finally, Wagner banished the tuneful aria to the wings. He avoids melodic repetition, symmetry, and regular cadences—all things that can make a tune "catchy"—in favor of long-flowing, nonrepetitive, not particularly song-like lines. As the tuneful aria decreases in importance, the role of the orchestra increases.

With Wagner the orchestra is everything. It sounds forth the main musical themes, develops and exploits them, and thereby "plays out" the drama through pure instrumental music. On stage the words and actions of the singers give the audience supplementary clues as to what the musical drama

FIGURE 14–9

Cosima Wagner (daughter of Franz Liszt and Marie d'Agoult), Richard Wagner, and Liszt at Wagner's villa in Bayreuth in 1880. At the right is a young admirer of Wagner, Hans von Wolzogen, who first coined the term "leitmotif" (see page 309).

Richard Wagner Museum, Bayreuth

in the orchestra is all about. In the 1850s Wagner drank deeply of the philosophy of Arthur Schopenhauer (1788–1860), who wrote that "music expresses the innermost basis of the world, the essence behind appearances." In music drama what happens on the stage is the appearance; what happens in the orchestra is the reality, the drama at a deeper level.

As had Beethoven and Berlioz before him, Wagner continued to expand the size of the orchestra. He called for triple woodwinds and greatly enlarged the brass section, requiring more trombones and tubas. A bigger orchestra demanded, in turn, more forceful singers. To be heard above an orchestra of nearly a hundred players, a large, specially trained voice was needed, the so-called Wagnerian tenor or Wagnerian soprano. Yet during moments of climax even these powerful voices are scarcely audible. Imagine an opera of Verdi in which the voice of the hero or heroine cannot be heard. Impossible! But in a music drama of Wagner, the virtual disappearance of the voice does not matter. By design the singer is ultimately consumed by the greater reality of pure music projected by an all-powerful orchestra. Let us see how the orchestra brings this about in Wagner's music drama *Tristan und Isolde*.

TRISTAN UND ISOLDE (1865)

Wagner began to compose *Tristan und Isolde* during 1857 when living in Switzerland and supported in part by a wealthy patron, Otto Wesendonck. Although still married, the composer began an affair with Wesendonck's wife, Mathilde—so fully did Wagner the man live his life as Wagner the artist that it was impossible for him to create an opera dealing with passionate love without being passionately in love himself. Eventually, his own wife, Minna, caused such a scene that the composer fled to Venice. By 1864 Wagner had made his way to Munich for the first production of the now finished *Tristan*. Having long since forgotten both Mathilde and his wife, he now fell in love with Cosima von Bülow, the wife of the man scheduled to conduct *Tristan*. Cosima was the illegitimate daughter of Franz Liszt and Marie d'Agoult (see Fig. 13–18 and page 291), and she and Wagner soon produced three illegitimate children of their own. The first of these, a daughter born on the first day of rehearsals for *Tristan*, was christened Isolde.

The story of *Tristan und Isolde* comes from an old Arthurian legend. Briefly, it is the tale of the love of a captive Irish princess, Isolde, betrothed to King Mark of Cornwall (England), and of Tristan, the king's trusted knight. Tristan is sent to conduct the reluctant Isolde to her wedding with King Mark. Wishing only for revenge and then death, Isolde asks for a deadly potion, but her devoted servant instead substitutes a love potion, which the unknowing Tristan and Isolde consume. On arrival in Cornwall this passionate, soon adulterous, love is revealed to the court. Despairing of any happy union with Isolde in this world, Tristan allows himself to be mortally wounded in combat and sails off to his native Brittany to die. Isolde pursues him but arrives only in time to have him expire in her arms. Knowing that their union will only be consummated through death, Isolde sings her *Liebestod* (*Love-Death*), an ecstatic vision of their love beyond the grave, and then she, too, expires next to her lover's body. This was the sort of all-consuming, sacrificial love so dear to the hearts of Romantic artists.

Wagner begins *Tristan*, not with a rousing, self-contained overture, but with a simple yet beautiful prelude that sets the general tone of the drama and leads directly to the raising of the curtain. The first sound we hear is a

Bayerisches National Museum, Munich

FIGURE 14–10

Original costume designs for the premiere of Wagner's *Tristan und Isolde*, June 1865.

plaintive call of the cellos, answered by one in the woodwinds. Each is not so much a lengthy theme as it is a short, pregnant motive. Wagner's disciples called each a **leitmotif** (signature-tune), a brief, distinctive unit of music that is designed to represent a character, object, or idea and that returns repeatedly in order to facilitate the progress of the drama. We have encountered a representational, or programmatic, theme before in the form of Berlioz's *idée fixe* (see page 274). But Wagner's leitmotifs are much shorter than Berlioz's lengthy melody, and there are many more of them. They are usually not sung but only played in the orchestra. In this way an element of the subconscious can be brought to the drama: The orchestra can give a sense of what a character is thinking even when he or she is singing about something else. By developing, extending, varying, contrasting, and resolving these representational leitmotifs, Wagner is able to play out the essence of the drama almost without recourse to his singers.

leitmotif: a short signature-tune

Leitmotifs in *Tristan* are associated mainly with feelings rather than concrete objects or persons. Typical are the leitmotifs representing "Longing," "Desire," and "Ecstasy."

EXAMPLE 14–2

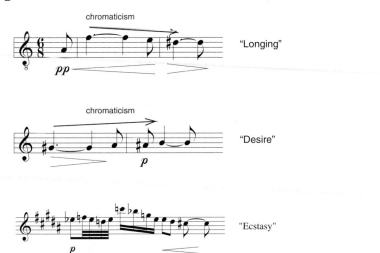

leitmotifs in Wagner's Tristan

Notice how both the "Longing" and "Desire" motifs involve chromatic lines, the first descending, the second ascending (see arrows). This sort of linear chromatic motion made it easy for the composer to wind continually through many different keys, not stopping long enough to establish any one as a home base, or tonic*. Wagner's intense use of chromaticism loosened the feeling of key and eventually led to the collapse of tonality as the main organizing force in Western music, as we shall later see (page 358). Here he uses twisting chromatic lines for a specific expressive purpose, to convey a sense of the anxiety and pain to be felt by the ill-fated lovers.

intense chromaticism

As you listen to the final scene of *Tristan* you can feel Wagner trying to draw you into his all-enveloping world of love, longing, desire, and death. Here Isolde cradles the body of the dying Tristan and prepares to share his fate. As she sings her justly famous *Liebestod* (*Love-Death*), four leitmotifs sound forth, each heard previously in the opera. They frequently appear in melodic sequences*, usually moving upward so as to convey a sense of continual longing and rising tension. Cadences are avoided, thereby increasing the restless mood. Dissonances are placed at points of climax to heighten the feeling of

a glorious conclusion

Leitmotifs in Star Wars

The technique of the leitmotif, as developed by Richard Wagner, has been borrowed by many composers of Hollywood film music. To name just one: John Williams, the creator of the music for George Lucas's *Star Wars* series. When Williams wrote the music for *Star Wars, The Empire Strikes Back,* and *The Return of the Jedi,* he composed for each main character (and theme or force) a particular musical motive. Below are two of Williams's leitmotifs, the first signifying the hero Luke Skywalker, the second (merely an insistent rhythm) symbolizing the evil Darth Vader.

Like Wagner, Williams also sets these leading motives in the orchestra and thereby tells the audience what the character is thinking or what the future may hold. When young Luke is confined to his uncle's farm, for example, we learn that greater things await him: The orchestra plays the heroic Force leitmotif in the background. In fact, *Star Wars* has more than just leitmotifs in common with Wagner's music dramas. Both Wagner and Lucas started with a core of three dramas and added a fourth as a preface or "prequel" (*Das Rheingold* was prefixed to the *Ring* and *The Phantom Menace* to *Star Wars*). Both drama cycles play out a succession of epic battles between larger-than-life heros and villains, mythical forces for good and evil. Lucas has gone on to add yet other episodes to his saga, but the leitmotifs remain the same.

Luke's Theme

Darth Vader's Theme

pain and anguish. Finally, the music reaches one last, glorious climax (4:42) and hereafter all is consonance and reduced movement—Isolde has joined Tristan in the world beyond. First listen to the *Liebestod,* concentrating on the leitmotifs as they are worked out by the voice but even more by the orchestra. Then play it once more, this time just drinking it in, like a love potion, all of Wagner's divinely inspired sound. If there is such a thing as a transcendental experience in Romantic music, you will have it here.

Listening Guide

WWW

Richard Wagner
Liebestod, from *Tristan und Isolde* (1865)

6CD 4/9;
2CD 2/5

Characters: The lovers Tristan and Isolde
Situation: Tristan's castle in Brittany; Isolde cradles Tristan in her arms as she prepares to join him in death.

0:00 Isolde, gazing at Tristan, slowly sings the "Love-Death" leitmotif, which is then taken up by the orchestra

Mild und leise wie er lächelt,	Oh how tenderly and gently he smiles
Wie das Auge hold er öffnet—	As he opens his eyes—
Seht ihr, Freunde? Seht ihr's nicht	Do you see, Friends, don't you see it?
Immer lichter wie er leuchtet,	Ever brighter, how he shines,
Stern-umstrahlet hoch sich hebt?	Glowing in starlight raised on high?

(Continued on next page)

1:07	The orchestra continues with the "Love-Death" motif as the singer goes her own way	Seht ihr's nicht? Wie das Herz ihm mutig schwillt, Voll und hehr im Busen ihm quillt?	Do you not see it? How his heart proudly swells, Full and brave beating in his breast?

1:37	The "Ecstasy" leitmotif enters, not in the voice, but in the high woodwinds and then the violins	Wie den Lippen, wonnig mild Süsser Atem sanft entweht— Freunde! Seht! Fühlt und seht ihr's nicht?	How from his lips, blissfully tender, Sweet breath gently flutters— Do you not see, Friends? Don't you feel and see it?
2:17	Reappearance of the ascending, chromatic "Desire" motif from the Prelude		

2:26	"Love-Death" motif returns in voice and orchestra, followed by "Ecstasy" motif and then "Desire" motif in voice	Höre ich nur diese Weise Die so wundervoll und leise, Wonne klagend, alles sagend, Mild versöhnend aus ihm tönend, In mich dringet, auf sich schwinget, Hold erhallend um mich klinget?	Do I alone hear this melody Which, so wonderfully and gently, Moaning bliss, expressing all, Gently forgiving, coming from him Pierces me, soars upwards, Blessedly echoing all around me?
3:33	"Transcendent Bliss" leitmotif appears in violins		

3:53	Tension increases as "Desire" motif rises by chromatic steps in the orchestra	Heller schallend, mich umwallend, Sind es Wellen sanfter Lüfte? Sind es Wolken wonniger Düfte Wie sie schwellen, mich umrauschen, Soll ich atmen, soll ich lauschen? Soll ich schlürfen, untertauchen? Süss in Düften mich verhauchen? In dem wogenden Schwall, in dem tönenden Schall.	Resounding clearly all around me, Are they waves of gentle air? Are they clouds of delightful fragrance? As they swell and envelop me, Should I breathe, should I listen? Should I sip them, plunge beneath them? Breathe my last in such sweet fragrance? In the growing swell, the surging sound.
4:42	Glorious climax with the "Transcendent Bliss" motif shining forth in the orchestra	In des Welt-Atems wehendem All— Ertrinken, versinken— Unbewusst— Höchste Lust!	In the vastness of the world's spirit To drown, sink down— Unconscious— Supreme bliss!

The orchestra then fades away into silence as the curtain descends

(Listening Exercise 33)

LATE NINETEENTH-CENTURY OPERA

Verismo Opera

If Wagner's operas center on the deeds of mythical heroes, and Verdi's "domestic operas" on those of the upper middle class, the late nineteenth-century works of Giacomo Puccini (1858–1924) and his competitors focus on the actions of the lower stratum of society. They depict the grimy, everyday life of industrialized nineteenth-century Europe and are tinged with just a hint of eroticism and the threat of violence. This turn to social realism on the musical stage produced what is called *verismo* ("realism") opera. **Verismo opera** was part of a general late-Romantic movement that held that in art and literature the ugly and the vulgar have their place because truth has aesthetic value. The goal for poets like Charles Baudelaire (1821–1867), painters like J.-F. Millet (1814–1875), and novelists like Charles Dickens (1812–1870) and Emile Zola (1840–1902) was to transform the mundane and commonplace into art, to find the poetic and mystical in even the most ordinary of human experience. No more do we hear of gods and goddesses, Nordic giants, or benevolent kings and queens. A gypsy girl who works in a cigarette factory (Carmen in Bizet's *Carmen*, 1875), a jealous clown who stabs his wife (Canio in Leoncavallo's *Pagliacci*, 1892), and a distraught singer who murders the chief of police (Tosca in Puccini's *Tosca*, 1900)—these are the heros and heroines of *verismo* opera.

realism in art, realism in opera

Giacomo Puccini (1858–1924)

Giacomo Puccini did not have to look far for a profession. He was the scion of four generations of musicians from the northern Italian town of Lucca. His father and his grandfather had both written operas, and before that his forebears had composed religious music for the local cathedral. But Puccini was no child prodigy. For a decade following his graduation from the Milan Conservatory he lived in poverty as he struggled to develop a distinctive operatic style. Not until the age of thirty-five did he score his first triumph, the *verismo* opera *Manon Lescaut* (1893). Thereafter, successes came in rapid succession: *La bohème* (1896), *Tosca* (1900), *Madama Butterfly* (1904). The heir to Verdi, the king of Italian opera, had been found. Growing famous, wealthy, and a bit complacent, Puccini worked less and less frequently. His last, and many believe his best, opera, *Turandot*, was left unfinished at the time of his death from throat cancer in 1924.

FIGURE 14–11
Giacomo Puccini.

Bettmann Archive

LA BOHÈME (THE BOHEMIAN GIRL, 1896)

the libretto

Puccini's most famous opera is *La bohème*. Indeed, statistics show that it is the most performed of all operas. *La bohème* is typical of *versimo* opera because the characters are portrayed as living a bohemian life in miserable poverty. The hero, Rodolfo (a poet), and his pals, Schaunard (a musician), Colline (a philosopher), and Marcello (a painter), are starving artists who inhabit an unheated attic on the Left Bank of Paris. The heroine, Mimi (the "bohemian girl"), their neighbor, is a poor, tubercular seamstress. Rodolfo and Mimi meet and fall in love. He grows obsessively jealous while she becomes progressively sickly. They separate for a time, only to return to each other's arms immediately before Mimi's death. In truth, this is not much of a plot, nor is there much character development. The theatrical setup on stage is merely a pretext to allow each of us to feel love, hope, and despair. The words of the singers and their particular dramatic situation, in the last analysis, don't matter. In a singers' opera such as *La bohème* it is the glorious sound of the human voice that carries the moment. When Rodolfo, for example, sings of Mimi's frozen little hand in the aria "Che gelida manina" we escape the cold, hopeless world of a Left Bank attic. The soaring sound of Rodolfo's high tenor voice, not his words, invites us to experience feelings and sensations far beyond the mundane. With the expansive arias of Puccini the golden century of Italian opera, which began with Rossini and embraced all of Verdi, comes to a fitting end. Thereafter, escapism would be found in the motion picture.

Listening Guide

Giacomo Puccini
La bohème (1896)
Aria, "Ah, what a frozen little hand"

6CD 4/10

Characters: The poor poet Rodolfo and the equally impoverished seamstress Mimi
Situation: Mimi has knocked on Rodolfo's door to ask for a light for her candle. Charmed by the lovely stranger, he naturally obliges. The wind again blows out Mimi's candle, and amidst the confusion she drops her key. As the two search for it in the darkness, Rodolfo by chance touches her hand and, then holding it, seizes the moment to tell her about himself and his hopes.

0:00	Rodolfo begins conversationally, much like in a recitative	Che gelida manina se la lasci riscaldar. Cercar che giova? Al buio non si trova. Ma per fortuna è una notte di luna, e qui la luna l'abbiamo vicina.	Ah, what a frozen little hand, let me warm it up. What's the good of searching? We won't find it in the dark. But by good luck there is moonlight tonight, and here we have the moon nearby.
	(Mimi tries to withdraw her hand)	Aspetti, signorina, le dirò con due parole chi son, e che faccio, come vivo. Vuole? Chi son? Sono un poeta. Che cosa faccio? Scrivo. E come vivo? Vivo!	Wait, young lady, I will tell you in two words who I am and what I do, how I live. Would you like this? Who am I? I'm a poet. What do I do? I write. How do I live? I live!
1:03	Voice increases in range, volume, and intensity		
	(Rodolfo proceeds to explain who he is and what he does)		
1:52	Return to conversational style	In povertà mia lieta scialo da gran signore rime et inni d'amore. Per sogni et per chimere e per castelli in aria, l'anima ho milionaria.	In my delightful poverty I grandiosely scatter rhymes and songs of love. Through dreams and reveries and through castles in the air, I have the soul of a millionaire.
2:30	Voice grows more expansive with longer notes and higher range; orchestra doubles voice in unison	Talor dal mio forziere ruban tutti i gioelli due ladri: gli occhi belli. V'entrar con voi pur ora, ed i miei sogni usati e i bei sogni miei tosto si dileguar! Ma il furto non m'accora,	Sometimes from the strongbox two thieves steal all the jewels: two pretty eyes. They came in with you just now and my usual dreams, my lovely dreams vanish at once! But the theft doesn't bother me
3:24	Orchestra sounds melody alone; then is joined by voice for climactic high note "hope"	poichè v'ha preso stanza la speranza!	because their place has been taken by hope!
	(As the music diminishes, Rodolfo asks for a response from Mimi)	Or che mi conoscete, parlate voi, deh! parlate. Chi siete? Vi piaccia dir!	Now that you know who I am, Tell me about yourself, speak. Who are you? Please speak.

Listening Exercises

32

Giuseppe Verdi, *La traviata* (1853)   6CD 4/7; 2CD 2/4
Act I, Scene 6: Aria "Ah, perhaps he's the one"
Recitative "Folly! Folly!"
Cabaletta "Always free"

In *La traviata* Verdi has created what is very much a "singers' opera"—the listener's attention is drawn almost entirely to the voices. The orchestra plays a subordinate role, often limited to setting up a background accompaniment with simple rhythms and regular meters. The following questions illuminate the way in which Verdi makes the voice the center of attention, pausing from time to time to enjoy a moment of vocal bravura, yet still keeps the tempo of the opera moving at a rapid pace.

1. (0:00–1:00) What are the meter and the mode at the beginning of this aria?
   a. duple and minor   b. duple and major
   c. triple and minor   d. triple and major
2. (0:12–0:33) What does the orchestra do while Violetta (soprano) sings?
   a. provides simple imitative polyphony
   b. provides simple chordal homophony
3. (1:24–2:11) Here Violetta sings the expansive "love" refrain introduced previously by Alfredo. The orchestral accompaniment now changes to the "big guitar" effect. How does Verdi create this big guitar in the orchestra?
   a. Strings play vibrato chords and flute plays arpeggios.
   b. Strings play pizzicato chords and clarinet plays arpeggios.
   c. Strings play tremolo chords and flute plays arpeggios.
4. (2:26–5:32) Violetta now sings the second strophe of her aria. When the expansive "love" refrain returns (3:42–4:36), does the orchestra still produce the "big guitar" effect?
   a. yes   b. no
5. (4:45–5:32) Toward the end of the second strophe Violetta ornaments her melodic line to give it more interest the second time around. The ornamentation concludes with a lengthy trill, during which time the orchestra is silent. At what moment does the trill begin?
   a. 4:55   b. 5:08   c. 5:23

6CD 4/8; 2CD 2/4

6. During Violetta's accompanied recitative "Folly! Folly!" there is a passage in which she expresses her fear at being merely "a poor woman alone, abandoned in this populated desert that they call Paris" (0:13–0:23). The orchestra helps heighten this feeling of fear by playing:
   a. string *rubato* and rising stepwise motion in the bass
   b. string pizzicato and falling stepwise motion in the bass
   c. string tremolo and rising stepwise motion in the bass
7. After her recitative, and following some vocal fireworks on the word *gioir* ("pleasure"), Violetta launches into her brilliant cabaletta "Sempre libera" ("Always free"). What characteristic identifies this as a cabaletta?

    a. The rhythm of the aria is like that of a galloping horse riding off the stage.

    b. It is a fast-concluding aria that Violetta will use to exit the stage.

8. Toward the end of the first statement of "Always free," the voice of Alfredo enters (at 2:01) with his familiar refrain "Love that animates the world." Which of the following is true about Alfredo's music?

    a. The tempo slows down and a harp accompanies the voice.

    b. The tempo speeds up and a guitar accompanies the voice.

    c. The tempo speeds up so as to be at the same speed as Violetta's aria.

9. (3:00–3:15) Again Violetta vows to dedicate herself to a life of pleasure ("gioir"). What does the orchestra do during this vocal flourish?

    a. nothing

    b. merely plays chordal homophony

    c. creates the "big guitar" effect

10. Now Violetta repeats "Always free" (3:17), swearing to remain free of the snares of love. Where does the vocal high point of "Always free" occur—where does the soprano go to the top of her range?

    a. at the end of the first time Violetta sings the aria (1:57–2:01)

    b. at the end of the second time Violetta sings the aria (4:34–4:49)

· ·

    Richard Wagner   6CD 4/9; 2CD 2/5

    Liebestod, from Tristan und Isolde (1865)

Isolde's *Liebestod (Love-Death)*, which brings *Tristan und Isolde* to a glorious conclusion, is a unique musical composition. It is written for soprano voice—indeed, for a dramatic Wagnerian soprano—with orchestra, yet it is a very different sort of piece from Giuseppe Verdi's aria "Always free" from *La traviata*, which we have previously heard.

1. Is there an easily perceptible duple or triple meter in the *Liebestod?*

    a. yes   b. no

2. When the soprano sings the "Ecstasy" leitmotif (2:48–3:11) she does so to rather square poetry—lines of 4 + 4 syllables with internal rhyme. (Try saying the German to yourself.)

Wonne klagend, alles sagend	Moaning bliss, expressing all
Mild versöhnend aus ihm tönend	Gently forgiving, sounding from within

    What is the course of the soprano line during this couplet?

    a. rises

    b. rises in a melodic sequence

    c. falls

    d. falls in a melodic sequence

3. Immediately after (3:12–3:30), the music rises toward a climax to reflect the sentiment of the next couplet:

In mich dringet, auf sich schwinget,	Pierces me, rises upwards,
Hold erhallend um mich klinget?	Blessedly echoing all around me?

How is this rising tension brought about in the music?
a. Tremolos are played by the strings.
b. There is a gradual crescendo.
c. The voice rises up chromatically.
d. all of the above

4. (3:53–4:42) Wagner now builds to a final climax with the "Desire" leitmotif churning in the orchestra. But along the way, on the word *"Lauschen"* (4:17, "listen"), he suddenly changes dynamics. To which does he change?
   a. *fortissimo*   b. *pianissimo*

5. (5:05–5:39) The great climax has been reached. How does Wagner now musically depict the final words of Isolde "to drown, to sink down, in supreme bliss"?
a. The vocal line continually falls.
b. The vocal line falls, then soars up and holds a note.
c. The vocal line soars up, then falls.

6. Which leitmotif is heard softly in the oboes (at 5:59) immediately before the final chord?
   a. "Ecstasy"   b. "Transcendent Bliss"   c. "Desire"

7. (5:05–6:26) In this passage Wagner brings us to the end of the opera. The nature of the music changes to suggest a feeling of winding down. Which one of the following does **not** occur?
a. The tempo of the music appears to get slower.
b. The "Transcendent Bliss" leitmotif no longer rises upward.

CULTURAL CONTEXT

The Habanera: A Popular Dance-Song from Cuba

The Romantic sensibility rejoiced in things foreign and exotic, a delight that only increased toward the end of the nineteenth century, as we shall see. The European imagination viewed non-European cultures as treasure troves from which to draw artistic stimulus. As early as 1829, the French poet Victor Hugo confessed to writing under the spell of the foreign, or the "Oriental," as he called it:

Oriental colors came as of their own accord to imprint themselves on my thoughts and on all my dreams. And all my dreams and thoughts found themselves in turn, almost without having wished it so, Hebraic, Turkish, Greek, Persian, Arab, even Spanish, because Spain is still the Orient; Spain is half African, Africa is half Asiatic.

For the Romantic spirit then, there was Europe, and there was the Other. Spain, as Hugo says, belonged to the Other.

Following Hugo's example, the French composer Georges Bizet (1838–1875) incorporated a number of Spanish themes into his stage works including, most famously, into his opera *Carmen* (1875). *Carmen* takes place in nineteenth-century Seville, the southern Spanish city closest to North Africa. The opera centers around, indeed is dominated by, a sensual young gypsy woman known only as Carmen. This sexually assertive, willful woman holds the populace in her sway. By means of alluring dance and song, she seduces a naïve army corporal, Don José. Hopelessly in love, Don José deserts his military posting, "marries" Carmen, and takes up with

    c. The orchestra drives toward its own *fortissimo* climax.

    d. The dynamic level gradually changes from loud to soft.

8. Who has the "last word" (who is heard at the very end of the *Liebestod*)?

    a. the voice   b. the orchestra

9. Which musical force could be omitted without serious loss to the overall effect of the piece?

    a. the voice   b. the orchestra

10. Wagner's *Liebestod* is composed in which musical form?

    a. through composed   b. *da capo* aria   c. sonata–allegro

Key Words

Bayreuth Festival Theater (307)	leitmotif (309)	*Ring* cycle (306)
bel canto (298)	*Liebestod* (309)	Risorgimento (300)
cabaletta (303)	music drama (307)	scena (303)
diva (299)	prima donna (299)	*Singspiel* (305)
Gesamtkunstwerk (307)	*recitativo accompagnato* (301)	*verismo* opera (311)
La Scala (299)		

her gypsy bandit friends. But Carmen, who refuses to belong to any man, soon abandons Don José to give herself to the handsome bullfighter Escamillo. Having lost all for nothing, the humiliated Don José stabs Carmen to death in a bloody ending. This "Love-Death" is very different from the idealized happy ending of the usual Romantic opera.

In fact, the lurid plot of *Carmen* stamps it as an early example of *verismo* opera*—avant-garde realism in the musical theater. *Carmen* embraces the underbelly of nineteenth-century society. The stage is populated with gypsies who work in a cigarette factory, prostitutes, and bandits. The heroine, Carmen, is a woman of easy virtue available to all, albeit on her own terms. This was

Sally Burgess sings the seductive role of Carmen in a 1998 production by the English National Opera.

revolutionary stuff for the Parisian theater in Bizet's day. During the first rehearsals in 1875, the women of the chorus threatened to strike because they were asked to smoke and fight on stage. The producers asked Bizet to tone down the more sensational aspects of the drama (especially the tragic ending)—to make it more acceptable as family entertainment—but he refused.

The foreign has always had a certain allure of the forbidden. To give his opera *Carmen* a flavor both foreign and forbidden, Bizet borrowed several Spanish folksongs and **flamenco** melodies (songs of southern Spain infused with gypsy elements). But by far the best-known

(Continued on next page)

CULTURAL CONTEXT (continued)

foreign music in the opera is the "Habanera" that he fashioned to introduce the character Carmen.

Literally, **Habanera** means, "the thing from Havana." Musically, it is a type of dance-song that developed in Spanish-controlled Cuba during the early nineteenth century. African and Latin influences on its musical style can perhaps be seen in the descending chromatic scale, and certainly in the static harmony (the downbeat of every measure is a "D" in the bass) as well as in the insistent, repetitious rhythm [$\frac{2}{4}$ ♪♫♩|♪♫♩]. The infectious rhythm of the Habanera gives it its irresistible quality—we all want to get up and join the dance. But the Habanera is a sensual dance, like its later descendant the tango, and it is the sensual quality of the music that greatly contributes to the seductive aura of Carmen herself.

The structure of Bizet's Habanera is straightforward. At first Carmen sings a stanza of text set to a descending chromatic line of four, four-bar phrases ("Love is like

an elusive bird"). It is the nature of the chromatic melodies to seem to have no tonal center. This one, too, is musically noncommittal and slippery, just as the character of Carmen is both ambiguous and evasive. The chorus immediately repeats the chromatic melody, but now Carmen voluptuously glides above it singing the single word *"L'amour"* ("Love"). As her voice soars, like the illusive bird of love, the tonality shifts from minor to major. To this is then added a refrain ("Love is like a gypsy child") in which the melody alternates between a major triad and a minor one. Against this refrain the chorus shouts "watch out," warning of Carmen's destructive qualities. This same structure—chromatically descending melody, followed by a triadic refrain with choral shouts—then repeats. Bizet wanted this Habanera to establish the character of Carmen as a sensual enchantress. In every way, the music *is* Carmen. And like Carmen, once this seductive melody has us in its spell, it will never let go.

Listening Guide

Georges Bizet
Habanera from the opera *Carmen* (1875)

6CD 4/11

Situation: The scantily clad gypsy woman Carmen, exuding an almost primeval sexuality, dances before José, other soldiers and the villagers. The Afro-Cuban music suggests that she is both foreign and forbidden.

(Continued on next page)

0:00	Bass ostinato with Habanera rhythm; minor mode
0:06	Carmen enters with enticing descending melody

L'amour est un oisseau rebelle	Love is like an elusive bird,
Que nul ne peut apprivoiser;	That cannot be tamed;
Et c'est bien en vain qu'on l'appelle,	You call it in vain
S'il lui convient de refuser.	If it decides to refuse.
Rien n'y fait, menace ou prière,	Neither threat nor prayer will prevail;
L'un parle bien, l'autre se tait;	One man talks a lot, the other is silent;
Et c'est l'autre que je prèfère	And it's the latter I prefer,
Il n'a rien dit; mais il me plait.	He hasn't said a word, but he pleases me.

0:38	Change to major mode; chorus repeats melody; Carmen soars above on the the word "Love"
0:53	Carmen sings the refrain

L'amour est enfant de Bohème,	Love is like a gypsy child,
Il n'a jamais connu de loi,	Who has never known constraint,
Si tu ne m'aimes pas, je t'aime;	If I love you, and you don't love me,
Si je t'aime, prends garde à toi!	Watch out!

1:09	Chorus shouts "Watch out!"
1:32	Chorus sings refrain with Carmen

Second stanza:

2:09	Bass ostinato with Habanera rhythm
2:17	Carmen enters with enticing chromatic melody

L'oiseau que tu croyais surprendre	The bird you thought you'd surprised
Battit de l'aile et s'envola;	Beat its wings and flew away;
L'amour est loin, tu peux l'attendre;	Love is far away, but expect it;
Tu ne l'attends plus, il est la!	You don't expect it, but there it is!
Tout autour de toi, vite,	All around you, quick!
Il vient, s'en va, puis il revient;	It comes, it goes, and then it returns;
Tu crois le tenir, il t'evite;	You think you've trapped it, it escapes;
Tu crois l'éviter, il te tient!	You think you've escaped it, it traps you!

2:50	Change to major mode; chorus repeats melody; Carmen soars above on the word "Love"
3:05	Carmen, the chorus (3:41), and then Carmen (3:58) again sing the refrain

When we speak of cultures we usually refer to civilizations of different geographic regions and their particular ethnic qualities. But we can also take culture to mean an aspect of training, refinement, and taste. Thus we talk about high culture, low culture, learned culture, popular culture, oral culture, and the like. Remarkably, Bizet's opera *Carmen* has relevance to both senses of the word "culture." Yes, *Carmen* portrays the cultures of different ethnic groups—French, Spanish, Afro-Cuban, and gypsy. But it also has contained within it two strata of musical cultures, learned and popular. The Habanera, for example, is not the usual "high art" of opera, but rather a refashioning of a popular song with origins in Cuba.

At its premiere in Paris in 1875, *Carmen* was a flop—the subject matter was thought degrading. But as the "every-day world" became a suitable subject for the increasingly realistic theater, the broad popular appeal of *Carmen* gradually became apparent. In the twentieth century alone, the music and story of *Carmen* served artistic projects with very different cultural expectations. It has been transformed into an African-American Broadway musical (*Carmen Jones*), into nearly twenty films including at least one pornographic one, into an ice escapade (*Carmen on Ice*), and used as the basis of more than one cartoon show. In an early episode of *The Simpsons*, for example, the family goes to the opera where it hears—what else?—*Carmen*, and Bart and Homer sing along with the music. Perhaps that explains why *Carmen* is arguably the most popular opera of all time. It connects with several ethnic cultures as well as with many different levels of artistic taste, each as valid as the next.

KEY WORDS

flamenco   Habanera

Chapter 15

Tretiakov Gallery, Moscow/SuperStock

Late Romanticism

When historians speak of "late Romanticism," they refer to the artistic developments that occurred in the West from about 1870 until 1900–1910, from the time of the Franco–Prussian War (1870) until shortly before the outbreak of World War I (1914). Of course, human activity, artistic or otherwise, rarely occurs within tidy chronological units. As we shall see, a strong anti–Romantic movement developed in France as early as the 1880s. Yet while some progressive artists began to turn away from Romanticism at this early date, other more conservative ones continued to compose in the late Romantic style into the 1940s. Romanticism had a strong hold on the consciousness of the listening public, one that it has not entirely relinquished even today.

During the last decades of the nineteenth century, orchestral music, especially German orchestral music, increasingly came to dominate the European concert hall. The continued growth in the size and color of the orchestra made listening to a symphony orchestra the most powerful aesthetic experience that a citizen of the late nineteenth century could enjoy. Not surprisingly, the force of the ever-larger orchestra affected the development of musical genres. We have seen that Wagner wrote operas in which the instrumental ensemble sometimes overwhelmed and absorbed the voice into its rich orchestral tapestry. Similarly, the orchestra began to infiltrate the realm of the art song, so that now the singer of a *Lied** was often accompanied not merely by a piano but by a full orchestra. So, too, the symphony orchestra expropriated the overture, taking it out of the theater and bringing it into the concert hall. And all the while the traditional four-movement symphony grew longer and more complex, a direct response to the increased number and variety of instruments. Let us review briefly the development of the symphony and concerto during the nineteenth century.

THE LATE ROMANTIC SYMPHONY AND CONCERTO

The four-movement symphony came into being during the Classical period, in the orchestral works of Haydn and Mozart (see page 205). Throughout the nineteenth century it remained a favorite with audiences everywhere, except in Italy, where opera was a national obsession. Symphonic composers in the Romantic period generally followed the four-movement format inherited from their Classical forebears—fast, slow, minuet or scherzo, fast. But now the third movement might be almost any sort of light, contrasting creation, while the finale increasingly took on a more serious tone. As we have seen (page 258), the movements of a symphony grew in length in the course of the nineteenth century. Perhaps as a consequence of this greater length and seriousness, composers wrote fewer symphonies. Schumann and Brahms composed only four, Mendelssohn five, Tchaikovsky six, Dvořák, Bruckner, and Mahler each nine. No one approached the 40-odd symphonies of Mozart, to say nothing of the 104 of Haydn.

composers write few, but long, symphonies and concertos

Similarly for the concerto, with expanded length came a reduction in number. A Classical concerto may last twenty minutes, a Romantic one forty; Mozart gave us twenty-three piano concertos, but Beethoven only five. Beethoven, Mendelssohn, Brahms, and Tchaikovsky penned just a single violin concerto, yet each is a substantial showpiece for the soloist. Despite its growing length, the Romantic concerto retained the three-movement plan established during the Classical period—fast, slow, fast.

For a Romantic composer contemplating the creation of a symphony or concerto, no figure loomed larger than Beethoven. Wagner asked why anyone after Beethoven bothered to write symphonies at all, given the dramatic impact of Beethoven's Third, Fifth, and Ninth. Wagner himself wrote only one, Verdi none. Some composers, notably Berlioz and Liszt, turned to a completely different sort of symphony, the program symphony*, in which an external scenario determined the nature and order of the musical events. But these works sometimes lacked the force, internal unity, and compelling logic of a Beethoven symphony. It was not until the late Romantic period, nearly fifty years after the death of Beethoven, that someone came forth to claim the title of successor to Beethoven the symphonist. That figure was Johannes Brahms.

the legacy of Beethoven

Johannes Brahms (1833–1897)

Brahms was born in the north German port city of Hamburg in 1833. He was given the Latin name Johannes to distinguish him from his father Johann, a street musician and "beer-hall" fiddler. Although Johannes's formal

FIGURE 15–1

Johannes Brahms in his early thirties. Said an observer of the time: "The broad chest, the Herculean shoulders, the powerful head, which he threw back energetically when playing—all betrayed an artistic personality replete with the spirit of true genius."

education never went beyond primary school, his father saw to it that he had the best training on the piano and in music theory. He was fed a heavy diet of the great masters: Bach's *The Well-Tempered Clavier* (see page 152), Beethoven's piano sonatas, and Haydn's chamber music. While he studied these by day, by night he earned money playing out-of-tune pianos in "stimulation bars" on the Hamburg waterfront. To get his hands on better instruments, he practiced daily in the showrooms of local piano stores.

Brahms first came to the public's attention in 1853, when Robert Schumann published a highly laudatory article proclaiming him to be a musical Messiah, the heir apparent of Haydn, Mozart, and Beethoven and their great legacy. Brahms, in turn, embraced both Schumanns, Robert and his wife Clara (see page 283), as his musical mentors. When Robert was confined to a mental institution in 1854, Brahms moved into the Schumann home for two years to help Clara raise her seven children. Not surprisingly, his respect and affection for Clara ripened into love, despite the fact that she was fourteen years his senior. Yet for whatever reason—they both later destroyed many of their letters to each other—their mutual affection did not culminate in marriage after Robert's death. Brahms remained a bachelor for the duration of his life.

Disappointed first in love and then in his attempts to gain an official position in his native Hamburg, Brahms in 1862 moved to Vienna. He contracted to conduct choral groups from time to time, but for the most part was able to maintain his modest lifestyle—"very un-Wagnerian" he called it—with fees earned as a concert pianist and with royalties accruing from the publication of his ever-growing list of compositions. His fame increased dramatically in 1868 with performances of his *A German Requiem*, which was sold to amateur choruses around the world. Honorary degrees were offered from Cambridge University (1876) and Breslau University (1879). After Wagner's death in 1883, he was generally considered the greatest living German com-

FIGURE 15–2

Brahms's composing room in Vienna. On the wall, looking down on the piano, is a bust of Beethoven. The spirit of Beethoven loomed large over the entire nineteenth century (see also the cover) and over Brahms in particular.

poser. His own death, from liver cancer, came in the spring of 1897. He was buried in the central cemetery of Vienna, thirty feet from the graves of Beethoven and Schubert.

That Brahms should choose Vienna as his home is not surprising—it was then a city of nearly a million people, the fifth largest in the world. But, more important, Vienna had been the home of Haydn, Mozart, Beethoven, and Schubert. In the music of these past masters the conservative Brahms sought inspiration. He returned again and again to the genres (symphony, concerto, quartet, and sonata) and forms (sonata–allegro, theme and variations, and rondo) that they had established or popularized. Most telling, Brahms composed no program music—what to other nineteenth-century musicians like Liszt and Berlioz was the very soul of Romantic music. Instead, he chose to write **absolute music**, chamber sonatas, symphonies, and concertos without any sort of program. In these, Brahms did not give free rein to his musical imagination as had Berlioz, Liszt, and Wagner, but maintained a sense of balance by setting Romantic themes within the tight confines of traditional musical forms. Brahms could write songful Romantic melodies, but he was at heart a contrapuntalist, a "developer" in the tradition of Bach and Beethoven. Indeed, soon he would be dubbed the last of the musically famous "three B's": Bach, Beethoven, and Brahms.

Brahms the conservative

VIOLIN CONCERTO IN D MAJOR (1878)

In 1870 Johannes Brahms wrote: "I shall never compose a symphony! You have no idea how the likes of us feel when we hear the tramp of a giant like him behind us." Brahms, of course, was referring to Beethoven. He was terrified by the prospect of competing with the symphonies of that "giant." But Brahms did go on to write a symphony—indeed, four of them, each in four movements. They were first performed, in turn, in 1876, 1877, 1883, and 1885. In the midst of this symphonic activity, Brahms also wrote his only violin concerto, a worthy rival of the earlier violin concerto of Beethoven.

By training and profession, Brahms was a pianist, not a violinist. For help with regard to violin bowing and fingering he turned to his long-time friend and playing partner Joseph Joachim (see Fig. 13–13). When the concerto received its premiere at the Gewandhaus (see Figs. 13–9 and 13–10), it was virtuoso Joachim who played the solo part while Brahms conducted the orchestra. One technical skill that Brahms required of the soloist is the art of playing **double stops**. Usually we think of the violin as a monophonic* instrument, capable of executing only one line of music. But a good violinist can hold (stop) two and sometimes more strings simultaneously and sweep across them with the bow. This imparts a richer, more chordal sound to the soloist's part. Example 15–1 shows how Brahms incorporates double stops into the melody of the last movement of his concerto.

a demanding violin part with double stops

EXAMPLE 15–1

When he arrived at the finale of his Violin Concerto, Brahms the conservative turned to a form traditionally used in the last movement of a concerto: the *a rondo finale* rondo. Recall that a rondo centers on a single theme that serves as a musical refrain. Here the refrain has the flavor of a gypsy tune, like the Hungarian dances Brahms often heard in the Prater Park in Vienna as he sipped beer and chatted with friends. What marks this refrain is its lively rhythm (𝄞). Above this foot-tapping motive the violin sometimes soars with difficult passage work (scales, arpeggios, and double stops). The technical demands placed on the soloist caused one musician of the day to complain that Brahms had not written a concerto "for" the violin but rather "against" it. To which a later virtuoso replied: "Brahms' concerto is not against the violin, but for violin against orchestra—and the violin wins."

Listening Guide

Johannes Brahms
Violin Concerto in D major (1878)
Third movement, *Allegro giocoso, ma non tropo vivace*
(fast and playful, but not too lively)

6CD 4/12;
2CD 2/6

Form: rondo

Time	Description	Section
0:00	Refrain played by violin and then by orchestra	A
0:56	Transition: racing scales in violin	
1:20	New theme moves up, and then down, a major scale	B
2:09	Violin returns with refrain; orchestra repeats it	A
2:51	Violin plays more lyrical theme built on arpeggio	C
3:55	Rising scale in violin, answered by falling scale in orchestra	B
4:46	Elaboration of rhythm of refrain	
5:07	Orchestra plays refrain *fortissimo*	A
5:35	Violin plays very brief cadenza*, then rhythm of refrain developed	
6:46	Another brief cadenza*	
6:55	Rhythm of refrain becomes march-like	CODA

(Listening Exercise 34)

VOCAL MUSIC FROM CRADLE TO GRAVE

Brahms was a very serious person and he usually wrote very serious music. When he wanted to "lighten up," he did so in his Lieder, songs for solo voice and piano. Brahms' most famous Lied, perhaps the best-known art song ever written, is his Wiegenlied (Lullaby). He drew the text from a collection of folk poetry, and fashioned the melody from a tune a girlfriend had once sung to him. The piano accompaniment is a syncopated waltz. Above it the voice sings a melody that is as profoundly simple as it is beautiful.

Listening Guide

WWW

Johannes Brahms
Lullaby (1868)

Intro CD/21

Meter: triple
Genre: *Lied*
Form: strophic

0:00	Piano introduction		
0:05	Soprano sings first strophe	Guten Abend, gut Nacht,	Good evening, good night
		Mit rosen bedacht,	Covered with roses,
		Mit Näglein besteckt	Adorned with carnations,
		Schlupf unter die Deck':	Slip under the covers.
		Morgen früh, wenn Gott will,	Tomorrow early, if God so wills,
		Wirst du wieder gewecht.	You will awake again.
0:50	Repeat of piano introduction		
0:56	Soprano sings second strophe of text to same melody	Guten Abend, gut Nacht,	Good evening, good night,
		Von Englein bewacht,	Watched over by angels,
		Die zeigen im Traum	Who in dreams show
		Dir Christkindleins Baum:	You the Christ child's tree.
		Schlaf nun selig und süss,	Now sleep blissful and sweetly,
		Schau im Traum's Paradies.	Behold Paradise in your dreams.

The serious—and conservative—Brahms can be heard again in his *A German Requiem*. The idea of composing a Mass for the Dead gradually coalesced in his mind following the death of his teacher, Robert Schumann, and then, in 1865, of his mother. What Brahms created was not a burial service for either the official Catholic church or the German Lutheran church. Nowhere can be heard the voice of the wrathful God of judgment. Rather, *A German Requiem* is a personal, nonsectarian confession of faith, full of sounds of solace for all who have suffered loss through death. For texts of consolation, Brahms drew equally from the Old and New Testament. For musical inspiration, he again turned to the music of past masters. Brahms had studied and conducted the motets* of Palestrina and the cantatas* of Bach. He wedded their old-style counterpoint to the sound of the large-scale nineteenth-century chorus.

A German Requiem

The emotional core of this hour-long, seven-movement work is its fourth movement. "How lovely is Thy dwelling place," says the text of Psalm 84, and before us looms an image of the heavenly House of the Lord. Imitating the blissful souls in heaven, a four-part chorus sings praises to the Lord in a skillful blend of homophonic and polyphonic textures. The interplay between chorus and orchestra is evident at the very outset. The opening phrase played by the woodwinds is immediately sung in mirror image by the sopranos (see musical example in the Listening Guide). Such contrapuntal details rest at the heart of Brahms' compositional style. The challenge to the listener is to hear the counterpoint in the midst of the richly soothing sound of the Romantic chorus and orchestra.

Brahms' counterpoint

Listening Guide

Johannes Brahms
A German Requiem (1868)
Fourth movement, "How lovely is Thy dwelling place"

6CD 4/13

Text: Psalm 84, verses 1, 2 and 4

0:00   Woodwinds play peaceful melody

0:07	Sopranos respond in same mood	Wie lieblich sind deine Wohnungen, Herr Zebaoth!	How lovely is Thy dwelling place, O, Lord of Hosts!
0:44	Tenors sing same text, basses, altos and sopranos follow in imitative counterpoint		
1:23	More imitative counterpoint sung by chorus	Meine Seele verlanget und sehnet sich nach den Vorhöfen des Herrn;	My soul longs and thirsts for the courts of the Lord;
1:56	Chorus sings homophony with strong accents in orchestra	Mein Leib und Seele freuen sich in dem Lebendigen Gott.	My body and soul rejoice in the living God.
2:26	Return of opening music in orchestra and then chorus	Wie lieblich . . .	How lovely . . .
3:15	Chorus quietly sings chordal homophony	Wohl denen, die in deinem Hause wohnen,	Blessed are they who dwell in Thy House,
3:38	Chorus declaims its praise of the Lord in forceful imitative counterpoint	die loben Dich immerdar.	where they praise you ever after.
4:27	Return of opening music and text	Wie lieblich . . .	How lovely . . .

FIGURE 15–3

Antonín Dvořák conducting: a painting now hanging in the Dvořák Museum in Prague.

Dvořák Museum, Prague/SuperStock

Antonín Dvořák (1841–1904)

"There is no doubt that he is very talented. He is also very poor." Thus Johannes Brahms wrote to the music publisher Simrock in 1876 describing the then-unknown thirty-five-year-old Antonín Dvořák. Dvořák, the son of a butcher, was a native of Bohemia, an area of the Czech Republic south of Prague. He, too, passed an apprenticeship to be a butcher, but a prosperous uncle saw musical talent in the teenager and sent him to study organ in Prague for a year. Thereafter, for nearly two decades, Dvořák eked out a living as a freelance violist and organist in Prague, playing in dance bands, the opera orchestra, and in church. All the while he composed tirelessly—operas, symphonies, string quartets, and songs, almost all of which went unheard.

Brahms's intervention with the publisher Simrock proved decisive in Dvořák's career. Soon the Czech composer's charming *Slavonic Dances* for piano duet were available in music stores across Europe, and they caught on like wildfire. Simrock's firm got rich from this publication, though Dvořák received only the equivalent of two months of his usual salary. (There was no such thing as artists' royalties at this time; the composer or author simply sold the work for a flat fee to the publisher, who took all risks and kept all revenues.) What Dvořák did receive from his publications was recognition. Commissions from various orchestras and conductors now came like a flood. During the 1880s his symphonies, string quartets, and choral works were heard in London, Berlin, Vienna, Dresden, Leipzig, Moscow, Budapest, and even Cincinnati, which then had a strong Bohemian component to its population.

In the spring of 1892 Dvořák received an offer he couldn't refuse. He was promised the astonishing sum of $15,000 per year (the equivalent of about $600,000 today) to become the Director of the newly founded National Conservatory of Music in New York City. So on September 17, 1892, Dvořák set sail for America and ultimately took up residence at 327 East 17th Street. It was here that he began work on his "American" Quartet and his Symphony "From the New World." Instead of returning to Prague that summer, Dvořák and his family traveled by train and carriage to Spillville, Iowa, spending three months among the mainly Czech-speaking people of this rural farming community. When he composed there he did so in part on the organ in the local Catholic church (Fig. 15–4). After two more winters in New York City as Director of the National Conservatory, he returned to his native Bohemia for good. He died in Prague in 1904, the Czechs' most famous and beloved composer.

Paul C. Bina, Milwaukee

FIGURE 15–4

The organ, built in 1875, in the Church of St. Wenceslaus in Spillville, Iowa. When Dvořák resided there during the summer of 1893, this was the only large-keyboard instrument available, and he used it to try out portions of his Symphony "From the New World."

SYMPHONY "FROM THE NEW WORLD" (1893)

The Symphony "From the New World" in E minor, Dvořák's ninth and last symphony, is by far his best-known work. It received a rousing premiere in New York City, at the newly built Carnegie Hall, on December 16, 1893. As Dvořák wrote to his publisher, Simrock, the following week:

> The success of the symphony was tremendous. The papers write that no composer has ever had such a triumph (Fig. 15–5). I was in a box. The hall was filled with the best New York audience. The people clapped so much that I had to thank them from the box like a king! You know how glad I am if I can avoid such ovations, but there was no getting out of it, and I had to show myself like-it-or-not.

The title that Dvořák gave to this symphony, "From the New World," might suggest that he placed within it musical elements that are distinctly American. Yet while Dvořák showed a keen interest in the indigenous music of African Americans and American Indians, none of the many tuneful melodies heard in this symphony can be identified as a pre-existing folk song. They came from Dvořák's own head and heart. And although these melodies, especially those of the famous *Largo*, do possess a "folk style" quality, they may be as much Czech as American in inspiration.

First movement (Adagio: Allegro molto; "Slow: Very fast"). A satisfying blend of forceful energy and tuneful lyricism mark

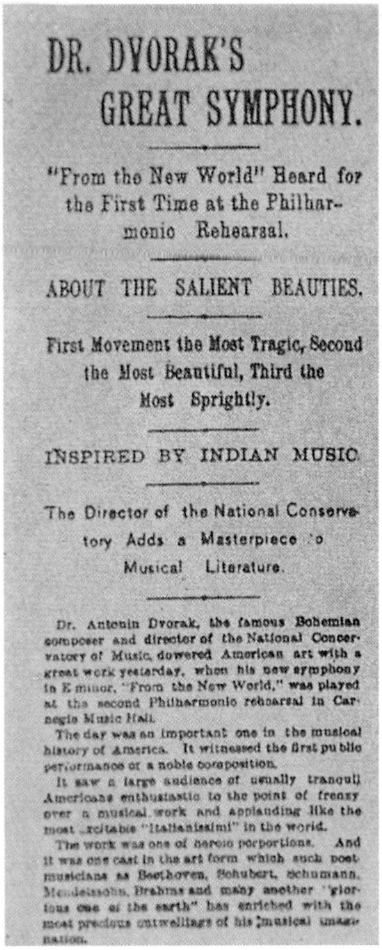

The New York Public Library

DR. DVORAK'S GREAT SYMPHONY.

"From the New World" Heard for the First Time at the Philharmonic Rehearsal.

ABOUT THE SALIENT BEAUTIES.

First Movement the Most Tragic, Second the Most Beautiful, Third the Most Sprightly.

INSPIRED BY INDIAN MUSIC.

The Director of the National Conservatory Adds a Masterpiece to Musical Literature.

Dr. Antonin Dvorak, the famous Bohemian composer and director of the National Conservatory of Music, dowered American art with a great work yesterday, when his new symphony in E minor, "From the New World," was played at the second Philharmonic rehearsal in Carnegie Music Hall.

The day was an important one in the musical history of America. It witnessed the first public performance of a noble composition.

It saw a large audience of usually tranquil Americans enthusiastic to the point of frenzy over a musical work and applauding like the most excitable "Italianissimi" in the world.

The work was one of heroic porportions. And it was one cast in the art form which such poet-musicians as Beethoven, Schubert, Schumann, Mendelssohn, Brahms and many another "glorious one of the earth" has enriched with the most precious outwellings of his musical imagination.

FIGURE 15–5

A review of the premiere of the Symphony "From the New World" in the *New York Herald*, December 17, 1893.

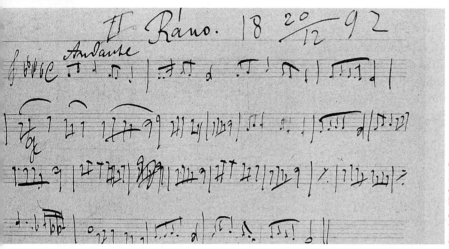

FIGURE 15–6

An autograph sketch of the famous English horn theme from the second movement of Dvořák's Symphony "From the New World." The tempo was later changed from *Andante* to *Largo* and some of the notes altered to give the movement a greater feeling of spaciousness.

this opening movement in strict sonata–allegro form. Solo wind instruments—French horn, oboe, and flute—introduce the principal themes, and then leave it to the strings to propel the music forward.

Second movement (Largo; "Very slow and broad"). Dvořák began his Symphony "From the New World" late in 1892 and continued to revise it during the following summer, which he spent with his family in Spillville, Iowa. Inspiration for the slow second movement apparently came from a popular American poem, Henry Wadsworth Longfellow's *Hiawatha:* specifically from the scene beginning "Pleasant was the journey homeward," in which Hiawatha travels across the great American plains. Dvořák, too, had experienced the vast expanse of the American prairie in his trip across Illinois and Iowa, and this apparently caused him to make changes to the draft of the slow movement to give it a greater sense of space, both temporal and sonic. The tempo, which was originally marked *Andante* (moving), was first slowed to *Larghetto* (slow but moving), and finally to *Largo* (very slow and broad). Several notes were changed in the famous English horn theme to make the intervals larger. Compare, for example, measure two of the original sketch of the theme (Fig. 15–6) with the finished version in the Listening Guide, where in measure two a higher A♭ replaces the original G♭. The final product is a movement infused with a sense of endless time and infinite space, as one might experience on the American prairie. Just as we speak of the Midwest as the "heartland" of America, so this slow middle movement constitutes the emotional soul of the Symphony "From the New World."

a famous English horn theme

Listening Guide

Antonín Dvořák
Symphony No. 9, "From the New World" (1893)
Second movement, *Largo* (Very slow and broad)

6CD 4/14

Form: ABCA

A

0:00	Solemn introductory chords by low brass choir, then timpani
0:47	English horn solo, the "Goin' home" melody

1:15 Clarinet joins English horn, then strings join as well

2:30 Introductory chords now played by high woodwinds and French horn, concluded by brasses and timpani

3:03 Strings play and extend "Goin' home" melody

3:57 Melody returns to English horn and is completed by woodwinds and strings

4:38 French horn echoes the melody

B

5:06 Faster tempo and new theme (**B1**) in flute and oboe

(Continued on next page)

5:32	Second new theme (**B2**) in clarinets above bass pizzicato	

6:20	Melody **B1** played more insistently by violins
7:15	Melody **B2** played more intensely by violins

C

8:20	Oboe introduces chirping of flute and clarinet
8:46	Brasses play *fortissimo* recall of first theme of first movement
9:00	Diminuendo and lovely transition back to

A

9:16	English horn brings back "Goin' home" melody
9:45	Pairs of violins and violas play melody but break off, as if choked by emotion
10:21	Solo cello and solo violin play melody, then full strings join
11:00	Quiet, monophonic soliloquy by violins
11:27	Final return and extension of opening chords

(Listening Exercise 35)

Third movement (Molto vivace; "Very fast and lively"). Dvořák said this scherzo was intended to depict "a feast in the woods where the Indians dance." Yet the only time Dvořák actually heard "live" American Indian music was when he saw a performance of Buffalo Bill's Wild West Show! Needless to say, the commercialized songs had little to do with authentic Indian melodies. For most listeners this scherzo is more suggestive of frolicking Bohemian peasants than dancing American Indians.

Fourth movement (Allegro con fuoco; "Fast with fire"). The stirring finale presents a succession of exciting themes in the brasses while also recalling melodies from the three previous movements, thereby binding the symphony into a satisfying whole.

LATE ROMANTIC PROGRAM MUSIC

Program music, as we have seen (pages 252–54), was at the very heart of the creative works of the early Romantics, like Berlioz, Mendelssohn, and Liszt. While Brahms, later in the century, held fast to the Classical ideal of absolute music*, most late Romantic composers continued to yield to the allure of music inspired by some sort of extramusical element—a play, an experience with nature, even a painting. The late-nineteenth-century composer who achieved the greatest popular success in writing program music was Peter Tchaikovsky.

Peter Tchaikovsky (1840–1893)

Tchaikovsky was born in 1840 into an upper-middle-class family in provincial Russia. He showed a keen ear for music in his earliest years, and by the age of six could speak fluent French and German (an excellent musical ear and a capacity to learn foreign languages often go hand in hand). As to his career, his parents determined that law would provide the easiest route to fame and fortune. Thus, young Tchaikovsky spent seven years, 1852–1859, at the School of

FIGURE 15–7
Peter Tchaikovsky.

Jurisprudence in St. Petersburg and four more years as a clerk in the Ministry of Justice. Then, like Robert Schumann before him, he realized that it was music, not law, that fired his imagination. He made his way to the St. Petersburg Conservatory of Music, from which he was graduated in 1866. That same year, he went to the newly formed Moscow Conservatory, where he assumed the position of professor of harmony and musical composition.

In truth, it was not his official position in Moscow that supported Tchaikovsky during most of his mature years, but rather a private arrangement with an eccentric patroness, Madame Nadezhda von Meck (Fig. 15–8). This wealthy, music-loving widow furnished him an annual income of six thousand rubles on the condition that she and the composer never meet—a requirement not always easily fulfilled, since the two sometimes resided at the same summer estate. In addition to this annuity, in 1881 Tsar Alexander III awarded Tchaikovsky an annual pension of three thousand rubles in recognition of his importance to Russian cultural life. Being a man of independent means meant that Tchaikovsky not only was able to travel extensively in Western Europe, and even to America, but could also enjoy the freedom he found so necessary to creative activity.

Tchaikovsky's creative output touched every genre of nineteenth-century music: opera, song, string quartet, piano sonata, concerto, symphony, and symphonic poem. It is, however, his large-scale works for orchestra that have best stood the test of time. Tchaikovsky's musical strengths—sweeping melodies, colorful instrumentations, dramatic contrasts, and grand gestures—could only be fully expressed by a large symphony orchestra. Not surprisingly, he also achieved unparalleled success as a composer of orchestral music for ballet, a type of music in which short bursts of colorful sounds and evocative rhythms are necessary to create distinctly different moods for each new scene. His *Swan Lake* (1876), *Sleeping Beauty* (1889), and *Nutcracker* (1892) are the most popular works in the entire repertoire of grand Romantic ballet, beloved by young and old alike.

Despite his considerable popular success, Tchaikovsky's life was not a happy one. He was a manic-depressive, a neurotic, and a hypochondriac. He was also a homosexual, and this was a time when there was little sympathy for homosexuality or awareness of its biological causes. He died suddenly in 1893, at the age of fifty-three, after drinking unboiled water during an epidemic of cholera.

Concert Overture: *The 1812 Overture*

Tchaikovsky was not an ultra-nationalist like Modest Musorgsky and the other members of the Russian Five*. Almost every year of his adult life he undertook at least one extended voyage to Germany, France, and/or Italy. Consequently, Tchaikovsky's musical style is more cosmopolitan than nationalistic. His six symphonies, for example, belong more to the German symphonic tradition than any purely Russian practice. Yet occasionally, when compelled by a royal command or an official commission, Tchaikovsky would don his Russian hat and produce a piece with a patriotic appearance. Such was the case with the creation of what has become his most popular work, *The 1812 Overture.*

In 1880 the leaders of Moscow asked Tchaikovsky to compose a piece to commemorate the Russian victory over the French army of Napoleon in 1812.

FIGURE 15–8

Nadezhda von Meck was the widow of an engineer who made a fortune constructing the first railroads in Russia during the 1860s and 1870s. She used her money, in part, to support composers such as Tchaikovsky and, later, Claude Debussy.

Novosti Information Agency, London

the cosmopolitan becomes a nationalist

The Russian Front and The 1812 Overture

In 1942, at the height of his power, Adolph Hitler drove the German army deep into Russia and up to the walls of Stalingrad. But the invaders went no farther. They were checked by tenacious Russian troops and an equally fierce Russian winter (these events are portrayed in the film *Enemy at the Gates*). The Germans began to retreat, and their tightly wound war machine started to unravel. Pushed first from the east by the Russians and, beginning in June 1944, from the west by the Americans, British, and Canadians, the once mighty Third Reich ultimately collapsed.

Hitler should have learned from history. One hundred and thirty years earlier a similar megalomaniac, Napoleon Bonaparte, had fallen into this trap. In the spring of 1812, Napoleon marched a huge army into Russia. Roughly 612,000 men, 333,000 horses and 3,000 cannons crossed the Polish-Russian border. The outnumbered Russians strategically withdrew deeper and deeper into the interior of their vast country. They fought sporadically, as at Borodino on August 20, 1812, and then retreated. Ultimately, Napoleon took Moscow. But it was a hollow victory, for the Russians had set ablaze their own city. Finding little sustenance in Moscow, and with his soldiers dying all around from starvation and disease, Napoleon began the thousand-mile trek back to Western Europe. During the retreat, temperatures reached 29 degrees below zero Fahrenheit. Of the 612,000

Bettmann/CORBIS

Napoleon and his French troops retreating from Russia during the Franco-Russian War of 1812.

troops who had started out in 1812, fewer than 100,000 returned. So weakened was the Grande Armée by this Russian fiasco that the European enemies of Napoleon easily invaded France and captured him. There would be no French domination of Europe and Western Asia in 1812, just as there would be no German hegemony under Hitler in 1942. Ironically, today our memory of the decisive Russian military victory of 1812 is kept alive mainly by the music of Tchaikovsky's stirring *The 1812 Overture*.

Immediately the composer formulated a plan of attack: He would enlist battalions of brass and percussion to simulate battle, joyful church bells to sound at the victorious climax, and even cannons to be fired by the conductor (via an electrical hookup). By simulating through sound the events of the Franco-Russian War of 1812, Tchaikovsky produced a splendid example of program music*. By incorporating melodies from both France and Russia, he also fashioned an example of musical nationalism*. The French national anthem, the **Marseillaise,** appears, and so too does a derivative of it to represent the French cavalry. For musical symbols of Russia, Tchaikovsky borrowed a Russian Orthodox hymn (*Save us, O Lord*), the Russian national anthem (*God Save the Czar*), a Russian folk song, and even a melody from his own first opera. This ragbag of themes he shaped into sonata–allegro form, holding back (like a battalion in reserve) the Russian national anthem for the climactic coda.

program music

Ultimately, *The 1812 Overture* was first heard in Moscow on August 20, 1882, the seventieth anniversary of the Russian victory at Borodino (see boxed essay). Because Tchaikovsky's piece opened the festivities on that commemorative day, it is called an overture. Today the work is heard in the United States on the Fourth of July to celebrate the American national holiday, and

Tchaikovsky's musical pyrotechnics are usually followed by fireworks in the night sky.

Is *The 1812 Overture* a great piece of music? Tchaikovsky had his doubts, for he wrote to his patroness Nadezhda von Meck soon after its completion: "The overture will be very loud and noisy, but I wrote it with no warm feeling of love, and therefore there will probably be no artistic merits in it." Certainly, there are moments that blare with showy noise; but there are also passages that shine with brilliant orchestration. Is this a work of noisy bombast or inspired genius? You be the judge.

beauty or bombast?

Listening Guide

WWW

Peter Tchaikovsky
The 1812 Overture (1882)

6CD 5/1

Form: sonata–allegro

INTRODUCTION

0:00   Russian Orthodox hymn in middle strings (cellos and violas)

1:24   Woodwinds extend hymn

1:58   Agitated strings and plaintive oboe offer portent of things to come

2:58   Brasses and percussion heighten tension; low strings release it

EXPOSITION

3:40   First theme part 1: French cavalry theme in French horns with snare drum

4:46   Confrontation: rapid counterpoint in the strings

5:29   First theme part 2: *Marseillaise* enters in French horns and then cornets

6:08   Transition, recall of *Marseillaise* (6:24) and fade out

6:53   Second theme in violins: tender memory of Russian home and hearth

7:44   Woodwinds take over second theme

8:34   Concluding theme: folk song in woodwinds accompanied by tambourine

DEVELOPMENT

9:25   Contrapuntal confrontation involving fragments of the *Marseillaise*

10:00   Bass drum, timpani, and cymbals suggest heavy artillery and swords

RECAPITULATION

10:36   First theme part 2: *Marseillaise* in brasses

11:05   Second theme (Russian home and hearth) slower and more expansive

11:52   Concluding theme: Russian folk song now in strings

CODA

12:18   *Marseillaise* starts in French horns and builds to loud climax in trumpets

12:53   Bass drum with optional cannons

13:04   Long downward spiral with ritard

(Continued on next page)

13:41 Russian Orthodox hymn played by brasses with joyous church bells

15:03 French cavalry returns in trumpets and snare drums

15:14 Russian National Anthem sounds in low brasses;
French cavalry in trumpets; cannons fire from both sides

15:48 French cavalry in retreat (descent with *diminuendo*)

(Listening Exercise 36)

THE ORCHESTRAL LIED

We began our discussion of Romantic music with two art songs* of Franz Schubert (pages 264–71), and we end it with an orchestral song by Gustav Mahler (1860–1911). This is an appropriate framework in which to experience Romantic music, for the nineteenth century was marked throughout by an exceptionally strong union between music and poetry. If poetry had the power to communicate feelings of love, grief, pain, or longing, these typically Romantic sentiments could not fail to be intensified when set to music. Thus, the art song came into being in the early nineteenth century. At about the same time, Beethoven incorporated song into the finale of his Ninth ("Choral") Symphony (1824), as Berlioz and Liszt would also do in their later programmatic symphonies. Naturally, it was only a matter of time before the genres of art song and symphony began to interact and influence each other, producing something new: the orchestral *Lied*. In its simplest form the **orchestral Lied** was an art song in which the full orchestra replaced the piano as the medium of accompaniment. Yet because the orchestra could supply more color and add a greater number of contrapuntal lines, the orchestral *Lied* grew to be longer, denser, and more complex than the piano-supported art song. Berlioz, Brahms, and Wagner all experimented with the orchestral *Lied* in various ways, but not until Gustav Mahler did this hybrid musical genre reach maturity.

an orchestrally accompanied song

FIGURE 15–9
Gustav Mahler.

CORBIS/Bettmann

Gustav Mahler (1860–1911)

Gustav Mahler was born in 1860 into a middle-class Jewish family in Bohemia, then part of the Austrian Empire but now encompassed by the Czech Republic. At the age of fifteen he was admitted to the prestigious Vienna Conservatory of Music, where he studied musical composition and conducting. Mahler felt his mission in life was to conduct—to interpret—the works of the masters ("suffer for my great masters," he said). Like most young conductors, he began his career in provincial towns, gradually working his way to larger and more important musical centers. His itinerary as resident conductor took him, among other places, to Kassel (1883–1884), Prague (1885–1886), Leipzig (1886–1888), Budapest (1888–1891), Hamburg (1891–1897), and finally back to Vienna.

In May 1897 Mahler returned triumphantly to his adopted city as director of the Vienna Court Opera, a position Mozart had once coveted. The next year he also assumed directorship of the Vienna Philharmonic, then and now one of the world's great orchestras. But Mahler was a demanding autocrat—a musical tyrant—in search of an artistic ideal. That he drove himself as hard as he pushed others was little comfort to the singers and instrumentalists who had to endure his wrath during rehearsals. After ten stormy but artistically successful seasons (1897–1907), Mahler was dismissed from the Vienna Opera. About this time he accepted a call from New York to take charge of the Metropolitan Opera and, eventually, he conducted the New York Philharmonic as well. Here, too, there was both controversy and acclaim. And here, too, at least at the Met, his contract was not renewed after two years, though he stayed on longer, until February 1911, with the Philharmonic. He died in Vienna in May 1911 of a lingering streptococcal infection that had attacked his weak heart—a sad end to an obsessive and somewhat tormented life.

songs and symphonies

his career

Mahler is unique among composers in that as a mature artist he wrote only orchestral songs and symphonies. These he managed to create during the summers when freed of his conducting duties. His five orchestral song cycles* typically contain settings of four, five, or six poems by a single author. *Kindertotenlieder* (*Children's Death Songs*, 1901–1904), for example, is a collection of five songs for voice and orchestra to words by Friedrich Rückert (1788–1866). They express the poet's overwhelming grief on the loss of two young children to scarlet fever. By tragic coincidence, no sooner had Mahler finished setting Rückert's painfully personal memorials than his own eldest daughter died of scarlet fever at the age of four, a loss from which the intensely sensitive composer never recovered.

songs influence symphonies

What is also unique to Mahler is the extent to which he borrowed from his own orchestral *Lieder* when he sat down to compose a symphony. It is as if the songs served as a musical repository or vault to which the composer could return for inspiration while wrestling with the problems of a large, multimovement work for orchestra. Mahler's First Symphony (1889), though entirely instrumental, makes use of melodies already present in his song cycle *Lieder eines fahrenden Gesellen* (*Songs of a Wayfaring Lad*, 1885). His Second (1894), Third (1896), and Fourth (1901) symphonies incorporate various portions of the *Wonderhorn Songs* (1892–1899) as solo vocal parts within the symphony. Symphonies Five (1902) and Six (1904) are again purely instrumental, but once more incorporate preexisting melodies, in this case from *Children's Death Songs* and *Five Rückert Songs* (1901–1902). Altogether Mahler wrote nine symphonies, seven of which make use of his own orchestral *Lieder* or other preexisting vocal music.

FIGURE 15–10

A cartoon of Mahler conducting his "Symphony of a Thousand" in 1910. A German caption says that there is no audience because everyone is needed on stage.

But to Mahler a symphony was much more than just an extended orchestral *Lied*. "The symphony is the world; it must embrace everything," he once said. And so he tried to embrace every sort of music within it. There are folk dances, popular songs, military marches, off-stage bands, bugle calls, and even Gregorian chant* at various points in his symphonies. What results is a collage of sound on the grandest scale, one achieved, in part, by employing massive forces and a greatly extended sense of time. Mahler's Symphony No. 2, for example, calls for ten horns and eight trumpets, and lasts an hour and a half. The first performance of his Symphony No. 8 in Munich in 1910 involved 858 singers and 171 instrumentalists. With good reason it has been nicknamed the "Symphony of a Thousand" (Fig. 15–10).

Life Among the Artists

In 1901 middle-aged Gustav Mahler married the dazzling Viennese beauty Alma Schindler (1879–1964). She was the daughter of a noted Austrian landscape painter and was in her own right a talented pianist and budding composer. As a precondition to their marriage, however, Mahler insisted that Alma give up her own career in music to serve his art. "You have only one profession from now on: to make me happy," he wrote her.

Given this attitude and the fact that she was just slightly more than half Mahler's age, it is not surprising that their marriage was not a tranquil one. At one point, in 1910, Mahler consulted the famous Sigmund Freud, father of psychoanalysis, in hopes of coming to a better understanding of himself and his union with Alma. (Freud declined to treat Mahler, apparently for fear of destroying the latter's creative process.) After the composer's death in 1911, Alma went on to have affairs with the conductor Bruno Walter and the painter Oskar Kokoschka, and later to marry the architect Walter Gropius and the novelist Franz Werfel. Obviously, Alma Schindler had a keen eye for talent. Her tongue was equally sharp, as can be seen in the following extracts from her memoirs *And the Bridge*

Photo by H. J. Nieman

Alma Schindler at the age of nineteen in 1899, the year she met Gustav Mahler.

Was Love, which describe Mahler's work habits at their lakeside summer home in southern Austria.

"Mahler got up at six or six-thirty every day. As soon as he was awake, he rang for the cook, who promptly prepared his breakfast and carried it up a steep, slippery trail to his forest study, two hundred feet above the house. (She was forbidden to use the regular road, lest he meet her on his way up; before work, he could not stand seeing anyone.) The study was a one-room brick hut with a door and three windows, a grand piano, a bookshelf with the collected works of Kant and Goethe. No music but Bach's. About noon he came down, changed, and went for a swim. . . . Our afternoons were spent walking. Rain or shine, we walked for three or four hours, or rowed around the gleaming, heat-spewing lake. . . . Often he stopped and stood with the sun burning down on his hatless skull, drew out a notebook, wrote, thought, wrote some more. Sometimes he beat time in the air before writing the notes down. This could go on for an hour or more, with me sitting on a tree trunk or in the grass, not daring to look at him. Mahler made sure that everything in his personal life revolved around his own genius."

Gustav Mahler was the last in the long line of great German symphonists that extended back through Brahms, Schubert, and Beethoven to Mozart and, ultimately, to Haydn. What had begun as a modest instrumental genre with a limited emotional range had grown in the course of the nineteenth century into a monumental structure, the musical equivalent, in Mahler's view, of the entire cosmos.

ORCHESTRAL *LIED, I AM LOST TO THE WORLD*, FROM THE *FIVE RÜCKERT SONGS* (1901–1902)

It is the everyday world, not the grand cosmos, that concerns Mahler in his setting of Friedrich Rückert's *Ich bin der Welt abhanden gekommen (I Am Lost to the World)*. Rückert was a minor German Romantic poet whose verse, nonetheless, enjoyed favor with Schubert, Schumann, and Brahms because of its structural regularity. During the summers of 1901 and 1902, Mahler chose to set five among the many hundreds of poems by Rückert. The subject of these five verses was dear to the composer because it expresses in various ways his outlook on life and on art.

I Am Lost to the World speaks of the artist's growing remoteness from the travails of everyday life and of withdrawal into a private, heavenly world of music, here signified by the final word *Lied* (song). Although the poem has three stanzas,

an artist withdraws into the world of music

FIGURE 15–11

Mahler conducted during the winter and composed during the summer, usually at a villa in the Austrian mountains. He made sure that each summer residence was supplied with a "forest hut" where he could go each morning to compose without distraction. The one at Maiernigg near Klagenfurt, Austria, was the hut in which he created the orchestral *Lied, I Am Lost to the World.*

Mahler chose not a strophic setting*, but a through-composed* one. The first strophe sets the mood of the song as a mournful English horn begins to play a halting melody, one then picked up and extended by the voice. The second stanza moves to a faster tempo and more rapid declamation in the voice, as if the mundane world should be quickly left behind. The final strophe returns to a slow tempo. It also sets the notes of the bass on the beat and on the roots of triads*, all of which help project a settled, satisfied feeling—the self-absorbed poet-composer has withdrawn into the peaceful world of art. Toward the end Mahler shows how music has the capacity to sum up in a few brief sounds the entire progress of the poem, the movement from the dissonance of the world to the peace of the inner self. First the strings (at 6:23) play an extended dissonance (F against E♭), which resolves to a consonance (E♭ against E♭), and this is repeated at the very end (6:39) by the English horn, "dying out expressively" as the composer requests. The desire to escape from this dissonant world into the consonant realm of art has been fulfilled.

I Am Lost to the World has been called Mahler's best orchestral *Lied.* That he made use of some of this same music in the beautiful slow movement of his Symphony No. 5 suggests that these musical ideas were important to him and express, as he said at the time, "his very self." Both song and symphony have a certain world-weariness about them, as if Mahler had a premonition that both the artist's life and the Romantic era were coming to an end.

Listening Guide

Gustav Mahler   6CD 5/2
Orchestral *Lied, I Am Lost to the World,*
from the *Five Rückert Songs* (1901–1902)

Form: through composed

0:00	English horn haltingly rises with the melody		
1:00	Voice enters and extends the melody	Ich bin der Welt abhanden gekommen, mit der ich sonst viele Zeit verdorben; sie hat so lange nichts von mir vernommen,	I am lost to the world, in which I've squandered so much time; it has known nothing of me for so long,
1:56	English horn returns with the melody	sie mag wohl glauben, ich sei gestorben!	it may well think that I am dead!
2:34	Triplets in harp; faster tempo, recitative quality in the voice	Es ist mir auch gar nichts daran gelegen, ob sie mich für gestorben hält. Ich kann auch gar nichts sagen dagegen, denn wirklich bin ich gestorben der Welt.	I don't really care, if it takes me for dead. Nor can I contradict, for really I am dead to the world.
3:39	Melody returns in English horn; slow, peaceful conclusion	Ich bin gestorben dem Weltgetümmel und ruh' in einem stillen Gebiet! Ich leb' allein in meinem Himmel, in meinem Lieben, in meinem Lied.	I am dead to the world's commotion, and rest in a world of peace. I live alone in my own heaven, in my love, in my song.
5:47	English horn returns with melody		
6:23	Dissonance–consonance in violins		
6:39	Dissonance–consonance in English horn		

Listening Exercises

34 . . . .

Johannes Brahms   6CD 4/12; 2CD 2/6
Violin Concerto in D major (1878)
Third movement, *Allegro giocoso, ma non troppo vivace*
(fast and playful, but not too lively)

We derive our term "concerto" from the Italian word *concertare*. A concerto involves a concerted effort, and sometimes a friendly competition, between a soloist and an orchestra. In the finale of Brahms' Violin Concerto, the violin and orchestra vie for control of the theme, and sometimes there is a real tug of war between the two. At other moments, however, the orchestra merely accompanies the virtuosic flights of the soloist. The following questions focus on the nature of the musical "struggle" between violin and orchestra. Who in fact does "win"?

At the beginning of the movement the refrain is heard three times. Indicate below which is true for each of the three statements.

    a. The solo violin has the refrain and the orchestra accompanies.

    b. The orchestra has the refrain and the solo violin is silent.

1. 0:00–0:11 _____
2. 0:12–0:22 _____
3. 0:38–0:49 _____
4. (1:09–1:20) At the end of the transition, what is the relationship between the forces?

    a. The violin plays runs against pizzicato accompaniment in the orchestra.

    b. The orchestra has the melody and violin plays counterpoint.

5. (1:21–1:25) Now a new theme enters, specifically a rising scale. Which is true?

    a. There is a true dialogue here: the violin goes up with the theme, the orchestra comes down with it.

    b. Only the orchestra has the theme, going both up and down with it.

6. (2:32–2:48) Once again, there is a transition to a new theme. Which is true?

    a. The violin plays difficult arpeggios to a background accompaniment of simple chords in the orchestra.

    b. The orchestra has the melody and the violin plays pizzicato.

7. (5:07–5:23) The refrain returns. Which is true?

    a. The violin has the melody and the orchestra is silent.

    b. The orchestra has the melody and the violin is silent.

8. Now an unusual moment (5:35–5:55):

    a. The orchestra plays alone and the violin gradually sneaks back in.

    b. The violin plays entirely by itself and the orchestra gradually sneaks back in.

9. Following the violin cadenza (6:47–6:54), the refrain is transformed into a march-like melody (6:55). Which is true?

    a. The violin plays the transformed refrain, and the orchestra provides an accompaniment.

b. The orchestra plays the transformed refrain, and the violin provides an accompaniment.

10. What, in your opinion, is the outcome of this musical contest (concerto)?
    a. It's a draw.   b. The violin is dominant.   c. The orchestra is dominant.

35

Antonín Dvořák   6CD 4/14
Symphony "From the New World"
Second movement, *Largo* (Very slow and broad)

With its passion, intense lyricism, grand gestures, and generally consonant sound, this movement conveys the essence of musical Romanticism. The following questions attempt to highlight the qualities of the Romantic musical style as well as the special colors of the large nineteenth-century orchestra. If you are uncertain about any of your answers, review Chapters 3 and 12.

1. The introduction played by the brass choir is a good example of the bold harmonic shifts that often mark Romantic music. This is also a good example of
   a. homophonic texture   b. monophonic texture   c. polyphonic texture

2. The low brasses begin the movement, specifically the low trombones and tuba. These instruments were introduced into the symphony orchestra during which century?
   a. seventeenth   b. eighteenth   c. nineteenth

3. The English horn was an instrument that came to prominence during the nineteenth century, primarily because of the distant, mournful quality of its sounds. In fact, the English horn belongs to which family of instruments?
   a. brasses   b. strings   c. woodwinds   d. percussion

4. Now the French horns play an echo of the English horn theme. The French horn, too, was beloved by Romantic composers because of the traditional association of the hunting horn with the outdoors, mountains, and nature generally. Which is true about the French horn?
   a. It is a brass instrument introduced into the orchestra during the Baroque period.
   b. It is a woodwind instrument introduced into the orchestra during the Romantic period.

5. (5:06–5:30) Here the music assumes a more agitated tone; the tempo increases and the flute and oboe play a new theme. Behind this the strings add an element of tension by employing which string technique?
   a. pizzicato   b. staccato   c. tremolo

6. (5:32–6:18) A second new theme appears in the clarinets and beneath it the low strings play a pizzicato bass. This style of bass line is not one particular to the Romantic era but first appeared in the Baroque period. It is called a
   a. vibrato bass   b. cabaletta bass   c. walking bass   d. pedal point

7. (6:41–7:12) Romantic composers traditionally conveyed a feeling of passion by having one particular instrument play with intensity and usually with vibrato in its highest range. This instrument, which can be heard here carrying the melody with a sense of passion, is the
   a. English horn   b. violin   c. cello

8. (8:20–8:38) The Romantics, as we have seen, were enamored with nature and the outdoors. As represented by this passage, they usually chose which family of instruments to suggest singing or chirping birds?
a. strings   b. brasses   c. woodwinds

9. (8:30–9:15) The nineteenth century was nothing musically if not the era of the grand gesture. Here we have a grand climax, which is brought about in no small measure by the use of dynamics. Which of the following symbols correctly indicates the progress of the level of volume (dynamics) throughout this passage?

a. $<$ b. $>$ c. $<>$

10. Let us assume, for the sake of argument, that Dvořák was not influenced in any way by Longfellow's poem *Hiawatha*. The *Largo* from the Symphony "From the New World" is then an example of
a. program music   b. absolute music   c. poetic music

Peter Tchaikovsky   6CD 5/1
Concert Overture, *The 1812 Overture*

How do you create a battle in music? This question must have run through Tchaikovsky's mind when he set about writing *The 1812 Overture*. His solution was to use a few basic gestures of musical expression to make the music sound out its meaning. A simple example: to represent fighting at its most intense, Tchaikovsky makes the music loud and full of cymbal crashes (swords) and bass drum thuds (cannons). He also, of course, evokes French and Russian melodies to symbolize the two opposing forces. The following questions ask you to think about the means by which a composer creates a piece of program music. How are musical gestures and symbols used to tell a story or recreate an event purely in sound?

1. (0:00) The overture opens with a view of which side, the French or the Russian?
a. The French, because a French hymn sounds in the cellos and violas.
b. The Russian, because a Russian hymn sounds in the cellos and violas.

2. (0:00–1:23) The people represented here appear to be peaceful and unified because
a. they have their act together. The music is all quietly monophonic.
b. there is no conflict (counterpoint). The music is all quietly homophonic.
c. there is no homophony. The music is all quietly contrapuntal.

3. (2:05–3:41) How does Tchaikovsky create a feeling of rising and then falling tension?
a. The music gradually rises in pitch and gets louder, then falls and becomes quiet.
b. The music starts *fortissimo*, drops in pitch through a quiet section, and ends *fortissimo*.

4. (5:29–5:43; and again 5:44–5:59) When the French, represented by the *Marseillaise*, enter they do so in the heroic brasses. Which statement is true about the presentation of the *Marseillaise*?

a. The French horns come in after the cornets and play each phrase three times in a row.

b. The French horns play one phrase of the melody twice and the cornets two phrases just once.

5. (6:53–7:46) Why is it reasonable for the listener to intuit that this is **not** a battle scene?

a. There are no crashing or banging percussion instruments.

b. There are no heroically blaring brasses.

c. The strings are playing the melody with a warm, lovely vibrato.

d. All of the above.

6. (8:34–9:00) This is another peaceful scene built around a Russian folk song. Which of the following is **not** true?

a. There are no heroically blaring brasses.

b. A percussion instrument, the tambourine, accompanies the folk song.

c. The strings are playing the melody with a warm, lovely vibrato.

7. (9:25–10:35) The development section is brief and it seems to be rather one-sided. The musical symbols of which country dominate the development?

a. France   b. Russia

8. One of the ways that Tchaikovsky suggests musical conflict is by the use of rhythmic syncopation* (playing off the beat) which throws the music into metrical conflict. At the height of the development section (10:21–10:25), which instrument is playing syncopation?

a. trumpet   b. flute   c. French horn   d. cymbal

9. (12:39–12:52) Again, Tchaikovsky uses a simple musical gesture to suggest growing tension and an imminent confrontation.

a. The music rises through the use of melodic sequence and grows louder.

b. The music falls through the use of melodic sequence and becomes *fortissimo*.

c. The music falls through the use of melodic sequence and becomes *piano*.

10. (13:45–15:00) How do we know the Russians have won?

a. The *Marseillaise* sounds below in the heroic brasses.

b. The *Marseillaise* sounds forth in retrograde* motion, signaling a musical retreat.

c. Simulated Russian church bells peal joyfully with the orchestra.

Key Words

absolute music (323)	*Marseillaise* (331)	orchestral *Lied* (332)
double stops (323)	Nadezhda von Meck	Alma Schindler
A German Requiem (325)	(330)	Mahler (335)

Bulloz

From Romantic to Modern: Impressionism

Romantic music reached its apogee during the late nineteenth century in the grandiose works of Wagner, Tchaikovsky, Brahms, and Mahler. But by 1900 this German-dominated musical empire was in danger of crumbling, shaken by forces both within and without. Some composers outside the mainstream of Romanticism were becoming downright hostile toward the German style, epitomized by the music of Wagner. Not surprisingly, the most powerful anti-German sentiment was felt in France. (France and Germany went to war in 1870 and would do so again in 1914.) After first embracing Wagner during the 1870s and 1880s, the avant-garde of French music had, by the 1890s, turned antagonistic. It began to ridicule the sentimentality of Romanticism in general and the grandiose structures of the Germans in particular. German music was said to be too heavy, too pretentious, too bombastic. Wagner's system of obvious leitmotifs* was now deemed overly simplistic—just as clumsy as one of his Nordic giants. Meaningful expression, they said, might be communicated in more subtle ways, in something other than sheer volume of sound and epic length.

IMPRESSIONISM IN PAINTING AND MUSIC

the Impressionists:
the most popular of all painters

The movement that arose in France in opposition to German Romantic music has been given the name **Impressionism** (Fig. 16–1). We are, of course, more familiar with this term as a designation for a school of French painters living and working in Paris during the last decades of the nineteenth century. That group included Claude Monet (1840–1926), Edgar Degas (1834–1917), Camille Pissarro (1830–1903), Alfred Sisley (1839–1899), Auguste Renoir (1841–1919), and the American Mary Cassatt (1844–1926). Impressionist painters were not overtly anti-German like their musical counterparts. There was no need to be, for French painting had a long and secure tradition (see Figs. 6–14, 12–2, and 13–14), one not subject to threat of foreign domination. Their rebellion was against the traditional, academic style of painting of their native land.

an act of rebellion

The Impressionist movement in painting began in the early 1870s when Monet and his colleagues were forbidden to show their canvases in the official Parisian Salon. Consequently, they launched their own exhibition. In the uproar that followed, the artists were jeeringly called "impressionists" for the sometimes-vague quality of their art. The painters accepted the name, partly as an act of defiance against the establishment, and soon the term was universally adopted.

It is ironic that this style of French painting generated such controversy, for no school of painters is now more popular with the general public than the Impressionists. Indeed, judging by museum attendance and the number of books and reproductions sold, there is an almost limitless enthusiasm for the works of Monet, Degas, Renoir, and their associates—precisely the paintings that the artists' contemporaries mocked and jeered. But what is it about the Impressionist style that then caused such a furor?

The Impressionists were the first to turn against representational art, the idea that a painting should exactly represent an object, as in a photograph. Instead, they tried to recreate the impression that the object produced on their senses. The key here is light: The Impressionists saw all objects as awash in vibrant rays of light and sought to capture the aura that the light-bathed object created in the eye of the beholder. To accomplish this they covered their canvases with small, dablike brushstrokes in which light was broken down into spots of color. This creates a sense of constant movement and fluidity. Shapes are not clearly defined but blurred, more suggested than delineated. Minor details disappear. Sunlight is everywhere and everything shimmers (Fig. 16-2).

As impressions and sensations became paramount for these painters, it is not surprising that they showed an intensified interest in music. What art form is more elusive and suggestive? What medium allows the receiver—the lis-

FIGURE 16–1

The painting that gave its name to an epoch, Claude Monet's *Impression: Sunrise,* was exhibited at the first group exhibition organized by Monet, Renoir, Degas, and Pissarro in Paris in 1874. The ships, rowboats, and other elements in the early morning light are more suggested than fully drawn. Said the critic Louis Leroy derisively of this painting at the time: "Wallpaper in its most embryonic state is more finished than that seascape."

Musée Marmottan, Paris/SuperStock

tener—more freedom to interpret the sensations he or she perceives? Painters began to speak in musical terms. Paul Gauguin (1848–1903) referred to the harmonies of line and color as the "music of painting," and Vincent Van Gogh (1853–1890) suggested "using color as the music of tones." Paul Cézanne (1839–1906) painted an "overture" in homage to Wagner, while James Whistler (1834–1903), an American who worked in Paris in the 1860s and 1880s, created "nocturnes" and "symphonies" (see Fig. 13–16). The artist envied the musician's good fortune to work in a medium in which flux and change could be continually expressed—rather than one that required the artist to seize the moment and fix it on canvas. At the same time Claude Debussy, the musician whose work most consistently displayed the Impressionist style in music, found inspiration for his work in the visual arts. He called various collections of his pieces *Sketches, Images,* and *Prints.* Rare are the moments in history when the aesthetic aims of painters and musicians were as closely allied.

Claude Debussy (1862–1918)

Claude Debussy, French musician and innovator par excellence, was born in 1862 into a modest family living in a small town outside Paris. Since neither of his parents was musical, it came as a surprise when their son demonstrated talent at the keyboard. At the age of ten he was sent off to the Paris Conservatory for lessons in piano, composition, and music theory. Owing to his skills as a performer he was soon engaged for summer work in the household of Nadezhda von Meck, a wealthy patroness of the arts and the principal supporter of Tchaikovsky (see Fig. 15–8). This employment took him, in turn, to Italy, Russia, and Vienna. In 1884 he won the Prix de Rome, an official prize in composition supported by the French government, one that required a three-year stay in Rome. But Debussy was not happy in the Eternal City. He preferred the Bohemian life of Paris, the atmosphere of the bistros and the cafes.

Returning to Paris more or less permanently in 1887, the young Frenchman continued to learn his craft and search for his own independent voice as a composer. He had some minor successes, and yet, as he said in 1893, "There are still things that I am not able to do—create masterpieces, for example." But the next year, in 1894, he did just that. With the completion of *Prélude à L'Après-midi d'un Faune (Prelude to The Afternoon of a Faun),* he gave to the public what has become his most enduring orchestral work. Debussy's later compositions, including his opera *Pelléas et Mélisande* (1902), the symphonic poem *La Mer (The Sea,* 1905), and his two books of *Preludes* for piano, met with less popular favor. Critics complained of a certain formlessness and a lack of melody. Today, with the advantage of a century of hindsight, these works are seen as early beacons pointing straight down the road to musical modernism. *La Mer* has become a staple in the repertoire of every professional orchestra, *Pelléas* is a standing production of every major opera house, and the *Preludes* form part of the required literature for every would-be concert pianist. Illness and the outbreak of World War I (1914) brought Debussy's musical productivity to a virtual standstill. He died of cancer in the spring of 1918 while the guns of the German army were shelling Paris from the north.

Peter Willi

FIGURES 16–2 AND 16–3

(above) Claude Monet, *Woman with Umbrella* (1886). The Impressionist canvas is not a finished surface in the traditional sense. Rather, the painter breaks down light into separate dabs of color and juxtaposes them for the viewer's eye to reassemble. Here bold brushstrokes convey an astonishing sense of movement, freshness, and sparkling light. (below) Claude Debussy at the age of twenty-four.

Visual Arts Library, London

FIGURE 16–4

The poet Stéphane Mallarmé, author of *The Afternoon of a Faun,* as painted by the great predecessor of the Impressionists, Edouard Manet (1832–1883). Mallarmé was a friend and artistic mentor of the composer Debussy.

a Symbolist poem

FIGURE 16–5

Mallarmé's *The Afternoon of a Faun* created something of a sensation among late nineteenth-century French artists. This painting by Ker-Xavier Roussel (1867–1944) is just one of several such representations of the Faun surrounded by woodland nymphs.

PRELUDE TO THE AFTERNOON OF A FAUN (1894)

Debussy spent his time more in the company of poets and painters than with musicians. His orchestral *Prelude to The Afternoon of a Faun,* in fact, was written to precede a staged reading of the poem *The Afternoon of a Faun* by his friend and mentor Stéphane Mallarmé (Fig. 16–4).

Mallarmé was the spiritual leader of a group of versifiers in *fin-du-siècle* Paris called the **Symbolists,** poets whose aesthetic aims were in harmony with those of the Impressionist painters. They worked to create a suggestive verse in which the sound of the word, and the associations that that sound might produce, were more important than the literal meaning of the word. Said Mallarmé: "To name an object is to destroy its poetic enjoyment; the idea is to suggest the object." Symbolism is certainly at the heart of Mallarmé's evocative *The Afternoon of a Faun,* which applies suggestive language to an ancient Greek theme. The faun of Mallarmé's poem is not a young deer but a satyr (a mythological beast that is half man, half goat). He spends his days in pursuit of sexual gratification at the expense of the nymphs who inhabit the forest. On this afternoon we see the faun, exhausted from the morning's escapades, reclining on the forest floor in the still air of the midday heat. He contemplates future conquests while piping listlessly on his flute. A passage from the poem suggests the dreamlike mood, vague and elusive, that Debussy was challenged to recreate.

> No murmur of water in the woodland scene,
> Bathed only in the sounds of my flute.
> And the only breeze, except for my two pipes,
> Blows itself empty long before
> It can scatter the sound in an arid rain.
> On a horizon unmoved by a ripple
> This sound, visible and serene,
> Mounts to the heavens, an inspired wisp.

Debussy wisely made no effort to follow Mallarmé's poem closely—the poem is just a succession of feelings, not a narrative program. Debussy, moreover, was no composer of programmatic music like Berlioz or Tchaikovsky. As he said at the time of the first performance in December 1894: "My *Prelude* is really a sequence of mood paintings, throughout which the desire and dreams of the Faun move in the heat of the midday sun." When Mallarmé had heard the music, he, in turn, said the following about Debussy's musical response to the poem: "I never expected anything like it. The music prolongs the emotion of my poem and paints its scenery more passionately than colors could."

Significantly, both musician and poet refer to *Prelude to The Afternoon of a Faun* in terms of painting (Fig. 16–5). But how does one create a painting in music? Here a tableau is depicted by using the distinctive colors of the instruments, especially the woodwinds, to evoke vibrant moods and sensations. The flute has one timbre, the oboe another, the clarinet yet a third. Debussy has said, in effect: Let us focus on the sound-producing capacity of the instruments, let us see what new shades can be elicited from them, let us try new registers, let us try new combinations. Thus a solo flute begins in its lowest register (the pipes of the faun), followed by a harp glissando*, then dabs of color from the French horn. These tonal impressions swirl, dissolve, and reform, but seem not to progress: There is no regular rhythm or discernible meter to push them along. All is languid beauty, a music that is utterly original yet shockingly sensual.

the tone color of the instrument is paramount

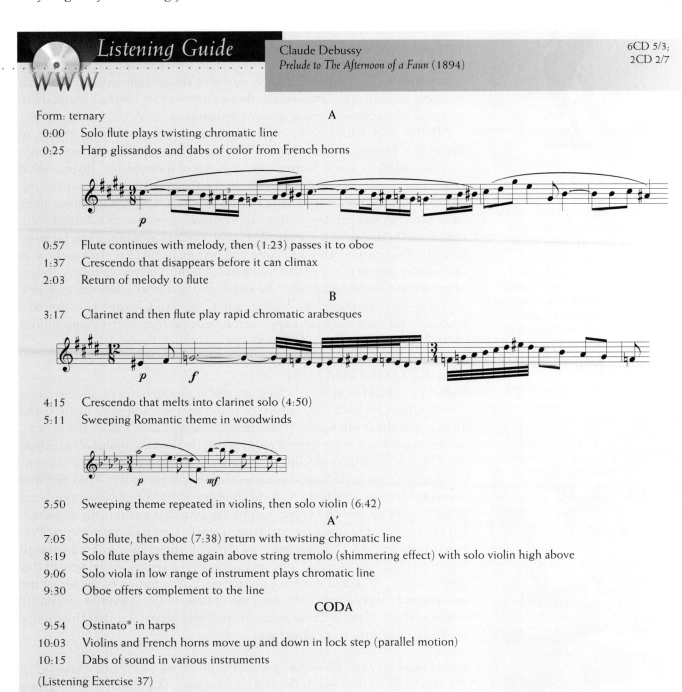

Listening Guide

Claude Debussy
Prelude to The Afternoon of a Faun (1894)

6CD 5/3;
2CD 2/7

Form: ternary

A

0:00   Solo flute plays twisting chromatic line

0:25   Harp glissandos and dabs of color from French horns

0:57   Flute continues with melody, then (1:23) passes it to oboe

1:37   Crescendo that disappears before it can climax

2:03   Return of melody to flute

B

3:17   Clarinet and then flute play rapid chromatic arabesques

4:15   Crescendo that melts into clarinet solo (4:50)

5:11   Sweeping Romantic theme in woodwinds

5:50   Sweeping theme repeated in violins, then solo violin (6:42)

A'

7:05   Solo flute, then oboe (7:38) return with twisting chromatic line

8:19   Solo flute plays theme again above string tremolo (shimmering effect) with solo violin high above

9:06   Solo viola in low range of instrument plays chromatic line

9:30   Oboe offers complement to the line

CODA

9:54   Ostinato* in harps

10:03 Violins and French horns move up and down in lock step (parallel motion)

10:15 Dabs of sound in various instruments

(Listening Exercise 37)

FIGURES 16–6 AND 16–7

(above) In 1912 the music of Debussy's *Prelude to the Afternoon of a Faun* was set as a ballet by the famous *Ballets russes* (see page 362). Here the dancer Vaslav Nijinsky assumes the role of the faun. (below) August Renoir, *Young Ladies at the Piano* (1892). Our present-day love of Impressionist art is due at least in part to the relaxed mood created by the pastel hues and diffused light. Also, because the Impressionists usually painted scenes from everyday life, a deep knowledge of religious symbolism and pictorial conventions is not a precondition for enjoyment.

Debussy's voluptuous *Prelude* creates an entirely new world of musical aesthetics, one very different from the German Romantic school of Mendelssohn, Wagner, and Brahms. Where a composer in the German Romantic tradition asserts a strongly profiled theme, a French Impressionist like Debussy will insinuate a tiny motive. Instead of clear meters and regular rhythms, the Impressionist favors constantly shifting accents that obscure the pulse. Instead of working toward a thunderous climax and a strong cadence, the Impressionist prefers to avoid a climax by placing a diminuendo before the cadence, thereby creating an anticlimax. Instead of moving purposefully along a well-directed harmonic progression, the Impressionist chooses to sit on a single static harmony and let the colorful instruments work their magic. Most important, instead of having musical color reinforce the musical theme, the Impressionist prefers to call on the instruments to demonstrate their sonorities independent of theme. What is different about Debussy's music is that beautiful sonorities are allowed simply to exist without having constantly to progress, by means of themes, to some distant goal.

All this was radically new. Think back to the orchestral music of Beethoven, Brahms, or Tchaikovsky. When a new theme enters in their works, it is presented by a new instrument or group of instruments. Instrumental color thus reinforces and gives profile to the theme. The exposition and development of themes create a musical form. With Debussy, on the other hand, color becomes independent of melody. Instruments enter with a distinct color but no easily discernible theme. The instrumental groupings can be more dense or less dense. In this way color and texture begin to replace melody as the primary agents in the creation of musical form. The revolutionary figures of twentieth-century music who use colors and textures exclusively to generate form—among them Ives, Varèse, and Cage (see Chapter 17)—found a precedent for their modernist approach to musical form in the compositions of the Impressionist Claude Debussy.

PRELUDES FOR PIANO (1910, 1913)

Debussy's last and most far-reaching attempt at descriptive writing in music is found in the two books of *Preludes* for piano that he published in 1910 and 1913. Here the challenge to create musical impressions was all the greater, for the piano has a more limited musical palette than the multicolor orchestra. The evocative titles of some of these short pieces allude to their mysterious qualities: *Steps in the Snow, The Sunken Cathedral, What the West Wind Saw,* and *Sounds and Perfumes Swirl in the Night Air.* Timbres and textures can be produced in music, and images and events can be suggested, if not actually depicted. But can music really stimulate our sense of smell? Can it create perfume? Perhaps for some. That Debussy suggests it might, shows how intent he was to create an ideal sort of music, one involving all the senses. As he says of this perfect music, "It would involve a mysterious collaboration of the air, of the movement of leaves and of the perfume of flowers along with music; music would serve to bind all these elements in a way so natural that their unity would seem to grow from all of them."

Voiles (Sails) (1910) *Voiles (Sails)*, from the first book of Preludes, takes us to the sea. In our mind's eye is implanted the vision of sailboats bobbing in a sea of fog. The sails flap listlessly in a fluid descent, mostly in parallel thirds.

The hazy, languid atmosphere is created in part by the special scale Debussy employs, the **whole-tone scale**. All the notes of the whole-tone scale are a whole step apart:

EXAMPLE 16–1

whole-tone scale

Because in the whole-tone scale each note is the same distance from its neighbor, no one pitch is heard as the tonal center—they all seem equally important. The composer can stop on any note of the scale and it will sound no more central, or final, than any other note. The music floats without a tonal anchor. Then, as if impelled by a puff of wind, the boats seem to rock on the now-rippling waters. Debussy creates this gentle rocking by inserting a four-note ostinato* into the texture. Ostinatos are frequently employed by Impressionist composers. They help account for the often static, restful feeling in the harmony. By definition, ostinatos involve repetition rather than dramatic movement.

FIGURE 16–8

Edgar Degas's *Beach with Sailboats Distant* (1869) is as much a fleeting impression of sailboats at sea as it is a realistic representation.

Réunion des Musées Nationaux, Art Resource, NY

EXAMPLE 16–2

A new ostinato now appears in the upper register (right hand), while a succession of four-note chords sounds in the middle register (left hand). Notice that all the four notes of each chord consistently move in what is called parallel motion. In **parallel motion** all parts move together, locked in step, in the same direction.

EXAMPLE 16–3

left hand

parallel motion

Parallel motion is the antithesis of counterpoint, the traditional musical technique in which two or more lines usually move in directions opposite to one another. Parallel motion was an innovation of Debussy, and it was one way he expressed his opposition to the German school of Wagner and Brahms, so heavily steeped in counterpoint.

Suddenly a gust of wind shakes the ships as the pianist races up the scale in a harplike glissando*. This scale, however, is different from the preceding whole-tone one. It is a pentatonic scale*. There are only five notes within each octave, here the five notes corresponding to the black keys on the piano. We have seen before that the pentatonic scale is often found in folk music (see page 251). Debussy first encountered it in the Southeast Asian music he heard at the Paris World's Fair of 1889 (see figure on page 349).

EXAMPLE 16–4

Following this energized whirl around the pentatonic scale, the seascape regains its placid demeanor as the whole-tone scale returns and, ultimately, the descending thirds with which the piece began. At the end Debussy directs the pianist to push down and hold the sustaining pedal (the right-most of the three pedals). Once the sustaining pedal is pressed and held, all notes sounded thereafter will blur into a vague haze, similar to the hazes and mists that envelop many Impressionist paintings (see Figs. 16–1 and 16–8).

Listening Guide

Claude Debussy
Voiles (Sails), from *Preludes*, Book I (1910)

6CD 5/4

0:00	Descending parallel thirds using whole-tone scale
0:12	Bass pedal point* enters
1:11	Ostinato enters in middle register
1:38	Ostinato moves into top register; chords move in parallel motion in middle register
2:14	Harplike glissandos using pentatonic scale
2:28	Chords moving in parallel motion above pedal point
2:51	Glissandos now employing whole-tone scale
3:36	Opening descending thirds return
3:57	Glissandos blur through use of sustaining pedal

THE EXOTIC IN MUSIC

One of the magical qualities of music is its capacity to carry us to distant lands. Far-off places can be experienced in our minds, if only through the strange and mysterious sounds we associate with them. Composers at the turn of the twentieth century delighted in such vicarious journeys, and their music is brimming with the "exotic." Claude Debussy, as we have seen, enjoyed the sounds of Southeast Asia at the Paris World's Fair of 1889. This exposure to Eastern elements accounts in part for the ostinatos, the static harmonies, the pentatonic and whole-tone scales, and the shimmering surfaces found in Debussy's music.

(continued on page 351)

CULTURAL CONTEXT

West Meets East: Music for Chinese String Instruments

In 1889 Claude Debussy, then an impressionable young man of twenty-six, paid several visits to the *Exposition universelle* (World's Fair) organized in Paris next to the newly constructed Eiffel Tower. There he not only saw newfangled inventions like electric lighting and electric-powered elevators but he also heard the colorful sounds of music from China and its Southeast Asian neighbors such as Cambodia, Thailand, and Indonesia. Debussy absorbed these sounds and later incorporated musical elements from Asia into his music. In 1903, for example, he composed a piano piece called *Pagodes* (*Pagodas*), which attempts to recreate the sounds and atmosphere of a pagoda, be it in China, Cambodia, or elsewhere—a musical pagoda of the mind. Debussy did so by basing all of the melodic and harmonic material on a pentatonic scale*, a scale found widely in and around China.

China is arguably the oldest and richest continuing civilization in the world. Many of the inventions and products that altered the course of Western history—gunpowder, printing, paper, silk, the nautical compass, and the dictionary, for example—were first developed in China. China also has a musical history that extends back thousands of years. A mathematical theory for generating all musical pitches was known in the third century B.C.; orchestras with twenty and more performers played at court during the T'ang dynasty (618–907); and full-fledged opera developed during the Yuan period (1271–1368) and continues to be popular today.

Central to the Chinese musical heritage are the traditional instruments. In general, Chinese instruments are more "natural" than those in the West, meaning that the materials from which they are made are readily found in nature. The Chinese flute, for example, is usually a section of bamboo with air holes (as opposed to the Western flute made of silver or platinum with an elaborate key mechanism) Among the string instruments three are of particular importance: the **pipa** (a four-string lute), the **yangqin** or **qin** (a seven-string dulcimer), and the **erhu** (a two-string fiddle, pronounced "R-who"). While the strings of the pipa are plucked and those of the yangqin struck with two bamboo sticks, those of the erhu are played with a bow. The player of the erhu passes the bow between the two fixed strings. A sound box, covered with snakeskin, helps the instrument to resonate with a vibrato-rich sound, a strange, veiled tone of great beauty.

The special quality of the sound of the erhu can be heard in *Erquan yingyue* (*The Moon Reflected on the Second Springs*) by Hua Yanjun (ca. 1893–1950), known today simply as Abing. Abing was a popular street musician from the city of Wuxi, about seventy miles west of Shanghai, who played both the erhu

Photo collection Sirot

The Cambodian Pagoda at the World's Fair in Paris in 1889. Here Debussy heard the music of Cambodia, China, Thailand, and Indonesia, and he began to formulate a musical aesthetic different from the prevailing German symphonic tradition.

Courtesy of Prof. Yu Zigang, Conservatory of Music, Beijing

The erhu is played by passing a bow between the two strings and continually twisting the instrument so that the bow can move from one string to the other. Playing is Min Hui-Fen of Shanghai, China.

(continued on page 350)

CULTURAL CONTEXT *(continued)*

and pipa. Like almost all Chinese folk musicians, he worked without benefit of written music, playing and improvising as he went. Abing's music survives in large measure because he recorded six of his creations shortly before his death in 1950. One of these, *The Moon Reflected on the Second Springs*, was originally conceived for erhu alone. Its subsequent history, however, is like that of a folk melody: It is known in many different versions and arranged for many different combinations of instruments including orchestra, string quartet, and even the Western piano. The title refers to an ancient pool, called the Erquan Pool, in a park near Abing's home city of Wuxi.

As we listen to Abing's composition several qualities of Chinese music immediately become apparent. First, Chinese bowed string instruments are infinitely flexible with regard to pitch. The solo erhu and the supporting orchestral strings seem to play as much between pitches as on them. (Compare this to the Western practice of moving from one separate and discrete pitch to the next.) Second, there is almost no harmony in Chinese music. What little there is usually results from two or more instruments playing the melody simultaneously in

different ranges. Thus Chinese music often resounds with parallel motion* (all parts moving together in lock step). Sometimes the melody is simply doubled at the octave or in unison with tremolos*, a technique that produces a shimmering effect. Finally, Abing's melody is constructed around a pentatonic scale*, the specific notes being G, A, B, D, E [G]. These five pitches, however, are only the point of departure. By using them in different registers and applying to them a multitude of rhythmic values, the composer extends his basic melody in a variety of subtle ways. The melody, or theme, has two parts. Usually the orchestra plays or varies part 1, and the erhu plays or varies part 2. What we have here is not so much "composition" as we in the West understand it, but rather continual improvisation and variation around a given theme, a musical practice found among street and folk musicians across the globe.

KEY WORDS

Abing   pipa
erhu   yangqin

Listening Guide

Huan Yanjun, known as Abing (ca. 1893–1950)
The Moon Reflected on the Second Springs

6CD 6/16

Form: two-part theme and variations

0:00   Bamboo flute plays six-note introduction
0:07   Full orchestra introduces melody, part 1

0:30   Erhu continues with melody, part 2

1:17   Erhu plays variation of melody, part 2
2:25   Orchestra with pipa plays variation of melody, part 1
2:46   Erhu and pipa play together different versions of the melody, part 2
3:16   Prominent "Western-style" bass emerges in low register
3:38   High bowed strings and plucked strings play variant of melody, part 2, in unison
3:52   Lower bowed strings and plucked strings play variant of melody, part 1, in unison
4:18   Erhu and high strings play variant of melody, part 2, against simple duple-meter accompaniment plucked in background
4:52   Erhu plays framents of pentatonic scale

But Claude Debussy was not the only artist to feel the allure of the "other" in these years. The painter Claude Monet lined the walls of his home in Giverny, France, not with his own canvases, but with prints and water colors from Japan. Their influence can be seen in the startling portrait of his wife in traditional Japanese costume (Fig. 16–9). Modernists like Pablo Picasso (1881–1973) and Georges Braque (1882–1963) began collecting African art in Paris during the years 1905–1908. Some historians believe that the Cubist movement in painting (see page 357) was born of Picasso's interest in African sculpture and ceremonial masks.

What was the exotic in music? Anything outside Western European musical culture. It might be a non-Western scale, a folk rhythm, or a musical instrument, like the tambourine* or gong* that signified the exotic. It might also be an alien subject matter. Giacomo Puccini fashioned operas using stories set in Japan (*Madam Butterfly*, 1904), China (*Turandot*, 1924), and even the American West (*The Girl of the Golden West*, 1910). For French Impressionists like Claude Debussy and Maurice Ravel, nearby Spain was thought to be exotic. Debussy composed an orchestral piece (*Ibéria*, 1908) and a piano work ("Evening in Grenada," 1903) using Spanish melodies. Ravel wrote his first orchestral work (*Rapsodie espagnole*, 1907) and his last ballet (*Bolero*, 1928), as well as an opera (*The Spanish Hour*, 1911) on Spanish subjects. Yet neither Debussy nor Ravel set foot in Spain. In art, the evocative powers of the imagination are often a more potent force than mundane reality.

Maurice Ravel (1875–1937)

"He was the eternal traveller who never went there," said an acquaintance of Maurice Ravel. Indeed, Ravel spent almost all of his life in Paris, a modest music teacher and composer earning a modest living. Only through his music did he journey to Spain, Arabia, ancient Greece, and the Far East—all lands he sought to evoke through exotic-sounding elements in his music. Yet there was one exception to Ravel's life of the imagination: In 1928 he embarked on a four-month concert tour of the United States. He heard jazz in Harlem with American composer George Gershwin (1898–1937), and had breakfast in Hollywood with Charlie Chaplin (1889–1977); he visited Niagara Falls and the Grand Canyon. Having performed and conducted his music in twenty-five American cities, Ravel returned to Paris with what was then the enormous sum of $27,000. He was financially secure for the remainder of his life.

RAPSODIE ESPAGNOLE (1907)

Ravel's first composition, written in 1895 at the age of twenty, was a work for piano entitled *Habanera*. A **habanera**, as we have seen, is a slow, seductive dance named after Havana, the capital of the then Spanish colony of Cuba. The rhythms that mark its progress are, however, West African, a musical legacy of the slave trade to Cuba. In 1907 Ravel arranged his *Habanera* for orchestra and added three additional pieces to it to form his four-movement *Rapsodie espagnole*. Like the progress of a Spanish day, the musical moods move from a mysterious, flower-scented night (*Prelude to the Night*), through two dances (*Malagueña* and *Habanera*), to the blistering brilliance of the noonday sun (*Feria*). Musical elements

FIGURE 16–9

Claude Monet, *La Japonaise (Madame Camille Monet in Japanese Costume,* 1876). America and Europe began to show an enthusiasm for things Japanese after the opening of trade with Japan in the 1850s. Fashionable Parisian women wore kimonos and furnished their homes with oriental furniture, prints, and *objets d'art.*

FIGURE 16–10

Portrait of Maurice Ravel playing the piano (ca. 1909) by Achille Ouvré.

of the exotic include the habanera rhythm, which involves alternating groups of three and two eighth-notes as well as syncopations (see Listening Guide). A **tambourine** (a small drum hung with jingles) from Basque (a region of Spain) is heard in *Habanera* as well as castanets* in *Feria*. Yet everywhere in *Rapsodie espagnole* there are glissandos*, hints of themes rather than sweeping melodies, and lines moving in parallel motion. This is exotic Spain, but Spain filtered through the musical sensibilities of a French Impressionist.

CORBIS

FIGURE 16–11

John Singer Sargent (1856–1925), *El Jaleo: Spanish Dancer*. Sargent was an American expatriate painter who got caught up in the European enthusiasm for all things Spanish during the late nineteenth century.

Listening Guide

Maurice Ravel
Rapsodie espagnole (1907)
Movement 1, *Prelude to the Night*
Movement 3, *Habanera*

6CD 5/5–6

Prelude to the Night (*Très modéré*, very moderate)

0:00	Four-note ostinato begins in violins and violas	
		ppp
0:09	Cellos and double basses provide pizzicato accompaniment	
0:43	Clarinets play eerie melody in parallel octaves	
		p
0:56	Four-note ostinato moves on	
1:28	Sudden rushes of orchestral color, but ostinato audible in background	
2:29	Sharp, dissonant *cadenza ad libitum* (freely played) for two clarinets	
2:55	Solo violin, viola, and cello play eerie melody	
3:22	Two bassoons now play cadenza	
3:51	Ostinato returns and fades away	

Habanera (*Assez lent et d'un rhythm las;* rather slow and with a jaded rhythm)

0:00   Introduction: syncopated rhythm  and glissandos in the strings

0:21   Habanera melody in oboe and English horn

0:47   Solo violin and viola continue Habanera melody

1:01   French horns move from minor triad to major triad against Habanera rhythm

1:13   Violins play Habanera melody in parallel motion

(Continued on next page)

1:42   Tambourine enters as woodwinds continue with Habanera melody
2:00   Violins continue Habanera melody with tambourine in background
2:09   French horns play Habanera melody
2:22   Trumpets slide from minor triad to major triad at the end

Listening Exercises

 37

Claude Debussy   6CD 5/3; 2CD 2/7
Prelude to The Afternoon of a Faun (1894)

Debussy, as we have seen, was a master at extracting new sonorities and textures from the traditional Western orchestra. The following questions, therefore, deal mainly with issues of color and texture.

1. (0:00–0:23) What is the musical texture at the beginning?
    a. monophonic   b. homophonic   c. polyphonic
2. (0:57–1:22) The flute returns with the chromatic line, but now the strings quietly shimmer behind them. The shimmering effect is created by rapidly repeating the same pitch with up and down strokes of the bow. It is called
    a. tremolo   b. obligato   c. pizzicato
3. (1:37–2:03) Here is an instance where Debussy avoids a climax by repeating a motive as it fades away. By continually repeating a motive on the same pitches Debussy is employing
    a. walking bass   b. an arpeggio   c. an ostinato
4. (1:37–2:03) Which dynamic markings does Debussy prescribe to create this feeling of an evasion and anticlimax?
    a. *diminuendo–crescendo*   b. *crescendo–diminuendo*
5. (2:03, 2:18, 2:40, and 7:05) When the flute returns with the twisting chromatic line, which instrument provides a colorful background?
    a. English horn   b. French horn   c. harp
6. Appropriately enough, what is this instrument playing to help create this background "wash of sound"? The playing is particularly clear at 7:05–7:20.
    a. arpeggios   b. chromatic scales   c. pedal points
7. (3:21–3:46) Which is a correct description of the music at this point?
    a. The violins sweep forward with a sensuous melody based on a whole-tone scale.
    b. Various instruments dart in and out with tiny motives, creating colorful sonorities but a discontinuous texture.
8. (5:50–6:35) In this beautiful passage Debussy comes closest to recreating the lush sentimentality more typical of Romantic than Impressionist music. Which statement is *not* correct?
    a. There is a solo for French horn and then violin at the beginning.
    b. There is a long, sweeping, rhythmically free melody.
    c. The melody is played expressively by the violins.

9. A passage with a prominent flute is stated (7:05–7:32) and then repeated at a lower pitch (7:36–8:09), now featuring an oboe. What happens to the texture and orchestration in the course of each of these two passages?
   a. Polyphonic texture and discontinuous orchestration give way to homophonic texture and unchanging orchestration.
   b. Homophonic texture and unchanging orchestration give way to polyphonic texture and discontinuous orchestration.

10. In a typical orchestral work of the Classical or Romantic periods it is usually the violins that present most themes. In Debussy's Impressionist *Prelude*, however, the instruments of which family introduce most melodic motives?
   a. strings   b. brasses   c. woodwinds   d. percussion

CULTURAL CONTEXT

From Cuba to Argentina: The Tango

We all know that "It takes two to tango." But what is a tango? The **tango** is a genre of urban popular song and dance that developed first in Cuba and then Argentina during the nineteenth century. Its most immediate ancestor was the Cuban habanera*. Like the habanera, the tango is a slow, sultry piece in duple meter with syncopation on the first beat. The tango, in addition, also has a steady four-pulse rhythm that works in conjunction with the syncopated pattern thus:

Unlike the habanera, however, the tango is not a solo or group dance, but one for couples in which two interlaced bodies glide as one across the floor. Indeed, this "forbidden" South American dance must be seen to be understood—the music alone does not convey the beautifully sensual, interlocking movements of the partners. The tango became something of a dance craze at the beginning of the twentieth century, was pushed aside by rock 'n' roll in the 1950s

Tango dancers convey some of the stylish élan of the dance. Today the tango is both an art form and an Olympic event.

and 1960s, but regained its popularity toward the end of the century. During the 1980s and 1990s the tango was featured in a Broadway musical (*Tango Argentino*) and in several films. Even Arnold Schwarzenegger took a turn at the tango in *True Lies* (1994). Recently the tango became an official Olympic event, having been introduced to the Sydney Games in 2000 under the classification of ballroom dancing.

The soul of later twentieth-century tango can be found in the music of Astor Piazzolla (1921–1992), an Argentinian who lived his life in Buenos Aires, New York, and Paris. Piazzolla not only composed and performed tangos, he was a virtuoso on the **bandoneon**, a poor-man's accordion played by pushing buttons instead of keys. During the late nineteenth century the bandoneon became the traditional instrument of the tango. Most established tango orchestras included strings (violins, cello, and bass), piano, and bandoneon. But Piazzolla was anything but a traditionalist. To the lilting melodies and captivating rhythms of tango he added dissonance,

Key Words

habanera (351)

Impressionism (342)

parallel motion (347)

Symbolists (344)

tambourine (352)

whole-tone scale
(347)

A checklist of the musical style of Impressionist composers is given on page 70.

Listening Guide

WWW

Astor Piazzolla
Tango Tragedy (1985)

6CD 6/17

0:00	Sixteen-bar unit; bandoneon, double bass, and piano emphasize tango rhythm
0:18	New sixteen-bar unit
0:34	New sixteen-bar unit; more dissonance, penny whistle added
0:49	New sixteen-bar unit; piano adds greater syncopation
1:04	New sixteen-bar harmony; brutal chords off the beat (syncopation)
1:19	Sixteen-bar unit raised to higher pitches
1:34	New sixteen-bar unit with low drum playing on second beat of each measure
1:49	New sixteen-bar unit; texture grows more dense
2:03	New sixteen-bar unit; low strings play twice as fast
2:18	New sixteen-bar unit; pitch is raised; tempo speeds up
2:31	New sixteen-bar unit; tempo becomes faster and the music more frenetic
2:43	Final dissonant chords

percussive effects, and an electric guitar to produce *tango nuevo* (new tango). Conservatives accused him of having murdered the tango. But the listening public soon warmed to his aggressive style, especially after his film music for *Tango* (1985) and *Sur* (1988). It was for the film *Tango* that Piazzolla wrote *Tanguedia* (*Tango Tragedy*), in which we can hear both the traditional rhythms of the tango and Piazzolla's own modernist style.

Astor Piazzolla once said that he was "only Astor Piazzolla trying to be Igor Stravinsky." In *Tango Tragedy* we hear the musical identity crisis that Piazzolla experienced as he tried to harmonize "low" and "high" culture. Yes, *Tango Tragedy* rests squarely in the popular tradition of the Argentinian tango. Yet it is popular music overlaid with the modern sounds of twentieth-century high-art music: biting dissonance, pounding percussion, urgent accents, and insistent rhythms. It is to these modern sounds that we now turn.

Joel Meyerowitz

Astor Piazzolla playing the bandoneon.

KEY WORDS

Astor Piazzolla   bandoneon   tango

Chapter

17

Peter Willi; Stadtische Galérie im Lenbachaus, Munich

The Twentieth Century

The twentieth century might best be called the Age of Extremes. Two world wars, a worldwide depression, the extermination of millions of people, the atomic bomb, biological weapons, and horrific acts of terrorism have marked this past century. At the same time, scientific advances have improved the quality and length of life: The automobile and airplane, radio and television, antibiotics, organ transplants, computers, and the Internet have had a profound impact on our daily lives. Some inventions—the radio, long-playing records, magnetic tape recorder, compact disc, and the Internet—have greatly affected our musical culture, bringing serious music to a much larger segment of the populace. At the same time they have discouraged musical education and music-making in the home: Why learn to play an instrument if you can hear it by just putting on a CD? For every step forward, there has been one backward; for every medical discovery, an act of terrorism. The anxiety and disjunction that you will feel in much of modern music is an artistic expression of the social tensions and underlying uncertainties of the past hundred years.

MODERNISM: DIVERSITY AND EXPERIMENTATION

Given the extremes of good and evil that have marked the twentieth century, it is hardly surprising to find that in matters of culture there was a lack of cohesion. Where was its artistic core? What were the main artistic currents? What path to the future was left to those of the new century?

Earlier periods in the history of music had a norm for the music of that time—there was a consensus as to how the music of that particular era should sound. Not so for the twentieth century. A bewildering variety of styles came and went: atonal music, twelve-tone music, electronic music, chance music, Neo-classicism, and Minimalism all enjoyed favor at various times. Composers themselves adopted one style or another as their careers evolved, just as the painter Picasso, for example, moved from Cubism (Fig. 17–1) to Neo-classicism (see Fig. 17–25). We will discuss each of these musical styles in this chapter, but no one of them can be said to be the mainstream of modernism. From the vantage point of a new century, the last hundred years appears as a time of alienation, fragmentation, experimentation, and diversity. It is the radically experimental quality of the music that allows us to call it modern or avant-garde.

Radical experimentation in music began shortly before World War I (1914–1918). The new music was not a further evolution of the German-dominated symphonic style of late Romanticism but a sharp turning away from it. It renounced the notion that music should be beautiful and pleasing, expressive or elevating, that it should delight or comfort the listener. Instead, it resorted to distortion, even violence, of sound, to shock the listening audience. Arnold Schoenberg's early experiments with dissonance were received with hoots by a hostile public in Vienna in 1913; Igor Stravinsky's dissonant chords and pounding rhythms caused a riot at the first performance of *Le Sacre du printemps (The Rite of Spring)* in Paris the same year. The intent of the avant-garde composer was to shake the listener out of a state of cultural complacency, just as the artist of the period offended middle-class sensibilities by means of radical visual distortions.

Indeed, there are clear parallels between the music and the art of the early twentieth century. The increasingly angular melody and discontinuous rhythm of the new music found analogous expression in an artistic style called **Cubism**. A Cubist painting is one in which the artist fractures and dislocates formal reality into geometrical blocks and planes, as in Pablo Picasso's (1881–1973) famous *Les Demoiselles d'Avignon* (1907), where the female form has been recast into angular, interlocking shapes. During the 1910s and 1920s, Picasso and Stravinsky were friends and occasional artistic collaborators in Paris. So disjointed did the musical line become in the works of Arnold Schoenberg that melody as we know it all but disappeared. At that very time a group of painters working mainly in Germany in a style called Expressionism (see page 369), because they expressed intense internal feelings, so distorted formal reality that objects in their paintings were sometimes barely recognizable. The women are discernible in Picasso's *Les Demoiselles d'Avignon* but where is the audience in Wassily Kandinsky's *Concert* (1911)

The Museum of Modern Art, New York

FIGURE 17–1

One of the first statements of Cubist art, Picasso's *Les Demoiselles d'Avignon* (1907). The ladies of the evening are depicted by means of geometric shapes on a flat, two-dimensional plane. Like much avant-garde music of the time, Cubist paintings reject the emotionalism and decorative appeal of nineteenth-century art.

Peter Willi, Stadtische Galérie im Lenbachaus, Munich

National Gallery of Art, Washington, DC

FIGURES 17-2 AND 17-3

(above) Wassily Kandinsky's *Impression III (Concert)* (1911). Kandinsky was one of the founders of the Expressionist movement, which was centered in Vienna and Munich. This painting of an audience at a concert does not depict the concert so much as a psychological state—the audience's reaction to the concert. (above right) The angularity and disjointed quality of much early twentieth-century melody can also be seen in contemporary painting. In Picasso's *Harlequin Musician* (1924), for example, the face of the musical clown, including his moustache, is entirely out of alignment. Compare the disjunct melody of Arnold Schoenberg given in Example 17-1.

(Fig. 17–2)? Cubism, Expressionism, Dadaism, Surrealism, and later Abstract Expressionism, Optical art, and Pop art are a few of the diverse artistic movements that have left their mark on the twentieth century. Diversity and radical experimentation are hallmarks of modern art no less than they are of modern music.

TWENTIETH-CENTURY MUSICAL STYLE

Despite its diversity, there are, nonetheless, several constant qualities of modern music that create a consistent musical style. These are most forcefully expressed in the elements of melody, harmony, rhythm, and tone color.

Melody: More Angularity and Chromaticism

Unlike the melodies of the Romantic period, many of which are song-like in style and therefore easily sung and remembered, there are very few themes in twentieth-century music that the listener goes away humming. In fact, melody per se is less important to the avant-garde composer than is a pulsating rhythm, an unusual texture, or a new sonority. If Romantic melody was generally smooth, diatonic*, and conjunct* in motion (moving more by steps than by leaps), early twentieth-century melody tends to be fragmented, chromatic*, and angular. The young avant-garde composers bent over backward to avoid writing conjunct, stepwise lines. Rather than moving up a half-step from C to D♭, for example, they were wont to jump down a major seventh to the D♭ an octave below. Avoiding a simple interval for a more distant one an octave above or below is called **octave displacement** and it is a fea-

asymmetrical, angular themes

ture of modern music. So, too, is the heavy use of chromaticism. In the following example by Arnold Schoenberg (1874–1951), notice how the melody
makes large leaps where it might more easily move by steps and also how
several sharps and flats are introduced to produce a highly chromatic line:

octave displacement

EXAMPLE 17–1

Harmony: The "Emancipation of Dissonance," New Chords, New Systems

Throughout the Baroque, Classical, and Romantic eras, the basic building
block of Western music was the triad*—a consonant three-note chord. All
music, in one way or another, was composed of a succession of consonant
triads. Dissonant notes could be inserted for variety and to add tension, but
the ancient laws of harmony required that they move (resolve) immediately
to a consonance. During the late Romantic period, however, composers like
Richard Wagner (1813–1883) began to enrich their music with more and
more chromaticism. This, in turn, created greater dissonance simply because
the added chromatic notes generated chords that were not consonant triads.
By the first decade of the twentieth century, some composers, such as Arnold
Schoenberg, were using so much dissonance that the triad almost disappeared. In a famous statement Schoenberg referred to this as "the emancipation of dissonance," meaning that dissonance was liberated from the requirement that it move to a consonance. Some of Schoenberg's works, when
measured according to the traditional rules of harmony, are composed of
nothing but dissonances. At first, audiences rebelled. But in the course of the
twentieth century listeners gradually came to accept a greater level of dissonance in both popular and art music. Were it not for Schoenberg and like-
minded composers, the heavy metal rock of Metallica would not have been
possible.

"the emancipation of dissonance"

In addition to creating dissonance by chromatically obscuring the triad,
twentieth-century composers created dissonance by means of new chords.
This was done mainly by superimposing more thirds on top of the consonant triad. In this way were produced not only the **seventh chord** (a seventh
chord spans seven letters of the scale, from A to G, for example) but also the
ninth chord and the **eleventh chord**. The more thirds that were added on
top of the basic triad, the more dissonant the sound of the chord:

EXAMPLE 17–2

seventh chord   ninth chord   eleventh chord

new chords

The ultimate new chord was the **tone cluster,** the simultaneous sounding
of a number of pitches only a whole step or a half-step apart. This highly
dissonant chord can be created by striking a group of adjacent keys on the
piano with the fist or forearm. Try it.

FIGURE 17–4

Lines of varying lengths can be seen as analogous to measures of different lengths caused by changing meters. Theo van Doesburg's *Rhythms of a Russian Dance* (1918) was surely inspired by the Russian sounds of Igor Stravinsky's *The Rite of Spring* (1913).

Chromatic dissonance, new chords, and tone clusters all weakened the traditional role of the triad in music. But more was at issue: Remember that the triad, and its network of related triads, had created a stable system of keys and tonality. As the triad disappeared, so too did a feeling of tonality in music. What were composers to do without the framework of tonality and the building blocks of the triad? Simply said, they invented new systems to give structure to music. As we shall see, Igor Stravinsky anchored much of his music in long ostinatos*, while Arnold Schoenberg invented an entirely new type of musical structure called the twelve-tone* method.

Rhythm: New Asymmetrical Rhythms and Irregular Meters

Most art music before the twentieth century, and indeed all of our pop and rock music down to the present day, is built on regular patterns of duple ($\frac{2}{4}$), triple ($\frac{3}{4}$), or quadruple ($\frac{4}{4}$) meter. Romantic music of the previous generation of composers had many qualities to recommend it: direct expression, broad themes, powerful climaxes, and moments of tender lyricism, to name a few. But only rarely was Romantic music carried along by an exciting, vital rhythm, staying instead within the comfortable confines of regular accents and duple or triple meter.

At the turn of the twentieth century composers of art music began to rebel against the rhythmic and metric regularity that had governed much of nineteenth-century music. Musicians such as Stravinsky and Bartók began to write music in which syncopations and measures with odd numbers of beats made it all but impossible for the listener to feel regular metrical patterns. Accents moved from one pulse to another, and meters changed from measure to measure. In abandoning the traditional structures of regular rhythms and consistent meters, these composers were no different from modern poets like Gertrude Stein (1874–1946) and T. S. Eliot (1888–1965), who dispensed with traditional poetic meters and repeating accents in favor of free verse.

Tone Color: New Sounds from New Sources

Twentieth-century composers have created a brave new world of sound. This came about mainly because many musicians were dissatisfied with the string-dominated tone of the Romantic symphony orchestra. The string sound, with its lush vibrato, was thought to be too expressive, perhaps too mushy and sentimental, for the harsh realities of the modern world. So the strings, which had been the traditional melody carriers, relinquished this role to the sharper, crisper woodwinds. Instead of playing a sweeping melody, the violinists might now be called on to beat on the strings with the wooden part of the bow or to take their hands and strike the instrument on its sound box. This preference for percussive effects was also expressed in the new importance assigned the instruments of the percussion family. Entire pieces were written for them alone. Instruments such as the xylophone*, glockenspiel*, and celesta* were added to the group (see Fig. 3–12), and objects that produced an unfixed pitch, like the cow bell, brake drum, and police siren, were also heard on occasion. The piano, which in the Romantic era had been favored for its lyrical

new percussion instruments

"singing" tone, came to be used as an orchestral instrument prized for the decisive way in which the hammers could be made to bang into the strings.

Producing new tones in novel ways, whether by new "instruments" or by traditional instruments using new playing techniques, is only part of the story of sound in modern music. A more fundamental development is the new way of thinking about musical color, or timbre, as an independent element in music. During the Classical and Romantic periods, sounds of different colors and different volumes had been used mainly as a way to highlight the progress of the themes and thus to articulate the form of a composition. When the second theme entered in sonata–allegro form, for example, it was usually assigned to a new instrument to tell the listener that this was, in fact, a new theme; when a final climax was near, more and more instruments, including the powerful brasses, were usually added to increase the level of sound, signaling that the end was close at hand. The use of tone color and volume as mere servants of melody came to an end at the turn of the twentieth century. Claude Debussy (see page 346) was the first to use color, independent of melody, to give form to a work. But this development was carried to radical lengths

FIGURE 17–5

Red runs amok in Henri Matisse's *The Red Studio* (1911). Here color is not a subordinate element employed to delineate the various objects in the room. Instead, color and line are separated, and color per se has gained unprecedented power. In 2000, *Time* magazine voted this the greatest painting of the twentieth century.

in the compositions of modernists such as Edgard Varèse (1883–1965), Charles Ives (1874–1954), and John Cage (1912–1992), whose pieces sometimes do nothing except progress from bright tones spaced far apart to dark tones densely grouped together. There may be no melody or harmony as we usually think of these, but only clusters or streams of sounds with changing colors. This approach to color and line is, of course, similar to the one followed by avant-garde painters who deconstruct recognizable objects so as to emphasize the emotional power of pure color (Fig. 17–5).

THE EARLY AVANT-GARDE: STRAVINSKY, SCHOENBERG, AND BARTÓK

Faced with the extraordinary diversity of modern music, today's conductors and performers have a difficult time selecting a musical repertoire for the listening public. What kinds of modern music should be performed and how much of it? Audiences are notorious for preferring the tried-and-true "chestnuts" of the Classical and Romantic periods to any sort of new or experimental music. The masterpieces by the composers discussed next are not only compelling works of art in themselves but they also have offered answers for other composers in regard to the fundamental question of modern music—how to create cogent new music in a world marked by increasing cultural diversity and artistic fragmentation. All of these works have now become accepted into the standard repertoire of concert music, though not all of the composers have become icons of popular culture like Beethoven or Mozart.

Igor Stravinsky (1882–1971)

Igor Stravinsky was arguably the most significant composer of the twentieth century, both for the music he produced and for his influence on other composers. He created masterpieces in many different genres: opera, ballet, symphony, church Mass, and cantata. His versatility was such that he could write a ballet for baby elephants (*Circus Polka*, 1942) just as easily as he could set to music a Greek classical drama (*Oedipus Rex*, 1927). Throughout his long life he traveled with the fashionable set of high art. Although reared in St. Petersburg, he later lived in Paris, Venice, Lausanne, New York, and Hollywood. Forced to become an expatriate by the Russian Revolution (1917), he took French citizenship in 1934, and then, having moved to the United States at the outbreak of World War II, became an American citizen in 1945. He counted among his friends the painter Pablo Picasso (1881–1973), the novelist Aldous Huxley (1894–1963), and the poets Dylan Thomas (1914–1953) and T. S. Eliot (1888–1965). On his eightieth birthday, in 1962, he was honored by President John Kennedy at the White House and, later in the same year, by Premier Nikita Khrushchev in the Kremlin. He died in New York in 1971 at the age of eighty-eight.

Stravinsky rose to international fame as a composer of ballet music. In 1908 some of his early work caught the attention of the legendary impresario (producer) of Russian opera and ballet, Sergei Diaghilev (1872–1929). Diaghilev wanted to bring Russian ballet to Paris, at that time the artistic capital of the world. So he formed a company, called the **Ballets russes** (Russian ballets), and hired, over the course of time, the most progressive artists he could find: Pablo Picasso and Henri Matisse for scenic designs, George Balanchine (later the force behind the New York City Ballet) as a choreographer, and Debussy, Ravel, and Stravinsky, among others, as composers. Stravinsky soon became the principal composer of the company, and the *Ballets russes* became the focus of his musical activity for the next ten years. Accordingly, the decade 1910–1920 has become known as Stravinsky's Russian ballet period. He would have others—a Neo-classical period (1920–1951) when he returned to classical forms and a smaller orchestra, and a twelve-tone period (1951–1971) during which he adopted the so-called serial style of composing (see page 371)—but his fame was made through his early ballets. Motion, whether of dancers or of musical performers, was always foremost in his mind's eye. As Stravinsky said in his autobiography, "I have always had a horror of listening to music with my eyes shut, with nothing for them to do. The sight of the gestures and movements of the various parts of the body . . . is fundamentally necessary if music is to be grasped in its fullness."

The three most important ballets Stravinsky wrote for Diaghilev's company were *The Firebird* (1910), *Petrushka* (1911), and *The Rite of Spring* (1913). All are built around stories taken from Russian folk tales—a legacy of musical nationalism*—and all make use of the large, coloristic orchestra of the

FIGURE 17–6
Igor Stravinsky, painted by Emile Blanche in 1921.

Giraudon, Art Resource, NY

FIGURE 17–7
Sergei Diaghilev in New York in 1916.

Roger-Viollett

late nineteenth century. Unlike symphonic music, however, music for ballet does not explore, or develop, carefully integrated musical themes. Rather, the composer creates a succession of short, independent vignettes designed to express the action being danced and mimed on stage in separate scenes. The dance of Diaghilev's *Ballets russes* is not the elegant, graceful classical ballet in the French and Russian tradition, the sort that we associate with Tchaikovsky's *Swan Lake* (1877) and *The Nutcracker* (1892). It is a new, modern style of dance influenced by "primitive" Russian folk dancing and folk art; it is heavier, more physical, more driving. Rhythm becomes the driving force of these Russian ballets and of Stravinsky's music in general.

LE SACRE DU PRINTEMPS (THE RITE OF SPRING) (1913)

The Rite of Spring has been called *the* great masterpiece of modern music. Yet at the premiere, *The Rite of Spring* provoked not admiration, but a riot of hostility. This opening, the most notorious "first night" in the history of music, took place on an unusually hot evening, May 29, 1913, at the newly built Théâtre Champs-Élysées in Paris. With the very first sounds of the orchestra, many in the packed theater voiced, shouted, and hissed their displeasure. Some called for a doctor, others for two. There were arguments and flying fists as opponents and partisans warred over this Russian brand of modern art. To restore calm, the curtain was lowered momentarily and the house lights were turned on and off. All in vain. The musicians still could not be heard, and the dancers had difficulty following the pulse of the music. The disorder was experienced first-hand by a visiting critic of the *New York Press*, who reported as follows:

> I was sitting in a box in which I had rented one seat. Three ladies sat in front of me and a young man occupied the place behind me. He stood up during the course of the ballet to enable himself to see more clearly. The intense excitement under which he was laboring, thanks to the potent force of the music, betrayed itself presently when he began to beat rhythmically on the top of my head with his fists. My emotion was so great that I did not feel the blows for some time. They were perfectly synchronized with the beat of the music!

In truth, the violent reaction to *The Rite of Spring* was in part a response to the modernist choreography of Vaslav Nijinsky (see Fig. 16–6), who sought to obliterate any trace of classical ballet. Nijinsky's dance was just as "primitive" as Stravinsky's musical score. But what, specifically, is there in Stravinsky's music that so many that night found shocking?

CORBIS/Burstein Collection

Hermitage Museum, St. Petersburg, Russia/AGE FotoStock/SuperStock

FIGURES 17–8 AND 17–9

(top) In 1909, Henri Matisse painted the first of two canvases entitled *Dance*. Here he achieves a raw primitive power by exaggerating a few basic lines and employing a few cool tones. Two years later he created an even more intense vision of the same scene (see Fig. 17–9). (bottom) *Dance* (1911) by Henri Matisse. Here the painter uses greater angularity and more intense colors, and thereby creates a more intense reaction to this later version of a primitive dance scene (see Fig. 17–8).

a percussive, metallic sound

Percussive orchestra. First, there is a new percussive—one might say "heavy metal"—approach to the orchestra. The percussion section is enlarged to include four timpani, a triangle, a tambourine, a guiro*, cymbals, antique cymbals, a bass drum, and a tam-tam*. Even the string family, the traditional provider of warmth and richness in the symphony orchestra, is required to play percussively, attacking the strings with repeated down-bows at seemingly random moments of accent. Instead of warm, lush sounds, the audience heard bright, brittle, almost brutal ones pounded out by percussion, heavy woodwinds, and brasses.

Irregular accents. Stravinsky intensifies the effect of his harsh, metallic sounds by placing them where they are not expected, on unaccented beats, thereby creating explosive syncopations. Notice in the following example, the famous beginning of "Augurs of Spring," how the strings accent (>) the second, fourth, and then first pulses of each four-pulse measure. In this way Stravinsky destroys ordinary 1, 2, 3, 4 meter and forces us to hear, in succession, groups of 4, 5, 2, 6, 3, 4, and 5 pulses—a conductor's nightmare!

EXAMPLE 17–3

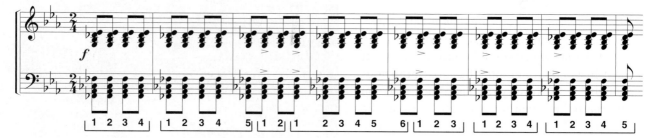

Polymeters. The rhythm of *The Rite of Spring* is complex because the composer often superimposes two or more distinctly different meters simultaneously. Notice in Ex. 17–4 that the oboe plays in $\frac{6}{8}$ time, the E♭ clarinet plays in $\frac{7}{8}$, while the B♭ clarinet is in $\frac{5}{8}$. This is an example of **polymeters**—two or more meters sounding simultaneously.

EXAMPLE 17–4

Polyrhythms. Not only do individual parts often play separate meters but they also sometimes project two or more independent rhythms simultaneously. Look at the reduced score given in Ex. 17–5. Every instrument seems to be doing its own thing! In fact, six distinctly different rhythms can be heard. This is a good example of **polyrhythms**—the simultaneous sounding of two or more rhythms.

EXAMPLE 17–5

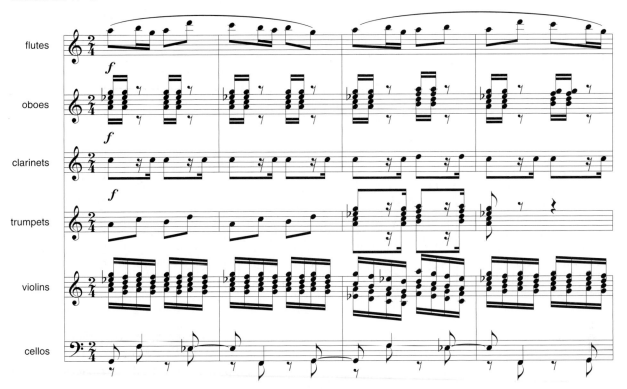

Ostinato figures. Notice also in Ex. 17–5 how most of the instruments are playing the same motive over and over at the same pitch level. Such a repeating figure, as we have seen, is called an ostinato*. In this instance we hear multiple ostinatos. Stravinsky was not the first twentieth-century composer to use ostinatos extensively—Debussy had done so earlier in his Impressionist scores (see page 347). But Stravinsky employs them more often and does so for longer spans. In *The Rite of Spring*, ostinatos give the music its incessant, driving quality, especially in the sections with fast tempos.

Dissonant polychords. The harsh, biting sound that is heard throughout much of *The Rite of Spring* is often created by having two triads*, or a triad and a seventh chord*, sound at once. What results is called a **polychord**—the simultaneous sounding of one triad or seventh chord with another. When the individual chords of a polychord are only a whole step* or a half-step* apart, the result is especially dissonant. In Ex. 17–6, the passage from the beginning of "Augurs of Spring," a seventh chord* built on E♭ is played simultaneously with a major triad built on F♭.

EXAMPLE 17–6

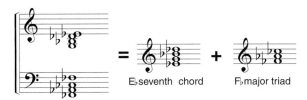

E♭ seventh chord   F♭ major triad

Stravinsky's dissonant polychord

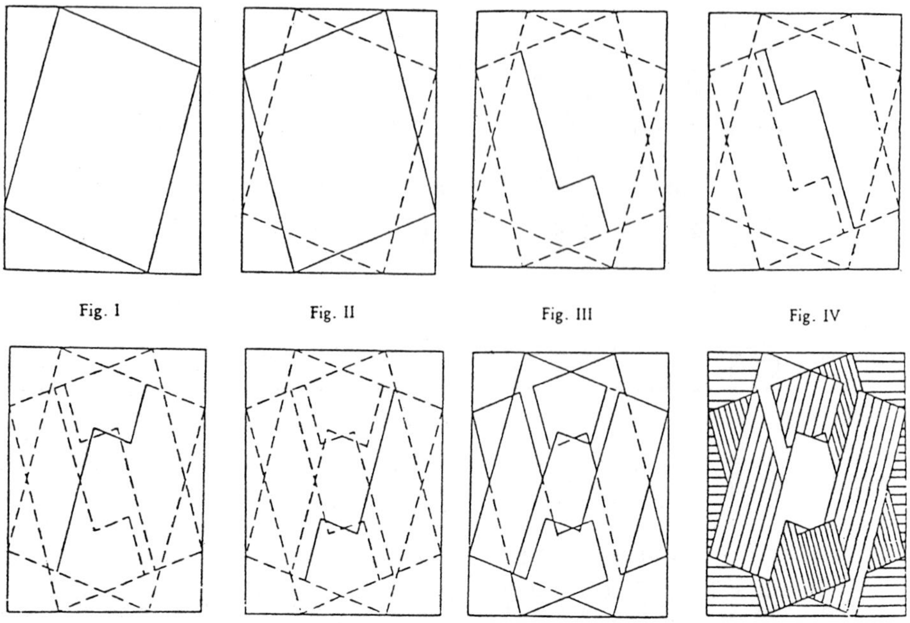

Fig. I   Fig. II   Fig. III   Fig. IV

Fig. V   Fig. VI   Fig. VII   Fig. VIII

FIGURE 17–10

In his *Schemes of Painting* (1922), the artist Albert Gleizes demonstrates that a Cubist work could be created by rotating a figure or line against itself, and then again and again until visual dissonance results. Similarly, a polychord is created by placing two or more triads or seventh chords off center and against one another, thereby creating musical dissonance.

The plot of the ballet *The Rite of Spring* is suggested by its subtitle: "Pictures of Pagan Russia." Part 1 is called "The Kiss of the Earth" and depicts the spring-time rituals of primitive Slavic tribes; part 2 is entitled "The Sacrifice," and here a virgin dances herself to death as an offering to the god of Spring. Stravinsky's music is sometimes lyrical and sensuous, but more often percussive, dissonant, and even violent. Throughout he makes use of Russian folk songs, fragments of folk songs, and his own brief imitations of these. Yet as Stravinsky said, he had little tradition or precedent to direct him: "I had only my ears to guide me. I heard and I wrote what I heard. I am the vessel through which *The Rite of Spring* passed."

Listening Guide

WWW

Igor Stravinsky
The Rite of Spring (1913)
Introduction and Scenes 1–3

6CD 5/7–10;
2CD 2/8–9

Genre: Ballet music
Introduction (the awakening of the earth; curtain still down)

0:00	Bassoon writhing in high register
0:20	Other winds (bass clarinet, English horn, another bassoon, high clarinet) gradually enter
1:37	Flutes play in parallel motion
1:53	Writhing woodwinds continue
2:34	Ostinato in bass supports gradual orchestral crescendo
2:57	Bassoon melody returns, clarinet trills

Augurs of Spring: Dances of the Adolescents (youthful dancers pound onto the stage; male and female groups entice one another; attention shifts to the more folk-like dances of the girls)

0:00	Elemental pounding of dissonant string chords punctuated by blasts from the French horns and trumpets (see Ex. 17–3)

(Continued on next page)

0:46   Bassoons and then trombones play stepwise motive

1:15   *Fortissimo* chords and timpani blows
1:39   French horn plays folklike melody

1:59   Flute plays melody
2:13   Trumpets play new folklike melody

2:47   Gradual orchestral crescendo

(2CD stops here)

Game of Abduction (macho gestures of "kidnapping" a girl)

0:00   Wild, chaotic playing in orchestra peppered with blows on the timpani and blasts from the French horn
0:53   Quickly changing meters; syncopated percussion blows

Spring Rounds (round dances by groups of male and female adolescents)

0:00   Flutes trill while clarinets play in parallel motion
0:26   Low strings set up mournful accompaniment
1:04   Folklike melody now played by violins and flutes, then French horns

1:59   Folklike melody played dissonantly by full orchestra
2:41   Dissonant, syncopated, percussive music for male dancers
2:58   Return of opening flute trill and opening melody

(Listening Exercise 38)

Following the *succès de scandale* that attended the premiere of *The Rite of Spring*, Stravinsky immediately removed the music from the ballet itself and had it played as an independent orchestral suite. The music alone was now recognized as an important, if controversial, statement of the musical avant-garde. Later, in 1940, the score of *The Rite of Spring* furnished the music for an important segment of Walt Disney's early full-length animated film, *Fantasia*. Musical modernism had become mainstream.

Arnold Schoenberg and the Second Viennese School

If Paris was the artistic capital of Europe before the First World War, Vienna was second in importance. The city of Mozart and Beethoven was blessed with strong musical traditions and a large, if conservative, audience. But the musical expectations of the Viennese were now challenged by a trio of native composers who were to take modern music on a radically different course: Arnold Schoenberg (1874–1951), Alban Berg (1885–1935), and Anton Webern (1883–1945). The close association of these three innovative musicians has come to be called the "Second Viennese School," the first, of course, being that of Mozart, Haydn, and Beethoven.

FIGURE 17–11
Arnold Schoenberg, *Self Portrait* (1910).

Arnold Schoenberg, the leader of this group, almost single-handedly thrust modern music on a reluctant Viennese public. Schoenberg was from a Jewish family of modest circumstances and was largely self-taught as a musician. As a young man he worked as a bank clerk during the day, but studied literature, philosophy, and music at night, becoming a competent performer on the violin and cello. He came to know the music of Brahms, Wagner, and Mahler, mostly by playing their scores and attending concerts. Having "left the world of bank notes for musical notes" at the age of twenty-one, he earned a modest living by conducting a men's chorus, orchestrating operettas—the Viennese counterpart of our Broadway musicals—and giving lessons in music theory and composition. Eventually, his own compositions began to be heard in Vienna, though they were usually not well received.

from bank clerk to musician

Schoenberg's earliest works are written in a typical late Romantic style, with rich harmonies, chromatic melodies, expansive forms, and programmatic content. But by 1908 his music had begun to evolve in unexpected directions. Having been strongly influenced by Wagner's chromatic melodies and harmonies, Schoenberg started to compose works in which there was no tonal center. If Wagner could write winding chromatic passages that temporarily obscured the tonality, why not go one step farther and create fully chromatic pieces in which there is no tonality? This Schoenberg did, and in so doing created what is called **atonal music**—music without tonality, music without a key center.

But Schoenberg not only abandoned music with a tonal center—a stable point of reference for the listener—he also dispensed with the triad as the basic building block of music. Earlier, tonal music had unfolded in chord progressions built mainly of consonant triads. Dissonance, which adds an element of tension and anxiety, was carefully controlled and required to resolve to a stable consonance, usually a triad. With Schoenberg's new atonal music, however, dissonance is freed from the necessity of resolving to consonance—it can wander off chromatically to another dissonance and then yet another. As we have seen (on page 359), Schoenberg referred to this as "the emancipation of dissonance." Most listeners today are at first hostile to atonal music, in part because there is no tonal center but more so because it is so highly dissonant. Small wonder that in Schoenberg's day some Viennese musicians refused to play his atonal music, or that when they did the audience's reaction was sometimes violent. (At one concert, March 31, 1913, the police had to be called out to restore order.) Despite the hostility, Schoenberg remained true to his own artistic vision:

> Whether one calls oneself conservative or revolutionary, whether one composes in a conventional or progressive manner, whether one tries to imitate old styles or is destined to express new ideas—whether one is a good composer or not—one must be convinced of the infallibility of one's own fantasy and one must believe in one's own inspiration.

Graphische Sammlung Albertina, Wien

FIGURE 17–12

This 1909 Viennese theater poster by Oskar Kokoschka shows the Expressionist affinity for the dramatic and grotesque. The effect is created by the use of strong, almost crude, lines and bold, contrasting colors.

Expressionism and Atonality

Arnold Schoenberg and his students Alban Berg and Anton Webern were not alone in creating a radically new style of art. As we have seen, there appeared at this same time a powerful movement in the visual arts called Expressionism. **Expressionism** was initially a German–Austrian development that arose in Berlin, Munich, and Vienna. Its aim was not to depict objects as they are seen but to express the strong emotion that the object generated in the artist; not to paint a portrait of an individual but to create an expression of the subject's innermost feelings, anxieties, and fears. In Edvard Munch's early Expressionist painting *The Scream* (1893), the subject cries out to an unsympathetic and uncomprehending world. Schoenberg's statement in this regard can be taken as a credo for the entire Expressionist movement: "Art is the cry of despair of those who experience in themselves the fate of all Mankind" (1910). Gradually, realistic representations gave way to highly personal and increasingly abstract expression. Artists such as Oskar Kokoschka (1886–1980) and Wassily Kandinsky (1866–1944) used harsh colors, macabre images, and distorted figures to show intense psychological states, sometimes with shocking results (see Figs. 17–2 and 17–12). Schoenberg, a personal friend of both Kokoschka and Kandinsky, was himself a painter and exhibited his works with the Expressionists in 1912 (Figs. 17–11 and 17–13). In fact, the music and art of this movement can be described in rather similar terms. The clashing of strong colors, the disjointed shapes, and the jagged lines of the painters have their counterparts in the harsh dissonances, asymmetrical rhythms, and angular, chromatic melodies of Schoenberg and his followers. It is surely not an accident that Schoenberg moved from tonality to atonality in music (1908–1912) at precisely the time Kandinsky and others turned away from realistic representation to abstract expression.

The Scream, by Edvard Munch.

Erich Lessing, Art Resource, NY

PIERROT LUNAIRE (MOONSTRUCK PIERROT) (1912)

Moonstruck Pierrot, Schoenberg's best-known composition, is an exemplary work of Expressionist art. It is a setting for chamber ensemble and female voice of twenty-one poems by Albert Giraud. Here we meet "Moonstruck Pierrot," a white-faced clown from the world of traditional Italian pantomime and puppet shows. Yet in this Expressionist poetry the fun-loving clown suffers the endless anxiety of a sensitive artist-lover whose only confidante is the moon. Pierrot's inner feelings are projected by means of a new vocal technique invented by Schoenberg called **Sprechstimme**—"speech-voice." *Sprechstimme* requires the vocalist to declaim the text more than sing it. The voice is to execute the rhythmic values exactly; but once it hits a pitch, it is to quit the tone immediately, sliding away in either a downward or an upward direction. This creates exaggerated declamation, even a feeling of hysteria, a sentiment appropriate for this hyperexpressive text.

Sprechstimme, a new vocal technique

Poems 6 and 7 of *Moonstruck Pierrot* reveal two different aspects of the clown's feverish state of mind. In number 6 Pierrot offers a hymn of solace to the suffering Madonna; and in number 7 he projects on the face of the moon his own love pains. Each poem is cast as a *rondeau,* an old musical and poetic form characterized by the use of a refrain (see page 197). Traditionally, composers had used the appearance of a textual refrain to repeat part or all of the melody as well. This helped create a unity of text and music and gave the work formal coherence. But Schoenberg, true to his iconoclastic ways, avoids musical repetition in his atonal works. His music unfolds in an ever-varying continuum, like a stream of consciousness. His dissonances, disjunct

musical repetition is avoided

rhythms, changing textures, and nonrepeating melodies place unprecedented demands on the listener. Your first reaction to the seemingly formless flow of dissonance in *Moonstruck Pierrot* may be decidedly negative. Yet with repeated listenings the force of the jarring elements of the atonal style begins to lessen and a bizarre, eerie sort of beauty emerges, especially if you are sensitive to the meaning of the text.

Listening Guide

Arnold Schoenberg
Moonstruck Pierrot (1912)
Number 6, *Madonna*
Number 7, *The Sick Moon*

6CD 5/11–5/12;
2CD 2/10

Number 6, *Madonna*, draws its inspiration from
the vision of the sorrowful Mother of Christ at the Cross. The traditional association of the image of the Cross with musical chromaticism, one extending at least back to Bach, may have given rise to the ascending chromatic line, played pizzicato, in the cello. The angular movement of the voice is typical of Schoenberg's atonal melodic line:

(*Sprechstimme* — "speech-voice")

Steig,   O Mut - ter al - ler Schmer-zen, auf den Al - tar mei - ner   Ver - se!

Steig, O Mutter aller Schmerzen	**Arise, O Mother of all sorrows**
Auf den Altar meiner Verse!	**On the altar of my verse!**
Blut aus deinen magern Brüsten	Blood from your thin breast
Hat des Schwertes Wut vergossen.	Has spilled the rage of the sword.
Deine ewig frischen Wunden	Your eternally fresh wounds
Gleichen Augen, rot und offen,	Like eyes, red and open,
Steig, O Mutter aller Schmerzen	**Arise, O Mother of all sorrows**
Auf den Altar meiner Verse!	**On the altar of my verse!**
(1:13) In den abgezehrten Händen	In your thin and wasted hands
Hältst du deines Sohnes Leiche	You hold the body of your Son
Ihn zu zeigen aller Menschheit,	To show him to all mankind,
Doch der Blick der Menschen meidet	Yet the look of men avoids
Dich, **O Mutter aller Schmerzen.**	You, **O Mother of all sorrows.** (2CD set stops here)

Number 7, *Der kranke Mond* (*The Sick Moon*), is a soliloquy for voice and accompanying flute. As do the Expressionist painters, here the poet transfers to the object (the moon) the internal feelings of the subject (the artist Pierrot). Thus, as Pierrot speaks, the moon begins to reflect his inner turmoil, becoming feverish, tormented, death-sick with love. The silvery tones of the flute help evoke an aura of moonlight, "death-sick" as it may be.

Du nächtig todeskranker Mond	**You nocturnal, death-sick moon**
Dort auf des Himmels	**There on heaven's**
schwarzem Pfühl,	**dark couch,**
Dein Blick, so fiebernd übergross	Your look, so feverishly swollen,
Bannt mich wie fremde Melodie.	Charms me like a foreign melody.
An unstillbarem Liebesleid	In unending pain of love
Stirbst du, an Sehnsucht, tief erstickt,	You die, in yearning consumed,
Du nächtig todeskranker Mond	**You nocturnal, death-sick moon**
Dort auf des Himmels	**There on heaven's**
schwarzem Pfühl.	**dark couch.**
(1:31) Den Liebsten, der im Sinnenrausch,	The lover who, in sensual frenzy,
Gedankenlos zur Liebsten geht,	Steals to the beloved without a care,
Belustigt deiner Strahlen Spiel,	Rejoices in your play of light,
Dein bleiches, qualgebornes Blut,	Your pale, tormented blood,
Du nächtig todeskranker Mond.	**You nocturnal, death-sick moon.**

Needless to say, this music of the extreme avant-garde did not sit well with the anti-intellectual Nazis who took power in Germany in 1933 and Austria in 1938. Hitler and his National Socialists not only harbored a hatred of Jews, but they also made it virtually impossible for "degenerate" modern art like *Moonstruck Pierrot* to be seen or heard. So Schoenberg fled the German lands, as did thousands of other progressive spirits, including Thomas Mann (1875–1955), Kurt Weill (1900–1950), and Albert Einstein (1879–1955). He ultimately made his way to this country and to Los Angeles, where he died peacefully in 1951 at the age of seventy-six.

SCHOENBERG'S TWELVE-TONE MUSIC

When Arnold Schoenberg and his followers did away with tonal chord progressions and melodies that repeated, they found themselves facing a serious artistic problem: how to write large-scale compositions in the new atonal style. For centuries musical structures, like fugue and sonata–allegro form, had been generated by means of a clear tonal plan and the repetition of broad musical themes. Forms created by repetition were useful to the composer and most welcome to the listener seeking to make sense of a new musical composition. But Schoenberg's chromatic, atonal, nonrepeating melodies made traditional musical forms all but impossible. What other formal plan might be used? If all twelve notes of the chromatic scale are equally important, as is true in atonal music, why choose any one note at a given spot in a piece and not another?

By 1923 Schoenberg had solved the problem of formal anarchy—or absence of form—caused by total chromatic freedom. He had discovered a new way of creating music that he called "composing with twelve tones." **Twelve-tone composition** is a method of writing that employs each of the twelve notes of the chromatic scale set in a fixed, predetermined order. The composer chooses the succession of twelve notes to achieve the desired "melody" and places them in a row. Throughout the composition the twelve notes must come in the same order. Music in which elements such as pitch, timbre, or dynamics come in a fixed series is called **serial music**. In twelve-tone music the twelve-note series may unfold not only as a melody but also as a melody with accompaniment, or simply as a progression of chords, since two or more notes of the row may sound simultaneously. Moreover, in addition to appearing in its basic form, the row might go backward (retrograde*) or upside down (inversion*) or both backward and upside down at the same time (retrograde inversion). While such arrangements might seem wholly artificial and very unmusical, we should remember that composers such as J. S. Bach in the Baroque era and Josquin Desprez in the Renaissance had subjected their melodies to similar permutations. The purpose of Schoenberg's twelve-tone method was to create musical unity by basing each piece on a single, orderly arrangement of twelve tones, thereby guaranteeing the perfect equality of all pitches so that none would seem like a tonal center.

TRIO FROM *SUITE FOR PIANO* (1924)

The first steps along this radical twelve-tone path were tentative and, not surprisingly, the pieces that resulted were short, very short. Among Schoenberg's first serial compositions was his *Suite for Piano*, a collection of seven

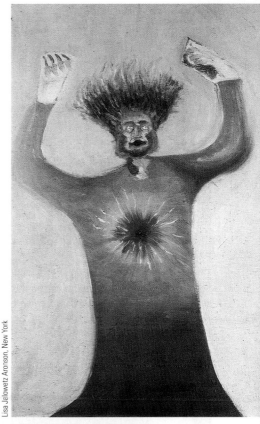

Lisa Jalowetz Aronson, New York

FIGURE 17–13

As a young man, Schoenberg was undecided whether his future lay in music or painting. Like many Expressionist paintings before World War I, his *Hatred* (ca. 1910) gives a sense of the subject's inner feelings.

serial music

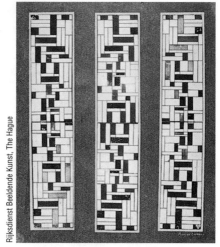

FIGURE 17–14

The same rational processes at work in Schoenberg's twelve-tone music can be seen in Theo van Doesburg's *Composition IV* (1917). Notice the retrograde motion: the pattern proceeding downward from the top left is the same as that upward from the bottom right.

Rijksdienst Beeldende Kunst, The Hague

brief dance movements, including the Minuet and Trio to be discussed here. The tone row for the *Suite*, along with its three permutations, is as follows:

Row   *Retrograde*

E F G D♭ G♭ E♭ A♭ D B C A B♭   B♭ A C B D A♭ E♭ G♭ D♭ G F E
1 2 3 4 5 6 7 8 9 10 11 12   12 11 10 9 8 7 6 5 4 3 2 1

Inversion   *Retrograde-inversion*

E E♭ D♭ G D F C F♯ A G♯ B B♭   B♭ B G♯ A F♯ C F D G D♭ E♭ E
1 2 3 4 5 6 7 8 9 10 11 12   12 11 10 9 8 7 6 5 4 3 2 1

Schoenberg allows the row or any of its permutations to begin on any pitch, so long as the original sequence of intervals is maintained. Notice in the Trio, for example, that the row itself begins on E but is also allowed to start on B♭ (see Listening Guide). In the second part, measures 6–9, the exact serial progression of the row breaks down slightly. The composer explained this as a "justifiable deviation," owing to the need for tonal variety at this point. Notice as well that the rhythms in which the notes appear may likewise be changed for the sake of variety. As you listen to the Trio, see if you can follow the unfolding of the row and all its permutations. Listen many times—the piece is only fifty-one seconds long! Its aesthetic effect is similar to that of a constructivist painting of an artist like Theo van Doesburg (see Fig. 17–14). If you like the painting, you should like Schoenberg's twelve-tone piano piece as well.

Listening Guide www

Arnold Schoenberg
Trio from *Suite for Piano* (1924)

6CD 5/13

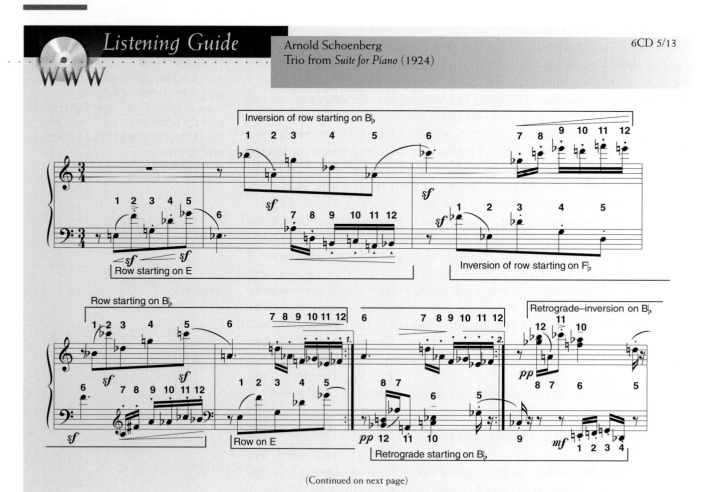

(Continued on next page)

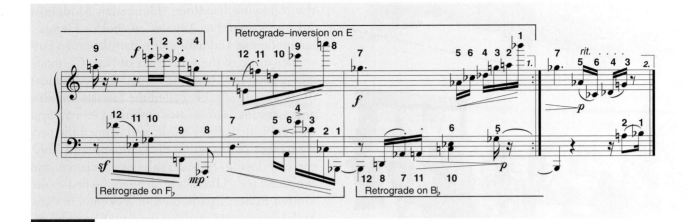

As the years progressed, Schoenberg used his twelve-tone method to construct longer compositions for larger forces. In 1932 he completed most of a full-length opera, *Moses and Aaron*, and in 1947 he finished a cantata*, *A Survivor from Warsaw*, that tells of Nazi atrocities in Poland. Both works are twelve-tone in style throughout. But the listening public never embraced Schoenberg's twelve-tone music. The style is still very much that of dissonant, atonal music. For most listeners, it sounds irrational and arbitrary, indeed completely "out of control." Indeed, the twelve-tone way of writing music has been called one of the two great failed experiments of the twentieth century, the other being Communism. Schoenberg was philosophical about the public's general dislike of his music: "If it is art, it is not for all, and if it is for all, it is not art."

Béla Bartók (1881–1945)

The music of the Hungarian composer Béla Bartók is decidedly modern, yet distinctly different in sound from that of Stravinsky or Schoenberg. While it can be atonal, like the music of Schoenberg, it is often highly tuneful, making use of sweeping melodies. And while it is frequently percussive and highly rhythmic, like the motor-driven sounds of Stravinsky, Bartók's rhythmic force derives mainly from folk music. Bartók's creative imagination was fired by folk materials of his native Hungary. He saw the return to the simple, direct style of folk music as a way to counter the tendency in Romantic music toward ostentation and sentimentality.

The life of Béla Bartók was strongly affected by the turbulent events that occurred in Eastern Europe during the first half of the twentieth century. He was born in 1881 in Hungary, but in a part of that nation that was later given over to Rumania at the end of World War I. Throughout his life he was an ardent Hungarian nationalist, and chose to develop his obvious musical talents at the Academy of Music in Budapest rather than at the German-dominated Vienna Conservatory, where he had also been admitted. As a student at the Academy in Budapest he studied composition and piano, quickly acquiring a reputation as a concert pianist of the highest quality. By the 1920s he had achieved an international reputation both as a pianist and as a composer of music in the modern vein. His tours even carried him to the western part of the United States, where one newspaper alerted the public to his coming with

FIGURE 17–15
Béla Bartók.

FIGURE 17–16

Béla Bartók recording folk songs among Czech-speaking peasants in 1908. The performers sang into the megaphone of a wax-cylinder recording machine invented by Thomas Edison.

the following headline: "Hungarian Modernist Advances upon Los Angeles." As both a Hungarian modernist and nationalist, Bartók was an outspoken critic of the supporters of Nazi Germany who gained control of the Hungarian government in the late 1930s. He called the fascists "bandits and assassins," cut off ties with the German firm that published all his music, and banned the performances of his works in Germany and Italy, thereby losing considerable performance and broadcast fees. Ultimately, in 1940, he fled to the United States. Bartók died of leukemia in New York City in 1945, and not until 1988 were his remains returned, at the request of his sons, to his beloved Hungary.

Béla Bartók is unique among composers in that he was as much interested in musical research, specifically in the study of Eastern European folk music, as he was in musical composition. He traveled from village to village in Hungary, Rumania, Bulgaria, Turkey, and even North Africa using the newly invented recording machine of Thomas Edison. In this way his ear became saturated with the driving rhythms and odd-number meters of peasant dances, as well as the unusual scales on which the folk melodies of Eastern Europe were constructed. If the cosmopolitan Stravinsky took his folk melodies from printed anthologies, Bartók found his among the people.

The musical heritage of Eastern Europe is heard continually throughout Bartók's music, from his first string quartet (1908) to his great final works for orchestra: *Music for Strings, Percussion and Celesta* (1936), *Divertimento for Strings* (1939), and *Concerto for Orchestra* (1943). This last-named work was commissioned by the conductor of the Boston Symphony Orchestra for the then substantial fee of $1,000. It remains Bartók's best-known and most alluring composition.

CONCERTO FOR ORCHESTRA (1943)

Normally a concerto is for a single solo instrument—piano or violin, for example—pitted against an orchestra. In Bartók's *Concerto for Orchestra*, however, the composer encourages many instruments to step forward from within the orchestra to serve as soloists from time to time. The spotlight switches from one instrument to another or to a new combination of instruments, each displaying its distinctive tonal color against the backdrop of the full orchestra. There are five movements: The first is "written in a more or less regular sonata form," as the composer says, and makes use of the folklike pentatonic* scale; the second is a colorful parade of pairs of instruments; the third is an atmospheric nocturne*, an example of what is called Bartók's "night music," in which the woodwinds slither around chromatically above a misty tremolo in the strings; the fourth is an unusual intermezzo; while the fifth is a vigorous peasant dance in sonata–allegro form. Let us focus our attention on the fourth movement, *Intermezzo interrotto* (*Broken Intermezzo*).

a modern-day concerto grosso

CORBIS/Archivo Iconográfico, S.A.

An **intermezzo** (Italian for "between piece") is a light musical interlude intended to separate and thus break the mood of two more serious surrounding movements. But here, as the title *Broken Intermezzo* indicates, the light intermezzo is itself rudely interrupted by contrasting music. A sophisticated mood is first established by a charming theme in the oboe. As is usual for Bartók, this melody shows the influence of the Hungarian folk song both in its pentatonic construction (the five notes that make up the scale of the melody are B, C♯, E, F♯, and A♯) and in the way the meter switches back and forth between an even $\frac{2}{4}$ and an odd $\frac{5}{8}$:

Hungarian melodies

EXAMPLE 17–7

After the tune is passed among several wind instruments, an even more ingratiating melody emerges in the strings. It, too, is Hungarian in style. In fact, it is Bartók's idealized reworking of the song *You Are Lovely, You Are Beautiful, Hungary.*

EXAMPLE 17–8

But the nostalgic vision of the homeland is suddenly interrupted by a new, cruder theme in the clarinet, and it also tells a tale. Bartók took this clarinet melody from the Russian composer Dimitri Shostakovitch's Symphony No. 7, a programmatic work depicting the German invasion of Russia (1942). Bartók borrowed the theme Shostakovitch had written to signify the invading Germans, believing its simple quarter-note descent to be appropriately heavy and trite.

EXAMPLE 17–9

Thus, Bartók's intermezzo can be heard as an autobiographical work in which, as the composer related to a friend, "the artist declares his love for his native land in a serenade which is suddenly interrupted in a crude and violent manner; he is seized by rough, booted men who even break his instrument." Bartók tells us what he thinks of these "rough, booted men" by surrounding them with rude, jeering noises in the trumpets and woodwinds. Ultimately, he brings back the idyllic vision of the homeland by returning to the opening two themes. As to the soloists in this movement of Bartók's *Concerto for Orchestra*, there are many: oboe, clarinet, flute, English horn, and the entire section of violas.

Bartók, an ardent anti-Nazi

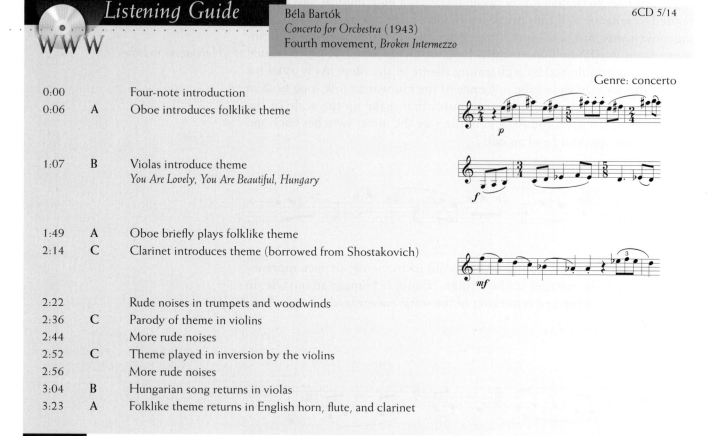

Listening Guide

Béla Bartók
Concerto for Orchestra (1943)
Fourth movement, *Broken Intermezzo*

6CD 5/14

Genre: concerto

0:00		Four-note introduction
0:06	A	Oboe introduces folklike theme
1:07	B	Violas introduce theme *You Are Lovely, You Are Beautiful, Hungary*
1:49	A	Oboe briefly plays folklike theme
2:14	C	Clarinet introduces theme (borrowed from Shostakovich)
2:22		Rude noises in trumpets and woodwinds
2:36	C	Parody of theme in violins
2:44		More rude noises
2:52	C	Theme played in inversion by the violins
2:56		More rude noises
3:04	B	Hungarian song returns in violas
3:23	A	Folklike theme returns in English horn, flute, and clarinet

THREE AMERICAN EXPERIMENTALISTS: IVES, VARÈSE, AND CAGE

anything is possible

There are times in the history of art when the rejection of a previously dominant system coincides with radical experimentation, as new ideas compete to fill a void. In music this happened at the turn of the seventeenth century, when many composers suddenly gave up on imitative polyphony, as well as at the turn of the twentieth century, when tonality and consonance no longer seemed important. Painting, too, experienced a revolution after the turn of the twentieth century, when artists determined that photographic realism was not the path to the future. Radical experimentation continued into mid-century. Painters Jasper Johns (Fig. 17–19) and Andy Warhol (Fig. 17–24), for example, explored a host of new ways that paint, and other materials, could be applied to canvas. Simultaneously, musicians sought new ways to organize pitch, density, and spacial relationships.

Among the most radical of these exploratory musical thinkers were Charles Ives (1874–1954), Edgard Varèse (1883–1965), and John Cage (1912–1992). By creating a novel style of collage art, Ives gave new meaning to traditional and popular music material; Varèse worked to remove the element of pitch from music so as to concentrate on color and texture; and Cage brought noises from the everyday world into the concert hall and asked why these, too, were not music, thereby questioning our very definition of this art. That all three of these experimental composers were American suggests the probing, independent, sometimes scientific quality of American musical thought during the twentieth century.

Charles Ives (1874–1954)

Charles Ives was the greatest, and most eccentric, of American composers. He was born in Danbury, Connecticut, the son of George Ives (1845–1894), a bandleader in the Union Army who had served with General Grant during the Civil War. The senior Ives gave his son a highly unorthodox musical education, at least by European standards. True, there was the obligatory study of the three B's—Bach, Beethoven, and Brahms—along with harmony and counterpoint, as well as lessons on the violin, piano, organ, cornet, and drums. But young Ives was also taught how to "stretch his ears," as he said. In one exercise he was made to sing *Swanee River* in E♭ while his father accompanied him on the piano in the key of C—a useful lesson in polytonality*! The sounds that stuck in his ears were those of marches, popular and patriotic songs, fiddlers' jigs, minstrel tunes, and church hymns.

Since his forebears had gone to Yale, it was decided that Charles should enroll there, too. At Yale he took courses in music with Horatio Parker (1863–1919), a composer of some capability who had been trained in Germany. But Ives's youthful, independent ideas about how music should sound clashed with Parker's traditional European notions of harmony and counterpoint. The student learned to leave his more radical musical experimentations, such as a fugue with a subject entering in four different keys, outside Parker's classroom. Ives became heavily involved in extracurricular activities, including fraternity musicals, and maintained a D+ average (a "gentleman's" mark before the days of grade inflation).

When he graduated with the class of 1898, Charles Ives decided not to pursue music as a profession. He realized that the sort of music he had in his head was not the kind the public would pay to hear. So he headed for New York City, and in 1907 he and a friend formed the company of Ives and Myrick, an agency that sold insurance as a subsidiary of Mutual of New York (MONY). Ives and Myrick grew to become the largest insurance agency in the United States, and in the year in which Ives retired, 1929, had sales of $49 million.

But Charles Ives led two lives: insurance executive by day, frantic composer by night. During the twenty years between his departure from Yale (1898) and the American entry into World War I (1917), Ives wrote the bulk of his 43 works for symphony or band, 41 choral pieces, approximately 75 works for piano solo or various chamber ensembles, and more than 150 songs. Almost without exception they went unheard. Ives made little effort to get his music performed—composition was for him a very private matter. Gradually, however, word of his unusual creations spread among a few influential performers and critics. In 1947 he was awarded the Pulitzer Prize in music for his Third Symphony, one he had written forty years earlier! In his usual gruff, eccentric way, Ives told the members of the Pulitzer committee, "Prizes are for boys. I'm grown up."

VARIATIONS ON AMERICA (1892–ca. 1905)
Charles Ives's great contribution to music was to create what might fairly be called "collage art" in sound. He borrows elements from traditional classical

FIGURE 17–17

Young Charles Ives in the baseball uniform of Hopkins Grammar School, New Haven, Connecticut. A better baseball player than student, Ives needed an extra year between high school and college to prepare for Yale. The photo was taken in 1893, a year after he had written the bulk of *Variations on America*.

insurance executive by day, composer by night

FIGURE 17–18

William Harnett's *Music and Good Luck* (1888) creates a satisfying collage by melding various objects from a horse barn and the world of music. Ives applied this same technique of "collage art" to music, bringing together all sorts of musical objects from classical and popular styles to create a new, unexpected medley.

music—fugue themes, polonaises*, snippets from Wagner, and others—and takes even more from American vernacular music—popular and patriotic songs, fiddle tunes, American hymns, band marches, and the like. Ives combines these familiar musical objects in a very unfamiliar way, piling one borrowed tune on top of another and thereby creating a collage of sound that is usually highly dissonant. In a manner akin to that of an avant-garde artist who reinterprets fragments of reality in surprising ways (Figs. 17–18 and 17–19), Ives defamiliarizes the familiar with sometimes shocking results.

Ives took an important step toward collage art in one of his earliest works, *Variations on America* for organ, written in 1892 at the age of seventeen. As the title indicates, this is a set of variations on the patriotic tune known in the United States as *America* or *My Country 'Tis of Thee*. It begins with a conventional introduction, followed by a statement of the well-known theme. Variation 1, filled with increasingly chromatic figuration for the right hand, is in no way exceptional, but Variation 2 ends with the close chromatic harmony popular with "barber shop" quartets during the gay '90s. Variation 3, with its quick puffs of sound, is reminiscent of a calliope, or steam organ, at a village fair, while Variation 4 introduces a most foreign element: a Polish polonaise*, here in a minor key. The fifth and final variation features a Bach-like walking bass* to be played by the pedals "as fast as they can go." Thus the collage here consists of a patriotic tune melded with allusions to a barber shop quartet, steam whistles, a Polish polonaise, and a Baroque organ toccata*.

Sometime during the first decade of the twentieth century, while working in the insurance industry in New York City, Ives revisited his *Variations on America* and inserted two interludes. Both are remarkable because they make use of **polytonality**, the simultaneous sounding of two keys or tonalities. In the first Interlude, for example, the right hand plays in F major (one flat) while the left and the pedal do so in D♭ major (five flats; see Listening Guide). Ives was the first composer in the history of music to employ polytonality, and the result is bracing yet highly dissonant. *America* had never sounded like this—in two keys at once! But America was not ready for Ives's ear-splitting dissonances. Not until 1949 was a publisher willing to print *Variations on America*—more than fifty years after Ives had composed it.

FIGURE 17–19

The American Optical artist Jasper Johns has taken a venerable object and created unexpected effects of light, motion, and color in his *Three Flags* (1958). In a similar way Charles Ives created an unexpectedly dissonant, polytonal effect when he superimposed the tune America upon itself in his *Variations on America*.

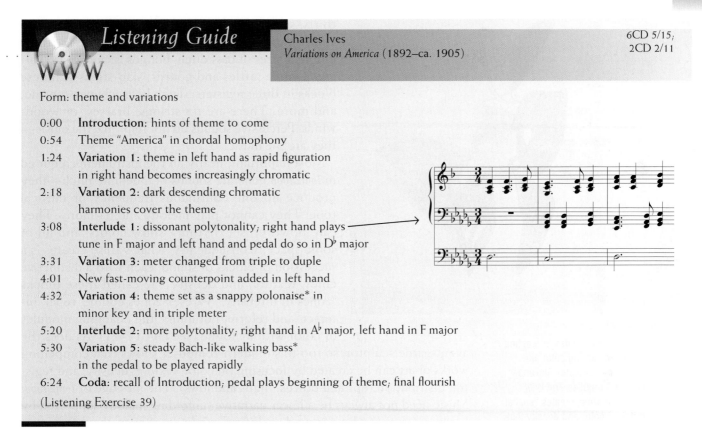

Listening Guide

Charles Ives
Variations on America (1892–ca. 1905)

6CD 5/15;
2CD 2/11

WWW

Form: theme and variations

0:00 **Introduction**: hints of theme to come
0:54 Theme "America" in chordal homophony
1:24 **Variation 1**: theme in left hand as rapid figuration
      in right hand becomes increasingly chromatic
2:18 **Variation 2**: dark descending chromatic
      harmonies cover the theme
3:08 **Interlude 1**: dissonant polytonality; right hand plays
      tune in F major and left hand and pedal do so in D♭ major
3:31 **Variation 3**: meter changed from triple to duple
4:01 New fast-moving counterpoint added in left hand
4:32 **Variation 4**: theme set as a snappy polonaise* in
      minor key and in triple meter
5:20 **Interlude 2**: more polytonality; right hand in A♭ major, left hand in F major
5:30 **Variation 5**: steady Bach-like walking bass*
      in the pedal to be played rapidly
6:24 **Coda**: recall of Introduction; pedal plays beginning of theme; final flourish

(Listening Exercise 39)

Edgard Varèse (1883–1965)

Passage to a land of new aesthetic frontiers was also the goal of Edgard Varèse.
Thus in 1915 this French musician left old-world Europe and sailed for the
United States. An accidental fire caused the loss of some of the scores he had
brought with him from Paris. He then destroyed the rest, obliterating in this
symbolic act all traces of his European musical past. Significantly, Varèse entitled his first work written in this country *Amériques* (1921), suggesting not only
a new geography but also a new world of musical sound. Besides the usual
complement of strings, brasses, and woodwinds, *Amériques* also requires a bat-
tery of new percussion instruments, including sirens and sleigh bells, most of
which had never before been heard in a symphony orchestra. Later compositions, such as *Hyperprism* (1923) and *Intégrales* (1925), likewise experiment with
percussion instruments, to the virtual exclusion of the traditional strings.
Eventually, Varèse did away entirely with conventional acoustical instruments,
creating something called **musique concrète** (see boxed essay on page 382).

Varèse not only uses more percussion instruments than any other composer, but he employs them in a most untraditional way. In earlier centuries,
orchestral composers customarily called on the percussion for purposes of
accent. By means of taps, thuds, and bangs these instruments helped delineate the main features, and especially climaxes, of the musical structure. Like
a spice, they added character, but did not change—and did not constitute—
the essence of the music.

FIGURE 17–20
Composer Edgard Varèse surrounded by a
light sculpture.

CBS/Sony

IONIZATION (1931)

In *Ionization*, however, Varèse completely turns the musical tables. Now there
are no instruments other than percussive ones. Thirteen performers play

FIGURE 17–21

Just as Edgard Varèse creates interacting "sound masses" of varying color and density, so American sculptor Alexander Calder, in his 1960 mobiles *The Wall Flower* and *Red Pyramid*, creates "spatial zones" of different color and density that, on the slightest breath of air, interact in unexpected ways.

thirty-seven different instruments, including two sirens, two tam-tams, a gong, cymbals, anvils, three different sizes of bass drum, bongos, snare drums, various Cuban rattles and gourds, slap-sticks, Chinese blocks in three registers, sleigh bells, chimes, a piano, and more. There are no strings, brasses, or woodwinds. Percussive sounds do not reinforce the music—they are the music.

Most important, nearly all the instruments required in *Ionization* generate sounds of indefinite pitch—they produce no one continuous frequency or musical tone. They cannot play melody and harmony. They can, however, set rhythms, show colors, and fill in sonic space. Consequently, what Varèse creates is a succession of blocks of sound, each with a distinctive color, texture, and density. He called these blocks "zones of intensity." Varèse's zones collide, repel, interact, and reform, not unlike the changing modules of color with a mobile (see Fig. 17–21). As does the avant-garde sculptor, so too this modern composer shows that compelling works of art can be created by focusing on color, texture, density, and registral distribution (ups and downs, highs and lows). The message of *Ionization*: Music need not always be a linear narrative (unfolding melody supported by harmony) but can be a "sound sculpture" made up of ever-changing sonic zones.

Listening Guide

Edgard Varèse
Ionization (1931)

6CD 5/16

WWW

0:00	Sound zone 1: shimmer of cymbals, drums, gongs, and sirens
0:27	Sound zone 2: snare drum and tam-tam create sharply defined rhythms, thin texture
0:42	Sound zone 1 returns briefly
0:52	Sound zone 2 expanded, becomes denser as more instruments added
1:47	Siren from sound zone 1 penetrates into sound zone 2
1:58	Sound zone 3: pounding intensity (*fortissimo*), denser texture in low register (bass drums)
2:33	Sound zone 4 (high-sounding anvils) interacts with sound zone 1
2:47	Sound zones 1–4 interact at various levels of intensity (louds and softs)
3:57	Sound zone 5 (piano and chimes) added to the mix
4:40	Fadeout: intensity diminishes, texture thins as accumulated sonority of five sound zones fades away

John Cage (1912–1992)

John Cage was born in Los Angeles, the son of an inventor. He was graduated valedictorian of Los Angeles High School and spent two years at nearby Pomona College before going to Europe to learn more about art, architecture, and music. Arriving in New York in 1942, he worked variously as a wall washer at the YWCA, teacher of music and mycology (the science of mushrooms) at the New School for Social Research, and as music director of a modern dance company.

From his earliest days as a musician, Cage had a special affection for percussion instruments and the unusual sounds they can create. His *First Construction (in Metal)* (1939) has six percussionists play piano, metal thundersheets, oxen bells, cowbells, sleigh bells, water gongs, and brake drums, among other things. By 1941 he had collected three hundred percussion objects of this kind—anything that might make an unusual noise when struck or shaken. Cage's tinkering with percussive sounds led him to invent the **prepared piano**: a grand piano outfitted with screws, bolts, washers, erasers, and bits of felt and plastic all inserted between the strings (Fig. 17–23). This transformed the piano into a one-man percussion band that could produce a great variety of sounds and noises—twangs, zaps, rattles, thuds, and the like—no two of which were exactly the same in pitch or color. In creating the prepared piano, Cage was merely going farther along the experimental trail first blazed by his spiritual mentor, Edgard Varèse: "Years ago, after I decided to devote my life to music, I noticed that people distinguished between noises and sounds. I decided to follow Varèse and fight for noises, to be on the side of the underdog."

Cage's glorification of everyday noise began in earnest during the 1950s. Rather than engage in a titanic struggle to shape the elements of music, as did Beethoven, he decided to sit back, relax, and just let noises occur around him. In creating this sort of purposeless, undirected music, Cage invented what has come to be called chance music, the ultimate in musical experimentation. In **chance music**, musical events are not carefully predetermined by the composer but come in an unpredictable sequence as the result of traditionally unmusical activities such as using astrological charts, tossing coins, throwing dice, or shuffling the pages of music any which way. In *Music Walk* (1958), for example, one or more pianists connect lines and dots in any fashion to create a musical "score" from which to play. Such "scores" only suggest in the most vague way what the musician is to do. The musical "happening" that results is the sort of spontaneous group experience that was to flower during the 1960s. More radical still is Cage's work o'oo" (1962), which allows the performer total artistic freedom. When performed by Cage himself in 1962, he sliced

Christopher Felver/CORBIS

FIGURE 17–22

"I have nothing to say and I am saying it." John Cage

The New York Public Library

FIGURE 17–23

John Cage's "prepared piano." By putting spoons, forks, screws, paper clips, and other sundry objects into the strings of the piano, the composer changes the instrument from one producing melodic tones to one generating percussive impacts.

Electronic Music: From Varèse to Radiohead

The effect of technology on recent classical and popular music has been nothing short of astonishing. Most classical music, of course, is **acoustical** music—music produced by instruments that make sound "naturally" by means of vibrating strings, pipes, or drums, for example. But shortly after World War II new developments in technology began to make possible **electronic music**—music produced by machines that generate sound using electronic circuitry.

The earliest experiments with the creation of electronic sound gave rise to *musique concrète*. **Musique concrète** is so-called because the composer works, not with sounds written for voice or musical instruments, but with those found naturally in the environment. Another term for *musique concrète*, then, might be "found sound." A car horn, a person speaking in a room, a dog's bark may be captured by a tape recorder and doctored

W. G. "Snuffy" Walden is an eminently successful TV composer, having created the theme for The West Wing *as well as scores for* The Drew Carey Show, My So-Called Life, The Street, The Wonder Years, *and many others.*

in some way—reassembled and repeated (spliced, mixed, and looped) to form an unexpected montage of sound. Edgard Varèse, working both in New York and Paris, was one of the first practitioners of *musique concrète*, his *Poème electronique* (1958) being a landmark in the history of this sort of synthetic music.

Pop artists, too, quickly began to exploit these musical-technical developments. The Beatles' John Lennon used "tape looping" to create a novel background ambience for his song *Revolution #9* (1968). As Lennon said about the making of this recording: "We were cutting up [tapes of] classical music and making different size loops, and then I got an engineer tape on which an engineer was saying, "Number nine, number nine, number nine." All those different bits of sound and noises were all compiled. . . . I fed them all in and mixed them live." Lennon also added *musique concrète* (found sound) to a few Beatles songs. *Strawberry Fields*, for example, has a piano crash followed by a dog's whistle played at fifteen kilocycles. Not to be outdone, the rock band Pink Floyd incorporated the sounds of a clanging cash register into their song, appropriately titled, *Money* (1973). And filmmakers, too, jumped on the electronic bandwagon. George Lucas used banging chains to create the sound of the Imperial Walkers for his *Star Wars* epics. To be specific, he recorded, and then modified and layered, the noise of a bicycle chain falling on a concrete floor—a literal example of the principle of *musique concrète*.

As the previous examples demonstrate, what had begun as an esoteric experiment of a few avant-garde scientists and composers soon transformed the world of popular entertainment. The technological development that made this possible was miniaturization. During the 1960s, the large-console tape machine was reduced to the portable tape recorder, and then, during the 1980s,

FIGURE 17–24

The Campbell's Soup Can (1965) painted by Andy Warhol (1930–1987) asks the fundamental question: What is art?

and prepared vegetables at a table on a stage, put them through a food processor, and then drank the juice, all the while amplifying and broadcasting the sound of these activities around the hall. In a funny way, Cage's attempts to elevate the random, ordinary noise of food processing to the level of art is rather like Andy Warhol's glorification of the Campbell's soup can (Fig. 17–24).

Naturally, music critics called Cage a joker and a charlatan. Most would agree that his "compositions" in and of themselves are not of great musical value. But he did have a philosophy about music that he articulated the computer became miniaturized within the keyboard synthesizer. Every fledgling composer and every aspiring rock band could own the hardware to create and doctor their own sounds. Take the keyboard synthesizer, for example. A **synthesizer** is a machine that creates, transforms, and combines (or synthesizes) electronic sounds. Within every synthesizer is a computer, and from it computer music can be created. The principle of **computer music** is this: all aspects of musical sound—pitch, duration, color, volume, attack, and decay—can be measured and expressed quantitatively in binary numbers. Such numbers can be stored and manipulated by the computer and, on command, turned into electrical voltages that can then be pushed through speakers to produce audible sound. (This same technology—the capacity to store and retrieve digital sound—allows music to be sent over the Internet as MP3 files.) By manipulating the numbers, the artist manipulates the sound. He or she can change the timbre of a clarinet into that of a trumpet, for example. Today the computer-driven synthesizer can produce sounds that are almost indistinguishable from those of a ninety-piece orchestra. Needless to say, this has revolutionized the world of commercial music. The computer-equipped recording studio now generates much of the music we hear on radio and television. The opening music for the TV series *Law and Order*, for example, begins with tones that sound like those of a clarinet. In fact, these are synthesized (artificially fabricated) sounds created by a computer-driven synthesizer.

Technology has recently created new genres and new processes for pop music. In the 1980s, rap and hip-hop artists begain using a technique called **sampling**, whereby the rapper extracts a small portion of pre-recorded music and then mechanically repeats it over

Radiohead in concert in Frejus, France, on 17 June 2000.

© AIM PATRICE/CORBIS SYGMA

and over as a musical backdrop behind the text that he or she raps. Most recently the technique of **scratching** (also called "cutting" and "spinning") has appeared. A creative D.J. with one or more record turntables manipulates the needle, scratching on the vinyl of the record while other pre-recorded sounds loop continually in the background. Perhaps no contemporary rock group has blended song writing with the manipulation of electronic audio more exhaustively than Radiohead. For their albums and concert tours they use not only analog and digital synthesizers but also computer software programs (such as Whammy-Wah), effects and distortion pedals, and compression filters to reform the audio of their voices and instruments. All these electronic devices and computer processes help give the music of Radiohead its sometimes disembodied, otherworldly quality.

by means of questions implied in his music. By focusing on the chance appearance of ordinary noise, Cage aggressively asks us to ponder the fundamental principles that underlie most Western music. Why must sounds of similar range and color come one after the other, why must music have form and unity, why must it have "meaning," why must it express something, why must it develop and climax, why must it be goal oriented, as is so much of human activity in the West?

Must music, too, be goal-oriented?

4'33" (1952)

The "composition" of Cage that causes us to focus on these questions most intently is his *4'33"*. Here one or more performers carrying any sort of instrument come out on the stage, seat themselves, open the music, and play nothing. For each of the three carefully timed movements there is no notated music but only the indication *tacet* ("it is silent"). With no organized sound to be heard during the four minutes and thirty-three seconds of silence that follows, the listener gradually becomes aware of the background noise in the hall—a creaking floor, a passing car, a dropped paper clip, an electrical hum. It turns out there is no such thing as absolute silence. Cage asks us to embrace these random, everyday noises—to tune our ears in innocent sonic wonder. Are these sounds not of artistic value too? What is music? What is noise? What is art?

Can random noise be music?

Needless to say, we have not filled your CDs with four minutes and thirty-three seconds of background noise. You can create your own, and John Cage would have liked that. Listen to *4'33''* with the following guide and note what you hear. Perhaps this experiment will make you more aware of how important conscious organization is to the art we call music. If nothing else, Cage makes us realize that music, above all, is a form of communication from one person to the next and that random background noise can do nothing to express or communicate ideas and feelings.

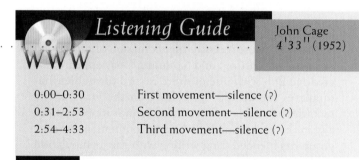

Listening Guide

John Cage
4'33'' (1952)

0:00–0:30	First movement—silence (?)
0:31–2:53	Second movement—silence (?)
2:54–4:33	Third movement—silence (?)

THREE TRADITIONALISTS: SERGEY PROKOFIEV, AARON COPLAND, AND ELLEN TAAFFE ZWILICH

music in traditional forms and styles

While experimental composers in this century, such as Varèse and Cage, have sought to break with the traditions of Western music, other musicians have tried to extend and invigorate the past by imposing on it modern idioms and styles. In this sense composers like Aaron Copland and Ellen Taaffe Zwilich, to name only two among the traditionalists, are more evolutionary than revolutionary. Their aim is to show that traditional values of form, balance, melodiousness, warmth, emotion, and meaning in music have validity in the modern sonic world. Modernity, of course, could never fully eradicate tradition. The two aesthetics continue to exist side by side. Each offers an ongoing critique of the other, and thereby further identifies and defines itself.

Toward the end of the first World War (1914–1918), a new artistic movement called **Neo-classicism** sought to revive the balanced forms and conjunct melodies of earlier music, specifically of the Baroque and Classical periods. The resourceful Igor Stravinsky turned away from his large-scale, colorful Russian ballets like *The Rite of Spring* to write for a much smaller, leaner orchestra of strings and woodwinds. "I attempted to build a new music on eighteenth-century classicism," he said. Neo-classicism rejected not only the large orchestra and the emotionalism of the Romantics but also the extreme sort of dissonance and atonality being advanced by modernists such as Arnold Schoenberg and his Second Viennese School (see page 367). Needless to say, the listening public, which had never taken kindly to the experimental works of the radical avant-garde, welcomed the greater simplicity, clarity, and even humor in the Neo-classical style. The earliest and perhaps most enjoyable example of musical Neo-classicism is Sergey Prokofiev's *Classical Symphony* (1917).

Sergey Prokofiev (1891–1953)

The career of Sergey Prokofiev is full of contradictions and ironies, caused in part by the place he occupied in Russian history. The son of a well-to-do farm administrator, he fled the Communist Revolution in 1917, only later to celebrate in music the most murderous of the revolutionaries, Joseph Stalin (1879–1953). He was known as the dissonant, atonal "bad boy" of the St. Petersburg Conservatory, where he received his musical education, but later wrote such pleasantly benign works as *Peter and the Wolf* (1936). He thought of himself above all as a serious composer—the author of seven symphonies, six operas and six ballets, five piano concertos, and nine piano sonatas—but today is remembered mainly for his lighter works: the *Classical Symphony*, *Peter and the Wolf*, and the film scores *Lieutenant Kijé* and *Alexander Nevsky*. He and Joseph Stalin died within minutes of each other on the night of March 5, 1953, but news of Prokofiev's death was withheld for days so as not to deflect attention away from the deceased dictator. No flowers could be bought for the great composer's coffin: The funeral of the supreme murderer, without exaggeration, had claimed them all.

CLASSICAL SYMPHONY (1917)

There is a sense of historical irony present as well in Prokofiev's *Classical Symphony*. It is the irony created by a clash of musical systems and values: those of the eighteenth century against those of the modern world. Prokofiev creates a model of Neo-classicism by invoking the orchestra and the musical forms of Joseph Haydn. He hypothesized: "It seemed to me that had Haydn lived in our day, he would have retained his own style while accepting something new at the same time." The "something new" in this four-movement Neo-classical symphony is the following: a melody that is more disjunct and angular than Haydn would have written, a harmony that slides suddenly to unexpected chords, and a dissonance so biting and so frequent as to be unknown to classical composers. What is more, Prokofiev distorts our traditional sense of timing and balance; in this very short symphony every musical idea seems to end before it has begun. Prokofiev uses classical forms and procedures, yet simultaneously mocks classical ideals by means of modern dissonance, imbalance, and unexpected brevity. By juxtaposing the classical and the modern in a single work, the composer demands that we address the question: "What makes musical style?" Thus, as we listen to the *Classical Symphony* we enjoy the music in and of itself, but we also think about the interaction of contrasting musical styles. Prokofiev's work is simultaneously art and a critique of art.

The Alex T. Hillman Family Foundation, New York

FIGURE 17–25

Just as Stravinsky, after the example of Prokofiev, entered a Neo-classical period during the 1920s, so the artist Pablo Picasso painted in a lighter, more transparent Neo-classical style in that decade. Although the figures in his *Mother and Child* (1921–1922) are somewhat extended and abstract, the formal composition of this painting, which harks back to a Madonna and Child of the Renaissance, is classical.

FIGURE 17–26
Sergey Prokofiev.

Bettmann/CORBIS

Listening Guide

Sergey Prokofiev
Classical Symphony (Symphony No. 1; 1917)
First movement, *Allegro* (fast)

6CD 6/1

Genre: symphony
Form: sonata–allegro

Exposition

0:00 Violins play racing first theme

0:23 Woodwinds lead lively transition
0:55 Violins softly play second theme above bassoon counterpoint

1:28 *Forte* closing theme

Development

1:44 First theme returns briefly
1:54 Transition material developed and extended to different keys
2:13 *Fortissimo* expansion of second theme
2:40 Closing theme used as retransition*

Recapitulation

2:54 First theme returns
3:04 Woodwinds lead transition
3:30 Soft violins bring back second theme above bassoon counterpoint
3:58 *Forte* closing theme

Aaron Copland (1900–1990)

The tradition embodied in the music of Aaron Copland is, simply said, our American musical heritage. He does not reuse materials taken from eighteenth-century Europe but instead employs American hymn tunes, cowboy songs, and jazz idioms. These he sets not in a collage of dissonant polytonality, as did his older contemporary, Charles Ives, but in a conservative backdrop of generally consonant harmony.

Copland was born in Brooklyn of Jewish immigrant parents. After a rudimentary musical education in New York City, he set sail for Paris to broaden his artistic horizons. In this he was not alone, for the City of Light at this time attracted young writers, painters, and musicians from across the world,

he discovered America in Paris

including Stravinsky, Picasso, James Joyce (1882–1941), Gertrude Stein (1874–1946), Ernest Hemingway (1898–1961), and F. Scott Fitzgerald (1896–1940). After three years of study Copland returned to the United States, determined to compose a kind of music that was distinctly American. Like other young expatriate artists during the Twenties, Copland had to leave his homeland to learn what was distinctive about it: "In greater or lesser degree, all of us discovered America in Europe."

At first Copland sought to forge an American style by incorporating into his music elements of jazz, recognized the world over as a uniquely American creation. His debt to the Jazz Age is especially apparent in his *Piano Concerto* (1926), written two years after George Gershwin's *Rhapsody in Blue for Jazz Band and Piano*. Then, beginning in the late 1930s, Copland turned his attention to a series of projects that had rural and western America as their subjects. The ballet scores *Billy the Kid* (1938) and *Rodeo* (1942) are set in the West and make use of classic cowboy songs like *Goodbye, Old Paint* and *The Old Chisholm Trail*. Another ballet, *Appalachian Spring* (1944), recreates the ambience of the farm country of Pennsylvania, and his single opera, *The Tender Land* (1954), is set in the cornbelt of the Midwest. Most recently filmmaker Spike Lee used Copland's music to fashion the soundtrack for his basketball movie *He Got Game* (1998). In the minds of some, the Copland sound is as American as basketball!

In his most distinctly American works, Copland's musical voice is clear and conservative. He uses folk and popular elements to soften the dissonant harmonies and disjunct melodies of European modernism. Copland's melodies tend to be more stepwise and diatonic* than those of other twentieth-century composers, perhaps because Western folk and popular tunes are fundamentally conjunct and without chromaticism. His harmonies are almost always tonal and often slow-moving in a way that can evoke the vastness and grandeur of the American landscape. The triad, too, is still important with Copland, perhaps for its stability and simplicity, but he frequently uses it in a modern way, as we shall see, by having two triads sound simultaneously, creating mildly dissonant polychords. But perhaps the most important component in the distinctive "Copland sound" is his clear, luminous orchestration. He does not mix colors to produce rich Romantic blends, but keeps the four families of instruments (strings, woodwinds, brasses, and percussion) more or less to their own group. And he distributes the instruments of the orchestra so as to construct a solid bass, a very thin middle, and a top of one or two high, clear tones. It is this separation and careful spacing of the instruments that creates the fresh, wide-open sound so pleasing in Copland's music.

The clarity and simplicity of Aaron Copland's music is not accidental. During the Great Depression of the 1930s, he became convinced that the gulf between modern music and the ordinary citizen had become too great—that dissonance and atonality had little to say to most music lovers. "It made no sense to ignore them and to continue writing as if they did not exist. I felt that it was worth the effort to see if I couldn't say what I had to say in the simplest possible terms." Thus, he not only wrote appealing new tonal works like *Fanfare for the Common Man* (1942) but also was attracted to traditional tunes such as *The Gift to Be Simple*, which he uses in *Appalachian Spring*.

AP/Wide World Photos

FIGURE 17–27
Aaron Copland.

Copland's musical style

a clear, wide-open sound

modern music for the ordinary citizen

APPALACHIAN SPRING (1944)

Appalachian Spring is a one-act ballet that tells the story of "a pioneer celebration of spring in a newly built farmhouse in Pennsylvania in the early 1800s." A new bride and her farmer-husband express through dance the anxieties and joys of life in pioneer America. The work was composed in 1944 for the great lady of American choreography, Martha Graham (1893–1991), and it won Copland a Pulitzer Prize the following year. It is divided into eight connected sections that differ in tempo and mood. Copland has provided a brief description of each of these orchestral scenes.

Section 1. "Introduction of the characters one by one, in a suffused light." The quiet beauty of the land at daybreak is revealed as the orchestra slowly spaces out the notes of the tonic and then dominant triad.

EXAMPLE 17–10

While this simultaneous presentation of two triads should be heard as a polychord, the effect is only mildly dissonant because of the slow, quiet way in which the notes of the two chords are introduced. The serene simplicity of the introduction sets the tone for the entire work.

Section 2. "A sentiment both elated and religious gives the keynote of this scene." The early calm is suddenly broken by a lively dance with a salient rhythm played aggressively in the strings. The dance has all the modern rhythmic vigor of Stravinsky's music, but none of the extreme polymeters. As the dance proceeds, a more restrained hymn-like melody emerges in the trumpet.

Section 3 is a dance for the two principals, in ballet parlance a pas de deux, accompanied by lyrical writing for strings and winds. Sections 4 and 5 are musical depictions of the livelier aspects of country life, with 4 including a toe-tappin' hoedown, while Section 6 recalls the quiet calm of the opening of the ballet.

Section 7. "Calm and flowing. Scenes of daily activity for the Bride and her Farmer-husband." For this section Copland chose to make use of a traditional tune of the Shakers, an extreme religious sect that prospered in the Appalachian region in the early nineteenth century and whose members showed their spiritual intensity in frenzied singing, dancing, and shaking. Today this tune is famous, having been featured recently, among other places, in a car commercial for General Motors. But the melody has become well-known only because of Copland's *Appalachian Spring*. The composer plucked it from folkloric obscurity in 1944 because he thought the simple, diatonic* tune (Ex. 17–11) fit well with the American character of the ballet and because the text of the Shaker song is harmonious with what is occurring on stage, which concerns "scenes of daily activity."

EXAMPLE 17–11

FIGURE 17–28

A scene from Martha Graham's ballet *Appalachian Spring*, with music by Aaron Copland. Here Katherine Crockett dances the role of the Bride (New York, 1999).

Julie Lemberger/CORBIS

a Shaker tune

'Tis the gift to be simple,
'Tis the gift to be free,
'Tis the gift to come down where we ought to be,
And when we find ourselves in the place just right,
'Twill be in the valley of love and delight.

Thereafter come five variations in which *The Gift to Be Simple* is not so much varied as it is clothed in different instrumental attire.

Section 8. "The Bride takes her place among her neighbors." Serenity returns to the scene as the strings, then the woodwinds, and then the strings and woodwinds together play a slow, mainly stepwise descent "like a prayer." The hymn-like melody from section 2 is heard again in the flute, followed by the quiet landscape music from the beginning of the ballet. Darkness has again descended on the valley, leaving the young pioneer couple "strong in their new house" and secure in their community.

an end like the beginning

Listening Guide

Aaron Copland	6CD 6/2–6/5;
Appalachian Spring (1944)	2CD 2/12–2/14
Sections 1, 2, 7, and 8	

Genre: ballet music

SECTION 1 (6CD 6/2; 2CD 2/12)

0:00	Quiet unfolding of triads by clarinet and other instruments
0:45	Soft violin melody descends
1:11	More triads in woodwinds and trumpet
1:36	Oboe and then bassoon solos
2:19	Clarinet plays concluding triad

SECTION 2 (6CD 6/3; 2CD 2/13)

0:00	Percussive rhythm (♫ ♩ ♫ ♩) in strings and rising woodwinds
0:19	Rhythm gels into sprightly dance

0:44	Trumpet plays hymn-like melody above dance

1:13	Rhythmic motive scattered but then played more forcefully
2:09	Hymn heard in strings, with flute counterpoint above
2:36	Rhythmic motive skips away in woodwinds

SECTION 7 (6CD 6/4; 2CD 2/14)

0:00	Clarinet presents Shaker tune

0:36	Variation 1: Oboe and bassoon play tune
1:06	Variation 2: Violas and trombones play tune at half its previous speed
1:51	Variation 3: Trumpets and trombones play tune

(Continued on next page)

2:16   Variation 4: Woodwinds play tune more slowly
2:31   Variation 5: Final majestic statement of tune by full orchestra

SECTION 8 (6CD 6/5)
0:00   Serene, stepwise string music
0:44   Woodwinds continue placid mood
0:58   Strings and winds together play more loudly
1:20   Flute enters with hymnlike tune from section 2
2:14   Clarinet plays triad from the beginning of ballet
2:29   Soft, mild polychords in strings

(Listening Exercise 40)

Ellen Taaffe Zwilich (b. 1939)

Brittain Hill

FIGURE 17–29

"I never have to work for themes; they can hit me at any time, and usually do." Ellen Taaffe Zwilich

Handel made modern

Like the late Aaron Copland, Ellen Taaffe Zwilich works to integrate musical modernism with earlier musical traditions. She draws not so much upon American folk music but more upon the traditions of the European concert hall. Her string quartet, four symphonies, and twelve concertos, among other works, reflect her desire to honor the traditional genres of classical music. Yet her aim is always the same: to communicate directly with the audience and thereby show that modern music can be enjoyed by the average listener. As she has said, "Most people have the mistaken impression that classical music is written by dead people."

The daughter of an airline pilot, Zwilich was born in Miami and educated at Florida State University. She then moved to New York City, where she played violin in the American Symphony Orchestra, studied composition at the Juilliard School, and worked for a time as an usher at Carnegie Hall. Zwilich's big "break" came in 1983, when she became the first woman to win the Pulitzer Prize in music. During 1995–1998 she was the first person of either sex to occupy the newly created Composer's Chair at Carnegie Hall—usher had become director. Today Zwilich enjoys a status to which all modern composers aspire: She is free to devote herself exclusively to writing music, sustained by her royalties and commissions. Recently, the New York Philharmonic and the Chicago Symphony Orchestra each paid five-figure sums for a single new piece from her pen.

The tradition of the Baroque concerto grosso* lies at the heart of Zwilich's five-movement *Concerto Grosso 1985*. Commissioned by the Washington Friends of Handel, this work honors the composer George Frideric Handel (see page 153), a leading exponent of the concerto grosso. Zwilich borrows a melody directly from Handel (the opening theme of his Violin Sonata in D major). She also embraces several elements of Baroque musical style: a regular rhythmic pulse, a repeating bass pedal point*, a walking bass*, and a harpsichord*. Yet Zwilich adds twisting chromaticism to Handel's melody (see Listening Guide) and sets it in a biting, dissonant harmony. Most important, she demands an insistent, pounding style of playing that would have shocked Handel. The composer says that the emotional core of this concerto grosso is its slow third movement, marked *Largo*. When Handel composed a largo, he invariably made it noble and serene. In Zwilich's *Largo*, everywhere lurks a brooding, menacing sound suggestive of the modern age.

Listening Guide

WWW

Ellen Taaffe Zwilich
Concerto Grosso 1985 (1985)
Third movement, *Largo* (Slow and broad)

6CD 6/6;
2CD 2/15

Genre: concerto grosso

0:00   Bass pedal point begins

0:05   Melody rises in oboes and violins

mp

Handel's original melody

mp

Zwilich's modernization of it

0:29   Bass finally begins to "walk" to lower pitches

0:59   Violins play melody *forte,* with dissonant chords added by harpsichord

1:04   French horns provide dissonant melodic counterpoint

1:39   Dissonant chords repeated *forte*

2:10   Cellos play melody above soft dissonant chords in harpsichord

2:42   Cellos and violins play melody above soft dissonant chords and bass pedal point

3:33   Bass and chordal accompaniment become more fragmented

3:52   Violins play melody quietly above fragmented chords

NEW TRENDS: MINIMALISM AND POSTMINIMALISM

Composers at the end of the twentieth century have faced a perplexing question: Where is the mainstream of musical modernism? Should they follow Arnold Schoenberg's dissonant twelve-tone* method and create works in which all aspects of melody and harmony are strictly predetermined? Or should they head in the opposite direction and travel the freely experimental route of John Cage, even though this more chancy path can sometimes lead to musical happenings that border on the silly? Should they recreate the warmth and sentiment of nineteenth-century music, a Neo-romantic sound produced by traditional acoustic instruments? Or should they try to create wholly new sonorities generated electronically by means of synthesizers and computers? One recent trend, which rejects all of these solutions, is a movement in composition called Minimalism. Minimalist composers, like their counterparts the Minimalist artists (Fig. 17–30), strive to do away with both time-honored processes and modern technical complexities.

Where's the path to the future?

   Minimalism is a style of modern music, begun in the early 1960s, that takes a very small amount of musical material and repeats it over and over to

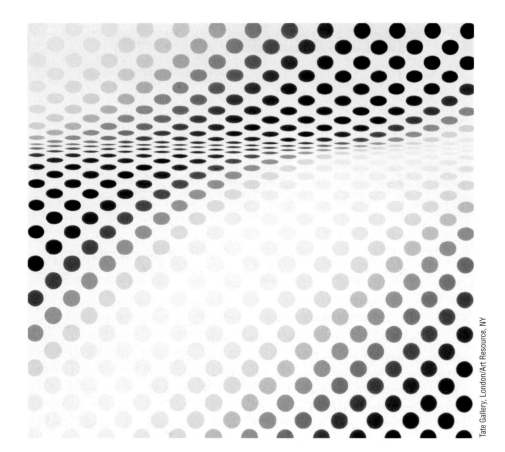

Tate Gallery, London/Art Resource, NY

FIGURE 17–30

Briget Riley's Minimalist *Hesitate* (1964) repeats a basic design again and again, much as does the score of Adams' *Short Ride in a Fast Machine*. Indeed the score itself could be taken to be an example of Minimalist visual art (see Ex. 17–12).

FIGURE 17–31

John Adams. In 2003 Lincoln Center, New York, held an eight-week "Absolutely Adams" festival to go along with its annual "Mostly Mozart" program.

Albright-Knox Art Gallery, Buffalo

form a composition. A three-note melodic cell, a single arpeggio, or two alternating chords is the sort of small, "minimal" element a composer will introduce, reiterate again and again, modify or add to, and then begin to repeat once more. The basic material is usually simple, tonal, and consonant. By repeating these minimal figures incessantly at a steady pulse, the composer creates a hypnotic effect—"trance music" is the name sometimes given this music. The trance-like quality of Minimalist music has influenced rock musicians (Velvet Underground, Talking Heads, and Radiohead) and spawned the new genre of pop music called "techno," or "rave," music. Minimalism, in both art and music, has been mainly an American movement. Its most successful musical practitioners are Steve Reich (b. 1936), Philip Glass (b. 1937), and John Adams (b. 1947).

John Adams (b. 1947)

John Adams (no relation to the presidents) was born in Massachusetts and educated at Harvard. As a student he was encouraged to compose in the twelve-tone style of Arnold Schoenberg (see page 367). But if Adams counted twelve-tone rows by day, he listened to the Beatles in his dorm room at night. Indeed, most of Adams' music has an eclectic quality about it, blending the learned with the popular. Certainly he is not a strict Minimalist, for from time to time a riff from a rock band or a funk bass line will creep into his constantly repeating, minimal patterns. Thus Adams might best be termed a "post-Minimalist"—a Minimalist who works other materials into his minimal sonorities. Moreover, the two works for which Adams is best known, the three-act opera *Nixon in China* (1987) and the two-hour oratorio *El Niño* (2000), are anything but minimal in length.

SHORT RIDE IN A FAST MACHINE (1986)

Let's take a brief excursion through a Minimalist work by Adams, one commissioned in 1986 by the Pittsburgh Symphony. *Short Ride in a Fast Machine* is scored for full orchestra and two electronic keyboard synthesizers*. Example 17–12 shows how the music is composed of short (mostly four-note) motives that continually repeat. There are five sections to this work (we'll call them laps). In each lap the machine seems to accelerate, not because the tempo gets faster but because more and more repeating motives are added. The effect created is that of a powerful, twenty-first-century engine firing on all cylinders. As Adams has said about his Minimalist work: "You know how it is when someone asks you to ride in a terrific sports car, and then you wish you hadn't?"

endlessly repeating ostinatos

EXAMPLE 17–12

![Listening Guide]

WWW

John Adams
Short Ride in a Fast Machine (1986)
Delirando (with exhilaration)

6CD 6/7

0:00	Lap 1: woodblock, woodwinds, and keyboard synthesizers begin; brasses, snare drum, and glockenspiel* gradually added
1:06	Lap 2: bass drum "backfires"; motives rise in pitch and become more dissonant
1:47	Lap 3: starts quietly with sinister repeating motive in bass; syncopation and dissonance increase
2:40	Lap 4: two-note falling motive in bass
2:55	Lap 5: trumpets play fanfarelike motives (this is the "victory lap")
4:03	Coda: return to sounds of the start

BACK TO THE FUTURE: POSTMODERNISM

Modern music before World War II emphasized stylistic consistency—the rigorous prosecution of one set of musical ideals from the beginning to the end of a piece. More recent "postmodern" music, however, is often an eclectic hybrid, mingling learned with popular idioms, or film music with classical styles, for example. One of the most recent trends in contemporary art music blends the newest of sounds with the oldest of musical materials. "Time travelers" such as Henryk Gorecki (b. 1933), Arvo Pärt (b. 1935), and John Tavener (b. 1944) have composed with an ear turned not ahead, but backward to the very distant musical past: to early Celtic hymns, the chants of the medieval Church, and the *a cappella** singing of the Middle Ages and Renaissance. They borrow from ancient Eastern and Western religious rituals to create spiritual music for a new age.

John Tavener (b. 1944)

FIGURE 17–32
John Tavener.

Sir John Tavener was born in London and received a musical education at the Royal Academy of Music, where his younger classmates included Reginald Dwight (Elton John). A closer friend, however, was John Lennon of the Beatles, with whom he hung out during the Swinging Sixties. Some of Tavener's earliest works were recorded on their Apple label. Yet Tavener's art shows little influence of pop music. Instead, it is infused with sounds of the ancient Roman Catholic and Greek Orthodox churches: chant, drones, open fifths, and singing in parallel motion*. Tavener views his art as spiritual music in the broadest sense. All music, like all nature, he believes, is a manifestation of God, and it is his aim to show God through his music. At its simplest, the Tavener sound is a cross between ancient chant and **New Age Music** (soothing, often repetitious, music performed on electronic instruments). At its best, his slow-moving, resonant sonorities create a mystical, otherworldly effect of unusual beauty. As the blocks of sound repeat, a feeling of religious ritual emerges, like the chanting of a prayer or mantra.

music for Princess Diana

Tavener's *Song for Athene* was originally composed in memory of a young family friend killed in a tragic auto accident in 1993. The piece gained worldwide fame, however, when performed at the funeral of Diana, Princess of Wales, in 1997. During the service for Diana in Westminster Abbey, Elton John sang his refashioned *Candle in the Wind*. Music for the final procession, however, was provided by Tavener's *Song for Athene*, the text of which, drawn from Shakespeare's *Hamlet* and the liturgy of the Orthodox Church, speaks of the celestial journey of a deceased maid. Heard by nearly a billion people around the world, this one performance made Tavener the best-known composer of art music in Great Britain.

a neo-medieval sound

Song for Athene begins with a bass drone* ("the eternal F," Tavener called it). From it a chant-like melody slowly emerges. Sometimes the melody appears in the major mode and sometimes in the minor. Like Gregorian chant, this melody proceeds without clear meter and rhythm. Both melody and drone are sung in the ancient *a cappella** style (without instruments). The piece processes dirge-like through a succession of Alleluia verses, moving gradually to a stunning climax (4:46). Suddenly low becomes high, minor becomes major, dissonance becomes consonance, darkness becomes light. At the climax, the spirit of the dead young woman seems to enter Celestial Jerusalem, a realm filled with the blinding brightness of divine light.

Listening Guide

John Tavener
Song for Athene (1993)

6CD 6/8

Genre: motet

0:00	Chant-like melody in major mode rises above drone	Alleluia. May flights of angels
0:18	Higher voices sing in parallel motion	sing thee to thy rest. (*Hamlet*)
0:42	Chant-like melody in minor mode rises above drone	Alleluia. Remember me, O Lord,
0:58	Higher voices sing in parallel motion	when you come into Your kingdom.*
1:39	Chant-like melody in major mode rises above drone	Alleluia. Give rest, O Lord, to Your
1:56	Higher voices sing in dissonant, contrary motion	handmaid, who has fallen asleep.
2:20	Chant-like melody in major mode rises above drone	Alleluia. The Choir of Saints have
2:36	Higher voices sing in dissonant, contrary motion	found the wellspring of life and
		the door of Paradise.
3:03	Chant-like melody in major mode in parallel octaves	Alleluia. Life: a shadow
3:23	Higher voices sing slowly in minor mode in parallel motion	and a dream. (*Hamlet*)
3:59	Chant-like melody in minor mode in parallel motion	Alleluia. Weeping at the grave
4:18	Gradual *crescendo;* change from minor to major	creates the song. (*Hamlet*)
4:46	*Fortissimo* climax: all voices sing in bright,	Alleluia. Come, enjoy rewards and
	dissonant chords in parallel motion; consonant final chord	crowns I have prepared for you.
5:36	Return to chant-like melody in major mode above drone	Alleluia.

*All texts not taken from *Hamlet* are drawn from the medieval liturgy of the Orthodox Church.

Listening Exercises

38

Igor Stravinsky
The Rite of Spring (1913)
Introduction and Scene 1

6CD 5/7–8; 2CD 2/8–9

Stravinsky, more than any other modern composer before the recent Mini-malists (see page 391), made use of the musical ostinato—the repetition of a motive, over and over at the same pitch. The ostinato imparts to his music a feeling of kinetic energy continually being recycled and renewed. At the same time, the static quality of a repeating motive allows Stravinsky to work against the functional chord progression* and "goal-oriented" melodic expansion of Romantic music. A stationary musical moment can be maintained and enjoyed in and of itself. The following exercise asks you to focus on the ostinatos heard in the Introduction and Scene 1 of *The Rite of Spring*. Listen to the listed passages, and state if an ostinato is or is not present. Sometimes this will require listening carefully to the inner parts.

Ostinato present? (yes or no)

1. 0:35–0:56 _____		6CD 5/8; 2CD 2/9
2. 2:08–2:20 _____	6. 0:24–0:36 _____	
3. 2:34–2:55 _____	7. 1:14–1:22 _____	
4. 2:57–3:10 _____	8. 1:23–1:36 _____	
5. 3:28–3:34 _____	9. 1:59–2:29 _____	

10. Judging from your responses, are there more moments in *The Rite of Spring* making use of an ostinato than those that do not? _____

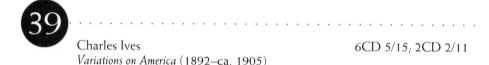

Charles Ives   6CD 5/15; 2CD 2/11
Variations on America (1892–ca. 1905)

We are all familiar with the tune *America* (known in Great Britain as *God Save the Queen*), but can you follow its progress as Charles Ives leads it through a jaunty, high-spirited set of variations? Below the times of eight portions of the piece are indicated. In these the tune can be heard clearly in the treble part of the texture (right hand of the organist), in the middle part of the texture (left hand of the organist), or in the bass (played by the organist's feet). Identify where in the texture the tune resides during these passages.

1. 0:54–1:23 Theme: a. treble   or   b. middle
2. 1:24–2:16 Variation 1:   a. treble   or   b. middle
3. 3:08–3:30 Interlude 1:   a. treble   or   c. bass
4. 3:31–4:30 Variation 3:   a. treble   or   c. bass
5. 4:32–4:57 Variation 4:   a. treble   or   c. bass
6. 5:30–6:15 Variation 5:   a. treble   or   c. bass
7. 6:32–6:40 Coda: a. treble   or   c. bass
8. 6:42–7:00 Coda: a. treble   or   c. bass
9. Judging from your answers above, the patriotic tune *America* is most often assigned to which range of the organ?
    a. treble   b. middle of texture   c. bass
10. Now listen to the entire piece one more time. Which of the following statements is true?
    a. The tune *America* can always be heard in Ives's set of variations.
    b. The tune *America* can almost always be heard in Ives's set of variations.
    c. The tune *America* can rarely be heard in Ives's set of variations.

Aaron Copland   6CD 6/2–4; 2 CD 2/12–14
Appalachian Spring (1944)
Sections 1, 2, and 7

The following questions focus on musical themes, textures, and colors. They also ask you to consider the ways in which Copland the conservative softens the sometimes biting sound of twentieth-century music.

Section 1 (6CD 6/2; 2CD 2/12): Introduction
1. (0:00–0:43) Indicate the simple musical gesture by which a composer can suggest a sunrise in music.
   a. The instruments play a rising melodic line.
   b. The instruments hold high in their ranges.
   c. The instruments play a falling melodic line.
2. (0:45–1:09) Why does this passage sound more like Romantic music than modern music?
   a. A lovely French horn call suggests nature.
   b. An exotic-sounding English horn suggests the love of adventure.
   c. A warm, primarily stepwise melody is played by the violins.
3. (1:10–2:31) Which family of instruments provides the bulk of the **soloists** for this lovely section?
   a. strings   b. brass   c. woodwinds   d. percussion
4. (2:17–2:31) As the clarinet rises to end the opening section, what do the strings do?
   a. continue with the melody
   b. hold a single note below allowing the clarinet to create open space above
   c. play a dissonant polychord* above the clarinet

Section 2 (6CD 6/3; 2CD 2/13): Joys and anxieties of pioneer life
This section is composed of two musical ideas: an energetic dance theme and a more restrained hymn-like tune (see examples on page 389).
5. The dance theme begins in the strings (at 0:19) and then the hymn-like tune enters in the trumpet (0:43). Which is more percussive and dissonant—hence more modern sounding?
   a. dance theme   b. hymn-like theme
6. (1:22–2:08) Now the lively dance theme dominates. This passage sounds a bit like the music of Igor Stravinsky, a composer whom Copland greatly admired. Which of the following cannot be heard in this section?
   a. strong, irregular accents
   b. a sweeping melody in the cellos
   c. a rhythmic ostinato in the flutes and harp
   d. violent, percussive strokes in the timpani, piano, and xylophone

Section 7 (6CD 6/4; 2CD 2/14): Variations on a Shaker tune *The Gift To Be Simple* (see Example 17–11 on page 388)
   0:00 Tune in the clarinet
   0:36 Oboe and bassoon present variation 1
   1:06 Violas and then violins present variation 2
7. During variation 2 (1:06–1:41), what do the woodwinds and percussion (piano, harp, and glockenspiel) do?
   a. establish a tinkling backdrop by playing an ostinato*
   b. play a flowing countermelody
   c. pound syncopated polychords*
8. At the end of variation 2 comes a brief transition (1:46) to variation 3 (1:51). Which of the following occurs in this transition?
   a. a rising scale in trombone and trumpet that produces a modulation to a new, higher key

b. a descending scale in trombone and trumpet but no modulation

9. In variation 3 (1:51–2:13) the Shaker tune appears in note values that are played at which speed?
   a. twice as slow as the previous variation
   b. the same speed as the previous variation
   c. twice as fast as the previous variation

2:16 Woodwinds quietly carry the tune in variation 4

10. (2:31–2:53) The full orchestra offers a fitting climax in the fifth and final variation. The bass is very clear and strong, which gives a "rock solid" feeling to this American musical vision. How would you describe the bass line?
    a. It rises slowly, mainly in large intervals.
    b. It descends quickly, mainly in large intervals.
    c. It descends slowly, mainly by step.

Key Words

atonal music (368)	*musique concrète* (382)	prepared piano (381)
Ballets russes (362)	Neo-classicism (384)	sampling (383)
chance music (381)	New Age Music (395)	scratching (383)
computer music (383)	ninth chord (359)	serial music (371)
Cubism (357)	octave displacement	seventh chord (359)
electronic music (382)	(358)	*Sprechstimme* (369)
eleventh chord (359)	polychord (365)	synthesizer (383)
Expressionism (369)	polymeter (364)	tone cluster (359)
intermezzo (375)	polyrhythm (364)	twelve-tone
Minimalism (391)	polytonality (378)	composition (371)

A checklist of musical styles of the twentieth century is given on page 71.

CORBIS/Lynn Goldsmith

American
Popular Music:
Blues, Jazz, and Rock

American popular music, including pop songs, jazz, rock, and Hollywood film music, now dominates popular musical culture around the world. But what is popular music? Is it music for all the people? Is it a commodity that can be mass produced and sold everywhere? Is it music more loved or favored than some other types of music and hence "popular," like a movie star or sports hero? Although lovers of classical music can be just as passionate about Bach as rock fans are about Bono and U2, the truth is that popular music is enjoyed by a much larger segment of society than is "serious" music. Popular music is heard everywhere. It is "broadcast" in the literal sense of the word. Popular CDs outsell classical discs by more than ten to one. For the most part, popular music is simple and direct. It requires little or no formal training in music. It is made to be enjoyed for the moment without concern for lasting artistic value.

Popular music is similar, but not identical to, folk music. Folk music, too, is enjoyed by all societies. But, unlike popular music, different folk songs are known to different groups. Moreover, true folk music is not created by an identifiable individual; it springs from the entire community and is part of that group's unique heritage. Popular music, on the other hand, is not only created by an "artist" but also is intended to be reproduced and sold as a commodity to a mass audience, usually in digital audio format as CDs. The homespun folk singer who wails a centuries-old ballad—like *The Streets of Laredo* (see page 31)—is a far cry from the professional pop singer, like Britney Spears, who performs her latest hit in Madison Square Garden. Yet from the folk music of both white and black Americans have sprung our most distinctive genres of popular music: blues, jazz, and rock.

BLUES

origins

Why, where, and how the blues originated is a story that will probably never be fully told. We cannot even hazard a guess as to who gave this style of singing the name "blues," though the expression "the blue devils" had been used to describe a melancholy mood since Shakespeare's time. All that can be said with certainty is that the **blues** are a form of black folk song that originated in the South sometime during the 1880s and 1890s. Like all true folk music, the blues were passed along by oral tradition, one performer learning directly from another without benefit of written music. Comparisons with other forms of folk music suggest that the blues had two immediate ancestors. First and most important was the work song and field holler (or cry) of the black laborers, which bequeathed to the blues a wailing vocal style, a particular scale (see later), and a body of subjects or topics for singing the blues. The second was the Anglo-American folk ballad, which imparted the regular, predictable pattern of chord changes that characterize the blues. Blues were first printed as sheet music in 1912 (*The Memphis Blues* and *The Dallas Blues*), and the first blues recordings, all made by black artists, were cut in 1920.

a succession of three-line stanzas

A singer sings the blues to relieve a melancholy soul, to give vent to feelings of pain and anger. Poverty, loneliness, oppression, family troubles, infidelity, and separation are typical subjects of the blues. The lyrics are arranged in a succession of stanzas, usually three to six to a song, and each stanza is made up of three lines. The second line normally repeats the first, and the third rounds off the idea and concludes with a rhyme. At the end of each line an instrument inserts a short response, called an **instrumental break**, as a way of replying to the cry of the voice. Thus, the blues perpetuates the age-old African performing style of "call and response," the form of which is shown in the following blues stanza:

Call	*Response*
The blues is a lowdown, achin' heart disease,	(instrumental break)
The blues is a lowdown, achin' heart disease,	(instrumental break)
It's like consumption, killin' you by degrees.	(instrumental break)

guitar accompaniment

By the 1920s the guitar had become the accompanying instrument favored by blues singers. It could not only supply a solid harmonic support but also provide an expressive "second voice" to answer in the instrumental break after the previous call in the vocal line. "Bending" the guitar strings at the frets produced a whining, mournful sound in keeping with the general feeling of the blues.

The object of the blues is not so much to tell a story, as in the white folk ballad, but to express emotion. The voice sometimes moans and sometimes shouts, it is often raspy or frayed, and it always twists and bends the pitch. Instead of hitting a tone directly, the singer usually approaches it by slide from above or below. In addition, a particular scale, called **blues scale,** is used in place of a major or minor scale. The blues scale has seven notes, but the third, fifth, and seventh are sometimes flat, sometimes natural, and sometimes in between. The three "in between" tones are called **blue notes.** The blues scale is an integral part of virtually all African-American folk music, including the work song and spiritual as well as the blues.

EXAMPLE 18–1

blues scale

⌐ = blue note

Good blues singers indulge in much spontaneous expression, adding and subtracting text and improvising around the basic melody as the spirit moves them. Such liberties are possible because these mournful songs are built above the bedrock of a twelve-bar harmonic pattern that repeats, over and over, one statement for each stanza of text. Singing the blues means singing in a slow $\frac{4}{4}$ above this simple I–IV–I–V–I chord progression in the following manner:[†]

Vocal lines:	Line 1		break		Line 2		break		Line 3		break	
Chord:	I ———————————————				IV————	I ————			V————	I		
Measure:	1	2	3	4	5	6	7	8	9	10	11	12

Sometimes additional chords are inserted between the basic ones for greater harmonic interest. Yet the simplicity of the pattern is its greatest resource. Thousands of tunes have been constructed over this basic harmonic progression, by solo singers, by solo pianists, by Dixieland jazz combos, and by rock 'n' roll bands.

Bessie Smith (1894–1937)

Although there have been and are many great blues singers—Blind Lemon Jefferson, Leadbelly, Muddy Waters, and B. B. King, to name just a few— perhaps the greatest of them all was Bessie Smith, called the "Empress of the Blues." A native of Tennessee, Bessie Smith was "discovered" singing in a bar in Selma, Alabama, and brought to New York to record for Columbia Records. The blues recordings she made between 1924 and 1927 catapulted her to the top of the world of popular music. In her first full year as a recording artist, her disks sold more than two million copies, and she became the highest-paid black artist, male or female, of the day. In fact, all of the great blues singers who achieved recording success during the 1920s were women, perhaps because so many of the texts of the blues have to do with male– female relations and are written from the woman's perspective. Tragically, Bessie Smith's career was cut short by a fatal automobile accident in 1937.

(Continued on page 404)

FIGURE 18–1

Bessie Smith, the "Empress of the Blues," was a physically powerful woman with an exceptionally flexible, expressive voice.

Photofest

[†]Chord progressions of this sort are discussed on page 30.

CULTURAL CONTEXT

African Influence in American Popular Music

The blues, as we have seen, were greatly influenced by the experiences of African Amercans in the rural South and reflect African musical practices. In fact, almost all forms of twentieth-century American popular music—blues, ragtime, jazz, rhythm and blues, rock 'n' roll, funk, rap, and hip-hop—show, in one way or another, ties to African music. Most of the slaves arriving in the United States came from the western part of Sub-Saharan Africa—from the western part of the continent below the Sahara Desert. Today the countries of Sub-Saharan West Africa have names such as Senegal, Guinea, Ghana, Benin, and Ivory Coast, though in fact the boundaries of most of these nations are more or less artificial lines drawn by nineteenth-century European rulers. Real unity and loyalty in Africa rests within the structure of the countless tribes, each of which possesses its own history, language, and music. It is the music of the West African tribes that was transported to the Americas and, in the course of time, came to influence and, in some cases, largely shape the traditions of American popular music. But what are the characteristics of African music that are manifest in American popular music?

Music as Social Activity

Music permeates every aspect of African life. It is sung or played while chopping wood, pounding grain, paddling a canoe, harvesting crops, weeding a field, burying a chief, or stamping letters at the post office. Singing keeps the workers together and makes their tasks go faster. When people perform classical music in the West, some play, others listen. Westerns have performers and an audience. In Africa, the audience and the performers are one and the same. Similarly, there is usually no class of professional musician: everyone participates. When transferred to the Americas, these traditions produced the field holler of the cotton or tobacco pickers and the line songs of the railroad gangs, all characterized by a call of the leader and the response of the group. The name of the "composer" is not known, for usually it is all the people.

Importance of Rhythm

Complex harmonies distinguish Western classical music. Subtle melodic gradations characterize traditional Indian and Chinese music. The distinguishing quality of African music, however, is rhythm. Yet rhythm in African music is not like that in Western art

(right) The continent of Africa, and (left) the country of Ghana situated in the western portion of Sub-Saharan Africa.

Both maps: Carto-Graphics

music. Western performers invariably start together at a beginning point, an opening downbeat*, and are guided by the regular recurrence of downbeats and up-beats. All musicians lock onto and play with or against this single, common, regulating pulse. In African music, by contrast, the individual parts are far more likely to start independently and to stay that way. There is usually no common downbeat around which the players gravitate. Each part has its own downbeat, pulse, rhythm, and often its own meter. What results is a complex of several layers of musical rhythms and me-ters—polymeters*. We have met polymeters before, specifically in the music of the European avant-garde (see page 365). The difference between the Western European and the African use of polymeter, again, is the absence in African music of a shared downbeat, as can be seen in this musical example.

Two African drumming patterns sounding together, each with its own downbeat, rhythm, and meter:

There are always at least two rhythms sounding in African music, and this accounts for its complexity. We Westerners perceive it as complex, indeed are often baffled by it, because we can't find a unifying beat to which to tap our feet. The African-influenced Latin pop music and the Afro-Cuban jazz of today seem ex-citing and energetic because there are so many rhythms and meters sounding at once.

Importance of Drums

Many musical instruments are indigenous to Africa—flutes, whistles, harps, bells, even trumpets—but it is the drum we immediately associate with African cul-ture. Drums are at the heart of almost all group music-making and all dances. African drums come in a stag-gering variety of shapes and sizes. There are hand drums, stick drums, water drums, slit drums (a hollowed-

out log with a long slit on top), and talking drums. **Talking drums** are those upon which tension can be placed on the drum head by tightening the skin around it. In this way the pitch of the drum can be changed and it can be made to "speak." African drum makers sometimes place charms within the drum—pebbles from the yard of the village gossip so as to make the drum talk freely, or a bit of skin of a lion to make it roar. When slaves ar-rived on the shores of America they were often forbid-den from using these talking drums because the masters were afraid that this secret musical language would be used to foment rebellion. Following the Civil War, African drums reappeared. Later, during the 1940s, the insertion of strong drum beats and back beats* helped transform the blues into rhythm and blues and, ulti-mately, into rock 'n' roll.

Bending the Pitch

Western classical music is one of the few musical cul-tures that places melody upon a rigid grid of pitches—the unvarying notes of the major and minor scales. Western melodies move directly from one specific fre-quency to the next with no sliding in between. In large measure this is because Western music, over the course of the centuries, has become heavily dependent upon written notaton and fixed-pitch instruments such as the piano and organ. Other non-Western musical cultures—those that rely on the oral rather than the written com-munication of music—are marked by melodies of far more subtle nuance of pitch. African music is among these orally communicated musics that allow for greater melodic flexibility or "bending of pitch." The most ex-citing part of the music is often what happens between the pitches, not on them. African slaves brought their traditional modes of singing with them to antebellum America. *Slave Songs of the United States* (1867) appeared shortly after the Civil War and in the preface the white editor remarked that black musicians "seem not infre-quently to strike sounds that cannot be precisely repre-sented by the gamut [scale]"—a suggestion that the bending blue notes of the blues scale (page 401) were already audible.

(continued on next page)

CULTURAL CONTEXT (continued)

Call and Response

The structure of African music is governed in large measure by a principle of performance called "call and response" (see also page 400). In vocal music a lead singer will announce an opening phrase, and the chorus will utter a short, simple reply. The soloist returns, extending and varying the call, to which the chorus responds again in simple, stable fashion. The soloist may enter and depart according to his or her whim. The chorus, however, responds at regular and predictable intervals. Instrumentalists can also engage in call and response. A master drummer, for example, can imitate a conversation with a chorus of subordinates. Sometimes the performing forces are mixed: A vocal soloist may engender a massed instrumental reply. Today call and response remains an important structural feature of African-American spirituals, blues, gospel, and soul. When James Brown, the "godfather of soul," sings "Get up" and we then hear a collective "Get on up," we have a classic example of African call and response.

A Praise-Song from Ghana

As a way of hearing what African music sounds like today—and what it might have sounded like before coming to America—let us examine a drum-accompanied song from Ghana. Ghana is a country in West Africa (see map) somewhat smaller than the size of Texas with a population of eighteen million people. In its northeast corner lies a territory called Dagomba, which supports a people called the Dagombas who speak a language called Dagbani, one of the forty-four official languages of Ghana. The primary musical instruments of the Dagombas are the drums, specifically the dondon and the gongon. The

John Miller Chernoff, Pittsburgh

A group of dondon and gongon drummers from Dagomba, Ghana.

John Miller Chernoff (both)

The dondon is a talking drum, so called because the player can pull on the leather thongs connecting the two heads to raise the pitch, as we do in our speech.

a highly expressive, flexible voice

Lost Your Head Blues, recorded in 1926, reveals the huge, sweeping voice of Bessie Smith. She was capable of great power, even harshness, one moment, and then in the next breath could deliver a phrase of tender beauty. She could hit a note right on the head if she wanted to, or bend, dip, and glide into the pitch, as she does, for example, on the words "days," "long," and "nights" in the last stanza of *Lost Your Head Blues*. In this recording Bessie is backed by Fletcher Henderson (piano) and Joe Smith (trumpet), and they

dondon (see figures) is a talking drum* shaped like an hourglass, with heads at opposite ends. Leather thongs connect the two heads. Pulling on the thongs increases the tension on the heads and raises the pitch. The **gongon** is a large, barrel-like drum that produces a deep tone. It can also create the rattlelike sound of a snare drum* because a snare string is stretched across the upper part of the face of the drum. Both the dondon and the gongon are struck with a stick in a wrist-flicking motion (see figures). Five or six dondons and one or two gongons typically constitute the "orchestra" for dance music and praise-songs in this region of Ghana.

Kasuan Kura is a praise-song of the Dagombas, a song that tells the history of an important member of the tribe. Its structure is call and response. The vocal soloist relates the history of the honored figure while the chorus repeats the name of this esteemed ancestor "Kasuan Kura" throughout. The piece begins with dondon drummers manipulating their instruments to make them speak. Immediately thereafter at (0:02) the gongons

enter, recognizable by their snare rattle and deeper sound. The gongons play throughout the song, while the higher-pitched dondons come and go. Whenever dondons and gongons are heard together, complex polyrhythms and polymeters result. When gongons merely support the choral response, a rather simple rhythm in a clear duple meter emerges. Thus two musical conversations develop: one between the solo singer and chorus, and a second between the complex dondon-gongon mixture and the simpler rhythmic texture of the gongons alone. In the course of this short piece the soloist's calls become more elaborate and exuberant, just as the drumming on the dondons grows more excited.

KEY WORDS

call and response	gongon
dondon	talking drum
Ghana	

Listening Guide

WWW

The People of Dagomba, Ghana
Kasuan Kura
(recorded in Ghana by John Miller Chernoff)

6CD 6/18

0:00	Dondons begin
0:02	Gongons enter
0:12	Solo vocal call accompanied by dondons and gongons
0:16	Choral response accompanied by gongons alone
0:21	Solo call accompanied by dondons and gongons
0:25	Choral response accompanied by gongons alone
0:29	Call and response continues, accompanied as before
1:25	Dondon and gongon patterns become more complex
1:32	Call and response continues to the end

begin with a four-bar introduction. Then the voice enters and the twelve-bar blues harmony starts up, one full statement of the pattern for each of the five stanzas of text. Each time Bessie Smith sings her melody above the repeating bass, she varies it slightly by means of vocal inflections and off-key shadings. Her expressive vocal line, the soulful, improvised responses played by the trumpet, and the repeating twelve-bar harmony carried by the piano are the essence of the blues.

for each stanza, one statement of the blues harmony

Listening Guide

Lost Your Head Blues
sung by Bessie Smith (recorded in New York, 1926)

6CD 6/9

0:00 Four-bar introduction

0:11 Line 1: I was with you baby when you did not have a dime. (trumpet)
      Chords: I ——

0:22 Line 2: I was with you baby when you did not have a dime. (trumpet)
      Chords: IV ——————————————————— I —————————————————————

0:32 Line 3: Now since you got plenty money you have throw'd your good gal down. (trumpet)
      Chords: V——————————————————— I ——————————————————————

(For the next three stanzas the chord changes and instrumental breaks continue as above;
in the last stanza the breaks come in the middle of the lines as well as at the end.)

0:44 Once ain't for always, two ain't for twice.
      Once ain't for always, two ain't for twice.
      When you get a good gal, you better treat her nice.

1:16 When you were lonesome, I tried to treat you kind.
      When you were lonesome, I tried to treat you kind.
      But since you've got money, it's done changed your mind.

1:49 I'm gonna leave baby, ain't gonna say goodbye.
      I'm gonna leave baby, ain't gonna say goodbye.
      But I'll write you and tell you the reason why.

2:20 Days† are lonesome, nights are long†.
      Days are lonesome, nights† are so long.
      I'm a good gal, but I've just been treated wrong.

†Note the vocal "slides" here.

(Listening Exercise 41)

The impact of the blues on the popular music of the twentieth century has been enormous. In addition to being in itself a genre of music of great feeling and power, the blues gave to jazz a much-used harmonic pattern and an expressive style of playing. Many jazz and rock greats—from Louis Armstrong (*Gut Bucket Blues*) to Wynton Marsalis (*The Majesty of the Blues*) to Tracy Chapman (*Give Me One Reason*) to Cream (*Strange Brew*)—have improvised around the blues. Equally important, it was from the blues and its offspring, rhythm and blues, that rock 'n' roll was born.

enduring influence of the blues

JAZZ

Jazz has been called America's classical music. Like America itself, jazz is an amalgam, a mixture of many different musical influences. Foremost among these, of course, are the traditional musical practices of Africa, as manifested in the spirituals and blues of American blacks in the South. But jazz also contains European elements, marches and hymns, in addition to fiddle tunes and dances from the British Isles as preserved in the folk music of white Appalachia. The complex rhythms, percussive sounds, and bending vocal style of African-American music merged with the four-square phrasing and strong, regular harmonies of the Anglo-American tradition to produce a dynamic new sound. Jazz originated about 1910 almost simultaneously in many southern and midwestern cities: New Orleans, St. Louis, Kansas City, and Chicago, to name a few. Because its style was different from city to city and because various other styles of jazz would later evolve—swing*, bebop*, cool*, and jazz-fusion* among others—jazz must be defined in rather general terms. *roots*

Jazz is lively, energetic music with pulsating rhythms and scintillating syncopations, usually played by a small instrumental ensemble (a combo) or a somewhat larger group (a big band). Jazz tends to be polyphonic, since several instruments play independent lines. And it also includes a strong element of improvisation that gives individual performers the freedom to follow their own flights of musical fancy. Tension and excitement are created as *jazz style* virtuosic soloists play off against a regularly changing harmony and a steady beat provided by the rhythm section (usually drums, piano, and a string bass). Playing jazz is like playing a competitive team sport: It requires teamwork, imagination, skill and endurance, and the outcome is never certain!

Ragtime: A Precursor of Jazz

Ragtime music was an immediate precursor of jazz and shares with it many of the same rhythmic features. To black musicians, "to rag" meant to play or sing music in a heavily syncopated, jazzy style—with "ragged time." Ragtime music originated in brothels, saloons, and dancehalls during the 1890s—the Gay Nineties—and the jaunty, upbeat sound of ragtime captured the spirit of that age. Most rags were written by black pianists who played in houses of ill repute because it was difficult in those years for black musicians to find employment elsewhere. Piano rags, which first began to be published in 1897, took America by storm, more than two thousand titles appearing in print by the end of World War I. Sold as sheet music of a thin page or two, piano rags quickly moved from the saloon into middle-class homes, where musically literate amateurs played them on the parlor piano.

The undisputed "King of Ragtime" was Scott Joplin (1868–1917) (Fig. 18–2). The son of a slave, Joplin managed to acquire for himself a solid grounding in classical music while he earned a living playing in honky-tonk bars in and around St. Louis. In 1899 he published *Maple Leaf Rag,* which sold an astonishing one million copies. Though he went on to write other immensely popular rags, such as *The Entertainer* and *Peacherine Rag,* Joplin gradually shed the image of barroom pianist and moved to New York to compose rag-oriented opera.

The *Maple Leaf Rag,* which was all the rage at the turn of the century, is typical of the style of Joplin and his fellow ragtime composers. Its form is similar to that of a traditional military march, consisting of a succession of sixteen-bar units, each of which is repeated. And its harmonies are also European in origin, moving purposefully from chord to chord with slight chromatic inflections—Joplin knew his Schubert and Chopin! But what makes ragtime so infectious is its bouncy, syncopated rhythm. Syncopation, of course, is the momentary displacement of an accent from on the beat to off the beat. In piano ragtime the left hand keeps a regular "um-pah, um-pah" beat, usually in $\frac{2}{4}$ meter, while the right hand lays on syncopations against it. In the following example from the *Maple Leaf Rag,* syncopation (S) occurs

CORBIS/Bettmann

FIGURE 18–2

One of the few surviving images of ragtime composer Scott Joplin.

when long notes (either an eighth note or two sixteenth notes tied together) sound off (between) the steady eighth-note beats of the bass:

EXAMPLE 18–2

New Orleans Jazz

New Orleans, a musical and cultural melting pot

Although jazz sprang up almost simultaneously in towns up and down the Mississippi River, its focal point and probable place of origin was New Orleans. Not only was New Orleans the home of many of the early jazz greats—King Oliver (1885–1938), Jelly Roll Morton (1890–1941), and Louis Armstrong (1901–1971)—but it enjoyed an exceptionally lively and varied musical life that encouraged the development of new musical styles. Culturally, New Orleans looked more toward France and the Caribbean than it did to the Anglo-American north. The city air was filled not only with opera tunes, marches, and ballroom dances from imperial France but also African-American blues and ragtime and Cuban dance rhythms. The end of the Spanish-American War (1898) brought a flood of used military band instruments into second-hand shops in New Orleans at prices that were affordable even to impoverished blacks. Musicians, black and white alike, found ready employment in ballrooms of the well-to-do, in the bars and brothels of Storyville (a thirty-eight-square-block red-light district in the center of the city), at parades, picnics, weddings, and funerals associated with the many New Orleans societies and fraternal orders. Music was everywhere. Even today in New Orleans bands of various sorts, some good, some bad, can be heard on the streets of the city's French Quarter at almost any hour, day or night.

What marks the sound of New Orleans jazz? Syncopation combined with a free treatment of melody. A given march, rag, blues or popular tune is played with off-beat accents and a spontaneous sliding into and around the pitches of the tune. The rag had phrases (strains) of sixteen bars, many popular songs of the period had four four-bar phrases, and the traditional blues, as we have seen, consisted of a steady stream of twelve-bar units. Within the square formal confines of these four-, eight-, twelve-, and sixteen-bar patterns, the New Orleans jazz combo found a security that allowed the solo instruments the greatest sort of freedom of expression. The melody was usually played in some jazzed-up way by a cornet or trumpet; a clarinet supported this lead instrument and further embellished the tune; a trombone added counterpoint against the melody in a lower

FIGURE 18–3

A New Orleans street band in the early 1990s. The tradition of playing jazz in the streets of New Orleans, at parades, funerals, and functions of fraternal orders, extends back to the late 1800s and continues today.

CORBIS

range; down below, a tuba set the harmonies if the group was marching, but if it did not, that job was handed over to a string bass, piano, banjo, and/or guitar. These same instruments (tuba, string bass, piano, banjo, and guitar), along with the drums, formed the **rhythm section** because they not only set the harmony but also helped the drums give out the beat in a steady fashion. Finally, New Orleans–style bands, then and now, never play from written music. They count, or feel, when the chords must change and they improvise and refashion the tune to make it fit those changes.

playing without written music

Louis Armstrong (1901–1971)

When the brothels and gambling houses of the red-light district of New Orleans were closed by the U.S. government in 1917, many places of employment for jazz musicians disappeared. Performers began to look elsewhere for work—in New York, Chicago, and even Los Angeles. One of those who eventually made his way to Chicago was Louis "Satchmo" ("Satchelmouth") Armstrong. Armstrong was born in New Orleans in 1901, and in 1923 followed his mentor, King Oliver, to Chicago to join the latter's Creole Jazz Band. By this time Armstrong was already recognized by his peers as the best jazz trumpeter alive. He soon formed his own band in Chicago, the Hot Five, to make what was to become a series of landmark recordings. When the vogue of classic New Orleans–style jazz gave way to the sound of the swing band around 1930, Armstrong moved to New York, where he "fronted"—played as featured soloist—in a number of large bands. He invented the practice of "scat singing"—singing nonsense syllables in jazz style—and eventually became known as much for the gravelly sound of his voice, in songs such as *Hello Dolly* and *Mack the Knife*, as for his trumpet playing. His last years were spent in almost continual travel, sent around the world by the U.S. State Department as "Ambassador Satchmo." He died at his home in Queens, New York, in 1971.

Profiles in History/CORBIS

FIGURE 18–4

Louis Armstrong in 1933 at the age of 32. His style of trumpet playing revolutionized the soundscape of jazz.

Although cut in Chicago, Armstrong's early discs are classics of New Orleans–style jazz. The tune *Willie the Weeper* was recorded by Armstrong's expanded band, the Hot Seven, in 1927. As to who "composed" the piece, we'll never know. Like much folk music, and African-American music in particular, *Willie the Weeper* was worked out by the entire group, following two basic chord progressions, the first in a major key, the second in a minor one. Certainly, none of *Willie the Weeper* was ever written down in musical notation. As Armstrong's drummer, Baby Dodds, said: "We weren't a bunch of fellows to write down anything." Instead, they relied on "head arrangements," a combination of aural memory (remembering the tune and the harmony) and spontaneous improvisation, in which each member of the group took his turn as a soloist with the tune. Here the tune in major is sixteen bars long, while the contrasting one in minor is eight bars in length. In a jazz piece of this sort each presentation of the tune is called a **chorus**, whether played by a soloist or the entire ensemble. The underlying chord progressions and the outline of the melody provide a framework for the spontaneous improvisations of the players during each chorus. Call it what you will—precision abandon, bonded independence, controlled chaos—the joyful exuberance of these extraordinary musicians cannot be denied.

chorus, a statement of the tune around which the performers improvise

Listening Guide

Willie the Weeper, played by
Louis Armstrong and his Hot Seven
(recorded in Chicago, 1927)

6CD 6/10

WWW

0:00   Four-bar Introduction
0:05   Chorus 1 (16 bars): full ensemble; trumpet (Armstrong) and trombone play the tune
0:25   Chorus 2: Armstrong varies the tune
0:46   Minor Chorus 1 (8 bars): trombone and tuba play the tune
0:57   Minor Chorus 2: trombone and tuba repeat the tune
1:07   Chorus 3: trombone solo
1:28   Chorus 4: extraordinary clarinet solo
1:49   Minor Chorus 3: trumpet solo
1:59   Minor Chorus 4: piano solo
2:09   Chorus 5: guitar solo
2:29   Chorus 6: Armstrong carries the tune
2:49   Chorus 7: trumpet, trombone, and clarinet improvise around the tune with wild abandon

(Listening Exercise 42)

What is music? When dealing with a symphony of Mozart or a sonata of Beethoven, we might say that the written score is the music. We can pick up the music of Beethoven, for example, and place it on the piano. But with New Orleans–style jazz, and indeed most jazz, there is no written score. As music, it exists only at the moment of performance, or as a recording, if that particular performance happened to be recorded. The music of Beethoven is more or less the same each time it is played, because the written document prescribes a certain performance. Jazz is never performed, or recreated, twice in exactly the same way. With classical music, then, music tends to be a time-honored written artifact leading to a definitive performance; with jazz, on the other hand, music is a living aural tradition, one to which each new performer is expected to add.

Big Bands and Swing

The recordings of Louis Armstrong and the Hot Seven sold as fast as they could be pressed. Jazz became the rage of the 1920s, just as ragtime had been the craze at the turn of the century. It was, in the words of novelist F. Scott Fitzgerald, the "Jazz Age." So popular did jazz become that it was now performed in ballrooms, large dancehalls, and movie theaters, in addition to the smaller bars and supper clubs where New Orleans–style jazz had its home. And just as the small supper club gradually gave way to the ballroom, so too did the small jazz combo cede pride of place to the big band—for to be heard above the stomping and swaying of many hundreds of pairs of feet, an ensemble larger than the traditional New Orleans combo of five or seven players was needed. Thus was born the big-band era, the glory days of the bands of Benny Goodman (1909–1986), Duke Ellington (1889–1974), Count Basie (1904–1984), and Glenn Miller (1904–1944).

Though not "big" by the standard of today's marching band, the **big band** of the 1930s and 1940s was at least double the size of the New Orleans–style

FIGURE 18–5

Benny Goodman, the "King of Swing," during a radio broadcast in the early 1940s.

Yale Music Library, Benny Goodman Archives

jazz combo. In 1943, for example, Duke Ellington's orchestra consisted of four trumpets, three trombones, five reed players (men who played both clarinet and saxophone), plus a rhythm section of piano, string bass, guitar, and drums—a total of sixteen players (Fig. 18–6). Most big-band compositions were worked out ahead of time and set down in written arrangements called "charts." The fact that jazz musicians now for the first time had to play from written notation suggests that a more disciplined, polished, orchestral sound was desired. The addition of a quintet of saxophones gave the ensemble a more mellow, blended quality. The new sound has little of the sharp bite and wild syncopation of the earlier New Orleans–style jazz. Rather, the music is mellow, bouncy, and flowing. In a word, it "swings." **Swing**, then, can be said to be a popular style of jazz played by a big band in the 1930s and 1940s. The present revival of "swing dancing" suggests that an elegant dance style that is distinctly jazzy can enjoy enduring popularity.

UPI/Bettmann

FIGURE 18–6

Duke Ellington (seated at the piano) and his big band in 1943. Unlike other band leaders of this time, Ellington was as much a composer and arranger as he was a performer.

Bebop

The craze for big-band swing jazz reached its peak immediately before and during World War II. It had become, in effect, the popular music of America. Swing jazz was heard at home on the radio, on jukeboxes, at college proms, in hotel ballrooms, in theaters, and even in New York's Carnegie Hall, the hallowed home of classical music. Then, for reasons that are not fully known, it fell out of favor. One cause was that many of the best young performers found that playing from written big-band charts limited their freedom and creativity. They wanted to return to a style of playing in which improvisation was more important than composition and where the performing soloist, not the composer, was king. Choosing their playing partners carefully, they worked or "jammed" in small, elite groups in clubs in midtown Manhattan and in Harlem, and in so doing created a new virtuosic style of jazz called bebop.

return of the jazz combo

Bebop is an angular, hard-driving style of jazz played by a small combo without written music. It derives its name from the fact that the fast, snappy melody sounds like the word "bebop, bebop" said quickly. Typically, bebop requires a quintet of trumpet, saxophone, piano, double bass, and drums. The best players, among them saxophonist Charlie Parker (1920–1955) and trumpeter Dizzy Gillespie (1917–1993), had astonishing technique and played at breakneck speed. Their love was improvisation, and the solos they created were more complex than those heard in either swing or New Orleans–style jazz. They overlaid the melody with so much rapid, jarring embroidery that the tune soon became unrecognizable. They also changed chords more rapidly than earlier jazz players and went to more remote keys. Only the most gifted performers could keep up and "make the changes." Bebop was for an elite few.

a frenetic style of playing

"far out" improvisations above oscure harmonies

Charlie "Bird" Parker (1920–1955)

FIGURE 18–7

Charlie "Bird" Parker about 1950. Parker developed a fast, snapping, syncopated style of playing that often sounds like the word "bebop" said quickly.

Perhaps the most gifted of the bebop artists was Charlie "Yardbird" or "Bird" Parker, the subject of Clint Eastwood's movie *Bird* (1988). Parker was a tragic figure, a drug-addicted, alcoholic, antisocial man whose skills as an improviser and performer, nonetheless, were greater than all other jazz musicians, save Louis Armstrong. Indeed, the lives of Armstrong and Parker make an interesting comparison. Both were born into the extreme poverty of the ghetto, Armstrong in New Orleans and Parker in Kansas City, and both rose to the top of their profession through extraordinary talent and hard work. But Armstrong was an extroverted person who viewed himself as a public entertainer as much as an artist. Parker didn't care whether people liked his music or not, and he managed to alienate everyone around him including, finally, his friend and longtime playing partner Dizzy Gillespie. He died of the effects of his many excesses, alone and broke, at the age of thirty-four. Parker's life may have been a mess, but his rapid, inventive style of playing changed irrevocably the history of jazz.

In 1950 Parker and Gillespie recorded a bebop version of a sentimental love song called *My Melancholy Baby* (1911). Like many popular tunes from the early part of this century, *My Melancholy Baby* is sixteen bars long and divided into four four-measure phrases (here **ABAC**). After a four-bar introduction by pianist Thelonious Monk, Parker plays the tune more or less "straight," with only moderately complex elaborations. But when Dizzy Gillespie enters for the second chorus, the ornamentation becomes more complex by means of racing thirty-second notes and continues to do so through the third and final chorus, which Monk and Parker divide. Try to follow the original tune of *My Melancholy Baby* as each soloist embroiders it. As you listen, notice that there is no group ensemble playing at the end and no strong beat. Instead, in bebop we find frenetic solos for a single instrument set against a quiet, relaxed rhythm section. What results is a music more for listening than for dancing. Bebop is the "chamber music" of jazz, a style designed to appeal to only a small number of aficionados.

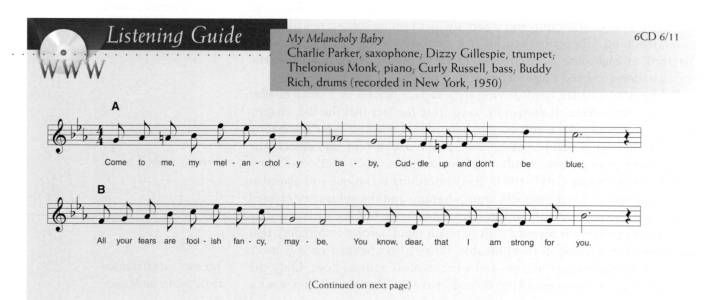

Listening Guide

My Melancholy Baby   6CD 6/11

Charlie Parker, saxophone; Dizzy Gillespie, trumpet; Thelonious Monk, piano; Curly Russell, bass; Buddy Rich, drums (recorded in New York, 1950)

A

Come to me, my mel-an-chol-y ba-by, Cud-dle up and don't be blue;

B

All your fears are fool-ish fan-cy, may-be, You know, dear, that I am strong for you.

(Continued on next page)

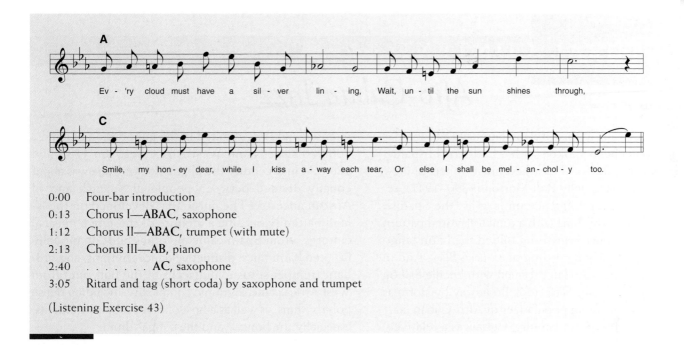

A

Ev - 'ry cloud must have a sil - ver lin - ing, Wait, un - til the sun shines through,

C

Smile, my hon - ey dear, while I kiss a - way each tear, Or else I shall be mel - an - chol - y too.

0:00   Four-bar introduction
0:13   Chorus I—**ABAC**, saxophone
1:12   Chorus II—**ABAC**, trumpet (with mute)
2:13   Chorus III—**AB**, piano
2:40   . . . . **AC**, saxophone
3:05   Ritard and tag (short coda) by saxophone and trumpet

(Listening Exercise 43)

By 1950 jazz was no longer young; indeed it had been around nearly fifty years. Moreover, by mid-century one could no longer speak of "jazz" and refer to one specific style. There was New Orleans–style, swing, bebop, Afro-Cuban jazz (see page 414), and a host of new sounds emerging. Maybe bebop, with its fast tempos and biting attacks, was too hot to handle. Soon a reaction against both bebop and the frenetic style of Afro-Cuban jazz appeared in the form of "cool jazz," which sought to soften their hard-driving sounds with more relaxed, less-frenzied solos. But experimentation was also in the air. Making the scene were "modal jazz" (using new modal harmonies), "electric jazz" (using electric instruments as well as acoustical ones), and "free jazz" (full of unpredictable improvisations). The principal practitioner of free jazz was saxophonist John Coltrane (1926–1967). Cool jazz, on the other hand, was made popular mainly by Miles Davis.

Miles Davis (1926–1991) and Cool Jazz

Miles Davis was born in St. Louis, the son of a well-to-do dentist. He took up the trumpet at age thirteen and two years later was already playing professionally. In 1944 he moved to New York to be near his idols, Charlie Parker and Dizzy Gillespie (on both, see page 412). Naturally, Davis at first emulated their intense, angular style of bebop. But Davis' own, more mellow voice became audible in a series of recordings he made in 1949 called *The Birth of Cool.* In brief, **cool jazz** rejects the aggressive style of bebop. Instead, it emphasizes lyricism, restraint, instruments in the lower part of their range, slower tempos, and quieter dynamic levels. Davis was not the only exponent of cool jazz—Gerry Mulligan (1927–2002) and Dave Brubeck (b. 1920) were two others—but he was by far the most influential.

(Continued on page 416)

FIGURE 18–8

Miles Davis in the 1950s, the decade during which he became the seminal force behind the development of cool jazz.

Mosaic Images/CORBIS

Afro-Cuban Jazz

Throughout its history the language of jazz has always been spoken with a Latin, or Hispanic, accent. One of the earliest practitioners of New Orleans–style jazz, Jelly Roll Morton (1890–1941), referred to the Latin influence on jazz as "the Spanish tinge," meaning rhythms with a rumba-flavored pattern of accenting. Louis Armstrong folded the Latin tango into a famous early recording of *St. Louis Blues.* And in 1939 Desi Arnaz, who later teamed with Lucille Ball on the famous *I Love Lucy Show*, took Broadway by storm as a conga drum–playing popularizer of Afro-Cuban jazz.

Until the nineteenth century, Cuba was a relatively underdeveloped island with an economy based on tobacco and cattle. The introduction of sugar cane, a labor

intensive industry, resulted in the importation of almost 400,000 slaves from West Africa between 1835 and 1864. At mid-century the population of Cuba was about equally divided between people of Spanish and of African ancestry. The music that developed on the island naturally became a mixture of these two musical cultures. From Spain came melodies built on modally flavored harmonies, distinctive dance rhythms, and brilliant trumpet solos reminiscent of the bull ring; from West Africa came rhythmic complexity, including dense polyrhythms, as well as a host of percussion instruments, especially the bongo* and the conga* drum.

Afro-Cuban music invaded the United States in a succession of waves during the twentieth century, landing with greatest impact in New York and Miami. First there was the tango rage in the 1920s, then the rumba craze in the 1930s, and finally mambo mania in the 1950s. During the 1940s, Cuban musicians such as Chano Pozo (1915–1948) began to play with New York bebop jazz musicians such as Dizzy Gillespie. What they created was a new style called **Afro-Cuban jazz** (also called **Cubop**). Up to this point jazz had been essentially monorhythmic. Now it was infused with intense polyrhythms, heavier percussion, and modal sounding melodies (melodies based on scales other than major or minor).

In *110th St. & 5th Ave.* we clearly hear the fusion of the traditions of American jazz with Cuban dance, folk, and popular idioms. The first sounds are those of a saxophone quartet, an instrumental section derived from the big swing* bands of the 1930s and 1940s. They are playing what is called a **jazz riff**—a short motive that recurs again and again in the course of one piece (see Listening Guide). The saxophones are supported by a composite drumming pattern and a bass line with a conflicting meter. Thus at the very beginning there are aleady several layers of rhythm superimposed in this piece, a characteristic of African music. Next a choir of trumpets gradually enters with a second jazz riff. The central moment of the piece, however, is an extended solo for saxophone. The saxophone melody sounds non-Western

Desi Arnaz (1917–1986), more of a show business personality than an innovative musician, was the product of New York's fascination with Cuban music. He came to New York in 1936 as a conga-playing rumba singer and met Lucille Ball on Broadway in 1940.

Underwood & Underwood/CORBIS

© Herman Leonard

Chano Pozo (1915–1948), a Cuban whose drumming and singing were rooted in Nigerian religious cult practices, did much to bring the rhythms of Afro-Cuban music to New York.

because it is based on a scale using the interval of an augmented second (three half-steps). Such an exotic interval is traditionally associated with the music of southern Spain, and probably arrived there from the Near East via North Africa. Soon the saxophone riff returns and this leads to another solo, this time by a blaring trumpet with a distinctly Spanish tinge. The title *110th St. & 5th Ave.* refers to a corner in Spanish Harlem (also called East Harlem and *El barrio*) in New York City. This location was home to two large theaters in which Cuban bands, such as that of Noro Morales, frequently played.

KEY WORDS

Afro-Cuban jazz
Cubop
jazz riff

Listening Guide

WWW

Paul Lopez and Noro Morales
110th St. & 5th Ave.
Noro Morales and His Orchestra
(recorded in New York, 1949)

6CD 6/19

0:00	Opening jazz riff played by four saxophones

0:08	Two, three, and then four trumpets enter with second jazz riff

0:31	Piano improvises
0:58	Saxophones return with their riff
1:06	Saxophone solo with exotic Spanish-North African sound based on scale

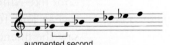

augmented second

1:38	Saxophones return with riff
1:50	Trumpet solo with a decidedly Spanish tinge; saxophone riff continues to the end
2:20	Piano returns to lead fade out

To hear the essence of the "cool" in jazz, we need only turn to Davis' creation *Night on the Champs Elysées*. It was recorded in 1957 as background music for a French motion picture, *Ascenseur pour l'échafaud (Elevator to the Scaffold)* starring Jeanne Moreau. Davis and the other members of his quintet gathered in a recording studio in Paris. As the film danced before them, they improvised and fleshed out music that Davis had only vaguely sketched, trying to match their sounds to what they saw. Needless to say, several takes were necessary, and indeed there are four different versions of the music of just one scene, *Night on the Champs Elysées*. Let us focus on the longest of the four.

In *Night on the Champs Elysées* Davis creates a melody around the notes of a D minor triad, bending them in a blues-inspired style of playing. Periodically, a four-bar unit built around an eleventh chord* on C interrupts the improvisations on the melody in D minor. Unlike "up-tempo" bebop, here Davis chooses a very slow tempo as well as a relaxed and constant $\frac{4}{4}$ meter. He also makes exclusive use of the middle of the trumpet's range, eschewing its more intense higher register. The resulting "cool" style is perfectly suited to the visual image of a cool misty night along the famous Parisian boulevard Champs Elysées.

a slower tempo, a lower range

Listening Guide

Miles Davis
Night on the Champs Elysées (1957)

see footnote*

WWW

0:00 Four-bar introduction played by rhythm section* (piano, drums, bass) and saxophone
0:13 Davis plays a trumpet solo around a D minor triad for sixteen bars
1:12 Change to eleventh chord* on C for four bars
1:26 Return to improvisation around D minor triad for twenty-four bars
2:54 Change to eleventh chord* on C for four bars
3:08 Return to improvisation around D minor triad for ten bars
3:45 Saxophone enters and improvises around D minor triad for fourteen bars
4:37 Change to eleventh chord* on C for four bars
4:53 Concludes with eight more bars of improvisation in D minor (fade out)

rock influences jazz

*Universal Music was unable to license this recording. You may wish to find it on the album *Ascenseur pour l'eschafaud* (Polygram ASIN B000004785), track 2. The publisher invites instructors to contact Wadsworth/Schirmer for a free copy of the music.

During the 1970s jazz began to assimilate some of the traits of rock. The cause of this stylistic change was simple: money. Jazz recordings—whether swing, bebop, or cool—were not selling. What was selling was rock. So jazz musicians, driven by economic reality, began to adopt the rhythms of the rock drummer and the simple, repetitious harmonies outlined by the bass guitar. **Jazz-fusion** is the name given this mixture of jazz and rock. Young trumpeters, such as Lew Soloff (b. 1943) and Chuck Mangione (b. 1941), stopped playing cool like Miles Davis and went off to form jazz-rock bands, such as Blood, Sweat, and Tears, Chicago, and the Chuck Mangione ensemble. Davis, too, saw the financial handwriting on the wall and began to release jazz-fusion albums. His *Bitches Brew* sold 400,000 copies in its first year, more than other Davis album. These musicians all made great music—and got rich—by blending the driving rhythms and repetitious harmonies of rock with the big-band brass sounds and the virtuosity of the jazz improviser. With his smooth style, popular saxophonist Kenny G extended the tradition of jazz-fusion into the 1990s. The moral of the story, as it pertains to the history of jazz and its listening public, is that any popular music without a catchy tune or a finger-snapping beat won't be popular for long.

Wynton Marsalis (b. 1961) Spokesman for Jazz Today

Today, our best-known jazz musician is Wynton Marsalis, appropriately enough, a native of New Orleans, the birthplace of traditional jazz. He is the son of pianist Ellis Marsalis and the younger brother of saxophonist Branford Marsalis (leader of the *Tonight Show* band during the 1990s). Being part of a musical family, Marsalis received his first trumpet at the young age of six. To build a virtuosic technique and to "know what makes music great," Marsalis studied the classical repertoire, enrolling at the Juilliard School in New York City in 1979. In 1984 he became the only person to win a Grammy simultaneously as a classical performer (for a recording of the Haydn trumpet concerto) and as a jazz performer (for his album *Think of One*). In all, he has garnered nine Grammys, including one for his jazz oratorio *Blood on the Fields*, which also won the Pulitzer Prize in 1997. Today Marsalis is a practicing jazz musician, an educator, and a frequent TV commentator and consultant. Obviously Marsalis' understanding of both classical music and jazz give him a unique insight into both the learned and popular traditions. Marsalis' observations about jazz, taken from an interview given in connection with the Ken Burns PBS series *Jazz* (2000), provide a useful summary as to what jazz today represents.

CORBIS/Lynn Goldsmith

FIGURE 18–9

Wynton Marsalis, performer and senior spokesman for jazz and its role in American musical culture.

What is the special genius of jazz?

The real power and innovation of jazz is that a group of people can come together and create art—improvised art—and can negotiate their agendas with each other. And that negotiation *is* the art. Like, you'll hear all the time that Bach improvised, and he did improvise. But he wasn't going to go to the second viola and say, "Okay, let's play [the cantata] 'Ein feste Burg.'" They were not going to do that. Whereas in jazz, I could go to Milwaukee tomorrow and walk into a bar at 2:30 in the morning. There'll be three musicians playing there and I'll say, "What you want to play, man? Let's play some blues." Well, all four of us are going to start playing and everybody will just start comping and playing and listening. You never know what they're going to do. So, that's our art. The four of us can now have a dialogue. We can have a conversation. We can speak to each other in the language of music. And that is art. That is our art.

jazz, a conversation through music

What would life be like without jazz?

You definitely can live without jazz. The only thing you need to live is water and some food. Art in general is nonessential to living. But now, the style that you're gonna be living in? Well, I don't know about that. You don't need a bed to sleep. You don't have to cook food to eat it. You don't have to have clothes of a certain style. You don't have to speak a certain way. Most of the things you are surrounded by you don't need. But when you have those things around you, it makes you feel good about living in the world. And it gives you something to look forward to, and it also gives you a way to connect with everything that has happened on earth. It's like real poor people in the country, on a Sunday, would get dressed up and they wouldn't have any money but just that little hat with the flower on it. You know, just what that flower represents. A certain thing. Just a little something to make you special and make you sweet. That's jazz music. That's what the jazz musician wants to give to the people.

art makes you feel good about living in the world

Source: Geoffrey C. Ward and Ken Burns, *Jazz: A History of America's Music,* © Alfred A. Knopf, 2000)

ROCK

Bursting on the scene in the mid-1950s, rock 'n' roll (and its later manifestation, rock) revolutionized popular music in America and indeed throughout the world. Its style is well known to all—the pounding beat, the heavy, amplified guitar sound, the driving bass, and the simple, repetitive harmonies. There is, to be sure, much harmonic repetition, noisy filler, and electronic distortion. But, of course, rock involves much more than just music. The style of dress of the rockers, their sometimes-outrageous behavior, both on and off stage, and their social and political beliefs are just as important to rock culture as is the music they produce. Rock was born as a music of protest and rebellion directed against the established musical and social orders.

The origins of rock can be found in a style of music called rhythm and blues that came out of the South around 1950. Like the blues, **rhythm and blues** makes use of the twelve-bar blues pattern, $\frac{4}{4}$ meter, and an expressive style of singing. But here the usually slow tempo of the blues is changed to a faster $\frac{4}{4}$, upbeats and downbeats are made stronger, a saxophone is added to the basic guitar sound, and the text is shouted as much as sung. All of this produces a raw, driving, highly danceable kind of music. At first rhythm and blues was created and played exclusively by black musicians for a black audience. But as many of these musicians and listeners moved to the urban centers of the North in the 1950s, a white audience began to hear and dance to this energized black music, mostly over the radio. Indeed, the term "rock 'n' roll" was first coined in 1951 by a white disk jockey in Cleveland, Alan Freed, who championed black rhythm and blues—that is the principal reason the new rock 'n' roll Hall of Fame was situated in Cleveland. Soon black artists like Chuck Berry ("Maybellene" and "Roll Over Beethoven"), Bo Diddley ("Bo Diddley"), Fats Domino ("Blueberry Hill"), and Little Richard ("Tutti Frutti" and "Lucille") found that there was a demand for their music in the white market. And white musicians like Bill Haley ("Rock Around the Clock"), Carl Perkins ("Blue Suede Shoes"), Jerry Lee Lewis ("Great Balls of Fire"), and Elvis Presley ("Jail House Rock") began to copy the black sound. Perkins, Lewis, and Presley had grown up in the South in the environment of black rhythm and blues. Presley's first manager said that he was simply "looking for a white boy who could sing colored."

Elvis Presley (1935–1977) became the "King of Rock 'n' Roll"; his singing electrified a white audience only then coming to know the sounds of black rhythm and blues. Presley's first national hit "Heartbreak Hotel" and subsequent "Love Me Tender" (both 1956)

CORBIS/Bettmann

FIGURE 18–10

Little Richard (Richard Penniman, b. 1932), one of rock 'n' roll's early stars. Along with Chuck Berry and Bo Diddley, he transformed early rhythm and blues into rock 'n' roll.

FIGURE 18–11

"The King is dead, long live the King." The hysteria surrounding Elvis has diminished only slightly since his death in 1977. His retrospective album *Elvis 30 #1 Hits*, released in 2002 on the twenty-fifth anniversary of his death, sold a million copies in the first month. Elvis' estate has generated more income than that of any deceased celebrity.

Bettmann/CORBIS

were in the tradition of the white country ballad, though sung in an expressive, throbbing style. But his "Hound Dog" (1956) and "Jail House Rock" (1957) continued the development of hard-driving rhythm and blues. Indeed, "Hound Dog" had been borrowed from blues singer Big Mama Thornton. Within two years of his first hit, Presley had become a national obsession, his every gyration the object of scrutiny by the media. Presley still holds the record for "top ten" pop singles (forty) and he continues to be the world's best-selling solo artist with total sales of more than one billion singles worldwide. He died young, of drug abuse, a bloated caricature of himself. The sad part is that, in spite of the rhinestones, the Cadillacs, and all the other silliness that attended his life, Presley was highly musical and blessed with an exceptionally rich and wide-ranging baritone voice. His was by far the best voice of any of the male rock singers, then or now.

from rhythm and blues comes rock 'n' roll

In the early 1960s American rock received a shot in the arm from an unexpected source, Great Britain. The reason for this is clear. England had recently become infatuated with the sounds of American blues players like Muddy Waters as well as rhythm and blues singers such as Chuck Berry and Bo Diddley, some of whom had toured there. As foreign imitators, British pop musicians embraced the new styles with greater fidelity to the original than did their American cousins. The pounding, swaggering style of Mick Jagger and his Rolling Stones is very much in the tradition of "shouting" rhythm and blues from Louisiana and Mississippi. And The Who, led by guitarist Pete Townshend, added more varied chord changes, notably in their two "rock operas" *Tommy* (1969) and *Quadrophenia* (1973). But of all the British groups, the most adaptive and most successful was the Beatles.

Photofest

FIGURE 18–12

Although they were together for only a few short years (1960-1970), no pop group has ever equaled the Beatles' musical originality and stylistic variety. Every No. 1 tune was fresh and wildly different from the last.

The Beatles were formed in Liverpool, England, in 1960 and achieved an almost overnight success in that country with their first single "Love Me Do" (1962) and the follow-up "Please Please Me" (1963). In 1964 they took America by storm, first with their best-selling single "I Want to Hold Your Hand" and then in person through their sensational appearance on the *Ed Sullivan Show* and a sold-out national tour. "Beatlemania" was born. But unlike the equally popular Elvis, a dynamic performer but not a composer, each of the Beatles was a songwriter in his own right. And two of them, bass guitarist Paul McCartney and rhythm guitarist John Lennon, were exceptionally creative. They wrote fresh lyrics and unpredictable tunes that the parents as well as the kids could enjoy. What is most remarkable about the Beatles is the variety of musical styles that they adopted and made their own: rhythm and blues ("Roll Over Beethoven" and "Twist and Shout"), country blues ("Oh, Darling"), gospel ("Let It Be"), Broadway show tunes ("The Long and Winding Road"), British music-hall songs ("When I'm Sixty-Four"), novelty songs ("The Yellow Submarine" and "Octopus's Garden"), Baroque instrumental styles ("Eleanor Rigby" and "Penny Lane"), Indian raga ("Love You

an enormous variety of musical styles

FIGURE 18–13

With Bono as the lead singer, U2 has enjoyed almost twenty years of popularity. Bono is a throwback to the early days of rock 'n' roll and folk-rock*, when the artists were often activists for social or political causes. Here, U2's Bono and The Edge perform the opening song at the 2002 Grammy Awards.

Reuters NewMedia Inc./CORBIS

To"), and psychedelic Rock ("Lucy in the Sky with Diamonds"). In 1970, after a decade of unprecedented popularity and financial gain, the Beatles disbanded, though each of them ultimately returned, with differing degrees of success, to the field of popular music with his own band. Thirty years later, in 2000, thirty of their "number one" hits were collected in an album simply called *1*. It sold 20,000,000 copies in two months. The long hair of the Vietnam era may have disappeared, but the novelty and freshness of the Beatles' sound seems eternally popular.

With the 1970s came a splintering of what had been the central tradition of rock 'n' roll. This tendency to turn rock 'n' roll into alternative forms of rock only accelerated during the last two decades of the twentieth century. As one band created an alternative sound it immediately provoked yet another alternative reaction from the next. Among the multitudinous types of rock that emerged in these decades were acid rock (Jefferson Airplane and the Grateful Dead), progressive rock (Pink Floyd), glam rock (David Bowie and Kiss), Latin rock (Santana and Los Lobos), jazz rock (Steely Dan and Frank Zappa), light rock (Phil Collins), heavy metal rock (Led Zeppelin and Metallica), punk rock (Ramones and Clash), blues rock (Stevie Ray Vaughan and Steve Winwood), working-class hard rock (Bruce Springsteen and John Mellencamp), goth rock (Marilyn Manson), and grunge rock (Pearl Jam and Nirvana), along with many others.

Having reached middle age, rock seems to be losing its vitality, perhaps a victim of too much stylistic fragmentation or too many alternatives. Old men like Mick Jagger and the other Rolling Stones still strut around the stage but look silly. Yet no one younger group has replaced them (or their near contemporaries, U2) in the field of worldwide arena rock. Today teen pop, rap, hip-hop, country music, and Latin song-and-dance dominate the "top ten" charts. Now progressive rock must compete with these other genres of music for public attention. And, just as many styles of classical music have crowded into today's concert hall, so too many genres and sub-genres of popular music battle for primacy. As to which will win out, only time will tell.

Listening Exercises

Lost Your Head Blues   6CD 6/9
sung by Bessie Smith (recorded in New York, 1926)

Lost Your Head Blues tells the tale of a "good old gal" who has "just been treated wrong." In a format typical of the blues, Bessie Smith belts out five stanzas of text, each with three lines. There are "classic" performances in every genre and style of music. With its blend of precision (changing chords in the blues harmony) and freedom (slides and "wah-wah's"), this rendition of *Lost Your Head Blues* is surely a classic.

1. How many performers are there in this recording?
   a. two   b. three   c. four   d. five

2. Which two instruments play during the four-bar introduction?

    a. piano and drums   b. drums and trumpet   c. piano and trumpet

3. Within each of the five stanzas of text, the twelve-bar blues harmony is heard how many times?

    a. once   b. twice   c. three times

4. Excluding the partial statement in the four-bar introduction, the full twelve-bar blues pattern, then, is played how many times?

    a. three times   b. four times   c. five times

5. Which instrument always sets the harmony (the twelve-bar blues pattern) beneath the soloists?

    a. piano   b. drums   c. trumpet

6. Which instrument always plays the instrumental breaks?

    a. piano   b. drums   c. trumpet

7. Which two instruments engage in a dialogue throughout?

    a. piano and trumpet   b. voice and piano   c. voice and trumpet

8. Which instrument does not appear on this recording?

    a. piano   b. drums   c. trumpet

9. Which two instruments continually slide into and around their pitches?

    a. piano   b. drums   c. trumpet   d. voice

10. Why does this recording last only three minutes?

    a. Because that is all the time needed to perform the twelve-bar blues pattern once.

    b. Because in the 1920s a single side of a 78 record could hold only about three minutes of music.

New Orleans Jazz   6CD 6/10
Willie the Weeper
Louis Armstrong and the Hot Seven
(recorded in Chicago, 1927)

As with blues, jazz is rarely written down in musical notation. Rather, it is created on the spot using a combination of aural memory and spontaneous improvisation. In large measure, the notes the musicians played were determined by the shape of the melody and the accompanying harmony, both of which the musicians had in their ears. At the same time, jazz musicians were usually constrained by the fact that the tune and its harmony would be the same length for each chorus. Is that practice followed here in *Willie the Weeper*? Do we have a very square durational pattern helping to hold together independent lines, or is the durational pattern (the length of each chorus) continually changing? Listen to the music. Conduct and count measures as you do. The piece is in duple meter and the first chorus has sixteen bars, the first minor chorus eight. For the other sections listed below, indicate the number of measures that each contains.

    (0:00) Introduction: four bars
    (0:05) Chorus 1 (all instruments): sixteen bars
1. (0:25) Chorus 2 (all instruments): _____ bars
    (0:46) Minor Chorus 1 (trombone & tuba): eight bars

2. (0:57) Minor Chorus 2 (trombone & tuba): _____ bars

3. (1:07) Chorus 3 (trombone): _____ bars

4. (1:28) Chorus 4 (clarinet): _____ bars

5. (1:49) Minor Chorus 3 (trumpet): _____ bars

6. (1:59) Minor Chorus 4 (piano): _____ bars

7. (2:09) Chorus 5 (guitar): _____ bars

8. (2:29) Chorus 6 (trumpet): _____ bars

9. (2:49) Chorus 7 (all instruments): _____ bars

10. Finally, which is true?

    a. The major chorus and the minor chorus always have sixteen and eight bars, respectively.

    b. The length of each chorus varies from section to section.

43

Bebop-style Jazz   6CD 6/11
My Melancholy Baby
Charlie "Bird" Parker, saxophone; Dizzy Gillespie, trumpet
(recorded in New York, 1950)

Bebop is a highly complex style of progressive jazz with difficult chord changes and dizzying flights of instrumental virtuosity. What makes *My Melancholy Baby* easy to follow is the form: a short introduction, three sixteen-bar choruses, and a short coda. The form is made clear to the listener because there is a change to a new solo instrument at the beginning of each chorus. From one chorus to the next, however, the playing becomes progressively more complex and the tune more heavily disguised by ornamentation. The first five questions that follow help illuminate the musical form, while the second five concentrate on aspects of the bass line.

1. (0:00–0:12) Which instrument solos during the introduction?
    a. saxophone   b. piano   c. trumpet

2. (0:13–1:11) What does the piano do during Charlie Parker's solo in chorus 1?
    a. plays its own frenetic melody against Parker's solo
    b. plays chords quietly in the background

3. (1:12–2:12) During Dizzy Gillespie's trumpet solo of chorus 2, what does saxophonist Parker do?
    a. plays his own frenetic melody against Gillespie's solo
    b. nothing

4. (2:13–3:04) During chorus 3, is Gillespie's trumpet heard?
    a. yes   b. no

5. Which of the forms often employed in classical music is embodied in this piece?
    a. theme and variations
    b. rondo
    c. sonata–allegro

6. Which type of bass instrument is playing the bass line in this quintet?
    a. the double bass of the symphony orchestra
    b. the electric bass of the rock band

7. Does the player use a bow or play pizzicato?
    a. bow   b. pizzicato

8. Which figure more accurately reflects the rhythm of the bass?

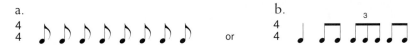

9. Which statement correctly describes the bass line?
   a. moves mainly in stepwise motion in regular, even notes
   b. moves by leaps in highly varied rhythms
10. This sort of bass line, then, can be said to be similar to which musical procedure of the Baroque era?
    a. the pedal point*
    b. the ostinato* bass
    c. the walking bass*

Listening to Contemporary Rock

This book was written as a text for music courses in colleges and universities. Although the author played piano in a rock 'n' roll band many years back, he is certain that you, the college student, are more familiar with the contemporary rock scene than he. This last listening exercise gives you the chance to demonstrate your expertise. Your task is to choose a piece of contemporary rock music, analyze it, and write a brief report. As you listen, you may wish to consider the following questions as a way of focusing your thoughts.

1. What instruments are playing?
2. Are they acoustical musical instruments or electronically amplified ones?
3. What do you think is the relationship between music and noise in your piece? Is there any "electronic filler"? If so, what purpose does it serve?
4. Is your piece an original composition by the artist, or is it a "cover" version (remake) of a pre-existing rock or pop song? If it is a cover, how does it compare to the original version?
5. What do you think is the single most important element in your piece? Is it the text, a catchy melody, a satisfying harmonic pattern, a driving rhythm, or something else?
6. What instrument is playing the bass line? Does the bass stand out in any special way? Is it, for example, played louder than the other parts? If so, why?
7. What about the form of your rock song: Is it through-composed* like Schubert's *Erlking* (page 268) or strophic* like *Lost Your Head Blues* (page 406)? Many pop tunes are strophic but each stanza ends with a text refrain. Is yours arranged in this fashion?
8. Is the mood and style of the music well suited to the text of your piece, or might this music be used just as well for another set of lyrics?
9. Has a music video been made to accompany your piece? If so, how do the visual images enhance the message conveyed by the music and lyrics?
10. Finally, how inventive is your work? Is it fresh and innovative, or is it simply a repackaging of the clichés of popular music? Do you think your selection will stand the test of time to become a classic? If so, why; if not, why not?

Key Words

bebop (411)
big band (410)
blue note (401)
blues (400)
blues scale (401)
chorus (409)

cool jazz (413)
instrumental break (400)
jazz (407)
jazz-fusion (416)

ragtime (407)
rhythm and blues (418)
rhythm section (409)
swing (411)

Glossary

absolute music: instrumental music free of a text or any pre-existing program

a cappella: a term applied to unaccompanied vocal music; originated in the expression *a cappella Sistina*, "in the Sistine Chapel" of the pope, where instruments were forbidden to accompany the singers

accelerando: a tempo mark indicating "getting faster"

accent: emphasis or stress placed on a musical tone or a chord

accidental: a sharp, flat, or natural sign that alters the pitch of a note a half step

accompagnato: see *recitativo accompagnato*

acoustical instruments: instruments that produce sounds naturally when strings are bowed or plucked, a tube has air passed through it, or percussion instruments are struck

acoustical music: music produced by acoustical instruments (see above)

adagio: a tempo mark indicating "slow"

Alberti bass: instead of having the pitches of a chord sound all together, the notes are played in succession to provide a continual stream of sound

aleatoric music: see *chance music*

allegretto: a tempo mark indicating "moderately fast"

allegro: a tempo mark indicating "fast"

allemande: a stately dance in $\frac{4}{4}$ meter with gracefully interweaving lines

alto (contralto): the lower of the two female voice parts, the soprano being higher

andante: a tempo mark indicating "moderately moving"

andantino: a tempo mark indicating "moderately moving" yet slightly faster than *andante*

antecedent phrase: the opening, incomplete-sounding phrase of a melody; often followed by a consequent phrase that brings the melody to closure

anthem: a composition for chorus on a sacred subject; similar in design and function to a motet

aria: an elaborate lyrical song for solo voice

arpeggio: the notes of a triad or seventh chord played in direct succession and in a direct line up or down

arioso: a style of singing and a type of song midway between an aria and a recitative

art song: an accompanied song or ayre with artistic aspirations

atonal music: music without tonality, music without a key center; most often associated with the twentieth-century avant-garde style of Arnold Schoenberg

augmentation: the notes of a melody held for longer, usually double, their normal duration

back beat: a drum beat or cymbal crash occurring regularly after a strong beat, as on beats two and four in a measure with four beats

ballad: a traditional song, or folk song, sung by a soloist that tells a tale and is organized by stanzas

ballet: an art form that uses dance and music, along with costumes and scenery, to tell a story and display emotions through expressive gestures and movement

Ballets russes: a Russian ballet company of the early twentieth century led by Sergei Diaghilev

bandoneon: a square-cut woodwind instrument much like an accordion, except it is played by pushing buttons rather than keys

banjo: a five-string plucked folk instrument of African-American origin

bar: see *measure*

baritone: a male voice part of a middle range, between the higher tenor and the lower bass

bas instruments: a class of soft musical instruments, including flute, recorder, fiddle, harp, and lute, popular during the late Middle Ages

bass: the lowest male voice range

bass clef: a sign placed on a staff to indicate the notes below middle C

bass drum: a large, low-sounding drum struck with a soft-headed stick

bass viol: see *viola da gamba*

basso continuo: a small ensemble of at least two instrumentalists who provide a foundation for the melody or melodies above; heard almost exclusively in Baroque music

basso ostinato: a motive or phrase in the bass that is repeated again and again

bassoon: a low, double-reed instrument of the woodwind family

Bayreuth Festival House: an opera house in the town of Bayreuth, Germany, constructed exclusively for the music dramas of Richard Wagner

beat: an even pulse in music that divides the passing of time into equal segments

bebop: a complex, hard-driving style of jazz that emerged shortly after World War II; it is played without musical notation by a small ensemble

bel canto: (Italian for "beautiful singing") a style of singing and a type of Italian opera developed in the nineteenth century that features the beautiful tone and brilliant technique of the human voice

big band: a mid- to large-size dance band that emerged in the 1930s to play the style of jazz called swing

binary form: a musical form consisting of two units (**A** and **B**) constructed to balance and complement each other

blue note: the third, fifth, or seventh note of the blues scale that can be altered to be sharper or flatter; helps produce the wail of the blues

blues: an expressive, soulful style of singing that emerged from the African-American spiritual and work song at the end of the nineteenth century; its texts are strophic, its harmonies simple and repetitive

blues scale: a seven-note scale in which the third, fifth, and seventh pitches are sometimes flat, sometimes natural, and sometimes in between

bolero: a popular, suggestive Spanish dance for a soloist or couple often performed to the accompaniment of castanets

bongo drum: a pair of small Afro-Cuban single-headed drums created in Cuba ca. 1900; they are often heard in Latin American dance bands

Brandenburg concertos: set of six concerti grossi composed by J. S. Bach between 1711 and 1720, and subsequently dedicated to Margrave Christian Ludwig of Brandenburg

brass family: a group of musical instruments traditionally made of brass and played with a mouthpiece; includes trumpet, trombone, French horn, and tuba

bridge: see *transition*

bugle: a simple brass instrument that evolved from the valveless military trumpet

cabaletta: the concluding fast aria of any two- or three-section operatic scene; a useful mechanism to get the principals off the stage

cadence: the concluding part of a musical phrase

cadenza: a showy passage for the soloist appearing near the end of the movement in a concerto; it usually incorporates rapid runs, arpeggios, and snippets of previously heard themes into a fantasylike improvisation

call and response: a method of performance in which a soloist sings and a group or another soloist answers; it is particularly favored in African music and genres of African-American music such as the blues

canon (round): a contrapuntal form in which the individual voices enter and each in turn duplicates exactly the melody that the first voice played or sang

cantata: a term originally meaning "something sung"; in its mature state it consists of several movements, including one or more arias, ariosos, and recitatives; cantatas can be on secular subjects, but those of J. S. Bach are primarily sacred in content

caprice: a light, whimsical character piece of the nineteenth century

castanets: percussion instruments (rattles) of indefinite pitch associated with Spanish music

castrato: a boy or adult singer who had been castrated to keep his voice from changing so that it would remain in the soprano register

celesta: a small percussive keyboard instrument using hammers to strike metal bars, thereby producing a bright, bell-like sound

cello (violoncello): an instrument of the violin family but more than twice the violin's size; it is played between the legs and produces a rich, lyrical tone

chamber music: music, usually instrumental music, performed in a small concert hall or private residence with just one performer on each part

chamber sonata: see *sonata da camera*

chance music (aleatory music): music that involves an element of chance (rolling dice, choosing cards, etc.) or whimsy on the part of the performers; especially popular with avant-garde composers

chanson: a French term used broadly to indicate a lyrical song from the Middle Ages into the twentieth century

character piece: a brief instrumental work seeking to capture a single mood; a

genre much favored by composers of the Romantic era

chorale: the German word for the hymn of the Lutheran church; hence a simple religious melody to be sung by the congregation

chord: two or more simultaneously sounding pitches

chord progression: a succession of chords moving forward in a purposeful fashion

chorus: a group of singers, usually including sopranos, altos, tenors, and basses, with at least two and often many more singers on each vocal part; also, in jazz, a full statement of the tune around which the performers improvise

chromaticism: the frequent presence in melodies and chords of intervals only a half step apart; in a scale, the use of notes not part of the diatonic major or minor pattern

church sonata: see *sonata da chiesa*

clarinet: a single-reed instrument of the woodwind family with a large range and a wide variety of timbres within it

clavier: a general term for all keyboard instruments including harpsichord, organ, and piano

clef sign: a sign used to indicate the register, or range of pitches, in which an instrument is to play or a singer is to sing

coda: (Italian for "tail") a final and concluding section of a musical composition

col legno: (Italian for "with the wood") an instruction to string players to strike the strings of the instrument not with the horsehair of the bow, but with the wood of it

collegium musicum: a society of amateur musicians (usually associated with a university) dedicated to the performance of music, nowadays music of the Middle Ages, Renaissance, and Baroque era

color (timbre): the character or quality of a musical tone as determined by its harmonics and its attack and decay

comic opera: a genre of opera that originated in the eighteenth century, portraying everyday characters and situations, and using spoken dialogue and simple songs

computer music: the most recent development in electronic music; couples the computer with the electronic synthesizer to imitate the sounds of acoustical instruments and to produce new sounds

concert overture: an independent, one-movement work, usually of programmatic content, originally intended for the concert hall and not designed to precede an opera or play

concertino: the group of instruments that function as soloists in a concerto grosso

concerto: an instrumental genre in which one or more soloists play with and against a larger orchestra

concerto grosso: a three-movement concerto of the Baroque era that pits the sound of a small group of soloists (the concertino) against that of the full orchestra (the tutti)

conga drum: a large Afro-Cuban single-headed barrel drum played in Latin American dance bands

conjunct motion: melodic motion that proceeds primarily by steps and without leaps

consequent phrase: the second phrase of a two-part melodic unit that brings a melody to a point of repose and closure

consonance: pitches sounding agreeable and stable

continuo: see *basso continuo*

contrabassoon: a larger, lower-sounding version of the bassoon

cool jazz: a style of jazz that emerged in the 1950s that is softer, more relaxed, and less frenzied than bebop

cornet: a brass instrument that looks like a short trumpet; it has a more mellow tone than the trumpet and is most often used in military bands

cornetto: a woodwind instrument that developed during the late Middle Ages and early Renaissance that sounds like a hybrid of a clarinet and trumpet

counterpoint: the harmonious opposition of two or more independent musical lines

courante: a lively dance in $\frac{6}{4}$ with an upbeat and frequent changes of metrical accent

crescendo: a gradual increase in the volume of sound

cymbals: a percussion instrument of two metal disks; they are made to crash together to create emphasis and articulation in music

da capo aria: an aria in two sections, with an obligatory return to and repeat of the first; hence an aria in ternary (**ABA**) form

dance suite: a collection of instrumental dances, each with its own distinctive rhythm and character

development: the center-most portion of sonata-allegro form, in which the thematic material of the exposition is developed and extended, transformed, or reduced to its essence; it is often the most confrontational and unstable section of the movement

diatonic: pertaining to the seven notes that make up either the major or the minor scale

Dies irae: a Gregorian chant composed in the thirteenth century and used as the central portion of the Requiem Mass of the Catholic Church

diminished chord: a triad or seventh chord made up entirely of minor thirds and producing a tense, unstable sound

diminuendo: a gradual decrease in volume of sound

diminution: a reduction, usually by half, of all the rhythmic durations in a melody

disjunct motion: melodic motion that moves primarily by leaps rather than by steps

dissonance: a discordant mingling of sounds

diva: (Italian for "goddess") a celebrated female opera singer; a prima donna

dominant chord: the chord built on the fifth degree of the scale

dondon: a two-headed pressure drum indigenous to West Africa

dotted note: a note to which an additional duration of fifty percent has been added

double bass: the largest and lowest-pitched instrument in the string family

double counterpoint: counterpoint with two themes that can reverse position, the top theme moving to the bottom and the bottom to the top (also called *invertible counterpoint*)

double exposition form: a form, originating in the concerto of the Classical period, in which first the orchestra and then the soloist present the primary thematic material

double stops: a technique applied to string instruments in which two strings are pressed down and played simultaneously instead of just one

downbeat: the first beat of each measure; it is indicated by a downward motion of the conductor's hand and is usually stressed

drone: a continuous sound on one or more fixed pitches

dynamics: the various levels of volume, loud and soft, at which sounds are produced in a musical composition

electronic instruments: machines that produce musical sounds by electronic means, the most widespread instrument being the keyboard synthesizer

electronic music: sounds produced and manipulated by magnetic tape machines, synthesizers, and/or computers

eleventh chord: a chord comprised of five intervals of a third and spanning eleven different letter names of pitches

encore: French word meaning "again"; the repeat of a piece demanded by an appreciative audience; an extra piece added at the end of a concert

English horn: an alto oboe, pitched at the interval a fifth below the oboe, much favored by composers of the Romantic era

episode: a passage of free, nonimitative counterpoint found in a fugue

erhu: an ancient two-string Chinese fiddle

"Eroica" Symphony: Beethoven's Symphony No. 3 (1803) originally dedicated to Napoleon but published as the "Heroic Symphony"

etude: a short one-movement composition designed to improve one aspect of a performer's technique

exposition: in a fugue, the opening section, in which each voice in turn has the opportunity to present the subject; in sonata–allegro form, the principal section, in which all thematic material is presented

falsetto voice: a high, soprano-like voice produced by adult male singers when they sing in head voice and not in full chest voice

fantasy: a free improvisatory-like composition in which the composer follows his or her whims rather than an established musical form

fermata: in musical notation, a mark indicating that the performer(s) should hold a note or chord for an extended duration

fiddle: a popular term for the violin

figured bass: in musical notation, a numerical shorthand that tells the player which unwritten notes to fill in above the written bass note

finale: the last movement of a multimovement composition, one that usually works to a climax and conclusion

flamenco: a genre of Spanish song and dance, with guitar accompaniment, that originated in southern-most Spain and exhibits non-Western, possibly Arab-influenced, scales

flat: in musical notation, a symbol that lowers a pitch by a half step

flute: a high-sounding member of the woodwind family; the instrument was initially made of wood but more recently, beginning in the nineteenth century, of silver or even platinum

folk-rock: a mixture of the steady beat of rock with the forms, topics, and styles of singing of the traditional Anglo-American folk ballad

folk song: a song originating from an ethnic group and passed from genera-tion to generation by oral tradition rather than written notation

form: the purposeful organization of the artist's materials; in music, the general shape of a composition as perceived by the listener

forte (*f*): in musical notation, a dynamic mark indicating "loud"

fortepiano (pianoforte): the original name of the piano

fortissimo (*ff*): in musical notation, a dynamic mark indicating "very loud"

free counterpoint: counterpoint in which the voices do not all make use of some preexisting subject in imitation

free jazz: a style of jazz perfected during the 1960s in which a soloist indulges in flights of creative fancy without concern for the rhythm, melody, or harmony of the other performers

French horn: a brass instrument that plays in the middle range of the brass family; developed from the medieval hunting horn

fugato: a short fugue set in some other musical form like sonata-allegro or theme and variations

fugue: a composition for three, four, or five parts played or sung by voices or instruments, which begins with a presentation of a subject in imitation in each part and continues with modulating passages of free counterpoint and further appearances of the subject

full cadence: a cadence that sounds complete, in part because it usually ends on the tonic note

gamelan: the traditional orchestra of Indonesia consisting of as many as twenty-five instruments, mostly gongs, chimes, drums, and metallophones

genre of music: type of music; specifically, the quality of musical style, form, performing medium, and place of performance that characterize any one type of music

Gesamtkunstwerk: (German for "total art work") an art form that involves music, poetry, drama, and scenic design; often used in reference to Richard Wagner's music dramas

Gewandhaus Orchestra: the symphony orchestra that originated in the Clothiers' House in Leipzig, Germany, in the eighteenth century

gigue: a fast dance in $\frac{6}{8}$ or $\frac{12}{8}$ with a constant eighth-note pulse that produces a galloplike effect

glissando: a device of sliding up or down the scale very rapidly

glockenspiel: a percussion instrument made of tuned metal bars that are struck by mallets

gong: a circular, metal percussion instrument of Asian origin

gongon: a large barrel-like drum indigenous to West Africa

grave: a tempo mark indicating "very slow and grave"

great staff: a large musical staff that combines both the treble and the bass clefs

Gregorian chant (plainsong): a large body of unaccompanied monophonic vocal music, set to Latin texts, composed for the Western Church over the course of fifteen centuries, from the time of the earliest Fathers to the Council of Trent

ground bass: the English term for *basso ostinato*

guiro: a scraped percussion instrument originating in South America and the Caribbean

habanera: an Afro-Cuban dance-song that came to prominence in the nineteenth century, marked by a repeating bass and a repeating, syncopated rhythm

half cadence: a cadence at which the music does not come to a fully satisfying stop but stands as if suspended on a dominant chord

half step: the smallest musical interval in the Western major or minor scale; the distance between any two adjacent keys on the piano

harmonics: the secondary tones above a fundamental pitch that taken in sum help form the totality of that sound

harmony: the sounds that provide the support and enrichment—an accompaniment—for melody

harp: an ancient plucked-string instrument with a triangular shape

harpsichord: a keyboard instrument, especially popular during the Baroque era, that produces sound by depressing a key that drives a lever upward and forces a pick to pluck a string

hauts instruments: a class of loud musical instruments, including trumpet, sackbut, shawm, and drum, popular during the late Middle Ages

"heroic" period: a period in Beethoven's compositional career (1803–1813) during which he wrote longer works incorporating board gestures, grand climaxes, and triadic, triumphant themes

Hindustani-style music: the traditional, or classical, music of northern India

homophony: a texture in which all the voices, or lines, move to new pitches at roughly the same time; often referred to in contradistinction to polyphony

horn: a term generally used by musicians to refer to any brass instrument, but most often the French horn

hornpipe: an energetic dance, derived from the country jig, in either $\frac{3}{2}$ or $\frac{2}{4}$ time

idée fixe: literally a "fixed idea," but more specifically an obsessive musical theme as first used in Hector Berlioz's *Symphonie fantastique*

imitation: the process by which one or more musical voices, or parts, enter and duplicate exactly for a period of time the music presented by the previous voice

imitative counterpoint: a type of counterpoint in which the voices or lines frequently use imitation

incidental music: music to be inserted between the acts or during important scenes of a play to add an extra dimension to the drama

instrumental break: in the blues or in jazz, a short instrumental passage that interrupts and responds to the singing of a voice

intermezzo: (Italian for "between piece") a light musical interlude intended to separate and thus break the mood of two more serious, surrounding movements or operatic acts or scenes

interval: the distance between any two pitches on a musical scale

inversion: the process of inverting the musical intervals in a theme or melody; a melody that ascended by step, now descends by step, and so on

invertible counterpoint: see *double counterpoint*

jazz: a lively, energetic music with pulsating rhythms and scintillating syncopations, usually played by a small instrumental ensemble

jazz-fusion: a mixture of jazz and rock cultivated by American bands in the 1970s

jazz riff: a short motive, usually played by an entire instrumental section (woodwinds or brasses) that appears frequently, but intermittently, in a jazz composition

Karnatak-style music: the traditional, or classical, music of southern India

key: a tonal center built on a tonic note and making use of a scale; also, on a keyboard instrument, one of a series of levers that can be depressed to generate sound

key signature: in musical notation, a preplaced set of sharps or flats used to indicate the scale and key

Kyrie: the first portion of the Ordinary of the Mass and hence usually the opening movement in a polyphonic setting of the Mass

La Scala: the principal opera house of the city of Milan, Italy, which opened in 1778

largo: a tempo mark indicating "slow and broad"

leading tone: the pitch a half step below the tonic, which pulls up and into it, especially at cadences

leap: melodic movement not by an interval of just a step but usually by a jump of at least a fourth

legato: in musical notation, an articulation mark indicating that the notes are to be smoothly connected; the opposite of staccato

Leitmotif: a brief, distinctive unit of music designed to represent a character, object, or idea; a term applied to the motives in the music dramas of Richard Wagner

lento: a tempo mark indicating "very slow"

libretto: the text of an opera

Liebestod: (German for "love death") the famous aria sung by the expiring Isolde at the end of Richard Wagner's opera *Tristan und Isolde*

Lied: (German for "song") the genre of art song, for voice and piano accompaniment, that originated in Germany ca. 1800

London Symphonies: the twelve symphonies composed by Joseph Haydn for performance in London between 1791 and 1795; Haydn's last twelve symphonies (Nos. 93–104)

lute: a six-string instrument appearing in the West in the late Middle Ages

madrigal: a popular genre of secular vocal music that originated in Italy during the Renaissance, in which usually four or five voices sing love poems

madrigalism: a device, originating in the madrigal, by which key words in a text spark a particularly expressive musical setting

major scale: a seven-note scale that ascends in the following order of whole and half steps: 1-1-½-1-1-1-½

Marseillaise, La: a tune written as a revolutionary marching song in 1792 by Claude-Joseph Rouget de Lisle and sung by a battalion from Marseilles as it entered Paris in that year; it subsequently became the French national anthem

Mass: the central religious service of the Roman Catholic Church, one that incorporates singing for spiritual reflection or as accompaniment to sacred acts

mazurka: a fast dance of Polish origins in triple meter with an accent on the second beat

measure (bar): a group of beats, or musical pulses; usually the number of beats is fixed and constant so that the measure serves as a continual unit of measurement in music

melisma: in singing, one vowel luxuriously spread out over many notes

melodic sequence: the repetition of a musical motive at successively higher or lower degrees of the scale

melody: a series of notes arranged in order to form a distinctive, recognizable musical unit; it is most often placed in the treble

meter: the gathering of beats into regular groups

meter signature: see *time signature*

metronome: a mechanical device used by performers to keep a steady tempo

mezzo-soprano: a female vocal range between alto and soprano

middle C: the middle-most C on the modern piano

Minimalism: a style of modern music that takes a very small amount of musical material and repeats it over and over to form a composition

Minnesinger: a type of secular poet-musician that flourished in Germany during the twelfth through fourteenth centuries

minor scale: a seven-note scale that ascends in the following order of whole and half steps: 1-½-1-1-½-1-1

minuet: a moderate dance in $\frac{3}{4}$, though actually danced in patterns of six steps, with no upbeat but with highly symmetrical phrasing

mode: a pattern of pitches forming a scale; the two primary modes in Western music are major and minor

moderato: a tempo marking indicating "moderately moving"

modified strophic form: strophic form in which the music is modified briefly to accommodate a particularly expressive word or phrase in the text

modulation: the process in music whereby the tonal center changes from one key to another, from G major to C major, for example

monophony: a musical texture involving only a single line of music with no accompaniment

motet: a composition for choir or larger chorus setting a religious, devotional, or solemn text; often sung *a cappella*

motive: a short, distinctive melodic figure that stands by itself

mouthpiece: a detachable portion of a brass instrument into which the player blows

movement: a large, independent section of a major instrumental work, such as a sonata, dance suite, symphony, quartet, or concerto

music: the rational organization of sounds and silences as they pass through time

music drama: a term used for the mature operas of Richard Wagner

musical comedy: a popular genre of musical theater designed to appeal to a general audience by means of spoken dialogue, songs, and energetic dances

musique concrète: music in which the composer works directly with sounds recorded on magnetic tape, not with musical notation and performers

mute: any device that muffles the sound of a musical instrument; on the trumpet, for example, it is a cup that is placed inside the bell of the instrument

nationalism: a movement in music in the nineteenth century in which composers sought to emphasize indigenous qualities in their music by incorporating folk songs, native scales, dance rhythms, and local instrumental sounds

natural: in musical notation, a symbol that cancels a pre-existing sharp or flat

Neo-classicism: a movement in twentieth-century music that seeks to return to the musical forms and aesthetics of the Baroque and Classical periods

new age music: a style of non-confrontational, often repetitious, music performed on electronic instruments that arose during the 1990s

ninth chord: a chord spanning nine letters of the scale and constructed by superimposing four intervals of a third

nocturne: a slow, introspective type of music, usually for piano, with rich harmonies and poignant dissonances intending to convey the mysteries of the night

nonimitative counterpoint: counterpoint with independent lines that do not imitate each other

oboe: an instrument of the woodwind family; the highest-pitched of the double-reed instruments

octave: the interval comprising the first and eighth tones of the major and minor diatonic scale; the sounds are quite similar because the frequency of vibration of the higher pitch is exactly twice that of the lower

octave displacement: a process used in constructing a melody whereby a simple, nearby interval is made more distant, and the melodic line more disjunct, by placing the next note up or down an octave

opera: a dramatic work in which the actors sing some or all of their parts; it usually makes use of elaborate stage sets and costumes

opera buffa: (Italian for "comic opera") an opera on a light, often domestic subject, with tuneful melodies, comic situations, and a happy ending

opera seria: a genre of opera that dominated the stage during the Baroque era, making use of serious historical or mythological subjects, *da capo* arias, and a lengthy overture

operetta: a light opera with spoken dialogue and numerous dances involving comedy and romance in equal measure ophicleide: a low brass instrument originating in military bands about the time of the French Revolution; the precursor of the tuba

opus: (Latin for "work") the term adopted by composers to enumerate and identify their compositions

oral tradition: the process used in transmission of folk songs and other traditional music in which the material is passed from one generation to the next by singing, or playing, and hearing, without musical notation

oratorio: a large-scale genre of sacred music involving an overture, arias, recitatives, and choruses, but sung, whether in a theater or a church, without costumes or scenery

orchestra: see *symphony orchestra*

orchestral score: a composite of the musical lines of all of the instruments of the orchestra and from which a conductor conducts

orchestral song: a genre of music emerging in the nineteenth century in which the voice is accompanied not merely by a piano but by a full orchestra

orchestral suite: a dance suite written for orchestra

orchestration: the art of assigning to the various instruments of the orchestra, or of a chamber ensemble, the diverse melodies, accompaniments, and counterpoints of a musical composition

Ordinary of the Mass: the five sung portions of the Mass for which the texts are unvariable

organ: an ancient musical instrument constructed mainly of pipes and keys; the player depresses a key that allows air to rush into or over a pipe, thereby producing sound

organum: the name given to the early polyphony of the Western Church from the ninth through the thirteenth centuries

oscillator: a device that, when activated by an electronic current, pulses back and forth to produce an electronic signal that can be converted by a loudspeaker into sound

ostinato: (Italian for "obstinate") a musical figure, motive, melody, harmony, or rhythm that is repeated again and again

overtone: see *harmonics*

overture: an introductory movement, usually for orchestra, that precedes an opera, oratorio, or dance suite

parallel motion: a musical process in which all of the lines or parts move in the same direction, and at the same intervals, for a period of time; the opposite of counterpoint

part: an independent line or voice in a musical composition; also, a section of a composition

pedal point: a note, usually in the bass, sustained or continually repeated for a period of time while the harmonies change around it

pentatonic scale: a five-note scale found often in folk music and non-Western music

phrase: a self-contained portion of a melody, theme, or tune

pianissimo (pp): in musical notation, a dynamic mark indicating "very soft"

piano (p): in musical notation, a dynamic mark indicating "soft"

piano: a large keyboard instrument that creates sound at various dynamic levels when hammers are struck against strings

piano transcription: the transformation and reduction of an orchestral score, and a piece of orchestral music, onto the great staff for playing at the piano

pianoforte: see *fortepiano*

piccolo: a small flute; the smallest and highest-pitched woodwind instrument

pickup: a note or two coming before the first downbeat of a piece, intending to give a little extra push into that downbeat

pipa: an ancient four-string Chinese lute

pitch: the relative position, high or low, of a musical sound

pizzicato: the process whereby a performer plucks the strings of an instrument rather than bowing them

plainsong: see *Gregorian chant*

point of imitation: a distinctive motive that is sung or played in turn by each voice or instrumental line

polonaise: a dance of Polish origin in triple meter without an upbeat but usually with an accent on the second of the three beats

polychords: the stacking of one triad or seventh chord on another so they sound simultaneously

polymeters: two or more meters sounding simultaneously

polyphony: a musical texture involving two or more simultaneously sounding lines; the lines are often independent and create counterpoint

polyrhythms: two or more rhythms sounding simultaneously

polytonality: the simultaneous sounding of two keys or tonalities

popular music: a broad category of music designed to please a large section of the general public; sometimes used in contradistinction to more "serious" or more "learned" classical music

prelude: an introductory, improvisatory-like movement that gives the performer a chance to warm up and sets the stage for a more substantive subsequent movement

prepared piano: a piano outfitted with screws, bolts, washers, erasers, and bits of felt and plastic to transform the instrument from a melodic one to a percussive one

prestissimo: in musical notation, a tempo mark indicating "as fast as possible"

presto: in musical notation, a tempo mark indicating "very fast"

prima donna: (Italian for "first lady") the leading female singer in an opera

program music: a piece of instrumental music, usually for symphony orchestra, that seeks to recreate in sound the events and emotions portrayed in some extramusical source: a story, a play, a historical event, an encounter with nature, or even a painting

program symphony: a symphony with the usual three, four or five movements in which the individual movements together tell a tale or depict a succession of specific events or scenes

Proper of the Mass: the sections of the Mass that are sung to texts that vary with each feast day

qin: an ancient seven-string Chinese dulcimer played with two bamboo sticks

quadrivium: a curriculum of four scientific disciplines (arithmetic, geometry, astronomy, and music) taught in medieval schools and universities

quadruple meter: music with four beats per measure

quarter tone: the division of the whole tone, or whole step, into quarter tones, a division even smaller than the half tones, or half steps, on the piano

raga: an Indian scale and melodic pattern with a distinctive expressive mood

ragtime: an early type of jazz emerging in the 1890s and characterized by a steady bass and a syncopated, jazzy treble

rebec: a medieval fiddle

recapitulation: in sonata-allegro form, the return to the first theme and the tonic key following the development

recital: a concert of chamber music, usually for a solo performer

recitative: musically heightened speech, often used in an opera, oratorio, or cantata to report dramatic action and advance the plot

recitativo accompagnato: recitative accompanied by the orchestra instead of merely the harpsichord; the opposite of *secco* recitative

recorder: an end-blown wooden flute with seven finger holes played straight out instead of to one side

relative major: the major key in a pair of major and minor keys; relative keys have the same key signature, for example, E♭ major and C minor (both with three flats)

relative minor: the minor key in a pair of major and minor keys; see *relative major*

rest: a silence in music of a specific duration

retransition: the end of the development section where the tonality often becomes stabilized on the dominant in preparation for the return of the tonic (and first theme) at the beginning of the recapitulation

retrograde: a musical process in which a melody is played or sung, not from beginning to end, but starting with the last note and working backward to the first

rhythm: the organization of time in music, dividing up long spans of time into smaller, more easily comprehended units

rhythm and blues: a style of early rock 'n' roll ca. 1950 characterized by a pounding $\frac{4}{4}$ beat and a raw, growling style of singing, all set within a twelve-bar blues harmony

rhythm section: the section within a jazz band, usually consisting of drums, double bass, piano, banjo, and/or guitar, that establishes the harmony and rhythm

Ring cycle: a cycle of four interconnected music dramas by Richard Wagner that collectively tell the tale of the Germanic legend *Der Ring den Nibelungen*

Risorgimento: the name given to the political movement that promoted the liberation and unification of Italy in the mid-nineteenth century

ritard: a gradual slowing down of the tempo

ritardando: in musical notation, a tempo mark indicating a slowing down of the tempo

ritornello: the Italian word for "return" or "refrain"; a short musical passage in a Baroque concerto grosso invariably played by the tutti

romance: a slow, lyrical piece, or movement within a larger work, for instruments, or instrument and voice, much favored by composers of the Romantic period

rondeau: see *rondo*

rondo: an ancient musical form (surviving into the twentieth century) in which a refrain alternates with contrasting material

rubato: (Italian for "robbed") in musical notation, a tempo mark indicating that the performer may take, or steal, great liberties with the tempo

Russian Five: a group of young composers (Borodin, Cui, Balakirev, Rimsky-Korsakov, and Musorgsky) centered in St. Petersburg, whose aim it was to write purely Russian music free of European influence

sackbut: a brass instrument of the late Middle Ages and Renaissance; the precursor of the trombone

Sanctus: the fourth section of the Ordinary of the Mass

sarabande: a slow, elegant dance in $\frac{3}{4}$ with a strong accent on the second beat

scale: an arrangement of pitches that ascends and descends in a fixed and unvarying pattern

scena: a scenic plan in Italian opera involving a succession of separate elements such as a slow aria, a recitative, and a fast concluding aria

scherzo: (Italian for "joke") a rapid, jovial work in triple meter often used in place of the minuet as the third movement in a string quartet or symphony

Schubertiade: a social gathering for music and poetry that featured the songs and piano music of Franz Schubert

score: a volume of musical notation involving more than one staff

secco recitative: dry recitative accompanied only by the harpsichord

Sequence: a Gregorian chant, sung during the Proper of the Mass, in which a chorus and a soloist alternate; see also *melodic sequence*

serenade: an instrumental work for a small ensemble originally intended as a light entertainment in the evening

serial music: music in which some important component—pitch, dynamics, rhythm—comes in a continually repeating series; see also *twelve-tone composition*

seventh chord: a chord spanning seven letter names and constructed by superimposing three thirds

sforzando: a sudden, loud attack on one note or chord

sharp: a musical symbol that raises a pitch by a half step

shawm: a double-reed woodwind instrument of the late Middle Ages and Renaissance; the precursor of the oboe

sinfonia: (Italian for "symphony") a one-movement (later three- or four-movement) orchestral work that originated in Italy in the seventeenth century

Singspiel: (German for "singing play") a musical comedy originating in Germany with spoken dialogue, tuneful songs, and topical humor

sitar: a large lutelike instrument with as many as twenty strings, prominently used in the traditional music of northern India

snare drum: a small drum consisting of a metal cylinder covered with a skin or sheet of plastic that when played with sticks produces the "rat-ta-tat" sound familiar from marching bands

solo: a musical composition, or portion of a composition, sung or played by a single performer

solo concerto: a concerto in which an orchestra and a single performer in turn present and develop the musical material in the spirit of harmonious competition

solo sonata: a work, usually in three or four movements, for keyboard or other solo instrument; when a solo melodic instrument played a sonata in the Baroque era it was supported by the *basso continuo*

sonata: originally "something sounded" on an instrument as opposed to something sung (a "cantata"); later a multi-movement work for solo instrument, or instrument with keyboard accompaniment

sonata–allegro form: a dramatic musical form of the Classical and Romantic periods involving an exposition, development, and recapitulation, with optional introduction and coda

sonata da camera (chamber sonata): a suite for keyboard or small instrumental ensemble made up of individual dance movements

sonata da chiesa (church sonata): a suite for keyboard or small instrumental ensemble made up of movements indicated only by tempo marks such as *grave, vivace, adagio*; originally intended to be performed in church

song cycle: a collection of several songs united by a common textual theme or literary idea

soprano: the highest female vocal part

Sprechstimme: (German for "speech-voice") a singer declaims, rather than sings, a text at only approximate pitch levels

staccato: a manner of playing in which each note is held only for the shortest possible time

staff: a horizontal grid onto which are put the symbols of musical notation: notes, rests, accidentals, dynamic marks, etc.

stanza: a poetic unit of two or more lines with a consistent meter and rhyme scheme

step: the interval between adjacent pitches in the diatonic or chromatic scale; either a whole step or a half step

stomp: a piece of early jazz in which a distinctive rhythm, with syncopation, is established in the opening bars, as in the opening phrases of the "Charleston"

string bass: see *double bass*

string instruments: instruments that produce sound when strings are bowed or plucked; the harp, guitar, and the members of the violin family are all string instruments

string quartet: a standard instrumental ensemble for chamber music consisting of a first and second violin, a viola, and a cello; also the genre of music, usually in three or four movements, composed for this ensemble

strophe: see *stanza*

strophic form: a musical form often used in setting a strophic, or stanzaic, text, such as a hymn or carol; the music is repeated anew for each successive strophe

style: the general surface sound produced by the interaction of the elements of music: melody, rhythm, harmony, color, texture, and form

subdominant chord: the chord built on the fourth, or subdominant, degree of the major or minor scale

subject: the term for the principal theme in a fugue

sustaining pedal: the right-most pedal on the piano; when it is depressed, all dampers are removed from the strings, allowing them to vibrate freely

swing: a mellow, bouncy, flowing style of jazz that originated in the 1930s

syllabic singing: a style of singing in which each syllable of text has one, and only one, note; the opposite of melismatic singing

symphonic poem (tone poem): a one-movement work for orchestra of the Romantic era that gives musical expression to the emotions and events associated with a story, play, political occurrence, personal experience, or encounter with nature

symphony: a genre of instrumental music for orchestra consisting of several movements; also the orchestral ensemble that plays this genre

symphony orchestra: the large instrumental ensemble that plays symphonies, overtures, concertos, and the like

syncopation: a rhythmic device in which the natural accent falling on a strong beat is displaced to a weak beat or between the beats

synthesizer: a machine that has the capacity to produce, transform, and combine (or synthesize) electronic sounds

tabla: a double drum used in the traditional music of northern India

talking drum: a drum having a head or heads covered with skin that can be made more or less tight so as to raise or lower the pitch and thereby approximate human speech

tambourine: a small drum the head of which is hung with jangles; it can be struck or shaken to produce a tremolo effect

tam-tam: an unpitched gong used in Western orchestras

tango: a genre of popular urban song and dance originating in Cuba and Argentina in the nineteenth century; it is marked by a duple meter with syncopation after the first beat and a slow, sensuous feel

tempo: the speed at which the beats occur in music

tenor: the highest male vocal range

ternary form: a three-part musical form in which the third section is a repeat of the first, hence ABA

terraced dynamics: a term used to describe the sharp, abrupt dynamic contrasts found in the music of the Baroque era

texture: the density and disposition of the musical lines that make up a musical composition; monophonic, homophonic, and polyphonic are the primary musical textures

theme and variations: a musical form in which a theme continually returns but is varied by changing the notes of the melody, the harmony, the rhythm, or some other feature of the music

The Well-Tempered Clavier: two sets of twenty-four preludes and fugues compiled by J. S. Bach in 1720 and 1742

through composed: a term used to describe music that exhibits no obvious repetitions or overt musical form from beginning to end

timbre: see *color*

timpani (kettle drums): a percussion instrument consisting usually of two, sometimes four, large drums that can produce a specific pitch when struck with mallets

time signature (meter signature): two numbers, one on top of the other, usually placed at the beginning of the

music to tell the performer what note value is carrying the beat and how the beats are to be grouped

toccata: a one-movement composition, free in form, originally for solo keyboard but later for instrumental ensemble as well

tonality: the organization of music around a central tone (the tonic) and the scale built on that tone

tone: a sound with a definite, consistent pitch

tone cluster: a dissonant sounding of several pitches, each only a half step away from the other, in a densely packed chord

tone poem: see *symphonic poem*

tonic: the central pitch around which the melody and harmony gravitate

transition (bridge): in sonata-allegro form the unstable section in which the tonality changes from tonic to dominant (or relative major) in preparation for the appearance of the second theme

treble: the uppermost musical line, voice, or part; the part in which the melody is most often found

treble clef: the sign placed on a staff to indicate the notes above middle C

tremolo: a musical tremor produced on a string instrument by repeating the same pitch with quick up and down strokes of the bow

triad: a chord consisting of three pitches and two intervals of a third

trill: a rapid alternation of two neighboring pitches

trio: an ensemble, vocal or instrumental, with three performers; also, a brief, self-contained composition contrasting with a previous piece, such as a minuet or a polonaise; originally the trio was performed by only three instruments

trio sonata: an ensemble of the Baroque period consisting actually of four performers, two playing upper parts and two on the *basso continuo* instruments

triplet: a group of three notes inserted into the space of two

trivium: a literary curriculum of three disciplines (grammar, logic, and rhetoric) taught in medieval schools and universities

trombone: a brass instrument of medium to low range that is supplied with a slide, allowing a variety of pitches to sound

troubadour: a kind of secular poet-musician that flourished in southern France during the twelfth and thirteenth centuries

trouvère: a kind of secular poet-musician that flourished in northern France during the thirteenth and early fourteenth centuries

trumpet: a brass instrument of the soprano range

tuba: a brass instrument of the bass range

tune: a simple melody that is easy to sing

tutti: (Italian for "all") the full orchestra or full performing force

twelve-tone composition: a method of composing music, devised by Arnold Schoenberg, that has each of the twelve notes of the chromatic scale sound in a fixed, regularly recurring order

unison: two or more voices or instrumental parts singing or playing the same pitch

upbeat: the beat that occurs with the upward motion of the conductor's hand and immediately before the downbeat

verismo opera: "realism" opera; Italian term for a type of late nineteenth-century opera in which the subject matter concerns the unpleasant realities of everyday life

vibrato: a slight and continual wobbling of the pitch produced on a string instrument or by the human voice

viola: a string instrument; the alto member of the violin family

viola da gamba (bass viol): the lowest member of the viol family; a large six- or seven-string instrument played with a bow and heard primarily in the music of the late Renaissance and Baroque eras

violin: a string instrument; the soprano member of the violin family

virtuosity: extraordinary technical facility possessed by an instrumental performer or singer

vivace: in musical notation, a tempo mark indicating "fast and lively"

vocal ensemble: in opera, a group of four or more solo singers, usually the principals

voice: the vocal instrument of the human body; also a musical line or part

volume: the degree of softness or loudness of a sound

walking bass: a bass line that moves at a moderate pace, mostly in equal note values, and often stepwise up or down the scale

waltz: a popular, triple-meter dance of the late eighteenth and nineteenth centuries

whole step: the predominant interval in the Western major and minor scale; the interval made up of two half steps

whole-tone scale: a six-note scale each pitch of which is a whole tone away from the next

woodwind family: a group of instruments initially constructed of wood; most make their sound with the aid of a single or double reed; includes flute, piccolo, clarinet, oboe, English horn, and bassoon

word painting: the process of depicting the text in music, be it subtly, overtly, or even jokingly, by means of expressive musical devices

xylophone: a percussion instrument consisting of tuned wooden bars, with resonators below, that are struck with mallets

yangqin: see *qin*

Credits

Page 1 © CORBIS; 2 (above) From "The Cortical Topography of Tonal Structures Underlying Western Music" by Peter Janata, et. al. *Science* Magazine, 13 Dec 2002, Vol 298, p. 2168, figure 2. Reprinted by permission of the AAAS; 2 (below) AP/Wide World Photos; 4 © Lynn Goldsmith/CORBIS; 5 © CORBIS; 6 Novosti Information Agency, London; 7 (right) © Bettmann/CORBIS; 7 (left) Photofest; 9 (left) *Rich Jew*, one of the "Pictures at an Exhibition" by Gartman (hartman), Viktor Aleksandrovich/Novosti/Bridgeman Art Library, London/NY; 9 (right) *Poor Jew*, one of the "Pictures at an Exhibition" by Gartman (hartman), Viktor Aleksandrovich/Novosti/Bridgeman Art Library, London/NY; 10 (above) *Sketch of a Gate* by Gartman (hartman), Viktor Aleksandrovich/Novosti/Bridgeman Art Library, London/NY; 10 (below) © Hugh Rooney/CORBIS; 13 Musée Nationale de l'Art Moderne, Paris; 14 AP/Wide World Photos; 16 Steve J. Sherman/Photofest; 18 CORBIS/Hulton-Deutsch Collection; 23 Josef and Anni Albers Foundation; 24 Musée Nationale de l'Art Moderne, Paris; 28 The Granger Collection; 30 © AFP/CORBIS; 31 © Réunion des Musées Nationaux/Art Resource, NY; 32 *Violinist at the Window*, 1918 by Henri Matisse/Musée National de l'Art Moderne, Paris, France/ Peter Willi/Bridgeman Art Library, London/NY; 39 © Bettmann Archives/CORBIS; 40 Photograph by Michael Macioce; 42 SuperStock; 43 (above) Musée d'Orsay, Paris/SuperStock; 43 (below) Decca/Andrew Eccles/Photofest; 44 © Sheila Rock/ICM Artists, Ltd; 45 (left) Courtesy of ICM Artists, Ltd.; 45 (right) Courtesy of Sony Classical; 45 (below) © Ira Nozik 1987/Jane Davis, Inc.; 46 SuperStock; 47 Courtesy of the G. Leblanc Corporation, Kenosha, WI; 49 (above) Martin Reichenthal; 49 (below) Courtesy of the Yamaha Corporation; 50 The Minnesota Orchestral Association; 51 PhotoDisc; 52 (below) © 1991 Steve J. Sherman; 53 (above) University of St. Thomas, MN; 53 (below) Yale University Collection of Musical Instruments; 53 (left) © 1991 Steve J. Sherman; 55 Michael Tenger; 57 (above) Tate Gallery, London/Art Resource, NY; 57 (below) Museum of Modern Art, NY; 62 © Louise Bourgeois/Licensed by VAGA, NY. © Whitney Museum of American Art; 63 (far left) Tate Gallery, London/Art Resource, NY; (left) Cosy-Verlag, Salzburg; 64 Charles and Josette Lenars/CORBIS; 67 National Gallery of Art, Washington. Photo Dennis Brack/Black Star; 72 Bibliothèque nationale, Paris; 74 (above) Otto Miller Verlages, Salzburg; (below) Biblioteca Statale, Lucca; 77 (above) Photo Researchers, Inc.; 77 (below) Biblioteca Lauren Ziana, Florence; 78 Craig Wright, New Haven; 80 Bibliothèque Nationale, Paris; 82 ARXIV MAS; 83 Bibliothèque Nationale, Paris; 84 Bibliothèque Nationale, Paris; 85 (left) Bibliothèque Nationale, Paris; 85(right) © Museo del Prado, Madrid; 76 (left and right) Angel Records, Hollywood; 88 © Jose Fuste Raga/CORBIS; 90 Sistine Chapel, Vatican, Rome, Italy/ Fratelli Alinari/SuperStock; 91 (above) Alte Pinakothek in Munich; 91 (below) *Virgin and Mary Magdalen at the foot of the Cross*, detail from the Isenheim Altarpiece, © 1510–1515 by Matthias Grunewald. Mathis Nithart Gothart/ Musée d'Unterlinden, Colmar, France/Bridgeman Art Library, London/NY; 92 *David* by Michelangelo Buonarroti, 1501–1504/Galleria dell' Accademia, Florence, Italy/Bridgeman Art Library, London/NY; 93 (above) *School of Athens*, detail of the center showing Plato and Aristotle with students including Michaelangelo and Diogenes, 1510–1511 by Raphael/Vatican Museums and Galleries, Vatican City, Italy/ Bridgeman Art Library, London/NY; 93 (below) © The British Library, London; 94 Sistine Chapel, Vatican, Rome, Italy/Fratelli Alinari/SuperStock; 97 Instituto dei Padri dell'Oratorio, Rome; 101 (above) Musées de la Ville de Bourges; 101 (below) Explorer, Paris/SuperStock; 98 Church of St. Frediano, Lucca; 99 Cott Dom A XVII f.74v Poor Clares at service/Richard II's Psalter/British Library, London, UK/Bridgeman Art Library, London/NY; 106 Scala/Art Resource, NY; 107 (left) Scala/Art Resource, NY; 107 (right) Archiv fur Kunst und Geschichte, Berlin; 107 (left) Musée NationaL des Chateaux de Versailles; 108 (left) Bayerische Staatsbemaldesammlungen, Munich, Alte Pinakothek; 108 (right) Chorherrenstift St. Florian, Austria; 108 (below) Yale University Music Library; 109 Galleria Borghese; 110 Barrie-Kent Photographers; 112 Gemäldegalerie Alter Meister, Dresden; 113 Precision Graphics; 114 (above) Scala/Art Resource, NY; 114 (below) CORBIS/Adam Woolfitt;

116 Tiroler Landesmuseum Ferdinandeum, Innsbruck; **117** Bibliothèque et Musée de l'Opera, Paris; **118** Bibliothèque et Musée de l'Opera, Paris; **121** (**above**) National Portrait Gallery, London; **121** (**below**) Scala/Art Resource, NY; **125** (**below**) Staatliche Schlösser and Gärten Berlin, Schloss Charlottenburg; (**above**) Violin, by Stradivari, Cremona, 1699/Victoria & Albert Museum, London, UK/Bridgeman Art Library, London/NY; **127** Civico Museo Bibliografico Musicale, Bologna; **128** Photo Costa; **129** The Frick Collection, New York; **123** McMullen/ Dozoretz Associates, Los Angeles; **135** Giraudon/Art Resource, NY; **137** The Norton Simon Museum; **139** Museo Civico di Torino, Italy; **141** The Collection of William H. Scheide, Princeton, NJ; **142** St. Thomas's Church, Leipzig; **143** Offenliches Kunstmuseum, Basel; **144** (**above**) Berlin, Deutsches Staadsbibliothek; **146** Bach-Archiv, Leipzig; **147** St. Thomas's Church, Leipzig; **148** CORBIS/National Gallery Collection; **153** Gesammtansicht des Bach-Skeletts in W. His, Anatomische Forschungen über Johann Sebastian Bach's Gebeine und Antlitz. . . Leipzig: S. Hirzel, 1895; **154** Staats-und-Universitätsbibliothek, Hamburg; **155** Giraudon/Art Resource, NY; **159** British Library, London; **162** (**above**) Yale Center for British Art, Paul Mellon Collection; **162** (**below**) West Side of Poet's Corner, plate 25 from *Westminster Abbey*, detail of the Funeral Monument of George Frederick Handel (1685–1759), engraved by J. Bluck (fl.1791–1831) pub. by Rudolph Ackerman (1764–1834) 1811 (aquatint) (detail of 97147) Private Collection, The Stapleton Collection/Bridgeman Art Library, London/NY; **167** Leopold Mozart and his two children, Wolfgang Amadeus and Maria-Anna, known as "Nannerl," by Carmontelle (Louis Carrogis)/British Library, London/Bridgeman Art Library, London/NY; **168** (**above**) Editoriale Museum, Rome; **168** (**below**) Courtesy of the University of Virginia, Charlottesville; **169** (**above**) George Nixon Black Fund, Museum of Fine Arts, Boston; **169** (**below**) Scene from *The Marriage of Figaro*, Act 1, Scene 11, by Wolfgang Amadeus Mozart by French School/Deutsches Theatremuseum, Munich, Germany/Roger-Viollet, Paris/Bridgeman Art Library, London/NY; **171** (**above**) Vienna, Kunsthistorisches Museum; **171** (**below**) The Iveagh Bequest, Kenwood, London; **173** (**above**) Precision Graphics; **173** (**below**) With the kind permission of Professor Daniel Heartz; **174** Pesci, Esterhása Castle, Orszagos Müemleki Felügeloség; **175** Mozart Museum, Salzburg; **176** (**above**) Leopold Mozart and his two children, Wolfgang Amadeus and Maria-Anna, known as "Nannerl" by Carmontelle (Louis Carrogis)/British Library, London, UK/Bridgeman Art Library, London/New York; (**below**) Civico Museo Bibliografico Musicale, Bologna; **177** Museum der Stadt Wien; **180** (**above**) © 1984 The Saul Zaentz Company. All Rights Reserved; **180** (**below**) CORBIS/Archivo Iconografico, S.A.; **182** Museum der Stadt Wien; **183** Museum der Stadt Wien; **184** CORBIS/Bettmann; **190** (**above**) Private Collection; **190** (**below**) Salzburg, Mozart-Museum. Inv. Nr. 90/4; **195** (**above**) Mozarteum, Salzburg; (**below**) Reproduced by courtesy of the British Museum, London; **197** The Granger Collection; **198** Collection of Musical Instruments, Yale University; **199** Photofest; **204** Mozart Memorial Collection, Prague; **205** (**above**) Museum der Stadt Wien; **205** (**below**) Museum der Stadt Wien; **206** Joseph Haydn at the first performance of his opera "L'Incontro Improviso" in the Esterhazy Theatre, 29 August 1775 by German School/ Deutsches Theatermuseum, Munich, Germany/Bridgeman Art Library, London/NY; **209** Kunsthistorisches Museum, Vienna; **210** Mozart Memorial Collection, Prague; **211** (**above**) Private Collection; (**below**) Historisches Museum der Stadt Wien; **214** Mozart Museum, Salzburg; **215** (**above**) Engraving by Johann Rudolf Holzhalb, 1777. Reproduced with kind permission of Oxford University Press; (**below**) Mozart Museum, Archiv, Salzburg; **222** © Winnie Klotz; **220** The Granger Collection, NY; **228** British Library, London, Collection Stefan Zweig; **229** Historisches Museum der Stadt Wein; **234** Gesellschaft der Musikfreunde, Vienna; **235** CORBIS/Burstein Collection; **238** Deutsche Staats, Berlin; **240** Museum der Stadt Wien; **243** Original lost; **245** British Library, London, Collection Stefan Zweig; **248** Private collection; **249** *The Wanderer Over the Sea of Clouds*, 1818 by Caspar-David Freidrich Kunsthalle, Hamburg, Germany/Bridgeman Art Library, London/NY; **250** National Portrait Gallery, London; **251** Giraudon/Art Resource, NY; **253** Private collection; **259** (**above**) © Victoria & Albert Museum, London/Art Resource, NY; **259** (**below**) CORBIS; **260** Bibliothèque Nationale; **261** (**above**) The Bettmann Archive; **261** (**below**) Sterling and Francine Clark Art Institute, Williamstown, MA; **262** (**left**) CORBIS; **264** *The Witches' Sabbath* by Francisco Jose de Goya y Lucientes/Museo Lazaro Galdiano, Madrid, Spain/Index/Bridgeman Art Library, London/NY; **265** Museum der Stadt Wien; **266** (**above**) Graphische Sammlung Albertina, Vienna; (**below**) Schaack-Galerie, Munich; **273** Academie de France, Rome; **275** Yale Center for British Art, Paul Mellon Collection; **276** *The Witches' Sabbath* by Francisco Jose de Goya y Lucientes/Museo Lazaro Galdiano, Madrid, Spain/Index/Bridgeman Art Library, London/NY; **277** The Louvre,

Index

Introductory CD Performers List

1. Musorgsky, *Promenade* from *Pictures at an Exhibition*, Montreal Symphony Orchestra/Charles Dutoit, ℗ 1985 Decca Music Group Limited (1:39)

2. Musorgsky, *Bydlo* (Polish Ox-Cart) from *Pictures at an Exhibition*, Montreal Symphony Orchestra/Charles Dutoit, ℗ 1985 Decca Music Group Limited (2:40)

3. Musorgsky, *Goldenberg and Schmuyle* from *Pictures at an Exhibition*, Montreal Symphony Orchestra/Charles Dutoit, ℗ 1985 Decca Music Group Limited (2:16)

4. Musorgsky, *The Great Gate of Kiev* from *Pictures at an Exhibition*, Montreal Symphony Orchestra/Charles Dutoit, ℗ 1985 Decca Music Group Limited (5:40)

5. Listening Exercise 3, Hearing Meters, ℗ 1992 West Publishing Company, Courtesy of Wadsworth/Thomson Learning (4:29)

6. Listening Exercise 4, Hearing Major and Minor, ℗ West Publishing Company, Courtesy of Wadsworth/Thomson Learning (5:03)

7. Listening Exercise 5, Hearing Melodic Structure, Beethoven, *Ode to Joy* from Symphony No. 9, IV, Karl Böehm, ℗ 1994 Deutsche Grammophonc (3:21)

8. Listening Exercise 6, Hearing the Bass Line and the Harmony, Barbara Strozzi, *Voglio morire* (I want to die), Glenda Simpson and The Camerata of London, ℗ 1988 Hyperion Records Ltd, London, Courtesy of Hyperion Records Ltd, London (1:44)

9. Listening Exercise 7, Hearing Chord Changes in the Harmony: Listening to Music: Blues, ℗ 1992 West Publishing Company, Courtesy of Wadsworth/Thomson Learning (1:19)

10. Instruments of the Orchestra: Strings, Courtesy of Wadsworth/Thomson Learning (4:02)

11. Instruments of the Orchestra: Woodwinds, Courtesy of Wadsworth/Thomson Learning (2:26)

12. Instruments of the Orchestra: Brasses, Courtesy of Wadsworth/Thomson Learning (2:22)

13. Instruments of the Orchestra: Percussion, Courtesy of Wadsworth/Thomson Learning (:44)

14. Listening Exercise 8, Identifying a Single Instrument, Courtesy of Wadsworth/Thomson Learning (3:14)

15. Listening Exercise 9, Identifying Two Instruments, Courtesy of Wadsworth/Thomson Learning (3:18)

16. Listening Exercise 10, Identifying Three Instruments, Courtesy of Wadsworth/Thomson Learning (2:19)

17. Handel, Hornpipe from *Water Music*, RCA Victor Symphony Orchestra/Leopold Stokowski, Courtesy of The RCA Victor Group, a Unit of BMG Music under License from BMG Special Products (2:03)

18. Handel, Minuet from *Water Music*, RCA Victor Symphony Orchestra/Leopold Stokowski, Courtesy of The RCA Victor Group, a Unit of BMG Music under License from BMG Special Products (2:55)

19. Handel, "Hallelujah" Chorus from *Messiah*, The Chicago Symphony Chorus/Margaret Hills, director/The Chicago Symphony Orchestra/Sir Georg Solti, ℗ 1985 Decca Music Group Limited (3:41)

20. Listening Exercise: Hearing Musical Textures, Craig Wright, Wadsworth/Thomson Learning (4:36)

21. Brahms, *Wiegenlied (Lullaby)*, Anne-Soffie von Otter, ℗ 1991 Deutsche Grammophone (1:51)

22. Mozart, Variations on *Ah, Vous Dirai-je Maman* ["Twinkle, Twinkle, Little Star"], K, 265: Theme and First Three Variations, Andras Schiff, piano, ℗ 1988 Decca Music Group Limited (3:33)

23. Haydn, Symphony No. 94, The "Surprise" Symphony, Second movement, *Audante*, Allegro, Sir Collin Davis, ℗ 1994 Phillips Int'l (6:14)

24. Tchaikovsky, *Dance of the Reed Pipes*, from *The Nutcracker*, Royal Philharmonic Orchestra, Vladimir Ashkenazy, ℗ 1992 Decca Music Group Limited (2:28)

25. Mouret, *Rondeau* from *Suite de symphonies* (1729), Wolfgang Hannes and Bernhard Läubin, ℗ 1986 Deutsche Grammophone GmbH (1:56)